D1477037

MANCHESTER UNITED 1958–68

Rising from the Wreckage

Iain McCartney

Foreword by David Meek

AMBERLEY

This book is dedicated to the memory of Jimmy Murphy, the man from Pentre who did so much for United in their time of need, and without whom there is every possibility that the Manchester United of today would not be the world-acclaimed club that it is.

First published 2013

Amberley Publishing
The Hill, Stroud
Gloucestershire, GL5 4EP

www.amberley-books.com

British Library Cataloguing in Publication Data.
A catalogue record for this book is available from the British Library.

ISBN 978 1 4456 1798 5 (print)
ISBN 978 1 4456 1812 8 (ebook)

Typeset in 10pt on 12pt Adobe Caslon Pro.
Typesetting and Origination by Amberley Publishing.
Printed in the UK.

CONTENTS

Acknowledgements

I would like to thank the following (in no particular order) for their help during the course of writing this book:

Mark Wylie (Manchester United Museum), Jimmy Nicholson, Reg Hunter, Alex Dawson, Bob English, Mel Nurse, Alec Govan, Barney Chilton (*Red News*), Maurice Setters, Jimmy Murphy Jnr, Phil Murphy, Nick Murphy, Gary James, Frank Colbert, Sandy Busby, Hugh McIlmoyle, Giles Oakley, Fred Eyre, Harry Gregg, Brian Leng (editor of therokerend.com), Johnny Crossan, Nicky Sharkey, Pete Molyneux, Tom Clare, Andrew (stretfordendarising website), Worried Turkey, Joe Glanville, John Camm, John Hewitt, Ray Adler, Jim Thomas, Tom Tyrrell, Jimmy Ryan, David Meek, and Tom Furby of Amberley Publishing.

FOREWORD BY DAVID MEEK

I am delighted to introduce Iain McCartney's latest book because it highlights what for me is the most significant chapter of Manchester United's history.

Rising from the Wreckage deals with the period between the Munich air crash of 1958 and the European Cup victory ten years later.

It was hardly a spectacular era in terms of winning trophies, certainly not compared with the conveyor belt of success enjoyed under the management of Sir Alex Ferguson. For me, though, it was always compulsive viewing as I set out, in the dark days after the accident, on my career as the local reporter covering United for the *Manchester Evening News*, a journey that was to last thirty-seven years, and indeed which still sees me involved in writing about arguably the most famous and successful football club in the world.

Before the Munich accident I was with the *Evening News* as a political correspondent and leader writer, but with our United man, Tom Jackson, one of the eight journalists who lost their lives, the editor asked me to help out in the emergency of finding someone to report those sombre and challenging days.

It was meant to be a temporary posting, but like a lot of people whose lives are touched by Manchester United, it's a difficult club to walk away from.

From the very first moment I was gripped by the drama of a club fighting for survival. Many thought it was the end. How could a club, not especially wealthy, carry on in the face of losing the Busby Babes, with not only eight players killed but with several more so badly injured that they never played again, at least at their previous level?

We know now of course that not only did they survive, but they flourished to the extent that just ten years later they became the first English club to become Champions of Europe.

This is the story that Iain tells. The further along the road we go, the more incredible it seems to me was the achievement of Sir Matt Busby and his trusty lieutenant Jimmy Murphy.

The tragedy cut right across the fabric of the whole club with not only so many players wiped out but the coaches and secretary as well.

Sir Matt and Jimmy, plus the people they gathered round them, like the long-serving trainer Jack Crompton and Les Olive, promoted overnight to become the new secretary, worked wonders.

Painstakingly they rebuilt, won the FA Cup five years after the accident and then in 1968 came the spectacular win at Wembley against Benfica.

I have long felt Sir Matt and company never received the credit they deserved for their part in ensuring that Manchester United rose again, almost literally from the dead.

They were traumatic times, and Iain McCartney is the right man to take us through the drama and also pay homage to another great player era that saw three European Footballers of the Year in Sir

Bobby Charlton, Denis Law and George Best, all playing in the same team at the same time. Brilliant, we didn't know at the time how fortunate we were.

Iain does, though, because here is another man who, despite living in Scotland, has never been able to walk away from Old Trafford. He reckons he has missed only one weekend home fixture in the last twenty-six years and I can quite believe it.

He is steeped in the place, producing biographies of stalwarts like Duncan Edwards and Roger Byrne as well as helping players like Norman Whiteside write his biography and producing numerous histories. He even has a distant relative who played for and captained Newton Heath!

I am delighted he has turned his love of Manchester United to focus on the period that he rightly describes as 'the most memorable decade in the history of the club', because that is exactly what it is.

David Meek

INTRODUCTION

For on-the-field success, the 1990s will undoubtedly be the decade that will eclipse all others in the long and colourful history of Manchester United Football Club. However, there is one ten-year period that could possibly outdo even those trophy-strewn years.

Between 1958 and 1968, Manchester United, the team and its supporters, experienced emotions that even the 1990s failed to match, and for those who were around at that time, whether they admired the team from afar or followed it religiously every week, it was a period that would live on in memories forever.

Munich will always be a pivotal episode in the history of Manchester United Football Club. It was something that almost brought to an end the inspirational work of the men from the carriage and wagon works of the Lancashire & Yorkshire Railway at Newton Heath, the founding fathers, the success of the Charlie Roberts and Billy Meredith era, and the contributions of J. H. Davis and James Gibson, men who did more than most for the Manchester United cause.

Offering the manager's job to Matt Busby in those immediate post-war years was a huge gamble. He was an untried figure in such a role, despite his creditable CV as a player. But Busby grew into the job and the club grew around Busby. For what he lacked in managerial experience, he made up for in vision.

There were moments, days of darkness, following the events of February 1958, when he felt he could not go on; the burden of Munich too heavy upon his broad shoulders. Had Jimmy Murphy not been endowed with man-management skills and an undoubted all-round ability to not just simply carry the flag, but to raise it high, to flutter proudly in the breeze, then Busby may well have called it a day.

His 'Babes' – a name Busby apparently disliked – were, to many who followed their fortunes, irreplaceable. Indeed, one or two undoubtedly were, but through time, trial and error, Manchester United was rebuilt and finally achieved that immortal dream of the European Cup success that Busby craved.

Manchester, and indeed all of Britain, suffered in the wake of the Munich air disaster, which deprived United of an even greater period of success than any history book shows. It is on the afternoon of that devastating accident that this book begins.

It then takes you on a roller-coaster ride of highs and lows as United, under the leadership of Jimmy Murphy, the man to whom Manchester United owe so much, somehow scraped together a team and marched to Wembley, surviving when many others would have collapsed. How, in the aftermath of the crash, having achieved the impossible and with manager Matt Busby having regained his health, they suddenly slipped downwards and were almost relegated to the Second Division.

Slowly, the team was rebuilt, bringing in the likes of Denis Law and Pat Crerand, and once again Manchester United rose to the top, with the emergence of one George Best, tantalising spectator and opponent alike.

This book paints a telling picture of football and indeed life in a totally different decade through the eyes of supporters who were around at the time, creating the definitive story of how Manchester United recovered from a terrible tragedy and went on to conquer Europe.

This is the story of that rebuilding, beginning at Munich and ending at Wembley, the good times and the bad.

The rising from the wreckage.

1

Munich to Milan

The footsteps echoing along the deserted Old Trafford corridors abruptly awoke Alma George from her deep, mind-numbing thoughts. The portly figure of United's assistant manager Jimmy Murphy passed her office door, bringing her crashing back to reality.

Her initial shout of 'Mr Murphy!' brought little response from Matt Busby's second-in-command, other than a 'Yes Dear?' as he headed upstairs towards his own office. But when he heard the emotive cry of 'Mr Murphy, you don't understand!' He stopped in his tracks, turning to face the secretary, who he now realised was in some form of great distress.

Enquiring as to what was troubling her, the tears began to trickle down her cheeks, retracing a path they had taken some time previously. She managed to bring Murphy's world crashing down around him with the words, 'You haven't heard the news? The United plane has crashed at Munich. A lot of people have died.'

It was four o'clock on the afternoon of Thursday 6 February 1958, and Jimmy Murphy had just returned to Old Trafford, having guided the Welsh international side to a 2-0 victory over Israel in a World Cup qualifier at Ninian Park Cardiff. He had suggested to Matt Busby that he could hand the international duties over to others and accompany him, prior to the United party flying out to Belgrade for their important European Cup quarter-final second-leg tie against Red Star, but the Scotsman told him that his presence was not required and it was more important that he fulfilled his managerial role in Cardiff with his national side. It was a decision that perhaps saved Jimmy Murphy's life. It was also a decision that was to change the Welshman's life for the next few months, but the pain he felt that afternoon would never go away.

As First Division Champions in season 1955/56, United had been invited to take part in the European Cup competition for 1956/57, a knock-out tournament and the brainchild of Gabriel Hanot, the football editor of the French daily sports paper *L'Equipe*.

With air travel and football played under floodlights becoming more popular, clubs were eager to pit their wits against others from further afield, and friendlies against foreign opposition soon became all the rage. These were all very well, but often lacked a true competitive edge, so a meeting was arranged in Paris between representatives from sixteen countries, and in April 1955, the European Cup was born.

Chelsea, as Football League Champions, had been invited to take part, but they were refused permission to do so by the Football League. Manchester United, twelve months later, received a similar invite, and like their First Division counterparts, were also told that they could not take part.

Matt Busby, however, was made of sterner stuff than Joe Mears, the Chelsea chairman who also had a similar position with the Football League. With the backing of his board, Busby stood up to Alan Hardaker and the Football League, defying their instructions not to take part in the competition and informed the organisers that Manchester United would accept the invitation to take part in the 1956/57 competition.

Indeed, a letter to United, from Sir Stanley Rous, secretary of the Football Association, dated 14 May 1956, actually asked if United 'would consider entering the competition'. It went on to point out that there were financial advantages in entering and a copy of the regulations of the competition was also sent. It ended, 'I think this could be an excellent opportunity for your Club and should show a good financial return.'

Matt Busby required little time to think about whether or not to accept and told his directors that this was indeed the way forward and the club must accept the invitation to take part.

This decision did not go down well in the corridors of power and a letter, dated 21 August 1956, duly arrived at Old Trafford from Jack Howarth, secretary of the Football League. It read:

> The Management Committee have considered your letters with regard to your entry into this (European Cup) competition and they quite understand that you entered the competition in good faith. Nevertheless I am instructed to write you as follows.
>
> The Management Committee consider that participation in such a competition is not in the best interests of the League as a whole, clashing as it does with the League competition. They therefore ask you to reconsider your decision to participate in the light of its possible effect on attendance at League matches, when you are playing at home.

The letter was given due consideration by the United directors and the following reply was sent by Walter Crickmer:

> Your letter of the 21st was submitted to my Directors at their meeting last evening (August 23rd).
>
> My Board very much regret that at this late date it is impossible to withdraw from the above competition. All arrangements have been made for our home and away games *v.* Anderlecht, tickets have been printed, and we the applications are now being dealt with.
>
> My Directors are pleased to note the Management Committee realise that we entered the competition in good faith, and, notwithstanding that the existing rule does not call for any payment to the Football League from the receipts of matches in the competition, my Board instruct me to say that they will in any event make the usual payment of 4% to the League, so long as our interest in the competition continues.

United had won their first European Cup victory.

That initial European Cup adventure saw Busby's team march through to the semi-finals, a journey no doubt eagerly followed by the Football League from a financial point of view and also from something of an underhand outlook, hoping that United would slip up somewhere along the way, so that they could haul the club up in for a little disciplinary chat.

A mind-blowing 12-0 aggregate win over Belgian side Anderlecht in the preliminary round was followed by a 3-2 success over the Germans of Borussia Dortmund in round one. But it was the 6-5 aggregate victory over Bilbao of Spain in the quarter-finals which thrilled not just the Manchester public, but also football lovers across the country.

That quarter-final tie, played like the previous home ties under the Maine Road floodlights as Old Trafford at that particular time did not possess the luxury of floodlighting, is still considered by many as the best ninety minutes of football that they witnessed from Matt Busby's 'Babes', with the Spaniards, having taken a 5-3 lead to Manchester, being completely overwhelmed in Moss Side.

But there was to be no appearance in the final for United, despite such a devastating performance, as a Real Madrid side, who are still talked about in awe by those who saw them and considered them the best-ever club side, won their home leg 3-1, leaving United with more than a mountain to climb in what was the inaugural European fixture under the recently installed Old Trafford floodlights.

A mountain it was indeed, and despite scoring twice, United also conceded twice and therefore went out of the competition 5-3 on aggregate.

Retaining their First Division title, the 1957/58 European Cup competition presented Matt Busby with a second opportunity to pit himself and his team against the cream of the Continental clubs, and once again they marched practically unopposed to the semi-finals.

The Irish part-timers, Shamrock Rovers, provided little in the way of opposition in the preliminary round, losing 9-2 on aggregate, while Dukla Prague, although claiming a 1-0 victory in the Czechoslovakian capital, had lost the first leg in Manchester 3-0. Red Star Belgrade provided a sterner task and were narrowly beaten by the odd goal in three in the quarter-final first leg at Old Trafford, and indeed fostered hopes of edging out United in the return in Yugoslavia.

With conditions far from perfect on a snow-covered pitch, both teams slipped and slid but the visitors, despite conceding three goals, held out for a 3-3 draw, which was enough to send them into the semi-finals once again.

The absent Jimmy Murphy had rejoiced in Wales at United's aggregate victory over Red Star and looked forward to the draw for the semi-finals, although the forthcoming First Division fixture against League leaders Wolves at Old Trafford was now in the forefront of his mind. Or at least it was, until the events in Munich.

Had the United assistant manager's train been late in arrival at Manchester's London Road station, or had he chosen to take a later departure from Cardiff, then news of the events in Munich would have hit him with even more force, either from the taxi driver who picked him up outside the station, or from the nearby newspaper sellers as they shouted the grim headlines to the unsuspecting public.

Both the early editions of the *Manchester Evening News* and the *Evening Chronicle* carried reports on the game against Red Star Belgrade, with Alf Clarke telling the newspapers readership in the 'Last Extra' of the latter, that

> Manchester United are almost certain to be without Ken Morgans (thigh injury), but both England left-half Duncan Edwards and £23,000 goalkeeper Harry Gregg are expected to be fit for the vital championship clash with Wolves at Old Trafford on Saturday.
>
> Both Edwards and Morgans carried on under difficulties against Red Star in the European Cup game in Belgrade yesterday after being injured in the first half, and Gregg was injured later in the game.
>
> The players will have a check-up at Old Trafford tomorrow morning, and if Morgans is not passed fit, manager Matt Busby will bring in Johnny Berry, who recently asked for a transfer, at outside-right. The team is likely to be: Gregg, Foulkes, Byrne, Colman, Jones, Edwards, Berry, Charlton, Taylor, Viollet and Scanlon.

On the front page of the same paper were the brief couple of paragraphs that Clarke had telephoned back to Manchester, delaying what was to be the fateful attempt at take off. The United correspondent's last despatch, under the heading of 'United are held up in Germany', read:

> The triumphant Manchester United footballers, on their way back from Belgrade to Manchester, are held up in Munich by engine trouble, and they may not be able to get away until tomorrow.
>
> United, who drew 3-3 with Belgrade Red Star (*sic*) and so qualified for the European Cup semi-finals, broke their journey at Munich, where they had lunch.
>
> They were due in Ringway this evening, but their plane developed engine trouble and it is doubtful if they will get away today as it is also snowing very heavily.

As many read Alf Clarke's updates from Munich, they were completely oblivious to what had already unfolded at the German airport, as the newspaper's 'Stop Press' column on the back page listed the result of the 3.15 race at Wincanton.

The *Evening News*, which rolled off the presses at a similar time to the above *Evening Chronicle*, carried Eric Thornton's report on the injuries to Edwards and Morgans on its back page (and the result of the 3.15 from Wincanton in its Stop Press column), but no sooner had the public paid their three pennies for that edition, than another arrived, this time carrying more attention-grabbing news than the winner of the 3.45 from Wincanton. The front page headline screamed, 'United Cup Team's Plane Crash: 10–15 Survivors.'

The brief report went on to say:

> Manchester United's European Cup team was in a BEA Elizabethan plane which crashed on take-off at Munich Airport today.
>
> British European Airways HQ in London said that the report gave no details. But from the spot, it was learned that the plane was 60ft up when it crashed.
>
> The plane was a complete write-off.

A BEA spokesman later said, 'It is understood there are ten to fifteen survivors out of forty people on board. This is not (repeat not) definitely confirmed.'

The same edition was also soon to be updated, as offices of both newspapers went from a winding-down mode into a frantic overdrive state of confusion, disbelief and panic as news from Munich began to filter through, with every available telephone being used in the attempt to discover any further crumbs of information. The latest edition of the *News* hitting the streets carried the new headline of 'UNITED CUP XI CRASH: 28 DIE.'

The *Evening Chronicle* was quick to follow suit, abandoning its earlier headline relating to the report of Dr Vivian Fuchs being in serious trouble about 28 miles south of Depot 700 on his trek from the South Pole, replacing it with 'UNITED AIR DISASTER – 28 KILLED' on a special 'Late Night Final 6 p.m. Edition'.

News of who had died and who had survived had yet to filter through from Germany, as despite the headlines there was at this particular time very little information relating to the events in Germany available, even to the newspapers.

Under the above headline, which stopped many in their tracks as they made their way through the streets of the city, was the following:

> ABOUT 28 PEOPLE, INCLUDING MEMBERS OF THE MANCHESTER UNITED FOOTBALL TEAM, CLUB OFFICIALS AND JOURNALISTS ARE FEARED TO HAVE BEEN KILLED WHEN A BEA ELIZABETHAN AIRLINER CRASHED SOON AFTER TAKE-OFF IN A SNOW STORM AT MUNICH.
>
> It is understood there may be about sixteen survivors. Four of them are crew members.
>
> THE PLANE HAD ACCELERATED ALONG THE RUNWAY IN THE NORMAL WAY AND WAS AIRBOURNE TO ABOUT 60FT, WHEN WATCHERS ON THE GROUND SAW IT SUDDENLY DIP, CRASH AND EXPLODE ON SOME HOUSES.

The article went on to relate the events as far as they were known, while also listing the names of all on board. To the left of the article, in the same bold letters as the above, were the names of those known to be saved: BOBBY CHARLTON, BILLY FOULKES, HARRY GREGG. Those believed saved: RAY WOOD, Peter Howard (*D. Mail*, Photographer), T. Ellyard (*D. Mail*, Telegraphist), Frank Taylor (*News Chron.*, Dispatch), Mrs Vera Lukic, Venana Lukic (22 months). It then listed those who were also on board, leaving the shocked public in a state of the unknown.

At the foot of the back page, in the blank area where any 'stop press' snippets could normally be found, was further news on the crash. Unfortunately, and unknown to those frantically working in the offices of the *Evening Chronicle*, the majority of the up-to-the-minute information was incorrect.

'Roger Byrne is among saved,' began the update and continued a few inches further down with, 'Byrne strove to make himself one of the death-defying heroes of the grim drama as fire flared.

'Rescue workers, red eyed from smoke told of the courage of Roger Byrne. They said he crawled from the wreckage, his clothes slashed.

'His hand fell on a fire extinguisher thrown clear in the melee of twisted steel. He turned it on small fires already leaping from the wreckage as passengers moaned beneath the tangled metal work.

'He beat back the flames, hauled people clear, not caring for the danger for the danger as the planes fuel tanks spilled fuel across yards of ground.

'This story was told from Munich to BEA in London who said, "Here is the story of a brave man."'

Fortunately, it was a story that escaped his wife Joy, as she waited at home, like all the other wives and relatives, for news from official sources.

The earlier mention that Ray Wood was safe was now also thrown into some disarray, with 'Ray Wood was earlier reported believed saved, but now fate not known.'

Back at Old Trafford, Jimmy Murphy, having slowly taken in the words of the now inconsolable secretary, hesitated only momentarily before snatching the telephone from its cradle and frantically dialling whatever numbers came into his head: the police, the newspaper offices, the BBC, wherever, in an attempt to find out more as regards to what had happened.

He was later to say that he had little recollection regarding the hours which followed, or what happened to the contents of a bottle of whisky which was kept in his office cupboard, as he tried to build a mental picture of what had actually occurred thousands of miles away, hoping like thousands of others that he would wake up and everything had been little more than a cruel nightmare.

By now, all the regional evening newspapers had picked up the story and similar headlines and stories were being read across the country. 'Manchester United Plan Crashes: 28 Dead' was on the front of the *Birmingham Evening Despatch*; 'Night Final', with a photograph underneath of the 1957 FA Cup final side that had narrowly lost to Aston Villa. The *Ipswich Evening Star*, with photographs of Bobby Charlton, Dennis Viollet, Jackie Blanchflower, Duncan Edwards, Tommy Taylor, Harry Gregg and Ken Morgans alongside, ran the headline 'Manchester United Team in Crashed BEA Airliner – 10 to 15 Passengers safe – First Report'.

The tragic news had filtered through to Old Trafford around half-past three, with chief scout Joe Armstrong the first to be told of the tragic events. He relayed the telephone conversation to assistant secretary Les Olive, who then had the unfortunate task of informing club chairman Harold Hardman, who had missed the journey due to illness.

The inconsolable chairman later told of how the news was broken to him: 'When Les Olive 'phoned me, he said he had some bad news. He said that he had just had word that the plane had got off from Munich after refuelling and crashed. So far as was known, there were only ten survivors.'

Hardman then said, 'The information had a terrific repercussion on us. It absolutely deadened you. You didn't know where you were.' He went on to replay the following message: 'I should like to convey a message to all those who may have lost anybody or had them seriously injured – the wives, sweethearts, children and families. To those, I extend my deepest sympathy and condolence.'

'To our supporters – I can only tell you, we shall carry on whatever our losses may be and we shall still have a good team ... Keep your hearts up.'

Some of the club's younger players were also among the first to hear the bad news, as they were passing the afternoon playing snooker in the players' games room, underneath the main stand, snatching a rare opportunity with the seniors nowhere to be seen. One of the youngsters brushing up his skill on the green baize was Alex Dawson.

'Yeah, we were up there,' the young reserve-team player recalled. 'We heard these little feet dash along the top, "God, it sounds like my little Pancho" (Mark Pearson). As he entered the room, I asked, "What's up with you, somebody chasing you mate?" "No Alex," he replied. "Haven't you heard? I've just heard the lads have been in a crash."

'We just put the cues down and couldn't believe it and started thinking: Duncan, Tommy Taylor, all of them.

'A reporter came to the ground and we opened the windows and asked him if it was true. "I've heard," came the reply. "But no, I don't know if it's true ... I'm just going to find out."

'Soon he came back to confirm our fears with a simple "yeah it is".

'Good lord, well we just sat there and listened to the news. It was so...'

As well as Jimmy Murphy and Alma George, young office boy Les Olive, along with scout Joe Armstrong and Fred Owen, was at the ground, as were a number of supporters, who were there to purchase tickets for the forthcoming FA Cup tie against Sheffield Wednesday; however, as the news filtered through, entry to the office area was barred and ticket sales were abandoned, with only those intimately associated with the club allowed entry.

Members of the United junior sides arriving at the ground were met with a hand-written message 'Training Cancelled' pinned to a gate. Little did some of those young hopefuls realise that their own playing careers were about to take on an entirely new perspective.

Jackie Charlton, Bobby's older brother, was in the showers after training at Elland Road, Leeds, when a teammate rushed in to tell him that United's plane had crashed at Munich and there were no survivors. He immediately got changed and headed for home after 'phoning his wife. He didn't dare to buy a newspaper, which carried the early news of the crash, but had he done so, this would have put his mind at rest. It wasn't until he reached Newcastle station that he happened to see the 'stop press' column of a newspaper tucked under the arm of a fellow passenger and was relieved to see that Bobby was listed as one of the survivors.

For one local youngster, who now goes by the name 'Worried Turkey', 6 February was a day when time stood still, and one that the eight-year-old would never forget.

Looked up at the school clock, not long now before Trevor (my best mate) and I would race home from school every day. First one home took their 'casey' down to the recreation ground for the match and would also be captain and select the teams. Trev could never understand why I always won. We lived on the same street, but Trev lived three doors up from me so I didn't have as far to run!

Anyway this day home and on to the 'rec' we went. It was a bloody cold and snowy day, but what the heck (I'm a hardened red). The match rules were first to twenty or five o'clock, whichever came first. Trev being a rich so and so had a Mickey Mouse watch so he was timekeeper. With the game well underway, and it must have been about fourteen-a-side, Trev informed everyone it was nearly five o'clock. We were leading 18-12 when I picked up the ball just inside their half, played a quick one-two and hit a screamer. I'd seen Duncan Edwards do this for United and England and I'd practiced for hours on end because of Dunc. The ball sailed into the bottom corner (well that's what I reckon), then the arguments started... 'Post! Post! The ball went over my jumper', said someone. 'No way, was a goal,' I replied... 'Blah blah blah.'

After the arguments had settled I looked up and who should be there but my uncle, 'The ball was in wasn't it Unc? Unc, why are you crying?' Unc beckoned me over and told me that United's plane had crashed.

He had come out for fresh air, a place to think, not really to find me. He'd forgotten we played football at the 'rec'. All the United fans amongst us ran off to listen to the latest news. Myself, Trev and Unc walked slowly back home and only realised how serious the situation was, more than I first thought, when I saw Unc with tears in his eyes. We're Manchester United ... big Dunc, Peggy, Tommy Taylor, Bobby Charlton, Bill Foulkes they're all superstars, nothing could happen to them ... could it?

We arrived at Gran's where everybody was crowded around the radio – it didn't sound good. News bulletins were being issued every five minutes – they were reporting fatalities, but nobody knew who for sure. Looking out of the window people were gathering everywhere. Houses had their windows open allowing people passing by to hear the latest radio update.

As time passed names were starting to be revealed, Matt Busby was alive but only just. Big Dunc was fighting for his life. Surely not Dunc, he was indestructible, built like a brick ... Muhammad Ali once said he was the greatest. I don't think so. Tommy Taylor was reported to have died (please, please be wrong … they weren't). So too was David Pegg, who had spoken to me once!

My Uncle was struggling more than I was. He had supported United for years, while I was only a child (though red mad), so never understood the full seriousness of the situation. I waited up that night for as long as possible. I stayed at Gran's with Unc, not for Unc's sake, but my own – I needed someone to understand. My dad was a City fan, what did he know about football? In the space of a few hours I'd grown up. Emotions don't normally come to kids (only as an excuse to get what they want), but I was very emotional on that night.

Waiting for bulletins was awful, nobody knew what to say. The latest bulletin informed us another player had died – if I remember correctly it was Liam (Whelan). Oh no, was he good or was he good … then we got a call to go around Geoff's as he had a television and the first pictures were coming through. It was horrendous and seemed worse as the pictures were in black and white.

Coming away from Geoff's it suddenly hit me that I wouldn't see the likes of Tommy, David and Roger Byrne again.

The last thing I remember for that night was the time being twelve o'clock with myself and Unc in the front room. He was crying his eyes out. I then realised a pillow which had been placed underneath me as I drifted off to sleep was drenched. Unc, realising I had woken, pulled himself together and said, 'You okay now, you've been crying and praying for Dunc.' In no way am I religious. Anyway, that is where we remained for the full night, just listening to radio bulletins.

The next morning Gran allowed me stay home, rather than go to school. Shows how serious the situation was, while Unc didn't go to work so we sat and sat and waited…

The name of Manchester United was now on everyone's lips, whether they were a United supporter, a footballer lover or neither. Who had survived? Who had died? What had happened to cause the crash? Slowly, the grim news began to tell a story of tragedy and heroics, with the newspapers of Friday 7 February revealing to the world the extent of the disaster.

A roll of the dead appeared in every newspaper, bringing home the severity and reality of the disaster: 'PLAYERS – Roger Byrne (captain), Tommy Taylor (centre-forward), Eddie Colman (right-half), Billy Whelan (inside-right), David Pegg (outside-left), Mark Jones (centre-half), Geoff Bent (left-back). OFFICIALS – Walter Crickmer secretary, Tom Curry trainer, Bert Whalley coach. JOURNALISTS – Tom Jackson (*Manchester Evening News*), George Follows (*Daily Herald*), Archie Ledbrooke (*Daily Mirror*), Henry Rose (*Daily Express*), H. D. Davies (*Manchester Guardian*), Alf Clarke (*Manchester Evening Chronicle*), Frank Swift (*News of the World*). CREW – W. T. Cable (steward). OTHERS – W. Satinoff, Manchester business man and racehorse owner, S. P. Miklos, travel agent.' Alongside, a similar listing could be found, naming those who had suffered injuries and their condition at the time of going to press.

The Manchester papers obviously had the upper hand with the latter, as they could give updates on those injured in their various issues, such as their 'Home Edition' and 'Late Extra'.

The *Evening Chronicle* 'Home Edition' had the headline of 'Matt Fights For Life: "We Hope To Save Him" Edwards and Berry are still critical'. With the condition on the United manager given as 'somewhat improved, but still critical'. Johnny Berry was 'very serious, in bad shape', while Duncan Edwards, like Busby, was 'somewhat improved'. There was 'no change' relating to Jackie Blanchflower, Ray Wood, Dennis Viollet or Kenny Morgans, with Albert Scanlon and Bobby Charlton in 'fairly good condition'.

The same newspaper, in its 'Last Extra' Ashton, Stalybridge and Hyde edition had changed its heading on Busby to 'A 50/50 Chance Now', with Dennis Viollet now 'seriously ill'. An hour and a half later, the 'Last Extra' available in the city centre had Duncan Edwards as now being 'serious'. Each issue of the *News* and the *Chronicle* was eagerly awaited, with sales reaching a level never previously recorded.

Around midnight, a knock came to the door of No. 9 Archie Street, a nondescript house like many others on the Ordsall estate, a short walk from Old Trafford. There were similar unwanted knocks at other doors in the Manchester, Yorkshire and Ireland.

Answering the door, Dick Colman came face to face with an airline official, who told him that his son had died instantly in the crash and that a plane would convey next-of-kin to Germany in the morning. It was an offer that Mr Colman declined. When asked why by a priest, who said he was flying out to give Matt Busby the last rites, he replied, 'My son is dead. Nothing can be done.'

Sadly, in later years, Dick Colman suffered again when vandals broke off the hands on the marble statue of the diminutive half-back, which stood beside his grave. Concrete was also poured over the grave. Later, on another anniversary of the Munich crash, they sawed through the neck and kicked the head around outside the cemetery gates. The statue was then removed and kept in Dick Colman's home in a high-rise flat.

While the condition of the injured and the memories of those who had died were obviously the main talking points in the immediate aftermath of the crash, thoughts began to drift as to what the future would hold for the club.

On the afternoon of Thursday 6 February, Manchester United were in the semi-finals of the European Cup for the second consecutive season and challenging for a third consecutive First Division championship, with some of the players also looking forward to the World Cup tournament in Sweden at the end of the season. Now, seven of the team had perished, the long-term extent of the injuries to a number of others was unknown. Could the club go on?

Sadness, shock, bewilderment and profound sorrow swept, not only across Britain, but the whole world in the wake of the disaster, but nowhere was it felt more than in Manchester itself and perhaps the mood around the city is best captured in 'Tanfield's Diary' in the *Daily Mail* the morning after the devastating news shattered the lives of so many.

'I have never known a city so stunned as Manchester was last night,' penned the correspondent. 'In every home, in trains and buses, in café's and public houses, the talk was about "our wonderful football team" ... the team that won glory against all-comers ... the team that will never be the same again.' He continued:

In the pubs it was rather like those days in 1940 when a hush came over the whole place as soon as the BBC news bulletins came on the air. Glasses stopped clinking. Everybody stopped ordering drinks as the latest casualty lists came over.

Saddest of all were the fervent cloth cap and raincoat supporters who paid their two shillings to watch their Old Trafford idols, through sunshine and rain, hail and thunder, week-in week-out, throughout the season.

Crowds stood outside Manchester United's ground in tears as they waited for news of the players they had known so well. Several times, anxious supporters – teenage girls among them – hammered on the main door for the latest news.

At eight o'clock, chief scout Joe Armstrong opened the door, held up his hand and said, 'Please go away. We can't tell you any more than what's on the news on the wireless.' Joe's face was grey, his voice was tired.

As he closed the door he told me 'I have just come back from seeing the relatives of the players and officials. They were all very brave. It was the worst job I have ever had to do, and I never want to do anything like it again. It was a nightmare'.

Still the crowd waited. Girls stood sobbing under the shadow of the giant stand.

Sandy Busby, Matt's son, was a twenty-two-year-old professional with Blackburn Rovers and was leaving Victoria station around four o'clock with a friend, who suddenly asked him if he had seen the news vendor's placard they had just walked past. Sandy hadn't and even when his friend mentioned that it said that United had been involved in a plane crash, he simply kept walking. Suddenly, the words sunk in and he dashed to a telephone booth, where he 'phoned home. 'My aunt, who was down from Scotland staying with my mother answered and frantically shouted, "Get home son, get home." That's when I realised things were a bit serious. I got a taxi and rushed home.'

On Friday 7 February, Jimmy Murphy, Matt Busby's wife, son, daughters and son-in-law, along with Mrs Frank Taylor, wife of the only surviving journalist, Molly Leach, the fiancée of Duncan

Edwards, and Jimmy Payne, a friend of the United left-half, boarded a BEA flight at Manchester's Ringway airport, heading for Paris, while an Aer Lingus Viscount made its way to Amsterdam with the wives of Ray Wood, Johnny Berry, Dennis Viollet, Jackie Blanchflower and Albert Scanlon onboard. Both flights were due to meet a connecting flight bound for Munich, but runway conditions at the German airport worsened and their flights had to be diverted to Frankfurt, where they were then faced with a seven-hour train journey before reaching their loved ones.

Eventually, the families arrived in Munich, heading straight for the Rechts der Isar Hospital and Jimmy Murphy, upon whose shoulders the responsibility of Manchester United now fell, spoke of his sad, uncomfortable meeting with friend and manager Matt Busby.

'Matt told me that he was feeling a little better, but I had to put my head under the oxygen tent to speak to him. He smiled slightly, his voice was faint, but clear and he said, "Take care of the things for me Jimmy."'

Arriving at the hospital, Sandy Busby recalled that he and his mother, along with the relatives of the other survivors, were met by Professor Maurer and an interpreter and they were told how serious things were. 'When he read out the name "Busby", the professor shook his head and my mother nearly fainted. We then asked, "How is he?" and were told "Bad, bad. Very bad." I walked ahead of my mother into the intensive care area to see how bad he was and get ready to help her and saw this old man lying in an oxygen tent and walked by him before I turned around and realised that it was my dad. I went back and managed to stop my mother and prepare her for what had happened.'

When asked what the future might, or would hold, Murphy admitted, 'I cannot say what will happen about the team. We must just take first things first.' One thing that was certain was the fact that the former West Bromwich Albion player was now the man at the helm of Manchester United Football Club, upon whose shoulders its entire future lay.

No one could have been better equipped to take over the reins than the tough, tenacious one-time wing-half, as he possessed the unflagging zest, drive and enthusiasm required for the painstaking job, while also knowing the players with whom he had to rebuild the ruins of the club as well as he knew his own sons.

Every Tuesday afternoon, Murphy would meet with Coach Bert Whalley and manager Matt Busby in the latter's Old Trafford office, pondering over the team selections for the forthcoming weekend fixtures, but now he would have to manage alone.

Any initial doubts as to the immediate future were soon allayed, following a meeting of the club directors at Old Trafford, with the club chairman, Mr H. P. Hardman, saying, 'We have a duty to football and to the public. We shall carry on with all our commitments – League, FA Cup and European Cup – even if it means we are badly beaten.' The latter certainly being a distinct possibility, considering the players who were at Jimmy Murphy's immediate disposal. It was also something that was unfamiliar to the supporters, with only half a dozen really bad defeats in the past six seasons.

Bolton Wanderers were responsible for two of those, at Old Trafford on 23 January 1954 when they won 5-1 and at their Burnden Park ground on 14 September 1957. They scored four without reply. Middlesbrough had recorded a 5-0 victory at Ayresome Park on 25 April, the last day of season 1952/53, while neighbours City had left Old Trafford with smug smiles on their faces following their 5-0 drubbing of the rivals in February 1955. Everton hit five on 20 October 1956, but at least United had scored two in reply. Arguably, however, the most embarrassing defeat for United during this same period came on 3 January 1956, when they were knocked out of the FA Cup 4-0 by Bristol Rovers.

So, who were the players available for selection for whatever the club's next competitive game was? Waiting in the wings were: goalkeepers – Gordon Clayton, David Gaskell, Tony Hawksworth. Full-backs – Ian Greaves, Jimmy Shiels, Barry Smith. Wing-halves – Bobby English, Wilf McGuinness, Freddie Goodwin, Joe Carolan, Bobby Harrop, Harold Bratt. Centre-halves – Ronnie Cope, Peter Jones, Reg Holland. Wingers – Reg Hunter. Inside-forwards – Mark Pearson, Seamus Brennan, John Giles. Centre-forwards – Alex Dawson, Colin Webster, Jack Mooney. Looking through the list, experience was not something that was in abundance. It was certainly something that nineteen-year-old

Reg Hunter, the only winger in the remaining squad of players at Murphy's disposal, was quick to admit that he didn't have: 'I was actually in the Army when the accident happened,' he recalled, 'and I was allowed to return to Manchester on compassionate leave, so that I could attend the funerals and also be with my colleagues, who like myself suffered immense shock and walked round in something of a daze in the aftermath of the accident.

'I wasn't doing too well at United at this time, at least I personally didn't think so, as I didn't get the same level of training as the others due to being in the Army and stationed down south. I found that the travelling took a lot out of me.

'Had I been at the club later in my career, when I had completed my National Service, then perhaps things would have been different and I would have coped better and enjoyed a higher level of fitness.'

The scheduled First Division match against Wolves on Saturday 8 February was obviously immediately postponed, as was the reserve team's Central League match at Aston Villa due to be played that same afternoon, but there was much debate as to whether the complete League programme should be abandoned on Saturday 8 February as a mark of respect.

Many of the players, from all divisions, backed by several club officials, notified the Players Union to say that they would prefer not to play, but the Union's secretary, Mr Cliff Lloyd said, 'We contacted the Football League today after some of the players had told me that they would prefer not to play tomorrow.

'We asked the League if their decision to carry on with the League programme could be reconsidered. They gave their reasons why they decided that the matches should be played. We will abide by their decision.'

The *Manchester Evening Chronicle* carried out a survey on the streets of the city, which revealed that three out of every four people interviewed thought that the complete Football League programme of forty-six games should be postponed as a mark of respect to United, while Mr Bert Tann, the manager of Bristol Rovers, whose team had recorded that memorable 4-0 FA Cup victory two years previously, was severely critical of the League's ultimate decision: 'The matches should be postponed out of respect for Manchester United and the wives and relatives of those killed or injured,' said the Rovers manager. 'If this had happened in any other organised sport in this country there would have been no thought of continuing with the programme. It smacks of complete disregard for the feelings of those who mourn.

'It is all very well to say the show must go on, but there is far more to it than that. Those who criticise professional soccer will be further fortified in their stand when they know the Football League have come to this deplorable decision.

'Critics will say the need to make money transcends all other feelings.

'Bristol Rovers will travel to Nottingham to play Notts County feeling numbed inside and we have very little stomach for playing football tomorrow.'

In response, Mr Alan Hardaker, secretary of the Football League and, ironically, the man who had voiced his opposition of United entering the European Cup in 1956, was quick to explain his organisations decision, saying, 'The chairman of United, Mr Harold Hardman, has authorised me to say that on behalf of his club he wholeheartedly agrees with the Management Committee's decision to carry on with the League programme.

'Mr Hardman asked that players should turn out and play the game in the normal way, which would be their best way of paying tribute to the players concerned in the tragedy.'

A Football League spokesman also added, 'There is a Management Committee meeting on 16 February, I expect that by then the club will have made a report and the Committee will decide whether or not to grant United an extension of time in which to play their League games. But until the club make a report, or ask for an extension, we can do nothing.'

At the League Management Committee meeting there was much to discuss in relation to the disaster which had cast up an unprecedented position, with no one exactly sure as to what steps to take.

With United being forced to field something of an under-strength team, how this would affect the remaining months of the First Division fixture list was something that the Committee had to look at very closely. It was suggested that United's record for the 1957/58 season would be deleted completely and all of their remaining fixtures, although fulfilled, would be nothing more than friendlies.

This was thought to perhaps be the best all-round decision, as it would not put any undue pressure on United, while it would relieve any of the clubs who had still to face United from a difficult and embarrassing position. It would also, of course, give United some necessary breathing space and allow them to rebuild at their leisure. However, there was nothing the League Management Committee could do until they had heard from United.

All clubs were notified that all the players should wear black armbands, all flags should be flown at half-mast and that there would be two minutes' silence prior to every game.

So, a few minutes short of forty-eight hours since that fateful attempted take-off, footballers, rugby players, officials, and supporters young and old, across the length and breadth of Britain, stood heads bowed for two minutes prior to their fixtures on a Saturday when the red shirts of Manchester United were conspicuous by their absence.

Although absent from that particular Saturday afternoon's fixture list, they were certainly not absent from the thoughts of football supporters across not simply England, but all of Great Britain and beyond, and just because there was no game at Old Trafford, it didn't stop many from making their way to the ground. Amongst those who treated that particular Saturday as a normal matchday was 'Worried Turkey' and his uncle.

They had already been to the ground on the day following the crash and were certainly not alone, as he recalled:

> People were walking around like zombies. One man had a cigarette in his mouth and one in each hand! The silence was eerie. Nobody spoke, you didn't have to. Nothing was real … My scarf was wet. I'd been crying, but never realised. Then someone came out of the offices with a piece of paper and read out the latest bulletin. People gathered more in hope and expectation than anything…
>
> After the bulletin Unc took me to the chippy and bought me a bag of chips. For some strange reason each chip felt like the size of a cucumber as I struggled to swallow. We returned to the ticket offices and waited for further news. The next bulletin was similar to the first – more would be known in the next twenty-four hours and when relatives had been informed. 'Come on, we're going home,' Unc said. As we were leaving I noticed a group of people with sleeping bags and candles. They were actually going to stay all night! The weather was so cold; they were true reds.

But on that particular Saturday, as sporting venues around the country stood in silence, 'Worried Turkey' received a message from his friend Trevor, telling him that his uncle wanted to see him at his grandmother's. Thinking that there was more bad news, he rushed over to be greeted by the words, 'Come on, we're going out. We're treating today like a matchday, we're going to Old Trafford.'

> We went through the same matchday routine – down to the pub, but in all honesty the atmosphere in there was a lot quieter. There was no joking and little drinking. As the weather was so cold, I was allowed inside the pub on the proviso I sat in the corner near the coat stand and stayed quiet.
>
> So the routine began, but again no pushing and shoving on the way to the station. It was just hands in pockets, heads down and putting one foot in front of the other. On the train the talk got around to the air crash and it was only then I realised who had died and who we wouldn't see again: Roger Byrne, Mark Jones, Eddie Colman, Tommy Taylor, Liam Whelan; David Pegg and Geoff Bent.
>
> We got off the train at Warwick Road and started that long walk. Normally, the walk is done in no time, but not today. The place was eerie, there were so many people, but you could hear a pin drop. A sheer silence. No vendors shouting the price, no little chants, nobody shouting across the street to people that they recognized from where they stood in the ground. There was nothing.

We arrived at the ground and people were walking around in a daze. Many wanting to pay their respects, men took off their flat caps and trilbys, said a few words and then returned home. It was then that I realised if United meant so much to me, who had only started to attend games – the older fans had lost everything.

We did a lap of the ground and as we neared the players' entrance the severity of the air crash hit home. No longer would I see those players again; how I wish I'd got their autographs when I had the opportunity. What this team could have achieved we'll never know. One thing is for sure, they would have brought an awful lot of happiness to those cheering them on, but through no fault of their own there was now only sadness.

Can you imagine what it was like going to Old Trafford as a kid, watching several players that were not a lot older than yourself, who you tried to replicate when kicking the front of your shoes, if you could afford 'em, as you kicked a tin can in the streets. Then try to feel the pain, the shock and the complete helplessness of not being able to do anything on hearing news about the smash. Words simply cannot do justice…

Another supporter who was outside the red-brick walls of Old Trafford to pay homage to his fallen heroes was Bill Simpson, who had not missed a home game since 1919 and had pedalled his old red-framed bicycle from his home in Cartwright Road, 2 miles away. With the League championship flag flying at half-mast high above him, the old-timer, in his battered cap and scarf, when asked why he was there, said simply, 'I come rain or snow. I just had to come. It draws you when you've been coming here so long. It's part of my life, is Saturday at Old Trafford.'

For many, however, Saturdays would never be the same, even if they were in their favourite spot on the terracing at Old Trafford, but it was something that they would just have to get used to, along with the sight of unfamiliar players running from the mouth of the tunnel wearing the red and white of United.

There were, of course, not just the remaining Football League fixtures to fulfil, but also a fifth-round FA Cup tie against Sheffield Wednesday on the not-too-distant horizon. In the aftermath of the crash, the Football Association, like their League counterparts, did not hold any emergency meetings, but a spokesman told the press that they would 'wait a day or two to assess the situation, as at the moment, it was difficult to contemplate Manchester United fielding a team'.

Mr Eric Taylor, the Sheffield Wednesday secretary-manager, was as uncertain as anyone: 'We do not know what will happen to our cup tie with Manchester United, but we shall gladly fall in with any suggestions the FA might make concerning the postponement of the game,' he said. 'But whatever happens there will be no heart for the match. We knew all the people on the plane. They were our friends. It is like losing members of your own family.'

United, however, had to address their future and it had to be done sooner rather than later. But it was a future of great uncertainty and one which caused many sleepless nights for those left in charge, although they quickly found out that many of their rivals were more than happy to offer whatever help they could.

One early offer of help arrived through the Old Trafford letterbox from Blackpool, with the Bloomfield Road club writing, 'If there is anything we can do to help you regarding the temporary transfer of players or in any way whatsoever to assist you in overcoming this sad loss we will be only too willing to do so.' This quickly raised the question of whether United would have to borrow players in order to fulfil their League and Cup programme, and whether the authorities would permit this, while some of the media had began to speculate as to what the first post-Munich United line-up would look like.

In the *Daily Express* of Saturday 8 February, Terence Elliott was confident that had United been forced to play their League fixture against Wolves, then no matter what sort of team they were forced to field, the new-look United would have put up a show that Matt Busby would have been proud of. Elliott also felt that United would fulfil their FA Cup tie against Sheffield Wednesday the following Saturday, and suggested that the following eleven players could pull on the red shirts: Harry Gregg (or David Gaskell), Peter Jones, Ian Greaves, Freddie Goodwin, Ron Cope, Wilf McGuinness, Tommy Spratt, Colin Webster, Alec Dawson, Mark Pearson and Jimmy Elms.

Of that XI, Jones, with one First Division appearance under his belt and Spratt, an England schoolboy trialist, had appeared in the 'A' team's last fixture on 1 February, a 2-1 defeat against Preston North End, while England Youth internatonal Elms, that same afternoon, was turning out for the 'B' XI. The remainder, with the exception of youth-team player Mark Pearson, were reserve-team players.

Terence Elliott's optimism was certainly not shared by someone much closer to the dilemma facing United, as Jimmy Murphy, while visiting the injured in Germany, admitted that he considered the club's plight as 'worse even as I thought'. He did, however, feel confident that the club would rise again, as he voiced his thoughts and concerns with a reporter from the *People* newspaper.

'The Red Devils will rise again,' Murphy was quick to emphasise. 'It took Matt Busby, Bert Whalley and myself twelve years to produce the 1958 Red Devils. It was long, tiring hard work, but we succeeded. We reached a perfect system. We had the best set up in football.'

Having just visited Matt Busby, he talked of the tearful reunion, during which time the slowly improving manager told his assistant, 'It's all in your hands now. Look after the lads. Go to it and don't worry.' Busby at this point was completely unaware as to the extent of the disaster and that most of 'his boys' were dead.

'Just sketching through the players we have left, it is obvious we shall need more to help us fulfil the commitments this season. But where are the Manchester United type players?' The deflated assistant manager continued: 'As soon as I return to Manchester I shall confer with our chairman, Harold Hardman, and directors to decide our future action. At the moment I'm so confused, so tired, so sad, I can't think clearly.

'What of the future? It will be a long, hard struggle. But the game must go on in tribute to all members of our staff who have left us and who did their job so nobly and so proudly.'

Before leaving Germany and heading back to Britain to begin the rebuilding, he added, 'If the FA Cup tie against Sheffield Wednesday is played on Saturday, I still haven't the faintest idea what our team will be. At this moment, I would say that only Harry Gregg has a real chance of appearing. He and Billy Foulkes have been examined by a German specialist, and we shall have a club doctor go over them again.'

As Jimmy Murphy prepared to travel back to England with Harry Gregg and Bill Foulkes, two players who were undoubtedly going to form the backbone of the new-look team and play a major part in re-establishing United as a force in football, speculation was already appearing in the media as to who might be reinforcing those depleted ranks.

Former United favourite Charlie Mitten, a member of Busby's 1948 FA Cup-winning side, and now manager of Mansfield, hinted that although Portsmouth were showing an interest in his Irish winger Sammy Chapman, himself a former United player, if his old club came along with an offer then they would consider it, even though they didn't really want to let the player go.

Another ex-United favourite and a former teammate of Mitten's, Grimsby Town manager Allenby Chilton, was even quicker off the mark, offering United any player on his club's books. Two of these were certainly very well-known to Murphy, as they, like their manager, were more than familiar with Trafford Park and its environs. They were half-back Jeff Whitefoot and forward Johnny Scott.

But before Murphy could contemplate any 'loan' signings, he would first have to navigate the FA red tape, as their permission would have to be granted before any short-time signings were made. Relations between the club and its overlords were not exactly cordial, but at this particular moment, all differences had to be put to one side.

On the afternoon of Monday 10 February, chairman Harold Hardman, deciding that there was little point in delaying the inevitable, called what must have been one of the most difficult board meetings in the club's history, stating, 'We must try and tackle a hundred and one tasks with very little chance of completing any of them at the moment.' It was certainly a difficult time for the chairman, who had lost one director prior to the League match at Highbury against Arsenal, when Mr George Whittaker had died on the morning of the game. But along with acting secretary, the inexperienced but enthusiastic Mr Les Olive, Mr W. H. Petherbridge, Mr Louis Edwards and the pyjama-, dressing-gown- and overcoat-clad Mr Alan

Gibson, who was suffering from a fractured ankle and who was brought to the ground by a neighbour, saw that the first post-Munich board meeting took place.

Louis Edwards had only been opted on to the board less than forty-eight hours previously and at the start of the meeting was welcomed by his fellow directors, replying that he was honoured to become a director of such a great club and that his services were at their disposal at anytime. The chairman's burden was eased slightly, as he commented on the wonderful way that everyone had rallied round with offers of help: 'Every club in Lancashire and many more outside have offered us loan players and we are deeply grateful, but if in fact we decide to accept their offers, we must first of all see what they have available and also if those players will meet our requirements.

'The FA have been very good and I am sure they will co-operate in every way possible, but quite honestly I just don't know what will happen about next Saturday. I have no doubt at all that we could field a fairly strong side, but it must be remembered that all our young players are still terribly shocked and as they will want to attend the funerals, there will be very little training done this week.

'It is also too early to say what we shall do about the European Cup, but here again my first reaction is we will carry on to the end even if we are heavily defeated. We are not after honour and glory nor plaudits. We just want to fulfil our commitments as best we can.'

During the three-and-a-half-hour meeting, Mr Hardman informed his fellow directors that on the advice of the Football Association, he had sent a letter requesting the postponement of the Sheffield Wednesday cup tie, suggesting Wednesday 19 February as a suitable date. Sheffield Wednesday had signified their agreement to the new date and during the meeting a telephone call was received from the Football Association, giving the sanction to go ahead with this. The scheduled First Division match, away to Aston Villa, due to be played on the 19th, would now be postponed and fitted in later in the season.

There was never really any doubt as to the outcome relating to the request for a postponement, as Sir Stanley Rous, the secretary of the Football Association, had been very supportive of Matt Busby when he made it known that United were going to enter the European Cup in 1956, urging him to take part as it would be good for the game. He was therefore obviously going to do all in his power to help the club when they most needed it.

It had also been decided to approach the FA Challenge Cup Committee to see if it would be possible for two of the qualification rules for the competition could be changed. The two questions raised were:

1. Would newly signed players, who had not been with the club for fourteen days, as the rule demands, be eligible for the cup?
2. Could the club sign and play a player who had already appeared in the cup for another club?

When questioned about the above, Mr David Wiseman, the chairman of the Committee, confirmed that the FA would grant a postponement of the tie against Sheffield Wednesday from Saturday to the following Wednesday, but that he was not in a position to say whether or not either of the other two points would be given the green light. Other points discussed at the board meeting were the sale of tickets for the cup tie, when it was agreed to suspend the programme token scheme and place all remaining tickets on open sale as from Sunday 16 February. Relating to the crash, it was resolved that temporary relief grants equal to their average wage should be paid to the next of kin of those killed at Munich until further notice. The question of insurance was also discussed, but this was held over until the next meeting.

On the morning of that first post-Munich board meeting, the cog-wheels of Manchester United had slowly began turning once again. Under the guidance of assistant trainer Bill Inglis, who decided not to damage the Old Trafford pitch, which was soft from heavy overnight rain, and watched by a handful of stadium workers, female canteen assistants and former United full-back John Aston, a group of twenty-two players left the ground and proceeded up Warwick Road, turning left into Chester Road and making their way to the White City Stadium, a couple of hundred yards further on.

Having limbered up around the greyhound track, the youngsters, who made up what was in effect the United Second and Third XIs, were split into two teams. With discarded maroon tracksuit tops for goal posts they were told by Inglis, who acted as referee, 'Remember, you are United players. This is just a practice game, but any one of you could be playing in the cup. I would also like you to remember what 'The Boss' and Mr Murphy have always told you: "Keep on playing football all the time."'

The thirty-minutes-each-way practice match was certainly a lively affair, with the two teams – one clad in green bibs, the other in white – lining up as follows: Gaskell, Greaves, Peter Jones, Goodwin, Cope, Bratt, Webster, Harrop, Dawson, Pearson and Hunter. Spiers, Smith, Shiels, English, Holland, Carolan, Stiles, Giles, Mooney, Brennan and Elms. With first-team places certainly up for grabs, the United youngsters and indeed some who already had First Division experience, treated the hour-long kick about as if it was a cup final, a game to be won at all costs. At times, it was not for the faint hearted, Inglis having on more than one occasion to shout 'steady on lads', with crunching tackles leaving bodies prostrate on the wet turf and one or two players limping slightly as they made their way back along Chester Road for a well-earned shower at the silent Old Trafford.

For one youngster, with the possibility of a first-team place dangling in front of him, his dreams were to be cruelly shattered by a knee injury, which would, at a later date, finish his football dreams altogether. Jimmy Shiels had crossed the Irish Sea to Manchester having played for Waterside Boys Club in Derry, and was earmarked as a successor to Roger Byrne's left-back position. Looking back, he recalled how, as a member of the first-team squad, he would train with the likes of Roger, Duncan Edwards and Tommy Taylor at Old Trafford, living on the other side of the cricket ground from Duncan and often catching the same bus as half the team for a night out in Manchester: 'We all used to go to the dogs at Salford on a Tuesday night. I was on £8 a week and felt I was a millionaire.' But there were also bad times, as he spoke of the afternoon of the crash. 'We were sitting in the digs – me, Joe Carolan and Jackie Mooney – resting ourselves after coming back from training. Joe and Jackie were half asleep in their chairs and I thought I heard something on the radio about Manchester United and a crash.

'I asked the boys and they didn't respond, so I presumed I'd misheard. But a few minutes later the announcer came back on with the same message and it was though the room started shaking.

'I tried to take in what I'd just heard. I roused the lads up. "Quick, quick, the United plane has gone down in Munich," I said. Within minutes we were scurrying up to Old Trafford. I think we were one of the first groups to arrive but before long droves and droves of people were coming from all corners with looks of disbelief on their faces.

'None of us wanted to train or play again,' added Jimmy. 'And to be fair, the club was very decent to us at that stage.'

For many, the past few days had been spent in little more than a daze, unable to believe what had taken place, but on the evening of Monday 10 February, the reality of it all certainly hit home, with the arrival back in Manchester of the bodies of those who had died on the slush-covered Munich runway.

The BEA Viscount freighter from Munich was expected at Manchester's Ringway airport at around 9.20 p.m., but was seventy-five minutes late due to a delay in London, where four of the coffins – those of David Pegg, Liam Whelan, the dead air steward and the Yugoslav passenger – were taken off.

On a clear, starlit night at the unusually quiet airport, where the 1955/56 League championship flag flew at half-mast above the terminal building, fifty-eight wreaths of red carnations and white tulips were carried out to the waiting hearses, as the lord mayor of Manchester, Alderman Leslie Lever, United chairman Mr Harold Hardman and directors Mr William Petherbridge and Mr Louis Edwards stood, heads bowed, at the foot of the plane's gangway.

Slowly, one by one, the coffins, covered in a mass of red and yellow carnations, roses, white lilies, and lilac and blue irises, were carried from the hold of the plane and placed in the seventeen hearses.

An hour later at 11.18 p.m., when the last door was finally closed, ten of the coffins headed for Old Trafford, accompanied by a police car and motorcycle, where they would lie for the night in the gymnasium. The others would drive off in the opposite direction for private destinations.

Despite the lateness of the hour, thousands packed the 12-mile route between the airport and Old Trafford, with the cortège going via Ringway Road, Shadow Moss Road, Cornishway, Portway, Rudd Park Road, Brownlow Road Brownley Road, Altrincham Road, Princess Parkway, Almouth Road, Princess Road, Mauldeth Road West, Barlow Moor Road, Manchester Road and Seymour Grove, with a police estimate putting the figure at near to a quarter of a million people.

As the doleful procession weaved its way through the chosen route, along the usually deserted streets, men and women knelt clasping their rosary beads, while all transport heading in the opposite direction came to a halt. Double-decker buses on their late-night journeys emptied their passengers as the cortège passed by. All along the route, people left their homes, despite the rain that now fell, or watched from upstairs windows. Others climbed vantage points such as walls or even telegraph poles in order to obtain a better view. Many stood stiffly to attention, even more with tears unashamedly running down their cheeks.

As a nearby clock chimed midnight, ten of the hearses slowly turned onto the Old Trafford forecourt, the others having drifted away from the procession at Trafford Bar, before moving towards the large wooden doors of the main entrance, with a slow-moving crowd closing in behind.

One by one, the coffins of Walter Crickmer, Tom Curry, Bert Whalley, Roger Byrne, Tommy Taylor, Geoff Bent, Eddie Colman, Mark Jones, Alf Clarke and Tom Jackson were removed from the hearses and carried into the club gymnasium, where they were placed on tables draped with black cloth. Along the wall bars lay numerous wreaths and other floral tributes.

Later that morning, even before dawn had broken over the industrial sprawl of Trafford Park, a steady stream of workers and lorry drivers made a slight detour to the main entrance of the ground, where they stood silently for a few minutes, heads bowed, deep in thought, remembering the players they worshipped, lying inside behind the large wooden doors. They were joined by schoolchildren and housewives and throughout the day, there was seldom a minute that there was not someone standing, gazing blankly at the wall of the stadium and at the numerous wreaths placed against it. The United players and staff also made their way to the stadium to pay their respects, filing into the gymnasium, where they stood in silence for a few minutes, as the morning light filtered through the small windows, casting eerie shadows around the room which, for once, was not filled with the usual laughter of the players as they trained.

Around 11.15, a hearse pulled up outside the double wooden doors and the coffin of Eddie Colman was removed and taken the short journey to the home of his parents on the Ordsall estate. Shortly afterwards, Tommy Taylor's was also removed, with the others following suit during the course of the day.

As if Jimmy Murphy, having returned from Munich along with Harry Gregg and Bill Foulkes and having to force his way through a surging crowd at London's Liverpool Street station before travelling north, did not have enough on his plate, he was suddenly hit with the news that Wilf McGuinness might be out for the rest of the season, as he was due to go into hospital for a cartilage operation after his knee failed to respond to treatment. McGuinness was one of the players that Murphy was depending upon, as he did have a smattering of first-team experience.

Also waiting for Murphy upon his return was a proposal that must have stopped him in his tracks and made him consider his options very seriously, as it was not every day that you were offered the services of three top-class international players. Ferenc Puskas, Zoltan Czibor and Sandor Kocsis, three members of the famous Hungarian team who had humiliated England 6-3 at Wembley in November 1953, made contact with United from Vienna through a third party, offering their services. Such quality players seldom became readily available and they would have undoubtedly been a tremendous asset to United. However, there were immediate complications to the possibility of any transfer taking place, as all three players were under a FIFA ban due to their refusal to return to their native Hungary after the 1956 uprising in their homeland.

As it was, the possibility of the three Hungarians moving to England failed to materialise, but United's immediate problems were eased slightly when the Football Association got back in touch to say that the fourteen-day qualification ruling, which affected newly signed players, would be waived, and any players signed who had already played in the FA Cup, might be allowed to play for the club, even if signed less than twenty-four hours prior to the match.

The signing and playing of the already cup-tied players, was not completely cut and dried, as each case, if any did arise, would be decided on its individual merit, with United also having to contact the FA immediately before they contemplated signing anyone. It was, however, considered highly unlikely that any such requests would be turned down. Had Jimmy Murphy been on an hourly rate of pay with United, then he would have been taking home a bulging wage packet as his Old Trafford office became a home from home, often burning the midnight oil. But did he ever spend the night there, working away into the small hours of the morning? 'Not to my knowledge,' said his son Jimmy Jnr. 'Although he was obviously away from home quite a lot.'

Murphy's job had always been a seven-days-a-week thing, with no regular hours. Little had changed except for those hours now being somewhat longer. Only when the football season came to a close did the Welshman find time for relaxation, often being found entering local tennis competitions in Whalley Range. On occasions, he would take his wife Winnie to the local cinema, but readily admitted that he found it difficult to relax and couldn't wait for the film to finish. Playing cards bored him, while a book might hold his attention for slightly longer. It was basically football or nothing.

But what of the Puskas thing? 'Oh yes, dad definitely wanted Puskas. Not just as a top player, but also as the old head for the youngsters. However, the maximum wage could not compete with the riches of Real Madrid.'

Training was still not back to any real regularity, as there were funerals to attend, with the players told to attend whichever ones they wished. Wednesday 12 February saw those of Liam Whelan (at Christ the King church, Carba, Dublin), Roger Byrne (at St Michael's church, Flixton) and David Pegg (at St George's church, Highfield, Doncaster). But before rushing off to the latter, Mr Harold Hardman, Mr William Petherbridge, Mr Louis Edwards, Les Olive and Jimmy Murphy attended a very brief emergency board meeting at the business offices of the United chairman.

An official statement released following the meeting read, 'Mr Jimmy Murphy, assistant manager, has been authorised to make enquiries regarding certain players.' The United chairman later expanded on the brief, two-line statement, saying:

We haven't yet come to firm decisions about everything, for the simple reason that there are so many problems to consider when one is planning to counter the many blows the club has suffered.

But we are determined to build again as quickly as possible and while giving our youngsters every chance of making good, we shall have to buy.

This does not mean that any of our up-and-coming boys will find their chances limited at all. It is because we have to insure against injuries in the first place. Just imagine if, say, three or four of our present players were hurt and unable to turn out, it could mean we would not be able to field two complete teams.

That is the point we have to bear in mind very closely. So that we shall not fail in our fixture commitments other players must be brought to the club.

That being so, it is vitally necessary that we don't just sign players for the sake of signing them and that we get the right type to fit into our plans. They must be experienced, but young.

Of course, there are many snags in effecting transfers. Generally, it is difficult to sign players without fairly lengthy negotiations.

Mr Murphy will now look into the matter of transfers, but you can't force clubs to part, and often the ones you want are just the ones you can't get.

So the position is that we shall pick a team from our present playing staff for next Wednesday's cup tie and see how we go. But we don't intend borrowing players, even though we recognise that offers to lend have been made in kindliest terms.

All new players introduced to Old Trafford will come here on a permanent basis, fitting into the general scheme of rebuilding.

The big question on everyone's lips now was who would be the main targets? There was money available, with the club bank balance showing £34,250.5/5*d* in its current account and £50,000 in its deposit account, but where would Jimmy Murphy turn his attention and how much could he pull from the club coffers?

The media was soon rife with speculation as to who would be making their way to Old Trafford. Early names thrown into the spotlight were Laurie Hughes of Liverpool, a strong-tackling centre-half who had won a League championship medal in 1947, an FA Cup runners-up medal in 1950, three full England caps and one England 'B' cap. He hadn't played a first-team game since September the previous year, but his experience would have been beneficial.

Jim Iley of Tottenham was another who was mentioned, as was former United player Jeff Whitefoot, now with Grimsby Town. While United had made it known that they were concentrating on only permanent signings, Jimmy Murphy did show a hint of interest when it was revealed that Grimsby were willing to let United borrow any of their players. The recently sold £8,000 wing-half would certainly make made an ideal replacement for the injured Wilf McGuinness.

One name that was prominent in more than one of the daily newspapers was Ernie Taylor of Blackpool. His teammate, Jackie Mudie, was another name being bandied about, but it was the diminutive, transfer-listed Taylor whose name was suddenly thrust to the fore.

Sunderland-born Taylor had made his name with Newcastle, winning an FA Cup winners' medal in 1951, before joining Blackpool that same year in a £25,000 deal. In a 217-game career on the Lancashire Riviera, he went on to win a second FA Cup medal in the 'Matthews Final' of 1953. Unsettled at Bloomfield Road for some time, the 5'4" inside-forward was a highly respected player, and despite being thirty-three years of age, he was still considered to have a number of seasons left in the top flight and had indicated that he did not want to move too far from his Lancashire home.

It was, however, not just the United first team that required rebuilding, but also the junior sides, as a number of youngsters in the 'A' and 'B' teams, would suddenly find themselves catapulted into a higher level of football. To counter this, the club contacted the Manchester & District Federation of Boys Clubs, asking all the secretaries to send names of any promising young players to Mr James Buckley, the secretary of the Federation, who would in turn pass them on to United.

The Federation secretary said, 'The boys whose names I am given will go to the United training ground at the Cliff on Saturday and next week for trial matches.

'The boys must be outstanding players. If United officials think any lad will make the grade he will be signed by the club for the rest of the season.

'Some members of our Federation have played for the England boys' team and we hope that these will offer their services.

'The Federation have a match against the Durham Federation on Saturday, but any boy in the team who might be of more use to United will be asked to go along and play at the Cliff instead. We will fill the gaps in our team with reserves.'

It would certainly not be the first time that United had been associated with the Federation, as Roger Byrne, Eddie Colman and Albert Scanlon were all former members.

But it was around the first team that all the attention centred, with the move for Ernie Taylor now more than newspaper talk, as Jimmy Murphy, having attended the funerals of Tommy Taylor and Bert Whalley, began moves to attempt to bring the Blackpool man to Old Trafford. Suddenly, however, the transfer, which seemed clean cut, developed a slight twist, as Sunderland came into the picture, Taylor's hometown club. It was an approach that Taylor could certainly not ignore, and as the Sunderland chairman had made Blackpool a definite offer, not knowing that United were poised to move, the player agreed to speak to them. He would, however, speak to Jimmy Murphy twenty-four hours previously.

'We don't want to cut across United in their grievous situation,' said Col J. Turnbull, the Sunderland chairman. 'But in fairness to ourselves I must say we discussed Taylor several weeks ago and we have been in contact with Blackpool more than once recently with reference to the price.' Vice-chairman Mr Sidney Collins added that his club knew nothing of United's interest in Taylor and indeed, Blackpool never mentioned that they had received any other offers, or had anyone else interested in their player.

Another of Jimmy Murphy's transfer targets looked to be a non-starter, with twenty-two-year-old Welsh international Mel Charles of Swansea Town reportedly uninterested in leaving the club. Charles, a quality half-back or inside-forward, would have been a tremendous capture, due to his ability to play in numerous positions, but a Swansea official told the press, 'Mel has not asked to leave the club. On the contrary he wants to stay in Swansea. Naturally we sympathise with United in their trouble but we are fighting a relegation battle.'

The media spotlight on the club had obviously been quite intense, but by now had eased off slightly following the funerals of Eddie Colman, Mark Jones and Walter Crickmer on 13 February. The club, however, were still very much in the spotlight; the daily news bulletins regarding the condition of Duncan Edwards and Matt Busby were read by all, with the big United left-half fighting for his life one day, having taken a turn for the worse, but suddenly showing signs of improvement twenty-four hours later. His physique and undoubted determination played a major part in his fight for survival.

Busby, on the other hand, showed a steady improvement and was moved from the emergency ward to a private suite, but was still under constant observation; as was Johnny Berry, who like Edwards, was considered to be in a 'most critical' condition.

Back in Manchester, chairman Harold Hardman made an appearance on the BBC *Sportsview* programme and in front of the cameras the United chairman told those watching that he would be very surprised if any of the injured players would be playing by the end of the season. However, he did think that the team would again reach similar heights to where it had been before the crash. He also added, 'We shall keep in the FA Cup and League. About the European Cup, everything seems to depend on whom we are drawn against in the next round. If the game involves long air travel, because of our present mental outlook of ourselves and our players, we do not feel we could possibly make the journey by air.'

Seven days had passed since the drama of Munich had unfolded. Seven days that for many had seemed like months. One day blended into the next with time meaning nothing. For many, there was never a moment's rest, and had the likes of stand-in manager Jimmy Murphy and acting secretary Les Olive been on hourly rates, then the Old Trafford wage bill would have gone through the roof.

There were moments, like back in Munich, when Harry Gregg found the genial Welshman sobbing on the stairs of the hospital, but there was so much for the former West Bromwich Albion half-back to attend to that there was seldom time to sit down and think about what had happened or indeed the enormity of the task that he had suddenly found himself encumbered with.

A smile did appear across his hardened features just after 6 p.m. on the evening of 13 February, when he made his first signing for the club, beating Sunderland for the signature of Blackpool's Ernie Taylor. The inside-forward playmaker, who took a size four in boots, reduced the United bank balance by around £8,000. With Sunderland also in the hunt, the transfer was never going to be straightforward, or without its problems. Indeed, Murphy would have had his doubts as to whether or not it would actually happen when he was informed by the Blackpool officials that his target could not be found anywhere in the seaside resort. Fears would have immediately set in that Taylor was at that moment on his way to the north-east.

Eventually the illusive playmaker was found and informed that Jimmy Murphy wanted to see him in Manchester that night. With little or no hesitation, off he went; his thoughts on little more than what the remainder of the evening would have in store.

Arriving at Old Trafford on a pouring-wet Mancunian night, Taylor made his way to Murphy's office inside the dimly lit stadium, to listen to what the United man had to say, and was immediately sold to the cause. Murphy had secured his first signing. Things were at last beginning to look up, as earlier that same day goalkeeper Harry Gregg and defender Bill Foulkes had trained for the first time.

Stepping from the warmth of Jimmy Murphy's office and back into the cold, dismal night, Taylor was met by the waiting press, alerted as to the unfolding events.

The following morning news of United's first post-Munich signing was blazoned across the back and front pages: 'United sign No. 1 – Ernie Taylor', proclaimed the *Daily Express*, while the *Daily Herald*'s headline read, 'Ernie Taylor signs for United – Murphy Steps in to Pip Sunderland'. The back page of the *News Chronicle* declared 'Capture No. 1 A £7,000 Bargain.'

United's newest recruit's story was also there for everyone to read: 'I met some grand people in Manchester last night. It is nice to know there are so many fine people like the United chairman Mr Harold Hardman and his fellow directors left in the game.

'I have never doubted Manchester United's courage would help them rise again. I am more certain than ever about it after my experience last night.

'I feel a proud man. In fact, when I walked into the Manchester United office and saw Mr Murphy and other members of the staff, then the directors, I felt a surge of confidence.

'This is a challenge I gladly accept, a challenge I shall meet with everything I have. And if I can only help in some way to put this great club back where they belong I shall be satisfied.

'I knew many of the boys in the crash ... and the first who springs to mind naturally enough perhaps because he has been my opponent so often, is Duncan Edwards. I have had my good days against him ... and he has had his good days against me. What a wonderful player!

'And thinking of Duncan makes me wish I were only a few years younger. For he exuded the spirit of youth if ever a player did.

'Most players would feel honoured to play for United. I have always admired them and naturally, if I were six or seven years younger I would be even happier. But experience and youth do not always come together in the one player. Combined on the playing field they can work wonders.

'On Saturday morning I shall met the boys. I am sure I shall like them. I hope they will like me.

'Lots of people may be surprised that I have not held on until I had a chance to go back to the north-east. It seemed at one time this week that this might happen. But I sat down to think things over. I thought about United's great traditions. I thought too, about the fine journalist friends from Manchester whom I knew so well. And my mind was quickly made up.

'I said to myself, "Ernie. It must be Manchester United. Let's see what can be done. I was brought up in the north-east. I was born there. Surely if they wanted me so badly they should have kept me there."

'To the fans I say: "I will do my very best." To the critics: "We cannot be good all the time. If I am on the receiving end. I can take it. Fair enough?"'

Of his new recruit, Jimmy Murphy said, 'I saw Ernie play only once ... when his side beat us. He was magnificent. That memory was quite enough to make up my mind.'

Taylor's signing for United was a bitter blow to Sunderland, who at one point had thought that they had a clear run for the player, with nothing better to do than drive down the 'Golden Mile' and sign their target. 'Perhaps public sentiment has had something to do with the way things have turned out,' said Sunderland manager Alan Brown, disappointed at missing out on his prime target. 'But that's how it goes.'

With the signing of Ernie Taylor wrapped up, Jimmy Murphy began to cast his net elsewhere, Cliff Jones, the Swansea and Wales right-winger, having been one of the names cropping up with much regularity. The Welsh connection between the manager and potential recruit was certainly a strong drawing-point and the possibility of a deal taking place took a sudden twist as the winger stalled on a move to Tottenham Hotspur. Twenty-four hours previously Swansea chairman Mr Philip Holden had returned from London stating 'the deal is wrapped up', but a delay in the winger making the move hinted that a late move by United had forced Jones into a rethink.

However, like his Swansea teammate Mel Charles, Jones decided against moving north, and said that the reason behind the delay in signing was down to wanting a last-minute chat with his wife before putting pen to paper, and as far as he was concerned, there was no other club that he had considered signing for.

The fee for Cliff Jones, and indeed for Mel Charles as well, would have been around £35,000. A considerable sum, but was it too much for one player at this time and would Jimmy Murphy be better spending the same amount on two or three players who might be more beneficial to the club in the long run?

With the FA Cup tie against Sheffield Wednesday drawing closer, training sessions were becoming slightly more intense, with the White City Stadium continuing to be used as a venue and the players falling under the watchful eye of Bill Inglis, who was now in sole charge of the fitness regime. As United's First Division opponents headed off for their scheduled First Division fixtures, or fifth-round FA Cup tie, the morning of Saturday 15 February found United's depleted squad head along Chester Road for a twenty-minutes-each-way practice match.

Not content to simply watch from the sidelines, Jimmy Murphy decided to don his boots and see at close quarters how the youngsters were shaping up, how Ernie Taylor fitted in to his new surroundings, and more to the point, how crash survivors Harry Gregg and Bill Foulkes were adapting to playing again.

With the likes of David Gaskell, Foulkes, Mark Pearson, Freddie Goodwin and Ernie Taylor on one side and Gregg, Colin Webster and Alex Dawson on the other, it was a combative forty minutes. But it was the fearless Harry Gregg who caught the eye, with a number of notable saves despite the kick about stature of the game. Freddie Goodwin, Mark Pearson and new recruit Ernie Taylor also impressed Murphy, who dashed off to a meeting with the United directors following a quick shower to discuss further transfer targets.

That same day, across the city at the club's training ground at the Cliff, the youngsters from the Manchester and District League clubs and the Federation of Youth Clubs gathered to be put through their paces, in the hope that one or two nuggets would be found in order to bolster the club's junior ranks. The latter, following United's request for help, sent nine youngsters – Arthur Sutton, John Brown, John Capper, John Barker, Charles Chadwick, Jack Dennis, Trevor Humphries, Robert Gow and Peter Harris – whom they considered as possibles for making the step up to a higher level of football. Of those named, eighteen-year-old John Barker suddenly found himself with a place in the United junior sides for the remainder of the season.

Another youngster who found himself very much involved at the club during these immediate post-Munich days was Phil Murphy, Jimmy's son. Phil had celebrated his eighteenth birthday four days after the crash, and under any other circumstances, finding himself on the books of Manchester United would have been an ideal present: 'I had played at school and with Manchester Boys alongside Nobby Lawton and also Roy Cheetham who went on to play for City,' recalled Phil. 'But I would only class myself as an average amateur footballer at the time of the crash.

'Due to the lack of staff at the club and because many of the players in the junior ranks were forced to move up a level, reinforcements were urgently required, and also because of my knowledge of local football, my father asked if I would go to the club on Saturday and Sunday mornings, as well as the odd evening and help Joe Armstrong sift through three tea chests full of letters from males of all ages who had offered their assistance in fulfilling the A and B team fixtures. The majority of those who had written to the club were mainly youngsters, although I must add that there were some ex-professionals in their thirties also offering their services.

'I also completed the somewhat surreal task of altar boy, along with Nobby Lawton and a fifteen-year-old Nobby Stiles, at several of the Manchester funerals.

'My involvement at the club did not simply involve looking for possible recruits, as due to the depleted ranks, I found myself playing for the B team around half a dozen times, although I was more than aware that it was simply as a stopgap and once better players were available I would go back to the local amateur ranks. To be honest, the quicker I could return to my usual haunts the better as it was not the most enjoyable of times.'

'B' team colleagues of Phil Murphy's at that time were the likes of Frank Haydock, Nobby Stiles, Jimmy Elms, Nobby Lawton, Johnny Giles and Reg Hunter, and the makeshift team of youngsters did not enjoy the best of times, suffering defeats that would do little to boost their confidence, such as 5-0 against Stockport County and 6-0 against Bolton Wanderers.

Phil Murphy played at left-half against Stockport, scoring an own goal, and right-half against Bolton, and remembered those 'B' team outings as being 'very intense and very quick'.

'I remember Jimmy Nicholson playing as a fourteen or fifteen year old, in a pair of borrowed boots two sizes too big for him. He was always so full of confidence, demanding the ball off players five or six years older than him.

'I must also add that the atmosphere around the club at this time was, as could be expected, very sombre, strained and quiet. As was training in the evenings.'

United's next signing was not one of Phil Murphy's suggestions, and although the new acquisition, which came as something of a surprise, would not make the first-team line-up, he would prove to be an excellent addition to Jimmy Murphy's Manchester United. Jack Crompton was the goalkeeper in Matt Busby's 1948 FA Cup-winning side and 1951/52 championship XI and had left United in October 1956 to join Luton Town, having played over 190 games for the club. Aged thirty-four, he was Luton's head trainer-coach, a position he had taken up some sixteen months previously and a position that he would resume upon his return to Old Trafford.

Luton chairman Mr Percy Mitchell, like countless others around the country, had approached United with offers of help, but Crompton was not someone he was exactly keen on losing; however, when Jimmy Murphy made his approach, Mitchell kept his word and gave the former United custodian the permission to leave. Crompton met Jimmy Murphy in Manchester a couple of days prior to signing and told the United man that he would rejoin the club following Luton's First Division fixture at Burnley that Saturday.

'I had been very happy at Luton,' said the former United 'keeper. 'Had things with United been otherwise, I might have hesitated about leaving. In the circumstances though, I feel I cannot do otherwise than accept United's call.'

Although veteran trainer Bill Inglis had been running the training side of the club, it was obviously a job that in the end would have proved too much for him, and he was happy to step back into the background, supporting Jack Crompton in whatever way he could.

Following the trials and practice games at the White City and the Cliff, Jimmy Murphy made his way to Burnley, not to meet up with his latest recruit, but to cast his eyes over other possible signings. Meanwhile, Les Olive and Harold Hardman travelled Manchester to watch City's game against Birmingham City, also in the hope that someone might catch their eye and that they would be available for transfer.

Jimmy Murphy's presence at Burnley's Turf Moor ground, where it was thought winger Brian Pilkington was the player under review, created back-page headlines. 'Burnley Chief Lashes Critics', proclaimed the *Daily Express*, with 'Is He Being Callous – Burnley Boss Hits at Sentimentalists' spread across the *Daily Herald*. Bob Lord, never one for mincing his words, had spoken out against those who had been critical of the other League clubs that had not rushed forward to offer players to United. The Burnley butcher dismissed such accusations as 'utter rubbish and tripe':

'I feel sure that when League clubs announced they would help Manchester United in any way possible, they never for a moment assumed Jimmy Murphy would plump for the star players of any club.

'Do United want to buy star players in order to win the League, the FA Cup, the European Cup, the Central League and the Youth Cup? If they do, why don't they ask Preston for their manager Cliff Britton and let him take Tom Finney with him under his arm, ask Manchester City for Trautmann, West Brom for Howe and Barlow, Newcastle for McMichael?

'Would Blackpool have allowed Ernie Taylor to go if he had been five or six years younger? I wonder.

'I am as sorry as anyone, but United went into this European Cup with their eyes open. They haven't been pushed into it. They have made a lot of cash out of it. They have won glamour and glory which has attracted a lot of youngsters.

'It's my belief that leading players are just what Jimmy Murphy wants. I have experienced that.

'I tell everybody now that Pilkington will not leave Burnley and give notice to every interested club to please keep off.'

Lord's comments offended many, even non-United supporters, but it was all water off a duck's back to the controversial chairman. While refusing United Pilkington, Bob Lord did say that if United should want a young player of eighteen or nineteen, they would be willingly released at a giveaway fee.

Across Manchester, many thought that the United duo at Maine Road were casting their eyes over Birmingham's Scottish left-winger Alec Govan, but it was later revealed that it was England under-23 left-half Dick Neal who was the target, with rumours rife that the £18,000 signing from Lincoln City only ten months previously was left out of the Birmingham side to save him from injury pending a move to Old Trafford.

It was the first game that Neal had missed since signing, but the reason for his omission was given as tactical. Any hopes that United had of signing the player, or his teammate Govan for that matter, were soon dashed when the Birmingham manager, Arthur Turner said, 'I cannot see how we can afford to release several players. Our League position is not by any means a strong one. We all feel sorry for United but I am sure they do not expect clubs to weaken their own position.' Messrs Olive and Hardman's afternoon was also spoilt by the City–Birmingham game being abandoned after thirty-seven minutes.

United were certainly not expecting any of their First Division rivals to sell them players they did not want to lose. Neither were they looking for any special treatment on the field of play once their fixtures resumed. Speaking to the *News of the World* in an exclusive interview, chairman Harold Hardman said, 'We have been flooded with messages of sympathy from all over the world and of course, from clubs in this country. For this we are exceedingly grateful. But we are determined to carry on in the true spirit of the game.

'That is why we do not want any of our opponents to show us particular consideration on the field, even though we shall be starting virtually from scratch.

'I have every confidence in the young players who already wear our colours and I know they are with me when I say we shall give as good as we receive. We do not want any "cissy" stuff in our future matches.'

The sympathy that the club had received in the wake of the crash was overwhelming and would in all honesty been given to any club suffering a similar fate. It is debatable however, if it would have been on the same scale of intensity, as this was during a golden age of football, when supporters thought nothing of going to watch other clubs when their personal favourites were not playing at home. United, due to their attractive style of football with their multi-talented side, pulled in more floating supporters than most, something signified within the words of the 'United Calypso': 'if they're playing in your town, you must get to that football ground, take a lesson come and see, football taught by Matt Busby'.

But the sympathy did not continue unabated, as five men and around thirty-six women were sacked by their employers for taking unauthorised time off to pay their respects to Eddie Colman, as his funeral cortège passed near to their factory. Employed by Boxmakers Ltd of Ordsall Lane, Salford, the workers, many of whom lived near to Eddie's Archie Street home and knew him personally, had asked for permission to leave the workplace for a few minutes to pay their respects, but the management refused, declining to give a reason why the request was turned down.

Around forty workers decided to disregard the management's decision and left the building to make the five-minute walk to Hulton Street, where the funeral would pass by on its way to Weaste Cemetery. Upon returning to the factory around twenty minutes later, they were told to leave the premises and return at 2.30 p.m. for their cards.

Much was made of the uncalled-for sackings, with the lord mayor, Alderman Leslie Lever, even stepping into the fray. His plea for their reinstatement certainly had some effect, as the company's production director was quick to say that if any of the sacked workers wanted their jobs back, then 'sympathetic consideration' would be given.

The cup tie against Sheffield Wednesday was now only five days away and the remaining tickets were due to go on sale on the Sunday morning at 10 a.m., but as midnight approached, James Chadwick of Coupland Street, Manchester, made his way across the Old Trafford forecourt to the door of the ticket office, where he was happy to stand until morning and await the ticket sales to begin. 'I want to make sure of seeing United's first game since the Munich tragedy,' he was to tell a newspaper journalist. By morning, he was not alone, as countless others had made their way across the city and indeed from other parts of Lancashire, desperate to get their hands on a ticket for that all important cup tie, with the queue stretching round the ground and back across the Warwick Road railway bridge.

Warwick Road itself was brought to a standstill around 10 a.m. and it took police reinforcements ten minutes to get the traffic moving again. Mounted police helped control the half-mile-long, six-deep queue, and because of the numbers, estimated at 20,000, the ticket office opened at 9 a.m., an hour earlier than planned. Although the sale of the 15,000 tickets was restricted to one per person, they were sold out within four hours, leaving many disappointed. Some youngsters did manage to evade the scrutiny of the mounted police and made several visits to the ticket office window, purchasing the much sought-after pieces of paper, which were quickly resold at double the price.

The clamour of the Sheffield Wednesday cup tie was now reaching fever pitch, and in order to prepare his players as best he could for the task ahead, and just as importantly take them away from the media spotlight, Jimmy Murphy and a squad of nineteen players left Old Trafford on the Monday afternoon prior to the game, heading for Blackpool's Norbreck Hydro Hotel, were they were to remain until the afternoon of the cup tie. The coach was strangely the same one that less than a fortnight previously had pulled up on the same spot, collecting the United party for the first leg of their ill-fated journey to Belgrade.

This time, there were a few fresh and unfamiliar faces taking their seats on the coach, with the following players heading off for the seaside resort: Ernie Taylor, David Gaskell, Jack Mooney, Tommy Spratt, Gordon Clayton, Ian Greaves, Barry Smith, Peter Jones, Freddie Goodwin, Harold Bratt, Ronnie Cope, Bobby English, Reg Holland, Colin Webster, Alex Dawson, Johnny Giles, Bob Harrop, Reg Hunter, Mark Pearson, and Seamus Brennan. A handful of ticket-hunting supporters hanging around the Old Trafford forecourt waved them on their way, wishing them luck.

Looking at that twenty-two-man squad (Bill Foulkes and Harry Gregg joined their teammates later) some of those who had watched them head off to Blackpool could have been forgiven in wondering how the club would fare, not only against Sheffield Wednesday, but in the remaining First Division fixtures that still had to be played in the weeks and months ahead. Harry Gregg, Bill Foulkes, Ernie Taylor, Colin Webster, Freddie Goodwin and Ian Greaves could all be considered experienced, while Alex Dawson, Ronnie Cope, David Gaskell, Peter Jones and Gordon Clayton could only muster a handful of appearances between them. As for the rest, they were little more than the best of the Manchester United players who were left.

Mark Pearson was a former north-east Derbyshire and England schoolboy player, and could fill any of the inside-forward positions. He had played in the FA Youth Cup-winning sides of 1955/56 and 1956/57, while also representing England at youth level in 1956/57. Despite being only 5 foot 6 inches, he was strongly built and difficult to shake off the ball. He was considered a certainty to line up against Sheffield Wednesday.

Seventeen-year-old Barry Smith was another England schoolboy international, who had recently played to youth international level. He had joined United from Spurley Hey County Secondary School in Gorton and progressed through the ranks, receiving creditable reports for his performances as full-back in the Central League side.

Another of those on the Blackpool-bound coach, who had made several Central League appearances this season, was nineteen-year-old, Stockport-born Bobby English, who had joined United straight from school and was described by an England youth-team selector as potentially the best wing-half on United's books.

Looking back to those days on the Lancashire coast, Bob recalled, 'It was somewhat amazing that Harry Gregg and Bill Foulkes actually made the trip. I think we were all in a daze, as well as still saddened by everything that had happened. But, we had to carry on regardless.

'I was only eighteen at the time and it all seemed unreal for the players who died not to be at training. I used to change next to Duncan Edwards and I was in total awe of Duncan and he is still the greatest player I have ever seen. He was the perfect soccer player – he had no faults.

'I remember playing in a youth-team game with Duncan, and Jimmy Murphy and Matt Busby told us to pass the ball around – everybody is a star. We were losing 2-1 at half-time and Jimmy and Matt told us to give the ball to Duncan – we won 3-2. Duncan scored the two goals.'

However, they weren't all home-grown youngsters who were dreaming of a place in the first team in a couple of days' time. Reg Hunter, another nineteen-year-old, was from Colwyn Bay, and had been playing for his home-town side while still a schoolboy. He signed amateur forms for United following a trial, taking up employment in a Manchester shipping office before signing professional in November 1956.

Tommy Spratt, a former north-east Northumberland county player and England schoolboy trialist; Harold Bratt, a Salford-born Lancashire schoolboy player, another who had had trials with England schools; Dublin-born and Republic of Ireland schoolboy international Johnny Giles; and Reg Holland from Sutton-in-Ashfield were all current members of the United youth team, while the names of Jack Mooney and Shay Brennan could be found in the team sheets of the United 'A' team; the former at outside-right, with the latter partnering him on the right flank.

At Blackpool, the players went through their paces on the golf course situated behind the hotel, while also enjoying the peace and tranquillity of the seaside town at this out-of-season time – walking along the almost deserted front, while also visiting the tower and its wrestling. 'One night we were there, we were introduced to the rest of the audience and had to stand up and receive a round of applause. Something that I found a little embarrassing,' recalled Reg Hunter. It also kept them well away from Old Trafford and the continual mourning in Manchester.

One interesting spectator at those somewhat impromptu training sessions was a novice *Manchester Evening News* reporter by the name of David Meek, who had been drafted into the paper's sports department, filling the desk left vacant following the death of Tom Jackson.

In his first of column, of what must have amounted to thousands, he updated the news-devouring public back in Manchester that the twenty-two players, dressed in dark maroon tracksuits, had taken part in 'a brisk six-a-side game' and exercises. The likes of Jackie Mooney, an Irish youth international, Shay Brennan and Peter Jones had all taken part, eagerly watched by a couple of dozen children.

Although partly away from the glare of the media spotlight, which had shone as brightly as the Blackpool illuminations on the club since the disaster, there was still much speculation on the back pages as regards to further signings. Birmingham City's Alex Govan, whose name had been mentioned previously, once again reappeared on the back pages, and it was thought that Jimmy Murphy had spoken to Birmingham's manager Arthur Turner about the player. Nearer to home, the Manchester City duo of Paddy Fagan and John McTavish were considered likely additions to the payroll 'before the week is out'. Had Alex Govan had been aware of United's interest at that time, or indeed, was there actually any grain of truth in the newspaper stories of the day?

Some fifty-odd years later, the Glaswegian-born Birmingham winger, who was noted for his speed and direct wing play, as well as the ability to score goals (he had netted 30 times during season 1956/57 – the only St Andrews winger to ever achieve such a feat) told me, 'I was well aware that Manchester United were looking for players to strengthen their depleted squad and were especially interested in players who were not cup-tied. A category that I certainly fell into.

'I had been a member of the Birmingham City who had lost to the "Babes" in the semi-final of the FA Cup in the previous season, and like everyone else, respected those marvellous players who had died.

'As the history books show, nothing came of the newspaper "rumours", but had Manchester United showed any hint of being interested in me, I would have walked all the way from Birmingham to Manchester to sign on the dotted line.'

According to the *Daily Herald* of Tuesday 18 February, Luton Town's Reg Pearce was another who was 'almost certain to become a Manchester United player in time for their history-making cup tie against Sheffield Wednesday at Old Trafford tomorrow night'.

The twenty-six-year-old Luton Town left-half had obviously come to the attention of the former Hatters trainer Jack Crompton, and it was the newly appointed United man with the magic sponge who was despatched to Luton to carry out talks with his former club. Crompton, having spent most of the day in talks with Luton, drove north for Blackpool, and upon his arrival immediately spoke to Jimmy Murphy, who wasted little time in contacting Luton.

'United have certainly inquired about Pearce,' said Luton chairman Percy Mitchell. 'But the player knows nothing of it yet. I have discussed it with my directors.'

Murphy's ears also perked up at the news that Bradford City's talented outside-left Martin Bakes had asked for a transfer, but confessed when asked if he had an interest in the player, 'I don't know. We have so little time and we are in a bit of fluster here. The trouble is I have to rely on other people's judgement as I am unable to see these players myself.'

No sooner had one name appeared as a possible United target than another was suddenly emblazoned across the back pages, and as the minutes continued to tick away towards that eagerly awaited cup tie, the newspapers continued to speculate as to last-minute signings.

A telephone call was made to Aston Villa's manager, Eric Houghton, enquiring about Stan Crowther, but their neighbours Birmingham City closed the shutters on the possibility of their wing-half Dick Neal moving north to Manchester. There was, however, still the possibility of the two clubs doing business regarding outside-left Alex Govan.

Two new names were also thrown into the pot, Ron Cockerill, the twenty-two-year-old Huddersfield Town half-back, and Jackie Henderson, Portsmouth's Scottish international centre-forward. The latter had refused a move to Newcastle United, but had admitted that he would have no hesitation in joining United if asked. 'You cannot refuse to go to a club like that, can you?' he said.

Cockerill's name suddenly came to the fore after a telephone call to Jimmy Murphy at the Norbreck hotel from Huddersfield manager Bill Shankly, asking if there was anything that he could do to help. It was a call that raised the stand-in manager's hopes a little, as he had taken another call earlier in the day from Aston Villa's Eric Houghton telling him that his club were not likely to consider selling Stan Crowther, as their squad was rather under-strength as it was and that they could not really let the player concerned go.

The move for Cockerill was not one that would go through before the cup tie and United were expected to speak to the player and his club once the cup tie was out of the way.

Under the watchful eyes of chief coach Joe Armstrong, assistant trainer Bill Inglis and the newly appointed trainer-coach Jack Crompton, twenty of the players spent their first day by the coast going through a three-hour limbering-up session followed by a kick about, with Jimmy Murphy again joining in. After lunch, having been joined by Bill Foulkes and Harry Gregg, some of the players went for a walk along the north shore sands, while others took advantage of the hotel's golf course.

Murphy, however, was happy the way things were going and told the press, 'The work-out is going well, but let's face it, we cannot expect miracles. We are doing our best to achieve the impossible.

'I hope Gregg and Foulkes will be fit to play but I'll know more tomorrow and I'll pick the team tomorrow (*Tuesday*) evening.'

It was thought by most that seven of the eleven places in the team picked themselves. Gregg was an automatic choice between the sticks, with Foulkes at right-back and Greaves partnering him at left-back. Goodwin would take the No. 4 shirt and Cope the No. 5. Ernie Taylor would make his debut at inside-right, with Dawson leading the line at centre-forward.

The speculation continued over the other four positions, with Pearson thought to be in the running for the other inside-forward place and English, Webster and Hunter the likely candidates to complete the starting XI. But only Jimmy Murphy and his two assistants knew for certain who would actually fill the red shirts hanging back at Old Trafford. Or did they? Reg Hunter certainly didn't expect to start: 'In all honesty, I didn't think that I would be selected to play, knowing the strength and quality of the other players who were there. For instance, Shay Brennan was in full-time training, while I was not, with this, I think a telling factor in Jimmy Murphy's eventual team selection.'

Jimmy Murphy left the Blackpool headquarters and returned to Manchester to meet with the United directors, spending four hours in deep conversation with those behind the running of the club. The main item on the meeting's agenda was the possibility of signing new players, with Murphy updating the board as to his ongoing enquiries. He revealed that Aston Villa were prepared to release their half-back Stan Crowther, and were asking for a fee of £25,000. Luton Town had also agreed to the sale of Reg Pearce for which they would want £18,000. Further negotiations would take place with both of the clubs concerned.

Other than an update on the medical reports of those still in Munich, other matters discussed had no effect on the club's actual future, and included the plans for a collection outside the ground by the unofficial supporters' club in aid of the Munich Memorial Fund prior to the Sheffield Wednesday match. Plans were also made for a new scoreboard to be built at the ground and the agreement that David Meek of the *Manchester Evening News* and Keith Dewhurst of the *Manchester Evening Chronicle* would be asked to contribute to the *United Review* in place of the late Alf Clarke and Tom Jackson.

Emerging from the Old Trafford offices just after 10 p.m., it was a more relaxed Welshman who informed the eight waiting reporters that he was 'sorry, but I've nothing to announce. I wish I could tell you more, but I am waiting for several "phone calls".' He then added jokingly, 'One word, you boys. All keep fit. I may need one or two of you tomorrow.'

Behind the smile, there was also nervousness, with the fear of failure lingering away at the back of his mind. The anxiety of the occasion was also felt by the players, with most of them trying to disguise the fact the best they could. It wasn't just the untried youngsters whose dream of running out of the Old Trafford tunnel wearing that famous red shirt was causing them much more than sleepless nights. The seasoned professionals were also finding it difficult to relax as the minutes slowly ticked away. Sitting on the cliff tops of Blackpool's north shore, overlooking the Irish Sea, veteran Ernie Taylor, back in familiar surroundings and who had played at the highest levels with both Newcastle United and Blackpool, was quick to admit how he felt as regards to the impending fixture.

'I'm honoured, but frightened,' he said. 'Scared for the first time in fifteen years of League football. 'I have never met anything like it,' he went on to say. 'I still feel something of an outsider, but the enthusiasm of these kids, their devotion to the club, is amazing.

'I know the team needs some more experience, but in three days I have found that it has got something that money will never buy. Something you feel right down inside as you play and talk and laugh with them. In the League, in cup finals, I have never wanted to be on the winning side as much.'

For another of those preparing for the all-important cup tie, there was also that same nervousness, but there were also countless other, different emotions to contend with.

Harry Gregg had been part of Manchester United for only a matter of months longer than his new teammate, but Gregg had experienced the horrors of Munich at first hand, and had much more to overcome than Ernie Taylor. With less than twenty-four hours to go before he would run out behind fellow survivor Bill Foulkes, Gregg spoke to Terence Elliott of the *Daily Express*:

Tonight we step out at Old Trafford for the cup tie with Sheffield Wednesday – the first match since Munich – and how grand it will be to have the famous turf beneath our feet once again.

Can we win? I think so. But there are far more important things on my mind at this moment than forecasting the result. This is the match of which I think I can fairly say the result isn't everything. Not by a long, long way.

Our main job tonight is to show the world that Manchester United will rise again, and we are determined with all our hearts that that ambition will be achieved.

Not only shall we have to play our hearts out. The older and more experienced players will have to set an example. That, too, we are determined to do.

I regard tonight's cup tie as a memorial to those boys we so well remember. I regard it as a match which I shall look back on and say: 'I'm glad I played.'

In fact, I regard it as the greatest and most important match of my life. And I am sure that goes too for the youngsters who will be stepping out tonight in those much-honoured red shirts.

Since my return home I have had an opportunity of getting to know these boys who now carry the Manchester United banner. And in every one of them I find the enthusiasm, pride and determination that have carried the club to such great heights.

Confidence? They have more than me! They could never have expected to have to shoulder such a tremendous responsibility so early in their careers. But take it from me they are not worried about that. Their only anxiety is to give their best.

We must regard tonight's game as a guide to the future. We shall win if we can, but it is not even necessary to discuss the outcome of this game to look into the future.

The way ahead may be studded with disappointments, but we shall have our successes too. What a wonderful thing if we can get off to a heartening start tonight. I think we will!

It's not necessary for me to say that I am ready to play the game of my life. But that isn't all. Believe me, there have been some wonderful boys with us at our Blackpool cup headquarters. Their confidence is terrific. Their skill is terrific. With experience they will be great.

And here's something. You may recall what some folk said - that we were too cheeky on the field, that we were cocky! What a mighty asset that is now.

But I think a better way of saying it is that the youngsters who go out tonight will be perky and raring to go.

So off we go. For us all I am sure a memorable occasion that will stay with us when United have again risen to the heights.

For this is the beginning of our fight-back. What greater incentive could there be. Nobody can read the future, but if enthusiasm and spirit are the necessary qualifications United will be great again.

In another interview, the burly United 'keeper admitted, 'Physically I have never felt better, but I'll know how I really feel when I go out into the lights with the boys tomorrow. I think I will be alright; there is so much to play for. There will surely never be another game like this.'

As Harry Gregg was giving his interview in Blackpool, further south in Birmingham, Stan Crowther was deliberating the biggest decision of his playing career. Should he move to Manchester United or remain with Aston Villa?

'I was asked by my manager if I was prepared to be transferred to Manchester United,' said the shy, twenty-two-year-old, England under-23 wing-half, 'but I replied that I wanted the night to think it over. I am not keen about leaving the Midlands, but any offer from Manchester United is worth thinking about.'

So, a sleepless night in Birmingham for Crowther, and yet another sleepless night for Jimmy Murphy, as he awaited a definite answer from the Villa man. He was, however, to miss out on his other target, Reg Pearce, who decided against a move to Manchester, opting instead to join Sunderland. The Wearsiders got their own back for United's capture of Taylor.

For those without tickets for the cup tie and fortunate enough to have access to a television, their hopes of catching some of the action on their screens looked to have been dashed when Football League officials expressed strong feelings against any pictures being shown on the BBC's *Sportsview* programme while the match was still in progress. What was it about Manchester United that the Football League did not like?

The programme would have been running as the match was being played and the BBC announced that they would be broadcasting a 'special report' on the game. No one was certain as to what this would actually be. Speculation varied between camera shots of the crowd or a brief glimpse of the play itself. With other games being played at the same time, it was thought that even five minutes' action from Old Trafford being shown on television would have some adverse effect on attendances.

As Blackpool Tower slowly disappeared from view in the fading afternoon light, the boyish joviality on the United team coach became slowly subdued. As the return to Manchester drew closer and closer with each passing mile, the thoughts on the task ahead and what awaited them upon their arrival at Old Trafford grew.

They were heading for a Manchester gripped in cup fever, a city, and its environs, that had awoken in the cold morning air; where everyone had a bounce in their step and a smile on their faces for the first time in a couple of weeks as they made their way to work, or to school, neither of which seemed to be a chore for once. Conversations were based around only one subject – United. It was also a Manchester where ticket touts asked £1 for their 6/6*d* (32p) tickets.

Jimmy Murphy had decided on his team, or at least ten of his eleven, as he awaited the arrival of Stan Crowther and his manager, Eric Houghton from Birmingham. The in-demand half-back had travelled to Villa Park early on the morning of the game and spoke to his manager before taking a telephone call from Old Trafford. Nothing was sorted out during the brief call, but it was agreed that the player and manager would drive to Manchester that afternoon for further talks with the United assistant-manager. Even if a deal could be struck, there was still the possibility that the FA would refuse United permission to field the player against Sheffield Wednesday a few hours later.

Of Murphy's other ten players, there was only one surprise, and that was the inclusion of twenty-year-old Seamus Brennan at outside-left. It had been thought, and even suggested by the man at the helm, that the No. 11 shirt would be worn by Reg Hunter, but following a conversation with Joe Armstrong and Bill Inglis, it was decided to play Brennan instead.

For the young Irishman, who had joined United straight from school, having been spotted by Joe Armstrong playing for St John's youth club side, it was a big step up, as he could be considered little more than an 'A' team player, with his selection coming as just a surprise to the player himself as it did to the United supporters.

'No one was more surprised than I,' confessed the youngster upon finding out that he was playing. 'I have only been out of the Forces since November and National Service has interrupted my form. However, I have been better recently and I am delighted at the chance to play for United. My dad will be delighted.'

It was only some nine hours prior to the game that Brennan actually found out that he was in Murphy's plans for the cup tie. 'At 10.30 on the morning of the game I got a call to go and see Jimmy Murphy,' he recalled. 'I thought he wanted to give me a telling off because I had been out in Blackpool the previous night for a couple of pints. I was stunned when I was told I was playing.

'The day just flashed by after that. It was all a big rush to get tickets for my dad and brother and sisters. There was no time to think about making my debut. The team was just thrown together really. We never met up with Stan Crowther, for instance.

'We went to Davyhulme Golf Club for a prematch steak and then to Old Trafford. Everyone was just lost in their own thoughts in the dressing room. There are always jokers in a football changing room but nobody was laughing or larking about.'

Stan Crowther and his manager left Birmingham at two o'clock to make the dash to Manchester by car, arriving at the city's Queens Hotel at 5 p.m., where they were met by Jimmy Murphy. As they travelled north, both clubs had been in prolonged talks and agreed on the terms of the transfer, with United also contacting the Football Association in order to obtain the necessary permission to allow the player to play that evening against Sheffield Wednesday. That was, of course, if he agreed to join United.

Sitting down face to face with Stan Crowther for the first time, Jimmy Murphy knew that he was up against the clock and so had to get straight to the point of persuading the player to leave Villa for a new career at Old Trafford. Looking back, Stan Crowther recalled the events of that afternoon, one that left him gasping for breath at the speed of how things unfolded:

When the move was first suggested, I immediately said 'no'. It wasn't as if I had anything against United. In fact, I had always admired them, particularly after their courageous fight with ten men against Villa in last year's cup final. But I've always been a Villa man at heart.

Mr Houghton told me to sleep on it and to give him my answer in the morning, but when Wednesday came, I still didn't want to leave Villa. Then I was asked if I would at least talk to Mr Murphy. How could I refuse this when such a great club had paid me the compliment of asking for my transfer?

Obviously, if I did sign, it meant that I could make soccer history by being the first footballer to play for two clubs in the cup in the same season. At that time, however, I'm afraid I wasn't thinking about football. I was so mixed up I hardly knew what I was doing.

Then, Mr Murphy told me why United wanted me. In fact, the way he put it they "needed" me. He said I could help them start the long climb back. I realised United could do a lot for me.

Gradually I began to like the idea of joining the famous Babes. Eventually Mr Murphy persuaded me to sign.

When I'd done so, I looked at the clock. It was nearly 6.30 p.m. and the match was due to start in an hour.

If things had been hectic before, now they became frantic. Within a few minutes we were out of the hotel, stepping into the car and on our way to Old Trafford with a police escort.

I'll never forget that journey. Imagine trying to cover 4 miles through a busy city along a road jammed with thousands of fans all going the same way and as anxious to get to the ground as we were.

The police driver of our escort car was magnificent. Without police help we could never have made it.

We got to the ground at 7.05 p.m. Just enough time to meet my new teammates and get changed.

At last, Jimmy Murphy could finally name his team and end the days of speculation surrounding who would play in this momentous game, one of the most important in the history of the club. His team read: Gregg, Foulkes, Greaves, Goodwin, Cope, Crowther, Webster, Taylor, Dawson, Pearson and Brennan. One of the youngsters amongst the passengers on the coach that had made its seemingly never-ending journey from Blackpool to Manchester and was disappointed not to have his name included in the starting line-up was Bob English: 'Going back to Manchester on the coach I did think I had a good chance of playing,' Bob was to recall. 'But, Jimmy Murphy had been working hard to sign Stan Crowther and he signed hours before the kick-off. I didn't think much to it at the time as I was only eighteen and I thought my chance would still come, but on reflection when Bert Whalley died so did my chances, as he was a big reason behind me signing professional forms. I just loved the man. He was such a great coach for young players. I was called up for National Service soon after Munich and when I returned United had signed a lot of players. I played in the reserves for two years and was later transferred to Southport.'

The scenes around Old Trafford were chaotic to say the least. Many had forsaken their form of transport in desperation as everything had come to a standstill on all the roads around the ground. One United supporter, George Watson, then a twenty-three-year-old from Flixton, remembered the scenes vividly: 'I worked in the industrial sprawl of Trafford Park and when the works' hooter blew at 5.30 p.m., I, like countless others, was out of the factory gates like a sprinter from the starting blocks. I must have covered the 2 miles or so to the ground in record time.

'I had arranged to meet up with a couple of mates on the stadium forecourt, but the closer I got, the more congested the pavements and roads became. When I eventually reached the ground, it became obvious that I would never find them, as cars were now bumper to bumper and there were thousands milling around.

'Many of them didn't have tickets, as I received numerous requests for one going spare from the emotional fans anxious to be inside. There were also a few ticket touts amongst the crowd offering two shilling (10p) ground tickets for thirty shillings (£1.50). Some seemed only too happy to pay the price.

'Once inside the stadium it seemed to be filled like never before. Many around me wore black ties or armbands, while others had sewn a piece of black cloth onto their scarves, beside the embroidered names of those who had died.'

Bob English, like the rest of his teammates, sat transfixed as the United team bus crawled at a snail's pace towards the floodlit Old Trafford stadium: 'I remember the coach arriving back at Old Trafford for the game with Sheffield Wednesday and it could hardly get to the ground as the crowds were enormous and there seemed more people outside the ground than what was inside. Could United win the game? I honestly don't think the players who sat around me knew what to expect. Shay Brennan was my best friend at the club at that time and our wives were friends and we both had young children. Shay had a dream game and never looked back – my story was quite the opposite.'

In the United dressing room, the minutes leading up to the kick-off provided the players with a time to reflect. For the survivors, Harry Gregg and Bill Foulkes, a glance around them must have provoked strange feelings without the likes of Roger Byrne, Eddie Colman or big Duncan involved in their prematch preparations. Their places were taken by untried youngsters barely old enough to shave, a couple of debutants and fringe first-team players.

For Bill Foulkes, the pressure was just that little bit more intense, with something of a weight upon his broad shoulders, as Jimmy Murphy had taken him to one side during a game of table tennis at their Blackpool retreat to tell him that he would be captain. The emotional ex-miner was later to say, 'It is a great honour. I shall do everything I can to carry on where Roger Byrne left off. We have a grand bunch of boys. I don't think we shall do well – I know it, because the spirit is in all of us.

'When I was a lad, I used to dream that one day I would captain a great team like United. Now my dream has come true, but I wish it hadn't.'

As the team prepared to make their way out of the dressing room, Alex Dawson, who was nervous as his colleagues, heard Jimmy Murphy's last words: 'I want you to get out there and now I've told you how to beat them. We're going to win this game for the lads. We're going to win it.'

In the Sheffield Wednesday dressing room, a few yards along the corridor, just what thoughts were running through the team's minds it would be difficult to imagine. They were preparing for a match that no one, except perhaps their own supporters, wanted them to win and one that they had actually little chance of winning.

At around 7.25, from the mouth of the tunnel below the main stand, a volley of camera flash bulbs silhouetted Bill Foulkes as he ran out in front of his fellow teammates, veering to the right towards the Warwick Road end of the ground, the section of the field where United always warmed up.

Squashed behind that goal was George Watson, who recalled, 'The programme contained eleven blanks where the United team should have been, but the printers had as much idea as anyone who Jimmy Murphy was going to pick, so we had to wait eagerly for those eleven names to be announced over the loudspeakers. I remember that Stan Crowther's got the biggest cheer.

'A minute's silence followed, and many around me cried unashamedly as they remembered those who had graced the empty pitch in front of us. That silence, however, was soon broken and amid a barrage of noise; out came the teams.

'I remember thinking that it was strange to see those unfamiliar faces in the red shirts. It was like watching a film, with actors taking on the part of someone more familiar.'

The programme did indeed have eleven blank spaces where the names of the United players should have been. 'It had to be done that way,' explained Jimmy Murphy. 'When the programme went to the printers I didn't know what the hell the team would be.' As regards to his final team selection, he said, 'Ernie Taylor was signed so that I could build a team around him. Stan Crowther was a big, strong boy and I wanted somebody in the middle of the field. The rest were square pegs in round holes.'

For the most seasoned professional within the Wednesday ranks it was difficult for them to focus on the game as it began to unfold, but it was actually United who showed the early signs of nervousness, with the visitors enjoying the best of those opening exchanges. Three times they came close to actually scoring and, undoubtedly, if any of those attempts had beaten Harry Gregg, then the outcome would have been so much different.

Centre-forward Johnson sent a long-range effort wide before Gregg saved from Cargill, but the big goalkeeper was beaten by a Wilkinson header, but was relieved to see Ronnie Cope, standing behind him, head the ball off the line.

Attacking the Warwick Road end, United slowly began to get their game together, growing in confidence, with Ernie Taylor seemingly involved in everything, causing Wednesday all sorts of problems. One minute he was sending Webster away on the right, the next he was swinging the ball to the opposite flank and into the path of the oncoming Brennan. There were also through-balls down the centre for either Dawson or Pearson to pursue. He even had time to have a shot at goal, his 25-yard effort through a crowd of players in the twenty-second minute rebounding off the post.

Play swung from end to end and even Bill Foulkes could be found pushing forward in search of that important opening goal, with a header from the United defender being punched round the post by Ryalls in the Wednesday goal.

From his corner-kick, over on the United Road side of the ground, Shay Brennan cunningly curled the ball goalwards, and as Ryalls grasped at the cold Manchester evening air, the ball dipped below the crossbar and into the vacant net. It was 7.58 p.m., Manchester United were reborn, and the capacity crowd of 59,848 greeted the breakthrough with ear-splitting noise. The noise was just as loud outside the ground as in, as those who had been unable to obtain tickets, but were simply wanting to be there, imagined and listened to the drama unfolding behind the red-brick walls.

In later years, Shay Brennan looked back at his defining moment in United's history and recalled, 'I went to take the corner and tried for an in-swinger by hitting the ball with my right foot. It swung beautifully under the glaring floodlights, wafted further towards goal by a gust of wind and curled over the 'keeper's head into the net.'

'It was a strange goal in many ways,' recalled George Watson. 'The ball seemed to hang in the air for a moment, and as the Wednesday goalkeeper jumped to grasp it, it dropped over his outstretched arms. You seemed to get the impression that the crowd behind the goal had sucked the ball into the net.

'There was silence for just a split second, before the stadium erupted. Hats and scarves flew into the air, many never to be seen by their owners again, but who cared? There were tears too, as never before could a solitary goal have meant so much to so many.'

Quixall was Wednesday's main threat, but the United defence stood firm against anything that came their way, although at times they did border on the unorthodox. A Crowther throw-in, which was intended for Harry Gregg who was coaxing and cajoling his defenders throughout the game, fell somewhat short, forcing the 'keeper to race from his area and head the ball out of play for a throw-in. As the game progressed, however, Gregg was to make three world-class saves to keep United in the game.

In front of him, centre-half Ronnie Cope played like a man possessed. His fearlessness saw him produce crunching tackles that many would have pulled out of, while on one occasion he landed in a heap on top of a crowd of photographers. On another he skidded into the barricades alongside the goal. Johnson, the Wednesday No. 9, rarely got a look in.

The pace of the game was immediately picked up as the second half swung into action. Ryalls managed to punch away a threatening cross from Webster, while at the opposite end Greaves managed to kick a Wilkinson shot off the goal-line, before Gregg did well to hold a powerful drive from Johnson.

Following a series of concentrated attacks, United scored a second goal twenty-five minutes into the second half. Ernie Taylor, always a thorn in the Wednesday side, found Pearson out wide on the left, but the inside-forward's shot from outside the penalty area cannoned off Ryall's leg. The ball, however, rebounded only as far as Brennan, who drove it home with his right foot from 10 yards out. The youngster was engulfed in a sea of red shirts and the noise that greeted the goal must have been heard in Manchester city centre.

Wednesday were now dead and buried, demoralised by this makeshift United side, leaving them with no hope whatsoever of a comeback.

Gregg leaped into the air to clutch a swerving corner from Cargill as it flew towards the top corner of his goal, but the majority of the action was in the opposite half of the field. Webster sent a terrific shot inches wide, as United continued to press forward, and with only six minutes remaining the visitors found themselves beaten for a third time.

It was Taylor again, this time sending Pearson through, with the youngster cutting the ball back from the byline for Dawson to slam home United's third of the night with a low hard drive, leaving Ryalls in the Wednesday goal utterly helpless.

To say that Ernie Taylor was inspiring is simplifying the player's contribution to the game and United's ultimate revival. From the opening whistle, he coaxed and urged the raw United recruits around him into action, supplying his new teammates with a never-ending supply of passes, ranging from the short but effective, to the 20- or 30-yard cross-field ball with pinpoint accuracy.

But what of Sheffield Wednesday? They were always on a hiding to nothing and although they were superior in experience, they were simply not good enough to compete against the strong-willed and ambitious United side on the night. Nor could they master the occasion that they found themselves a part of. At no point was there any sympathy in their play, as they certainly tried to compete, but at the end of the day they were beaten for skill, strength and above all the teamwork of an inspired Manchester United side.

In the aftermath of an incredible ninety minutes, which could not have been scripted by any Hollywood screen mogul, there were countless tears shed in the confines of the United dressing room. Tears of joy, tears of relief and tears for those whose red shirts they now wore.

Bill Foulkes wept unashamedly, having made his way up the tunnel to the sanctuary of the dressing rooms. 'The lads played their hearts out,' he said. 'They couldn't have given more. I like to think they did it all for our colleagues who died at Munich.

'I have never cried since I was a kid, but I cried tonight. As soon as I got back to the dressing room it affected me.

'It was wonderful to be skipper of such a grand side. They fought every inch of the way and no one can say we didn't deserve our win.'

Inside that packed United dressing room, Shay Brennan gave his first post-match interview, telling the reporters, as he pulled off his mud splattered shirt, 'I never thought it would finish up like this. I was terrified before I went on the field, but once I kicked the ball and found my feet I was ok.

'From then on I forgot the crowd and played it like any other game.'

Looking back at a much later date, he added, 'Before that game, I had not appeared before a crowd of more than 20,000. That was when I was a member of the United youth team which won the FA Youth Cup. And I had never played at outside-left before!'

During those incredible ninety minutes, standing only a few feet away from the corner flag, where Shay Brennan wrote his name into Manchester United folklore, was his proud father who attended the game with family friend Joseph Brown.

Joseph himself could have been a United player a decade earlier, as he was to explain:

In March 1947 I was demobbed from the RAF at the age of twenty-two and took up an appointment at Ringway Airport as a radio technician. I played football for a local amateur club; St John and St Thomas club of Woodhouse Lane in Wythenshawe, where one of my colleagues was Kevin Brennan, Shay's brother, who was just over ten years old at this time.

Kevin was a star player and we all thought he would make the grade to senior football. However, he was not too keen on that and always talked of his young kid brother being a much better footballer.

In August 1948 I received a letter from Louis Rocca pp Matt Busby, to provide my physical details and inviting me for trial spins with Manchester United. I had a few trials at Fallowfield and Jimmy Delaney, who I knew personally as he had lived only a few doors away from me in Omoa Road, Cleland, in Scotland, advised me to continue my studies at Manchester College of Technology, as he was of the opinion that I was not up to the grade for senior football.

I continued to play in the Mid Cheshire League until I returned to Scotland in December 1950.

I returned to the Manchester area in 1955 and took an interest in looking after the youth team of St John's. Shay was now a bit older and was quite an accomplished footballer, we all knew he would do well and it was no surprise when one day at Didsbury, Jimmy Murphy and Matt Busby came along to see him. Shortly after this Shay signed for United, but was not considered good enough for the big time. We were all very much great fans of United and I together with Shay's father and my father-in-law went to Old Trafford by bus to see the home game against Red Star Belgrade which United won 2-1.

We never thought they would be able to turn out an XI for the big fifth-round tie of the FA Cup against Sheffield Wednesday but after some arrangements and slackening of the rules the match was arranged for Wednesday 19 February. Jimmy Murphy had taken charge of the team and he persuaded Ernie Taylor from Blackpool and Stan Crowther from Aston Villa to join the depleted United side. This was now the chance for Shay to make his debut appearance for the first team. His father invited me and my father-in-law to go to the game. We got a bus from Wythenshawe to Stretford via Barlow Moor Road and we all paid our half crown to get in at The Warwick Road end. We were just above the corner flag where Shay took the corner kick when it happened. He was playing outside-left and won the corner, to our amazement he scored direct from the kick. We were overcome with excitement and his dad hugged and kissed us. Mr Brennan had some difficulty in walking, but that night he was jumping up and down with excitement. When Shay scored again it was more than we could take and we left the ground in state of euphoria.

Shay Brennan had been the undisputed Man of the Match, but the victory was mainly due to the tireless work of one man. A man who had spent many a long night debating the ability of the players at his disposal, selecting countless team formations in his head before deciding on his final line-up. The night belonged to United and Shay Brennan, but it was all down to Jimmy Murphy at the end of the day.

The 1955/56 and 1956/57 League championship flag once again flew at full-mast high above the Old Trafford stand, but this was only the first step on a long and winding road as Manchester United sought to regain a foothold on the domestic game.

The emotions at Old Trafford were also felt thousands of miles away in Munich, where Albert Scanlon, Ray Wood, Dennis Viollet and Kenny Morgans listened to the game via a telephone link, courtesy of the *Manchester Evening Chronicle*, with each player taking a five-minute turn at the handset. They were loud in their acclaim at the final whistle, but not too loud, as a short distance along the corridor lay Matt Busby. Although making slow but steady progress, the United manager was still completely unaware of what had unfolded at Munich, nor was he told that United were involved in the cup tie. He had recently asked for glasses so that he could read to pass the time, but his request was politely delayed in case he happened upon newspapers which carried news of the tragedy that had befallen his club.

The celebrations back in Manchester continued long into the night, but the joy and happiness which surrounded the victory over Sheffield Wednesday was soon to turn to tears, thrusting Manchester and beyond back into mourning, as the news broke that Duncan Edwards had died in the early hours of Thursday 20 February.

His condition had worsened over the past twenty-four hours and he had been reported as being 'rather weak and showing some signs of distress', but the boy from Dudley, a player and indeed a person that everyone loved and admired, had been fighting against the odds since his admission to the Rechts der Isar Hospital fifteen days previously. His death, however, was described as 'unexpectedly sudden' by BEA medical officer Dr J. Graham Taylor. The day prior to his death had seen the United No. 6 under an oxygen tent after his slight setback, but he was later removed from this and his condition was reported as unchanged. However, his circulation failed, his ongoing kidney condition worsened, and at 1.26 a.m., he partly went to sleep and died.

For many, if they had failed to hear the early morning news, they would have been stunned as they pulled their newspapers from letterboxes, with the front-page headlines breaking the news that no one wanted to hear.

'EDWARDS OF UNITED DIES' led the *Daily Mirror*, while the *Daily Herald* told its readers '4 a.m. News. Duncan Edwards is dead'. The middle of the *Daily Express* front page proclaimed '3 a.m.: After Fight For Life That Amazed Doctors – Duncan Edwards, England's Giant, Dies In Hospital.' The tributes took up even more column inches.

One United supporter, who did not see those newspaper headlines, was John Hewitt as he hurried to get ready for school: 'I was due to sit my eleven-plus exam that morning,' he recalled. 'An important exam which would determine which senior school I would attend.

'I usually had a quick look and the morning newspaper, well, the back pages at least, but on this particular morning, my father managed to hide it from me, telling me that I should concentrate on my exam. Thinking nothing untoward, I had my breakfast and set off for school.

'Before I reached school, I soon discovered why I had not been allowed to see the morning paper, as my friends told me that it had been announced that Duncan had lost his fight for life. Something that my father had not taken into account.'

So, the flag above the stand was again lowered. Tears were shed for the player who epitomised the Busby Babes, and whose name would be revered for eternity. For Jimmy Murphy, who loved Duncan like a son, it was devastating news. 'The last words he said to me were when he lay in a semi-conscious state in hospital,' said the distraught Welshman. 'He said, "What time is kick-off tomorrow, Jimmy?"

'This news is the final blow.'

But as he had done in the days following the crash, Jimmy Murphy pulled himself together despite his affection for the player and got on with the job in hand, as everyone relied upon him and the future of Manchester United depended on him. With that initial post-Munich fixture out of the way, it was time to look at the domestic League programme, with Nottingham Forest due to visit Old Trafford on Saturday 22 February.

On the Saturday following the crash, United occupied fourth position, three points behind Preston North End, who had beaten Chelsea at Stamford Bridge 2-0, and one point behind West Bromwich Albion, who had taken both points following a narrow 3-2 home win over Nottingham Forest. They were, however, six behind the leaders, Wolverhampton Wanderers, the team they were due to meet that afternoon three days after the trip to Belgrade. Had that particular fixture taken place, it would have given United the opportunity to reduce the leeway, keeping the pressure on the leaders, but now the pressure was on them and they would have to maintain the form of the Sheffield Wednesday cup tie for the remainder of the season if they wanted to retain their League title.

Due to their inactivity on the League front, Forest's visit to Manchester found United now in fifth place, with Luton Town having now moved into the top four, two points in front, but having played two games more. But Jimmy Murphy was once again faced with selection problems, this time due to injuries, as Ronnie

Cope had a calf strain, Mark Pearson a bruised foot and Shay Brennan a bruised shin, all picked up in the Sheffield Wednesday cup tie. Thankfully all three players recovered, shrugging off their aches and pains and declared themselves fit, allowing Murphy a little breathing space, although he continued his search for reinforcements. The game against Forest would see Pearson and Brennan make their First Division debuts.

What proved a more difficult task for Murphy was selecting a team for the Central League fixture against Sheffield Wednesday at Hillsborough, as he had only two players who could be considered regulars, David Gaskell and Bobby Harrop, to choose from. In the end, he selected a side with the average age of seventeen years and nine months – Gaskell, B. Smith, L. Cummings, English, Holland, Bratt, T. Spratt, Harrop, Mooney, Giles and Hunter. Of the eleven, Johnny Giles, Reg Holland and Leslie Cummings were making their Central League debuts. The latter, an unfamiliar name to most, was a local lad from Wythenshawe and had only joined the club a few months earlier.

With things now beginning to take on some form of normality, United had to take a look at the long-term picture, with their continued interest in the FA Cup throwing up fixture congestion as well as additional work for those behind the scenes. The announcement that the forthcoming cup tie against West Bromwich Albion would be an all-ticket game added more work to the already heavy load and forced overtime payment onto the wage bill.

For the cup tie, the club decided to revert back to their tried and trusted programme token scheme, with supporters requiring thirty-five tokens in order to claim either a 7s 6d (37p) seat, a 5s (25p) paddock, or a 2s 6d (12p) or 2s (10p) ground-side ticket. This system had been introduced the previous season, with a numbered token printed in each issue of the club programme, the *United Review*. They were then collected and stuck onto a sheet in the correctly numbered square and presented at the ticket office when all-ticket games arose, allowing the regular attendees with the highest number of tokens the first options to purchase a ticket.

Tokens would also be issued in reserve-team programmes and youth-team programmes, which could prove difficult to obtain if you followed the first team away from home and they had a game that same day. Those reserve and youth programmes were sold at the turnstile, one per person. Many, however, would attend those non-first-team fixtures, pay their money at the gate and then leave through the emergency exit and go home. Others, having been subsidised by absent friends, would leave through the same exits and pay again at the turnstile in order to get another programme. Those tokens soon became a form of currency, eagerly sought after, to be begged for, exchanged or sold in pubs, schools and streets around the ground. Such was the desperation of many to gain entry to those important fixtures.

Possibly, if time had permitted, the visit of Nottingham Forest should also have been an all-ticket affair. With a vast number of supporters outside the ground as early as eleven o'clock, it became obvious that problems would arise and, with an estimated 20,000 outside by 1 p.m. and with still two hours to go before kick-off, it was decided to open the gates.

Despite the vast numbers, there was something of a subdued atmosphere both inside and outside the ground, as those present were there just as much to pay tribute to their lost heroes in the memorial service due to be held prior to the kick-off, as they were to cheer the new United towards another victory.

With the kick-off drawing nearer and the buses and trains offloading their passengers beside and in the vicinity of the ground, things became even more frantic. As one by one the turnstiles began to shut due to the different sections of the ground becoming full, stewards were quickly despatched around the outside of the stadium in an attempt to guide the latecomers towards the few gates where admission could be obtained.

Around 2.30, as the snow began to fall, Old Trafford was full. The gates were firmly shut, with thousands still rushing about frantically outside, hoping to find a turnstile that was still open and would enable them to gain entry. Their attempts were to prove fruitless.

Inside was a post-war record crowd of 66,123, stood unmoving, almost frightened to breathe, during the one-minute silence of the inter-denominational service conducted out on the muddy Old Trafford turf by the Dean of Manchester, the Very Revd Herbert A. Jones. This service was also attended by the lord mayor of Manchester, Alderman Leslie Lever, and the mayors of Salford and Stretford.

There were more than a few tears shed during the service, as short prayers were said for the dead, the injured, the mourning families and those connected with the club. Missing were the United and Nottingham Forest teams, who remained in the dressing rooms, shut away from the emotions of events taking place not far from where they sat, deep in their own thoughts.

The silence around the ground was soon broken as the two teams made their way onto the pitch, but the question on everyone's lips and in their minds was, could United match their performance of three days previously, or was the Sheffield Wednesday result little more than a one-off?

As the ninety minutes unfolded, the makeshift United side proved that the cup tie performance was no fluke. Wednesday had not simply stood aside and allowed the misshapen United side a victory in order to ease their sorrows. Forest were soon to find themselves on the end of a hammering and were indeed more than a little fortunate to leave Manchester with one point at the end of the afternoon.

It was one-way traffic for the majority of the ninety minutes and had the United youngsters been a little more composed in front of goal, the 1-1 scoreline would certainly have been much different.

Thomson in the Forest goal was called into action as early as the ninth minute, doing well to save a powerful Dawson header. Sixty seconds later, the visitors' 'keeper was again tested, this time stretching to push a Pearson lob over the crossbar, although he was rather fortunate soon afterwards, when Brennan, through on goal, shot directly at him.

But it was Forest, in a quick movement that Robin Hood himself would have been proud of, who snatched the lead on the half-hour mark. Wilson gained possession out on the right and as he moved forward, he spotted the upraised arm of centre-forward Stewart Imlach. An inch-perfect cross picked out the Scot and before any United defenders could react, the ball was sent beyond Gregg and into the United net from around 20 yards out.

The second half opened in practically identical fashion to the first, with United throwing everything at the Forest goal. Dawson shot on the turn, but Thomson was once again equal to the effort, pushing the ball round the post for a corner. A minute later, the Forest 'keeper knew little as Pearson's shot cannoned off his chest and bounced to safety. The 'keeper was eventually beaten by Dawson in the fifty-sixth minute, but Thomas was on the line to kick clear.

No matter what United tried, they just could not break down the visitors' defence, or beat the fortunate Thomson standing between the posts. Their all-out attacking play, however, almost cost them a second goal, as a break by Gray brought Gregg into the action, the Irishman pulling off a superb save to keep United in the game.

Forest were more mature, confident and systematic about their play as the game wore on, but there was little they could do to prevent the equaliser when it finally materialised. With fifteen minutes remaining, United gained a corner and from Brennan's flag kick, Dawson lunged as the ball eluded two Forest defenders, and the ball flew past Thomson into the net.

There were, however, to be no last-minute heroics, although it was not without trying on United's part. But in reality, this and subsequent games were not about results, they were about survival against the odds and rebuilding a team when all seemed lost. The necessity to win games and success were for another day.

Over the Pennines in Sheffield, the Wednesday second string gained something in the way of revenge for their first team's recent cup defeat by beating the young United reserve side 4-0, although at times the visitors did play the better football. Had their finishing been better, then they may well have been three goals in front after half an hour, as Harrop, Giles, English and Bratt controlled the game, splitting the Wednesday defence apart with a fine array of passes, prompting a Wednesday supporter in the crowd to shout, 'Don't let this lot of kids take the mickey out of you as well!'

Eventually, the heavy-going physical build of the home players, along with their wealth of experience, told against the United youngsters, although it must be noted that two of the four goals they conceded were done so when they were reduced to ten men, with a defender off the field.

The youngsters returned to Manchester obviously disappointed, not just with the defeat itself, but also because they had been knocked off the top of the Central League, but like their senior counterparts, results were now of secondary importance.

Kenny Morgans and Dennis Viollet were allowed to leave hospital on 21 February and both players decided, after much debate, that neither of them would be flying back to Britain. Viollet was first to imply that he would seek an alternative route after he admitted that while having a very brief chat with Matt Busby, his manager had said that he did not really want him to fly home, but the final decision was that of the player. Viollet himself was also quick to admit that he didn't feel brave enough to fly at the present time.

In the end they decided that the journey would be made by rail and boat, but their arrival back in Manchester did little to lessen the load for Jimmy Murphy, as both had been told by the hospital doctors that they should not contemplate playing again this season. There was, however, some good news for the United stand-in manager: Bobby Charlton, who had returned to his Ashington home a few days prior to the Sheffield Wednesday cup tie, was almost ready to return to first-team duty. But it was thought that his first game following the crash would possibly be for the Army, as he was wanted for the RAOC Cup final prior to United's next fixture, a sixth-round FA Cup tie against West Bromwich Albion. Fortunately for Murphy, the Army Cup final was postponed due to snow.

Charlton had returned to Beatrice Terrace, Ashington still feeling the mental strain of the crash. Physically, he could have returned home around the same time as Bill Foulkes and Harry Gregg, but it was decided that he wasn't quite ready to do so and remained in Munich under observation. Behind the closed doors of the family home, he wanted to shut himself off from the rest of the world, not wishing to see anyone, but with reporters and photographers practically camped on the doorstep, it was a case of having to venture out at some point to speak to them and the sooner he got it over with, the better it might be.

His mother, sensing the despair, anguish and emotional strain her son was under, made an appointment with the family doctor, an appointment that went a considerable way to pushing him onto the road to recovery. He was perhaps a little taken aback when Dr McPherson told him that there was nothing at all wrong with him. The doctor proceeded to reveal that he had served in the RAF during the war and had lost friends who had been shot down beside him. After a while, he said, it was something that you learned to take in your stride.

'You are serving as a soldier,' the doctor continued. 'There is no war on now, but it's just the same as if you lost your pals on active service. You have been spared this time – the accident didn't have your number on it, and you've got to carry on. That's the way to look at it.

'What you must do now is this. Get hold of a ball, take it out in the park and kick it around as you used to do. Get back to what you know and love best.

'I shall expect to see you at Wembley in May.'

With Charlton still in the Army, and three months to go before his demob, there was always the immediate fear of him not being released for a United game, or indeed the Army stepping in front of his club to ensure that playing for them was his first priority. Such fears, however, were eased slightly, when an officer at the War Office issued a statement saying, 'We at the War Office feel the tragedy of Manchester United as much as any outsiders. It was a terrible thing.

'At the moment, all I can say is that Charlton should see his Commanding Officer and Manchester United should write to the CO if they want his demobilisation rushed through.

'If they write, a copy of their letter will reach us at the War Office. At the moment, I can promise nothing. But I can say that the Field Marshal will get to know about it and that the case will be dealt with as quickly and as sympathetically as possible.'

The kick about with the local youngsters had eased Bobby Charlton back into the swing of things, if not exactly exorcising the demons, and with snow having put paid to the Army Cup final, Charlton's first important game under the belt since the crash was at Old Trafford on the morning of Tuesday

25 February. A full-scale practice match took place prior to the eleven players who played against Forest, along with Bobby Harrop and Peter Jones, heading back to the Norbreck at Blackpool. After his outing, which saw him momentarily struggling, Charlton said, 'I felt as slow as an old carthorse.' But his presence was required by Jimmy Murphy, and the Welshman's coaxing and encouragement soon saw some of the old vigour and enthusiasm return. He was soon to tell reporters, 'I feel fine and would like to play in the cup game at West Brom on Saturday.'

Murphy was eager to have Charlton back in the fold and also fit for selection, and unlike a few years earlier, when he had delayed the former England schoolboy's promotion to the first team, as he felt the needed to toughen up both mentally and physically before he made the step up; he had little hesitation in selecting the player on this occasion.

There was still much debate as to possible new signings, but the club had to make it known that they no longer wanted any aspiring players to write to the club requesting a trial. It was reported that they had received over 300 letters from young – and some not so young – hopefuls, but there were to be no more trials as there were now enough youngsters at the club to fulfil the remaining fixtures for the season.

The name of Bradford City's outside-left, Martin Bake, had once again surfaced as a possible signing, but the club issued a statement that they would not be making a move for the player, although it was felt that this was a position that would need filling, with the likes of Portsmouth's Jackie Henderson considered another possible candidate. But with little actual activity, it was thought that Jimmy Murphy was waiting on a fuller medical update on Albert Scanlon before making any definite move.

With the focus firmly on the Albion cup tie, United broke with the norm and possibly went into the record books as being the first club ever to sign a player solely to play in their reserve team, with the signing of Bishop Auckland's, thirty-seven-year-old centre-half, Bob Hardisty. Old enough to be the father of many of his soon-to-be-teammates, the amateur defender, who had won three Amateur Cup medals and countless international caps with the North East side, had been retired since the previous April, but decided to rummage in his cupboard and find his old boots in order to help the Manchester United cause. 'I was quite content. I felt my active soccer days were over,' said the balding defender. 'But I could not turn down this appeal.'

Following a light training session, Hardisty, who was to be joined at Old Trafford by Warren Bradley and Derek Lewin, two of his Bishop Auckland teammates, spoke of his new role, saying, 'I didn't feel too bad after doing a spot of training. I felt I could play this weekend at a push, but with more training I should be in a better position to help the following Saturday.

'Naturally, I will do everything I can do to help, even though I am not as fit as I would like to be. I hope to be of some use, perhaps more on the coaching side.

'Matt Busby and Jimmy Murphy are old friends. I first met Matt when he was running an Army team during the war and got to know them both very well in 1948, when Matt was made team manager of the Great Britain Olympic team. Matt, Jimmy and the late Tom Curry all helped us a great deal then. It is good to be able to do something in return.

'I will play centre-half in the reserves on Saturday. There will be less running around to do and I should be able to help the youngsters better from that position.'

It was obviously Hardisty's presence and experience that had attracted Murphy, with the United man clearly stating to his new recruit, 'I want you in the reserve team even if you just stand around prompting the youngsters.' He went on to praise his three new recruits, who were set to make their Central League debuts against Burnley at Old Trafford, having been cleared to play by the FA: 'First I approached Bishop Auckland and their officials were kindness itself. Then I approached the players and their reactions were spontaneous. Grand chaps, all of them.

'I know they will be a great success with our youngsters, especially Bob Hardisty, an old and respected friend. And Derek Lewin is almost one of the United family, as he has trained with us so often.'

Derek Lewin actually worked in Manchester, but lived in Lytham St Annes, while Warren Bradley was an education officer at an RAF station near Darlington. Neither player upon signing would have felt that they had the possibility of a long-term career at United, simply glad to be helping out in the short term, but for one of the pair, their time at Old Trafford was going to exceed all expectations.

The scars of the disaster were still tender and would, in reality, never heal properly. Certainly not for those involved. But, as the build-up to the West Bromwich Albion cup tie grew, there was something of a sigh of relief amid the immediate worry, when news filtered through from Munich that Matt Busby had finally found out the true extent of what had happened on the slush-covered runway.

Newspapers had been banned from the vicinity of his hospital room, but it was the visit of a priest that led to the United manager learning the truth, or at least having his thoughts on the matter confirmed. Busby asked the priest, 'How's Duncan Edwards?' The visitor decided that he could not continue telling white lies and simply replied, 'Dead.' Busby did not pursue the matter, but when his wife visited that evening, he demanded to know the truth. The tearful Jean Busby could not answer when the names of his players were spoken in hushed tones. All he then asked for was his wife to simply nod or shake her head after each name was read out. The truth was out. There were no more secrets.

A friend accompanying Mrs Busby was then asked about the Sheffield Wednesday cup tie and who had played. Over the next few minutes, the manager was brought right up to date with what had been happening back in Manchester.

As everything unfolded, the whole scenario suddenly became too much for Busby and he told his family that he was going to call it a day. Walk away from both Manchester United and football. But, as Sandy Busby recalled, it was his mother who managed to convince her husband otherwise.

'"Matt, I don't think that the boys who have gone would want you to finish. They would want you to go on," were her words to my father and he listened to her and took his time to think the whole thing through.'

Snow threatened the cup tie at the Hawthorns, and as roads were blocked over hundreds of square miles, the journey to Blackpool took the United party more than four hours. But thankfully their already rescheduled fixture list did not need further reworking, as there was something of a thaw by the weekend of the cup tie, with a full complement of the League and cup fixtures taking place.

For Jimmy Murphy, all the bumps and bruises had healed and his only selection headache was whether to continue with the novice Shay Brennan and hope that his early performances were not simply beginner's luck, or whether to reintroduce Bobby Charlton to the team, playing him in the rather alien position of outside-left. In the end, he decided to go with the more experienced Charlton, who assured him that he was fit and raring to go.

By the time the team reached the Midlands, they knew what was in store for them, as the Albion manager Vic Buckingham had told all and sundry, via the morning newspapers, that United were in for an awakening that afternoon, going on to say, 'With every respect for what Manchester United are, what they have been and what undoubtedly one day they will be again, we are going to try and keep them in the waning stage.' He continued, 'Yes, the new United will be treated at the highest level and I don't think they will have the answer. The crowd, the background of Old Trafford, the desire to live up to the great men who are gone, and carried them through against Sheffield Wednesday and Nottingham Forest. But that cannot go on indefinitely. Talent does what it can. Genius does what it must.

'We have worked out no special plan and we are not watching any particular player. We shall be fighting all eleven United men, and there will be no singling out crash survivors or lads who had never played in a first-class match ten days ago.'

Inspiration was something that the United players did not require, but Buckingham's words were certainly taken onboard, and in his prematch team-talk, Jimmy Murphy, himself a former Albion player, told his charges, 'Get out there and fight. Show 'em we don't need any sympathy. Go and win.'

And win they almost did, as it was not until the eighty-sixth minute that the home side managed to secure an Old Trafford replay with a 2-2 draw.

The clock was showing that a mere five minutes had passed when United opened the scoring. Ernie Taylor pushed the ball out wide to Dawson, whose cross found Charlton. It could have been a dream return to action for the lad from Ashington, but his shot was blocked by Howe. Blocked, but not cleared, and in stepped Taylor to fire United into the lead.

The United contingent in the 58,250 crowd, estimated at between 14,000 and 15,000, went wild, but their celebrations were muted when Derek Kevan broke through. Although his centre evaded Harry Gregg, it was also too powerful for any of his Albion teammates. The travelling support was, however, well and truly silenced within five minutes, when Albion did draw level.

Kevan was again the threat and his powerful drive was only parried by Gregg. In the scramble that ensued, Allen managed to get to the ball and shot past the unsighted United 'keeper. Play became fast and furious, with the United youngsters keeping their more experienced opponents stretched to their limits and unable to play the type of football that had taken them to third place in the First Division.

With three minutes remaining before the interval, the visitors regained their lead, thanks again to the sterling work of their midfield general Ernie Taylor. The former Blackpool man was the inspiration behind United's rebuilding and had it not been for him, not just in this important cup tie, but throughout the remainder of this campaign, then things could have been so much different.

Moments before the goal, Taylor had wriggled his way past a static-looking Albion defence before sending Dawson through on goal. The burly centre-forward, however, shot wildly over the bar when he should have done much better. In their next attack, the robust No. 9 certainly redeemed himself, rising to head the ball firmly past Sanders in the West Bromwich goal, after Taylor's 25-yard drive rebounded off the crossbar.

With half-time beckoning, United had a huge let-off, as Kevan ran through with only Gregg to beat, but from 10 yards out, he could only watch in anguish as his shot rebounded off the post.

In the second pulsating forty-five minutes, which was certainly not for the faint-hearted, the United defence stood firm as Albion surged forward time and time again, but much to their disappointment and frustration, they could find no way through. With Albion leaving themselves exposed due to their seemingly constant attacks in search of an equaliser, United were always a danger and liable to mount a counterattack and in one such movement, Pearson should have put the game beyond any doubts late on, but he blazed the ball over the top of an open goal.

Slowly, with the game easing towards full-time, Albion's experience and constant attacking began to take its toll on United and with only four minutes remaining, Ronnie Allen pounced on a loose ball to volley goalwards. Gregg, for the first time in the match, failed to hold the ball and in stepped Horobin to slip the ball towards goal. Gregg reacted quickly and dived again for the ball, scooping it away with the help of Cope.

Without hesitation, the referee awarded a goal and hundreds of schoolboys quickly invaded the pitch as the United players surrounded the referee protesting that the ball had not crossed the line. Gregg in his disagreement threw his glove at the official, but escaped a caution and a couple of minutes later the whistle sounded the end of the match.

Afterwards, the disappointed United goalkeeper admitted that the ball had indeed crossed the line: 'The ball hit me on the leg and rolled toward goal. Ronnie Cope scooped it clear, but it had been over the line alright. The tension and excitement made me appeal. It was a terrible thing to happen with us so close to winning.'

Manager Jimmy Murphy had no real complaints: 'On the run of the play and abilities of the teams, I think a draw was correct. Every player did his part nobly. That is good enough for me.'

So, United had to wait until the following Wednesday and endure a further ninety minutes' football before they could look forward to an FA Cup semi-final, but they were already in another semi-final, one that had been more or less pushed to one side and forgotten about amid all the hectic goings on of the past three weeks or so.

The European Cup had been only thought about on the odd occasion, with the subject of flying having been brought up with those who had survived unscathed in Munich. When questioned on the subject, Harry Gregg was quick to say 'No', but admitted, 'To put it bluntly, I don't want to fly. How I shall feel later, I do not know. I am not afraid of flying but what happened at Munich was terrible to see.' Bobby Charlton was of a similar opinion, saying, 'I don't fancy it yet. And Bill Foulkes feels the same.'

Chairman Harold Hardman was uncommitted as to both a mode of travel to their semi-final tie, or indeed if the club would actually fulfil their European commitments: 'We are not keen on the prospect of long train journeys across the Continent. If we draw Borussia Dortmund and Milano (*the two clubs still having to play*) and Borussia get through, our tie will be quite definitely on.'

'If we have to go to Milan, Budapest or Madrid, I would say the chance of continuing is 50/50, but United do not plan to fly to any of the remaining European Cup games.'

Representing United at the European Cup semi-final draw in Brussels was the Scottish FA secretary Sir George Graham, and he was given some surprising and most welcome news after he spoke to the organising committee of United's reluctance to travel by air, as it was decided overwhelmingly, by both the committee and officials of the other clubs left in the competition, that the draw would be 'fixed' in United's favour.

In reality, there was no actual draw, as it was simply decided that United would play either Borussia Dortmund or Milan, enabling them to remain in the competition and travel to the away leg by train. It was some 640 miles to Dortmund and 1,024 miles to Milan, but both were considered reachable by train. United were certainly most grateful to the organisers for this tremendous gesture, but it was not something that went down well with everyone. David Jack, the former Arsenal player and columnist with the *Empire News and Sunday Chronicle*, who only a short while earlier had advocated that League clubs should have done more to help United, was stinging in his comments as far as the European Cup was concerned.

'This is carrying sentiment too far,' read the headline on his article. He went on to write that although he was in favour of helping United, he wanted to know why the rules were ignored, with only four of the five clubs agreeable, as the Hungarians of Vasas Budapest could not be contacted.

Jack felt that Real Madrid had the beating of anyone and were more than happy to play Vasas. Both Milan and Dortmund would be happy to play United, as with fourteen of their best seventeen players no longer available, they should be able to beat them over the two legs. As for the Hungarians, he felt that they had received a raw deal and would certainly not be happy at being 'allocated' Real Madrid.

United and Jimmy Murphy were quick to point out that they had not looked for any favours and would have happily taken a straight draw, but certainly appreciated the 'wonderful gesture'.

The FA Cup semi-final draw, on the other hand, was a simple, straight-forward affair. Four numbered balls into the velvet bag, a quick shake and then pulled out one by one. The first two numbers drawn paired Blackburn Rovers with neighbours Bolton Wanderers, while United, if they could overcome West Bromwich Albion, were left with Fulham, with the tie scheduled for Villa Park Birmingham.

The bookmakers made Bolton favourites to lift the trophy at 7-4, with United listed as 11-2. Their Midland opponents were 7-2. Many took a liking to the United odds.

Obviously, the Old Trafford faithful had every confidence in their newly enrolled heroes making it through to the semi-finals, but it was not a view shared by everyone, and not just those from the Midlands. Terence Elliott of the *Daily Express* put his head on the block by stating 'I Must Pick Albion,' but he was also quick to point out that he would be just as happy if he was to be proved wrong. He wrote, 'I think Manchester United's interest in the FA Cup will end tonight under the Old Trafford lights. To win, United must miraculously find another untapped source of physical strength and stamina.'

Fellow journalist Keith Dewhurst of the *Manchester Evening Chronicle* was equally uncertain of the outcome: 'If the issue is still undecided at about the seventieth minute, or if the game goes into extra time, I fear that West Brom will pull out that little bit extra and win.'

Defeat was not part of Jimmy Murphy's make-up or vocabulary, and once again he pondered long and hard with his team selection for the West Bromwich replay. This time, many thought that he would leave out Colin Webster, who had not shown the form that he was capable of producing over the past three games, with recent recruit Warren Bradley tipped as his possible replacement.

As it turned out, Murphy did make a change to his selected XI, but it was the experienced Stan Crowther who was omitted, not Webster, with the former Villa player left on the sidelines with a heel injury, forcing the stand-in manager to bring in twenty-year-old Bobby Harrop at left-half for his first-team debut. The actual severity of United's situation and the problems surrounding Jimmy Murphy were again highlighted with Harrop's selection, as the former Wolves amateur had been playing mainly at inside-left and had even turned out for the reserves at centre-forward the previous Saturday.

For those who attended the Sheffield Wednesday cup tie, that absorbing ninety minutes of football and the evening as a whole would be etched forever into their memories. The same could also be said for those who ventured to Old Trafford on the evening of 5 March, but for many, they would narrate a completely different story to that surrounding the previous round. The ninety minutes itself was possibly on par to that of the Sheffield Wednesday game, but the scenes outside the ground were as unforgettable as those played out on the opposite side of the red-brick wall, and not for the first time in recent weeks did the name 'Manchester United' appear on the front pages of the national press as well as the back.

'90,000 in Cup Storm – Locked Out Fans Miss Last Minute Victory', proclaimed the *Daily Express*, while 'Chaos for a Mile Around Manchester United Ground' appeared on the front of the *News Chronicle* and *Daily Despatch*.

Beneath the *Express*'s headlines, a photograph, taken outside the ground prior to the game, showed little more than a sea of heads, with the caption beneath reading, 'Still an hour to kick-off last night, the gates are shut and 60,000 are INSIDE Old Trafford. But OUTSIDE – a milling 30,000 crowd ... turned away.'

By 6.25 p.m., the gates were firmly locked, as latecomers, including West Bromwich Albion supporters, pushed frantically forward in the hope of making the turnstiles, having picked up tickets from the spivs who were doing a brisk trade in selling 7/6d (38p) stand tickets for £7. Others never even managed to get within sight of the ground, as announcements were made at Central station, informing them that the gates had been closed and that there would be no more trains running. Strangely, many decided to make their way to Maine Road, to watch City play Birmingham City!

A number of youngsters tried to gain access to the ground by scaling the walls, but were unceremoniously pulled down by police officers and led away, creating unwanted scenes of violence, with objects being thrown in the direction of the police, and as three mounted police officers attempted to regain some form of control, one was almost pulled from his saddle. The attention was then turned to the locked gates and two were pulled off their hinges, but those hoping for entry were repelled by a wall of policemen situated inside the ground.

Chief Superintendent Frederick Waddington, head of the Manchester Division of the Lancashire County police, said, 'In twenty-two years controlling crowds at Old Trafford I have never seen anything like it. My officers tell me the trouble was caused by youths and a few hotheads. There was no need for drastic action and all of the men, I believe, handled themselves extremely well in what could have been difficult circumstances.'

Unaware of the unfolding drama outside, Murphy prepared his troops for the battle ahead, but even he was unprepared for the early onslaught from his former team, as Albion pushed forward from the first whistle, shooting on sight, but finding Harry Gregg in superb form.

Slowly United found their feet, with Cope and Harrop gradually coming to grips with the thrusting Albion attacks, while Charlton left the imprint of the ball on the foot of the post in the thirty-eighth minute. But it wasn't until the opening ten minutes of the second half that they came close to breaching the visitors' defence and breaking the deadlock, with Taylor, Goodwin and Dawson all coming close. Albion, however, failed to succumb and the trio of Barlow, Kevan and Robson continued to push United to the limits.

It began to look as though Keith Dewhurst's prematch prediction was spot-on, as the minutes began to tick away and United found themselves stretched in all directions, but with sixty seconds remaining Jimmy Murphy had one last card to play.

Having shuffled his forward line continuously throughout the match – Charlton and Webster moving inside, Pearson and Taylor going wide – Murphy, sensing that it was now or never, left his seat in the stand and made his way down to the touchline where he shouted to trainer Jack Crompton, 'Now, Jack, now.' Knowing what was required, Crompton immediately caught the attention of Bobby Charlton, telling him to once again switch positions with Colin Webster.

As Albion attacked once again, Foulkes shouldered Horobin off the ball before despatching it somewhat un-stylishly down the wing towards Charlton. Albion centre-half Kennedy attempted to bundle the Munich survivor off the ball, but as the linesman's flag fluttered in the cold evening air, signalling a free-kick for United, the referee allowed play to continue and, having found the necessary space and also having avoided Williams, Charlton crossed the ball towards the feet on the oncoming Webster, who repaid his manager's faith in him by side-footing the ball past the helpless Sanders from 2 yards out.

A deafening roar thundered through the night air as the referee signalled full-time, with trainer Jack Crompton sprinting from his touchline post, making a beeline for Colin Webster, lifting him off his feet and kissing him firmly on the cheek, before congratulating the rest of the mud-stained, red-shirted heroes.

As the champagne corks popped in the dressing room, Bill Foulkes said, 'This was the toughest game of them all. Now we have achieved the impossible – and I can tell you plainly that we at Old Trafford fancy our chances for the cup. Footballers never try to count their chickens before they are hatched and I would not be so foolish as to say we shall win the cup – or even get to Wembley. But we have a good chance, and any other cup club who have other ideas had better be prepared for a hard fight.'

For hero of the hour Colin Webster, having come in for some rather unjust criticism prior to the game, scoring the only goal was a much-needed confidence-booster and confessed to 'being in a whirl ever since I saw the ball go into the net. Although it was only from 3 yards' range, it was a strain at the time. But it all looked so easy on television.'

It wasn't only in Manchester that there were celebrations following the dramatic cup victory; there was also jubilation hundreds of miles away in Munich, as the match was broadcast to those survivors still in hospital, with chairman Harold Hardman making a telephone call to Ray Wood minutes after the final whistle. 'Tell Matt that the lads have played their hearts out for him here tonight,' the seventy-eight-year-old chairman said. 'It was a magnificent match and a wonderful finish.'

The victory over West Bromwich Albion was particularly pleasing for Jimmy Murphy, not because it was against his former club, but because of the prematch press comments of Albion manager Vic Buckingham, who had suggested that Murphy's boys were not going to become men at the expense of his team and if the opportunity arose, they would score seven or eight goals against United. Following the self-satisfying victory, Murphy said, 'That will teach people to talk about seven or eight goals. That will show them not to go about predicting.'

At home, Jimmy Murphy was an entirely different person. 'He rarely spoke about his work at United,' said Jimmy Jnr. 'He would, on the odd occasion, talk about his "golden apples" – the youngsters in the youth team. After Munich we saw even less of him. Even on a Sunday, he was out, as the coaches would meet for lunch in a pub near the ground, where they would report on each team's performance the previous day. What you must remember is that Matt Busby would rarely, if ever, see some of the reserves play unless they had a midweek fixture.

'This was why Jimmy's role was so crucial to the club, as the promotion of players was 100 per cent his decision. He would say that so-and-so was ready for the first team and Matt would put them in.

'The first team had their own dressing room and the other players had to knock on the door before they entered. Matt was in charge of those first-team members, while Jimmy had the remaining twenty-four professionals and all the amateurs and juniors and along with Bert Whalley they would work two nights a week with these younger players.'

Those youngsters would have jumped through fire for Jimmy Murphy, such was his influence on them and their love for man. He would put an arm around their shoulder when it was required, but he also instilled what was required of them to become a Manchester United player. 'If you play for Manchester United, you never shirk a tackle,' they were told. 'You always chase a loose ball. No game is ever considered lost. Get it? And never forget it!'

Strangely, when the Welshman's fourteen-hour day was over, he enjoyed nothing better than to turn to his second love – music. He enjoyed listening to Chopin or Greig.

West Bromwich Albion returned to Old Trafford three days later, this time on Football League business, but once again, in front of a packed stadium, they found themselves upstaged. This time, however, it wasn't by the red-shirted United players, but by a party of twenty-five doctors and nurses from the Rechts der Isar Hospital in Munich, who along with Professor Maurer had been invited to Manchester by the lord mayor as something of a thank you for all that they had done for Matt Busby and his players.

One person who wasn't present for Albion's visit to Old Trafford was the match official selected to referee the First Division fixture, Kevin Howley, who suddenly found himself dropped from taking charge of the game, with League secretary Alan Hardaker saying, 'This must not be taken in any way as a reflection on Mr Howley's refereeing of the cup ties.' Other felt differently.

A crescendo of noise greeted the doctors and nurses as they emerged from the Old Trafford tunnel, growing louder as they made their way onto the pitch accompanied by chairman Harold Hardman and surrounded by countless photographers, rather shyly waving in acknowledgement, before Foulkes, Charlton and Gregg presented the nurses with bouquets of flowers.

With snow swirling around the stadium and the visitors now happily out of the spotlight, there was an instant hush, as suddenly, the words of manager Matt Busby echoed out from the loudspeaker system: 'Ladies and gentlemen, I am speaking from my bed in the Isar Hospital, Munich, where I have been since the tragic accident of just over a month ago.

'You will be glad, I am sure, that the remaining players here, and myself, are now considered out of danger, and this can be attributed to the wonderful treatment and attention given to us by Professor Maurer and his wonderful staff, who are with you today as guests of the club.

'I am obliged to the *Empire News* for giving me this opportunity to speak to you, for it is only in these last two or three days that I have been able to be told anything about football, and I am delighted to hear of the success and united effort made by all at Old Trafford.

'Again it is wonderful to hear that the club have reached the semi-final of the FA Cup, and I extend my best wishes to everyone.

'Finally, may I just say God bless you all.'

Albion, still smarting from their cup defeat, were in no mood to be beaten on a second consecutive occasion, and under the rather severe playing conditions took the game to United almost from the offset, eventually going in front through Ronnie Allen in the ninth minute.

An injury to playmaker Ernie Taylor, forced off the field to receive treatment, clearly unsettled United, and with the advantage of having an extra man, the visitors increased their lead in the thirty-fourth minute when Ian Greaves deflected a shot, which was clearly going wide, past a helpless Gregg.

Back to full strength, United tried to make up the lost ground, but were clearly struggling and were fortunate not to go further behind when Gregg brought down Kevan. The Albion forward was to gain revenge twelve minutes into the second half, when he put the visitors three in front after Cope failed to clear. A fourth, an Allen penalty, after Goodwin brought down Kevan, made the revenge even sweeter.

With Dennis Viollet and Kenny Morgans having returned home prior to the cup replay, Albert Scanlon, with his right leg in plaster, and Ray Wood, still having problems with his sight, were the next of the injured to wave goodbye to the staff of the German hospital, leaving Jackie Blanchflower, Johnny Berry and Matt Busby still occupying beds at the Rechts der Isar. Blanchflower would remain in the German hospital for another fortnight before being transferred to Manchester for an operation on his broken elbow.

Although both the fixtures for all United teams were now back on track, there was still something of a depleted look about the selected XIs, especially at lower levels, where youngsters were being rather hastily introduced to a higher level of football than they were sometimes equipped for. It was, however, a quick learning curve, which would certainly not do them any harm.

With one eye on the future as much as the current situation, Jimmy Murphy moved into the transfer market to secure the services of a young Scot from Irvine in Ayrshire, Tommy Heron. The twenty-one-year-old ICI clerk had began his career with Airdrie Recreation, before going into the Royal Artillery for two years, and guesting for Millwall whenever leave permitted. Upon his demob, it was expected that he would join the London club, but decided instead that he would return north and join Queens Park, for whom he played eight games the previous season. Due to being unable to hold down a regular place with the amateurs, he crossed the Irish Sea and joined Portadown. Suddenly, two months and seven games later, he found himself a £5,500 purchase for United, having been recommended to the club by Irish scout Bob Harpur.

Meanwhile, Kenny Morgans declared himself fit to play for the reserves against Newcastle United, as Bobby Charlton took further steps to regaining his match fitness by firing home a hat-trick for the 17th Company, Nesscliffe's in their 7-0 RAOC Cup final at Dicot. Slowly, things were returning to normal in the Old Trafford dressing room.

But not everything was rosy, as the short journey to Turf Moor, Burnley, not only produced a 3-0 defeat, but also some unwanted headlines, as the national press who had heralded the rebirth of the Babes reported on the ninety minutes in an entirely different manner, with one of the press corps squashed into the press box viewing the ninety minutes as something that 'might have taken part in a boxing ring'. Unfortunately, the football itself only took up a couple of paragraphs in many of those reports in the Sunday and Monday newspapers.

The early exchanges saw both sides evenly matched, but the powder keg was lit in a furious four minutes as the game approached the half-hour mark. Harry Gregg unwittingly triggered off the explosion as he tangled, fists raised, with Burnley centre-forward Alan Shackleton, and was fortunate not to find his way into the referee's notebook. Newlands and Crowther were not so fortunate: the former for a rather heavy tackle on Ian Greaves, while the latter having squared up to Shannon.

Following Crowther's offence, Smith launched the free-kick into the United area and it struck the post before being cleared out towards the Burnley right, where Mark Pearson's challenge on Shannon saw the Burnley player slump to the ground. Without hesitation, the referee pointed to the dressing room and amid jeers and boos and the intervention of the police, the United youngster trudged, head down, off the pitch.

With ten men and still around an hour left to play, United were now up against it, and although a man short, they did match the home side when it came to skill. However, it was of no surprise that Burnley soon gained the upper hand, taking the lead one minute after the interval and adding a further two goals in the seventieth and seventy-second minutes, as the resilient United side finally began to tire.

Bob Lord, the Burnley chairman, had of course stirred things up between the two clubs with his comments relating to United in the immediate aftermath of Munich, and following the game he did little to help the already brittle relationship, saying, 'They were running around like Teddy Boys. Let this lot run roughshod and it could upset the whole of organised football. It looks as if they don't like losing. If Manchester United continue to play like this they'll lose the sympathy the public have for them. They must remember there are other clubs in football than Manchester United.

'Manchester people are still swayed by what happened at Munich. It isn't a good thing for the game. There is too much sentiment about Manchester United in Manchester.'

'All they have had to withstand in recent weeks seems to be a bit too much for some of these young men.'

He also described United as 'unsporting' and said 'they didn't like getting beaten'. As the saying goes, 'it takes two to tango' and by all accounts Burnley were no angels, playing their part in the rather unsavoury scenes, with Shackleton actually turning on Pearson with his fists raised prior to the United player being sent off.

Obviously put out by the Burnley chairman's rather harsh criticism, his United opposite number, Mr Harold Hardman replied, 'It is a shocking thing – disgraceful coming from the chairman of a football club.

'After the Munich disaster, we did not expect to win a match. All we wanted to do was to keep the flag flying until the end of the season when we could start to reconstruct. So the question of losing does not enter into it.

'Since Munich there have been no untoward incidents in any of our matches until now. They have all been played in a sportsmanlike manner.'

Jimmy Murphy was, as could be expected, infuriated by the criticism and comments coming out of Turf Moor, and entered the fray with, 'In defence of my team I must say we object most strongly to the remarks about Teddy Boys. They were totally unjustified.

'I had to reply on behalf of the boys. Otherwise, I wouldn't bother even to answer this outburst, which is not worthy of the game.

'Despite everything that happened and though I was sorry to see young Pearson suffer, in my opinion, for what had gone before. I was ready to call it a day.

'I was busy thinking about our semi-final plans. But my attention was brought to that remark. I had to defend my players.'

He continued, 'We have played five matches since Munich, games that we didn't expect to win and until the Burnley game I cannot recall one incident anyone could take exception to. Our club has a record on and off the field almost all over the world as second to none in sportsmanship.

'Doesn't like losing? When defeat comes we are not upset. Why should we be? I have been on the losing end many times over thirty years and I have always been taught to accept defeat. That is what I tell my lads.'

'When things happen on the field, you forget them later. You shake hands as many did on Saturday. We have no excuses for our defeat.'

As for his thoughts on Mark Pearson, he simply said that the player was young and it was a pity this had to happen, but he would get over it, although he was later to admit, 'I was tagged a dirty player, and believe me, when once you are branded like that, it takes some shaking off.

'I suppose the sideburns I wear helped people to associate me with being a Teddy Boy. But then appearances can be deceptive. After that Burnley game, things went from bad to worse. Playing mostly in the reserves, I had two cautions then had my name taken.

'I had always tried to play the game on the field, but I think I suffered in the end from older players trying to provoke me, and after my first spot of bother, I think some referees had me marked down as a troublemaker and came gunning at me at the first opportunity.'

Despite the FA Cup semi-final against Fulham looming on the horizon, the Turf Moor fixture continued to hog the back pages, with reports confirming that Burnley had sent in a protest to the Football League, with claims being made of 'a scene between a United player and a Burnley official', and that 'United refused to accept the customary sandwiches sent down to the visitors dressing room'. Thankfully the whole thing died an early death and was soon forgotten about or at least until the next meeting between the two, as more important matters took over. However, for the unfortunate scapegoat, seventeen-year-old Mark Pearson, the memories lingered on for some time, while many felt that the referee simply sent him off to try and defuse the hostility that was seeping into the game.

Semi-final preparations took United back to the familiar surroundings of Blackpool, although there were no reports of visits to any of the fortune tellers scattered long the famous 'Golden Mile', in order to find out what lay in store in the Villa Park meeting with Second Division Fulham.

Reaching the semi-final had never been an expectation, with the over-used, present-day saying of taking each game as it comes proving very correct back in the early spring of 1958. Nerves had not been experienced, but with Wembley and a cup final appearance only ninety minutes away, this was a different Manchester United from that many had witnessed in the previous couple of months; something that was confirmed by Malcolm Brodie in his report for the *Belfast Telegraph*: 'This was not the Manchester United, who after the Munich air crash, who gave Sheffield Wednesday a soccer lesson. It was not the glorious United which defeated West Bromwich Albion in the sixth round. It was a mere skeleton of a once-great side.'

Despite the Irishman's observations, the semi-final was a gripping encounter, with both the goalkeepers vying for the Man of the Match award as the ball swung from end to end.

Fulham enjoyed the best of the early exchanges, but they were to find themselves a goal behind after twelve minutes, when a Taylor pass found Charlton, some 20 yards from goal. Taking the ball on the half turn, he gave Macedo little chance with a blistering shot, confirming that his recent selection for the Football League side was far from an act of sentiment.

United's lead, however, was short lived, as Fulham pushed forward straight from the restart, with full-back Langley sending a cross into the United penalty area, where Stevens snatched the opportunity from 8 yards out, prodding the ball over the line despite Gregg's desperate attempt to close him down.

Slowly, Fulham began to dictate the play, with Foulkes and his fellow defenders pushed to their limits, and it came as little surprise when the London side took the lead seven minutes before the interval. Hill took a through pass from Dwight, before working his way through the United defence and beating the advancing Gregg from close range.

Having taken the lead, and clearly looking the better side, many felt that this would prove to be the turning-point of the game, with Fulham going on to claim a place in the final. It was, however, another incident minutes later that played a definitive part in who would grace the Wembley turf in a few weeks' time.

Langley, the Fulham left-back, was injured just before the interval, and with their opponents reduced to ten men, United made the most of their advantage; Bobby Charlton putting United in front during the time added on for Langley's injury, latching on to a rebound which left him with little else to do but score.

Fulham never looked the same following the defender's injury and many thought that United would run out clear winners, but to their credit, the Craven Cottage side battled away and somehow managed to keep danger man Bobby Charlton at bay. Macedo produced two world-class saves from the United forward, while ten minutes from time it was the crossbar that came to their rescue when Charlton's drive rattled against it.

Langley bravely returned to the fray a few minutes after the second half had kicked off and was soon switched from his defensive position to outside-left. Rather surprisingly, he managed to cause United the odd problem, and on one occasion Gregg had to stretch himself to keep the ball out. A clash with Dawson, however, brought an end to the involvement of the Fulham full-back and he was again carried off towards the dressing rooms.

Dawson, unperturbed by the boos from the Fulham support, continued to cause havoc in the Londoners' defence. On one occasion he slipped as he attempted to centre the ball after outpacing Stapleton, and soon afterwards missed the target by inches with a flying header.

As the minutes ticked away, there were near misses at both ends, with goalkeepers Gregg and Macedo both making notable saves. Gregg snatched the ball off the feet of Dwight after stopping Chamberlain's shot and Macedo punched a Taylor header over the bar before clutching a stinging drive from Charlton.

Frank McGhee of the *Daily Mirror* reckoned that 'for seventy minutes, it was easily their (*United's*) worst display since Munich.' He was, however, 'equally convinced that United can and will win the replay. They can't play as badly again.'

The replay was scheduled for Arsenal's Highbury Stadium, with United voicing their complaints at the choice of venue. They complained that it was (a) unfair that they should have to travel to London when Highbury was only a 1/4*d* (less than 6p) tube ride from Craven Cottage, (b) it would cut down the level of their support because of the time and money involved, Fulham again benefiting here, and (c) some Fulham people had thought it unfair that if West Bromwich Albion had beaten United then they would have had to face them at nearby Villa Park.

In reply, the Football Association said that they had considered all the above points, but there could be no alterations to their plans, leaving the United supporters who decided to travel with the choice of two trains south, at 6.42 a.m. and 7.32 a.m. on the morning of the match, at a cost of £1 18/3*d* (approx. £1.90). Even then, there was no guarantee that they would get in, as the game was not an all-ticket one!

Entry to Highbury was not a problem, as United's call to the FA to reconsider its selection of the venue was justified, when just over 38,000 clicked through the turnstiles of a ground that could comfortably hold 68,000. It was the lowest cup semi-final crowd for twenty-nine years, and the major reason behind the lack of interest was the decision to televise the game. However, in the *News Chronicle*, Ian Wooldrige also suggested that the rumours of supporters queuing since dawn helped to keep the attendance down, as many felt that it could well be a wasted journey.

Some, however, did brave the cold and the rain, with a reported 200 queuing outside Highbury as early as 6 a.m., and when the gates opened at 12.30 p.m., there was a queue stretching some 300 yards up Highbury Hill.

United supporters who made the journey complained about having to travel the 200 miles to London. 'It will cost me £6,' said one supporter. 'But it will be worth it to see United through to the final. I have already booked my Wembley trip.' There were claims from Old Trafford that they had sold around 2,800 tickets, but transport officials estimated that no more than 1,000 made the journey south.

Police were standing by for vast numbers of supporters converging on the ground, but as kick-off approached, those supporters never materialised, with ticket touts having great difficulty in selling their wares, asking 25*s* for a 15*s* ticket, £1 for a 10*s* ticket, and £1 10*s* for a £2 3*d* one. Arsenal secretary Bob Wall assessed the loss in revenue at around £5,000, clearly citing television as the blame. United were also a little unhappy at the attendance, as they would have received a cut of the actual gate money, losing around £1,250.

But for those who did decide to travel to north London, they were treated to an eight-goal thriller and certainly received value for money, with John Camkin in his *News Chronicle* report writing, 'The nerves and indecision, so marked in Saturday's 2-2 draw at Villa Park, were swept away in the first twelve minutes of this critical game. Six powerful shots and five corners almost swamped Fulham.

'United, I believe, would have won without the help of unfortunate Tony Macedo, Fulham's brilliant goalkeeper. His first serious blunders in top-class football cost three first-half goals.'

United lost possession right from the kick-off and Fulham surged forward on the well-sanded pitch, with Gregg forced to race from his line in order to beat Stevens to the ball. But play quickly switched to the opposite end and Macedo's confidence took a severe dent in those opening minutes when he fumbled a 20-yard shot from Freddie Goodwin, just managing to grab it at the second opportunity as it rolled precariously towards the line. A minute later, the Fulham 'keeper was powerless and indeed fortunate, as Goodwin, once again in the thick of the action, drove a rising shot against the crossbar.

Jimmy Murphy had sprung something of a surprise on his opponents by playing Dawson, although wearing the No. 9 shirt, at outside-right, with Webster moving inside, and bringing Shay Brennan back into the side at outside-left, replacing Mark Pearson who was in the unfortunate position of finding himself dropped.

With fourteen minutes gone, the nervous Macedo was finally beaten as United took the lead. Fulham centre-half Stapleton pushed Webster in the back and from the resulting free-kick, United won a corner. Taking it short, Brennan passed to Webster and for some unknown reason, the Fulham 'keeper moved out from his goal in an effort to narrow the angle. But the shot he was expecting failed to materialise, and as the cross came over, Dawson nipped in unmarked from the right and his diving header flashed into the net past the outstretched hand of a helpless defender on the goal line.

Fulham, to their credit, weathered the storm and fought back, drawing level in the twenty-seventh minute through Stevens, who beat Gregg with a first-time cross-cum-shot from a Haynes pass. But seven minutes later, the Londoners were again behind when the Dawson–Webster switch paid off, with the latter swinging the ball out to the right and the burly centre-cum-winger suddenly switching the ball to his left foot before crashing it home from the 18-yard line when there seemed to be little danger. Macedo, perhaps slightly unsighted, allowed it to slip through his hands, mainly due to the power of the shot, rather than poor goalkeeping.

It was a lead that United did not hold for long, as within three minutes Fulham were again level. Always looking dangerous in their breakaways, Langley, fully recovered from his injury received in the first game, raced down the left and from his cross, as the United defence held back for some unknown reason, Chamberlain side-footed the ball past Gregg.

With two minutes remaining until half-time, Ernie Taylor, having something of a quiet game by his usual high standards, suddenly sprung into action, dribbling his way through a bemused Fulham defence, beating left-half Lawler, then right-half Bentley and centre-half Stapleton, before pushing the ball through towards Dawson and Brennan. Macedo dived for the ball, but failed to grasp it, presenting Brennan with the easiest of opportunities to put United in front.

As the second half got underway, Gregg, as he had done in the opening minutes of the first half, had to race from his line, as Dwight ran through the middle of the United defence, and smother the ball before the Fulham forward could reach it. Dawson then raced half the length of the field but shot wide, while at the opposite end, Hill and Chamberlain tried on three occasions to force the ball over the line as Gregg lay on the ground. Even if they had succeeded, the goal would not have stood, as the referee blew for offside.

For United, Crowther and Goodwin in particular were in exceptional form. The former Aston Villa man was strong in defence, while Goodwin was not only an able assistant, but also a danger to Fulham when combining defence with attack.

Macedo saved on the line from Brennan, as play swung relentlessly from end to end, but it looked all over for Fulham eleven minutes into the second half, when Bobby Charlton ran down the left, waltzing past one defender after another, before passing to Dawson who accepted the opportunity to put United 4-2 in front and complete his hat-trick.

For many lesser sides, that would have signalled game over, but to their credit, Fulham plodded away and were rewarded with a third goal in the seventy-third minute. A Stevens centre from the right was chested down by Chamberlain, and as Gregg failed to reach the ball, Dwight won the goalmouth scramble and dribbled round the stranded United 'keeper sprawled on the ground, before squeezing the ball over the line. Did Fulham have enough in reserve to snatch an equaliser and perhaps force the game into extra time?

With four minutes remaining, Haynes had the ball and was in the United net, but as the Fulham players and supporters celebrated, the referee signalled a free-kick to United, as he had judged that the Fulham player had controlled the bouncing ball with his hand before scoring.

As fog shrouded the pitch and full-time beckoned, Charlton put the game beyond any doubt, when he scored United's fifth, shooting past an unsighted Macedo. Frank McGhee, in the *Daily Mirror* described the result as 'the greatest Manchester United win of them all. This was their five-goal triumph return to the days when Manchester United were a complete, controlled footballing outfit.

'This was the victory which owed nothing to hysteria from the terraces or tough desperation on the field.

'This was soccer science, cold and surgical and deadly.

'And how appropriate that they should do it at Highbury, the last League ground their great Busby Babes played on before the Munich tragedy.'

Although Macedo's goalkeeping errors had a bearing on the result, no one could deny United the glory of reaching Wembley for the second successive season, in what was only the second time that eight goals had been scored in the semi-final of the FA Cup in its eighty-six-year history, equalling West Bromwich Albion's 6-2 victory over Nottingham Forest in 1892.

For Alex Dawson, it was the highlight of his Manchester United career. 'Fulham had a good side at that time,' recalled the barrel-chested Aberdonian. 'So it was great to score three against them and get through to the final. Strangely, before the game, Jimmy Murphy took me to one side and said, "I think you will score three today", something I just laughed off.

'Did I get the match ball? No, just the pleasure of scoring three in an FA Cup semi-final.'

Sitting on the touchline chain-smoking, Jimmy Murphy had been unable to have a major influential say in United's performance, but it was the Welshman's prematch masterstroke that won the day. After an intense ninety minutes he told the waiting reporters, 'I had already decided to bring back Shay Brennan to outside-left. But that wasn't enough. Then just before kick-off, something clicked. Centre-forward Alex Dawson and Colin Webster, the outside-right had stripped and I called them aside.

'I told them I wanted them to switch positions. I had to find a way to take the attention of the Fulham defence from Dawson.

'It worked out magnificently for it gave him more room in which to work and the boy took his chances like the good player he is.'

The exhaustions of the FA Cup semi-final and indeed the past couple of weeks in general, finally caught up with 'Murphy's Marvels', as they failed to overcome bottom-of-the-table Sheffield Wednesday at Hillsborough. Only one goal separated the two sides, scored by Shiner five minutes before the interval, but it was a deserved victory, as the home side did far more in the way of attacking than their visitors. Two days later, there was an equally uninspired performance at Villa Park, where third-from-the-bottom Aston Villa secured both points with a 3-2 victory.

At this particular time, no ninety minutes involving United seemed to pass without some form of controversy rearing its head. The Villa defeat, for example, saw a last-minute goal earn the home side a precious two points in their fight for relegation, but when Sewell fired the ball past Gregg, McParland (once again, if you remember the cup final of twelve months previously) was standing at least 2 yards offside!

Seven days after the FA Cup semi-final clash against Fulham, cries of 'we were robbed' began to echo northwards from the banks of the Thames. Both Fulham's manager, Duggie Livingstone, and general manager, Frank Osborne, made belated cries that their team had been denied what would have been a dramatic equalising goal seven minutes from time, for handball against Johnny Haynes.

There had been no Fulham protests during or immediately after the game, but following a rerun of the ninety minutes at the BBC studios, the Londoners made their belated complaint and pointed fingers at what they felt was a refereeing error. What they hoped to achieve was anyone's guess, but if they had studied the television pictures a little more closely, then they would have seen that the referee was 100 per cent correct, and not only did Haynes handle the ball, but Dwight was also in an offside position, thus leaving the Londoners with red faces.

Why the likes of Burnley, and now Fulham, had to indulge in such trivial activities, which at the end of the day earned them nothing, is something of a mystery. Was it simply a case of being 'bad losers' or perhaps the embarrassment of losing to something of a patched-up team? While United continued to struggle to some degree, there were many, some silently, who felt that they enjoyed a certain degree of favouritism, as well as overindulgence in the support shown towards the club as a whole, leaving opponents in something of a no-win situation, fighting against the odds from every angle.

There were also others, however, who felt that the outcome of some United fixtures could be decided by other, ulterior motives, as Harry Gregg revealed that he had received a letter, offering him £250, a sum not to be dismissed in the days of wages of around £12 per week, if he 'contributed' to United's semi-final defeat. Following the 2-2 draw at Villa Park, a further letter was sent to Harry at Old Trafford, upping the figure to £500.

'Written by a crank,' was the goalkeeper's response.

Some form of normality was resumed on the field of play over the Easter period, with four points from three games. Back-to-back home fixtures, against Sunderland on Good Friday and Preston North End twenty-four hours later, saw the points shared with a 2-2 and a 0-0 draw respectively, while the return fixture against Sunderland on the Monday brought the first win in seven League games, Colin Webster scoring twice in the 2-1 victory.

Having reached their second cup semi-final, there were now doubts over the first, as speculation mounted concerning United's forthcoming European tie with AC Milan. Newspaper reports suggested that they were now unable to play the semi-final on the provisional dates put forward due to the FA Cup final, and would withdraw from the competition. Club sources denied this, as did Jimmy Murphy, who said that such a scenario had never even been suggested, nor would the club contemplate withdrawing from the competition.

But, completely without warning, a telegram was received at Old Trafford from Milan insisting that the first leg should be played at Old Trafford on 16 April, with the return leg in Milan on 14 May, throwing United's already packed domestic fixture list into turmoil. The Italians strangely enough faced a similar scenario, stating that if they agreed to play the semi-final ties on 14 and 21 May, then they would be playing seven games in seventeen days.

United insisted that they simply couldn't accommodate the proposed first-leg date into their schedule, with an official saying, 'If Milano are allowed to persist on playing on one of the dates they propose, we just can't go on. It is as simple as that.'

Dennis Viollet and Albert Scanlon had by now returned to full training, as Matt Busby continued to recover in Munich. He had instructed the doctors to have him ready for Wembley, with only his shattered ankle causing any real concern. Wilf McGuinness, a reserve-team player who had been out for a few weeks with an ankle injury, was another on the road to recovery and was almost ready for a place in Murphy's starting line-up. The immediate future was beginning to look a little brighter.

Having discovered the painful reality of the crash, Busby had at first shown little interest in returning to football management, but thanks mainly to his wife Jean, he had slowly begun to show an interest in football and everyday affairs. By early April, he was even on the telephone to Old Trafford for an up-to-date summary of what was happening.

Busby, who had known little of what was going on back in England until someone had told him that they had beaten West Bromwich Albion in the FA Cup replay at Old Trafford, took his first steps to recovery on Sunday 13 April, taking the arm of a nurse for a few tentative steps, his first since the disaster, as his wife Jean looked on. With a walking plaster on his leg, those slow, measured steps were massively important, as Busby was due to leave his room in the Rechts der Isar Hospital, which had been home for the past ten weeks, four days later, heading back to Manchester via rail and boat.

The BBC television programme *Sportsview* had hoped to capture something of an 'exclusive' interview with the United manager on the eve of his homeward-bound journey, with the broadcast, scheduled for 9.15 p.m. on the evening of 16 April. Alongside him was expected to be Professor Maurer and the nursing sister who had cared for him throughout his stay. However, the live link to Munich had to be abandoned, with the programme's host, Peter Dimmock, explaining that Busby had previously promised to meet the press in an interview arranged by BEA, and because of this he felt that he was unable to do the live programme.

So, the following morning, a volley of flashbulbs met Matt and Jean Busby as they emerged from the glass-fronted Munich hospital to begin the journey back to England. He had already said his goodbyes to the nurses, doctors and nuns who had helped him so much during those long, dark days when all seemed lost. But before he headed to the station and the Rhinegold Express, for the first part of that long and daunting journey, he had to face a press conference in a Munich hotel.

Many of those newspaper men, familiar faces to the United manager, were surprised at how good he looked, considering the physical and mental pain that he had endured over the past few weeks. It was the Busby of old, as he answered all but one of the questions fired in his direction. The only one that failed to bring a positive response: 'Will you fly again with Manchester United?'

He paused, held his head in his hand and replied quietly: 'I would not like to answer that. Maybe in a little while things might seem different. Only time can tell. Yes, only time can tell.'

Sitting with his right leg resting on a chair, Busby talked about his plans for the club as the reporters quickly scribbled his replies into their notebooks:

'When will you take over your job again?'

'At the moment I say next season. This season lasts only three more weeks and it's impossible for me to take over in this short period of time. Beside Jimmy Murphy's doing a wonderful job. He'll keep it at least until the Cup Final and I will not attempt to take any part in management until after that. Jimmy had to take over when things looked extremely black, and the boys have responded wonderfully well to him. The development of Manchester United had a great influence on my recuperation and helped me quite a bit.'

'What about the cup final?'

'At the moment, it's too early to say whether I'll be able to go to Wembley, but I hope so. If I can I'd like to lead United into the stadium.'

'What of the future?'

'I think I will go for nursing the Babes and plan to buy other players to replace the lost ones, like Tommy Taylor, but I'll continue to rely on young players. There is a big gap to be filled and it'll take a little time.'

Soon it was time to call a halt to the proceedings, as there was a train to catch, and as the United manager and his wife settled down in their compartment, their thoughts drifted home to Kings Road, Chorlton-cum-Hardy.

It was 3.10 p.m. the following day when the black Humber that had collected the couple at Harwich pulled up outside the Busby home, where around thirty children and neighbours had gathered, awaiting its arrival.

The Boss was home.

Thankfully, Busby wasn't fit enough to travel the short distance from his Kings Road home to Old Trafford the following day to watch United face Birmingham City. Had he done so, he would have found the red-shirted XI unrecognisable from the last one he had cast his eyes over in Belgrade. The occasion might also have proved to be too much too soon.

Some hesitant defending by United allowed the Midlands side to score two first-half goals, which in the end were enough to take both points and cast further clouds over the capabilities of Jimmy Murphy's team in the forthcoming FA Cup final and European Cup semi-final.

To the north of Manchester that same afternoon, a small chink of light managed to make a fleeting appearance through those darkening clouds. In front of a sparsely populated Gigg Lane, United Reserves defeated Bury Reserves 1-0. The victory, and the game, meant very little, or indeed nothing at all, but that solitary goal was greeted with more enthusiasm and warm applause than many other scores at the ground by visiting teams.

With many of the crowd still settling down for their afternoon's entertainment and with a mere three minutes left on the clock, United's No. 10 latched on to a through-ball from Barry Smith, getting the better of two Bury defenders who appeared closer to the ball, before firing the ball past the outstretched arms of home goalkeeper from the edge of the area. Dennis Viollet was back in the groove.

Playing his first game in eleven weeks, and scoring into the bargain, not only gave the player a boost, but also eased the headache of Jimmy Murphy; giving the United manager another option and some much needed experience with the crucial games of a truly demanding season drawing ever nearer.

'I felt tired,' confessed Viollet after the game. 'But I feel confident that with a couple of games, I can be fully match fit for Wembley … if I am selected. If I played in one of the midweek matches, then again on Saturday, I would be ready to play in the final.

'I think it will all depend on these two games,' he confessed. He was quick to admit, 'I am desperately keen to play at Wembley, because I had to drop out of last year's final with a groin injury.

'But, if Mr Murphy thinks I am not ready, then I shall have no complaints. I realise the lads have done well enough without me, and that the cup final team will be picked entirely on merit and current form. If the club think someone else can do a better job, then I shall sit another Wembley out, knowing that it is in the best interests of Manchester United.'

Two days later, Viollet was back in action, this time for the first team, as United entertained League Champions Wolverhampton Wanderers, but his presence did little to sway the game United's way, with the Champions running out 4-0 winners.

With little to play for, Murphy took the opportunity to rest players crucial to any hopes of success at Wembley, which was now only two weeks away, with Gregg, Crowther and Taylor all missing, replaced by Gaskell, McGuinness and Brennan, and Viollet replacing Mark Pearson. Such team selections certainly kept the players fresh, while also keeping everyone guessing as to what eleven players Murphy would eventually select for the cup final.

Having returned to Manchester four days earlier, Matt Busby considered himself well enough, in both mind and body, to make the relatively short, but in all probability painful, car journey from his home to Old Trafford on the morning of 23 April, where he was warmly greeted by United staff. With a First Division fixture that same evening against Newcastle United, Busby did not linger too long in the offices and corridors that no doubt produced haunting, painful memories of the not-too-distant past, but much to everyone's total surprise, and indeed delight, he reappeared a few hours later, intent on watching his boys in action once again, making his way slowly to a seat in the directors' box as a tremendous cheer echoed around the rather sparsely filled stadium.

'It is great to be back at Old Trafford again and see so many familiar faces,' Busby told the numerous members of the press following the 1-1 draw. 'The welcome was tremendous. During my last fortnight in Munich, I got terribly homesick. I wanted to see a match at Old Trafford as quickly as I could. This has been a real tonic for me. I am certainly hoping to be fit to get to Wembley. This has helped me considerably.'

One problem had been solved by the time that penultimate fixture of the season against Newcastle United had been played, and that was the ongoing dilemma over the dates for the European Cup ties against AC Milan. Acting secretary Les Olive had reached the stage that he was about to have two sets of match tickets printed, one showing the date of the Old Trafford first leg as 8 May, the other 14 May. But it wasn't until Monday 7 April that news filtered through that the European Committee of the European Football Union in Luxembourg had looked at the matter, due to the two clubs failing to come to any form of agreement, and said that the first leg would be played in Manchester on the 8th, with the return in Italy on the 14th. All it required now was the Football Association to give those dates the go-ahead.

With that major concern out of the way, the League campaign was wound up with a 2-1 defeat at Stamford Bridge, with the final table showing United finished in a respectable ninth place, although they were some thirty points behind the Champions. They were, however, only seven points away from fourth spot. But for Munich, it would certainly have been a much different scenario and the

Midlands side would have been more severely challenged for their crown and there would have been the possibility of United claiming a third successive title. But it was Wembley that was now foremost on everyone's mind.

The scramble for cup final tickets had begun immediately after the semi-final victory, with some 15,000 converging on Old Trafford for the Central League fixture against Stoke City on Saturday 29 March. With United at Sheffield Wednesday, a token would be printed in the Stoke programme, and with forty-five tokens required for the chance to purchase a cup final ticket, the programmes sold like the proverbial hot cakes, while outside the ground other tokens from previous first- and reserve-team programmes were sold and exchanged.

In those distant days, many supporters would attend games at Old Trafford one Saturday, and then go to Maine Road seven days later. On the afternoon just mentioned, it was reported that many of the latecomers for City's game with Leeds United had the United reserve-team programme in their possession.

With cup final tickets changing hands at over twenty times face value, the black market seemed to be centred on Manchester, where shillings were swiftly turned into pounds, with a 25s stand ticket selling at £25. Terrace tickets, costing 3s 6d, had a slightly higher exchange rate, selling for £8. Begging letters flooded Old Trafford from those not fortunate enough to obtain tickets through the United token scheme. But in that week leading up to the Wembley show piece, letters of a different and more worrying kind plopped through the Old Trafford letterbox. A stream of poison-pen letters had been sent care of the club to comeback boy Dennis Viollet, and all covered an identical theme: that it would be unfair to consider the inside-forward as one of the XI who would line up to face Bolton. The writer stated that the youngsters and the reserves who had played so well in the earlier rounds deserved to play in the final itself.

Although stunned by the letters, Viollet was determined to put the unnecessary and certainly unfounded abuse to the back of his mind, and at first did not report them to Jimmy Murphy. He also felt that should he be included in Murphy's XI, then he was there on merit, having earned his place as the best man for the job. Surprisingly, such letters were not uncommon at the time, as Ernie Taylor revealed in his weekly column in the *Manchester Evening Chronicle* 'Saturday Pink'. The United inside-forward wrote that envelopes would often arrive at the ground addressed to 'whom it may concern' and contained 'language that is earthy to say the least, listing our sins and those of our parents'. They would continue to say 'you are only playing on sentiment. The other sides are letting you win.' Such letters were pinned on the Old Trafford notice board for the amusement of the players.

Speculation was rife as to Murphy's cup final team, with supporters debating the matter at every opportunity, and numerous different combinations being put forward. The goalkeeper and two full-backs, Harry Gregg, Bill Foulkes and Ian Greaves, picked themselves and were in everyone's starting XI. Goodwin, Cope and Crowther were popular choices for the half-back line, but what about Wilf McGuinness and Bobby Harrop? It was the forward line, however, that caused the most arguments in the works canteen and around the public bars, with Dawson, Taylor, Charlton, Viollet, Webster, Pearson, Brennan and Morgans all having their backers.

But the players were by now well away from the cup fever that was gripping Manchester, as Jimmy Murphy had taken them to the familiar surroundings of Blackpool's Norbreck Hydro. In the fresh spring air, under the watchful eye of the Welshman, clad in a royal-blue shirt with the No. 10 on the back, the squad were put through their paces on the adjacent golf course. Two inquisitive coalmen on their rounds gave little thought to their customers, stopping their lorry and climbing out to watch as Murphy pulled Goodwin, Crowther, Taylor, Charlton and Viollet to one side, emphasising point after point in a forty-five-minute-long tactical conversation. Had he at last revealed half of his cup final side?

Also present as the United players went through their paces were the usual collection of local youngsters who somehow knew when United were in town. 'We had inside information,' confessed Jack

Robinson, one of those who found their way onto the golf course beside the Norbreck, as he recalled those happy days. 'I had an aunt who worked at the hotel as a cleaner and she always knew when United, or any other team for that matter, stayed there. My friends and I were obviously Blackpool supporters, but football mad, so any chance we got to see the top players of the day, we were there.

'United were regular visitors and we would even skip school just to get the autographs of those great players. When they went through their paces with the trainers, we would line up as close as possible to them and go through the same routine, much to the amusement of the players.'

This time, the mood was more serious for the United players and it wasn't until the end-of-session eight-a-side kick about that this mood lightened, as the game they were preparing for was more than simply the FA Cup final. It was the chance to complete the fairytale; to lift the famous trophy and dedicate it to those who should have been there and to give Matt Busby a special 'welcome home' present.

If there were nerves within the camp, then they were not visible to the naked eye and certainly did not show when Murphy's selected XI, Gregg, Foulkes, Greaves, Goodwin, Cope, Crowther, Dawson, Taylor, Charlton, Viollet and Webster donned the cup final kit for the Wembley showpiece to pose for the press photographers on the Norbreck golf course. It was a strange move four days before a major game, revealing your hand to your opponents, but Jimmy Murphy felt that he simply could not hold back any longer.

'I was hoping to hold it back until the Friday to keep Bolton guessing,' admitted Murphy. 'But I couldn't hold out any longer. Every night since the semi-final I have been going to bed and seeing a new team line up at Wembley. I reckon I would have finished up having eighteen players trotting out there. Picking this team was the toughest job I have ever had to do.'

In common with cup final tradition, the red United shirt carried a badge, but unlike the shirts of 1948 and 1957, this was not the official club badge – an incorporation the city of Manchester coat of arms. It was something completely different and even today it is still brought up on conversation as to what it does actually represent. The most common perception is that it shows a phoenix rising from the flames, symbolising United rising from the disaster of Munich. Wrong.

Others thought, upon closer observation, that the letter 'M' and the eagle was a tribute to both Munich and Germany. Wrong.

Although not part of the official coat of arms, the badge had recently been granted to the city of Manchester. The eagle was a symbol of Manchester's association with ancient Rome, and what looked like the letter 'M' was in fact the *'fesse dancettee'* recording the association with an ancient family who were lords of the manor. The ring around it was symbolic of Ringway. The crown was the symbol of a municipal corporation and could be shown in either gold or white, meaning cotton or clean air, in which Manchester had played a pioneering role.

On the Wednesday afternoon, with Wembley only three days away, a car pulled up outside the Norbreck Hydro, and into the hotel foyer hobbled none other than Matt Busby, having been driven over from Manchester by a family friend. His surprise appearance added to the speculation that there was a distinct possibility that the United manager would lead his team out at Wembley.

'I'd love to lead my team out at Wembley on Saturday and take Jimmy Murphy alongside me,' confessed the Boss. 'Whether I do or not has not yet been decided. I'll know on Saturday morning when a doctor tells me if I can walk that long stretch from the dressing room tunnel to the centre of the pitch.

'If I am not allowed to lead out the team, then the alternative will be taking part in the official presentations before the kick-off.'

The manager was also quick to point out that he would not be taking the prematch team talk, leaving that in the hands of Jimmy Murphy.

Enjoying the sunshine on the Lancashire Riviera, Busby watched closely as the players went through their final training session, before doing a little 'training' of his own, slowly walking up and down the terraced steps outside the hotel. He also enjoyed a slow walk around the hotel grounds with his assistant, discussing the forthcoming game and football matters in general. There was one other topic, a rather awkward and painful subject for both men, which was brought up in the conversation; that was the circulating rumours that two big clubs, one from the North and the other from the Midlands, were preparing to offer the United No. 2 the position of manager, with a high salary to go along with the post. Only the proximity of the cup final prevented either club from coming out in the open with their offers of employment, but it was reported that so keen were both clubs in securing Jimmy Murphy as their new manager, that they were more than willing to let the United man name his own salary.

Murphy made no comment as to the rumours, but he was more than aware that the manner in which he had taken up the reins at Old Trafford and not simply kept the momentum going, but also taken the team to Wembley, was going to attract the attention of clubs searching for new man at helm.

Busby, Murphy and the players left the Norbreck on the Friday morning heading for their cup final headquarters in Weybridge. Their opponents, Bolton Wanderers, also headed south, to Hendon, but rather surprisingly, on the eve of the game they travelled to Wembley, where they proceeded to have something of an impromptu kick about, testing the texture of the turf and stealing a march on United.

The debate of whether Matt Busby would lead out United, or more likely accompany his assistant Jimmy Murphy, was finally put to rest when the United manager announced that it was only fitting that the genial Welshman would walk ahead of the eleven heroes who had achieved the impossible. The United manager felt that he would hold up the ceremonial procession from the tunnel to the halfway line. The Queen, however, who was to miss the game with a cold (obviously not football fan), had insisted that Matt should be presented to Prince Philip in the tunnel under the Royal Box, prior to kick-off.

Busby had joined his players for lunch at their Weybridge hotel, having a quiet word with each one, before heading for Wembley by private car, arriving half an hour prior to kick-off and being driven right into the ground via the royal tunnel entrance. Looking well, he walked to the mouth of the tunnel beneath the royal box with the aid of a specially constructed walking stick, where a wicker chair had been placed for him. While awaiting the arrival of the Duke of Edinburgh, he was met by numerous individuals who all greeted him warmly. Prior to kick-off, he moved to a touchline seat, just behind Jimmy Murphy, having declined a seat in the royal box, as he felt he would be unable to climb the stairs.

Outside, there was the usual pandemonium as latecomers rushed for their respective turnstiles and ticket touts did their best to tempt ticket-less supporters to part with their hard-earned cash. Some, however, got more than they had bargained for, as large numbers of Bolton and United supporters staged a revolt against the touts, refusing to pay the prices asked, leaving them with handfuls, even after the match had started. One supporter, however, was quite happy to pay out £50 for a 50s (£2.50) ticket. Prior to the United supporters leaving Manchester, one tout had been attacked by five men outside London Road Station and robbed of four 3s 6d tickets.

There was something of a lively start to the game, with Stevens of Bolton requiring attention in the opening minutes, following a challenge from behind by Crowther, but it was the white-shirted Wanderers who had the first real goalscoring opportunity. A high ball in the United area from outside-right Birch was collected by Gregg, and rather uncharacteristically, the goalkeeper dropped the ball, but was relieved when it went out of play rather than falling to the feet of the lurking Lofthouse.

But with only three minutes gone, United suddenly found themselves behind. Edwards made progress down the left and managed to thread the ball through to an unmarked Lofthouse, hovering around the penalty spot. Before Gregg could get close enough to smother the ball, or Crowther could get a tackle in, the Bolton centre had hit the ball firmly into the back of the net.

United's defence were being stretched and outplayed in those early stages, with the ball seldom seen in the Bolton half. Lofthouse found Birch in space down the right and the ball was almost immediately despatched to Holden on the opposite wing. His shot, however, was well blocked by Foulkes.

Crowther, never one to shirk his responsibilities, was certainly making his presence felt and was spoken to by the referee after another crunching tackle on Stevens, which even dislodged a couple of pieces of turf. From the resulting free-kick, Gregg once again gathered the ball, only to drop it, with the stuttering United defence managing to scramble the ball away to safety.

Bolton were happy to shoot on sight, but United were clearly struggling, and in one rare attacking move, Ernie Taylor lobbed the ball forward to Webster, who beat a defender before crossing towards Viollet. Although in a good position, the United inside man fired over. Goodwin started a move that produced another opportunity for United to draw level, his long pass out of defence finding Webster, who in turn passed to Viollet, before Taylor forced a fine save out of Hopkinson.

At the opposite end, Gregg had pushed his errors behind him and pulled off a couple of good saves as Bolton continued to keep pushing the United defence, but as half-time approached, United were slowly settling down following that rather uncharacteristic shaky start, and they began to push the Wanderers' defence.

A low shot from Charlton forced Hopkinson to his knees, while Dawson, having returned to his starting position on the right after a spell on the left side, managed to force a corner. From the flag kick, the diminutive Taylor managed to get his head to the ball, but it flew harmlessly over.

Despite having a pin in his shoulder from a recent injury, Lofthouse was clearly a thorn in United's side and looked dangerous every time he got the ball. Within minutes of the restart, he twice came near to increasing Bolton's lead. Gregg managed to hold a header, while another effort, after he had shaken off Goodwin, went narrowly over.

United were still searching for a way through in order to snatch the equaliser and they came close on a couple of occasions in the opening stages of the second half. Following neat play between Viollet, Charlton and Webster, the latter was closed down by Higgins as he prepared to shoot. Then came the most amazing escape for Bolton, when a Charlton drive from the edge of the penalty area beat Hopkinson, but hit the post and rebounded back into the 'keeper's arms.

Almost on the hour mark, United's hopes took a second knock. From just inside the left corner of the penalty area, Stevens drove the ball towards goal and, due to the power behind it, all Harry Gregg could do was palm it high into the air before catching it as it came down. As he did so, Lofthouse raced in and unceremoniously bundled the United 'keeper and ball into the back of the net.

Bill Clarke, in the *Manchester Evening Chronicle* wrote, 'Although the charge was rather robust, it was quite fair because Gregg was in possession. Unfortunately for United, Gregg was injured and it was some time before he was able to resume after attention from both United and Bolton trainers.

'Gregg erred in not turning the ball over the bar. He was, in fact, a 'sitting duck' for Lofthouse, who quite fairly took advantage.'

In the *Sunday Graphic*, Basil Easterbrook saw the incident as follows: 'A United player was sold a dummy to let Stevens in on the left. He let fly with every ounce of power in his lithe young body. Gregg pushed the ball up in the air. He could have flicked it over the bar, but his side were one down and he wanted the ball to belt back upfield and send his forwards in search of the equaliser.

'Off balance, Gregg reached backwards and grabbed the ball. Lofthouse had the situation sized up in a trice. He raced forward, hurtled through the air – and at the very moment Gregg was making sure his grip on the ball and fighting to regain his balance, sent the goalkeeper and ball spinning between the posts.'

Following the incident, Lofthouse was loudly booed by the United support every time he touched the ball, while the burly forward later claimed, 'I headed the ball over the line as it came down and before Harry caught it.'

Gregg, on the other hand said, 'I remember nothing of the second goal. I had to turn round to catch the ball. All I could see was the crowd. Then something hit me. I don't blame Nat; I'd have done the same.'

It was around four minutes before Harry Gregg could resume his duties between the posts, but the goal seemed to kill the game as a contest, with United struggling to gain any form of control on the proceedings. Taylor, having been much involved in the early stages, now faded into the background. Of the few opportunities that were to come United's way in the closing stages they fell mainly to Dennis Viollet and were either blotted out by the Bolton defence, put wide, or saved comfortably by Hopkinson.

Bolton now seemed content to see out the game at their own pace, with United realising that there was to be no fairytale finish to such a dramatic season, and for the second time in twelve months they would simply be remembered as FA Cup runners-up, although few could forget the events that enabled them to make that return trip up Wembley Way.

In the *News of the World*, Frank Butler summed up the afternoon as follows: 'Let me brush aside all sentiment right away and say that these happy wanderers from Bolton deserved to win. They were the more complete and sturdy side, and in their captain Nat Lofthouse, who scored both goals, they had a complete winner.

'The Busby Babes were never quite good enough, but they failed gloriously and, with just a little luck, they might have won.'

Jimmy Murphy, the chain-smoking United stand-in manager, gave his own thoughts on the outcome to Butler, saying, 'I am still very proud of the way these United boys got to Wembley and the way they performed today. A lot of people said it was emotion that got us to the cup final. That's rubbish. A crowd helps, but we played most of those games away from Old Trafford. You can't win five matches with bloody emotion. You have to play a bit as well, and they certainly did that, magnificently. But there is no question that the better team won.'

United returned home to Manchester twenty-four hours later, with a crowd of some 75,000 lining the streets of the city, and a further 20,000 packed into Albert Square outside the Town Hall, where they were greeted by the lord mayor, Alderman Leslie Lever.

Busby remained, once again, in the background, despite the chants of 'We want Matt' from the packed crowd. The manager was more than content to offer a simple wave as he sat on a chair just inside the Town Hall doors, as he felt a speech would be too emotional amid such an electrifying atmosphere. Instead it was down to captain Bill Foulkes to acknowledge the supporters. 'The boss, Mr Busby, Jimmy Murphy and the boys want to thank you very much for giving us such a welcome home.

'In the circumstances I think it was a really good try. We'll try again next season.'

Bolton Wanderers, however, were not so fortunate in their homecoming the following day. For some unknown reason, they had decided to make the final few miles of their journey to Bolton by coach, having travelled by train from London to Manchester's London Road Station. Equally strange was their decision to sit on the roof of the coach instead of simply making the last lap of the journey somewhat indiscreetly.

In the city centre, they were given polite applause, but once they crossed the boundary into Salford, all hell broke loose and the coach was suddenly under siege, with stones, tomatoes, flour bags and lumps of turf being thrown by a number of locals, reported to be mainly children.

Nat Lofthouse said, 'There were a number of hooligans along the route. One of the boys was hit by flour just after leaving London Road station and other things were thrown en route. But the real trouble came in Salford.'

'Cheyenne Country' was how Bolton coach George Taylor described the scene.

The season, however, was not over for United, as there was still a minimum of 180 minutes left to play. AC Milan were totally convinced that it would certainly not exceed that time scale, as their trainer, Gyppo Viani, was convinced that 'Manchester are tired. We will knock them out of the cup with our smarter play and more varied attacking moves.'

Although obviously disappointed by the defeat in the cup final, the United players were more than ready for the European Cup semi-final, with goalkeeper Harry Gregg quickly confirming that he was fit to play, despite suffering back and arm injuries, not to mention a black eye, in the collision with Nat Lofthouse that lead to that controversial second goal. Ronnie Cope was the only other possible doubt through injury, but there was certainly going to be one change to the cup final line-up, one that was certainly nothing to do with any niggling injury.

If you suspect the Football Association of today of being totally unpredictable, while performing some head-scratching antics, they have little on their 1958 counterparts.

At the end of season 1957/58, the Football Association had arranged to play three friendly internationals, against Portugal at Wembley on 7 May, Yugoslavia in Belgrade four days later and then the USSR in Moscow on 18 May, as warm-up fixtures for the forthcoming World Cup in Sweden. Included in the squad for that trio of fixtures was the new 'golden boy' of English football – Bobby Charlton. Having survived Munich with minor injuries, he not only returned to the United side, but found his way into the England set-up, making his debut against Scotland at a packed Hampden Park two months later, and stunning the 134,000 crowd with a spectacular volley from a Finney centre.

With the Portugal friendly due to be played twenty-four hours prior to United's semi-final first leg against AC Milan, there was no way that Charlton could play in both fixtures, and if the Football Association had any feelings or indeed consideration for anyone but themselves, they would have released the United inside-forward from international duty and allowed him to not only play for United in their more important and crucial cup tie, but also remain with his teammates for the second leg in Milan. Did they not consider the prestigious effect that United winning the European Cup (a long shot in all honesty with Real Madrid waiting in the wings) would have had on the English game? Obviously not.

Charlton played against the Portuguese and also featured in the Yugoslavia match, a confidence-shattering 5-0 defeat, but was not included in the third and final friendly against the USSR. Neither did he appear in any of England's World Cup Group Four games in Sweden, making his selection for the first two friendlies and eventual disappearance all the more disappointing to United supporters up and down the country. Perhaps even more so, when you consider that the England coach at the time was Walter Winterbottom, himself a former Manchester United player!

As his Manchester United teammates relaxed at home contemplating the Milan cup tie, Bobby Charlton was at Wembley for the second time in a matter of days; this time, however, in the white of England, scoring both goals in a 2-1 win over Portugal. The following evening, it was something of a reversed role, as Charlton could only watch the events from Old Trafford unfold on the flickering black-and-white television screen in the England team hotel; kicking every ball and wishing that he was there with his friends, doing their utmost to beat Milan.

It was back in September that the European campaign had begun, in the preliminary round – something of an insult really, having reached the semi-finals the previous season, with the draw pairing them with Irish side Shamrock Rovers. Having seen off the likes of Anderlecht and Bilbao last time, the Irish part-timers were certainly not going to cause any real problems and United ran up a 6-0 scoreline over the water. In a much more closely fought encounter at Old Trafford, Shamrock managed to score twice, although United managed three, going through 9-2 on aggregate.

Round One brought another illustrious name from European football, Czechoslovakian side Dukla Prague, but they were no match for Matt Busby's side, returning home after the first leg at Old Trafford having conceded three goals without reply, leaving them with a difficult job in the return leg. Three goals were just too many to pull back, and although they did manage to reduce the leeway by one, the United defence stood firm.

In the quarter-finals, it was the experienced Red Star Belgrade who stood between United and a second consecutive semi-final place, with the first leg scheduled for Old Trafford. Had the draw been the other way round, who knows what the future would have held.

Under the Old Trafford lights, United, playing in their all-white change strip, managed to gain some form of advantage over Belgrade, winning by the odd goal in three, but realising that they had something of a mountain to climb in the second leg.

In Belgrade, the game was played out on a muddy, slush-covered pitch, where United showed why they were beginning to be thought of as one of the best teams in Europe. Not only did they have to master their opponents and the difficult conditions, but they found another, equally difficult opponent in referee Karl Kajner, whose somewhat poor decisions almost saw United forced into a replay.

Two of the Red Star goals came from the referee's incompetence, and back in the dressing room, the United players admitted that they were beginning to fear making any form of physical contact with their opponents.

Despite the conditions under foot, United were three goals in front by the interval, with the semi-finals clearly in their sights; however, with the help of the over-officious referee, they pulled it back to 3-3. Had Cokic taken his time when well positioned to score, a third game would have been required to decide the winner. As it was, United held on, maintaining their advantage and going through to the semi-final.

For the first leg of the semi-final, Jimmy Murphy made a couple of other changes to his line-up. Colin Webster moved from outside-left to centre-forward to replace the otherwise occupied Bobby Charlton, while Mark Pearson took over at outside-left. On the opposite flank, Murphy left Alex Dawson, bringing in Kenny Morgans.

For Morgans, it was something of a bittersweet return. He had come back into the side towards the end of the League campaign, and looking back, the winger confessed that he perhaps should not have returned to the side so soon, and might have been better postponing his return until the following season. The Welshman reflected that 'Jimmy Murphy came down to Swansea to see me and said that I had to come back, as he didn't have any wingers. What else could I do?'

But much to Morgans' disappointment, having played in seven of the final eight League fixtures, Murphy had left him out of his Wembley line-up, as the stand-in manager believed that due to his loss of weight and the actual occasion, it would all have been too much for him. Morgans, however, was 'heart broken' as he had wanted to win the cup for his friends who had died. Rather ironically, Morgans was the best player on the park in the first leg against Milan, a mere five days after having had to endure his team's defeat from a seat in the Wembley stand. A few days later, however, Murphy called him into his office and held up his hands, admitting that he was sorry and that he had been wrong to leave his fellow countryman out of the cup final side. Had he played, United would have probably have won the cup.

The emotions of Munich had carried Jimmy Murphy's roughly assembled side through the FA Cup and on to the final itself, but Europe was a completely different scenario, although with the voracious Old Trafford crowd behind them, anything was possible.

As the first leg of the semi-final against Milan got underway, it looked as though it would take more than emotion, luck and the backing of their own supporters to carry United through to the semi-finals, as the Italians showed their pedigree, with Cucchiaroni and Bredesen causing numerous problems, and a defeat for United looking more than a possibility.

Indeed, it was the visitors who took the lead in the twenty-fourth minute, although it was only the courage and strong tackling of the United defence, sometimes bordering between fair and foul, that had kept them on level pegging up until that point. Having broken down yet another Milan attack, Crowther's intended pass to Greaves was intercepted by Bredesen and before any United player could react to the danger, the ball had found its way to Schiaffino, who steered it past Gregg with ease.

Although Milan continued to dominate, United found themselves back on level terms five minutes prior to the interval. Maldini rather uncharacteristically mistimed a pass back to his 'keeper and in-stepped Dennis Viollet to seize upon the half-chance.

A challenge between goalscorer Schiaffino and Harry Gregg resulted in the Italian centre-forward receiving a cut head, with the injury curtailing his effectiveness in the second half of the game, forty-five minutes that saw something of the United of the past few weeks, no doubt inspired by a rousing half-time team-talk from Jimmy Murphy.

According to Terence Elliott in the *Daily Express*, however, the United players needed little in the way of rousing, as he wrote, 'Some of United's first-half tackling made me wonder how these Milan boys could take it without retaliation.'

Galvanised as ever by the diminutive major that was Ernie Taylor, United proceeded to bombard the Italian goal, with Buffon forced into making excellent saves to keep efforts from Goodwin and Taylor out, then Webster fired over, when he possibly should have done better.

It was by now a typical cup tie, with both sets of players giving their all and the crowd on their toes or the edge of their seats, kicking every ball in earnest and urging on their favourites in the hope that they could snatch a second and ensure victory.

From end to end the ball flew, but still that much hoped-for breakthrough would not materialise. The remaining minutes were now slowly decreasing and with only eleven remaining, Dennis Viollet set off down the right, beginning yet another assault on the Milan goal. This time, however, instead of looking for a fellow teammate, he decided to go it alone and, after beating a defender, cut inside and headed for goal.

Centre-half Maldini, sensing the danger, moved in for the tackle, but Viollet stood his ground and as the two players moved into the Milan penalty box shoulder to shoulder, a nudge from the tall Italian saw the United No. 10 go sprawling on the Old Trafford turf.

Immediately, referee Helge from Denmark pointed to the spot, much to the surprise and disgust of Maldini, who threw himself to the ground in anguish as his protesting teammates surrounded the official to voice their disdain at the decision.

Standing well back from the melee was Ernie Taylor, ball in hand, patiently waiting for all around him to be restored to some form of normality. Eventually the Italians were dispatched to behind the 18-yard line and Taylor coolly placed the ball on the spot.

Despite his calmness in the face of the explosive situation, Taylor had decided as he waited for some sort of order to be restored around him that now was not a time for the finesse side of penalty taking. Instead, he stepped forward and hammered the ball high into the roof of the net, hitting the underside of the crossbar in the process and almost uprooting the whole structure.

As the net bulged, the Old Trafford crowd went wild, sensing yet another miraculous victory in the wake of the fateful events of Munich. Somehow, United managed to hold on to their solitary goal advantage, and despite the Italians feeling more than a little disgruntled and having conceded what they considered to be a rather dubious penalty award, when an indirect free-kick would have been more acceptable, they sportingly accepted the handshakes of the United players at the end.

Six days later, it was off to Milan, but it was certainly no ordinary trip, as a look through the players' itinerary for the game shows:

SATURDAY 10 MAY

P. M.
1.0 Report Old Trafford.
1.15 Depart Old Trafford.
2.0 Depart London Road station.
5.54 Arrive Euston Station. Coaches to Lancaster Court Hotel.

SUNDAY 11 MAY

A. M.
10.15 Depart Lancaster Court Hotel.
11.0 Depart London Victoria station.

P. M.
12.32 Arrive Dover.
1.00 Depart Dover. Lunch on steamer.
2.20 Arrive Calais.
2.42 Depart Calais. Dinner in restaurant car.

MONDAY 12 MAY

A. M.
8.20 Arrive Milan Central Station. Coaches to Principe d' Savoia Hotel

Needless to say, the return journey was an equally prolonged affair.

FRIDAY 16 MAY

P. M.
4.30 Coach from Hotel.
5.22 Depart Milan Central. Dinner in restaurant car.

SATURDAY 17 MAY

A. M.
7.25 Arrive Paris Nord. Breakfast at Paris buffet.
8.12 Depart Paris Nord.
11.55 Arrive Calais.

P. M.
12.15 Depart Calais. Lunch on steamer.
1.45 Arrive Folkstone Harbour.
2.20 Depart Folkstone Harbour.
4.50 Arrive London Victoria station. Coaches to Euston station.
6.00 Depart London Euston.
9.40 Arrive Manchester London Road station.

If getting to Milan had not been testing enough for the United party, reaching the Milan stadium on the evening of the game was equally daunting, as Harry Gregg recalled: 'We had given ourselves plenty of time to reach the ground from our hotel and to strip in leisure. Ninety minutes from the kick-off we were trying to get in ... an hour and ten minutes later we were still trying.

'With less than twenty minutes to the kick-off we made it, but now it was a rush to change. We got on the pitch breathless and hardly had time to get our breath back before the crowd began to barrack us. It was the most hostile crowd I have ever seen.

'After the game, they had to call the militia to help get us out of the place.'

As for the match, Terence Elliot of the *Daily Express* wrote that it was 'the dirtiest and most foul-studded game it has been my misfortune to see'.

Milan got off to the best possible start, opening the scoring as early as the second minute through Schiaffino, who hit the ball past Gregg from 12 yards. But despite this unwanted setback, United fought on bravely, with Ronnie Cope and his fellow defenders weathering the storm.

Six minutes into the second half, however, they went 2-0 behind on the night. A Milan attack saw Gregg move out of his goal to meet the advancing Italians, but he was beaten by Schiaffino's shot.

Cope, running back to cover, could do little to avoid the ball bouncing and hitting his hand before he managed to kick the ball off the line. The referee immediately pointed to the spot, with Liedholm converting the resulting penalty.

Danova beat Gregg from close range for a third in the seventieth minute, with a fourth coming ten minutes from time, when Schiaffino claimed his second of the night.

With half an hour remaining, one of the strangest events ever to be witnessed during a United match took place.

Although the ball was still in play, the referee blew his whistle to stop the game and the players and spectators stood respectfully for a minutes silence in memory of an Italian FA official. Not only that, but on three separate occasions, Italian officials ran onto the pitch to complain about decisions which did not go their team's way. On the touchline, however, Alex Dawson and Jack Crompton sat wondering what indeed would happen next.

'The San Siro, what a stadium,' recalled Dawson. 'But I can remember Jack Crompton saying that he was glad that there were fences around the ground, as the Italian crowd were something else.'

If such incidents unsettled the United players, not to mention those on the touchline, it made no real difference, as the game was well out of their reach and no matter how they had overcome adversity in the past couple of months, their march to the European Cup final had come to an end. Hopes of revenge against Real Madrid would have to wait.

Quite possibly, if it had not been for the events of Munich, Milan would have been brushed aside and victory over Madrid would have been achieved, but United would have to wait a few more years before they could claim both success in Europe and indeed entry into this elite competition. Despite being invited to take part in the competition the following year, once again, the stiff-collared members of English football's governing body stood in United's way. Off the field of play, United had little chance of success.

The Northern Ireland Football Association, on the other hand, unlike their English counterparts with Bobby Charlton, never even contemplated denying United access to goalkeeper Harry Gregg for those European Cup ties against Milan, considering the two ties to be sufficient warm-up games for the heroic custodian prior to the World Cup finals. Gregg went on to turn in superb displays as Northern Ireland progressed through to the qualifying stages, where they lost 4-0 to France. He was voted 'goalkeeper of the tournament'.

It was the World Cup that possibly saved Jimmy Murphy's life, or at least spared him from serious injury, and despite having earned a well-deserved summer break, he was off to Sweden with his international charges, a squad of only eighteen players, to compete against the world's best.

Preparations were far from ideal for Jimmy and his meagre squad, with an incident in a Stockholm hotel involving Colin Webster causing further unnecessary problems. Wales, however, surprised everyone, including their own office-bearers, by qualifying for the knock-out stages where they met Brazil. Had John Charles been fit to play, then Murphy's men might well have found themselves in the semi-finals. Instead they lost by a solitary goal to the eventual winners.

Murphy, though obviously disappointed, was soon to find himself a wanted man.

The two previously mentioned rumours of possible managerial job offers never materialised, but Murphy was certainly in demand, with Brazil, Juventus and Arsenal all keen to have his gruff Welsh tones echoing around their dressing rooms. A telephone call from a Brazilian official offered him £30,000 a year, while an indirect approach from John Charles, a key member of the Welsh squad, revealed that Juventus would happily pay £20,000 a year to have him as manager. Arsenal, on the other hand, simply made enquiries to see if Murphy might be interested in moving to north London.

With Busby already on a recuperation holiday, the Welshman, for whom United would be eternally grateful, could now put football to one side and take a well-deserved rest from the trials and tribulations surrounding Manchester United, as he prepared himself for the continued rebuilding which lay ahead.

2

CHALLENGERS AGAIN

'Some of our finest players, together with some of the most experienced members of our staff, are no longer with us. Matt Busby regains his strength, but the team you cheer today is about to start one of the most testing seasons in the history of the club,' wrote chairman Harold Hardman in the first issue of the club programme for season 1958/59, when Chelsea visited Old Trafford on Saturday 23 August.

'What has the future in store for us?' the United chairman wondered, as did the supporters who had shed their tears and urged on the new United during their whirlwind journey to Wembley, while they scrapped for League points to maintain a respectable position and jousted with Milan on the European stage.

There had been no summer activity in the transfer market, but Munich survivors Albert Scanlon and Ray Wood had been welcomed back into the fold, both of whom were included in the squad to face a Munich XI and Hamburg in the two pre-season tour games.

The return to Germany, and Munich in particular, was something that Matt Busby had thought long and hard about as he lay, fighting his injuries in hospital. 'It became my wish to bring United to play here, to try and repay some of the debt of gratitude we owe the people of Munich.' Obviously making the poignant return to the German city by plane, where United took on a combined Bayern Munich and Munich 1860 side, was out of the question, so it was a similar prolonged journey by train as to that of the trek to Milan a few months earlier.

Leaving Old Trafford at 2 p.m. on Saturday 9 August, it was 10.45 a.m. on the morning of Monday 11th when they arrived in Munich, having sailed from Dover to Ostend, where a special coach was added to the Corinthian night express train for the United party on their long journey to Germany.

Many of the players had found sleep difficult on the journey as the train rattled along, but upon arrival at their destination, they soon forgot their fatigue, as they were warmly greeted by a host of photographers, autograph hunters and civic officials.

Matt Busby limped down from the train to rapturous applause and walked proudly to the platform to be met by Munich officials, who presented him with a large bouquet of red and white carnations, while each member of the party was presented with a small silver monk – the symbol of the city.

No sooner had their feet touched German soil and their baggage been dumped at their hotel, than those who had survived the turmoil of Munich were off to the Rechts der Isar Hospital, with huge bunches of flowers for the sisters and nurses who had cared for and nursed them back to health during those traumatic days in the not-so-distant past.

Such was the attraction of United to the city of Munich that the crowds flocking towards the stadium prior to kick-off caused traffic jams, the likes of which had never been seen before, with many latecomers finding the gates locked with a capacity crowd inside, amongst whom were several doctors and nurses from the Rechts der Isar.

On the field, the Germans proved to be just a little too strong for the visitors, running out winners by the odd goal in seven. It was a game that Albert Scanlon was pleased to get out of the way. 'I'm glad it is over,' he said. 'I felt terrible. I felt very nervous and strange playing in my first proper match since the crash'.

While Scanlon was relieved the ordeal was over, Matt Busby was far from happy with his team's performance. 'Something will have to be done,' he said. 'I am not satisfied.' Neither was the United manager happy with the performance in Hamburg, where United lost 2-0.

At least passion had once again become part of Matt Busby's repertoire, as many had held the suspicion that the United manager might call it a day and walk away from football. It was a thought that Busby himself had certainly contemplated on more than one occasion. He was to confess, 'After the Munich disaster I had been afraid to look at the famous old Manchester United ground. I didn't think I could stand the sight of other players on a pitch on which so recently those wonderful "Babes" had romped.

'But the grand old chairman, Mr Harold Hardman, a United director for half a century, had faith, the entire board had faith, and United made another great signing in new director, Mr Louis Edwards, whose coming in itself was a sign of his faith in the future. I must not let them down.

'The name Manchester United had come to mean so much. It must carry on. It would carry on whether I played any part or not. I must play my part.

'Most of all, I owed it to the memory of those who had done so much to emblazon the words "Manchester United" all over the globe.'

Busby was well aware that having won only one of their last fourteen League games the previous season a lot of work had to be done in order to re-establish Manchester United as one of the best, if not the top side, in English football. He readily admitted that Jimmy Murphy had concentrated more on the FA Cup run, something that he certainly did not disagree with, but he also felt that, before plunging into the transfer market, the players who had carried that enormous weight upon their shoulders deserved the opportunity to play their part in the rebuilding of the team.

The manager also insisted that diving into the transfer market would do little for team morale, and neither would it do much to encourage the players who were perhaps not at their best in what had of course only been a couple of friendly fixtures.

Prior to the match in Hamburg, Dennis Viollet walked slowly round the empty stadium with his manager and was more than aware that Matt Busby was far from happy with his team's performance in that opening fixture, despite it only being a friendly: 'I know that he was aware that there were some players wearing the famous red shirt of United's first team that normally wouldn't have been given a run out in the "A" team. It was a desperately harsh fact, but it was there just the same. But most of all, I had the feeling that something had gone that could never be replaced ... the team spirit.

'Matt Busby wanted Manchester United, already acknowledged as the greatest team in Britain, to fulfil their destiny. He wanted them to be the best in Europe.

'"Will you ever be the same?" was the mocking challenge thrown down from those silent stands in Hamburg. I didn't think so, but suddenly Busby stopped. He turned to me and looked me steadily in the eyes and said quietly, "Denis, I have had the best and I tell you, I will have the best again," before walking away.'

With Busby back at Old Trafford and having taken up residency in his old office for the start of season 1958/59, many wondered if he would make any sweeping changes for the opening First Division fixture against Chelsea at Old Trafford, compared to Jimmy Murphy's XI that had finished the previous campaign in Milan. There was also much debate as to how United would fare during the coming campaign, with many of the opinion that although having weathered the storm following Munich, they would find things slightly different this time around, with the possibility of being involved in a struggle against relegation.

As the season got underway against Chelsea, neither the prospect of a relegation battle nor the slightest hint that they would fail to cope were evident, as Busby's selected XI, showing four changes to the side that played against Milan, tore the Londoners apart, with Bobby Charlton notching a hat-trick and Dawson a double in the 5-2 win.

Into the side came McGuinness, Dawson, Charlton and Scanlon, replacing Crowther (whose reported request for a transfer was deemed as totally untrue), Morgans, Webster and Pearson, with Viollet wearing the No. 9 shirt instead of 10, a line-up that Busby stuck with for the opening four fixtures.

One young player who should have been challenging for a place in the United staring line-up was Derry youngster Jimmy Shiels. The former Waterside Boys Club player had been understudy to Roger Byrne and could well have been called upon following the crash, but he was struck down with a knee injury. 'At that time, there wasn't the same degree of expertise around the medical end of things and I was misdiagnosed, which meant I would rest, come back in to play and end up being crocked again,' said the young defender who rubbed shoulders and exchanged passes and tackles with those who had perished.

Being part of the United family at that time was an experience that Shiels would always remember, but he recalled with sadness how he had heard about the crash and dashed up Warwick Road to the ground with fellow lodgers Joe Carolan and Jackie Mooney: 'It really hit us all a few days later when he watched the cortège of coffins being driven to the gym. None of us wanted to train or play again, and, to be fair, the club was very decent to us at that stage. They sent all the Irish boys home to Liam Whelan's funeral and I remember going to another two or three.

'I'll never forget the day Matt Busby came back to the club for the first time after the crash. He tried to meet us all individually but he broke down and no one could carry on a conversation with him. We were all in tears too.'

'I might have made it in 1959,' continued Shiels. 'But cartilage operations were iffy things. I was all set to make a big play for a first-team place, but a clash with a colleague who fell down on the wounded knee with all his weight meant that I was gone again for another season. The club brought over Tony Dunne and I left United and signed for Southend and I got a grand for a signing-on fee.

'When I saw I wasn't going to make it at United, I readjusted my sights. I had only ever played once for the first team, against City in the Lancashire Cup final.'

Whether Manchester United would have won the European Cup in that traumatic 1957/58 season is something that will never be known, but because of the circumstances evolving around the disaster, an invitation had landed on the Old Trafford doorstep in early June from Dr E. Schwarz, president of the European Football Union, asking the club if it would like to participate in the 1958/59 competition.

The invite from the Executive Committee said that it had decided in view of the loss suffered by United in the Munich disaster that the invitation might be helpful to them and their young players to become re-established in the football world. It was an invite, not simply made out of sympathy, but one that had also been taken with some financial consideration, as United would obviously have to dip into their bank balance at some point in the weeks and months ahead in order to rebuild the team to a similar standard to what it was before the crash.

It was a gesture which was warmly applauded by everyone. Everyone, that is, except the football authorities, who rather callously refused to give the club permission to compete. Clubs competing in the European Cup could be expected to earn around £20,000 from the first-round ties, with the sum obviously increasing as progress was made. Such a sum was not to be brushed aside, as the opportunities of making vast amounts of cash through the game in the late 1950s were few and far between.

A look at the club accounts from this time reveals £100,701 in the Deposit Account and £12,051 in the Current Account: not exactly vast sums of money, although the profit of £97,957 was a record for a football club at that time. The income from a few European Cup ties in the months ahead, however, would certainly have been more than welcome.

When the invitation arrived at Old Trafford, there was only one word to the RSVP and that was 'yes', despite the team's overall lack of experience. But unfortunately saying yes to UEFA was not all that was required. United immediately contacted the Football Association and the Football League, requesting permission to take part, and in answer to United's request, the Football Association responded positively, as it had done back in 1956, with that initial request to make the venture into the European unknown; however, their Football League counterparts once again stood firm and said that United would not be allowed to take part.

Matt Busby, as he had done in the summer of 1956, advised his board of directors that they should accept such a generous invitation and a letter was sent to UEFA to that effect. With the club accepting the invitation and despite the huge debate surrounding the matter, the name of Manchester United was included in the draw for the opening round of the competition, made in Cannes on 2 July. They were paired with Berne in Group Two, along with the likes of Juventus, Schalke and Wiener Sports Club.

Despite this positive step, correspondence continued to be exchanged almost daily between United, the Football League and the Football Association, and at the United board meeting on 8 July a letter from the Football League was read out which refused to give the club permission to participate in the forthcoming season's European Cup competition. It was a decision that angered the board, and secretary Les Olive was immediately instructed to reply.

Seven days later the board made the decision to appeal against the Football League's decision, with a letter sent to the Management Committee. On 29 July it was reported that the appeal had been upheld, with the decision of the Board of Appeal as follows: 'The Board of Appeal has come to the conclusion that whatever the intention of the Football League was, they have not the power under League Regulation 33 to refuse permission to the Manchester United Football Club to compete in the European Champion Clubs' Cup competition for season 1958/59. In these circumstances the Board of Appeal has decided to allow the appeal and the appeal fee will, therefore, be returned.'

Any thoughts, however, that Manchester United had secured yet another famous victory were soon thrown into disarray as on 8 August, a statement was released from Mr J. Richards of the Football League, which read, 'The position is that Manchester United have made and won their appeal and naturally so far as they are concerned, the matter is at an end. The Management Committee has decided to pursue the questions, but there is nothing to say on that point at this stage. We have certainly not inferred that United are about to be expelled from the League.

'There is a meeting of the League Management Committee on Sunday 17 August. It has been called to deal with the usual business, but at the meeting, the Manchester United question will also come under discussion.'

But before the Football League's meeting took place, the Football League Appeals Committee announced that it 'upheld United's right to take part in the European Cup' and that 'the Football League had no power to refuse the club permission to take part'.

This in turn brought an instant reaction from the League's ruling body, the Management Committee, with its president and secretary J. Richards and A. Hardaker issuing a joint statement which read, 'The decision of the Appeals Board has raised again questions of principle which affect fundamentally the whole structure of the Football League and which, in the opinion of the Management Committee, are of far greater importance than whether or not Manchester United play in the European Champion Clubs' competition.

'The Management Committee has asked for a meeting of the Joint Standing Committee of the Football League to be called as a matter of urgency to discuss the situation, and until that meeting has been held, no further statement will be issued by the League.'

The League Management Committee meeting on 17 August saw the Football Association also involved, but it still failed to see any conclusion or agreement reached. It was decided to refer the questions to the Football Association Consultative Committee for the final decision. A joint statement read, 'A special meeting of the joint committee of the Football Association and the Football League discussed the entry of Manchester United into the European Champions Cup competition. The representatives of the Football League made it clear that they did not wish to challenge the decision of the board of appeal. It was decided that the application of Manchester United to take part in the competition under FA Rule 18b (*clubs wishing to play foreign teams had to ask the FA for permission to do so at least fourteen days prior to the proposed date*) should be referred to the Football Association Consultative Committee.'

So, United simply had to sit and wait, as had their prospective European Cup opponents Berne Young Boys. It wasn't until the morning of 30 August that the outcome was finally known, when amongst the mail on that particular morning the United management received a letter from the Football Association Consultative Committee, and it was not good news.

The letter read, 'The Consultative Committee of the Football Association has considered an application by Manchester United FC, under FA rule 18b, for consent to take part in the European Champion Clubs' competition during the season 1958/59.

'The committee is of the opinion that as by its name, this is a competition of champion clubs, Manchester United FC does not qualify to take part in this season's competition. Consent is therefore refused.'

This was a dramatic reversal of opinion by the Football Association, who had at first been sympathetic to United's cause and backed their inclusion, as did the Appeals Board of the League which consisted of three FA councillors, but they had now turned their back on the club and surprisingly jumped into bed with the Football League.

Despite being stunned by the outcome and the club's 'no comment' stance there was no possibility of an appeal, as the Consultative Committee had the powers to act on behalf of the full FA Council. There was now nothing that United could do; the decision had been made.

A major reason behind United's decision to simply let the matter rest was that they felt they would receive little support from some of their First Division stable mates, with jealousy being mentioned as a major factor behind this.

Three days after United's path into the European Cup was blocked, the United board held their weekly meeting and, following this, they issued a statement which read:

Manchester United FC Ltd, while accepting the decision of the Football Association Consultative Committee, feel they must in justification of their attitude and actions state the following facts: The Football Association in their letter of 5 July 1958 stated they had no objection to Manchester United FC entering the European Champion Clubs' Cup competition for season 1958/59.

The Football League wrote the club that they could not give consent to the club entering this competition. The club appealed to the Board of Appeal of the Football League. The Board of Appeal upheld the club's appeal. The decision of the Board of Appeal is, by the rules of the Football League, FINAL.

Therefore, the club were allowed by the Football Association to enter the competition. By the decision of the Board of Appeal which is FINAL, the Football League were prevented from interfering with our entry.

In these circumstances there was no reason why the dates we submitted to the Football Association should not be approved, nor why the Football Association should depart from the terms of their letter of 5 July 1958 in which they stated as before mentioned 'The Football Association has no objection to your club taking part'.

The actions of both the Football League and the Football Association were certainly hard-hearted, and despite the support from the Continent, there were some within the domestic game that, even in those distant days, had little love for Manchester United.

Strangely, the truth of why the Football Association went back on their word has never been revealed, but it was suggested at the time that Mr Joe Richards, the President of the Football League, threatened that the whole of the League Management Committee would resign if the Football Association did not back them in their stand against United taking part.

David Meek, the United correspondent of the *Manchester Evening News* even went as far as to suggest that the club should call for a court of enquiry, in an effort to reveal the facts behind the decision. The matter, however, was allowed to drop.

The draw for the first round of the competition, however, had already been made, with Manchester United included, their name coming out of the hat along with that of Young Boys of Berne. At that time, as far as United were concerned, they were in the competition and the initial arrangements to play the ties had been confirmed by both clubs. When the news broke that United had been refused permission to take part, it was requested that the two fixtures could still go ahead as friendlies, with the Swiss side being given a bye into the next round of the competition.

At the club AGM on 4 September, chairman Harold Hardman added fuel to the fire as he addressed the shareholders: 'A grave injustice has been done by the FA's failure to indicate that they didn't oppose when the invitation was given and the Football League had no right to interfere. There is nothing in the rules of either the FA or the Football League to deal with the matter. Personally I think they are in the wrong.'

Matt Busby told the shareholders at the same meeting that 'United would be top of the tree again. The future of the club is rosy, although it will take time to fill the gaps.'

Having failed to make an appearance during the opening four games of the season, Colin Webster decided that despite having held down a regular first-team place following the disaster, his days at Old Trafford were numbered, and he subsequently handed in a transfer request.

He had returned to first-team duty, replacing Alex Dawson, scoring a goal in the 6-1 thrashing of Blackburn Rovers on 6 September. Although playing wide on the right, he kept his place. But a month later, in what was something of a bruising, physical encounter, he was sent off ten minutes from time in the friendly against Berne Young Boys at Old Trafford for kicking an opponent.

Webster had already earned something of a bad-boy image, following an incident in a Swedish nightclub during the Welsh World Cup campaign, but his grit and determination made him a favourite with Jimmy Murphy. However, it came as no surprise when the player, having lost his place against Preston North End, and having played in the previous seven games scoring five goals, found himself 'surplus to requirements' and was transferred to Swansea Town for £7,500 a few weeks later.

So, with some uncertainty surrounding one or two of the established names, the need for reinforcements to help bolster the ranks took on even more importance, with the press, as it had done in the aftermath of Munich, quick to throw countless names into the hat. Tom Finney of Preston North End was one unlikely candidate touted for a move to Old Trafford, while two United officials were spotted at a Middlesbrough fixture, with centre-forward Brian Clough the reported target.

With the season only a matter of weeks old, Matt Busby, while considering his options for the home fixture against Tottenham Hotspur, received the news that one name that he had kept pencilled in as a future possibility for one of his line-ups could now be erased for good, with Jackie Blanchflower finally conceding defeat in his six-month battle to regain fitness and resume playing.

Having suffered a fractured right arm, six broken ribs and a pelvic injury at Munich, it was the latter that had been causing the Irishman most concern. Despite the six-week stay in hospital and continued treatment and specialist examinations, he still found walking difficult and limped badly. He had also still to regain full use of his broken arm.

'The hardest thing has been these months of trying to make up my mind since February. I have been secretly hoping I would be able to play professional football again,' said the dejected Blanchflower. 'But I feel a lot better now that I have finally decided.

'I don't know what I am going to do by way of another job, but at least I have got over the first hurdle in deciding that it cannot be soccer. I have to find myself a future. I don't even have an idea what I can expect compensation wise, but now I suppose they will be able to do something.'

Up until now, Blanchflower had been on full wages and lived in a club house, so there was much to consider. United secretary Les Olive said, 'We shall do anything we can to help. His decision to retire will have to be considered by the board.'

As previously mentioned, transfer speculation in the late 1950s, certainly where Manchester United were concerned, was little different to that of the present day, and taking into account Matt Busby's plans for rebuilding his raw and inexperienced team, any possible transfer target was back-page news.

Mid-September thrust the name of Albert Quixall onto those back pages, hinting at the possibility of a move across the Pennines from Second Division Sheffield Wednesday. The inside-forward had certainly not asked for a move from his home-town club, but told reporters, 'If I leave Sheffield Wednesday there is one club above all I would like to join. That is Manchester United.

'There is another thing which makes any chance of going to Old Trafford so attractive. I might get permission to keep my house in Sheffield. This is my native city.'

Perhaps Quixall had not requested a transfer, but his statement certainly alerted United, and other clubs for that matter, letting them know that he would indeed consider a move, pushing the ball firmly into Matt Busby's court. The United manager, however, was quick to defuse any possible transfer talk – a wise move as this would supply Wednesday with enough fuel to complain that their player had been subject to an illegal approach. 'He is not on the transfer list,' the United manager replied. 'When he is, we would be very interested.'

This 'interest' soon became much more, when Quixall handed in a transfer request on Thursday 18 September, forcing Matt Busby to pounce as it soon became clear that a number of clubs, including neighbours City, were keeping an eye on the situation. The United manager quickly made the short journey across the Pennines and signed the twenty-five-year-old for what was a British record fee of £45,000, or £48,000 as reported in some sources. This was a fee, it must be added, that almost saw the transfer failing to go through, as Busby was rather wary about dipping into the Manchester United coffers and thought the figure required by Wednesday was too much, even when it came to rebuilding his shattered side.

Busby, however, bit the bullet. The cheque was signed and the player moved to Manchester.

Quixall, a dyed-in-the-wool Sheffield Wednesday supporter, had won the first of his five England caps against Wales in 1954, but the following year had lost his England place as his beloved Wednesday were relegated to the Second Division. Although they managed to immediately bounce back to the top flight, there was to be no return to the international set-up for one of the golden boys of the English game.

With the 1958/59 season still in its infancy, rumours circulated that there would soon be a parting of the ways between player and club, with Wednesday coming forward with claims that illegal approaches had indeed been made to Quixall. However, they failed to back up their pleas with any concrete evidence. Soon afterwards, Quixall was a Manchester United player!

The signing of Quixall came as something of surprise to many, as inside-forward was not considered as a 'priority' position when looking at the rebuilding of the team. Centre-forward, half-back and full-back were thought to be the major areas that Busby would be looking to strengthen. The manager, at the end of the day, decided that Quixall was worth the record £45,000 fee and that he was 'a player I have always admired on the number of occasions that I have seen him and a player of Quixall's undoubted class is invaluable to us in strengthening our inside-forward department.' Busby, however, was quick to extinguish any thoughts that he was going to attempt to buy success, stressing that there were still a number of promising youngsters in the Central League and junior sides.

Quixall, who had captained Sheffield Wednesday in that dramatic first game after Munich, had been with the Yorkshire club for ten years and was quick to emphasise that his reasons for moving were simply in order to further his playing career: 'I didn't have a row with anybody, or anything like that. It was a big pull leaving after ten years, but I had to make the break to better myself.

'I reckon I have got about eleven years of soccer left in me. It was a big disappointment not going to Sweden for the World Cup. Who knows – if I had been with United then I might have made it.

'There's the financial aspect too. I would be better off in the England side. Last season at Hillsborough we were all getting little dispirited at the way things were going. The bonuses weren't coming in, and so on.

'I have always admired United and once I decided to ask for a move there was only one club for me.

'I always enjoyed playing against them. The man who used to mark me was, of course, Duncan Edwards. I knew him as a friend.'

Looking back on that emotional night when football returned to Old Trafford for the first time following the crash, the former Wednesday captain said, 'Normally once a game has started, I am oblivious to the crowd. But not that night. It was a bizarre game. The atmosphere was electric.

'It was like playing against two teams – against the promoted players, determined not to let down their own mates, and also against the memory of the lads who were killed. That game drove home for me the tremendous spirit that exists at Old Trafford.

'I am looking forward to a long and happy future at United.'

Quixall's move to Manchester was not exactly straightforward, as the Football League once again felt that it had to become involved in United's affairs, showing some concern over the record fee that they had agreed to pay, a sum that was considered the equivalent to that of a Member of Parliament for nine years! But after consulting both clubs they announced that there would be no enquiry, as both clubs and the player were satisfied that the deal went through according to the transfer regulations.

The Yorkshireman's signing put immediate pressure on Ernie Taylor, but the diminutive former Blackpool forward was quick to say, 'I think this is great news. Am I despondent? Not on your life. I'm prepared to do anything the boss asks – anything. What he says is good enough for me.'

Albert Quixall's debut against Tottenham Hotspur brought the crowds flocking to Old Trafford, and the gates were locked prior to kick-off for the second consecutive home fixture. Some three hours before kick-off, supporters were queuing for the unreserved seats, and when the new signing arrived at the ground at 11 p.m. he was immediately besieged by eager autograph hunters.

In the United dressing room before the game, Quixall, who had looked a picture of confidence as he made his way into the stadium, was a completely different person. As he undressed, it was noticed that his back had come out in a rash, not through being allergic to the red shirt he was about to pull on, but due to nerves and the actual thought of pulling it on.

Under the spotlight, he took the credit for making United's first goal, but overall, he was closely marked by sometimes three white-shirted visiting defenders. Much like some of his teammates, he failed to stamp his authority on a game that so desperately required someone to do so. The future, however, looked bright for both player and club, although the likes of Dennis Viollet felt that his teammate was given a raw deal by both the press and the public and, due to his sensitivity, any adverse reaction to his on-the-field displays had an effect.

Football today is governed not so much by the likes of the Premier League or the Football Association, but by Sky TV, who enjoy the monopoly of televised football, dictating who plays who on a particular day and at what time. Back in the 1950s, kick-off times for League fixtures were generally 3 p.m. on a Saturday afternoon, certainly in the top division. But lower down the leagues, if a club did not have floodlights, then an earlier kick-off time would prevail during the winter months.

However, on Saturday 4 October, looking at the Saturday evening sport results paper and scanning down those of the First Division, the very last fixture – Wolves *v.* Manchester United – fails to give the result. Underneath was printed 'kick-off 7 p.m.'. The reason behind this was nothing more than an experiment, but one that would not be repeated in a hurry.

Disappointingly for the Molineux club, the attendance was some 10,000 down on average, and not even Manchester United could persuade the locals to forget about their regular Saturday night out at the theatre, cinema, dogs or pubs. Despite the drop in attendance, Wolves chairman Jim Baker said, 'We made football history and that's what Wolves are out to do all the time. Maybe we made a mistake by not making it an all-ticket game (*what difference this would have made is very debatable*), but this is unlikely to be Wolves' last attempt at Saturday night soccer.'

Matt Busby, on the other hand, was far from enthralled by the occasion, saying, 'We would have preferred an afternoon kick-off, but were quite happy to oblige when Wolves made the offer.

'It's most unlikely that United would agree to play a League match again on a Saturday night.'

Thankfully the encounter between the two First Division heavyweights was not shown live on television. Although certainly providing plenty of 'entertainment', the often bruising encounter did little to emphasise the quality of football in the top flight of the English game.

The match bubbled away right from the kick-off and in the twentieth minute, a bottle was thrown from the terracing towards Ian Greaves, following a hard but completely fair challenge on Norman Deeley. But it was a tackle by Stan Crowther, which left Bill Slater lying crumpled on the ground, that lit the blue touch paper, and in the ten minutes that followed there was a rash of hacking, body-checking and elbowing.

Mark Pearson made a couple of untimely tackles, while Freddie Goodwin and Gerry Harris were spoken to by referee Alf Bond following a scuffle. Clamp was then spoken to after bringing down Quixall.

United struggled for most of the match and were no match for the reigning Champions, losing 4-0. This was a result that left them in eighth place, two points behind early leaders Arsenal, but failure to win any of the following five fixtures saw them drop to fourteenth, leaving Busby with much to contemplate.

The defeat was not the only matter to concern the United manager, as he was also troubled with opposition supporters and certain quarters of the media tagging his team as 'dirty'. Both the Wolves encounter and a friendly against Wiener Sports Club had produced an unusually high number of fouls, bringing a comment from David Meek of the *Manchester Evening News* that 'there was too much tackling, which went for the man and not the ball. It is the urge to retaliate which causes the problems.'

It wasn't just at first-team level that disciplinary problems seemed to arise, as Mark Pearson once again found himself in the spotlight for all the wrong reasons, after being sent off in a Central League fixture against Leeds United at Elland Road on 11 October and then missing training on the Monday morning. Matt Busby refused to comment, but Pearson felt that he was now a marked man and actually began to dread playing, as the 'dirty player' tag seemed to follow him around.

Busby took great pride in his team's focus on attacking football and although many of the players he nurtured through the ranks, and indeed others that he introduced into the side from other clubs, were more than capable of handling themselves, he venomously disliked the thought of outsiders considering any of his players as being 'dirty'.

But away from the negativity, general opinion was that the United manager should build a team around recent signing Albert Quixall, and that the former Sheffield Wednesday golden boy was being wasted in his current role. His ability was never in question, but without a quality partner, a centre-forward to match his guile as an inside-forward, Manchester United were not getting the best out of their big-money signing.

There were still the rumours that further ventures into the transfer market were imminent, with the Welsh duo of Mel and John Charles both being mentioned by more than one source. Busby, however, was quick to state that he had put away the cheque-book and was more than happy with the playing squad that he had. Others would certainly not agree, and it wouldn't be long before the young reserves, who had performed admirably in the wake of Munich, were considered to have over-achieved. Some would also go on to regret their rapid rise and spell under the spotlight, feeling that a more relaxed and gradual approach would have been more beneficial.

A 2-1 victory at Elland Road on 1 November halted the run of seven games without a victory, but it was something of a false dawn, as seven days later the Old Trafford faithful were subjected to their second successive home defeat – 3-1 at the hands of Burnley. Unlike a few seasons ago, Busby did not have the resources to fall back on, but a fortnight later, in a week which saw last season's First Division Champions Wolverhampton Wanderers knocked out of Europe by German side Schalke (going out 4-2 on aggregate), United finally secured a home victory, defeating Luton Town 2-1 thanks to goals from Charlton and Viollet.

Briefly returning to the Wolves defeat in the European Cup, it was perhaps something of a blessing in disguise that United had been refused permission to enter the competition, as with current form being what it was, they may well have been spared much embarrassment.

Matt Busby had resumed his part-time managerial duties with the Scottish international side, as he 'enjoyed a challenge', but following a draw against Northern Ireland, coming on the back of an emphatic 3-0 victory over Wales in Cardiff, there were calls, not for his sacking, but for his appointment on a full-time basis in order to boost the credentials of Scotland as a footballing power.

Busby was quick to extinguish any such hopes of the hugely nationalistic Scottish supporters, stressing that he was duty-bound to put United first in his loyalties. This brought a huge sigh of relief from all United supporters, who had feared that the manager would, perhaps, following the events in Munich, enjoy a more relaxing and stress-free managerial environment: 'As the main parties concerned are happy with the present arrangements. That should end all speculation on any change in the set-up which would involve me leaving Old Trafford.'

Thankfully the Scotland job was not a time-consuming one, and unlike that of a present-day international manager, did not entail travelling around the country watching numerous players who might or might not be worth including in the national side. If it had been, the voices of discontent that were slowly beginning to be heard around Old Trafford would have been considerably louder.

In all honesty, they certainly did have something to be vocal about. By mid-November, with the 6-3 defeat at Bolton – where it was perhaps a blessing in disguise for the travelling United support that, even with the floodlights on, fog made it nigh impossible in the second half to follow the ball or players – United had won only five of their eighteen League fixtures. If the League results of the previous campaign, since Munich, were taken into consideration, then the picture was considerably worse, with six victories out of thirty-two fixtures nothing short of relegation form.

One thing that those supporters who peered through the Burnden Park fog were indeed aware of was that the 6-3 defeat cast more gloom over Old Trafford than at any time in the past few years – from a playing perspective at least. Confidence was now approaching an all-time low, as the team found themselves fifteenth in the table with fifteen points from their eighteen games. They were four away from bottom club Aston Villa and eight adrift of leaders Arsenal.

Suddenly though, instead of a mere flicker of light at the end of the tunnel, there was a full-on glare of countless headlights.

For the visit of Luton Town to Old Trafford on 22 November, Busby dropped Alex Dawson and handed Dennis Viollet, returning after injury, the No. 9 shirt, after having previously deployed the Munich survivor at outside-right. Joe Carolan, making his United debut, took over at left-back in place of Ian Greaves, while Warren Bradley, who had recently signed professional forms and had made his League debut the previous Saturday, retained his place at outside-right.

Twenty-one-year-old Carolan was surprised at his inclusion, as he had been bypassed previously when Greaves was injured. But following impressive displays in the reserves, the former Home Farm and Irish schoolboy and youth international was considered worthy of his promotion

The 2-1 defeat of Luton was considered by Eric Todd of the *Guardian* as only a victory due to the sense that United had scored more goals than their visitors, but it was a victory that Matt Busby's team had waited a considerable time for and one that would mark the turning-point of this particular season.

Seven days later, United travelled to St Andrews to face Birmingham City, where a Bobby Charlton-inspired performance gave United both points in a 4-0 win; and suddenly they were on a roll. Leicester City also conceded four at Old Trafford, while the short trip up the A6 to Preston made it twelve goals in three games. However, having conceded three at Deepdale could still be considered as something of a worry.

Indeed, not only was it twelve goals in three games, it suddenly became twelve League games without defeat, taking United from twelfth with seventeen points, to second and level on thirty-eight points with Wolves, although they had played a game more. The only blip was the shock 3-0 FA Cup defeat at the hands of Third Division Norwich City. On the other hand, it may well have been a blessing in disguise, as it kept the focus on the First Division programme, allowing Matt Busby and Jimmy Murphy to work on re-establishing Manchester United as a force to be reckoned with.

There were, however, distractions along the way, and it was only loyalty that kept the United management pairing together, as once again overtures were made towards Jimmy Murphy, on this occasion from Aston Villa. Having sacked Eric Houghton, Villa wanted Busby's No. 2 to take over the reins. Italy, Juventus, Leyton Orient and Arsenal and now Villa – who would be next to try and tempt Murphy away?

Rebuilding was still very much a priority, despite no further signings being made, and Busby, having seemingly settled on the side that had now struck that rich vein of form, found himself with one or two players who were now discontent with Central League football.

Goalkeeper Ray Wood had failed to return to the first team following Munich, and with Harry Gregg now well established as the No. 1 choice, the £5,000 signing from Darlington in December 1949 decided that, after finding himself left out of the Central League side, he would have to leave, as there were now five goalkeepers on the books – himself, Gregg, Gaskell, Clayton and Hawksworth – and only four teams. 'I do not want to leave,' he was quick to add. 'But obviously someone will have to go.'

The beginning of December saw the former England 'keeper courted by Third Division Southend United, with a fee of £3,500 agreed between the two clubs. Wood and his wife travelled to the South Coast to look at houses. Three were offered to the couple, but Betty Wood was far from impressed, with none of them up to her expectations, and the proposed transfer was off.

News of the collapse of Wood's move to Southend soon spread, and three days later Bill Shankly, manager of Second Division Huddersfield Town, stepped in and offered a more suitable and attractive option – and a £3,500 deal was soon struck. 'I think he can soon be challenging for an England cap,' enthused the Scot. 'But he won't play until he is match-fit.'

Although Wood failed to gain an England recall, he made 223 appearances for Huddersfield Town before spells with Bradford City and Barnsley, which were followed by a successful worldwide coaching career.

Rather ironically, Tony Hawksworth also left the club shortly after Ray Wood. However, had he stayed, the Munich survivor would still have struggled to obtain the first-team football that he felt he was still more than capable of playing.

Within a fortnight, two other players had disappeared off the Manchester United payroll with the transfers of Ernie Taylor and Stan Crowther to Sunderland and Chelsea respectively. Selling the two post-Munich heroes did not go down too well with some United supporters, as it was felt that both individuals, who had come into the side in the wake of the disaster and carried out such a monumental task, had been given something of a raw deal. Some also felt that Matt Busby had not exactly been enamoured with their style of play, particularly the more robust former Villa man. An orphan and someone who had endured a tough upbringing, his uncompromising style was perhaps taken by many in the wrong context. Both individuals had been brought to Old Trafford by Jimmy Murphy to do a specific job, which they had carried out admirably in a difficult environment, but as season 1958/59 progressed, the parting of the ways became more of possibility, especially for Ernie Taylor.

Sadly, the diminutive inside-forward could no longer be relied upon to deliver the goods at a level and pace required in the First Division – hence the foresight in the signing of Albert Quixall – but there was still little need for him to leave and he would have been ideal in something of a coaching capacity, playing mainly in the reserves, unless injury or loss of form to others dictated otherwise.

'I am happy at Old Trafford,' Taylor declared. 'And can see that Mr Busby had to buy Quixall, as he looks to the future. I'd play at right-back in the reserves if he wanted.' Sunderland, his home-town club, had been in talks with United for a few weeks as regards to his availability and what would be required in way of a transfer fee. When a firm offer was eventually made, Busby left the final decision up to the player himself.

The pull of the heart strings were to prove too strong, as the player's father still lived there, coupled with his sights still focused on regular first-team football and the possibility of the assistant manager's job once he retired. He returned to the North East for £7,000 (*only £1,000 less than United had paid for him*), taking with him 'a golden trail of memories'.

Stan Crowther on the other hand, was perhaps a little more unfortunate. As more of an attacking half-back, he had been expected to adjust his game to a more defensive role, something he actually struggled to do and eventually lost his place to Wilf McGuinness. He was also ignored by Matt Busby when Freddie Goodwin was going through a loss of form, and had the United manager made the change, it could easily have made a difference to the team and results.

Crowther also came with some baggage, from talk of not seeing eye-to-eye with teammates, to unprovoked fits of temper. One teammate of the time, while not wanting to name names, said that Matt Busby, although having a team considered to be capable of rough play if the occasion arose, would often call individuals into his office if he felt that a particular player was provoking trouble. Those who showed such a tendency did not last long at Old Trafford.

The club, as they had done in the case of Taylor, had not made any attempts to sell the player, but when the approach by Chelsea materialised, with of course the promise of first-team football, Crowther grasped the challenge, as he had done with United, with both hands. 'This was too good a chance to turn down,' said Crowther. 'Back in the first team and with a top club. My wife comes from down south as well.'

Interestingly, United approached the Football League, seeking approval to pay the departing player £300 from the £10,000 transfer fee, as he had not asked for a transfer.

It was also a little ironic that Crowther's first outing in the blue of Chelsea was against his former teammates at Stamford Bridge, but he could do little to stop United from recording their fifth successive victory with a 3-2 win.

Determined to prove that he still had much to offer and that United had been somewhat hasty in getting rid of him, he showed little in the way of friendliness towards his former teammates as he charged around the pitch with a vengeance, catching Bobby Charlton with one crunching challenge which saw the United forward fail to reappear for the second half.

The end of a traumatic year for many also brought an end to Jackie Blanchflower's association with Manchester United. Having announced his retirement from the game back in September, Blanchflower told the club that he no longer wanted to accept his weekly wage – something he was entitled to – until his contract was up at the end of the season. This was despite his current inability to do a full-time job.

'I used to kid myself that I'd be able to play again,' Blanchflower told *Empire News* reporter Ron Evans in his club house, where the roar of the crowd can be heard from the back garden. 'But it's just impossible.

'What can I do? I don't know. All I know is football. I've been at Old Trafford since I was a boy. The club have been very good to me of course.' This was despite having been told that he would have to vacate the club house on 6 February, a year to the day of that fateful afternoon in Munich.

'I'd like to get some sort of business,' Blanchflower continued, his right arm still in a sling. 'At one time I thought about butchering. But I don't know anything about it. And it's so easy to go wrong in business isn't it.

'How do I spend my time? Just mooch around the house. I'm a babysitter you know. Then the dog takes me for walk. Sure I can walk a distance. It's just that it takes time to get there.

'Saturdays, of course, I go to Old Trafford. I sit on the side with Johnny Berry. We kid on that they aren't so good as the old boys.

'It's the sitting around that's the worst. The filling in time, wondering what to do.'

The other recovering Munich survivor, Johnny Berry, also confirmed that he would never play football again towards the end of January. The former Birmingham City winger said that he had prolonged the final decision, as 'what had really convinced me that I'd had it was a kick-around I had with my children on the beach at Blackpool during the summer.

'We were playing with an ordinary rubber ball and the things I couldn't do with it!

'Now I have to settle down and think of my future. I am wonderfully well really and I am very thankful for that. But whatever job I do for a while will have to be a light one. I have to be careful not to get too tired.'

The retirement of both individuals had not been entirely unexpected, but Busby could certainly have done with both players, as he continued his rebuilding plans. Blanchflower, equally at home as a half-back and an inside-forward, not to mention as a stand-in goalkeeper, was the type of player that all managers coveted. Meanwhile Berry, having taken over the mantle of the evergreen Jimmy Delaney, had made the outside-right position his own.

Retirement was also something that Busby had been forced to consider, but the rumours being bounded about that he was set to relinquish his post at United were totally unfounded. However, after much consideration he decided that his managerial role with the Scottish national side would have to come to an end.

'It is because the dual task is too heavy a strain at the moment,' Busby reluctantly admitted after consultation with medical advisors. 'I have informed the Scottish FA that I should like to be relieved of my duties as manager of the Scottish team on medical advice, but have also expressed my willingness to help in any way I can.

'I pointed out that when my health further improves I should be willing to reconsider the whole position if they still required my services.'

Thankfully for United, the call from the Scottish Football Association never came.

Football in the 1950s was obviously a far cry from the game we know today. The switching of the kick-off time for the game at Wolves from afternoon to early evening caused much furore, with other occurrences that we simply take in our stride today bringing cries of anguish and raising considerable debate.

3 January brought Blackpool to Old Trafford, and United continued their fine run of form with a 3-1 victory which consolidated their position within touching distance of leaders Wolves. But it was not the performance in a 'bubbling, boiling Football League match' that captured the headlines, but the fact that sections of the 61,720 Old Trafford crowd actually had the temerity to boo Stanley Matthews!

W. R. Taylor, writing in the *Guardian*, penned, 'A similar lamentable experience can never have befallen the incomparable Matthews and before the match it would have seemed as unlikely as the pelting of Sir Laurence Olivier with rotten eggs for fluffing a line.' But what was behind the condemnation of the Blackpool icon?

Shortly after the interval, with United leading 2-0, the Seasiders' winger brushed past Carolan and moved towards the United goal, but as the United full-back made a second attempt at stopping his opponent, Matthews went down in the penalty area and Fenton scored from the resulting kick.

To the majority of spectators on that particular side of the ground, they thought that Matthews had made a meal of things – taken a dive even – although the *Guardian* correspondent appeared to side with the visiting winger, writing, 'Anyone would have thought the outside-right had made the decision instead of the referee.' The winger had been subjected to some vocal abuse early in the game, but following the penalty incident the volume was certainly turned up a few notches, and while the press had plenty to say on the matter, Matt Busby and chairman Harold Hardman remained tight-lipped about the whole episode.

Never ones to keep their thoughts to themselves, the United support were once again on their soapboxes a few weeks later prior to the club's friendly against Wiener Sports Club, with the decision to show the game on television at the heart of problem.

Having initially asked the joint committee of the Football Association and the Football League if they had any objections to the Wienar friendly being shown on television, the positive reply (would it have been anything else following the fiasco surrounding the European Cup entry?) saw the club approach both the BBC and Granada Television in confidence to see if either were interested.

The reason behind the hush-hush approach was to ensure that ticket sales would not be affected due to the televised showing, but due to United's intentions being revealed by the Football League, who had informed Accrington Stanley that their forthcoming fixture against Swindon Town would have to be postponed because of United's plans, the final decision regarding the proposed showing was put on hold.

Plans to show the whole game live were soon dropped, although Granada voiced an interest in televising at least some of the ninety minutes, and following discussions with United, it was decided that the second half would go out live. However, to do so, the kick-off would have to be changed to 7.45 to fit in to their planned schedule. It was to be shown between 8.30 and 9.30, following *Criss-Cross Quiz*.

With not every household having the luxury of a television, a good gate could still have been expected, but many supporters felt that the price of a stand ticket was a little expensive at 10/- (50p). secretary Les Olive, however, was quick to reply to those critics, saying, 'Our ground charge is 2/- (10p), which after all is the bulk of our capacity, and remains the same.

'The primary consideration was to get a top team here, and to do that, we had to make an attractive offer. We had to make a big guarantee to cover two matches in this country.

'We are not out to make a big profit, but we are looking to the future.

'United undertook a guarantee of £1,500 for their match and £1,200 for a second, or 50 per cent of the net gate, whichever was the greater.

'The 5/- (25p) seating is up to 7/6*d* (37p), while the 6/6*d* (32p) seats are up to 10/- (50p). 10/- is still cheaper than some First Division clubs charge.'

Despite ground admission charges being kept the same, the Wiener fixture attracted a mere 37,834, some 11,000 less than had attended the match against Newcastle United just over a week previously. It was a game won by United thanks to a solitary Dennis Viollet goal, but it was a guideline as to how far United had progressed over the past few months, as the Austrian club were far from being some 'unknown' club side, as they were one of the quarter-finalists in the European Cup (due to face Real Madrid) and had previously defeated both Dukla Prague and Juventus. A further test awaited Busby's team ten days later when League leaders Wolverhampton Wanderers travelled to Manchester for what promised to be an intriguing top-of-the-table encounter.

Against the League leaders, play flowed from end to end as the game gathered momentum, with play of a standard that would not normally have been expected on a slippery surface amid some heavy drizzle. But, as the visitors began to gain the upper hand, it was Dennis Viollet who gave United the advantage five minutes prior to the interval.

Starting the move which led to his goal, Viollet pushed the ball out to the right and from Charlton's centre, which was nodded down by Harris; he quickly pounced to half-volley the ball through the narrowest of gaps and into the net.

Wolves plodded away admirably, but it was not until the sixty-fourth minute that they managed to breach the United defence, Mason shooting past a partly unsighted Gregg from 25 yards.

As the minutes slowly ticked away, both sides continued to miss chances and, as the sands of time ebbed away, Bradley, a revelation on the United right since his step up from the amateur ranks, waltzed down the touchline, pushed the ball to Viollet, who in turn found Charlton, who on this occasion found the target to give United both points.

Twelve games without defeat and there was a distinct buzz around Old Trafford once again. But for one individual, February was something of a testing time.

One year on since the disaster, Matt Busby relieved Bill Foulkes of the club captaincy and left him out of his starting line-up after a run of eighty-eight consecutive appearances, stating, 'I have given him a rest to help him regain his form.

'Foulkes has led the side over the past twelve months in very trying circumstances and seen us through some difficult times. Now he feels he would like to concentrate on his own game and that is what we shall let him do.'

'I must admit I had grave doubts about my future with the club the day the boss decided to drop me,' admitted the former St Helens miner. 'I'd been playing under a strain as right-back and captain and I knew I'd had a bad game in our last match (*a 4-4 draw against Newcastle United at Old Trafford*), but I still had to swallow hard when I knew United were dropping me.

'The captaincy was a job I never wanted. It's a worrying job at the best of times. In the critical months on our road back, it was doubly so. It got me down and, in no small way, was responsible for my loss of form.'

But the Munich survivor was soon back in the spotlight when Mel Charles, a name linked with United on numerous occasions during the past twelve months, handed his current club Swansea Town a transfer request, and their manager, Trevor Morris hinted at an exchange deal.

It was a transfer that was doomed from the start and never entered the head of either Foulkes or Busby. 'We don't want Mel Charles or any player,' declared the United manager. 'There are a lot of suggestions, through no fault of my club or the players concerned, that United are signing certain players. My directors and I wish to state that we have decided to make our challenge for the championship with the present staff of players, who have got us into this happy position whether we are successful or not.'

With the first anniversary of Munich past, United, as they had been at the time of the crash, were in an ideal position to challenge for the First Division championship as the final weeks of the season appeared on the horizon. Matt Busby had struggled over the past twelve months, fighting an often lone personal battle, mentally as well as physically. He had long since thrown the crutches away, and with the walking stick now in the back of a cupboard there was barely a hint of a limp when he walked. Stairs could be taken briskly, while the old football boots had been dubbined and slipped back on, passing the ball to his players during training sessions.

In a rare moment away from football, he told Donald Gomery of the *Daily Express*, 'Surely it is the purpose of life to build, to create, to conquer set-backs when they come, to hope. If everything goes smash, then there must be the will to build again and again.

'When I knew it all, I was in despair. It was the end. There was nothing left. It was the doctors who told me off, who shook me out of that despair, who made me – forced me to – realise that I had to build again and succeed for the sake of those who had died.'

Through those darkest of days, there had always been a rock at Matt Busby's side, someone who had shared the strain and also the triumph of the last twelve long months, his wife Jean; a woman who kept herself out of the spotlight, but who was always there.

Speaking about her husband, when he wasn't within earshot, she told Donald Gomery, 'He has this tremendous determination to get better, completely better again.

'He never talks of being in pain. But I see it in his face. Only the next day, perhaps, he will say – "didn't feel quite so good yesterday".

'Matt and I never talk of the crash, though we often talk of the boys. He always calls them his boys. He lives for his team, but I suppose it is like that with all football managers.

'Last weekend (*the anniversary of the crash*) I saw the terrible upset on his face.'

Busby also spoke of the aftermath of Munich in a more revealing interview with another *Daily Express* journalist, Herbert Kretzmer, telling the South African, 'There was a time, when I gradually became aware that some of my boys must have been killed. I did not know for certain. I just knew something dreadful had happened. I was in that tent, barely alive myself.

'Twice I had been given the last rites of the Roman Catholic Church. I just wanted to stay inside that tent and die there, rather than come out of it and learn the truth. So I prayed for the end to come quickly. I have never said this to a living soul before...

'Strange how you hold on, the things you clutch at. In the middle of it all I found myself seeing visions of the ones I loved most in the world. Then I would fight back.'

He also spoke of life back in Manchester: 'Deep down, the sorrow is there all the time. You never really rid yourself of it. It becomes part of you. You might be alone, and it all comes back to you, like a kind of roundabout and you weep...

'The first time was when I went to the football ground at Old Trafford after the accident. I don't know. I just looked at the empty field and I tell you I have never in all my life felt such a terrible vacuum. And so I cried; and afterwards, I felt better for the tears and because I had forced myself to go back there. It was something I'd done, something I'd conquered. The first rung of the ladder…'

Back amongst the on-field action, all good things must obviously come to an end, and United's unbeaten run was brought to a halt seven days after their notable victory over Wolves, with a 3-2 defeat at Highbury on the last day of February. Two days later, the defeat was simply shrugged off with a 3-1 victory at Ewood Park, Blackburn, kick-starting the push for the championship and a further run of victories when it mattered most. Further victories – 2-1 at home to Everton, 3-1 at West Bromwich Albion and 4-0 against Leeds United at Old Trafford – helped United remain within touching distance of leaders Wolves as the fixtures became fewer, with one solitary point all that kept the two teams apart. The Midlands side did, however, have the added cushion of a game in hand over their rivals.

A 6-1 win against Portsmouth at Old Trafford on 27 March, a goal spree which included an own goal, a penalty and two shots which went in off the post, took United into top spot, one point in front of Wolves, but the Midlanders now had two games in which to overhaul their title rivals.

Twenty-four hours later, the destination of the First Division championship flag was more or less decided; as United's visit to Burnley saw the Turf Moor side complete the double over their near neighbours in a game that fortunately did not carry the same malice of the previous season's encounter. Hordes of United supporters flocked to Burnley expecting another victory along with the hopes that Preston North End might do their fellow Lancastrians a favour and send the Wolves back to the Midlands with their tails between their legs.

It was United, however, who returned home deflated, as they found themselves two down within the opening twenty minutes, and despite pulling it back to 2-1 through Goodwin, before the interval, setting up a storming second forty-five minutes, they simply couldn't put the ball in the net when it mattered most.

Scanlon missed two golden opportunities after the restart, which proved costly, as the home side added a third in the sixty-eighth minute and a fourth a few minutes later. Viollet scored a second for United fifteen minutes from time, but this was little more than a token gesture.

It was certainly a more sporting encounter than last season's impetuous display, but a few bumps, bruises and indeed bookings would have been gratefully received if it had meant two points for United. A few miles across Lancashire, Wolves headed for home two points better off and well and truly in the driving seat.

With five games remaining, Busby called Foulkes into his office and, following a ten-game lay-off, which had seen the former captain further demoralised with a sending-off in a Central League fixture against Chesterfield, told him that he was back in the side in his preferred position of centre-half.

Portsmouth were beaten again, for the second time in three days, but only 3-1 on this occasion. However, it was enough to take United back to the top, although only for twenty-four hours, as Wolves notched up a similar scoreline against Leeds United at Molineux.

The normally defiant Bolton were defeated 3-0 at Old Trafford, while Wolves could only draw 3-3 at home to Burnley. Perhaps…

Seven days later the nerves were beginning to show, as Wolves dropped another point at home to Bolton. But that same afternoon, United waved goodbye to any slim hopes they still held in snatching that championship crown in a goal-less, ill-tempered ninety minutes at Kenilworth Road, Luton.

With Bobby Charlton on international duty at Wembley, Busby brought Mark Pearson into the side for what was only his fourth senior outing of the season (his last way back in December) with the England man, who had scored five in his previous four outings, being sadly missed.

Luton, with one eye on their forthcoming cup final appearance, were undoubtedly there for the taking, but Pearson's sky-high effort in the twelfth minute, with Luton 'keeper Baynham lying helpless on the ground, set the tone for the afternoon.

As the game progressed, tempers became frayed and as the players lost their cool, United lost the championship, which in all reality had been little more than a dream since the defeat by Burnley.

McGuinness and Bingham were booked and one correspondent was surprised that only Luton's Pacey was a casualty of the afternoon, receiving a deep cut above his right eye. The same reporter claimed that neither side deserved even the point they won through the 0-0 draw!

The following Saturday, Wolves showed United how a championship-winning side should perform, defeating Luton 5-0, before rounding off their campaign with a 3-0 victory over Leicester City in their penultimate fixture, followed by a 1-0 win against Everton. United, on the other hand, finished their season with a 1-0 win over Birmingham City, but on that final afternoon lost 2-1 at Leicester, ensuring that the Filbert Street side would continue to enjoy First Division football the following season.

Despite losing out on the title, runner-up was a position that few could have envisaged twelve months previously. The strong vein of form between mid-November and the end of March proved that Manchester United no longer needed sympathy to win games and that Matt Busby had the nucleus of a promising side.

'We've won neither cup nor League – but we have achieved something greater either than either of these honours hold,' proclaimed the United manager. 'We've concertinaed into a single season a period of rebuilding which I imagined might extend over three or four years.'

They had weathered the storm, but the future was far from plain sailing, as the months ahead were soon to reveal.

Although the domestic season was complete, United had one more fixture to play: a friendly in Rotterdam against Feijenoord arranged, with a short break, as something of a 'thank-you' to the players for their endeavours throughout the past season. But for two individuals, the short, seventy-minute cross-Channel journey could just as well have been a round-the-world, non-stop journey, as it filled them with dread and anxiety.

For Matt Busby and Bill Foulkes, it would be their first flight following the events of Munich. The other survivors – Harry Gregg, Bobby Charlton, Dennis Viollet and Albert Scanlon – had all exorcised the demons, taking their tentative first flight on a previous occasion. But despite the flight being little more than an hour, it was going to be a real test for Busby and Foulkes.

Many would never have set foot inside an aeroplane again and this was something that the United manager had indeed contemplated, struggling in coming to terms with the mental barrier that such a scenario produced.

'I swore that I would never fly again,' he said. 'Once at the hospital, I remember they wheeled me on a stretcher into the sunshine of the veranda. As we left the door I had a sensation of flying again. Before I knew it I was screaming. They had to hold me down.'

But he knew that he would, one day, have to endure flying again and he continued, 'There was something else. Something that made me fly again.

'One of the teachings of the Roman Catholic faith, as I understand it, is that your life is in the hands of God ... that when your time comes to go, you must be ready and prepared for you will surely not miss it.

'Why then, I asked myself, was I avoiding the air? Was I so uncertain of my trust in God?

'So, I flew again. It was only a short hop from Manchester to Rotterdam. But it was long enough. Every second of that flight was like an endless torture. Along the runway I actually relived the whole crash, saw the whole thing.'

Prior to travelling, the United manager had been asked if he had considered sending his team to Holland on two different flights, but he waved the suggestion aside, saying, 'We are a team when we are playing and when we are travelling I do not want to spilt the team up.'

In the friendly itself, Alex Dawson once again showed his capabilities, scoring three in the 5-3 win, a performance that once again highlighted his calibre. But trying to secure a first-team place was so much harder than scoring goals for the Aberdonian.

3

Jekyll and Hyde United

Having finished season 1958/59 on a high, with the runners-up spot being something that could never have been imagined eighteen months previously, no one could have visualised that the following campaign would get off to such a disappointing start, with the pre-season build-up nothing short of disastrous.

To get his players into tune, Matt Busby took United back to Germany, now something of a favoured destination, as the Bundesliga sides could always be relied upon to provide a competitive ninety minutes. However, following the two fixtures against Bayern Munich and Hamburger SV, the United manager was wishing that he had taken his team to a different destination, where two more relaxed and incident free games would have been on offer.

In the first of the two workouts, United defeated Bayern Munich 2-1, taking a 2-0 lead within four seconds of the second half getting underway, as Quixall scored from some 58 yards out. But as the second half progressed, the fixture quickly lost its 'friendly' tag.

Five minutes after that second United goal, Zsamboki scorned the opportunity to put the Germans back in the game, blasting a penalty kick wide. A second penalty should have been awarded to the home side a quarter of an hour later when Foulkes appeared to bring down Zsamboki, but much to their disgust, the referee waved play on. Suddenly, the match spiralled out of control.

With twenty-five minutes remaining, the aggrieved Zsamboki clashed with Charlton and then proceeded to take out some of his frustration on Carolan, whom he had tormented for most of the game. The United full-back immediately retaliated, catching the German with a glancing blow to the back of the head, leaving the referee with little option but to send the United man off.

Instead of serving as a warning, the referee's actions seemed to light the blue touch paper, and two minutes later all hell broke loose. Zsamboki tussled with Quixall on the touchline, over the possession of the ball according to one newspaper, but according to another, the United man ran down the pitch, barged into the winger and kicked out at an opponent. This resulted in a cameraman rushing onto the pitch, gesticulating with the linesman and the United inside-forward.

The incident and the frantic waving of the linesman's flag caught the referee's attention and, after a heated discussion, Quixall was ordered off the pitch.

Bayern officials tried to persuade the referee to change his mind, but to no avail, and amid all the pushing and shoving, United trainer Jack Crompton threw his towel onto the pitch in disgust. Then, without consultation with either Matt Busby or Jimmy Murphy, he sent Jimmy Shiels on in place of the sent-off Quixall.

Play resumed and several minutes had elapsed before a linesman noticed that United had ten men on the pitch instead of nine. After attracting the referee's attention, the official tried to make Bill

Foulkes leave the pitch. Eventually United captain Dennis Viollet stepped in and asked Shiels to go back to his touchline seat.

Eventually calm was restored.

The events that blotted the ninety minutes upset Matt Busby, due more to where the game was being played than anything else, saying, 'We owe so much to the people of this city and I wanted the game to go off smoothly. The Bayern officials were particularly upset about the harsh decisions. We do not feel – and neither do Bayern – that our friendship has suffered in any way. It is my opinion, and theirs, that neither of these boys should have been sent off, though they may take some of the blame.'

In the second of the double-header warm-up games in Germany the only embarrassment that Busby was to suffer was watching his team soundly beaten 3-1 by Hamburg.

The League campaign, with United considered to be one of the favourites for the title following their overall performance of the previous season, failed to get off to the best of starts, leaving the United management shocked following two consecutive defeats: 3-2 to West Bromwich Albion and 1-0 at home to Chelsea. Busby had made no additions to his playing staff, relying on the players he had, making only one change in personnel to the XI who had played in the final game of 1958/59, bringing in Wilf McGuinness at left-half in place of Shay Brennan.

At the Hawthorns, Dennis Viollet gave United the lead, but according to one report, United 'shuddered and creaked in defence and the forward line played pretty, pretty patterns which were ruthlessly and constantly wrecked by two master wing-halves – solid Ray Barlow and prowling fierce-tackling Maurice Setters. Matt Busby and his directors have just announced a handsome £26,000 profit from last season. They already have a proud bank balance. My advice to Matt on this showing ... spend soon.'

There was also little in the way of excuses for the home defeat by Chelsea, as Terence Elliott in his match report for the *Daily Express* felt that 'that old Matt Busby magic was missing' and that United had been beaten on merit.

Despite those two defeats, Busby was quick to insist that he would stand by his statement of last season when he said that he was satisfied with his current squad: 'Just because we lose a couple of early games there's no need to think the world's come to an end. We have got to give the lads who finished second in the League last season a fair chance.'

He wasn't, however, entirely convincing, nor in his heart of hearts believed his own words, as when grilled further as to whether he would buy top-class players if and when they became available, he replied, 'That is something the club and myself would have to consider. The younger material in the club is very encouraging and I think time will show United will be alright.'

'Viollet, Quixall and Charlton made a fine goal-producing trio,' admitted Busby. But at the same time, he confessed, 'But I knew in my heart that this high place (*finishing second in the League last season*) was false. We were just not that good. The players were going all out, but the leaks were beginning to show. We had to buy. We couldn't wait now for youth, though our youth policy was going on. The players of the quality we needed were not in the quantity we needed.'

It was perhaps rather fortunate that the following fixture was at Old Trafford against fellow strugglers Newcastle United, who had also failed to win either of their opening fixtures. In order to capitalise on the Tyneside club's misfortune, Busby reshuffled his pack. Out went Ian Greaves and Freddie Goodwin and in came Ronnie Cope and Shay Brennan. Albert Scanlon replaced the injured Alex Dawson. But instead of making the most of the Magpies' equally poor start, United stuttered through the ninety minutes, and had it not been for Viollet's two goals in the opening twelve minutes, then things could well have been different.

White pulled a goal back for the visitors in the twenty-fifth minute, only for Charlton to increase United's lead seven minutes later. Allchurch reduced the leeway again midway through the second half, but United managed to hold on for their first points of the season.

The majority of the newspaper reports focused on United's poor defensive display – 'United Must Plug This Leak' and 'United Defence Is Sluggish' were only two of the headlines that followed the rather disappointing ninety minutes. In the *Daily Express*, Derek Hodgson asked 'what improvements Tommy Docherty, Mel Charles and Andy Kerr, all of whom have been available for transfer, could have brought to that defence?'

Strangely, the name of Mel Charles once again comes to the fore. Jimmy Murphy had fancied bringing his fellow countryman to Old Trafford, but there must have been something that failed to attract the Welsh internatonal to Busby, as despite the constant speculation in the press, there was no official interest and the cheque-book remained locked away in a desk drawer.

If you scan through United's illustrious history there is a continuous thread that forewarns those critics who are quick to write them off, to do so at their peril. No matter how United were playing, they still possessed that unique capability of attracting large crowds. Both factors were clearly in evidence at Stamford Bridge on the evening of Wednesday 2 September 1959.

There was, however, as much action off the field as there was on it. As kick-off approached, thousands remained outside, and with the terraces filling to overflowing, there was still no decision from the Chelsea hierarchy to close the gates. The turnstiles clicked merrily away as the gatemen continued to accept the 2*s* from supporters who were oblivious to what they were about to encounter on the terraces awaiting them.

Cars outside the ground were damaged as fans surged towards the gates, while inside, others scaled the floodlights, using the power cables as a rope, risking life and limb in an effort to see the game. Policemen struggled to keep supporters from surging through the stands, while all around them were scenes of utter chaos.

Forty-year-old Victor Smith, a Chelsea regular, said, 'They were laying out fainting cases and women were screaming inside the ground, while they were still letting people in. We hadn't a chance to see the game.'

Booing crowds followed the gatemen carrying bags of money from the turnstiles, shouting 'thieves', while others who never saw a ball kicked waited to speak to Chelsea secretary John Battersby. 'We have had about 80,000 in here,' said the Stamford Bridge secretary. 'Thousands are bound not to see if early arrivals don't move forward. It's up to them.' The official attendance was actually given as 66,579!

Another Chelsea official added, 'Reports from inside the ground gave no indication that arrivals would not get a view of the match. So we did not lock the gates. We have no power to refund the money.'

Play commenced with the players oblivious as to the goings-on only yards away. At half-time, when the situation was clearly beginning to get out of hand and take on a serious outlook, hundreds of those still outside were taken through the players' entrance and onto the dog track surrounding the pitch, where they were allowed to sit and watch the game.

On the pitch, United blew away both the early-season cobwebs and the Londoners with a devastating display, hitting them for six.

Greaves gave Chelsea the lead in the twenty-fifth minute, but twelve minutes later United were 3-1 in front with goals from Quixall, Charlton and Bradley. Sillett pulled one back five minutes before the interval, but Viollet increased United's lead a minute after the break, while Bradley added his second in the seventy-second minute to make it 5-2. Brennan needlessly handled a minute later, allowing Sillett to convert the penalty and make it 5-3, but with ten minutes remaining, Viollett scored United's sixth to round off a truly remarkable and memorable encounter down the Kings Road.

Was the scoreline something of a fluke, or had United well and truly turned the corner?

Three days later, they were held to a 1-1 draw at Birmingham City – a game they should have in all honesty won – but United soon confirmed that the 6-3 victory at Stamford Bridge was indeed no one-off, humbling Leeds United 6-0 at Old Trafford with more or less ten men. Albert Quixall played seventy-nine minutes of the game as a passenger on the right wing with his knee heavily bandaged.

But the show was certainly not 'back on the road' and the doubters were soon convinced that both the Chelsea and the Leeds victories were indeed nothing more than luck.

No matter how Manchester United's season had started, Matt Busby was a wanted man. An indirect approach came his way from a Scottish club, asking him to become their manager, with a salary of £4,000, but it was an offer that he not only kept from United; he also kept his wife Jean in the dark.

'Yes, there was an approach,' Busby confirmed. 'But it was an indirect approach, which I never even hesitated about. My life is with Manchester United and there it is going to remain.

'I told them, "I have no desire to leave. Manchester United have always been very good to me and so far as I am concerned, they are the only club I shall ever be with".'

The club who made the approach? It remains a mystery to this day.

When I asked Sandy Busby, Matt's son, if he knew anything about this particular subject, it came as something of a surprise to him and he confessed that he knew nothing about it: 'No, it is something that he never ever mentioned. I know that when he was a young player, Rangers wanted to sign him, but when they found out that he was a Catholic … But nothing was ever mentioned about a Scottish club wanting him as manager.'

So, that ruled Rangers out of the equation, while the newspapers of the day reveal that Partick Thistle were without a manager at that particular time. Shortly after season 1959/60 got underway, Third Lanark were to change managers, so the 'Hi-Hi' were also a possibility. A Thistle director, however, threw cold water on the suggestion that the Firhill club were behind the audacious move, quickly pointing out that the salary mentioned should have made most people realise that it was certainly not Thistle who were attempting to lure Busby from Manchester. Third Lanark could have been possible suspects, but although they were a First Division side they were hardly one of the big boys of Scottish football.

Celtic then? Indeed, they were a possibility, as the Parkhead club were trailing Rangers and had not won anything for several years, with manager Jimmy McGrory not getting any younger. He was eventually replaced by Jock Stein in 1965, but appointing Busby in 1959 might have brought success to the east end of Glasgow that little bit sooner.

The Edinburgh 'big-two' were also possible suitors. Hearts were on the wane, and were more of a selling club, with Tommy Walker possibly finding it difficult to adapt to the changing game of the time. Hibs, on the other hand, were perhaps the nearest contenders for attempting to secure Busby's services. He had, after all, played for the Easter Road side during the war, so was well known to officials, while Busby was just as familiar with the club and the city. As a club, they were yet another fading force north of the border after their success of the mid-fifties. They were to change their manager in November 1961, but had there been thoughts about doing so prior to this?

We can do nothing but speculate.

On 12 September Tottenham Hotspur travelled to Manchester, three days after the thumping of Leeds United, and inflicted a 5-1 defeat upon their hosts, with United's defence taking on the appearance of a deflated balloon.

'No panic buying' was again the Busby mantra, insisting that although he recognised that his defence was not playing well, they deserved to be given time. He did, however, hint that he had been keeping an eye on the market, by adding that 'there isn't anyone available'.

In his 'Matt Busby Talking' column in the *United Review*, the manager wrote, 'With only eight points from our first ten games, we have made a very disappointing start to the season that on paper, held high promise of sweet success in view of our performances last term.

'I make no excuses for saying here that in the last few weeks we have not had "the run of the green". We've had a little luck in the past – and we will get our share in the future, particularly when the boys break out of the recent poor patch that has brought a crop of "wrong" results.

'What I would like to make clear is that we are not sitting back Micawber-like and "waiting for something to turn up". That there are weaknesses I am fully aware – but good players are not often available for transfer in these days as many other clubs in addition to United have found out recently.'

In the *Daily Mirror* following the Tottenham defeat, Frank McGhee wrote, 'The patient voice of Matt Busby sounded a bit tired yesterday – tired of trying to provide a reasonable answer to the semi-hysterical scream that he must buy to bolster up his defence, that he must buy BIG and buy SOON.

'He knows the defence is suspect. He makes it clear that as soon as a top-class defender who can meet his standards of skill and strength comes on to the market Manchester United will be the financial pacemakers in the race to sign a star.'

McGhee's condemnation of the United defence was echoed by the United manager: 'We're obviously not happy with the way the defence is playing,' he confirmed. 'But they deserve to be given time.'

Leeds, who seven days earlier had leaked six, regained some respectability on home soil by holding United to a 2-2 draw at Elland Road. The short trip across Manchester to Maine Road brought a 3-0 defeat, which according to Busby was 'a bit disappointing'. This was followed by a 4-0 hammering at Preston, where they were considered 'lucky' only to concede four!

If there were to be no panic buys, and money was certainly available to finance such a scenario, it was certainly panic stations, as United were now only three points above bottom club Birmingham City, but seven points adrift of leaders Tottenham. Surely 'Busby will act now' was the general opinion of the United support.

Although the support were becoming frustrated, Busby had certainly not been idle and had identified twenty-five-year-old Eric Caldow, the Glasgow Rangers and Scotland full-back and a player with whom he was more than familiar with through the Scotland international set-up, as one individual who could add some stability to his rather lacklustre defence.

Despite his credentials, Caldow had lost his place in the Rangers first team, and on the afternoon that saw United crumble at Preston, the United manager had the full-back watched in a Rangers reserve game. But despite Caldow's demotion, something that had nothing at all to do with his transfer request, he would not come cheaply, as the directors of the Glasgow club, who had still to give their decision regarding the defender's request for a move, were well aware of interest from other clubs along with that of Manchester United, and they would be quite happy to allow the situation to develop into an auction if need be.

It soon emerged that the reason behind Eric Caldow's decision to leave Rangers was entirely down to his wife. 'Eric is doing it for me, because I am so unhappy in Scotland,' she explained. 'Rangers mean a great deal to him and I realise how difficult it is for him to break away from them. But there is nothing I can do about this feeling I have. I am so terribly homesick (*she hailed from Co. Durham*). Anywhere in England would suit me, though naturally I would like to move near to my family.'

Tommy Muirhead, a journalist with the *Scottish Daily Express*, hinted that Rangers would be more interested in a cash-plus-player deal and the Glasgow club should ask United for Bobby Charlton as the player part of the deal!

As September drew to a close the two clubs agreed a fee for the full-back, initially believed to be around £28,000, but a day later dropped to £25,000. It was now more or less a case of Caldow saying 'yes' or 'no' to United's offer. But it wasn't quite so clear-cut, as the full-back was still somewhat uncertain as regards to actually making the move.

'I have not decided yet,' he said after Scotland's 12-0 victory at Ballykinlar Camp, near Belfast against the 2nd Greenjackets. 'I must contact Rangers manager Mr Symon before making my decision and I may 'phone him tomorrow.

'Mr Busby wants to meet me in Manchester on Saturday to discuss the move and look at houses, but I must have things sorted with Mr Symon before meeting Mr Busby – even if it means postponing the Manchester meeting.'

The reason behind Caldow's hesitancy became clear when it was discovered that Newcastle United manager Stan Seymour missed his team's home match against West Ham United in order to travel to Belfast in an effort to hijack the deal. Rather ironically, the international fixture was the reason why the transfer had not been finalised during the talks between the two clubs, as there had not been enough time for all the details to be ironed out.

Busby was unruffled by this late in the day move by the St James' Park manager, saying, 'The transfer was arranged between my club and Glasgow Rangers last Tuesday. So far as I am concerned that arrangement holds good.

'There is nothing more I wish to say about the situation at this stage, but I am 100 per cent confident Caldow will become a Manchester United player on Monday.'

While making the telephone call to Caldow to arrange the meeting in Manchester, the United manager told the player that Rangers would deal with his share of the transfer fee and that United would be paying him a signing-on fee of £10, and maximum wages once he had signed. This, however, might throw a further spanner in the works, as Caldow, having already enjoyed a benefit with Rangers, was due a three years' accrued share of £450.

Like Matt Busby, as far as Rangers were concerned, the deal was done, and apparently even the player was happy. 'There is nothing now to stop me from signing for Manchester United. I went to Turnberry (*where Rangers were training*) to discuss what had taken place during my absence with Scotland, and left perfectly happy about my position.'

'Caldow signs today', proclaimed the headlines on Monday 5 October as the player arrived in Manchester, but his arrival was the only thing which went as planned. Following two two-and-a-half-hour sessions at Old Trafford with Matt Busby, and being shown a couple of houses – better homes compared to what they had back in Glasgow, his wife admitted – he asked for twenty-four hours to 'think it over'.

Everton, Middlesbrough and Sheffield Wednesday had now picked up the scent and the possibility of a move by Middlesbrough must have weighed heavily on his and more so his wife's mind, as it was only a few miles from her parents' home.

Speculation then became rife that Middlesbrough or even Newcastle United had indeed thrown the spanner into the works and put the transfer into jeopardy, although it was something that both clubs strongly denied. Why then, did the full-back want a further twenty-four hours to decide on a move to one of the top sides in the world, a move that had been in the pipeline for at least seven days, with everything agreed money-wise between the two clubs and the player?

Think it over he certainly did, and the following day announced that he had decided against the move south. In an exclusive interview with the *Scottish Daily Express*, under the headline 'Why I Won't Become a Babe', he went on to explain his reasons for not becoming Matt Busby's second post-Munich signing: 'It's off. First of all, the money has absolutely nothing to do with my decision. I knew before I went to Manchester on Monday what my financial end of the deal was to be.

'Ever since I asked Rangers for a transfer, I have made it clear that the only thing that mattered was my wife's happiness. She wanted to go back to the North of England to be near her parents in Willington, Co. Durham.

'Right until we left Willington on the day to see Mr Busby in Manchester and look at houses, I was certain that Manchester would suit us.

'But that travelling, at more than three hours, made me realise that my wife would be about as far in travelling time from her parents as she was in Glasgow.

'We still must get away from Glasgow. The only reason we asked for twenty-four hours to consider our decision was because we had to weigh up every aspect of the journey to Manchester as against the trip to Glasgow.'

Back in Manchester, a disappointed Matt Busby issued a statement which read, 'The deal has fallen through. Caldow will not sign. It is something neither club can understand.'

So, was it really the distance between Manchester and Co. Durham that caused the deal to fall through? Time-wise, it took ninety minutes, while from Middlesbrough to Willington was only twenty, with Newcastle a further four. Why, after he had said that he was looking forward to joining Manchester United, did he change his mind? Why, after his personal affairs had been settled with Rangers, did he change his mind?

Three days later, Middlesbrough stepped in with an offer of £20,000, which Rangers immediately turned down, while Newcastle, after the initial interest, failed to show any further inclination in signing the player. Rangers at the same time announced that Caldow was no longer up for sale and would stay at Ibrox. Was this a punishment for turning down the move to Manchester?

Strangely, Eric Caldow didn't leave Rangers until 1966, after 265 appearances for the Ibrox club, winning five championship medals along with Scottish Cup and League Cup medals, as well as captaining the side. It later transpired that he had expected better terms from United and that they had stood firm on their original offer of wages and accommodation.

Rather surprisingly, Busby, however, did not simply let his interest in the Scottish international defender drop, and made another move for Caldow later in the season, but was again knocked back by both club and player. Even a fee of £30,000 failed to bring a positive response.

So, it was back to square one for the United manager in his plans to rebuild the side which was, as results showed, beginning to struggle. With his former club Liverpool dropping hints that they were more than interested in taking Jimmy Murphy along the East Lancs Road to become their next manager, and a wage of £2,500 mentioned, it was not the best of times around Old Trafford.

Tony Knapp of Leicester City was a player who fitted the Busby identikit, with Blackpool's Roy Gratix and Jimmy Armfield also fitting the bill. Stoke City's Tony Allen also found his name linked with United, while there was also another individual that, had the move actually materialised, could have solved the United manager's problems for some considerable time.

The player in question was Jackie Charlton, then a twenty-four-year-old, who had shown great potential with Leeds United. Busby did indeed make enquiries as regards to his availability. He was, however, just as Liverpool had been following their enquiry relating to Jimmy Murphy, told there was nothing doing and the search had to continue.

It wasn't until April that the Manchester United manager managed to bring a defender to the club. It was certainly no big-money buy, but one for the future, signing eighteen-year-old Tony Dunne from Irish side Shelbourne for a fee of around £2,500.

Such was the unpredictability of United in the early weeks of the 1959/60 season that it was nigh impossible to forecast their results, leaving punters little hope in amassing a fortune should they care to wager money on the outcome of any of their fixtures.

Having conceded seven goals without reply in the final two September fixtures, they scored eight, conceding three, in the opening two games of October against Leicester City and Arsenal, which saw a five-place jump in the League table. Progress, however, was limited, as form continued to be haphazard, with five wins, three draws and four defeats in the following twelve games, up until the turn of the year.

Despite the indifferent League form, United travelled to Madrid on 11 November and turned in a truly memorable display against Real Madrid, losing by the odd goal in eleven in front of a 65,000 crowd, having led 3-2 at the interval. Had it not been for a highly dubious penalty decision, given for handball against Bill Foulkes, then United would have come away with a creditable 5-5 draw, a much-improved performance following the 6-1 humiliation back in Manchester the previous month.

The result in Spain did instil some much-needed confidence, with Dennis Viollet inspiring a 3-1 win over Blackpool and a 5-1 win over Nottingham Forest, scoring five over the two games. But true to form, the following two fixtures against West Bromwich Albion and Burnley were lost – 3-2 and 2-1 respectively.

Prior to the 3-1 victory over Blackpool at Old Trafford on 5 December, United had lost 2-1 against Everton at Goodison Park, forcing Busby to ring the changes for the short trip to Merseyside, banishing around £100,000 of talent to the Central League side for the reserve fixture against Aston Villa. Out went Harry Gregg. Out went Wilf McGuinness. Out went Warren Bradley. Out went Bobby Charlton. 'These four players have been out of form in recent games and can recover confidence with a run in the reserves,' explained Busby.

With the United second string enjoying a three-point lead at the top of the Central League, and due to the often indifferent displays from those holding down first-team places, it was perhaps not before time that Busby rang the changes. Such moves would not only give the team a much needed reshuffle, but it would also give the manager the opportunity to judge whether or not the youngsters he had at his disposal were in fact good enough to not simply step up, but hold on to a first-team place.

Admittedly, those who did come into the side – goalkeeper David Gaskell, half-back Shay Brennan and forwards Alex Dawson and Mark Pearson, were not exactly unknowns, having stepped into the void following Munich, but in more recent times, they had lacked an extended run in the side.

Pearson gave United a twenty-fifth-minute lead against the Seasiders, and a Dennis Viollet double was enough to give United victory, despite Kaye equalising for the visitors two minutes after half-time. This ensured that Busby's gamble, or last throw of the dice, whichever way you look at it, paid off. But only in the short term.

Four games was all that Pearson managed before Charlton returned to the fold, while Gaskell and Dawson managed only 180 minutes longer. Shay Brennan was the only one who managed to hold on to his place for the remainder of the campaign.

The downfall for Gaskell, who had been acclaimed for a superb performance at the Hawthorns, and Dawson, was the 7-3 defeat against Newcastle United on Tyneside, 2 January. It had been twenty years since United had leaked seven and fingers pointed in Gaskell's direction as being the fault behind at least three of the Newcastle goals. Busby was forced once again to reshuffle his pack.

Not only did the St James' Park defeat force Busby into making changes, it also forced Busby into the transfer market; although a broken leg suffered by Wilf McGuinness against Stoke City reserves on 12 December played just as big a part in the United manager's search for a player to strengthen is squad.

Maurice Setters was a name that sprang to the fore as a possible signing, but the rumours were quickly nipped in the bud by the United manager, who insisted that there was no interest in the player. However, as a new decade beckoned, the headlines proclaimed, 'United Back in the Market for Setters.'

Busby's change of heart was undoubtedly prompted by Manchester City's interest in Setters, with the Maine Road side happy to meet the West Bromwich asking price of £25,000. City manager Les McDowell had already met the Honiton-born and former Exeter City player, but the wing-half wanted further talks with McDowell before finally agreeing a deal. There was, of course, the possibility that United's re-emergence on the scene was enough to make Setters stall on the move, with the player admitting that he had spoken to a friend and a move to City was not going to materialise. Everton, who had also hinted at being interested, also received a polite 'thanks, but no thanks'.

United took up the chase. 'My club have reconsidered the position and we have been in touch with West Bromwich Albion today (*4 January*),' said Busby. 'And I hope to be in touch with the club and player again tomorrow.'

Setters now had his eyes firmly set on a move to Old Trafford and Busby, true to his word, returned to the Hawthorns and gave the tough-tackling wing-half his wish, paying West Bromwich Albion around £30,000 in order to add him to the Manchester United payroll.

Having lost some of the steel in the heart of the United team with the selling of Stan Crowther, a player who it could be debated would have made a difference to the current dilemma, the purchase of Setters, in many ways identical to the former Villa man, was a shrewd move by the United manager and one that would play a major part in the continual reconstruction of the team.

Although an excellent signing, Setters came north with something of a reputation. He had been sent home midway through West Brom's recent close-season tour of Canada, which led to him handing in his first transfer request. This, however, was withdrawn after manager Vic Buckingham had left the Hawthorns. A further confrontation, this time with trainer Dick Graham during pre-season training and over what was deemed a 'petty issue', saw the transfer request once again handed in. Many felt that Setters was in the wrong, but the incident clearly unsettled the player, with his difficulty in seeing eye to eye with one or two of the West Bromwich directors doing little to ease the ill-feeling which was simmering away.

Setters announced that he would happily go to any First Division club, but with so much friction hanging in the air, the Albion directors would be more than content to see him go anywhere.

Having signed for United, Setters quickly attempted to play down his 'bad boy' image and start his spell at Old Trafford with a clean slate; a move that he was rumoured to have wanted for the past eighteen months, but it is likely to have been nothing more than that. Had it been so, then Busby would surely have made his move much sooner.

'This is a wonderful day for me,' said Setters. 'I have had some sleepless nights since I asked Albion for a move – and it was a damned sight worse when I read that Manchester United were not interested in my future.' His nerves became slightly more frayed when Matt Busby and Jimmy Murphy were late with their scheduled appointment in the Midlands due to fog on the journey south. 'I am not a rebel or a troublemaker. I've tried to do my job as skipper by acting as spokesman for others with a grievance and because of that, I have been carpeted and for that alone acquired a reputation.'

Regarding his reason for wanting to leave the Midlands club: 'Why? For the past three seasons I have been unsettled with Albion and three times in the last twelve months I asked them to list me and give me a chance to move elsewhere. But I want to make this point clear – I am not a rebel or a troublemaker.'

Some forty years on, Maurice Setters, when asked if he was ever close to having signed for Manchester City, replied with a simple 'no', as he always lived in the hope that United would return with a definite offer and cement his move to Manchester.

Moving on to his reputed 'bad-boy' image, the strong-tackling, defensive half-back was quick to play down this unwanted reputation, and when asked if it was something that Matt Busby spoke to him about when he signed, he simply replied that such a topic was never brought up in any conversations and he was simply told to play his normal game.

Having paid out around £30,000 on Maurice Setters, Matt Busby was given the opportunity of not only recouping his outlay less than a fortnight later, but adding a further £90,000 to the Old Trafford coffers. Today, such a possibility might well have created much in the way of debate around the corridors of Old Trafford, but £90,000 belonging to any one of six Italian clubs did little to persuade Matt Busby to part with Bobby Charlton.

With the likes of Milan, Juventus, Roma and Torino more than eager to make the England player their latest acquisition, and Italian agent Piero Trisaglio having watched Charlton in recent outings, the slightest hint of a possible transfer would have seen a flurry of international activity. Perhaps if the player was not about to get married, then United might have found themselves certainly richer, but much worse off personnel-wise.

'I do not want to leave Manchester United,' said Charlton. 'But when you hear of the fantastic cash inducements overseas, you have to think twice about your future. Footballers have only a short life, but I will accept whatever decision from the club. My future wife does not want to live abroad. We'll be satisfied with any success we can find here.'

Despite Charlton's insistence that he was not interested in moving to Italy, or anywhere else for that matter, it did not deter the Italians. Milan came forward with an offer of £90,000 plus former Charlton Athletic forward Eddie Firmani. Clearly, the continuality of such talk was not completely ignored by the player despite his earlier claims, although he did not believe that such offers were indeed 100 per cent genuine, insisting that 'if they do materialise into something definite, I would naturally have to give them some consideration. A footballer's life is a short one.' His manager, however, was quick to point out that his player was under contract and that he was in the process of building a team and would not allow for any of his players to leave.

Busby gave new signing Maurice Setters the No. 4 shirt for his debut against Birmingham City at Old Trafford, replacing Freddie Goodwin. The former West Bromwich Albion player's initial performance was considered a 'workmanlike start', with Derek Hodgson in the *Daily Express* stating that he was only given a sentence in his match report, as 'he will be having the whole story soon'.

Setters soon realised that his Old Trafford career was going to be no smooth ride, as the 2-1 debut victory against Birmingham City was followed by United's eleventh League defeat of the season, a 2-1 defeat against Tottenham Hotspur at White Hart Lane, and United continued to stutter along in a strange, inconsistent fashion. A mistake by the new signing also contributed towards the twelfth defeat, a 3-1 reversal at Leicester City a month later. His early mistake allowed the home side to take the lead.

In between those defeats against Tottenham and Leicester were home draws against Manchester City, 0-0, and Preston North End, 1-1. Neither of the fixtures kept the supporters enthralled, especially the goal-less, practically football-less, but certainly not foul-less local 'derby' against Manchester City at Old Trafford, with the game described by journalist David Jack as 'scrappy', with entertainment as being of 'minor consideration'.

Analysing United's performance, he wrote, 'City, definitely the underdogs in the prematch wagers, surprised even their keenest supporters by matching United in all departments. Was this due to City's greatness or United's decline? Let's be kind and say the combination of both.

'United's biggest headache is the loss of sparkle by those dazzling inside men, Bobby Charlton, Dennis Viollet and Albert Quixall.

'Dennis Viollet has a hint of genius about his football. On his day, he is the finest centre-forward in England. Now, he seems to be sluggish, and even slow-thinking. He is caught in possession when, not very long ago, he showed his heels to all.

'Perhaps when Viollet regains his greatness, so too will Manchester United.'

Setters made amends for his Filbert Street error which sowed the seeds of defeat three days later on 27 February, when United travelled to Blackpool and fired six past the dazed Seasiders, the newcomer taking all the plaudits for his superb, all-round performance. Dennis Viollet even rediscovered something of his true form by notching a couple, but was outshone by Bobby Charlton's hat-trick.

Hopes of a decent FA Cup run to banish some of the gloom surrounding Old Trafford were extinguished the week prior to the trouncing of Blackpool, with a 1-0 fifth-round home defeat by Sheffield Wednesday, following victories at Derby and Liverpool. The season continued to career along like the Big Dipper just along the road from Bloomfield Road.

Two days prior to United making the familiar journey from Manchester to the Golden Mile, some 250 people, including parents, relatives and friends gathered in the pouring rain, along with the present playing staff, outside the main entrance at Old Trafford for the unveiling of the Munich Memorial.

The plaque, designed by local architect M. I. Vipond, and constructed by Messrs Jaconello Ltd of Manchester, showed a complete plan of the ground measuring 7 foot 9 inches by 6 foot. Green slabs of faience marked out the pitch incised with black and gold glass letters forming an inscription and names of those who lost their lives. The terraces, gangways and steps were also in faience to scale, and were in a memorial colour of mauve and grey. The stand roofs and perimeter path had been worked from solid quartzite, enclosed by red Balmoral granite forming the boundary wall of the ground. Two teak figures representing a player and spectator stood either side of a laurel wreath and ball, inscribed 1958.

After pulling back the velvet drapes, Matt Busby, who was clearly moved by the occasion, made a brief speech, saying, 'I know that those who are near and dear have a memorial in their hearts which will last for all time.

'But now our many friends will also have an everlasting memorial here to the lads who helped make this such a great club.'

Mr Dan Marsden, chairman of the Ground Committee, unveiled a clock, which was situated at the Warwick Road end of the ground, high up on the wall and inscribed above and below the two-faced dial, 'February 6th 1958, Munich'.

Inside the stadium, a bronze plaque in the press box, bearing the names of the eight journalists who died, was unveiled by the only surviving journalist, Mr Frank Taylor.

Even the 6-0 thrashing of Blackpool failed to instil confidence into the side and just as the 6-0 victory over Leeds United back in September had been followed by a defeat, the latest six-goal triumph did likewise, with Wolves winning 2-0 at Old Trafford, and the headlines making grim reading for any United supporters who did not witness the encounter at first hand.

'This United attack is like a shambles,' proclaimed one. 'This United attack needs a shakeup,' said another. The first of the two headlines preceded David Jack's report, and the correspondent, who was unimpressed by United's recent performance against City, was equally unmoved by his latest look at Matt Busby's team, describing them as little more than 'third raters'.

Once again, Jack was critical of Messrs Viollet, Charlton and Quixall, but now added Dawson and Scanlon to the trio of misfiring individuals. He admitted that the quintet represented star quality, but wrote that 'not for many a day have I seen any real glitter from these stars'.

He continued, 'How much longer will promising reserves like Mark Pearson and John Giles have to play second fiddle to these out-of-form first-teamers. Something will have to be done.'

It wasn't as if United were struggling near the foot of the table, dicing with relegation as the season moved towards its final weeks. They were in the mid-table 'comfort zone', ten points from the bottom and thirteen points off the top, but there was indeed something not quite right at Old Trafford.

Having lost eight players of renowned quality two years previously, no one could expect Manchester United to scale similar heights so soon. Neither could United expect to be able to prise players of outstanding ability from other clubs to rebuild their shattered team. However, the previous season had indeed been a false dawn and it was grossly unfair to some of those who had stepped up from the Old Trafford reserve ranks to be suddenly expected to become First Division superstars.

Setters had been bought, but the hard-tackling half-back was only one man. Quixall had at times failed to live up to his own high standards. Warren Bradley had moved from the amateur ranks and although his step up and contribution had been notable, he had begun to find the level of football and the constant demand for five-star performances something of a struggle.

Upon his return to the club, Busby should have bought, as new blood was certainly required, not simply to strengthen the rather weak squad, but also to bring some consistency to the erratic team that Manchester United had become.

Matt Busby, as he scanned the reports and the daily papers, must have noted the comments of David Jack, as a blank Saturday, due to their non-involvement in the FA Cup, saw them travel across Manchester to face neighbours City in a friendly. Reshuffling his team, he brought into the side Mark Pearson and Johnny Giles at the expense of Alex Dawson and Albert Scanlon. Meanwhile he moved Viollet from the right wing to centre-forward and Charlton from inside- to outside-left. It was a move that paid off, Viollet notching a double and Charlton another in the 3-1 win, while Giles and Pearson retained their places for the visit of Nottingham Forest to Old Trafford.

Busby had also played Tommy Heron and Frank Haydock in the City friendly, but both were omitted for the visit of Forest, a game that United won 3-1, with Pearson one of the goalscorers.

Hibs were hammered 4-0 at Easter Road, and Fulham beaten 5-0 at Craven Cottage, but true to form, as the season moved into its final eight weeks, United continued to confuse not only their own supporters, but the football public in general. Four days after scoring five at Craven Cottage, they lost 4-2 at Hillsborough, against Sheffield Wednesday.

Thankfully, relegation was not an issue, but at times it was surprising that the team was not fighting for its life at the foot of the table, as one sterling victory would be followed with a totally abysmal and inept display.

In the final ten games of the season, United managed seven victories, which were enough to ensure a respectable seventh spot in the First Division, although it was their lowest finish since League football had resumed following the Second World War. Their season as a whole is perhaps best summed up in the final three fixtures: West Ham United at Old Trafford, Arsenal at Highbury, and Everton, also at home.

Against the Hammers, who had beaten United 2-1 at Upton Park three days previously, two goals apiece for Charlton and Dawson and another by Quixall gave United a 5-3 win. However, five days later, two goals from the teenage duo of Pearson and Giles made little impact on the five scored by Arsenal. On the final day of the campaign, Alex Dawson notched his fiftieth United goal and claimed the match ball, with a hat-trick in the 5-0 win over Everton. This was the seventh time United had scored five or more that season, but worryingly, they had failed to win any of the games that followed!

Tucked amongst those end-of-season fixtures was a somewhat nondescript ninety minutes against Luton Town at Kennilworth Road on 9 April, which resulted in a 3-2 victory for United. But it was a match which was to end in controversy, conjuring up events not associated with football from those distant days.

With the second half ten minutes old and United leading 3-1, with goals from Bradley and a Dawson double, Harry Gregg fumbled a speculative shot from Luton full-back Dunne, allowing Cumming, who had scored an equaliser for Luton in the twentieth minute, the easy opportunity to snatch the half-chance that allowed the home side back into the game, with the majority of the second half still to play.

United managed to hold on to their solitary goal advantage against the bottom-of-the-table club, but as the players left the pitch, there was a flurry of activity that was only spotted by a small number of the 21,242 crowd.

One of those who were watching the players leave the pitch was Giles Oakley, attending only his second United game, who recalled:

As everyone started heading for the exits I happened to turn round to watch my idols as they left the field. I was at the far end but the famous red shirts, with the 'Busby Babe' V-necks, held a special attraction for me, and I was savouring every moment, it all being so new to me. Then suddenly I was astonished to see the green-jerseyed figure of Harry Gregg launch a massive punch into the face of one of the many fans who'd run onto the pitch. The man went down as if pole-axed. Suddenly everyone was gasping, 'Did you see that!' 'That was Gregg, wasn't it?' 'Did he just hit that man?' 'What's going on?'

Then opinion turned nasty. 'Typical bloody United, think they can get away with anything.' 'Yeah, they think they're above the law', 'They're all teddy-boys, they've got no discipline', and so forth.

With ever-louder booing in his ears, Gregg was hurried away from the pitch by teammates, led by the skipper, Maurice Setters, himself a bit of a hard man. Police could be seen heading towards the pitch and someone helped the felled spectator to his feet, clutching his face. All the participants in this extraordinary scene were quickly moved out of the public gaze, and those of us still left on the terraces could do nothing but guess what had happened. I was shocked. This was one of the people I respected most in the entire world and he'd done something outrageous. This was not what I expected from United players. I wanted them to uphold the finest traditions of the club, not to start throwing punches at people. Surely there must be some reason for him to hit a fan like that, but what was it?

So as I left Kenilworth Road with the crowd buzzing with talk of Harry Gregg, no one really knew quite what had happened. I knew I'd almost certainly have to wait until the next day for the newspapers for more details of what I'd just witnessed.

In fact the press coverage was relatively restrained, the story only gaining prominence on the Monday, by which time the reporters had dug out the bones of what had happened.

The man Gregg had punched was a local Luton factory worker, although he originated in the North and claimed to be a United fan merely wishing to congratulate Harry on a fine performance. He said Gregg had been 'a bit jittery' because of the 'rude comments' Luton fans had been making behind his goal. He was as surprised as anyone when Gregg decked him, leaving him dazed and with a badly bruised face. When the 'misunderstanding' had been cleared up the two men supposedly shook hands and exchanged apologies. Harry also apologised to the Luton chairman, who told him 'not to worry'.

The story made headlines for a few days, including the fact that he had threatened a press photographer who tried to take his picture on his return from Luton with the team to Manchester, saying he would smash his camera and push him under a train if he didn't stop. What made it worse was that the photographer was a fellow Munich survivor, Peter Howard. It looked as though Harry's nerves were fraying. Maybe all that pent-up guilt and anger inside him was becoming a problem.

On the Monday morning following the incident, which manager Matt Busby had not witnessed having been absent from the game, Gregg was hauled into his office and asked to explain what had exactly taken place at the end of the game. The 'keeper did admit to hitting the man, saying, 'There had been a bit of horseplay during the match and a few things were thrown onto the pitch. And as I was leaving the field a man barred my way.

'Three times I tried to evade him, but I didn't have much luck. Then I got the impression he was going to hit me. So I banged him first. Real hard.

'By the time I had reached the dressing room I had cooled down somewhat and was sorry that perhaps I had been too hasty.

'I apologised to Jimmy Murphy, to Luton officials and to the fan who was nursing a "shiner".'

A summons was issued against Gregg by the Bedfordshire Police, but despite Busby giving his goalkeeper the 'biggest verbal roasting of his life', the manager informed the police that the club backed their player 100 per cent and nothing more was heard of the incident.

Nothing, that was, until United's visit to Luton the following season, when upon alighting from the team bus, Gregg was approached by a man, who the United 'keeper felt that he should recognise. Perhaps it was through not having the black eye that Gregg failed to identify the man, as he was indeed his on-field sparring partner. Hands were shaken and nothing more was said about the incident.

Despite the favourable finish to that 1959/60 season, there was still much work to do, giving Busby many sleepless nights in his search for a defender, or even two, while also attempting to stabilise his forward line.

But the only financial outlay during the summer of 1960 went on the ground rather than the playing squad; with contractors battling to beat the deadlines set and have the stadium ready for the opening match of 1960/61 against Blackburn Rovers on 20 August. Rebuilding and repairs were carried out at the Stretford End and neighbouring Paddock, at a cost of between £20,000 and £25,000. This gave the ground a capacity of 66,500, with admission prices for the new section of 3/- (15p) for adults and 1/6d (8p) for juniors.

Perhaps it would have been better if those stadium improvements had been something major, with the contactors falling behind with their work, forcing that opening fixture of the new campaign to be played away from home, as United struggled in front of a packed Old Trafford.

A Ronnie Cope back-pass, intended for Harry Gregg, was intercepted by Derek Dougan, who gave Blackburn the lead with little more than ten minutes played. A spate of missed opportunities by United's lacklustre forwards were to prove costly, and although Bobby Charlton snatched a seventieth-minute equaliser, the visitors stepped up a gear, with Dougan notching his second of the afternoon four minutes later, completing his hat-trick in the final minute as many of the crowd made their way towards the exits.

Into the United side for that opening-day fixture against Blackburn came nineteen-year-old Frank Haydock, a former Blackpool amateur, and for those who had followed the youngster's progress through the ranks it would have come as no surprise that there was a flurry of goals on his first-team debut.

'When I played my first game for United's "B" team against Manchester City, the opposition centre-forward, Bert Lister, scored five,' recalled the player who somewhat unusually for a Manchester United youngster failed to play at a high-school level, moving to Old Trafford as a seventeen-year-old from the local side Park Villa who played in the Eccles League. But on his first-team debut, he had fared much better, facing his brother Bill in a friendly against Manchester City. 'I like to think that I came off pretty well,' said the younger of the Haydocks. 'As we won 3-1 and it wasn't Bill who scored the City goal.'

Looking back on his introduction to League football, Haydock was to say, 'It was just my luck Dougan had one of his good days, scoring a hat-trick. Busby didn't lose faith, however, and he kept me in the side for a few more games. But eventually I was back in the Central League.'

Four days later, things went from bad to worse, for both Haydock and United, with the short journey to Merseyside resulting in a 4-0 defeat at Goodison Park.

Cope's error in the opening fixture cost him his place in the starting line-up against Everton, with Shay Brennan moving from left-half to No. 2, allowing Jimmy Nicholson to make the step up from the Central League side for his debut. It wasn't, however, one to remember, as the 4-0 defeat, which could have been even heavier had it not been for Harry Gregg, sent United crashing to the foot of the table.

The seventeen-year-old Irishman's performance was perhaps the only plus point of the entire ninety minutes as far as Manchester United were concerned, and he not only retained his place for the next game, but kept it until injury ruled him out in February.

So, another youngster had rolled off the 'Busby Babes' conveyor belt, but what was life like for a youngster like Jimmy Nicholson at Old Trafford at this particular time?

As an apprentice professional at United from age fifteen to seventeen, you were expected to perform all kinds of manual tasks, maintaining the ground with your fellow apprentices.

Things like brushing the terracing, cleaning out toilets, cleaning the stands and dressing rooms and boot room duty. It was something which I felt that could be at times soul destroying and not balanced enough with the need to train to play and become a good professional footballer.

I had dreamed, as a kid playing football in the back streets of Belfast, of the day that I would be able to develop my footballing skills at the club that I loved: to be able to do this day-by-day in order to attain the high levels of skills required by such a world-famous club.

One Wednesday morning, when I was out working on the terracing, Jimmy Murphy walked round the track around the ground to where I was working and stopped in front of me and said, 'I want you to go home now, get changed and come down to the ground at 4.30 p.m.'

I arrived back at the ground at the appointed time and was taken to Davyhulme Golf Club for a prematch meal and it was then that Jimmy Murphy told me that I would play that night. I could not contain my excitement and virtually every player came over to congratulate me and wish me all the best.

I made my League debut at Goodison Park against Everton and we were beaten 4-0 that night. We played them again seven days later and defeated them by the same scoreline.

Another night that remains ingrained in my memory was against Real Madrid when we won 3-2, especially as I scored a goal.

Real Madrid were an aging team, having won five European Cups in succession, but they still had the fantastic skills, playing highly skilful, one-touch football, lightning movement, and opened my eyes forever to the development of young players, working everyday to develop the high skills necessary to play this highly exciting brand of football.

That same year I also made my international debut at Hampden Park against an excellent Scottish team; Denis Law scored a hat-trick, and went down 5-3! Again, an incredible thrill and an unforgettable experience.

If ever there was an ideal opportunity to kick-start the season, it was 27 August and the third fixture of the new season. It wasn't simply just another ninety minutes and the opportunity to secure that vital first victory of the campaign; it was 'derby day', with the trip across Manchester to Maine Road, where two points would lift United, not simply off the bottom, but up seven places.

However, as the afternoon unfolded, there was to be no two points for Busby's team, and they had to endure the embarrassment of propping up the table for longer than they would certainly have wanted to. The first local derby of the season was abandoned after seventy minutes.

City were a goal in front when many were still clicking through the Maine Road turnstiles on what was a truly miserable Manchester afternoon and, following several flashes of lightning which brightened up the overcast sky, the game itself exploded into action when Denis Law opened the scoring in the fourth minute.

But as the rain poured down, United acquitted themselves better to the conditions than their opponents and surprised even their own followers by going in at the interval with a 2-1 lead, with goals from Dennis Viollet and Alex Dawson in the thirty-fifth and thirty-seventh minutes. It should, however, have been 3-1, but Quixall fired wide from the penalty spot after Charlton was obstructed by Oakes and Betts.

As the sky darkened in the late afternoon, so did United's hopes of victory as the thunder and lightning continued to provide an unfamiliar backdrop. Another piece of Law magic conjured up the equalising goal for Hayes in the fifty-fourth minute.

Three minutes later a long, shrill, totally unexpected blast from the whistle of referee Arthur Ellis surprised the crowd, as did his actions of stamping his foot and pointing to the sodden turf and calling the two teams into the centre circle, before marching them off the pitch.

Speaking to the officials of both clubs, Ellis indicated that he considered that the pitch was no longer playable due to the amount of surface water, but that he would inspect it again in a few minutes before making a final decision on whether or not the game would continue.

There was to be no improvement, as the downpour worsened, and at 4.25, with sixty-three minutes played, the referee finally called a halt to the proceedings, with many having already headed for home.

Across the city, the 'mini-derby' between the reserve XIs lasted for twelve minutes longer, before it too became a casualty of the weather.

While Matt Busby sat and agonised over his team's lowly League position amid the deluge, he was also wondering what reports his scouting staff would deposit on his office desk on Monday morning, having sent them to take in various fixtures, not only in England, but also north of the border to Scotland and across the water to Northern Ireland. His priority was still a full-back, and such was his determination to strengthen this department that he had once again made a telephone call to Glasgow in the hope that Eric Caldow, not to mention his wife, would reconsider a move to Manchester. The Rangers defender once again gave the United manager a negative reply.

If he couldn't persuade the Scottish international full-back to move south over Hadrian's Wall, could he fare better in an attempt to bring the English equivalent – Ray Wilson of Huddersfield Town – across the Pennines.

Wilson, who had made his Huddersfield debut against United in 1955, enjoyed a favourable summer tour with the national side, and had suddenly begun to attract attention from clubs of a higher status than his Yorkshire employers. Huddersfield, however, were in no need to sell, although a cash-plus-player deal would have been favourable, with manager Bill Anderson an admirer of United's Ronnie Cope, a player he had made enquiries as regards to signing last season.

Huddersfield were not exactly rolling in money, and although they were more favourable to a player exchange, they were also in the hunt for a winger, so Albert Scanlon was being mentioned as another possible piece in the transfer jigsaw (whether or not he would be prepared to make the move was another story); however, if United had actually produced the cheque-book and written one for around £35,000, then there was every possibility that a deal could have been done including either Scanlon or Cope, or even both, which would have been no great reduction to the playing staff.

The move for Wilson failed to come to any conclusion, most probably due to the financial side of things, and the defender remained with Huddersfield until 1964 when, at the age of thirty, his £40,000 move to Everton broke the existing transfer record.

Another full-back who fell under the United spotlight was Heart of Midlothian left-back George Thomson, who was watched against St Mirren at Paisley in a Scottish League Cup tie, following impressive reports. The home side's 3-1 win did little to enhance Thomson's prospects of a move south, and his was another name that was scribbled off the list of 'possibles'. A similar 'wasted journey' was made to Belfast, where Glenavon's full-back pairing of Bobby Armstrong and Fred Clarke failed to catch the eye.

Old Trafford had dried out, as had those United supporters who had ventured to Maine Road, in time for the visit of Everton on the last day of August. Revenge for the 4-0 defeat, as well as the search for the first points of the season, was very much a priority and not for the first time in recent weeks the Old Trafford regulars headed home at the end of the ninety minutes scratching their heads and wondering where the logic behind some of their team's performances was.

Busby had decided on changes in personnel for the Toffees' visit, as well as completely reorganising his forward line. He left out full-back Joe Carolan and outside-left Albert Scanlon, switched Shay Brennan from right- to left-back, and handed Bill Foulkes the No. 2 shirt. Up front he brought in Alex Dawson at centre-forward, switching Johnny Giles from outside- to inside-right. As well as this, Albert Quixall was switched from inside-right to outside-right, Dennis Viollet from centre to inside-left and Bobby Charlton from inside- to outside-left.

It was a juggling trick that certainly paid dividends, with Dawson picking up where he left off the previous season (when he scored three on the final day against Everton), notching a double, with Bobby Charlton and Jimmy Nicholson scoring one each. United picked up their first win of the season, two points that nudged them a couple of places up the table.

Unfortunately, the 4-0 victory over Everton did little to instil confidence into the beleaguered red shirts, as they failed to win any of their following three fixtures, losing 4-1 at Tottenham, 2-1 at West Ham and drawing 1-1 at home to Leicester City.

With six games played, United were now eleven points adrift of early leaders Tottenham. Not that anyone had expected them to be challenging for the title, even at this early stage of the season, but there was something not quite right at Old Trafford, and Matt Busby knew that he had to retune his team, sooner rather than later, or United could find themselves embroiled in a dog fight at the foot of the table, with relegation always at the back of everyone's mind.

The 1-1 draw against Leicester City at Old Trafford was a game that saw the home support in the 34,493 Old Trafford crowd finally lose patience with their favourites, giving them the slow hand-clap during what was described by the *Manchester Evening News* reporter David Meek, as 'a poor quality game in which reputations went by the board and the game looked what it was – a clash between two teams near the bottom of the table'. The impatience of the Old Trafford crowd was matched, although in an entirely different manner, by the management, when it came to bringing new players into the fray, with a move made to sign Mel Nurse, Swansea Town's Welsh international centre-half.

Nurse, who had reportedly made something of a poor start to the season, was considered to have great potential, something which sparked the move, but despite making an official move to secure his transfer, United's undisclosed offer, believed to be around £20,000, was turned down by the directors of the Second Division club.

It was thought that a player-exchange deal might have swung the move in United's favour, although Swansea would probably have wanted the likes of Alex Dawson as part of any deal – a player who, while the defence was leaking goals, was very much in Matt Busby's plans to score them, despite finding it difficult at times to hold down a regular first-team place.

Busby was criticised for not only failing to use Dawson as part of the bait in order to secure a player he obviously wanted, but for also attempting to dictate the terms of the transfer, but he explained that with injuries playing as much a part in the current predicament as poor form, he felt that selling the bustling centre-forward was a gamble that he just could not take, as any further injuries to his forward line following any transfer of Dawson, would simply mean that he had to go out and buy yet another replacement.

United's interest in Nurse, as so often happens, clearly unsettled the player, but who is to say that such tactics were never unintentional? When Busby returned with an increased offer of £30,000, the Welshman, sensing that a golden opportunity awaited, was forced to speak out, saying, 'I am not happy about the way I am making progress. I think my standards would improve in the First Division.'

Even the increased offer of £30,000 was rejected by the Swansea directors, who stated that there was little point accepting the offer, as they would have difficulty in bringing a top-class replacement to the Vetch Field. But suddenly, the transfer was very much on, as on Saturday 24 September, Swansea manager Trevor Morris made an overnight dash to Rochdale with plans to sign leading Fourth Division scorer Frank Lord. The Swansea manager, once the ink was dry on that deal, then planned to travel the few miles south to Old Trafford to negotiate the transfer of Mel Nurse to United.

Everything suddenly went pear-shaped, however, with Lord's proposed transfer collapsing, producing a knock-on effect on Nurse's move to United. The Swansea directors were left regretting their decision of not selling the player to United when the initial interest was shown, as Busby's interest cooled, despite being given first refusal on the player, and two years later, the Welsh side sold Nurse to Middlesbrough for £25,000, which although £5,000 less than United's offer, was still a club record. Nurse, at this point, did not want to leave the Welsh side, but was told that he had no future there, so had little alternative.

So, what did Mel Nurse think about the proposed £30,000 move to Old Trafford falling through?

'£30,000? It was £35,000,' recalled the Welsh international defender. 'Obviously, I knew of the interest United had in me and of course Jimmy Murphy was well aware of my capabilities through his duties as the Welsh team manager. But that was about as far as it went. Manchester City were also interested in me back then.

'I remember getting a telephone call one day from one of the local Manchester newspapers asking me if, when I signed for United, I would write a few columns for them. I was totally bemused and asked them what they were talking about. 'You're signing for United aren't you?' came the reply. I had to tell them that nothing had been agreed. I would have to have been given permission from the club to do this anyway, as you were prevented from talking to the press in those days, never mind write a newspaper column.

'Nothing was agreed, and I stayed at Swansea, although two years later, one Friday morning I was asked to go to the manager's office, where I was told that I was being sold to Middlesborough.

'Middlesborough! No disrespect to the club, but it was like being sent to the end of the world.

'I had no choice in the matter either, as I was told, in no uncertain terms, that if I didn't sign for Middlesborough, then I would not play football again. Simple as that! You couldn't even speak to the press in those days to let your feelings be known. Such a thing would have brought you a fine and probably a suspension.

'£20 per week was what I was paid when I moved, same as what I was getting at Swansea. My brother and father were earning more than me doing ordinary jobs. You signed a one-year contract and at the end of each season you had to renegotiate terms with the club.

'Do I have regrets about not becoming a Manchester United player? Who knows what would have unfolded if I had moved to Old Trafford, it would have been interesting, but no, I have no regrets. I am grateful for my career in football.'

For many clubs, the panic bells would have been ringing merrily away, but Matt Busby refused to be ruffled. Yes, he was as concerned as the next person as to United's early-season performances, but he was happy within his own mind that the corner would be turned and the players under his command were more than capable of obtaining the results that would see them climb the First Division table. Others, however, felt otherwise.

Many thought that an improvement was on its way following the demolition of West Ham United on the evening of 14 September, when the Hammers were well and truly hammered 6-1, with many now questioning if United really needed Mel Nurse, or anyone else for that matter despite their worst start to a season since 1953/54 and one that was similar to that of season 1933/34 when the club almost found themselves in Division Three had it not been for a last-day victory at Millwall.

But it soon became obvious to even the most staunch supporter that victories like that 6-1 against West Ham and the earlier 4-0 against Everton, were little more than a false dawn, with three defeats and a draw in the next four games, keeping the club amongst the strugglers at the foot of the table.

Against Wolves at Old Trafford on 24 September, a 3-1 defeat, the headlines screamed, 'United Lose the Will to Fight', 'Another Drab United Show', with reports detailing that 'defenders kicked wildly and without the slightest hint of purpose', while 'the attackers wandered about blaming each other'.

One reporter, Jack Wood, wrote, 'It would be easy to raise the "sack the lot" cry, but a look through the reserve strength suggests that such a drastic move is impossible. I doubt if the playing resources at Old Trafford have been weaker.'

So, what was the problem at Old Trafford?

Matt Busby, never one to hide when the going got tough, held up his hands and confessed that even he did not think the poor patch would be as bad as it was, and at the end of the day it all boiled down to the fact that the team as a whole were playing badly, or to be more exact, there were too many players off form at the same time: 'This is something that has been visualised because we lost the services of ten great players in that awful Munich disaster and I only signed two as replacements. Whatever patching up was done after that black day, it was obvious that it would leave some impression eventually.

'In a way I consider it unfortunate that we had so much artificial success immediately after the crash. Had we slumped to the Second Division, people would have only nodded their heads in sympathy, as such a fall was expected. But instead we continued with success that on the cards looked impossible to get.'

The manager also said that he had tried to prevent the current lapse in form by signing players, such as Albert Quixall and Maurice Setters, but had been frustrated in his attempts to secure others, having made at least a dozen enquiries in the past eighteen months in order to bring his squad up to strength, and had also failed due to the fact that the quality required by the club was not there.

Obviously the current predicament was down to the players themselves, but some considered that the root of the problems was more to do with their nocturnal habits than their performances over the course of ninety minutes on a Saturday afternoon. This was a suggestion that Busby quickly dismissed, saying that once a player finished his 'work' at Old Trafford, then he was entitled to do relax as he wished. If he was married, then why not take his wife out for the night, or if he was single, he should find some other interest, such as a greyhound meeting: 'There is nothing wrong if such things are done in moderation.'

In the modern game, such a start would have sent not only the alarm bells ringing, but also the possibility of a change in management. Such a move by the directors of Manchester United was never mentioned, either in the press or behind closed doors at Old Trafford, such was the faith everyone had in Matt Busby to turn things around.

With the name of Mel Nurse no longer on the list of 'maybes', United had to look elsewhere if they wanted to recruit a centre-half, although in an effort to bring some stability to the centre of the defence, Busby called Bill Foulkes into his office and told him that he had decided to move him back to centre-half. Bishop Auckland amateur, twenty-two-year-old Laurie Brown, was one possibility, and securing his signature should not have been too difficult, as United had a good relationship with the North East side. There was a problem though: Brown, who had played for Great Britain in the 1960 Rome Olympics and was also at home as a striker, had signed a contract to join Northampton Town.

Now that United were on the scene, Brown hastily attempted to get the 'Cobblers' to cancel the amateur forms that he had signed only three weeks previously, but to no avail, and with a dream move to Old Trafford blocked, he signed professional forms with Northampton. However, he was soon to achieve his dreams of wearing a red shirt in the First Division, although it was not to be with United, but with Arsenal.

Another trip north of the border was also made by one of United's scouts, on this occasion to watch Dundee United's Ron Yeats. 'We cannot consider parting with Yeats at any price,' the Tayside club told United, but a £22,000 bid from Liverpool the following August was enough to take the 6 foot 2 inches defender south.

With Caldow deciding to remain in Glasgow, and the eventual transfers of Nurse to Middlesbrough, Wilson to Everton and now Yeats to Liverpool how had Manchester United failed in securing at least one of these players?

A move to sign Blackpool's England international full-back Jimmy Armfield also hit the buffers, with the Seasiders, following several enquiries by Matt Busby – which always received the same negative reply, although there was always hope of a cash-plus-player deal materialising – finally disappearing with the Bloomfield Road side's injury problems clearing up, leaving them in a more comfortable position, with little need to sell their coveted defender.

There was little in the way of luck to be had on and off the pitch, with injuries adding to the manager's ongoing problems. But how was this indifferent period viewed from the inside?

'After Munich, I felt that the development of younger players was put to one side for quite some time,' explained Jimmy Nicholson. 'United were buying players, some of whom were bought quickly to fill gaps left by the devastation of Munich.

'I felt that most of those buys were not of the standard required. They were short term and not in the interests of building another great team.

'I think that there were many good youngsters at the club who, if United had persisted, would have made United great again. Twenty-five years without a championship was the legacy of the short-term planning which I felt was the wrong route to take.

'Johnny Giles and Mark Pearson were the two best players at the club, along with Nobby Stiles, and were both later transferred out to Leeds and Sheffield Wednesday. I played with these three players through the "A" and "B" teams, youth team and reserve team and eventually into the first team, and I know that they were superior to any of the players brought in e.g. Albert Quixall. A £45,000 record fee bought us a midfield player, but only trusted to play on the wing.

'The same happened to Johnny Giles, one of the best midfielders in the country and again only trusted to play on the wing.'

Despite the urgency to sign players in an effort to bring the squad up to a standard comparable to that of the pre-Munich days, although finding a Duncan Edwards, Roger Byrne or Tommy Taylor clone was always going to prove impossible, Busby, despite Jack Wood's condemnation of the club's strength in depth, was slowly beginning to integrate his 'new Babes' into the Manchester United first team.

Jimmy Nicholson had not only forced his way into the first team, but held his place, while also making his international debut for Northern Ireland against Scotland just over a dozen games later.

Against Real Madrid, eighteen-year-old former Shelbourne youngster Tony Dunne replaced the injured Shay Brennan, no veteran himself, for a notable debut, while the 1-1 draw at Bolton on 1 October saw Busby hand the No. 4 and No. 7 shirts to yet another two home-produced teenagers, Norbert Peter Stiles and Ian Moir.

Stiles, a diminutive Collyhurst-born half-back, would become an integral part of Matt Busby's United side in the years to come, as well as becoming one of the first names Alf Ramsey would pencil into his England team. In later years, he earned something of a reputation as a hard-tackling, no-nonsense individual, and following his debut, it wasn't long before the newspaper reports of United games contained the likes of 'Stiles was given a long lecture by the referee following a tackle on Douglas' or 'Stiles clashed with Smith and received a talking to from the referee'. Moir, on the other hand, failed to command a regular place and joined Blackpool four years and forty-five games later.

Today, televised football, and indeed any sport (or events classed as sport), is taken for granted, and although bringing untold fortunes into the game, is also held responsible in many quarters as the root of everything that is wrong with what was, at one time, regarded as the working man's game. One certainly does not associate live Saturday televised tea-time football with the 1960s; indeed it was a time when many households did not have such luxuries as a television in their living rooms, but yes, there was live football broadcast in those now distant days.

Back in the sixties, however, the clubs did have a say in the matter and were not quick to grab the money without any thoughts to their supporters or any other 'trivial' matters. Arsenal were approached by the Football League at the start of the season and asked if they would consider allowing their fixture against Newcastle United on 17 September to be shown live on ITV. The directors of the London side quickly notified the Football League by letter, with a copy circulated to all First and Second Division sides, that they would not allow the game to be televised. Tottenham had also rejected plans to screen their forthcoming game against Everton.

Blackpool and Bolton, however, paid little heed to Arsenal's decision, or their letter, as did two-thirds of the clubs, and agreed for ITV to show the Bloomfield Road clash on 10 September, the first live showing of a Football League match, but it was a far cry from Sky Sports, as the programme started at 7.30 and finished at 8.30, leaving viewers something of a wait for the news later in the evening to find out the ultimate outcome of the fixture.

It had been agreed that some twenty-six games would be shown live, nineteen on a Saturday evening and seven on a Friday, but discussions were held to change this to twelve on a Friday and eight on a Saturday.

United rather surprisingly, however, were like Arsenal – one of the clubs who did not agree to this new innovation – having already told ITV 'no' when asked to allow their fixture against Wolves at Old Trafford on 24 September to be shown live. They informed the Football League that 'there were difficulties because Manchester Transport Department could not provide extra buses in the evening to take supporters to and from the ground'.

Chairman Harold Hardman said that televising games would 'do the game not the slightest bit of good', but it was not a view shared by his manager, who claimed that 'television would be a shot in the arm for football'. Strange how some fifty years on, the words of both men ring true!

But the £150,000 deal was soon thrown into chaos when clubs stated a preference for Friday night football rather than a Saturday, as they thought that the former would attract larger crowds. At the end of the day, ITV withdrew their original offer and the plans were discarded as quickly as they had been drawn up.

United and chairman Harold Hardman in particular, however, backed down slightly in his views on televised football, when the club approached Granada and asked them if they would like to show part of the forthcoming friendly fixture against Real Madrid. Despite United's current League predicament, the television company were quick to finalise a deal and it was agreed that the second half of the fixture would be shown live.

There was obviously money in it for United, but it also provided something of a safety net, as Madrid required a £10,000 guarantee, but at that time, there was a strict government currency regulation in place, which decreed that foreign clubs could not take more than half of the proceeds from a game out of the country. This meant that United had to take at least £20,000 on the night (with a police-set 'ceiling' of 64,000), forcing the cost of the cheapest seat up to 17/6*d* (87p).

In all honesty, the capacity dictated by the local police was something of a joke, as there was no way that United could have expected such numbers to click through the Old Trafford turnstiles, even with the opposition being the current European Cup-holders following their memorable 7-3 victory over Eintracht Frankfurt at Hampden back in May, their line-up including the likes of Di Stefano, Puskas and Gento.

Current attendances at Old Trafford were actually something of a concern for the United directors, as they were down almost 12,000 per game, with seats, normally sold out, easily obtainable on matchdays. The first eight home fixtures had attracted 311,241, compared to 405,617 for season 1959/60, with the average attendance down from 50,702 to 38,905. Losing around 95,000 paying customers was something that no club could sustain, but it was hoped that it was only a matter of time before results improved, which in turn would see those 'missing' supporters return to the fold.

As it turned out, the Real Madrid friendly, with the Spaniards on £60 a man to beat United, inspired a vastly improved team performance on the night and a narrow 3-2 defeat. The game attracted 51,506 spectators, most probably including many 'neutrals' happy to pay to see the visitors. It was still 312 less than the highest of the season – 51,818 against Everton.

19 October brought United some relief from the rigours of First Division football and the chance, many felt, to discover some of that missing self-belief, with their inaugural fixture in the Football League Cup against Fourth Division side Exeter City. Like their more illustrious visitors, Exeter were floundering around the foot of their division, but on the night there was little to choose between the two sides, with the Fourth Division side earning a memorable 1-1 draw.

The home side thought they had the ball in the net after eleven minutes, but much to United's relief, Stiles managed to scramble it off the line. However, the locals had only to wait a further three minutes to pump up the volume when Rees collected a long through pass, and brushed off a challenge from Stiles, before pushing the ball past the helpless Gregg.

To their credit, Exeter held on to their lead until the seventy-ninth minute, but at times rode their luck. Dawson shot over the bar and was also bundled off the ball as he prepared to shoot with the goal at his mercy. But it was the burly centre who saved United's blushes, pivoting on his right foot before sending a powerful 20-yard drive past Exeter 'keeper Lobbet to take the game to a replay.

Only 15,662 bothered to turn up at Old Trafford for United's first home tie in the League Cup, 662 more than had watched the first encounter seven days earlier, and although Quixall gave United the lead in the seventh minute, an equaliser from a Thompson penalty in the fourteenth, after Stiles had handled, hinted that a giant-killing could possibly be on the cards.

It was soon to prove little more than a hint, as a second from Giles and a third from Pearson on the half-hour put the result beyond doubt. A Quixall penalty, five minutes from time, rounded off the scoring and United were into the second-round draw.

Back in the First Division, Jekyll and Hyde United actually managed to win two successive games for the first time in thirteen outings, defeating Newcastle United 3-2 and Nottingham Forest 2-1, but then blotted their copybook by travelling to Highbury where they slumped to a 2-1 defeat. Fourteen games played and ten points, only four more than bottom-placed Nottingham Forest.

Four days later came the fixture that summed up the Manchester United of the early 1960s. Having struggled to nudge Exeter City out of the Football League Cup, after a replay, Round Two produced an away trip to Bradford City.

On a narrow, muddy pitch and played in torrential rain and fading light, the Third Division side took the game to their visitors and recorded a memorable 2-1 victory.

The home side weathered the conditions better than their illustrious visitors, who attempted to pass the ball around the muddied surface to little avail, despite Giles frequently tormenting the Bradford defence. Surprisingly though, against the run of play, United took the lead in the twenty-fifth minute. Pearson and Dawson worked the ball forward and the latter's pass found Viollet who had the simple job of tapping the ball home.

Following the break, United continued in their attempt to play football on the atrocious surface, but paid for their folly when the Valley Parade side scored twice in quick succession within twelve minutes of the restart. Smith rounded off good work from Webb and Jackson to grab the equaliser in the fifty-fifth minute and two minutes later Gregg fumbled Smith's header and Webb forced the ball home.

Despite a brave effort to snatch an equaliser, with Downie making a desperate save from Pearson in the dying minutes, the Bradford defence stood firm and the spotlight on the beleaguered United was now switched on to full beam. It was a defeat that took three fixtures to shake out of the system.

By now, supporters were totally bewildered. Attendances had continued to drop, with only 23,628 scattered around Old Trafford for the visit of Nottingham Forest, and any rumours as regards to impending transfers were now ignored, as they would now only be believed when a photograph appeared in the local and national newspapers of the individual in question wearing a red shirt, or better still actually signing a contact.

Arsenal's David Herd was a long sought-after target, with Albert Quixall touted as part of any deal in yet another player exchange or cash-plus-player deal. The former Sheffield Wednesday player, however, was quick to state that he was 'not interested in joining Arsenal', while the likes of Derek Dougan (Blackburn Rovers), Alex Young (Heart of Midlothian) and Brian Clough (Middlesbrough) were also thrown into the pot as possible transfer targets. However, it wasn't until 21 November that Matt Busby could announce that he had indeed managed to secure the transfer of a player to Manchester United.

Ever since the European Cup carrot was dangled in front of Matt Busby's nose, he was smitten; like a teenager suddenly discovering that girls were indeed different, he wanted to embrace the opportunity of tangling with the unknown whenever possible. The pre-season friendlies in Germany and the fixtures at home and away against Real Madrid were all part of a learning curve, as was the invite to Bayern Munich to visit Old Trafford to play a friendly on 21 November.

There was certainly a buzz around Manchester on that particular evening, but it was certainly not created by the visiting Germans, as only a meagre 15,769 bothered to turn up, an attendance that would have been even smaller had it not been for a new face in the red shirt.

Four days earlier, Matt Busby had agreed terms of around £25,000 with West Ham United for the transfer of twenty-eight-year-old defender Noel Cantwell. The final decision was, however, down to the player himself, or in this case, with echoes of the Eric Caldow transfer being clearly heard, the Irishman's future wife. Much to Busby's relief, the future Mrs Cantwell had no qualms about moving to Manchester and a telephone call on the morning of the Bayern Munich match confirmed that at long last, United had managed to conclude a deal. Cantwell then headed north and, within a space of three hours, had arrived in Manchester, signed for United and run out at Old Trafford in a red shirt for the first time.

The capture of Cantwell, although more than welcomed by the United support, left more than a few wondering why the Eire international captain had opted to leave the east end of London after eight years. Was there a hidden agenda somewhere?

Much to the relief of those who queried the move, there was a simple explanation behind the transfer, which was nothing more than Cantwell having been out of the side due to a leg injury for around seven weeks, and had failed to regain his place due to the form of his replacement John Lyall. It was also thought to be a move instigated by the Hammers' bank manager.

'I was quite happy at Upton Park and never thought I would leave,' explained the skilful defender. 'And I wasn't looking for a transfer. It came as a surprise, when out of the blue I was asked if I would like to join Manchester United.

'I think I was in a rut at West Ham. Eight years is a long time, and perhaps I had lost some of my drive.

'But I think the move is the best thing that could have happened to me. United are a famous club back home in Ireland and I have admired them for a long time.

'I was a schoolboy fan and the club's post-war feats filled a number of my soccer scrapbooks.

'I had a secret wish when dreaming of football as a career – and that was to be considered good enough to join United.

'I had a few personal things to discuss, first with my girlfriend because we are getting married in February, but then I jumped at the chance to come and work for Matt Busby.

'I now feel that I've been given a new lease of life. I think the move will help my football a lot.

'I feel that my footballing life is beginning again.'

The transfer fee paid to West Ham, although undisclosed, was undoubtedly a record for a full-back, as was confirmed by Matt Busby. The previous record was £21,000, paid by Tottenham Hotspur to Southampton in the summer of 1949 for Alf Ramsey, and following the Cantwell deal, the United manager told the press, 'You can say that we have paid just a bit more than that.' Some sources actually give the figure as £29,500, rounded off by others to £30,000.

Noel Cantwell, like the previous newcomer, Maurice Setters, proved to be an excellent acquisition, and strangely enough both were to become future Manchester United captains. The latter, best known as a tough-tackling, no-nonsense midfielder, found himself making a few of his appearances during 1960/61 at right-back in a move that not only strengthened the right flank, but also released Bill Foulkes to play in his best position of centre-half. This was only a temporary arrangement, as the arrival of Cantwell saw Shay Brennan take over the No. 2 shirt and move to the left side, with Cantwell taking over on the right.

Signing the former West Ham player, however, was something of a master stroke by Busby, as Cantwell, who also represented the Republic of Ireland at cricket, was an intelligent player, an excellent reader of the game and an inspiration to those who came in contact with him. He was a cross, perhaps, between Johnny Carey and Roger Byrne, and like those two former United captains and to a certain extent Maurice Setters, he also showed his worth as a utility player, turning out as a makeshift centre-forward in the months ahead.

Cantwell, however, although happy to be a Manchester United player, was shocked by what greeted him upon his arrival and his first few training sessions with his new teammates. Having grown accustomed to being a member of the West Ham 'soccer school', where previous games were digested and replayed and moves and tactics were thought out on the tabletop of a nearby café using sugar cubes and salt and pepper pots, he found there was certainly nothing like this down Old Trafford way, with training basic and actual tactical talks practically non-existent.

For those who ventured to Old Trafford for the Bayern Munich friendly, they witnessed Cantwell giving the impression of being an excellent acquisition, with a typically polished game, while almost scoring with a fierce left-footed drive in the second half. He was, however, outshone on the night by Alex Dawson, as the burly Scot claimed all of United's goals in the 3-1 win.

The faithful few on the Old Trafford terraces, while watching the initial United appearance of Cantwell, were also witnessing the final curtain call of a player who, having suffered the trauma of Munich, had returned to play First Division football but found himself frequently mentioned as 'the player' whenever one of those 'cash-plus-player' transfer deals materialised.

Albert Scanlon had been out of the United side for a few weeks prior to the Bayern Munich friendly, having appeared in only eight of the seventeen fixtures, but was thrust under the microscope by Busby for this particular match, as the United manager, having decided that Bobby Charlton was now his first choice to wear the No. 11 shirt, knew that a favourable performance by the Salford-born winger could open the door to a possible move and regular first-team football, something that Busby could not guarantee.

As it turned out, former United player and then manager of Newcastle United Charlie Mitten was in the crowd, along with his chairman Stan Seymour, and a performance only eclipsed by Dawson's hat-trick saw the St James' Park side table a £15,000 bid for the winger following the match. By the time Scanlon had showered and changed, a deal was done.

Seven days later, with some money in the bank, having recouped some of the outlay in the purchase of Cantwell, United were on the verge of clinching the transfer of another sought-after individual, David Herd, but it was a transfer in which the Arsenal directors held all the aces. The Highbury hierarchy had formally agreed to allow Herd to return to his native North West, as long as they succeeded in their attempts to sign George Eastham from Newcastle United, a player viewed as an ideal replacement. Eastham, whose name would soon be familiar to everyone and grace both the front and back pages of the national newspapers, was duly signed, and made his initial Gunners appearance in the reserves. However, the Highbury board were now caught in two minds as regards to releasing Herd, especially after the Scot hit a hat-trick in twelve minutes against Everton as the on-off transfer was debated. Adding further twists to the ongoing saga, an injury to Geoff Strong and the failure to sign Blackburn's Peter Dobing saw any immediate decision failing to be made.

The proposed move rumbled on into the New Year, with Matt Busby finally giving up hope in signing his target. 'The prospect of signing him seems as far off as ever,' said the United manager. 'In view of the fact that the player is now cup-tied, my club have decided to withdraw our offer.'

United's season was plunged into further disarray when captain Dennis Viollet broke his collarbone in the 3-0 defeat at Cardiff City on 26 November. Having already lost Johnny Giles a fortnight earlier with a broken leg sustained against Birmingham City, Matt Busby's options were slowly becoming fewer, adding to the frustration of his teams recent League form.

But rather surprisingly, Viollet's injury and the subsequent reshuffling of the team heralded the club's best run of results for two years, winning six and drawing one of their following seven League games, including resounding 6-0 and 5-1 victories against Chelsea and Manchester City respectively; with Alex Dawson notching hat-tricks in both, a feat unsurpassed since August 1951, when Jack Rowley did likewise in the opening two fixtures of the 1951/52 season against West Bromwich Albion and Middlesbrough. It was a run that by the end of the year had found the name of Manchester United occupying eighth spot in the First Division, and although still twenty-two points behind leaders Tottenham Hotspur, it showed a remarkable change in fortune for Busby's side.

Strangely, hat-trick hero Dawson could have been plying his trade a few miles from Old Trafford, as Blackburn Rovers had inquired about his availability. But it was a proposed transfer that had countless ifs and buts, and for the time being at least, Dawson would remain at Old Trafford.

One player, however, who did leave the club, was defender Ian Greaves who joined Lincoln City. Greaves had not featured in the first team since August 1959, due mainly to a knee injury and a cartilage operation.

With the mega-buck wages earned by the players of today, it is difficult to make any comparison to the wages earned and indeed the conditions that the players of four decades ago played under. Like life itself, the sixties would see countless changes throughout the game and the players of the period somewhat disgruntled by their far-from-happy lot. So much so that they had threatened to strike on 21 January in an effort to have the maximum wage abolished. However, with two days of 1960 remaining, it was announced that the Ministry of Labour had set out a new peace plan, with the lifting of the £15 per week wage to a new maximum wage of up to £30 per week in two years' time.

Other key points that were set down were that the 'benefit' rule was to be abolished and the maximum payout for a player who remained with one club would be £150 a year for the first five years and £200 a year for each year thereafter, depending on what was on a player's contract. Players would also be free to negotiate with their clubs on contracts of up to three years. There would also be a joint committee set up to settle disputes between players and the Football League.

United's upsurge in form, boosting their standing in the First Division, also ensured something of an easy passage over what could well have been a difficult FA Cup third-round tie against Second Division Middlesbrough. The fixture list also worked in United's favour, as immediately following the cup tie came a real test to see just how much of an improvement had taken place, with the visit of First Division leaders Tottenham Hotspur to Old Trafford.

The game, originally scheduled for 14 January, was postponed forty-eight hours due to fog, although the majority of the statistical records still give the former date. United, inspired once again by Alex Dawson in front of a 65,295 crowd, won a pulsating ninety-minute 2-0, only the second defeat that Tottenham had suffered all season.

Dawson's role in the outcome of the game was different from his usual wholehearted and determined contribution, with United's goals on this occasion coming from Mark Pearson and Nobby Stiles. Instead of his usual swashbuckling role, causing havoc in the middle of the opposition defence, Dawson's contribution on this occasion was made as a stand-in goalkeeper rather than a goalscorer, following a forty-fourth-minute injury to Harry Gregg.

Having on occasion swapped places with the United 'keeper in training, Dawson volunteered to take over between the sticks, and Gregg was shunted up front, simply to cause some confusion around the Tottenham goal. The centre-forward-cum-goalkeeper dealt comfortably with everything that came his way. The reversal of roles was later completed, when Gregg, to the wonderment of the crowd, back-heeled the ball into the path of Pearson for what was United's second goal.

United were later criticised for their rather physical approach to the game, but this had been a part of their game that had been missing earlier in the season, and although one or two of the challenges were somewhat robust, with even Bobby Charlton being spoken to by the referee, United were worthy of their victory.

Sadly, the 2-0 victory over Tottenham was to little avail, as five days later it was back to the 'same old, same old', with United slumping to a 6-0 thrashing at the hands of Leicester City. With injuries to Harry Gregg and David Gaskell, Matt Busby was forced to give seventeen-year-old Ronnie Briggs his first-team debut, but had the United manager foreseen what the ninety minutes would produce, he would have been more than happy to leave Alex Dawson between the sticks.

Was this something that Matt Busby had even considered? 'No,' said the centre-forward with an urge to pull on the green jersey. 'I doubt if it was something that the manager even gave a minute's thought to. I often played in goal in training, with Harry running about up front, kicking lumps out of everyone, and taking over in goal against Tottenham was just something that happened. Actually, Bobby Charlton wanted to take over between the posts, but the boss said no. He must have thought that he could do without me more, as he told Bobby that he had to stay up front.'

Leicester had only dropped one point in their previous four games, and were currently enjoying their best League position for thirty years. However, it was a fixture that United should have won given their current form. Yet it was not to be, with the debutant goalkeeper having an afternoon to forget.

Despite a misjudged cross there was little sign of early nerves from Briggs and he certainly could not be faulted for either of Leicester's two first-half goals. After the interval he tried his best as the visitors took the game to United and scored a further four, with the unfortunate Briggs given little in the way of help from his more experienced teammates.

Busby kept faith with the young Irishman for the fourth-round FA Cup tie away at Sheffield Wednesday, but at times it certainly looked as though the six-goal defeat by Leicester had knocked his confidence, and he could certainly be faulted for Wednesday's goal in the 1-1 draw, allowing the ball to squirm from his grasp and roll over the line. On over occasions he looked decidedly uncertain and nervous.

For the Old Trafford replay, there was little option but to play Briggs again, but it was a disaster waiting to happen and the United manager would have been better recalling Jack Crompton than allowing the stand-in 'keeper to be subjected to an evening of career-shattering proportions.

Old Trafford was packed for the 'Battle of the Roses' part two, and Wednesday picked up where they had left off and opened the scoring in the second minute through Fantham, who make no mistake from 5 yards out. But with latecomers still trying to squeeze their way down the packed terracing and with only another 120 seconds on the clock, United were level. Setters found Stiles, who pushed the ball through towards Pearson, and the inside-left skipped past a couple of defenders before unleashing a low, left-footed drive into the corner of the visitors net.

Suddenly, it was all United. Johnson cleared a Dawson header from underneath the crossbar, while Springett pulled off excellent saves from Charlton and Pearson. Confidence was now high and a cup run would have done everyone the world of good.

With half an hour gone, things changed dramatically. Wednesday outside-left Finney tried a shot at goal from 20 yards and, although it looked harmless enough, Briggs, who appeared to have the ball covered, allowed it to slip from his grasp and trickle over the line.

Three minutes later it was 3-1, Ellis heading home a Wilkinson free-kick following a rather crude and vicious foul by Setters.

It was now all Wednesday, with the United defence at sixes and sevens. Ellis made it 4-1 four minutes later when Craig got the better of Cantwell, leaving Briggs severely exposed, and although the 'keeper managed to get his hand to the ball, it spun away and crossed the line just inside the post.

There was now virtually no way back for United and with the second half still in its infancy, Stiles gave away a free-kick on the edge of the penalty area and although the kick was blocked by the defensive wall, Fantham reacted quickest and blasted the ball past Briggs for a fifth. It wasn't entirely one-way traffic, as Springett in the visitors' goal was called upon to make saves from Dawson, Pearson and Quixall, but Wednesday were soon back on top, adding a sixth and seventh through Ellis and Finney. Dawson scored a rather meaningless second for United, but thirteen goals conceded in two games was a poor showing by anyone's standards.

While the stand-in 'keeper's handling was at times suspect, Briggs, who ran off the Old Trafford pitch hiding his face with his hands, wasn't totally at blame for United's heaviest home defeat for thirty years. There is always a risk in throwing youngsters into the fray, and on this occasion it was a necessity rather than a gamble. However, on the night, there were more experienced players in front of him who could have helped prevent such a humiliation. Conceding fourteen goals in his first three senior games was not an ideal start for the red-haired goalkeeper, but the following day he told reporters, 'I think I have got over it now. And if I am selected for Saturday, I'll prove myself.'

Saturday, however, did not come and it was not until twelve months later that Ronnie Briggs reappeared in the United first team.

With Harry Gregg and David Gaskell still sidelined with injuries, the goalkeeping position now left Matt Busby in something of a dilemma, and although he had shown enough faith in the youngster to pitch him into first-team action, the manager was shrewd enough to realise that exposing Briggs to yet another defeat could do more harm than good. 'I gave the matter a great deal of thought,' said Busby. 'He had a terrible ordeal and it would have been more than unfair to have played him again so soon. Indeed, it would have been cruel.'

So, Matt Busby decided not to risk Ronnie Briggs against Aston Villa three days later, but he had to find a goalkeeper from somewhere, as there was no one on the books who was anywhere near up to the standard required. In any case, it was also a struggle to find a suitable custodian for the Central League side.

Eddie Lowery had been recruited from Oldham Batteries following the promotion of Ronnie Briggs, but he had received an injury during his debut against Barnsley's second string, forcing United to scourge the lower local Leagues for yet another replacement. Onto the books came Reg Adie, from Brinnington, a Stockport Sunday League side, but postponements and the demotion of Briggs saw the eighteen-year-old make his claim to fame as a United player in the 'A' team.

Perhaps Busby had not considered playing Alex Dawson in goal against Leicester City, but he certainly had contemplated hauling his trainer, Jack Crompton, out of retirement and casting him back into the First Division lime-light against Aston Villa, some five years after his last appearance. It had been 22 October 1955 when Jack Crompton last played first-team football for United, keeping a clean sheet in the 3-0 victory over Huddersfield Town at Old Trafford, but with an injury crisis on his hands, and knowing how fit his trainer kept himself, Busby asked the 1948 FA Cup winner if he felt like making a return against Villa.

Crompton's response was obviously positive, but his dreams of making a return were dashed by red tape, as upon retiring he had taken his pay out from the pension fund, and even when United had offered to repay the whole amount, the Football League refused to budge, stating that the rules were made to be enforced and it was something that they could not, and would not, change, even in what amounted to an emergency.

Gregg and Gaskell were obviously competent and reliable goalkeepers with a future at the club, so it was somewhat pointless in splashing the cash on a replacement, if indeed one could be found at such short notice. Having three first-class 'keepers on the books contesting the No. 1 shirt was just as big a waste. It was simply nothing more than a temporary replacement that was required and Busby knew the very man: a 'phone call to London secured the services of Great Britain Olympic 'keeper Mike Pinner.

Twenty-seven-year-old Pinner, long regarded as the country's leading amateur goalkeeper, was currently with Queens Park Rangers, and the Loftus Road club readily agreed to cancel his registration in order to allow the solicitor and serving RAF man to travel north to Manchester. Again, he would sign amateur forms, which would be cancelled by United as soon as their goalkeeping situation was resolved.

Signing the amateur custodian, who had thirty England international caps, was never considered a gamble, as he was a highly experienced individual, and as well as having the experience of playing in the Football League with QPR, he had also enjoyed spells in the spotlight with Aston Villa and Sheffield Wednesday. Prior to his United debut against one of his former clubs, Aston Villa, on 4 February, he said, 'I shan't be any more nervous than usual. Even so, tomorrow will be a grand day in my life.' No big deal then for the amateur goalkeeper, stepping up from Loftus Road to Old Trafford, and in the 1-1 draw, where he wore a sky-blue top, forsaking the regular green United goalkeeping jersey, he performed well and could certainly not be faulted for the Villa goal

His brief United 'career' was not, however, without its problems. Prior to his second appearance against Wolves, United had to obtain special permission from the RAF to play him, and during this fixture he damaged a finger, once again throwing United's goalkeeping position into disarray. With neither Harry Gregg or David Gaskell fully recovered from injury and with Pinner due to turn out for the RAF four days after the visit to Molineux, Matt Busby again moved into the amateur ranks and signed Harry Sharratt from Bishop Auckland on Central League forms. This was due to the fact that the 'keeper was also signed on Football League forms with Stockport County, and in doing so, could play for the reserves if no other 'keeper was available.

Mike Pinner made a trio of appearances before Harry Gregg returned to first-team duty, but the Irishman only managed two games before a shoulder injury forced him onto the sidelines for the remainder of the season. Pinner therefore made the journey north for one more game, before David Gaskell returned to the fray.

January 1961 was a momentous month in English football history, not because Manchester United had conceded six goals in one game without reply, but due to the threat of a players' strike, one that those at Manchester United clearly backed, as they called for the abolition of the maximum wage. Up until now, the clubs had always held the upper hand in controlling their players, and certainly the wages that they earned. This currently stood at £20 per week, and after much debate and consideration, the Football League somewhat reluctantly decided that the maximum wage was no more and clubs could pay what they liked, giving players the opportunity to negotiate a more lucrative contract.

Fulham raised the crossbar considerably by making their England inside-forward Johnny Haynes the first £100-a-week player, but others were reluctant to or simply had no intentions of following a similar path. United were certainly one of those clubs and felt that £50 per week was more than enough for their star performers, although this was a figure that they had no intentions of matching.

This was despite Matt Busby giving his support to this ground-breaking decision, saying, 'It must in the end bring better football. The improvement may not be spectacular and immediate, but football now becomes a specialist career. They (*the players*) now have the incentive to become outstanding at their job.'

With victories being few and far between and two-thirds of the season having been completed, the paying out of a winning bonus had not done much damage to the club's bank account if money was indeed an issue at this time, but as the season moved into its final two months, there was suddenly a bit more cash circulating around the Old Trafford dressing room.

At the beginning of March, with United safe from the fear of relegation, Matt Busby returned to hospital for a spinal operation, part of his continuing recovery from the events at Munich, and following his discharge, he left the dark, leaden sky of Manchester for the sunshine of the Riviera for some recuperation, once again leaving Jimmy Murphy as the man in charge.

Strangely, the inconsistency that had blighted the campaign seemed to disappear over those final twelve games, and although there were a couple of defeats – one of those ironically a 5-1 defeat at the hands of Sheffield Wednesday with David Gaskell this time the man facing the onslaught – performances did indeed show a vast improvement; especially the last four games, which saw United play what was arguably their best football of the season, scoring seventeen goals in the process, including a 6-0 hammering of Burnley at Old Trafford with double hat-tricks from Dennis Viollet and Albert Quixall. Although on the minus side seven were conceded, that run of results nudged United into a respectable seventh place, a position that was not conceived possible back in August.

It was crystal-clear that despite the flood of goals amid the end-of-season flourish, there was still considerable rebuilding work to do, as there was little strength in depth, with many of those who came into the team from time to time not up to the standard required by Manchester United. There had also been departures that had left gaps within the ranks. Ian Greaves had left for Lincoln City in December, as had fellow defender Joe Carolan, who had joined Brighton and Hove Albion, both players having played an important part in the clubs struggle to survive in the wake of Munich.

Another player to leave was Kenny Morgans, one of the Munich survivors, who moved back to his native Swansea in March. The Welshman had returned to the United first team against Bolton Wanderers on 18 February (two months after his first outing since the crash in a behind-closed-doors practice match), his first outing in over two years, but had only managed a couple of appearances before finding himself in the Central League side. Morgans readily admitted that things were never the same following the crash and that he 'didn't really care anymore'.

'I was unhappy for the two years following Munich. I just didn't want to play football again as I missed the boys so much. I was never the same player.'

Obviously Busby and Murphy were well aware of this predicament, but the abolition of the maximum wage had now put additional financial pressure on United, as well as on most other clubs, with the competition to sign players now even greater. United's reluctance to pay high wages certainly didn't help their cause, neither did their on-the-field failings. The Scot and his Welsh side-kick had a lot of work to do.

4

GOING DOWN –
AND NOT JUST WEMBLEY WAY

It certainly wasn't a pregnancy, but it took Matt Busby nine months to finally deliver an individual that he had long since coveted, paying out £35,000 to sign Arsenal's Scottish international forward David Herd, as the build-up to season 1961/62 got underway. The United manager had come within inches of signing the player during the previous campaign, but Arsenal's injury problems threw the transfer into disarray and it eventually failed to materialise.

Hamilton-born Herd, a free-scoring centre-forward, had enjoyed the unique distinction of playing alongside his father in May 1951 while on the books of Stockport County, and had joined Arsenal for £10,000 in August 1954. With the Gunners, he topped their scoring charts for four straight seasons, but those goals failed to bring the Scottish internatonal the success he craved, and then a telephone call urged him to travel to Highbury as there was a club coming to sign him. The centre-forward covered the distance between his home and the north London ground in double-quick time when he discovered it was none other than Matt Busby and Manchester United, as he was only too willing to return to the city where he was brought up and considered home.

Busby had also made a speedy journey to Highbury, following a late telephone call that had informed him that the player was now available, not wanting anyone else to step into the equation and perhaps jeopardise the transfer with a bigger financial incentive to both Arsenal and Herd.

The £35,000 paid out by Busby was actually £5,000 more than United's initial bid the previous November, and the close friend of his new signing's father had no misgivings in relation to the additional few thousand, proclaiming, 'Now we are all set at Old Trafford for the new season. It's third time lucky in our bids for Herd.'

'My chance to buy Herd came after I had given up hope. I tried very hard for him last season, then two weeks ago I contacted Arsenal again. They said there was nothing doing.

'I've been keen on Herd for years, particularly when I was managing the Scottish team.'

The player himself was just as happy with the move, 'phoning his father immediately after signing, telling him, 'It's all over. I'll be up at the weekend.' He was later to add, 'I was bitterly upset when I couldn't join United last season, now I am the happiest footballer in the country. I'm delighted to be going back north.'

Despite the form of Alex Dawson the previous season, scoring sixteen goals in twenty-eight League appearances, including consecutive hat-tricks against Chelsea and Manchester City, Busby had always been more than eager to add Herd to his line-up. Back in January, he had said, 'Alex is playing brilliantly, but we are keen as ever on Herd. It would be nice to have the two of them playing together. Herd was Arsenal's top scorer last season with twenty-nine in forty games.' The pairing of Dawson and Herd would have given United a powerful spearhead and a goal machine to challenge the best, but unfortunately, they would only start one fixture together, against Birmingham City in October, and the impending deluge of goals failed to materialise with United floundering to a 2-0 defeat!

Inconsistent performances were numerous the previous season, but despite this, United were tipped as possible championship challengers. Desmond Hackett of the *Daily Express* went as far as to say they 'would win the League and proceed far in the cup', adding that 'their forward line will score more goals than any other attack'.

Matt Busby, now totally pain-free following another close-season operation, also tipped his team to do well, although not going as far as the outspoken Hackett in proclaiming that the First Division championship trophy was heading for Old Trafford. 'I am very optimistic about United's prospects,' said the manager, while also tipping Tottenham Hotspur, Burnley and Everton to be amongst the top four. 'After Munich we estimated that it would take three to five years to rebuild,' Busby admitted. 'Three years have now passed and I think we can now detect the signs that our rebuilding is almost over.

'I have been watching our reserves and youngsters too, and I am very pleased with their progress. I do not visualise any more signings before the start of the season.'

This was perhaps little more than a confidence-booster for his players, although the form at the end of the previous season had indeed hinted that United were more than capable of winning games, and winning them well with the additional goal power of David Herd. Perhaps yes, they were capable of once again mounting a championship challenge.

A pre-season victory in Munich and a draw in Vienna provided satisfactory warm-ups, and when the First Division got underway, the only differences to the team that had finished the previous campaign was Harry Gregg in goal instead of David Gaskell, Nobby Stiles and Maurice Setters changing flanks, Johnny Giles dropping out and Albert Quixall moving to outside-right in order to accommodate new signing David Herd.

Herd had opened his scoring account against Bayern Munich, earning the nickname 'die Bombe' due to his shooting prowess – one effort going just wide, but felling a ball-boy behind the goal – however, it was Nobby Stiles who scored United's opening goal of season 1961/62, in the 1-1 draw with West Ham United at Upton Park.

Four days later, Herd was on the mark in the 3-2 win over Chelsea and again, with a double in the 6-1 trouncing of Blackburn Rovers, but United's failings were soon to be exposed with the visit to Stamford Bridge, where a Chelsea side that had cost a mere £130 not only beat United 2-0, but embarrassed them into chasing the ball around the pitch like mongrels on the beach.

Unlike last season, one defeat didn't suddenly materialise into three or four, as United immediately bounced back with a 3-2 win over Blackpool at Bloomfield Road, before securing a 1-0 home win over current League Champions and FA Cup-holders Tottenham Hotspur.

With the abolition of the minimum wage, United suddenly found themselves floundering in the 'who-pays-what League', with the likes of Sheffield Wednesday, Tottenham and even Burnley paying higher wages than those at Old Trafford. This caused some concern with the usually money-cautious Busby, and he advocated to the United board that the contracts of each player should be revised with immediate effect, even though none of the players had come knocking on his office door requesting a raise which would put them on par with other fellow professionals.

But the United board were not simply going to be over-generous and simply hand their players a better deal just like that, if the players wanted the money, then they had to earn it, with the club also benefiting from the new contracts. For those in the first team, their basic pay would rise to £35, with appearance money going up £5 to £10. The rewritten contracts now included a crowd bonus scheme, which guaranteed £1 per thousand between 37,000 and 45,000 and then £2 per thousand over 45,000. The ground capacity at this time was 65,000. There was also a win bonus of £4 and incentive pay determined by the team's actual League position. A far cry for the maximum £20 per week!

It was also a far cry from what players at other clubs were making. Johnny Haynes and his £100 per week at Fulham was certainly not the norm, but there were individuals at rival First Division clubs who could claim to be on at least double what the United players were taking home. Even some Second Division clubs were paying their players more.

As it turned out, with the new and improved contracts, Albert Quixall's goal which secured the 1-0 victory over Tottenham Hotspur, earned the scorer and his fellow teammates £85!

It wasn't just footballers who were beginning to sense an up-turn in their fortunes, many of those who watched them from the Old Trafford terracing and stands were also enjoying a better lifestyle, as Britain finally awoke from the grey post-war years of the 1950s.

Although Manchester wasn't exactly the most glamorous of cities to visit, or indeed live in, at this particular time, it could certainly stake a claim at being one of the most vibrant. There seemed to be plenty of jobs, if you wanted one, in the manual, commercial and retail sectors. Manufacturing, engineering, electrical and printing trades were all offering apprenticeships. Office workers were attracted in greater numbers to banks and insurance institutions, and the boutique and retail trade was booming. This in turn spawned the restaurant, café and coffee bar culture in the city. The university and many colleges in the area were busy with youngsters studying towards qualifications and careers, all those youngsters now wishing to make their own choices and decisions as to how to spend their time and money.

With money to be made, the United players were certainly going to do their utmost to swell their pay packets and followed their victory over Tottenham with a 2-1 win at Cardiff, with the two points that it brought being enough to leapfrog Sheffield Wednesday into third place in the First Division and treat the other half to something nice.

If Matt Busby had created the blueprint for building a team using mainly home-produced players, then he must have left a copy of his original plans lying around for others to see, as his good friend Joe Mercer, soon to become his cross-city rival at Maine Road, had decided to take a similar route to success at Villa Park.

Throwing caution to the wind, in the 18 September meeting between the two clubs, Mercer decided to include six youngsters under the age of twenty-one in his line-up to face an in-form United. Although a gamble, it was one that paid off, and it was only the brilliance of goalkeeper David Gaskell that earned United a share of the points in the 1-1 draw.

A 3-2 win in the first 'derby' of the season, seven days later, took United up to second, but it was little more than a ray of sunshine peeking through the grey clouds as they plummeted down the table just as quickly as they had climbed, taking them to within three points of leaders Burnley, with a game in hand.

A 2-0 defeat at Wolves followed the victory against City at Old Trafford, but the 1-1 draw at West Bromwich, where they were denied two obvious penalties, gave little indication as to what lay ahead.

From the following ten games, Busby's team collected only two points, courtesy of draws against West Bromwich Albion away and Leicester City at home. The other eight fixtures were an embarrassment of defeats, with the goals against column taking a real battering with twenty-eight conceded.

Forced into making six changes, two of them positional, against Birmingham City at Old Trafford on 14 October, United turned in their worst performance of the season against the First Division's bottom club. Missing the strengths of Foulkes, Viollet and Quixall, United struggled and Busby's hoped-for goal avalanche in playing Herd and Dawson together (only for the second time) failed to materialise. Long before the referee decided that the Old Trafford crowd had suffered enough, many had already headed for home.

If ever an opportunity was at hand to not simply gain a further two points, keeping tabs on leaders Burnley, but to score a handful of goals against a side who had already conceded thirty-four goals in their dozen fixtures to date, then this was it. But there was no one to take the lead. No one with the know-how to unlock the Birmingham defence, while the United defence itself was totally disorganised.

Things went from bad to worse seven days later with a visit to Highbury, where the 5-1 scoreline was neither a fluke nor undeserved, although again Busby was forced into making yet another half-dozen changes as the confidence slowly ebbed away from his downhearted players. He had begun the season, some thirteen games previously, with a line-up that read Gregg, Brennan, Cantwell, Stiles, Foulkes, Setters, Quixall, Viollet, Herd, Pearson and Charlton. Against the Gunners that had changed to Gregg, Brennan Cantwell, Nicholson Foulkes Lawton, Moir Giles Herd Viollet and Charlton, with others such as Warren Bradley, Alex Dawson, David Gaskell, Tony Dunne and Frank Haydock all taking a peg in the first-team dressing room.

A disastrous run of results was to follow, catapulting the team from being within touching distance of that top spot to second-bottom, with sixteen points from nineteen games, a solitary point keeping them above Chelsea, with the Stamford Bridge side having better goal difference. Things were beginning to look serious at Old Trafford. The results certainly did not create a false picture, as performances were indeed poor.

Following the 3-0 defeat at home to 'bogey team' Bolton Wanderers, one reporter wrote, 'There is a new meaning to that old but once-proud tag – "the Busby Babes". They are babes ... in action, in skill, and in heart. Bustling Bolton took the points from them like a mother removes the nappie from her helpless offspring.

'United could do nothing to stop the execution. They could only contribute to it.'

A week later they lost 3-1 at Sheffield Wednesday, before salvaging a point in a 2-2 draw at home to Leicester City. Then there came two consecutive 4-1 defeats at Ipswich and at home to Burnley.

Against leaders Burnley at Old Trafford, they seemed to lift their game, turning in an excellent opening forty-five minutes, having taken the lead in the sixth minute through Herd. Against the run of play, Burnley equalised with ten minutes of the first half remaining and, as play resumed after the interval, United suddenly found themselves under fire and unable to match their visitors in any department. As their confidence slowly ebbed away, Burnley scored a further three goals to consolidate their position at the top.

While they had started the game promisingly, there was no escaping the wrath of the press box, with the *Manchester Guardian* proclaiming, 'Manchester United Pushed Further into the Basement', and their correspondent writing, 'What can one say of United that has not been said already?

'The old sparkle and artistry have gone. A month away from football would do the whole side good, but that of course is impossible. One step towards improvement might be the inclusion of two capable inside-forwards with the physique of Herd. Giles and Quixall, against Burnley's well-built defenders looked far too small for the task confronting them.'

Any chinks of light that appeared through the gloom of that fourth home defeat of the season were totally extinguished on 2 December when United visited Goodison Park. The 5-1 defeat sending them down into that second from bottom spot.

In a matter of weeks, United had suddenly gone from being an outside tip for the First Division title to candidates for relegation, but despite the problems which were clearly surrounding the club, Matt Busby refused to be drawn into any panic buying.

'No, we aren't going to charge into the transfer market,' he told reporters. 'We have some fine players on the books and when the luck turns, as it most certainly will, they will show their ability once more.

'It was very disappointing the way things went in the first half against Everton, but nothing goes right for the boys at the moment as anyone must agree.

'Yet with any luck we could have turned round 3-2 down and the way the lads tightened up in the second half showed that the spirit is there, only luck is missing although Everton are a tip-top side and were worthy winners.'

At Goodison, David Herd had scored his second goal in two games, but those were his first since his double strike against Blackburn Rovers on 26 August, some fourteen games previously, although it must be added that he had missed five games through injury. United, however, were now short of firepower when the former Arsenal man was either out injured or lacking in form, as stand-in centre-forward Alex Dawson, who had an outstanding scoring record of forty-five goals in eighty appearances, had given up on securing a regular first-team place and left in a £18,000 deal to join Preston North End.

The signing of David Herd was obviously the beginning of the end for the burly centre-forward, but a spearhead of Dennis Viollet, David Herd and Alex Dawson, although a luxury, would have produced countless goals. However, it was Preston who were to reap the benefits of goals of the 'Black Prince', with Dawson scoring 114 goals in 197 outings.

'It was obviously disappointing to leave United, having been there since March 1957,' recalled the Aberdeen-born forward. 'But to be honest, I sort of knew that my time had come and it was perhaps time to move on. United were going through a transitional period and Matt Busby was determined to get back into the European Cup.

'When you were called into the office you'd either done something bad, or someone had enquired about you. Matt said that Preston had been in touch with him, but was also quick to state, "You don't have to go if you don't want to go." I didn't really want to, but I wanted to play football and I told him that I would leave and join Preston.

'I certainly had no regrets in joining Preston, where I had a good five years and enjoyed an excellent rapport with the supporters. I was very happy there. But looking back, Munich did not exactly help my career, or that of some of my teammates, as we had to grow up quickly, even though I had played a few times prior to the crash, and I often think that had it not been for the events that February afternoon, my days at Old Trafford might have been slightly longer.

'I certainly don't complain and wouldn't have it any different.'

If the defence was going to leak goals, then the forwards were going to have to work overtime to ensure that they scored more than their teammates behind them were conceding, and with Dennis Viollet out of favour, Busby, in an effort to revitalise his beleaguered team, had promoted Phil Chisnall to the first team and took a gamble in moving Nobby Lawton from half-back to inside-forward.

The change made little difference against Everton in what was described in one newspaper as a 'one way work out until Everton eased up and gave battered and dizzy United a chance to gather their shattered wits', with the United defence described as 'such a shambling, unimaginative, leaden-footed bunch that scoring in the first half became a mere formality for Everton'.

Not for the first time, Busby's astute decisions paid off and suddenly sunshine broke over the leaden Old Trafford skyline, with the doom and gloom replaced by a wave of newfound hope, as the introduction of Chisnall, according to Bill Fryer in the *Daily Express*, 'changed United from a scratching, scraping, low-spirited intermediate lot of units into a team of tearaways who knew what they were about'.

Another report tells of the roar returning to Old Trafford after eleven weary weeks, a healthy roar of a crowd cheering a team on top. But that same gathering of terrace worthies would still utter the groans of despair as the supporters were indeed wary of too much adulation. They were now more than familiar with sudden changes of fortune that could see all good work undone in a matter of minutes of on-field madness.

Despite having conceded five against Everton, United sprang back with a 3-0 home win over Fulham, with David Herd notching a double and finally finding that scoring touch which had eluded him since his return north. The former Arsenal man then scored another double under the Old Trafford lights, on an evening when everyone finally believed that the corner had indeed been turned, when the mighty Real Madrid arrived in town and were soundly defeated 3-1. Puskas was missing from the Madrid line-up, while Di Stefano and Santamaria were replaced at half-time, with United 2-1 in front, but victory was indeed deserved, with nineteen-year-old Phil Chisnall, scorer of United's first goal, receiving most of the plaudits.

'This is the most wonderful thing that has happened to me in my life,' proclaimed the youngster, who went to school a mere 300 yards from Old Trafford. 'I never dreamed that I would actually play in such a match myself. But it has happened and when I wake in the morning I shall pinch myself and ask if it really is true.

'I did not feel any nerves at all. Before the match the boss told me "when you go out there tonight remember that they are only flesh and blood like yourself".

'Those words were in my mind all the time and I was astonished not so much at my goal, as at myself. I had no nerves, I just enjoyed it.'

But dreams of a revival were over before they had begun with such hopes disappearing in the Manchester fog following a 2-1 home defeat against West Ham United, a game that saw one correspondent writing, 'For most of this game, I felt like a man who arrives at a party to find the drinks are finished.' Ten days later, the supporters must have thought that they had indeed been to the party, getting there early and consuming the drink on offer, leaving them with something of a hangover as they watched the Boxing Day fixture against Nottingham Forest, not really believing that what was unfolding in front of them.

On an ice-bound pitch, which was fortunate to actually host the game, United were four up by the half-hour mark, but had seen Forest peg a goal back prior to half-time. With twenty minutes remaining it was 4-2, leaving the frozen supporters to think 'here we go again'. But they were wrong. Nobby Lawton claimed his hat-trick in the seventy-second minute and although Palmer scored a third for Forest seven minutes later, Brennan rounded off the scoring two minutes from time to make it 6-3.

This result took United up to eighteenth, three points ahead of Chelsea, who were still rooted at the bottom with Burnley still twelve points away at the top. The sudden upturn in fortune was also blighted with the odd dark cloud over Manchester, with controversy never far away.

As 1961 moved into 1962, United saw yet another familiar face leave for pastures new; a player who had become a firm favourite with the United support since his emergence in first team back in season 1952/53. Dennis Viollet had not started a game since the 2-2 draw with Leicester City, when he scored United's equaliser and, despite having missed three games, was still United's second-top scorer for the season, with seven goals from thirteen games. He found it difficult leaving the club he had joined as a fifteen-year-old, but added that he had 'no regrets'.

'The truth is, that I was tired of playing second-team football.

'It's not just the extra money I shall be able to earn and it will be much more than I have been earning with United. I felt I needed a challenge and on their recent form, Stoke must have a great chance of getting into the First Division.'

Upon losing one of his original 'Babes', Matt Busby said, 'I do believe that the move will do Dennis a great deal of good. It may be that a new club was just what he needed to regain the form of which we all know he is capable.

'He has been part of all the trophies of this club in the past twelve or thirteen years and we are very grateful to him for his service. He has been a great player for Manchester United.'

Dennis Viollet's relationship with Matt Busby, however, had soured during the course of the past few months, and his unpublished book *The Kings Have Gone*, although full of praise for the United manager, included the statement, 'I will never forgive him for the heartless way in which he handled my leaving Old Trafford.'

Recalling his departure from Old Trafford, Viollet wrote:

The 'phone rang. I rose from the chair and went over to answer the call. I was not to know that it was about to be the end of my career with Manchester United.

On the other end of the line was Stoke City manager Tony Waddington, who said that he wanted to come over and have a talk with me.

Surprised by this out-of-the-blue approach, I said it was okay with me as long as he had spoken to Busby.

He said he had, and within half an hour or so, Tony was knocking on the front door. I still couldn't grasp what was happening.

As I let in Tony, I again asked him, 'Have you really spoken to Mr Busby about this?'

'Of course I have,' was his reply, and he went on to tell me as we chatted in front of the fire that he needed me at Stoke City.

This was a great offer and I felt thrilled and a little honoured, yet there was another feeling going through my mind.

After fifteen years at Old Trafford, I wasn't wanted. Alright, I know all good things have got to come to an end. Of course any club has the right to tell players, 'sorry and all that, but we can do without you now. Thanks for your efforts over the years.'

Yes, when you come into soccer you know that the parting of the ways can always be just around the corner, but why couldn't Busby have told me? Why couldn't he have taken me on one side and said just a word or two. Or maybe all those victories, all those big games, the thrills, were just for the record books.

Still feeling in a slight daze, with all those thoughts running through my mind, I went over to the 'phone and dialled Busby's number. The boss's Scottish tones came over the line. Yes, he said, Tony Waddington had been onto him, but he hadn't mentioned it to me as he had been rather busy.

The conversation, as far as I was concerned was pointless and I wound it up as quickly, although politely as I could.

It felt to me as if I had become to Busby like an old pair of boots that had been flung into a corner and ignored. Was it asking too much for Busby to say, 'This is the situation Dennis. Stoke City want you. How do you feel about it?'

Oh, Busby was nice enough when it came to the final farewell, but that didn't mean very much to me. I remember that, as I replaced the receiver after speaking to him, I saw in my mind a young team standing round Busby and listening to his every word. Now these words seemed hollow.

I simply shrugged my shoulders and said to Tony, 'Right. This sounds great, where are the forms. I'll sign for Stoke.'

And so I left Manchester United and headed for the Potteries.

It has also been hinted that the departure of United's record League goalscorer had more to do with his nocturnal habits than anything else, but no matter what, the highly talented forward, a candidate for any all-time United XI, was no longer on the Old Trafford payroll.

Fixtures played over any holiday period usually saw club directors rub their hands in anticipation of packed terraces and stands, but Christmas 1961 proved rather disappointing in that aspect for the men in the Old Trafford boardroom. Although the 31,366 who paid to watch the Boxing Day fixture against Forest was an improvement of 2,000 on that for the previous home fixture against West Ham, attendances had fallen as quickly as the team, with the eight defeats in ten games bringing a drop of some 163,759 spectators.

But it was not only attendances that had fallen. The players' take-home pay had also been dramatically reduced due to the incentives for League position, attendances and, of course, wins. Some players had actually lost their first-team place and this also affected the wage packet, which was now, on average, around £50. During this particular period, the United players had dropped around £1,700 in bonuses between them!

For one player, the bonuses and appearance money were no longer an addition to his wages from Manchester United. Upon returning to action from a cartilage operation, Wilf McGuinness was enjoying a run out against Stoke City in a Central League fixture when tragedy struck in the form of a double break to his left leg. Operations and bone grafts by skilled surgeons attempted to save the wing-half's career, but it was to no avail and, at the age of twenty, he was forced to finally give up the hope of returning to United's first team.

Charting the former Mount Carmel schoolboy's time as a footballer reads like a true 'Roy of the Rovers' story, as at thirteen, Wilf McGuinness was captain of the Manchester Boys under-14 side. At fourteen, he was still with Manchester Boys, but had progressed to both the Lancashire Boys and England Boys XIs. At sixteen, he was captain of the England youth team and a year later he signed for United, making his League debut against Wolves. By the age of nineteen, he had won a First Division championship medal and was an England under-23 international. His first full cap came against Ireland in Belfast the following year.

But now, he would never again enjoy the experience of running down the tunnel and out into a packed Old Trafford with its voracious crowd. He was, however, still employed by the club, beginning a career as assistant trainer, so perhaps he would one day share in further triumphs.

Despite the sometimes torturous results and performances, many had considered United to be a good bet for the FA Cup. An outside bet was perhaps better, but away from the week-to-week pressure of the First Division, who knew what could be achieved, although being paired with near neighbours and reputed 'bogey team' Bolton Wanderers in Round Three did little to see large amounts of money being placed on United progressing, never mind going all the way.

To win any cup competition, luck is something that is more often than not required, and it was certainly something that United needed to defeat Bolton who, for this particular game, were considered 5:2 outsiders. The visitors, never a side to let a visit to Old Trafford cause them any concern, took the game to United straight from the kick-off, with the home side rarely showing any cohesion. Once Bolton had opened the scoring in the thirty-fifth minute, after coming close on two occasions in the opening quarter of an hour, there only looked like one winner.

Once ahead, Bolton played with confidence, often toying with their opponents, but as the second half got underway, they appeared more than content to play a more defensive game. David Herd tested Hopkingson twice in those early second-half exchanges, but as the game wore on, the visitors were more than happy to waste time and play out the closing minutes by simply keeping United at bay. But the terraces were suddenly reignited as the game spun it on its axis.

With eight minutes remaining, United swept forward, as if on a final attempt at snatching an equaliser. From the right, Chisnall swung the ball teasingly towards the Bolton goalmouth. Up rose Herd and his powerful header flew towards goal. Hopkingson was again equal to the United No. 9, throwing himself across the goal and getting his hand to the ball, although unable to actually hold it. Like a cat leaping at a mouse, Herd quickly pounced and the ball was prodded over the line. The ground erupted, as did the Bolton players.

Silence suddenly enveloped the ground, as the white-shirted Bolton players voiced their complaints to the referee: the linesman had flagged for offside against Herd, who had certainly looked a good 5 yards in front of the nearest defender. Referee Denis Howell ran over to his fellow colleague, but following a brief discussion, allowed the goal to stand.

Sensing victory and definitely not wanting a replay, United seemed to come alive and pushed forward. With a minute remaining, they achieved the impossible.

Herd, wide on the right, collected the ball and sent it through to Nicholson who had pushed forward from his midfield position as the Bolton defence backtracked. From the edge of the area, Nicholson let fly, and although Hopkingson appeared to have the ball covered, it suddenly took a deflection off Farrimond and spun slowly into the net for the winner.

To say that Bolton were aggrieved was an understatement. So incensed were their players at full-time that the referee required a police escort off the pitch, something that gave him little concern.

'I don't care what 40,000 people think,' he said. 'I am the one to give the decisions and I did so.

'In my opinion, Herd was not offside when the ball was last played. I am paid to make decisions; the linesmen are there to assist me.'

Blackpool at home on 13 January was a game that was lost before the referee's whistle signalled the start of the ninety minutes, as United virtually kicked off with only ten men. In the prematch warm up, David Herd jarred a muscle in his thigh and had to go off to have it tightly strapped up, but as the game got underway, the United centre-forward seemed to be moving quite freely. That was until the ninth minute, when he aggravated the injury while shooting at goal. Limping slightly to begin with, Herd was soon severely restricted in his movement and was little more than a passenger on the left wing. Two minutes prior to this, Armfield had set up Hauser to score what turned out to be the only goal of the game,

Matt Busby must have thought it was Friday 13th, rather than twenty-four hours later, as with an hour still to play, Tony Dunne collided with Peter Hauser and both players were knocked out. Dunne was moved to centre-forward as United were again forced into a reshuffle. Dunne was obviously out of his depth up front, and the couple of opportunities that came his way – one from a mere 6 yards out early in the second half – would certainly have been seized upon by a fit David Herd.

Dunne was soon restored to his normal defensive position, with Lawton taking over the centre-forward role, but he was perhaps a little enthusiastic in his new role, wandering constantly into offside positions, thus halting promising attacking moves.

Despite the handicaps, United put up a determined fight, but could do little to prevent the visitors from taking both points back to the seaside.

Rumours abounded that Busby was looking for a top-class outside-left, so that he could move Bobby Charlton inside, but no matter where the England man played, he caused opposition defenders problems: as January came to a close, his goals against Aston Villa and Tottenham contributed to three valuable points.

Quixall added a second against Villa in the comfortable 2-0 win, while Giles joined Charlton on the score-sheet against Tottenham in a power-charged 2-2 draw.

Tottenham could be found two points behind leaders Burnley, although the Lancastrians had two games in hand, while United languished some ten points behind the north London side in seventeenth position. So, in reality, the draw at White Hart Lane was a creditable performance in a game that the *News of the World* correspondent Joe Hulme considered to be not just 'thrill packed', but 'the most niggly, bad-tempered game I have seen this season. There were far too many sly kicks at opponents, too many players pointing warning fingers at others, too many free-kicks.'

Despite the opinion of Joe Hulme, the performances against Villa and Tottenham produced the first back-to-back unbeaten games since September, and instilled some confidence into the beleaguered red shirts, setting off an unbeaten League and cup run of twelve games.

Tottenham's north London neighbours Arsenal travelled to Old Trafford on FA Cup business on the last day of January, having already made the journey a few days earlier, only to be defeated by a dense fog which forced the postponement of the game. In what many perceive as typical Mancunian weather, the rearranged fixture was played amid monsoon conditions, with both sides contributing to a closely fought, full-blooded cup tie, which embraced some splendid football.

With the centre of the Old Trafford pitch doing a superb imitation of a small pond, glistening under the floodlights, the young United side battled against their more experienced opponents, in a ninety minutes that were certainly not for the faint-hearted. Only one goal separated the two teams and it came in the twenty-eighth minute. A Chisnall shot was superbly saved by Kelsey, but from the resulting corner Chisnall swung the ball over and Maurice Setters ran in to power a header past the helpless Arsenal 'keeper.

Charlton thought he had made it 2-0, but his effort was disallowed for an earlier infringement, while Eastham, with thirteen minutes remaining, beat Gaskell, but could only stand open-mouthed as his effort hit the foot of the post.

The visitors put up a spirited fight, with their half-back line, which included the one-time United target Laurie Brown at centre-half, adding more than just a little bite to a closely fought cup tie.

Back to the week-by-week gruel of League football, an ageing Cardiff City arrived at Old Trafford on 3 February and were no match for an improving young Manchester United, inspired by Johnny Giles. The two points earned from the 3-0 victory, coupled with a further two from the 2-0 'derby' win at Maine Road the following Saturday, gave Busby's side a little breathing space, as both the Cities were precariously placed, along with United in that bottom section of the table.

The draw for the fifth round of the FA Cup was greeted with a little dismay in the Old Trafford dressing room and indeed around the red half of Manchester. The smiles of a home draw were quickly wiped off the faces, when Sheffield Wednesday followed Manchester United out of the maroon velvet bag. This was the third consecutive season that the two clubs had been drawn together in the competition and the fourth time since 1957/58. The 7-2 defeat in the previous season's fourth-round replay was still a little too fresh in the memory.

Cup ties can often be compelling and highly entertaining affairs, with any fears that a defeat could see a downwards movement in League position banished to one side. Of course a defeat would see the dreams of playing in a Wembley final dismissed for another year, but there had to be a winner at the end of the day, so it was best to cast your fate to the wind and simply go for it.

On this particular occasion, neither United nor Sheffield Wednesday adopted such an outlook, much to the disappointment of the 65,623 crowd, therefore producing a rather dull and dreary affair which, not surprisingly for those in attendance, ended goal-less. It could, however, have ended as the previous two cup ties between the two sides had, with a victory to the Yorkshire club, had referee Jim Finney viewed a Setters tackle on Ellis differently.

Midway through the second half, with Bill Foulkes off the field, receiving attention for a cut head, the visitors pressed forward, seeking to make the most of their extra-man advantage. Wednesday centre-forward Keith Ellis chased a through-ball into the United penalty area, more in hope than anything else, and as goalkeeper David Gaskell was about to gather it, Maurice Setters rushed forward and sent the Wednesday No. 9 crashing to the ground.

It was a tackle that Setters did not need to make, but one that had the striped jerseys screaming for a penalty. Much to their annoyance and United's relief, the referee viewed the challenge differently and awarded an indirect free-kick to Wednesday a few feet outside the area. The kick came to nothing as the Wednesday players continued to protest.

'What else could it have been but a penalty,' proclaimed Wednesday captain Tony Kay after the game.

This set up an interesting replay four days later, with fears that it could turn into something of an over-physical encounter, as there had been one or two close calls during the Old Trafford meeting.

Such fears were unfounded, as the game at times lacked the fire of the previous ninety minutes, with Sheffield Wednesday failing to reach the standard set by the visitors.

United took an eighth-minute lead, which gave them the confidence to settle down and dictate the play to their advantage and brought a comforting sigh of relief, as well as a loud roar from the 20,000 travelling support. Charlton moved the ball forward to Giles, and the in-form Irishman, after skipping past one defender, flicked the ball back to David Herd. Playing a one-two, the ball was quickly back at the feet of Giles and a low drive sent the ball past the outstretched arm of Ron Springett in the Wednesday goal.

Wednesday lacked the solidness in defence that was visible in the previous encounter, with centre-half Swan putting his goalkeeper under pressure on several occasions. At the opposite end, Gaskell kept United in the cup with three first-class saves, as did Tony Dunne with a goal-line clearance from an Ellis header.

With only one goal separating the two sides, the game was obviously far from over, but with thirteen minutes remaining, the result was finally put beyond any doubt with a landmark strike from Bobby Charlton. Picking up the ball some 30 yards from goal, Charlton began one of those trademark jinking runs across the pitch, beating two players in the process, before unleashing a tremendous drive from all of 25 yards past the helpless Springett. This was his 100th goal for the club.

The Sheffield Wednesday FA Cup jinx was broken and United, to the surprise of many, were in the quarter-finals. The victory also earned those in the mud-splattered red shirts £207 each through appearances and bonus payments.

Back on League business, a 4-1 victory over West Bromwich Albion at Old Trafford and two draws – 2-2 against Wolves at Molineux and 1-1 a short distance away at Birmingham City's St Andrew's – extended the unbeaten run to ten games, something that had not been experienced since season 1957/58.

It is worth noting, purely as a matter of interest and also in helping restore some credit to the blemished career of Ronnie Briggs, that the goalkeeper returned to first-team duty in that 4-1 victory against West Bromwich Albion and held his place for five consecutive League fixtures.

His appearance against Albion was watched with an initial nervousness, but he was given an encouraging cheer when he first handled the ball and went on to produce a few creditable saves. He was to blot his copybook slightly against Wolves, when he fumbled the ball and allowed it to roll across the line to earn Wolves a share of the points, although again he made some fine saves. The 1-1 draw at St Andrew's the following Saturday, however, produced headlines such as 'Wonder Show By Briggs', earning standing ovations from the crowd, both at half-time and full-time. However, true to form, he dropped a centre from Helliwell which enabled Leek to score Birmingham's goal.

Briggs was to make a further three appearances towards the end of the season, keeping a clean sheet in the 5-0 thrashing of Ipswich Town.

That seven-game unbeaten run in the League saw United climb up into tenth place, a mid-table position, eleven behind leaders Burnley and eleven in front of bottom club Fulham. With a dozen games remaining, there was little possibility of United actually contesting the championship, but there was more than a possibility of striding to Wembley and winning the FA Cup.

Drawn away at Preston North End in the quarter-finals, expectations were high as supporters and team headed up the A6, but as the ninety minutes unfolded, the journey back to Manchester was filled with talk of United's lucky escape at the hands of the Second Division side.

Matt Busby was forced into making several changes to his team, the most notable being Noel Cantwell's appearance at centre-forward, but even taking this into perspective, United were more than fortunate to survive to fight another day.

Thompson missed a glorious opportunity to give the home side the lead in the fourteenth minute. Briggs hit the bar on the half-hour and had former United forward Alex Dawson not squandered two golden scoring opportunities, one of which saw him shoot wide when only 6 yards from goal and only Gaskell to beat, then United would have been 4-0 behind at half-time.

United showed a little more promise in the second half, but even when Preston were reduced to ten men, after Cunningham was carried off with twelve minutes remaining, they still could not claim the advantage.

So, it was back to Old Trafford four days later and, as so often happens in cup ties, if the lesser team does not snatch those golden opportunities in the first tie, then their moment has passed. The 2-1 scoreline, in United's favour, fails to give a true reflection on the ninety minutes, dominated for most by the home side on a pitch which was frozen and rutted, making skilful football somewhat difficult.

Preston, without the injured Cunningham and with United inspired by the return of David Herd up front, were two of the main reasons for this cup tie to swing so decisively in United's favour. They took a firm hold of the game in the twenty-eighth minute when Bobby Charlton gave them the lead with a goal similar to the one he had scored against Sheffield Wednesday in the previous round, moving in from the wing and beating two players, before unleashing the ball past a helpless goalkeeper.

Within a couple of minutes, Nobby Lawton twice had the ball in the Preston net, but both 'goals' were disallowed: the first for a push on the goalkeeper, the second for a rather debatable offside. The subsequent cheers and boos left the 5,000 supporters locked outside in complete disarray as to what the actual score was.

There was no doubting that their favourites were indeed in front seven minutes prior to the interval, when a loud cheer filled the cold evening air following United's second. David Herd, collecting a pass from Charlton, coolly lobbed the ball over the head of Singleton before running round him to crack the ball past Kelly in the Preston goal from the edge of the area.

Biggs sliced the ball wide as Preston fought back and Gaskell pulled off an excellent save from a Wilson free-kick, but even when the visitors did equalise in the sixty-fifth minute, Spavin pouncing on a headed clearance by Foulkes, there was little danger in United throwing the game away.

The performance not only took United into the semi-final – their first since 1958 – but also fired out a warning to opponents Tottenham Hotspur, with many confident that United could indeed go all the way to Wembley and FA Cup success. It was a confidence that was soon to be shattered, as the following three fixtures, against Bolton Wanderers, Nottingham Forest and Sheffield Wednesday, produced only one solitary point, from the 1-1 draw against the latter; the away trips to Bolton and Forest both ended in 1-0 defeats. Not only was United's unbeaten run to fall at the thirteenth hurdle at Burnden Park, it had been thirteen long years since they had actually returned to Manchester with a victory from that particular neck of the woods.

Against Forest, it was a slip by Ronnie Briggs that gifted the home side the points, while against Wednesday, who were practically reduced to ten men following an injury to centre-forward Young, they should have had the game sewn up prior to the interval, but in the second half stuttered against the handicapped visitors.

And so the FA Cup semi-final dawned, with United's only real trepidations centring on the choice of venue – Sheffield Wednesday's Hillsborough ground. Oh, and a small matter of yet another goalkeeping injury crisis with the possibility of Ronnie Briggs reliving his FA Cup nightmare against the side who only last season hit seven past him.

Disappointment and relief met the announcement of the United line-up, with David Gaskell, having recovered from an ankle injury received in training, taking over in goal. Meanwhile, another injury doubt, Shay Brennan, was not considered fit enough to face Tottenham, so his place was taken by Noel Cantwell.

Despite having beaten last season's double-winners at Old Trafford and drawn in the away fixture at White Hart Lane, Busby's side knew that they would have to be on top form if they were to progress to the final, as the north London side, marshalled by Jackie Blanchflower's older brother Danny, and inspired by the ferocity of Dave Mackay and the silky skills of the superbly talented John White, were a formidable force.

But those Wembley hopes were proved to be little more than just that – hopes – as United's chances disappeared as quickly as the falling snow that failed to make an impression amid the pouring rain.

Nobby Lawton missed a golden opportunity to give United the lead after only forty seconds, while David Herd was denied by Bill Brown in the Tottenham goal before Jimmy Greaves – that goal-poaching maverick – opened the scoring for Tottenham in the third minute. From then on it was always going to be an uphill struggle. Lawton fouled Blanchflower and from the resulting free-kick, the Spurs captain found the head of Bobby Smith, leaving Greaves the simple task of placing the ball past Gaskell.

Nineteen minutes later it was 2-0. White's inch-perfect cross was headed over Dunne and into the roof of the United net by Jones. By now, Tottenham were so much in control that they could relax a little in an effort to conserve some of their energy for their forthcoming European Cup tie with Benfica.

Against the adverse weather conditions, United had something of an excuse, but Derek Hodgson in the *Daily Express* told something of the true story: 'This United were neither devils nor angels. Apart from Bobby Charlton and Noel Cantwell, they were pretty ordinary footballers.

'They reached the semi-finals on faith, hope and fortune, and then found they had no right on the same turf as Spurs.

'All Spurs did was to hold a powerful magnifying glass over every crack, every little weakness, exposing all United's pretensions of greatness.'

The player upon whose shoulders a considerable portion of United's hopes of cup success were heaped was Johnny Giles, but his match-winning ability was seldom on view. Lawton, another United hope who had been playing well of late, also failed to make any telling impression on the game as Tottenham toyed with their opponents, exposing a wide gulf between the two teams.

With six minutes remaining and the rain turning into a blizzard of sleet and snow, Charlton provided Herd with the opportunity to pull a goal back, and on this occasion the United centre-forward took it, having shunned two earlier, possibly just as easy opportunities. But any hopes of snatching another and a replay were shattered within three minutes, as another White cross was converted, this time by Medwin. And the Spurs went marching on.

In the dying minutes, Greaves had a shot kicked off the line, but by that time, many were already heading back to Lancashire.

'We looked young and raw at times,' said a disappointed Matt Busby. But reflecting on the game at a later date, the United manager took a more positive view: 'Spurs beat us 3-1, but I saw the pieces of the jigsaw beginning to fit. I felt we were getting within reach of the great Spurs. But one vital item was missing. We had plenty of the ball and used it well, except when it came to the final thrust. There was no end product in the penalty box.'

With only nine games remaining, as the season drew to a welcome close, any transfer activity was out of the question, but Busby had already began planning for the following campaign, being firmly focused on adding some firepower to his lacklustre squad. Relegation wasn't entirely out of the question, as although United were in fourteenth place with thirty-two points, they were only eight in front of the bottom two clubs, Fulham and Chelsea.

A trip to Leicester in the aftermath of that semi-final defeat provided the opportunity to bounce back and secure two valuable points, which would ease any gnawing fears of Second Division football, but they were reduced to ten men after only sixteen minutes, when Nobby Lawton was carried off with a cracked knee bone, sustained as he twisted awkwardly. It was back-to-the-wall stuff.

The Filbert Street side took advantage of United's mishap and stormed into a three-goal lead. Cheesbrough, with two thunderous drives in the fifth and twenty-first minutes, and Keyworth seven minutes before half-time, put the home side firmly in the driving seat and looked to have the match sewn up. But for those who decided that it would be a good idea to seek their half-time refreshments earlier than normal, they were soon to be choking on their fare, as United quickly turned the game around with two goals in the space of two minutes, through McMillan, playing his first League game in four months, and Quixall, from the penalty spot after McLintock had brought down McMillan, setting up an interesting second forty-five minutes.

Three minutes after play resumed, the ten men had pulled it back to 3-3. McMillan claiming his second, awakened Leicester from their trance, which led to a constant bombardment of the United goal. Setters and Stiles stood firm against the onslaught, while Gaskell pulled off four outstanding saves, but a tangle between the latter two players allowed Keyworth to snatch his second of the afternoon and what was to be the winner.

United dropped to fifteenth, the point margin remained at eight, but it was only a temporary setback and any fears of relegation were finally dismissed three days later, when Ipswich were emphatically brushed aside 5-0.

'It was embarrassing to watch,' wrote Bill Fryer in the *Daily Express*. 'United didn't just beat top-of-the-table Ipswich, they ignored them. No exaggeration, it could have been 24-0.

'It should have been 12-0.

'It was the most exciting United show I've seen since Rowley and company beat Burnley 5-0 one famous New Year's Day (1947/48).

'Even when three-goal Albert Quixall was off for ten minutes it looked like fifteen red ants against eleven wingless bluebottles.'

For Quixall, it was perhaps the most pleasing moment since his £45,000 move from Sheffield Wednesday, as too often in the past he had become the 'whipping-boy' for his critics. However, during this particular seventy minutes, he hobbled off to a standing ovation with half an hour remaining, receiving another as he limped back into the fray for the final ten minutes. The blond-headed inside-forward finally showed that it had been money well spent.

Giles and McMillan enjoyed a field day against a rather poor Ipswich defence, with the latter setting up Quixall for his first in the thirteenth minute. Six minutes later, he claimed his second with a 25-yard drive. Five minutes after the interval he claimed his third, pouncing on a Dunne shot that the over-worked Bailey in the Ipswich goal could only half parry.

Bailey, whose son Gary was to grace the same stage many years later, pulled off a string of first-class saves as United continued to press forward, but he could do little to prevent further goals from Stiles and Setters in the eighty-fifth and eighty-sixth minutes.

Quixall was absent for the trip to Blackburn three days later, as was Bobby Charlton who was on international duty, but in all fairness, the home side were also prevented from selecting their preferred line-up, although it was not noticeable throughout the ninety minutes.

With David Herd also missing from the United line-up, Matt Busby surprised everyone by once again selecting Noel Cantwell at centre-forward, a distinct clue as to the need for strengthening in this particular position. Whether the burly Irish defender could give his manager that final thrust in the penalty area he was looking for, if only on a temporary basis, was open for debate, but at least Cantwell was still available for selection, as the out-of-favour full-back had been the subject of a £30,000 bid from relegation-threatened Chelsea.

Having been squeezed out of the team by fellow countryman Tony Dunne and despite having only moved north last season, it did look as if Cantwell's days at Old Trafford were numbered and perhaps a move back to London was his best option. Matt Busby, however, was not in any hurry to see the back of the player, particularly as the Chelsea offer had come when United were still involved in the FA Cup. 'Cantwell is such very fine player that I am not sure that we can afford to part with him now,' said the United manager at the time. 'He has been unlucky with injuries this season and Dunne has been playing so well that Cantwell can't get back into the team. But that doesn't mean that we don't want him, or that Chelsea are going to get him.'

The presence of Cantwell up front made little difference, except for a few bruises to the Rovers defenders, and United slumped to a 3-0 defeat. But four days later, just a few miles across country, he justified his appearance in the No. 9 shirt with a goal in the 3-1 win against Burnley, as the 'Teddy Boy' taunt continued to dominate this particular fixture.

As always, it was a robust, physical encounter, which boiled over in the second half. On one side of the pitch Giles and Harris were involved in a scuffle, while on the opposite flank, Dunne and Towers had a couple of violent disagreements. One journalist went as far as to write, 'Halfway through the second half of this game in which player had sent player crashing to the ground in a flood of fouls, there came one of the most disgraceful scenes I have ever seen as violent punches were exchanged. When I want to see all-in wrestling, I'll go to Belle Vue Manchester.

'And with players, now reaping rich dividends for their feats, to start acting in such an atrocious manner, it is time someone told them where to get off.'

The stand-in centre-forward put United in front in the fortieth minute and, as the second-half battle raged, McMillan was already lying injured in midfield following one rather physical challenge, when Joyce brought down Pearson inside the area. Shay Brennan made no mistake from the penalty spot for United's second.

Burnley hit back almost immediately as Connelly slipped the ball past Foulkes for Pointer to shoot past Briggs, but with two minutes remaining, Giles went round Elder for the umpteenth time before crossing into the goalmouth for Herd to score a third. This was much to the annoyance of the Burnley support, who considered that the visitors were too physical in their approach and, having already subjected the referee to a barrage of missiles, forced the official into seeking police protection as he left the field.

Cantwell scored again, at both ends, and Arsenal left Old Trafford with both points following a 3-2 win, with the Gunners snatching the winner eleven minutes from time in front of a disappointing crowd of 24,788. The season petered out in disappointing fashion.

On a muddied Old Trafford pitch, with the only hint of grass being down the wings, where Giles excelled, United and Everton fought out a 1-1 draw in a sometimes over-physical encounter. Two days later, and in yet another home fixture, the last of the season, just under 30,000 witnessed a dour encounter against Sheffield United thankful that they would not have to endure any more miserable afternoons down by the ship canal, as the visitors went back over the Pennines with both points from a 1-0 win thanks to an eleventh-minute header from Pace.

In true United fashion, the return Easter holiday fixture at Bramall Lane saw United claim a 3-2 victory with goals from Nobby Stiles and a double from Sammy McMillan. Nineteen-year-old Northern Ireland under-23 international McMillan had come into the team following five months on Central League duty against Leicester City, and kept his place in the injury-hit United line-up, but at Sheffield, he had found himself wearing the No. 9 shirt, rather than the customary Nos 10 or 11, and revelled in the role.

There was, however, to be no repeat performance in the final game of the season against a Fulham side flirting with relegation. Although United began brightly, they gradually disintegrated as the home side increased the momentum, eventually running out 2-0 winners; a victory that ensured their First Division status for at least another twelve months.

United on the other hand finished in fifteenth place, six points above second-bottom Cardiff City and eleven above the also relegated Chelsea. They were, however, seventeen adrift of Champions Ipswich Town.

So why was there so much inconsistency at this particular time? One player well positioned to give an opinion was Jimmy Nicholson, as the Northern Ireland internatonal had spent long spells watching from the stands due to injury and loss of form.

'United during this time were very disappointing,' he recalled. 'And I was not happy with my own contribution during this period. But my gut feeling overall was very simply that the quality of the players was not up to the high standards required by Manchester United.

'This may seem to be a very easy explanation for the demise of this great club, but I recall many games where we were outplayed and increasingly outclassed by average teams. A sure sign that we were just not good enough.

'I do not want to blame individuals, or name players, as I think this would be unfair and unprofessional, but I felt that defensively we were conceding far too many goals.

'With most great teams you will find that they concede very few goals and build from a solid base.'

So, there was still work to be done at Old Trafford, as United continued to blow hot and cold with no two fixtures running the same. On a good day, they could hammer the likes of Ipswich 5-0, while still managing to concede thirteen goals in three consecutive games.

Despite the overall performances not exactly pulling the crowds in, the United board decided that they were putting the admission prices up for the following season, a decision based on the fact that since the maximum wage had been abolished, there had been an increase to the Old Trafford wage bill. The money to pay for this had to be found from somewhere and it was decided that it would be the supporters who would foot the difference.

It was a decision that did not go down well with the man on the terrace, and who could blame them, as United's home record over the past season had been far from impressive, losing eight of their twenty-one fixtures. Only third-bottom Fulham had lost more (ten). If goals scored were also taken into consideration, there were nine clubs who had scored more than United's tally of forty-four. Only seven had conceded more. But there was nothing they could do, except stay away as season tickets were increased by £1, while general admission prices went up by six old pennies.

Busby had already pinpointed the need for a forward with proven goalscoring ability, but he also required someone in the engine room; someone who could dictate the flow of the game at a pace to suit both himself and his teammates. Both were soon to arrive in Manchester 16, but battling for the First Division crown was still a long way off.

It had taken Matt Busby nine months to secure the signature of David Herd, but when it came to bringing a player to Old Trafford who he knew would make the difference between defeat and victory, it was ten long years. It was also a transfer saga that would transform itself into something akin to a television thriller, or indeed a soap opera.

Busby first set eyes on the slimly built, blond-headed, sixteen-year-old youngster in November 1956, when he lined up in an FA Youth Cup tie for Huddersfield Town against Manchester United at Heckmondwike. He saw enough in those ninety minutes to make an audacious £10,000 move soon afterwards for the talented teenager.

Huddersfield manager Archie Beattie knew that the cross-eyed, bespectacled 5-foot 3-inch figure that had sheepishly walked into his office in April 1955 was something special, and he simply laughed off Busby's offer, but the United manager, a friend of Beattie's, was to keep a close watch on the career of Denis Law as the years passed by and the player's reputation grew.

As manager of Scotland, Busby introduced Law onto the international scene, but when Huddersfield finally decided to trade in their prized asset, the United manager was in little need of a goalscoring forward, even the much-coveted Law, as his team had scored over 100 goals as the 1959/60 season moved into its final few games, and the Aberdonian moved to Manchester City for a fee of £55,000. It was also a sum of money that United could ill afford in the wake of the Munich disaster.

At Maine Road, Law scored twenty-one goals in forty-four games, before attracting the attention of Torino and Milan, as the Italians began casting their eyes towards the Football League in their search for new players. But the grass wasn't greener on the other side, despite the signing-on inducement of £20,000 and the possibility of earning £200 per week with Torino. Life in Italy was not all roses and despite the defensive play within the Italian League, where scoring opportunities were few and far between, Law still managed to notch ten goals in twenty-seven games, before everything turned sour.

To say Law's time in Italy was turbulent is simply skimming the surface. He was fined £10 and suspended for a week following an incident with a Lanerossi player, which was followed by a £200 fine for not turning up for the next game against Inter Milan, even though he was suspended. He even managed to get sent off, or to be more exact, taken off by his own coach, during a cup tie with Naples – for attempting to take a throw-in!

Denis, fuming from the 'dismissal' against Naples, was told that he had also failed to show the correct competitive spirit and was accused of saving himself for a Scottish international fixture. This was the last straw as far as the Scot was concerned and as he sat fuming for fourteen days in his luxury flat, before making up his mind that he simply had to leave Italy.

Busby had already been given a hint that signing Denis Law could be a possibility, following an opportune meeting with the player after a Football League *v.* Italian League fixture at Old Trafford, when the glum-looking striker revealed that all was not well in Italy. Not long afterwards, a call from George Sturrup, an agent connected to Real Madrid who Busby knew well, informed the United manager that Denis Law was indeed available if he was interested.

It was an interest that had never waned and a meeting was arranged in Amsterdam, on the eve of the Real Madrid–Benfica European Cup final, between Busby and Signor Angelo Fillipone, the president of Torino. Following an hour-long talk, the basics of the deal were put together, with the fee thought to be around £100,000. The United manager assumed all that now remained was a simple case of dotting the 'i's and crossing the 't's, telling Desmond Hackett of the *Daily Express*, 'The price for Law may seem excessive by English League standards, but it is not excessive on today's market with the tremendous rewards from European Cup games.

'Football is in urgent need of personalities and I think Law is among the top three in Britain.'

Also in the United manager's favour was the impending transfer of Real Madrid's inside-forward Luis Del Sol to Torino. The incoming payment for the Scotsman went a little way to finance the reported £250,000 for the Spaniard. Law's transfer, however, was far from cut and dried.

Torino president Angelo Fillipone suddenly took complete charge of the negotiations, with a figure of £143,000 now being mentioned in some quarters, but within hours of returning to Italy from Holland, Fillipone sent a telegram to Old Trafford which read, 'Regret unable to accept your offer. Transfer only possible on terms explained to your directors and Matt Busby.' Those 'terms' were 'not a lira less than £150,000'. The Torino president Fillipone explaining, 'Matt Busby, United's manager and I are on friendly terms, but his bid is appreciably short of the figure we want.

'We do not really wish to transfer Law. He is a brilliant player, almost impossible to replace.'

Within minutes of receiving the telegram, Busby was on the 'phone to Fillipone and told him, 'We are not budging an inch. Our bid stands.' Explaining to a *Daily Express* staff reporter, he said United had made a very big offer, one which would have been a new British record, and that the club were not prepared to increase this.

Three weeks later, with United in Majorca, amid a trio of friendly fixtures, a second meeting was held in Italy, when the United manager was accompanied by chairman Harold Hardman and director Louis Edwards, in the hope that the transfer would be concluded. As it turned out, the Manchester United trio walked out, as the Italians attempted to hike up the price from their original fee.

Following yet another breakdown of the transfer, Busby told Derek Wallis of the *Daily Mirror*, 'There is nobody more surprised than we are. We came to sign the player and again something has cropped up and we have just walked out.

'We are disgusted with the whole thing. I cannot say what the complication is at the moment. I may do that in my own time.

'All I can say is that it is something away from other things that have been discussed. We knew nothing about it until we got here. Our offer has not altered by one penny from the original.'

Torino secretary Renato Ghisti explained: 'For the moment, negotiations between the clubs have come to a halt. Divergences of a financial nature have arisen.' He added that he hoped that the difficulties could be worked out 'within a week'. Other sources in Italy were less optimistic, stating that the deal was already off.

It soon became crystal clear what that 'something' was.

Had it been for any other player than Denis Law, then Busby would undoubtedly have called the whole thing off, telling the Italians to simply forget about any possible deal. But Law was someone that Busby wanted, and certainly needed. He was not the last piece of the jigsaw, but he was a piece that completed most of the picture and if there was a possibility that he could become a Manchester United player then Busby was interested. His determination to secure the Aberdonian's signature was not something that he made totally clear to the Italians.

Suddenly, the ongoing on-off transfer took yet another twist with the action moving to Lausanne, where Torino were playing the local club in a Friendship Cup fixture. In a hotel overlooking Lake Geneva, Busby and Law, who had caused something of a scare by arriving late due to a missed flight, sat for hours talking over the proposed move, with the Italians finally thought to be near to agreeing a deal. 'I've every hope of getting him,' said Busby, with Law adding, 'I hope it won't be long now. I've waited so much for this moment. Manchester United are the club I've wanted to join all my life.'

Breathing a huge sigh of relief, Denis, already dreaming about a new life in Manchester, returned to Turin, for what he thought was only going to be a short stay while the Torino directors met in order to approve the transfer. Two days later he was summoned to meet the club president, expecting to be told that his transfer to United had been cleared, but was stunned to discover that he had instead, been sold to Juventus for £160,000.

The move from Juventus had exploded completely out of the blue, coming on the rebound of an illegal approach for the Tottenham Hotspur duo of Dave Mackay and Cliff Jones, which had been exposed in the *News of the World* (where else?).

Despite being told that he had little say in the matter and the possibility of picking up £8,000 in his first year, Law had no intentions of remaining in Italy, never mind signing for Juventus, and left the Torino president and Signor Umberto Angelli standing open-mouthed as he headed back to his flat, hurriedly packed a few clothes and headed for Milan airport courtesy of a friend who owned a taxi.

Thanks to more friends at the airport, he managed to obtain a 'Single to Aberdeen please' and was soon back in the more welcome surroundings of Printfield Terrace, intending to stay for only a few days until the whole sorry business was sorted out once and for all.

'I'm here for a quiet weekend to get away from it all,' said the runaway Scot. 'I'm going to sign for Manchester United. I'm not going to play for Juventus and it's impossible for Turin to transfer me over my head. My family want me to come home as well – that's natural.'

Two days in Aberdeen soon became four and quickly became weeks, with Law completely uncertain as to what developments, if any, had or were taking place. The only news was that he had indeed been sold to Juventus. Even the news from Manchester did little to cheer him, as he now found himself out on a limb.

'If Denis came to see the club, we would tell him "Look, son, we cannot help you. You'll have to sort out your problems with Turin",' said the United chairman Harold Hardman.

'But how can we help him? We have had nothing but friendly negotiations with Turin and we refuse to break that relationship with the Italians.

'Law has broken his agreement with Turin and now he is entirely on his own.

'If Denis came to see me I would give him this personal advice. "You know we are an interested party, but you must face up to your responsibilities."'

The eighty-two-year-old United chairman added, 'So far, nobody from the Italian club has contacted us. Turin know what we consider Law is worth and we will not increase that figure by one penny.

'We have never divulged that figure and so far, everyone has been wide of the mark.'

Unknown to either Denis Law or Manchester United, the proposed transfer of the player from Torino to Juventus was about to fall through, as the latter set a deadline for signing the Scot, which was never likely to be met as the player was still in Aberdeen, with no intentions of venturing outside the city limits. An Italian director added, 'Law cannot be sold in Italy because none of our clubs would have him. His registration would not be accepted again by the Italian League.'

So, if Torino wanted the cash from the transfer of Denis Law, then there was only one club who might be prepared to help them out, but relations between the Italians and Manchester United were now precariously balanced, although Matt Busby still coveted his fellow countryman and would be more than happy to agree a deal for the player despite all that had taken place over the past three weeks.

In an effort to salvage some of their lost dignity and resurrect the transfer and, more importantly from their point of view, finance the Del Sol transfer, Torino decided that the best person to do this was Gigi Peronace, the club's business manager and sporting director, who was despatched to Britain with the instructions to sell, not only Law, but his fellow teammate Joe Baker – the latter having roused some interest from Manchester City.

Peronace flew to Glasgow, not Manchester, where he met the two players in a city-centre hotel, with the talks taking on a more positive air than those of before. Nothing could, of course, be finalised there and then, but upon leaving the hotel, a smiling Denis Law told waiting journalists, 'I don't want to say too much just now, but it looks as though we are getting somewhere at last.'

Law returned to Aberdeen, while Peronace headed south to Manchester for a head-to-head with Matt Busby, a meeting that would either see the player finally signing for United or the deal collapsing for good.

Arriving in Manchester, Peronace gave little away: 'To say that anything is settled is not correct. I cannot say, but I think United's offer will be the same as they made before.

'You see, I had nothing to do with the transaction some weeks ago. That was nothing to do with me.

'Now I am only here to get the thing straightened out after much confusion. And I shall send the decisions to my directors. It is entirely up to them.'

For three long hours the transfer was debated, with United refusing to budge from their original offer of £110,000. The Italians, on the other hand, stood by their valuation of what was now quoted as £140,000.

'In my talks with Mr Peronace, we reached an agreement, and all it needs is ratification of the Turin board,' Matt Busby said as he emerged from the meeting. 'All I can say is that an offer has been made in detail which cannot be made public. It is very much on the lines of the offer we had previously made. The decision now rests with the Torino board.

'I think the fact that they have come over here to talk business must indicate that they want to get something moving. Now I am going on holiday to Spain and I do not anticipate that there will be any quick solution to the problem. But we shall just have to hope.

'Everything has been arranged between Denis and myself. It is only a matter of signing the forms once we get the okay from Turin.

'I want Denis Law. He is one of the greatest players in the world. Always looking for the ball.'

Back in Aberdeen a nervous Denis Law sat awaiting news of the latest developments and, when informed of the latest episode in the long, drawn out saga, he said, 'I hope now there are no more snags. I want to play for Manchester United and under Matt Busby.'

But still the deal was not finalised, and indeed anything could still happen as it had in the past. 'Whether the transfer goes through is like tossing a coin. It is anyone's guess,' Peronance sighed as he left the meeting, while thousands of miles away, the Torino directors were apparently split over the whole business.

Before the prolonged transfer could draw towards its conclusion, there was still one dramatic twist to the tale. In everyone's eyes, the outcome would firmly rest in the hands of the Torino directors, but in reality, Denis Law's future would be decided much nearer home, a mere cross-town bus ride from Old Trafford.

It transpired that, when Manchester City sold Law to Torino, they had an option in the contract that if the player was ever transferred back to England it must be to City! Relations between the two clubs, and in particular the managers, Matt Busby and Les McDowall, were thankfully excellent, and the Maine Road club made it clear from the start that they would not stand in the way of United's proposed deal.

On 10 July, Matt Busby picked up the telephone in his office to be told the news that the Torino directors had finally agreed to sell Denis Law to Manchester United, with the fee believed to be £115,000. £40,000 of that would, however, remain in Manchester, as this sum was still owed to City by the Italians.

So at long last, Denis Law was a Manchester United player: a transfer that left Matt Busby drooling at the thought of what lay ahead when the trawlerman's son pulled on the red shirt of his team.

'If my plans materialise, the six-figure transfer fee will be cheap at the price,' Busby enthused. 'I have no doubts that such a figure can be justified, provided the player has the class, brain and spirit to bring the best out of the rest of the team.

'His effect on the United team will be felt immediately, but I am more interested in the progressive effect over the next few years.'

If the United directors had thought Matt Busby's financial outlay for Denis Law was excessive, despite yielding to the manager's request for the money, they could quite easy have recouped the fee paid to Torino, while at the same time increasing their bank balance by £185,000, due to Barcelona's interest in Bobby Charlton. Charlton's stock had risen following impressive displays against Hungary and Argentina during England's World Cup ties in Chile, with Barcelona poised to make a £300,000 move for the player. 'I like Charlton's rhythm and flair and ball skill and natural instinct. He also has a wonderful shot,' declared Barcelona manager Ladislav Kubala. But despite his undoubted interest and the urging of his chairman to get in touch with Matt Busby, offering him the world-record fee, the transfer was always one that would never materialise.

'I am quite satisfied with what I am getting and it is Manchester for me,' the Barcelona target emphasised. 'In any case, England players who have gone abroad have found nothing but trouble.'

Although disappointed in their failure to land Charlton, it was to prove something of a blessing in disguise for Barcelona, as the player was ruled out of the first fifteen games of the new season due to a hernia operation. This also stalled Matt Busby's plans of pairing Charlton alongside Denis Law, with Mark Pearson also losing out, as Newcastle United and Middlesbrough's interest in the inside-forward had to be put on hold.

There was also the possibility of Matt Busby losing one his coveted back-room staff as the new season approached, with trainer Jack Crompton on the verge of returning to Luton Town, the club he had left four and a half years ago in the wake of the Munich disaster, following Jimmy Murphy's SOS as the Welshman struggled under the weight of what had fallen upon his shoulders. This time, however, Crompton was expected to join Luton, not as trainer, but as manager.

'This is the second time Luton have tried to get my services,' said the former United goalkeeper. 'This time I felt that it was an opportunity of progress in the game that I could not refuse.'

Surprisingly, or perhaps not, given Crompton's strong United connections, the former goalkeeper had a change of heart, much to the relief of Matt Busby, and decided that his future, for the time being at least, belonged at Old Trafford.

With Denis Law on board, Matt Busby's obsessive ambition of Manchester United returning to the European stage had hopefully taken a step closer to being achieved. But as West Bromwich arrived in Manchester to herald the start of season 1962/63, the blond head of the Lawman stood out in the warm afternoon sunshine, as he ran out to make his first Old Trafford appearance in the red of United. There was a hint of despondency due to the omission of Bobby Charlton from the United line-up.

Busby's ambition, something that had driven him on since those dark, foreboding days in the Recht der Isar hospital in Munich, was shared by many, but it was a dream which would be interwoven with demonic undertones as the weeks and months unfolded.

Denis Law's Manchester United debut came amid very familiar surroundings for the Scot, at Hampden Park, Glasgow, a ground where he had played a major part in his country's defeat of the 'auld enemy' England only a few months previously. Despite treating the 80,000 crowd to a few of his wide array of skills, Law failed to get himself on the score-sheet, upstaged by fellow countrymen Ian Moir and David Herd, with the former notching a double, the latter giving United the lead in their 4-2 victory.

The majority of the 51,685 packed into Old Trafford on Saturday 18 August were there to see only one man – Denis Law – and the new signing certainly did not disappoint, taking a mere six minutes to head United into a 2-0 lead.

United caught the Albion cold, taking the lead with only ninety seconds played. Stiles pushed a free-kick forward into the penalty area, where Herd shot home with a powerful low drive. Four minutes later, it was 2-0. Giles, who was to outshine the new signing, dribbled past two defenders before sending a pinpoint cross into the Albion goalmouth towards the lurking Law. His header evaded the outstretched arms of Millington and dropped in just under the bar.

It was a perfect start to the campaign, but as the Old Trafford faithful had seen only too often in recent seasons, United failed to capitalise on their two-goal advantage and, as the game progressed, they not only allowed the visitors to claw themselves back into the game, but surrendered a point in a rather impotent display.

United held on to their lead until the seventy-fifth minute, having had a Giles 'goal' disallowed for offside, but once Derek Kevan had pulled one back, it was backs-to-the-wall stuff for the home side.

Busby, attempting to keep a hold on the now one-goal advantage, reshuffled his troops, moving Giles inside, with Quixall taking over on the wing, but it only strengthened Albion's grip on the game, and with five minutes remaining, Setters committed defensive suicide when he took too much time intercepting a through-ball from Drury, allowing Smith to step in and slip the ball past Gaskell.

Four days later, things certainly went from bad to worse, as the short journey down the East Lancs Road to Goodison Park brought nothing but boos and slow hand-clapping from sections of the packed house of 69,501.

Alex Young, a one-time Busby target, opened the scoring in the twelfth minute, heading down a Stevens centre before hammering the ball past a helpless Gaskell. Sixty seconds later, it was 2-0, Young again, this time heading a Bingham corner past the clawing fingers of the United 'keeper.

Two minutes prior to half-time, Parker made it 3-0. A back-pass from Setters beat Gaskell and hit the post, before being scrambled behind. From the resulting corner, which was only partly cleared, the Everton full-back made no mistake with a rasping drive from all of 25 yards.

Law caused confusion wherever he went, while Setters set up enough scoring opportunities to win a handful of games, but it wasn't until the sixty-fourth minute that United managed to claw a goal back. A tantalising cross from Giles was only partly cleared by West in the Everton goal and as the ball dropped to the feet of Moir, it was instantly despatched into the roof of the net. Despite a late rally from the visitors, there was no way back and already, United were struggling to find any sort of rhythm in their play.

But true to the form of recent seasons, United confounded their critics, with the trip to Highbury producing the first two points of the season and headlines such as 'Law Joins the Immortals', 'Law Magic Worth Million To Manchester United', 'Law Fee Well Worth It' and 'Giles Outguns Highbury Boys'.

One correspondent, Alan Hoby of the *Sunday Express* wrote of Law: 'I have seen Alex James, my boyhood idol, operate his match-less magic on this classic stretch of turf. I have seen such brilliant individualists as Wilf Mannion, Raich Carter and Len Shackleton perform their tricks. But Law, the Scot with the elegant grace and shimmering pace, ranks right up there with all of them.'

Admiration, however, was all Law managed to gain in north London, as United's goals in their 3-1 victory came from Phil Chisnall and former Arsenal favourite David Herd with a double.

With the gates locked before kick-off, many missed United's emphatic display, although the home side almost took the lead in the opening minutes. First, Skirton forced Gaskell into making a rather unorthodox stop with the sole of his boot, then Strong, only 2 yards from a gaping goalmouth, shot over.

One minute from the interval, United should have had a penalty. Giles, forever a threat to the Arsenal defence, moved towards goal and, in desperation more than anything else, goalkeeper McKechnie hauled him down by the ankles. An obvious spot-kick to all but the referee simply waved play on.

So, United had to wait until thirteen minutes into the second half before taking the lead, when a casual Eastham pass was snatched upon by Giles and the winger's cross was headed home by Herd. A further thirteen minutes on, it was 2-0: another Giles centre, finding Chisnall on this occasion, with the inside-forward stabbing the ball home.

Sixteen minutes from time, Herd added his second from yet another Giles pass, leaving Arsenal well beaten, with Clamp's 30-yard drive past the helpless Gaskell, little more than a consolation, which many of the home support missed as they were already on their way home.

Bringing Nicholson, Lawton and Chisnall into the side, in place of Stiles, Setters and Pearson, had made a big difference, but true to the form of the previous two seasons, United failed to maintain any sort of equilibrium and secured both points in only one of their following four fixtures, a 2-0 victory over Birmingham City at Old Trafford.

An enthralling ninety minutes in front of a packed Old Trafford saw Everton snatch both points with a Roy Vernon penalty, after Shay Brennan had tripped Johnny Morrissey. Meanwhile, away days at Bolton Wanderers and newly promoted Leyton Orient saw United draw a blank in both the goals and points categories. The Wanderers won 3-0, a victory that had seen a United side fail to win at Burnden Park since 1945, and newcomers Orient won 1-0 with a last-minute goal, a scoreline that could easily have been more, had it not been for the goalkeeping of David Gaskell.

In an effort to transform his inconsistent side, Busby made further changes for the visit of bogey team Bolton Wanderers to Old Trafford. Maurice Setters, who had been switched from wing-half to inside-forward, returned to his usual position, with Nobby Lawton also reverting back to his more familiar inside-forward spot. Stiles was reinstated at right-half, but the United manager took something of a gamble, while also showing his real lack of reserve strength, by once again playing Noel Cantwell in the forward line, this time at outside-left.

Despite the 'local derby' tag, Old Trafford was far from full, with the attendance 2,100 down on that of the last home fixture against Birmingham City and 25,716 less than the midweek Everton fixture had attracted. Those who stayed away were probably justified in doing so, missing nothing more than a United victory in a poor ninety minutes.

'Herd goals flatter Manchester United', proclaimed the *Daily Telegraph*, with its man at the match, R. H. Williams, writing, 'If there be such a man as a connoisseur of soccer, this was no match for him. Manchester United beat Bolton Wanderers soundly enough in a meaningless scramble from which the Old Trafford crowd of 37,721 extracted a good deal more than at least one of the few neutrals present.

'United scored three times and deserved to win because they were not as bad as Bolton.'

Another, 'unnamed' correspondent who watched the ninety minutes unfold wrote, 'There was no lack of endeavour or spirit in United's efforts but the harmony and rhythm desired were never fully achieved; however, it would be churlish indeed to expect immediate perfection from such a reshuffled combination.'

It was a victory that left United in fifteenth place, a mere three points above bottom club Birmingham City.

The following fixture, three days later on 15 September, brought a Manchester City side to Old Trafford, who were also in something of a predicament and to date had been poor, even by their own standards, propping up the First Division with a mere four points from their eight games and a goals ratio of nine for and twenty-seven against. If ever there was a 'derby' that promised an odds-on two points for United then this was it, and the red half of Manchester made their way to their spiritual home contemplating that their cross-city rivals were about to be on the end of a real hiding.

But around 4.45 p.m., those same United supporters shuffled out of the ground, finding it difficult to believe what they had just witnessed.

The game opened in a lively manner, with close calls in both goalmouths, before Bill Foulkes, having been beaten by Harley, handled the ball inside his own penalty area in the seventeenth minute. From the resulting spot-kick, Peter Dobing beat David Gaskell from the spot.

Denis Law ferreted and tormented the City defence, but to little avail, and could only look on in dismay from the opposite end of the pitch as his former team once again surged forward. Harley tapped the ball to Dobing, who in turn found Hayes. Although the inside-forward was closely marked, he still managed to pivot on the spot before firing an unstoppable shot past Gaskell.

Twenty-three minutes gone: United 0, City 2.

There was no further scoring in the first half, although both teams continued to push forward, but within a minute of the restart, United had clawed a goal back. A back-heel from Herd saw Law race forward to thump the ball past Trautmann for what should have heralded a red revival; but try as they might, United failed to make any sort of impression until fifteen minutes from time.

Giles sent a high centre into the City area and, uncharacteristically, Trautmann dropped his catch. To his dismay, the lurking Law sent the ball high into the roof of the City net.

Old Trafford erupted, with the scent of United snatching a late winner swirling around the ground. The red shirts pressed forward, but City repelled whatever came their way. As the minutes and indeed seconds ticked away, United won yet another corner, but once again Trautmann leaped and caught cleanly, quickly hurling the ball towards Kennedy.

A long ball upfield was chased by Harley, and with Foulkes in close proximity, the City centre-forward powered the ball past the advancing Gaskell, for the decisive goal.

Another defeat and strangely, in the *Manchester Evening News* for that particular Saturday, trainer Jack Crompton spoke of the general disappointment around the club. 'Of course I am disappointed with Manchester United this season,' said the former United goalkeeper. 'But then I am always disappointed if Manchester United are not always top of the league. I must admit we set out with high hopes that this season we would really do something, and in terms of results, I am afraid we have not obtained all we were hoping for.'

From Old Trafford to the Bernabeu and from the embarrassment of a home defeat against their dreaded rivals to becoming the first English side to defeat Real Madrid on their own patch. That was the Manchester United of the early 1960s.

Four days after losing to City, United once again silenced a home crowd, but on this occasion, it was some 70,000 Spaniards, rather than the best part of 56,000 Mancunians, as Denis Law laid claim to becoming one of Europe's top players, with even the masterful Di Stefano unable to match the Aberdonian.

The first forty-five minutes gave little hint as to the outcome of the game, with Madrid's frequent match-winner, Di Stefano, being closely marshalled by Nobby Stiles. However, it was Law who caught the eye with a display of skills that would certainly have not gone amiss in the white of Madrid.

Herd could, and probably should have, given United the lead in the twenty-seventh minute, as Santamaria faltered, but Vincente was equal to the centre-forward's effort. However, within three minutes of the second half getting underway, United were in front. The Madrid goalkeeper dived and managed to stop an 18-yard drive from Mark Pearson, but to the amazement of the packed stadium, he allowed the ball to squirm from his grasp and roll over the line.

Twelve minutes later, it was 2-0. Law sent Giles scurrying down the right and, having dummied Casada, his finely tuned cross found David Herd, standing unmarked, to head into the net to seal a notable success.

Such a victory would have inspired most teams, but as we have already seen in the opening weeks of this 1962/63 campaign, Manchester United were not one of them.

'Shambling, niggling and often sterile,' was how United's 5-2 defeat at home to Burnley was reported by Leslie Duxbury in the *Daily Sketch*, referring to them as 'a struggling, unhappy outfit', while a fellow scribe penned, 'They had looked no more than a bunch of enthusiastic amateurs.' One headline proclaimed, 'Burnley Expose the Flaws', and indeed there were plenty of them, as United trudged off the pitch at half-time, heads down, having conceded thrice.

Connelly and Lochhead gave the visitors a two-goal advantage, and then Shay Brennan scorned the opportunity to pull a goal back from the penalty spot, after Angus handled, but his kick was comfortably saved by Blacklaw. Minutes later, McIlroy made it three, as Gaskell allowed his shot to sneak in at the post, thinking the ball was going wide.

By now, David Herd was little more than a passenger, hobbling around on the left wing, but fifteen minutes after half-time, following a stern talking to from Matt Busby, Law set up Stiles to make it 3-1, before reducing arrears further five minutes later.

There was, however, to be no heroic comeback, as United crumbled, allowing Burnley, last season's runners-up, to score two more in the sixty-sixth and eighty-fifth minutes, as John Connelly claimed his hat-trick. His was a name that Matt Busby would not forget, and one that would be filed away for another day.

United were now one of five clubs on seven points, only one more than Lancashire rivals Bolton Wanderers and Blackburn Rovers, who were anchored at the foot of the table. Busby's team looked what they were, a team lacking in confidence and a far cry from the Manchester United of old.

Although finding it hard to maintain any form of consistency at League level, the 2-0 victory over Real Madrid showed that on their day United could turn it on, and in the absence of competitive European football on a regular basis, Matt Busby once again looked at playing top European sides in friendlies, building on match fitness, while also gaining experience for when the real thing would once again surface. So it was that three days after the defeat by Burnley, Portuguese giants Benfica arrived at Old Trafford.

Despite the four goals and the performances of goalscorers Denis Law and Ferreira Eusebio in the 2-2 draw, the game as a whole was disappointing, with Benfica failing to do anything remotely different from any recent visitors to Salford, while the emerging talent of Eusebio was clearly outshone by Law.

Austrian side First Vienna were another to visit Manchester in late October, but by then watching domestic League fixtures was enough for most to endure, without having to suffer friendlies as well, and only 15,035 bothered to turn up to watch United win 3-1.

If there were problems on the pitch, equally there were problems off the pitch, with Albert Quixall becoming the first to ignore the loyalty within the ranks, and amid his anger, point a finger at Matt Busby for the predicament that the club currently found itself in.

'I am determined to leave United,' said the one-time 'Golden Boy' of British football and a £45,000 buy from Sheffield Wednesday. 'Nobody has a chance of playing well here when there is so much chopping and changing. If I can't get in the team now, when they are playing so badly, when can I get in?

'After we had drawn 2-2 with Benfica I thought I was there to stay. But I've still had only three League games this season. It gives nobody a chance.

'I firmly believe that I warrant a first-team place.'

His lack of first-team appearances at Old Trafford had not gone unnoticed and only last month Stoke City had made an approach, only for Quixall to turn down the chance to move to the Potteries. 'That was the biggest mistake of my life,' he declared and regretted it so much that he went to see Matt Busby, demanding a transfer. The manager, however, despite the player's feelings, refused to bow to his demands and told him, 'No. You are needed here.'

Not to be deterred, Quixall told reporters, 'I can't see where I am needed, or why. I must leave. Anywhere will do, as soon as possible.'

If indeed his presence was required, then why, with only three wins in the opening ten fixtures, had the Yorkshireman only started two games? Even more strangely, following his verbal outburst, he was to find himself back on first-team duty and was soon to justify his selection, while perhaps making his manager regret not giving the player the opportunity to re-establish himself with an extended run in the team.

Matters on the field failed to improve as, over the course of the following quartet of fixtures, United were to gain only one solitary point, losing 1-0 at Sheffield Wednesday, 3-0 at home to Blackburn Rovers, before being hammered 6-2 at White Hart Lane against table-topping Tottenham. Sandwiched in between the Wednesday and Rovers defeats came the only glimmer of light, inspired with a visit to the Golden Mile and the Illuminations. Even then, they should have soundly beaten Blackpool, but shoddy defending gave the home side a share of the points.

In his report of the 3-0 home defeat by Blackburn Rovers, David Meek of the *Manchester Evening News* wrote, 'Manchester United's rapidly fluctuating soccer stock touched rock-bottom today and Old Trafford was set for a take-over by Messrs Gloom and Despondency.' While in the *Manchester Guardian*, under the heading 'Manchester United at Their Lowest Ebb', Brian Crowther penned, 'United against ten men for twenty-seven minutes and they were still well beaten. Indeed, one has never seen United reach such depths, and one can but hope that the realisation of their present plight will prove remedial.'

Despite his outburst against Busby, Albert Quixall surprisingly didn't become a permanent fixture in the Central League side, before being shipped off another team. He reappeared in the Manchester United first team against Tottenham Hotspur on 24 October, scoring in the 6-2 defeat. Keeping his place, he scored twice seven days later in the 3-1 win over West Ham, but despite the goals and the run in the team that he had craved for, he was still far from happy.

Friends ask me what more do I want when I tell them that I am still unhappy with Manchester United. They point out that the club has refused to let me go, that I am back in the first team, that I am playing reasonably well and that we have even won one or two matches!

All very true and certainly I am usually neither an unhappy player nor a discontented one. I am not champing at the bit to get away from Old Trafford and I shall put my heart and soul into the game for United as long as I am here.

In fact I have no quarrel with the club at all. The manager has his job to do and must plan for the future in the way he thinks best. But at the same time I must also plan for my future and ask myself just exactly what are my prospects with Manchester United

Everything is going fine at the moment of course, but my in-and-out experience with the team over the past twelve months has made me consider my position very closely.

Look at it from my point of view. United have paid a British record fee of £115,000 for Denis Law, who in anyone's book must rate as a world-class player. United are also fortunate to have Bobby Charlton on their books.

So where does that leave Albert Quixall? I reckon that at twenty-eight I have six more years of football at a reasonable level left in me. I know there are promising youngsters pressing up from the juniors, but the World Cup and our old friends of Real Madrid have proved that you can't beat experience. In fact too much is made of youth.

Having looked after myself I am sure that I will remain a first-class proposition for a long time. I figure, however, that I do not rank in United's plans for the future.

I had a fair run in the reserves last season and accepted this as part of the game. I knew for one thing that I was not playing well at times and probably deserved it. But this season was a little different, dropped after only the opening game and then in and out with no time to settle and only three first-team games before the present spell.

This is why I shall seriously consider my future when contract time comes round again. In the meantime I am certainly not at war with the world and I shall play my best for United.

Was there friction between player and manager? Not according to Sandy Busby: 'How did the two get on? Dad loved Albert and the feeling was mutual. I remember when dad had a small stroke. Albert was round at the house, almost in tears, wondering how "the Boss" was.'

The extended run in the team was to keep Quixall happy and the transfer request was forgotten about, with the player conceding that he was happy to stay at United and that he was also glad that the reported interest from Genoa did not progress beyond friendly talks with Gigi Peronace.

If Albert Quixall was back on something of a high, recent weeks had seen United slip slowly downwards, and following that 6-2 defeat by Spurs, they were at rock-bottom, a point adrift of Fulham and Leyton Orient. The home side actually led 6-0, but eased off somewhat, allowing United back into the game to score two in the final nine minutes – one of those goals coming from Albert Quixall. Although scored from the penalty spot, it was a goal that gave the player much encouragement, not to say confidence.

United's latest run of poor form could be defined in the failure of Denis Law to find the back of the net, but perhaps it is better to look at the whole picture, as the Scot was trying to carry United on his own, defending, attacking and doing everything bar leaving the pitch a few minutes before the interval to make the half-time cuppa. His effort could certainly not be faulted, but it was of little use to the team if their star striker was plodding forward from midfield with the ball already pinging around the penalty area.

Clearly a word was needed in Law's ear, and prior to the visit of West Ham, Busby took his star pupil to one side and told him to concentrate on tormenting the opposition defence and leave the defending and midfield grafting to those employed to carry out those particular duties.

Busby was, of course, only too aware of what the critics were saying, as well as knowing without being told that his team were not playing well. 'We shall get out of this,' he confidently told Alan Hoby of the *Sunday Express*. 'We're having a bad run but there is nothing wrong that a couple of good victories won't put right.

'Naturally, some of the boys have lost confidence in themselves. That happens in a losing spell. But we've played some really good football too. Earlier in the season we beat Real Madrid and drew with Benfica, Champions of Europe.

'You must remember that although we bought a £100,000 player in Denis Law during the close season, we also lost a £100,000 player in Bobby Charlton when Bobby had to go into hospital for his hernia operation.

'When fully fit of course, I'd play Bobby anywhere. He is a great player. But we have no outside-left, so that's where he stays.

'Maurice Setters also went down with appendicitis. He had his first League game since his operation against Spurs. But for weeks now we have never been able to put out our strongest team.'

Hoby then put the United manager firmly on the spot and asked him if the stories doing the rounds were true: that he regretted buying Denis Law? 'Matt Busby looked at me incredulously, as if he had not heard me correctly,' wrote Hoby. 'Then shook his head and said, "Denis is a GREAT footballer – by any standards in the world. He would be an asset to any team. Indeed, as I see Denis, he is a cheap player, cheap at the price."'

The *Sunday Express* man, however, felt that although Busby had not lost his touch, as many others had suggested, he did feel that the United manager had to apply the whip, as many of his players were not pulling their weight; something Hoby said would never have happened in the pre-Munich days under the leadership of Roger Byrne, who had famously chastised his teammates when leading 10-0 against Anderlecht.

Hoby rounded off his article by writing, 'The Manchester United of late 1962 need a new awareness of this old spirit. They must be reminded that nothing else and nothing less will do. They are niggling too much on the field and one or two seem to lose heart too soon.

'But most of all, every United player must remember that he is playing for a club – and a manager – which lit the torch and carried the flag of British football in triumph to the furthermost capitals of Europe.'

Heeding the words of his manager, the change in not only Law's game but that of the team as a whole was instantaneous, and the smallest Old Trafford crowd of the season to date (29,204) witnessed a display that went a long way to lifting some of the dark clouds around the Salford docks, although 'Immature United Lack Confidence and Luck' was one of the following days' headlines, despite United defeating West Ham 3-1.

But it wasn't the Scot who captured the headlines, it was Albert Quixall. 'Quixall Clears Those Clouds', 'A Quixall Double Lifts That United Gloom', 'No Release For Quixall After Restoring Esteem' and 'Quixall Spurs Power Show' screamed the headlines, with head cook and bottle washer Denis Law having to take something of a back seat. He would, however, be more than content to get back onto the score-sheet, with his first in six games. Quixall made it three in two games.

Against West Ham, it was a totally different Manchester United, even though Matt Busby had made no changes to the side who had conceded six against Tottenham Hotspur. The two major factors were Busby telling Law to concentrate on what he did best and Quixall taking the game by the scruff of the neck, answering his critics with a display of superb accuracy, with practically every pass finding its intended target. There was also a confidence, particularly in defence, that had been clearly missing in previous weeks.

Perhaps he had been outshone by Albert Quixall against West Ham, but Denis Law did not take kindly to being a support act, craving centre stage, and he quickly reclaimed that position under the spotlight with an emphatic four-goal performance against Ipswich Town at Portman Road in United's 5-3 victory. Despite the dreadful weather, the game was played as if it were a cup tie; a winner-takes-all ninety minutes of near-classic football.

But the following Saturday, his old mentor, Bill Shankly, manager of First Division newcomers Liverpool, employed a man-marking system which paid off in harnessing his fellow Scot. It didn't, however, curtail United's ongoing improvement.

David Herd cranked up the Old Trafford atmosphere in the thirty-eighth minute, when he put the home side in front with a well-taken goal. But amid a swirling wind, which played its part in curtailing the game as a showpiece, as well as causing problems for both sets of defenders, St John equalised for Liverpool five minutes into the second half.

Brennan and Cantwell were troubled by A'Court and Callaghan, while Foulkes had his work cut out by the wily St John. At the opposite end, Herd kept Yeats on his toes, while Quixall once again displayed the form that had not been in evidence for some time and was always a thorn in Liverpool's side.

United regained the lead in the sixty-eighth minute – courtesy of a Quixall penalty – after Melia had tripped Stiles about a foot inside the area, following the diminutive half-back's surge forward from midfield. It was a goal that looked to have sealed the points for United.

There were close calls at both ends when the ball ricocheted off the underside of the crossbar before being cleared to safety. Liverpool, to their credit, never gave up gaining reward for their endeavours, and with five minutes remaining they equalised for the second time. Melia made amends for his foul on Stiles, by steering home a Yeats header.

With two minutes remaining, the game suddenly spiralled away from United when Moran fired a free-kick past Gregg, for what should have been the winner; however, as many disappointed United supporters began the long trek home, Giles appeared from nowhere to divert a Cantwell free-kick past Lawrence with only twenty seconds remaining.

The goals continued to flow over the next couple of weeks, with five the following Saturday as Wolves were beaten 3-2 at Molineux, followed by four in a 2-2 home draw against Aston Villa, making it thirty-five in six games. But that point from the Villa fixture was of little benefit, as it saw United slip three places in the table to nineteenth, having clawed their way off the bottom thanks to the recent favourable results. With sixteen points, they were six above bottom club Leyton Orient and four above second-bottom Ipswich Town.

The points were shared again in a 1-1 draw at Sheffield United, thanks mainly to a Harry Gregg penalty save, but the visit of Nottingham Forest to Old Trafford on the second Saturday in December saw the floodgates reopened, with Tom Holley of *The People* writing, 'Since those glorious pre-Munich days, Manchester United have often flattered to deceive. Now, if I'm a judge, they have made it at last – through discipline.

'Their side of big-money stars has ceased to be a collection of individuals and is blossoming into a combination in which every man is using his talents for the good of the team.

'And with men like Quixall, Charlton and Law turning it on with that thought in mind, it would have taken a better side than Forest to halt their seven game run without defeat.'

Forest were beaten 5-1, with Herd notching two and the others coming from Charlton, Giles and Law. The sports pages told everyone that United were on the crest of the wave, a victory that took United up to a more respectable fourteenth.

Riding the crest of the wave they may have been against Forest, but this was the Manchester United of the early 1960s, a team that was totally unpredictable, often rudderless, and seven days later they were well and truly sunk at the Hawthorns. West Bromwich Albion toyed with them as the game moved towards full-time with the home side leading 3-0. For fully a minute, the Albion players walked the ball around the bemused red shirts, as if they were playing a team wearing blindfolds, whose boots were so clogged down in the mud that they had become immobile.

There was considerably more to the ninety minutes than United's poor display and the three goals that they conceded, as the game soon became embroiled in controversy.

Following the lacklustre performance it was revealed that Denis Law had reported referee Gilbert Pullin to the Football Association for alleged misconduct during the 3-0 defeat. At half-time and again at full-time, he had spoken to Matt Busby about the conduct of the match official and remarks that had been made towards him.

'Law was very upset,' said the United manager. 'In all my years at Old Trafford this is the first time I have been associated with a protest of this description.'

The forty-six-year-old official from Bristol, when asked to comment on the matter, said he was 'amazed' at Law's complaint. 'Of course a referee speaks to players in the course of the game, but I can recall no disparaging remarks of any kind. I did not threaten Law with any disciplinary action.'

Strangely, Pullin was no stranger to such matters, as on 5 October he was reported after making a threat to Houghton, the Oxford United centre-forward, during a match at Torquay. However, he was later cleared by an FA enquiry, after giving evidence along with six Oxford players.

At their weekly board meeting, Matt Busby and his fellow directors discussed the matter that had been brought to their attention, as well as the statements of Denis Law and teammate Albert Quixall, for almost two hours before deciding that a strong protest should be made to both the Football Association and the Football League.

Following an FA Disciplinary Commission hearing in Birmingham, which lasted an hour and a half, the referee, who had been officiating for eight years and was in his last year before reaching the compulsory retirement age, was severely censured for what were described as 'unnecessary remarks' to Law during the game. A statement was issued which read, 'The commission has decided that Mr Pullin be severely censured and warned as to his future conduct and informed that he must not make unnecessary remarks to players during a match.

'Manchester United officials and players were informed their action in making press statements before the complaint had been considered by the committee is deprecated and their attention has been drawn to the letter sent to all clubs in 1957.'

'We feel that the Commission has been very fair all round,' said Matt Busby, who had supported his forward, as had Albert Quixall, adding that 'we have no complaints'. Law himself simply added, 'I am very happy with the decision.'

All the referee was willing to say following the hearing was that he would consider taking the matter further through other channels, but it appeared that he had little in the way of support, as Bill Rogers, the secretary of the Referee's Association said, 'A Football Association Commission does not censure referees without due cause. It does seem Mr Pullin left himself wide open.'

After the hearing the referee had declined Denis Law's offer to shake hands.

Around this time, one or two of the United playing staff found themselves in a similar situation to that of Mr Pullin, although it was not an FA Commission that they found themselves in front of, but a local court.

'Soccer Star In Police Chase', screamed the headlines, with the story below revealing that 'Seamus (Shay) Brennan, 25, was arrested yesterday after a 60 mph chase through the city, a court was told.

'Inspector Wilfred Cunliffe, prosecuting at Salford, Lancs, said: "He was ordered to stop, but carried straight on."

'Brennan, who admitted driving his mini-car while unfit through drink, told the court: "I am very sorry."

'He was fined £35 and banned from driving for twelve months.'

Jimmy Nicholson had also fallen foul of the law and had been fined £15 for speeding; he was doing over 45 mph in a 30mph area, and driving without third-party insurance.

They were not the only United players to add a court appearance to those of their League and cup ties, with goalkeeper David Gaskell also finding himself in trouble. For Gaskell, however, it wasn't anything to do with driving that earned him an appearance in court but rather diving.

On this occasion, the headline read, 'A wiggle in goal makes mother "livid"', reference to a rather peculiar incident during the Central League fixture between Sheffield United and United on 24 November at Bramall Lane.

The accompanying article read, 'Blonde Mrs Patience Savage, standing behind the goal with her five-year-old son, complained that the goalkeeper pulled his pants right down and wiggled his bottom at the crowd.

'Mrs Savage, a detective's wife, added, "He was not wearing anything under his pants – or if he was, it was pulled down as well."

'So, David Gaskell, of Manchester United, playing at Bramhall-lane (*sic*) against Sheffield United in a reserve match, appeared in court to explain the wiggle. Mrs Savage said it made her "absolutely livid".

'Mr J. Steele Carr, defending the twenty-two-year-old goalkeeper, who was being prosecuted under the town's by-laws, said, "I suggest he was just pulling up his knickers."

'Mrs Savage, an industrial nursing sister, replied, "Do you suggest that I have been nursing all these years and I do not recognise a bare back-side?"

'She wrote down words that Gaskell used after a retaken penalty goal – he saved the first attempt – scored for Sheffield.

'Gaskell told the court, "When I dived to try and save the ball my shorts fell down a bit and I had to pull them up. I am always pulling my shorts up."

'Gaskell then demonstrated his wiggle to the court. His explanation, "The crowd got over-excited because we were doing well."

'There was nothing offensive in the wiggle and he did not use bad language.

'Sir John Green, the magistrate's chairman, dismissed charges against Gaskell of making an insulting gesture and using insulting language.'

Gaskell was also to find himself in front of the Football Association, due to a separate incident in the above game against Sheffield United, when he had been booked by the referee and had given a false name! Appearing in front of the FA disciplinary board, the 'keeper was severely censured and fined five guineas (£5.25).

Others in previous years had found their way into the newspapers on the inside pages rather than the back ones, with Duncan Edwards fined £1 for riding his bicycle without a light and Albert Scanlon being ordered by magistrates to pay 30*s* a week to a barmaid that he got pregnant! Although the two recent matters gave the supporters something different to talk about over their pints and in the works canteen, performances of late were still subject to much debate, but boredom was soon to set in.

The 3-0 defeat against West Bromwich Albion at the Hawthorns on 15 December marked the end of an Old Trafford career for a disappointed Jimmy Nicholson. Having made just short of seventy first-team appearances, the Northern Ireland internatonal failed to reappear in the United first team even though it was another year before he left Old Trafford. Over the years, Jimmy had seen many players leave the club, but what of his own circumstances?

For myself, I felt that my career at Old Trafford was wrecked by a back injury which affected both my hips and buttocks and persistent dead legs, cold feet, while my toenails started to grow dead and black and drop off.

I could not persuade the physios at Old Trafford that I had a serious problem.

After a match, my hips used to swell up and my body felt bloated, giving the impression of weight gain. I struggled to put my trousers on after games and eventually found it difficult to walk 20 yards without pain.

The physios felt that I was 'swinging the lead' and didn't want to train!

The opposite applied. I loved training and used to come back in the afternoons to train by myself.

I was transferred to Huddersfield in this condition, but fortunately, Ian Greaves and Henry Cockburn, two former United players, were coaches at Huddersfield and persuaded the manager, Tom Johnson to buy me.

I was x-rayed from head to toe in Leeds and found a curvature at the base of my spine which was causing an imbalance on my leg length, which in turn was causing the pain and inflammation as well as pins and needles in my feet. No explanation for my toenails turning black and falling off!

Shortly after joining Huddersfield I had a manipulative operation on my spine, which caused me further pain and a series of smaller manipulations and deep massage which eventually allowed me to train and play again.

Eventually I began to enjoy football again and started to train very hard and using techniques which were recommended to me by specialists in spinal chiropractor. The fluid which had built up in my body gradually went and I began to really enjoy my football.

Ian Greaves and Henry Cockburn were so supportive and encouraging and I will always be eternally grateful to them for giving me the opportunity to once again play and eventually having a good degree of success, returning to the First Division and re-gaining my place in the Northern Ireland side after a gap of some three years.

While one individual's Manchester United first-team career had come to a close, another's was just beginning. Matt Busby had managed to persuade sixteen-year-old former junior bank clerk David Sadler to move north instead of joining one of the many clubs closer to his Maidstone home who had expressed an interest in signing him. The highly rated Maidstone United inside-forward could have taken his pick from the likes of Tottenham Hotspur, West Ham United or Arsenal, but even though the United manager told him 'you'll have to take it as it comes. There'll be no promises and no favouritism', he still decided to forsake his £16 per week banking career to join United's ranks of budding stars on an amateur contract.

Although informing the youngster that he would have to bide his time, Matt Busby had high expectations for the youngster. 'We're overjoyed at signing David,' he said. 'He's a great prospect.' But was this the start of a new bunch of 'Busby Babes? 'Yes, you can say that with the advent of young Sadler the Babes are on their way back again. We have many fine young lads maturing up here.'

Sadler, already an England amateur internatonal, was soon to go from playing in front of 1,200 or less with Maidstone United in the Isthmian League, while still a schoolboy, to the First Division and crowds of 40,000 plus. But why did he take the big step of moving north, when he had the pick of the big clubs much nearer to home? 'I can only tell the truth. I ran away from home to join Manchester United,' he was to admit.

'I was scared and I was having the life pestered out of me by talent scouts from here, there and everywhere. They were all after me and I didn't know which way to turn until I met Jimmy Murphy, Manchester United's assistant manager.

'One day when my mood was at its blackest and most despairing he asked, "Why not drop in at Old Trafford just to see the set up David?" And from the moment I set my eyes on the club I knew it was Manchester United for me. Every brick and board on the ground breathed atmosphere. Old Trafford looked like my idea of a footballer's heaven.'

Three days before Christmas, Arsenal travelled north to Manchester, with United hoping that dear old Santa Claus would bring them an early present in the form of two points that would help improve their rather precarious position of late.

Despite his liking for wearing red and white, early indications for many inside Old Trafford that afternoon was that Mr Claus must have had leanings towards the north London club rather than United, as the Gunners took the lead five minutes into the second half through John Barnwell, although play up until that point had been relatively even. However, within six minutes those letters to Santa had been well and truly answered.

That particular Saturday afternoon in Manchester 16 had been one of thick fog, and along with smoke from the trains travelling along the nearby railway line, visibility was getting worse by the minute. It was on the verge of becoming farcical, with many in the sparse 22,559 crowd having great difficulty in seeing the halfway line, never mind the opposite goal.

Not only could those in the stands and on the terracing make out little of the action, the referee was struggling to see either of his linesmen, and therefore decided to call both sets of players into the centre circle, where he informed them that he was suspending play for five minutes to see if visibility would improve. As the players and officials left the field, many thought that the game had been abandoned and headed for the exits.

Following the adjournment, conditions had improved slightly, but just as soon as the referee headed down the tunnel to call the teams back out onto the pitch, another bank of fog enveloped the Stretford End, once again reducing visibility, giving the referee little option than to abandon the match.

Boxing Day saw United travel to Craven Cottage, where Bobby Charlton's forty-first-minute goal was enough to secure both points, but none of the travelling support in the 23,928 crowd would have thought for one minute that this would be the last time they would see their favourites in action until 23 February.

Cold weather set in on 22 December and was followed by heavy snow on Boxing Day, which lasted for most of the next twenty-four hours. A blizzard over the South West of England during 29–30 December brought up 20 feet of snow in places, although Manchester city centre saw only 6 inches, and a further 3 inches fell a few miles further south in Wythenshawe. By the turn of the year, areas of the country began to freeze solid, with temperatures dropping as low as -16 °C, while February brought more snow and gale-force winds, with a thirty-six-hour blizzard causing further drifts of 20 feet in places.

With parts of the country at a standstill, football and all other sporting activities were far down in the list of people's priorities, curtailing much of the activity around the country's football grounds. Bolton Wanderers failed to kick a ball in a competitive fixture between 8 December and 16 February, while some FA Cup ties had to be rescheduled ten times.

United's third-round FA cup tie against Huddersfield Town didn't quite manage to reach double figures in postponements, but it was continually a case of 'yes, the ground is playable, it is on tomorrow as there has been a thaw', while overnight frost would leave large areas of the pitch frozen and the tie was again called off. Training at Old Trafford was difficult, with the pitch frozen, although the area behind the Stretford End had always been put to use as an ideal area for a kick about.

Things didn't quite come to a standstill at Old Trafford, as there was some activity, if only behind the scenes, with the lull in fixtures allowing Matt Busby to put pen to paper on a new seven-year contract, estimated to be worth more than £5,000 a year. Strangely, Busby had been working without a contract, as his last one had run out almost a year ago and according to chairman Harold Hardman: 'We just did not get around to drafting a new one.'

Also negotiated by the United board was the club's claim against British European Airways, which was raised in the aftermath of the Munich air disaster. On 8 January, it was announced that the 'huge compensation claim' had been settled out of court, with a spokesman for BEA saying, 'The claim is for between £250,000 and £300,000 and broadly speaking is compensation for the loss of the services of the players involved in the crash.' It was estimated that the present transfer value of the players killed and injured was around £300,000.

An agreement was also made between each party not to divulge the details of the agreement, with United chairman Harold Hardman saying that he could not say how much the club had received. When asked about what the money would be used for, he replied, 'We have not decided. But part of it is expected to be earmarked towards helping a speedier development of the ground.'

BEA had already paid out around £150,000 to relatives in personal claims, while United had collected around £200,000 on an insurance policy coming from the flight of their players and officials. All the money that United had so far received had gone to the relatives of those who had been killed or injured.

The *Daily Express* for some reason estimated the total to be 'less than £100,000', publishing the following quote from the BEA solicitor: 'We have agreed terms of settlement, but they are shrouded in secrecy.' Another quote from Manchester read, 'The action has been settled and will be withdrawn.'

Three days after the announcement of the out-of-court settlement came the bombshell. Instead of the estimated £200–300,000 that had been mentioned, it was revealed that United had agreed on a figure of £35,000. So, what had happened?

United chairman Harold Hardman said, 'Our original claim was certainly a lot higher (*it was in fact £273,000*) and our settlement figure does seem to have come as a surprise. We had to make it public because in view of the high figures suggested, our supporters might well have expected us to do more with the money than we obviously can.

'We are disappointed in the sense that we accept the figure.

'We are satisfied that if we had pressed for a higher amount and gone to court, we did not know what would have happened. We had to consider the merits and demerits of our case.'

A BEA spokesman said, 'The club has agreed to drop unreservedly all allegations of negligence and wilful misconduct made against BEA, and BEA in its turn will pay the club £35,000 and costs in settlement of the club's claim which totalled £273,000.'

Why United had decided to accept the sum of £35,000 is difficult to grasp, as there is every possibility that they could have obtained more had they persevered with the claim. The Lord Mayor of Manchester's relief fund raised £57,000! Perhaps they did not want the subject of Munich dragged through the courts, as it was coming up to the fifth anniversary of the crash. But on the other hand, the £35,000 was not much more than they had paid for Tommy Taylor and what sort of value would you have placed on the former Barnsley forward and the rest of his teammates today. A total of £285,500 had already been paid out on team-building since the crash.

This figure was soon to increase, as no sooner had Busby added his signature to a new contract than he was pushing another under the nose of Glasgow Celtic's Scottish international wing-half, Pat Crerand. Crerand, who had supported the Glasgow East End club since he was a boy, had been a key member of the Celtic line-up until recently, with feelings between the player and his employers having became somewhat strained, as the player himself explained in an article which appeared in the *Scottish Daily Express* on 30 January. In the article, under the heading 'Why I Want To Go', the Scottish international said that in a half-time dressing-room row during the 1 January fixture with Rangers at Ibrox, in which Celtic were losing 1-0, a club official told him that he was playing too far up the field. Soon stronger words were exchanged, but everything was soon forgotten as the teams were called out for the second half.

For the next fixture against Aberdeen, Crerand was omitted, although the official statement made by the Glasgow club said that he was 'being rested', as he was for the Scottish Cup tie against Falkirk. These decisions pushed him closer to the edge and finally prompted him to ask for a transfer. 'The toughest decision I have ever had to make,' he was later to say.

Crerand was a player that Busby had admired for some time, and when news filtered south that the often-volatile wing-half had been dropped by Celtic for the first time in his career, the situation was one that would be continuously monitored, especially as Celtic had beaten Aberdeen 5-1 without the influential playmaker.

In the *Scottish Daily Express* for 29 January, Jimmy McGrory told the paper, following the Scottish Cup victory over Falkirk, that 'as far as Crerand being dropped, we didn't think it was the type of ground that suited his style of play'. But reporter David Allister wrote that he felt that the player had been dropped for the two successive games due to Celtic abandoning their all-out attacking style and developing a more defensive attitude, something that didn't quite suit the player, and that the 'toast of the Parkhead terraces' could find himself struggling for a place in the Celtic side for a long time.

But that night, whether or not Allister's words gave Crerand much to think about, the Gorbals-born player had handed in his transfer request, and Celtic manager, Jimmy McGrory told the press that it would be 'considered by the board this week'. Crerand himself had 'absolutely no comment to make' about the letter, but it all came as something of a surprise, as it had been thought that a meeting between the player and Celtic chairman Bob Kelly had ironed out all the problems. Apparently not.

Crerand said, 'I spent a lot of time yesterday pondering my decision. Finally, without consulting my fiancée or my mother, I wrote my transfer letter. I don't think there is any future for me at Parkhead. I have always tried my best, but it is becoming increasingly obvious that my style does not suit the club.'

On 31 January the Celtic supporters awoke to be greeted with the headline in the *Daily Record*, 'Pat Crerand Says – I Want to be a Busby Babe'. Written by John McPhail, himself a former Celtic player, the article proceeded to reveal the thoughts of the disgruntled half-back. 'I have always had a great admiration for United's manager Matt Busby,' admitted Crerand. 'I'd like to go to Manchester – if my request is granted that is.' 'If' was the big question. There was the possibility that the Celtic board would refuse the player's request and Crerand would have to remain in the green-and-white hoops, but in the knowledge that the love affair would never be the same.

When asked about he possibility of adding Crerand to the Manchester United payroll, all Matt Busby would say was 'I have seen Pat Crerand play several times and I think he is a great player.'

That same morning, the *Scottish Daily Express* carried a different story by the player, under the headline 'How it Feels to be a Rebel', with Crerand saying, 'The most difficult day of my life is over – the day I had to report to Celtic Park after asking for a transfer – and coming face to face with the fans in the street. It turned out to be a normal day at training yesterday, with no difficult reaction to my transfer letter from Jimmy McGrory or the other Parkhead officials.'

There was no immediate reply to the transfer request, but after much deliberation, Celtic agreed to Crerand's transfer on 3 February, with the player saying, 'Glasgow Celtic have agreed to my transfer and I hope to join a new club this week. And it looks as though that club will be Manchester United.

'If I do sign for United, I will be proud to become a member of the Busby brigade. We in Scotland have a great respect for the Manchester United manager and we know what a wonderful chief he is.

'Do you know something? I have never met or even spoken to Matt Busby in my life! However, I am likely to meet him for the first time tomorrow in Manchester.

'I understand that Celtic and United have agreed terms on my transfer. Now it is up to me, or I should say my fiancée Noreen. I hope to bring her down to Manchester tomorrow to have a look around. If Noreen likes the place then Matt Busby will have made a double signing.'

Noreen Ferry, the future Mrs Crerand, however, was not too enamoured about moving south, telling the *Daily Express*, 'Manchester? Wait and see. I have not seen Manchester, but somehow, I am not keen.'

On Monday 4 February, the *Daily Record* carried a picture of Crerand and his 'two biggest fans' – his mother and his fiancée – alongside the heading 'Crerand to Join Busby Babes'. The article reported, 'Celtic star Pat Crerand could be a Busby Babe within the next twenty-four hours. Both Celtic and Manchester United have agreed on a fee. The decision is up to Crerand and last night it seemed certain to be "yes". But Pat got the surprise of his life when he heard that United manager Matt Busby was interested. "I didn't even know Celtic had granted my transfer request," he said.

'For his two ardent fans – his mother and his sweetheart, pretty twenty-one-year-old Noreen Ferry, it was an even greater shock. She buried her head into his shoulders and sobbed, "Oh Pat, will you go to Manchester? Must You?"' The article also revealed that Crerand had 'phoned his Scottish international teammate Denis Law to tell him that United had made a move for him.

In the same newspaper, another reporter, 'Waverley', revealed that the figure Busby had agreed was around £50,000 after travelling to Glasgow for a secret meeting with Celtic officials. Celtic manager Jimmy McGrory told the reporter, 'We have decided to grant Crerand's request for a transfer and we have come to an arrangement with Manchester United. It's up to the player to decide.

Strangely, the player told yet another *Daily Record* reporter, Jim Rodgers, that 'I still have to make up my mind and I'll have a talk with Mr McGrory tomorrow.' Was the player now having doubts about leaving the Gorbals and Celtic Park?

The meeting, however, was far from secret and the *Scottish Daily Express* reporter David Allister caught Matt Busby before he travelled back to Manchester, with the United boss saying, 'Unfortunately, we had no time to see the player himself in view of the possibility of an English cup tie with Huddersfield going on tomorrow night. I shall either be coming to Glasgow again or Crerand will have to come down to Manchester.' When asked if he envisaged any snags, Busby replied, 'No, not really. I think I have landed the lad I want.'

The following day the news broke that the transfer was indeed on hold, a situation brought about by the player himself. The three-hour lunch meeting between Matt Busby, Jimmy McGrory and Bob Kelly had agreed the fee, but the player, following a meeting with McGrory, had refused to commit his future to Manchester United. 'I had a talk with Pat this morning,' said the Celtic manager. 'There has been a hitch and at the moment the transfer is in abeyance.'

The Celtic manager told reporters that the player had got in touch with Matt Busby and said he would think things over, have another talk with Celtic and then decide if he would travel to Manchester to meet the United boss. McGrory added, 'Pat Crerand asked for the transfer. We had an amicable talk with Mr Busby – terms were agreed on and now Pat can't make up his mind.

'I can warn Pat that he won't be put up for auction. It's up to himself entirely today.'

When contacted, Matt Busby said, 'The player has certain matters to discuss with Celtic and then he will let me know the situation.' He did, however, add, 'Manchester United's policy has always been to provide the best for their supporters. That's why we want Celtic and Scotland's right-half Pat Crerand.

'Crerand is the inspiring mixture of strength, enthusiasm and command that can help us achieve our aims.

'I have never met Crerand, except for a few words on the telephone. But I have seen enough of him and know enough about him and realise that he is the type of player who can be an influence on our team. The bigger the occasion, the better he plays. No one who has not got a great love for the game could possibly play it with such verve and enthusiasm. Of all those things, great players are made.

'I went for Crerand because I judge him to have just the sort of personality and skill to bring the greatness out of forwards of that calibre. I am confident that Crerand will turn out to be, as Law will turn out to be, a very good investment.'

So, the ball was clearly in Pat Crerand's court, as the Celtic support held their breath in the hope that the player would stay, while further south Matt Busby could only wait for the telephone call that would tell him if he had a new player or not. The only thing that was stalling the deal was what Crerand classed as 'personal and financial' which obviously meant how much Celtic were paying for the remains of his contract.

The call finally came, giving the United manager the answer he had hoped for: 'Yes, I'll sign.' Crerand and his fiancée flew south to Manchester, being stopped at the airport by Derek Hodgson of the *Daily Express* who asked if the £56,000 fee bothered him: 'Well, I'll feel a bit of a fool if I don't play as well as expected. I think I can hold my place.'

The *Daily Record* reporter John McPhail, never one to miss an 'exclusive', had travelled south with the player and his fiancée and, under an article 'The Magic of Busby', Crerand told the reporter, 'I have always been Celtic daft, only Manchester United could make me change my mind, but I am still not sure.' But McPhail added, 'But today, Crerand met soccer's magic man Matt Busby and like so many other great players fell under his spell and became a Busby Babe.

'Not the city, not the contract, but the magic of Busby. He (*Crerand*) told me just after the transfer, "John, I just sat and gazed at this marvellous man. Even if the terms had not been what I wanted, I still would have signed."'

McPhail also spoke to the United manager, someone he had known for over twenty years, and said that he had never known the United boss feel so happy about signing a player. Busby told him, 'This is wonderful. I've always wanted to sign Pat and now he is a Babe. I have known and admired Pat as a player. Now as a person he has impressed me deeply. I feel, once settled in at Old Trafford, he will become a tremendous asset to our club. Pat will play against Burnley, if the Burnley field is ready for Saturday.'

Crerand only took twenty minutes to put pen to paper and sign the two-year contract, stating that he was 'happy with the deal, content with the terms and looking forward to Noreen and I looking over a house in Manchester shortly. I only hope I can be as happy at United as I have been with Celtic.

'Why did I leave? I don't want to be cruel about it, but if you take Celtic and Rangers away, there's not much left.'

Matt Busby finally had his man, but if the deal had fallen through, there was the likelihood that he would have added another Scot to his playing staff, with Billy Bremner of Leeds United looking for a move away from Elland Road. The ginger-haired midfield terrier might have added grit to the United team, but of the two, the silky skills of Crerand were better suited to their style of play.

Due to the severe weather and the lack of actual training facilities, clubs, including United, began to look at ways of overcoming such problems. One option which United considered and decided to explore was playing in the Republic of Ireland.

Saturday afternoon football in Dublin had, according to the local newspaper, 'died a death' some two years previously due to the declining interest of local supporters, but when the news broke that Manchester United, and to a much lesser extent Coventry City, were crossing the water to play a friendly at Milltown, home of Shamrock Rovers, all hell broke loose.

Normally a visiting United side would have played a local select XI, but with League of Ireland games scheduled for 2 February, Third Division Coventry were only too happy to come face to face with United.

Played in freezing conditions, as an Arctic wind blew around the ground, Coventry, despite their lowly status, certainly gave United the workout they sought, and were indeed unlucky not to record a memorable victory.

Quixall gave United the lead after twenty-six minutes, but within minutes, the sky-blues were level, Farmer lobbing the ball over the head of the advancing Gregg. With ten minutes of the first half remaining, Coventry took the lead when Whitehouse headed home a Humphries centre.

Bravely, the Midlands side held on, but with only eight minutes remaining, United equalised as Charlton ran on to a loose ball to shoot past Weeson in the Coventry goal, immediately prompting a mini-pitch invasion.

Although the referee said that, had the game been a League or cup tie, he would never have considered going ahead with it as conditions were atrocious, United decided they were better than nothing and continued with such ventures, returning to the Emerald Isle eleven days later to face Bolton Wanderers at the Flower Lodge ground in Cork. Such was the desperation for games that Spain was even considered, with Real Madrid, Valencia and Bilbao having been contacted. However, conditions there were not much better than in Ireland, as Spain had been exceptionally wet.

A crowd of 6,000, fewer than had been anticipated but a good turnout despite the weather, turned up at the Cork venue for what was in effect a local derby, despite the distance from Lancashire and although Matt Busby described the playing conditions (a heavy, sodden pitch, covered with water in parts) as 'appalling'. They were treated to a fine exhibition of football, plenty of goals and the first sight of Pat Crerand in a red United shirt.

Crerand marked his debut with a notable goal, a right-footed 40-yard drive in the thirty-fourth minute, cancelling out Bolton's sixteenth-minute opener. Further goals from Quixall with a penalty, Law and Charlton for United and Lee, scoring a second for Bolton, gave the crowd value for money despite the dreadful conditions. Indeed, the conditions delayed the taking of Lee's penalty kick, as the referee could not find the actual spot and had to pace it out before the kick could be taken.

With no let-up in the conditions at home, although the Sheffield Wednesday game at Old Trafford on 16 February was declared as being definitely 'on' two days before, overnight frost on the Thursday produced yet another cancellation, as areas of the pitch were covered in ice. Ground staff spent ages chopping the frozen surface with forks and also brought in a harrow machine in an effort to get the game played. But it was all to no avail.

So, United once again sought match fitness across the Irish Sea, returning to Dublin on 19 February to face a select side. With twenty minutes gone, the rather sluggish game suddenly bubbled into life after Cantwell sent O'Neill crashing to the ground with a tackle that forced the winger out of action and off to hospital for stitches in his gashed leg. The game suddenly developed into something of a cup-tie affair.

Amid a crescendo of boos, United weathered the storm, and in the end strolled to a 4-0 victory, having at least regained some of their missing match fitness over the course of the three games. They were now prepared as best they could for the resumption of domestic football.

It could, however, have been at a price, as Matt Busby sat biting his nails as he awaited the referee's report on the conduct of Maurice Setters and Pat Crerand, who were both booked during the sometimes robust ninety minutes in that final game in the Irish trilogy. The United manager tried to pour water on the flames by stating, 'Our players, after such a long lay-off, went into the match as a serious means of helping themselves to get back to match fitness.

'The match was of some importance to us. Perhaps our players mistimed some tackles in a way they would not have done had they been fully match-fit. This is the only explanation.'

Thankfully referee Kevin Richmonds' report went only as far a the Emergency Committee of the FAI who, after examining its content, decided that no further action was necessary, with the Football Association having no need to become involved.

Back on home soil, United finally got back into League action on 23 February, when Blackpool travelled to Old Trafford and, having waited longer than anticipated to make his home debut, Pat Crerand wasted little time in showing the Old Trafford faithful that Busby had spent his money wisely.

If the supporters were impressed, then the national press were likewise, as 'Crerand can be the Spur' and 'Crerand Lays on a Super Service' were just two of the headlines following the 1-1 draw, with his performance described further as intelligent and economical.

It was disappointing, however, not to return to action with a victory, but due to the predicament that the team found itself in at present, a point was certainly welcome. However, had Quixall's penalty not been saved by Waiters, then it could have been an entirely different story.

Quixall was almost the villain of the piece again seven days later, when an attempted back-pass to Harry Gregg had been intercepted by Freddie Pickering, the Blackburn Rovers centre-forward, who blasted the ball past the United 'keeper to give his team a 2-1 lead. Fortunately, the United man was to redeem himself sixty seconds later, when he pushed the ball out to David Herd, whose centre was crashed into the Rovers net by Bobby Charlton for a goal that earned United another point in their fight to keep clear of the relegation zone.

The point saw United move up one place, to thirteenth, with twenty-three points, five above second-bottom Ipswich Town, but with a game in hand. Was the tide finally turning?

If asked two days after the 2-2 draw against Blackburn, then the answer was an emphatic 'yes', as Huddersfield Town were hammered 5-0 at Old Trafford in the third round of the FA Cup, making it an unhappy return to his old stomping ground for goalkeeper and Munich survivor Ray Wood.

But if one player did not enjoy the best of afternoons when facing his old club, then another gave the matter little thought, as Denis Law took the game by the scruff of the neck and notched a hat-trick against the team who had given him his big break in the Football League.

The Second Division Yorkshire side were no match for United, in a game where every man and move clicked into place, giving the home side a formidable look and one that had not been seen for some time. Indeed, if it had not been for the heroics of Ray Wood, then the scoreline would have been something completely different, sending Huddersfield back over Saddleworth Moor in a state of shock.

But the party was soon to grind to a halt, before it had actually started.

Due to the weather causing havoc with the fixture list, as well as life in general, the last three months of the season were going to be nothing less than chaotic and, in United's case, they had to somehow squeeze eighteen League fixtures into that timescale. Depending on progress in the FA Cup, then there was the possibility of them playing almost every other day!

Five days after the five-star triumph against Huddersfield, Tottenham travelled to Old Trafford on League business and, in the early stages, United looked to have picked up where they had left off.

Crerand split the Spurs' defence with considerable ease, creating opportunities for his teammates, but they found Brown in the visitors' goal in excellent form, denying the home side time and time again. Indeed, they had enough chances to win not only this game but another half-dozen.

'It seems unbelievable,' wrote Terence Elliott in the *Express*. 'That scoreline looks crazy now when one recalls what Manchester United were doing to Spurs for forty minutes of the first half and much of the second.

'But the stark reality of this football business is that Spurs got two goals while Matt Busby's lads were bringing tears to the eyes of their fans by failing spectacularly in that vitally important job of getting the ball into the net.'

Those misses, however, were to prove fatal at the end of the day, as Elliott wrote. Tottenham scored twice without reply, and it was a result that was start a run of four consecutive defeats (West Ham United away – 3-1, Ipswich Town home – 1-0 and Fulham home – 2-0), which would send United down to seventeenth, a mere two points above second- and third-bottom Birmingham City and Manchester City. Even more worrying was the fact that the two Cities both had a game in hand. Bottom club Leyton Orient were thankfully eight points worse off.

Squeezed in between the defeats against Tottenham and West Ham was the fourth-round FA Cup tie against Aston Villa at Old Trafford and away from the pressure keg of the First Division, United raised their game in what was a typical cup tie, played at a vigorous pace with a tinge of viciousness thrown in.

Stiles and Setters, who had travelled back from the Midlands following a family bereavement, supported their forwards time and time again. Law and Herd both missed from close range, while Charlton's usual accuracy was nowhere to be seen. Eighteen free-kicks were given against United, with Villa conceding fifteen, and when it came to goals scored it was United who also held the advantage.

There were never going to be many goals for the 52,265 supporters to savour, as the visitors kept things tight at the back, hoping perhaps for a replay at Villa Park, while the United back line were just as solid, with Gregg having a reasonably easy night. As it turned out, one goal was enough to win the tie, and it came in the thirty-third minute.

A Giles–Law move down the right put Quixall in the clear just outside the Villa penalty area, with the inside-forward's half-hit shot looking an easy one for Sidebottom to save, but somehow the 'keeper allowed the ball to slip underneath his body and it rolled into the net.

One solitary goal, but enough for United to progress into Round Five.

There was little time for treatment to the bumps and bruises, as that fifth-round tie against Second Division leaders Chelsea was scheduled for Saturday 16 March, five days later, and once again it wasn't so much United's form on the day which procured victory, but a helping hand along the way.

Albert Quixall was continuing to show something like the form that had secured him the move to Old Trafford, and he was by far United's best player, having a hand in both their goals. With sixteen minutes gone, he chased a long Setters pass to the goal line and sent a hopeful cross into the Chelsea area. England under-23 international goalkeeper Peter Bonetti should have dealt with the high ball comfortably, but let it drop from his grasp and Law was on hand to prod it over the line to give United the lead.

One minute into the second half, Setters once again sent Quixall away, and his speculative drive from all of 25 yards slipped from Bonetti's grasp. On this occasion, it hit the post before trickling over the line.

Chelsea's midfield toiled manfully, but with little reward, while Bonetti redeemed himself slightly with fine saves from Law and Charlton. Gregg at the other end was also kept on his toes, but was beaten by Sorrell in the seventieth minute, setting up a nail-biting finale for the red support. Thankfully they managed to hold on.

Matt Busby now felt that Wembley was a possibility, but the defeats by West Ham and Ipswich – 'a pathetic performance', wrote one reporter – did little to boost the confidence of players and supporters alike, with slow hand-clapping echoing around Old Trafford during the latter of the two fixtures.

Both performances were noted by FA Cup quarter-final opponents Third Division Coventry City, who lay in wait for United on 30 March at their Highfield Road ground. It was a trip that must have given anyone with a connection or allegiance to United sleepless nights, and the prematch conversation outside the Old Trafford boundaries was generally all about a Coventry victory.

Urged on by the voracious backing of their supporters, Coventry surged into the attack from the first whistle, leaving their illustrious visitors floundering around the muddied pitch and within five minutes they had taken the lead. Sillett passed the ball wide to Humphries on the right, and as the winger's cross reached the United goalmouth, Foulkes, in an attempt to clear as Bly moved in, sliced the ball past Gregg to give the home side the initiative.

The switching on of the Highfield Road floodlights seemed to awaken the visitors, and Charlton snatched an equaliser in the twenty-seventh minute. A throw-in from Setters to Quixall was quickly switched to Law, who in turn found Charlton, who right-footed the ball into the bottom right-hand corner.

The goal certainly settled United's nerves and they began to enjoy most of the play, taking the lead five minutes into the second half. Charlton took the ball wide on the left and before anyone knew what had happened, the England winger had raced inside and hammered the ball past Weeson.

Coventry never gave up despite being behind and fought bravely for the equaliser, and indeed thought they had actually scored it when Humphries forced the ball home. The referee, however, had other ideas and pulled play back for a handball against Bly. The Norwich forward himself also came close minutes later, but was foiled by an acrobatic save from Gregg.

With twenty minutes remaining, the outcome of the game was decided once and for all, when a mix-up between Weeson and Bruck allowed Quixall to tap home United's third. Wembley was only one step away.

The semi-final, however, was a month away, and before the ninety minutes against Southampton on 27 April could be contemplated, there were seven vital First Division fixtures to be played in the space of twenty-two days. Those three weeks would go a long way to determining where United would be playing their football the following season.

For the first of the seven, Fulham travelled north to Manchester, and for those supporters who did not venture to Coventry for the cup tie, United failed to convince that they were on the road to recovery and indeed better things.

United were poor in the first half, even by their own dismal standards of late, and went behind to an O'Connell goal in the thirteenth minute. It wasn't until six minutes after the interval that they threatened the Fulham goal for the first time, Setters heading past Macedo from close range, but his effort was correctly disallowed for offside.

Graham Leggat added a second for the visitors ten minutes from time, and by then many in the sparse 28,124 crowd had either gone home, or wished that they had never ventured out into the cold Mancunian night in the first place.

There was a break of eight days until the trip to Villa Park, where rather surprisingly they secured two vital points in something of a shabby ninety minutes.

Following action around both goalmouths in the opening minutes, it was United who gained an early advantage, taking the lead in the sixth minute when an unmarked Charlton on the edge of the penalty area picked out Stiles, deputising for the injured Denis Law, who side-footed the ball home. Stiles returned the compliment eight minutes into the second half and Charlton crashed the ball home from the edge of the area.

But in common with the season to date, it was a case of one step forward and two back, with the visit to Liverpool on 13 April ending in a 1-0 defeat, and two days later they could only manage a 2-2 draw at home to Leicester City.

At Anfield, United struggled, mainly due to the failure of Denis Law to make not only an impact on the game, but to rediscover his shooting boots. His main contribution to the ninety minutes was a scuffle with Ian St John towards the end. In fact, it would be true to say that the major reason for United's current predicament was the failure of the blond striker to find the back of the net. Much had been expected of the Aberdonian front man, as was shown by the fee that Matt Busby paid out to secure his services, but although on occasions his overall performance had been good, there had been a distinct lack of goals.

After scoring on his debut, it took him eight games to notch his second, and of United's nine victories to that date, Law's goals only ensured two of those. United had also played out ten League fixtures where they had failed to score: certainly not the best of statistics.

Liverpool, a Second Division side last season and fellow FA Cup semi-finalists, should have been two down at the interval, but Stiles, on both occasions, failed to find the back of the net. They were misses that were to prove costly, as eighteen minutes from time St John collected a Hunt pass before firing the ball past Harry Gregg.

Two days later Leicester City visited Old Trafford in the first of a double-header against the Filbert Street club, and goals from Charlton and Herd gave United a share of the points in a game where the men who penned the newspaper reports felt that, during the ninety minutes, United had put up their best performance for many months.

Leading 1-0 from a Herd goal in the sixteenth minute, they then lost Stiles for a quarter of an hour due to a leg injury, and when he did return, his capabilities were severely restricted. Even so, United should have been 3-0 up by the interval, Sjoberg kicking a Setters volley off the goal line and Banks saving superbly from the subdued Stiles.

Eight minutes into the second half, the possible cup final opponents had equalised, with Cross taking advantage of a hesitant defence, but Charlton re-established United's advantage in the sixty-fourth minute when, after being fouled on the edge of the Leicester penalty area in full flight, he latched on to Quixall's free-kick to shoot past Banks.

It was a lead that they were to hold for only sixty seconds, as full-back Norman moved upfield for a corner and brought the ball down with his chest, before volleying home from all of 30 yards.

Twenty-four hours later, play resumed at Filbert Street, with a certain Denis Law in the thick of the battle, ending his seven-match barren spell with a hat-trick. Three goals, on any other day, would have earned United both points, but the Scot was outgunned by a resilient Leicester side who did more than match his every move.

Nineteen year-old Leicester reserve inside-forward Terry Heath opened the scoring on the half-hour. Law equalised two minutes later, only for Keyworth to put the home side back in front five minutes into the second half. It took Law again only two minutes to put United level for a second time, but once again his effort was cancelled out, not once, but twice, as Keyworth claimed his hat-trick.

As the roars of the table-topping Leicester City support in the 37,002 strong Filbert Street crowd were echoed by the listening thousands locked outside, United continued to plod away in the hope that Lady Luck would at last smile on them, as the games became fewer and fewer and the need for points increased.

With twenty minutes remaining, Law claimed a share of the match ball, but his goals were not enough to earn United anything other than praise for their endeavour, with the 4-3 defeat leaving them nineteenth in the First Division, level on points with neighbours City, one ahead of second-bottom Birmingham City, and eight clear of Leyton Orient, who were still cemented firmly at the bottom.

Law struck again in the 1-1 home draw against Sheffield United in a rather disjointed performance, and in the 2-1 win, also at home, against Wolves: three points that lifted them up one place and gave them the advantage of a one-point gap over City.

Not only did the three points offer a little breathing space in the fight for First Division survival, it helped boost the confidence of Busby's side leading up to their FA Cup semi-final against Southampton at Villa Park. It was certainly much needed, as the lack of belief was never more obvious than in the 1-1 draw against Sheffield United, when referee William Handley pointed to the penalty spot in the sixty-third minute after Quixall went down after a challenge from Shaw, and none of the United players wanted to take on the responsibility of taking the kick.

Law picked up the ball and asked several teammates, with the referee attempting to hurry things up, before Charlton took the ball and placed it on the spot. Minutes later, he regretted his actions, as his kick rolled gently towards Hodgkinson and the 'keeper pushed the ball round the post.

Busby had kept faith with his struggling stars, reluctant to make wide-scale changes as points were lost with much regularity, but on the eve of the quarter-final replay between Nottingham Forest and Southampton, a game that would determine United's semi-final opponents, the United manager emphasised that not only had his team to reach Wembley, but they had to lift the cup as well.

'We must win the cup or else our season – our season of big signings – will have been a failure,' said the United manager, while also making the point that those 'big signings' were partly responsible for the team's current predicament.

'When you buy new players you need time to for them to fit in,' said the United manager. 'No matter how great an individual player a man might be, he still needs time. We've slipped in the League because of all the diversions when we've been fitting in the new players.

'Now they're beginning to fit and with the extension of the season we've got that extra time to help us.'

Going into the semi-final on the back of a vital win, Busby was clearly reluctant to make any changes, but the manager certainly had much to think about on the journey south to Birmingham. He had left Harry Gregg out of the side which had defeated Wolves, allowing David Gaskell the opportunity to stake his claim, while Noel Cantwell and Johnny Giles were both left to sweat on places in the cup line-up, travelling with the party, but not having played recently. Injuries, however, were to save Busby the job of telling two of the above three that they were not in the side.

And so United headed to Villa Park on Saturday 27 April to face Southampton in the semi-final of the FA Cup; a fixture that could well produce a ray of sunshine amid the dark clouds that had continuously floated across the Manchester skyline for the past eight months, bringing little in the way of excitement for the long-suffering support. But with only two victories in the last dozen games, it was more a case of the travelling support packing the lucky rabbit foot and avoiding ladders and black cats than packing the cigars and champagne.

A crowd of 68,312 clicked through the Villa Park turnstiles that afternoon, paying record gate receipts of £28,499 7s 6d, but they were certainly not treated to ninety minutes of entertainment in exchange for their hard-earned cash. The game was as drab as the stone-coloured Birmingham sky.

At times, the stretcher-bearers, sprinting around the ground to deal with fainting victims due to the pushing and shoving on the terracing, showed more urgency than the players, who seemed somewhat overawed by the occasion and contributed to what became a total anticlimax.

Injuries had forced Busby to leave out Shay Brennan and Albert Quixall, allowing club captain Noel Cantwell and Johnny Giles to come into the side, but there was to be no place in the line-up for Harry Gregg. On paper, at least, United should have been able to overcome the Second Division side without too much of a problem.

But play was substandard, with players from both sides either too concerned about making mistakes, or perhaps more to the point, making too many, as the game started and stopped, with poor passes, miskicks and clumsy play so much in evidence.

United almost opened the scoring in the eighth minute, when Crerand sent Stiles away, but the ball bounced out of control on the edge of the Southampton penalty area, and three minutes later Herd headed down a long clearance from Cantwell. Giles, latching on to the ball, drove narrowly past the post, with goalkeeper Reynolds well beaten.

With twenty-one minutes gone, the deadlock was finally broken. Giles, wide on the right, nodded down a bouncing ball towards Herd, who immediately launched it towards the Southampton goal, the ball passing over the head of centre-half Knapp and on to Law. At first the United man missed his header, but Reynolds in the Southampton goal was hesitant, allowing Law a second bite. The United man scrambled the ball home while almost on his knees.

Law thought he had added a second ten minutes before the break, but the referee disallowed it for a foul on Reynolds. A minute before the interval he was denied again as the ball nestled in the back of the net: this time it was a linesman's flag that cancelled out the goal.

Southampton never gave up, and it wasn't until five minutes from time that they had an opportunity to salvage something from the jaws of defeat. A pinpoint pass from Wimshurst found O'Brien with only Gaskell to beat, but the inside-forward simply flicked the ball into the hands of the grateful goalkeeper, with reporters divided between a glaring miss by the Southampton man and an outstanding save from the United 'keeper.

So, United were at Wembley, but all thoughts of a new suit and cup final tickets could be forgotten as there were more important things on the horizon, with a little matter of seven First Division fixtures to complete. These three weeks would decide whether it was First or Second Division football that Manchester United would be playing next season.

As United prepared to entertain Sheffield Wednesday at Old Trafford, they were still in nineteenth place, with twenty-nine points from their thirty-five games. Above them, in eighteenth, was Ipswich Town, with thirty-one points, but they had played thirty-eight games, while below them were City with twenty-eight points from thirty-six games, and Birmingham City with twenty-six points from thirty-six games.

Of United's remaining seven fixtures, two were probably going to be more crucial than the others, if that was at all possible: the game at St Andrew's on 10 May and short trip across Manchester five days later.

Let the battle commence.

The month of May certainly did not get off to the best of starts, with Sheffield Wednesday leaving Old Trafford with both points from a 3-1 victory, and the following morning's *Daily Mirror* proclaimed, 'United Slip to the Brink'.

'Manchester United's most deplorable failures this season must have looked positively brilliant compared with their appalling performances at Old Trafford last night. I did not think that a team with so much talent could sink so low,' wrote the *Mirror*'s United follower Derek Wallis, while Derek Hodgson in the *Express* called it a 'May-Day massacre'.

United might be going to Wembley, but their supporters were heading for the Old Trafford exits half an hour before the final whistle following Wednesday's third goal. They missed Setters heading home a Crerand free-kick eight minutes from time, but they had seen enough in the previous eighty-two. The only plus point was that City had also lost, 4-1 at Blackburn. Birmingham, however, had won by the odd goal in five at home to West Ham United. There was still one point in it!

Four days later, United made the short trip to Turf Moor, not the most pleasant of venues for United in recent times, and as they travelled north out of the city, Busby and his players contemplated the tough ninety minutes ahead.

Shay Brennan, who had returned to the side against Sheffield Wednesday, found himself left out, with Tony Dunne taking the No. 2 shirt and Noel Cantwell continuing at left-back. Johnny Giles was also back in favour at outside-right, while Quixall moved into the centre in place of Herd.

It was certainly not a game for the connoisseurs, as could well be expected with United fighting for their First Division lives, but the atmosphere was the only thing that was electric, as there were few moments of excitement, or indeed class, as mistake was matched by mistake and scoring opportunities few and far between.

The United contingent on the terracing and on the touchline breathed a huge sigh of relief in the eighth minute, as Simpson's 25-yard drive smacked the crossbar. They were also relieved to see Gaskell spring across his goal to hold a half-volley from Lochhead midway through the second half.

Four minutes after that Gaskell save, United took the lead. With Johnny Giles lying injured, and Quixall hesitant as to what course of action to take, the referee allowed United to continue going forward, and United's No. 7 decided that his team's need, certainly on this occasion, was greater than that of his teammate and from around 40 yards out, as the Burnley defence momentarily hesitated, he sent a long, floating centre towards Law. Rising like a salmon, the blond head met the ball firmly, sending it past Blacklaw and just underneath the bar into the net.

Constantly burdened by the spectre of defeat, United had twenty minutes to hold on to their precious advantage, and only occasionally moved to within shooting distance of the Burnley goal. The home side, allowed to press forward, threatened on a couple of occasions, but they were a poor imitation of the Burnley side of recent times, and much to United's relief they failed to cause any damage. The visitors were more than relieved to hear the final whistle. Back in the dressing room they were to learn that City had been beaten 4-0 at home to Blackpool, while Birmingham had salvaged a point in a 3-3 draw at Craven Cottage against Fulham.

The laundry ladies were kept busy as the kit was required again two days later, and with neither of their fellow relegation candidates playing, it was down to United to move further away from the dreaded dropzone.

Encounters against Arsenal have produced some memorable moments, and this meeting was to prove little different from many others; however, surprisingly, it attracted one short of 36,000. That, however, was on par to recent attendances with 50,000 gates clearly a thing of the past. With the second home game of the season having been watched by 63,437, United's performances are clearly defined by the drop in supporters passing through the turnstiles.

Denis Law's stablemate from the Italian adventure, Joe Baker, gave the Gunners the lead in the thirty-first minute, as Arsenal's defence stood firm while United pressed forward seeking a way through on goal. Law hit the bar with a rasping 25-yard drive, and had another blocked by Clarke, who had also kicked clear from Charlton, whose shot had beaten 'keeper McClelland.

After the interval, the game suddenly erupted, with the force of a volcano, in ten second-half minutes that produced four goals.

In the fifty-third minute, a through-ball from Johnny McLeod to Geoff Strong saw the latter give the visitors a two-goal advantage. Three minutes later, McClelland could only parry a Charlton piledriver, and the lurking Law hooked the rebound over the line.

Baker and Strong combined on the right to produce the opportunity for Skirton to re-establish Arsenal's two-goal advantage in the sixty-first minute, but within two minutes, Law had clawed a goal back, launching himself almost horizontally at a Giles cross, to hook the ball over his head and into the net.

In between this flurry of activity, Quixall had a shot brilliantly saved, and ten minutes after Law's strike the Scot again had the ball in the net, but was denied a hat-trick by the linesman's flag.

As the minutes ticked away, tempers became frayed, as they often did when United and Burnley met, and the referee had to step in between Stiles and McCullough. As the game moved into its final throes, Charlton twice beat McClelland, once with a header, the other with a lob, but on each occasion Arsenal centre-half Brown was standing on his goal line to clear.

With four games now remaining, United were eighteenth place with thirty-one points. Bolton Wanderers now slipped into the equation, although having played one game more they were one spot below and also on thirty-one. Birmingham City had twenty-nine points from their thirty-eight games, while City had twenty-eight with the same number of games played.

Aston Villa beat City 3-1 on 8 May, with Liverpool beating Birmingham City 5-1 that same night. United now had a one-game advantage. Obviously every fixture in recent weeks had been crucial, but the next two outings were going to be the be-all-end-all of United's season: the defining moments of a long, agonising campaign, as they made the precarious journey to both Birmingham City and Manchester City.

Against the former, on a slippery, mud-covered surface, both goalmouths saw plenty of activity in the early stages of the first half. But it was the home side who took the lead in the twenty-sixth minute, Lee pushing the ball through to Bloomfield, who beat Gaskell with a low shot just inside the post.

The goal gave Birmingham a boost and they continued to take the game to United, but the visitors controlled the game for a twenty-minute spell and should have scored twice, Giles and Herd both blasting wide when in good positions.

Slowly, with so much at stake, tempers began to fray. Law was spoken to for a foul on Auld and several others went near to overstepping the mark before Stiles and Leek found their way into the referee's notebook within five minutes of the second half getting underway.

In the seventy-fourth minute, Leek gave Birmingham a 2-0 lead, but Law put United back into the game two minutes later with a header from a Quixall centre. It was too little, too late, and United, however much they tried, were unable to find that elusive equaliser as conditions underfoot worsened.

City, hanging on to a thread of hope, beat Tottenham 1-0 on 11 May, but then Birmingham lost 3-1 at Burnley on 14 May, leaving everything still very much up in the air.

On Wednesday 15 May 1963, with United due to visit Maine Road that night, the bottom of the Football League First Division table read as follows:

18th – Ipswich Town – played 40, points 32.
19th – United – played 39, points 31.
20th – Birmingham City – played 41, points 31.
21st – City – played 40, points 30.
22nd – Leyton Orient – played 41, points 21.

With each club playing forty-two games, a victory over on Moss Side was crucial for both sides, making it a 'derby' of major importance, with much more than the bragging rights and being able to walk into one's workplace with head held high up for grabs. United had the advantage of still having two games to play following their visit to Maine Road, with one of those against already relegated Leyton Orient; the other was away at Nottingham Forest, but nothing could be taken for granted, especially when a City victory would give them a one-point advantage. City on the other hand, had only ninety minutes against West Ham United following the 'derby' encounter if they wanted to save their season. Anything short of a victory for the home side would see them doomed to the Second Division.

So, with so much to play for, it was obviously not going to be ninety minutes for the faint-hearted. The excitement and tension around the vast open stadium was akin to those European nights some seven years previously, when United borrowed City's home for the initial sojourn into European football.

To say the tension was high around Moss Side on that May evening is something of an understatement, as it was probably the most highly charged game between the two sides since the 1926 FA Cup semi-final, a game that City won 3-0. By the end of the ninety minutes, it had also been described as not simply the most important, but also the most thrilling and dirtiest of the seventy-four games between the two local rivals.

City, on this occasion, once again deserved victory, as they played the better of what football there was and had the edge on United when it came to skill, endeavour and determination. What they didn't have was luck.

In both dressing rooms prior to kick-off, there was none of the usual chatter and banter, as everyone knew that the second relegation spot was a straight choice between United and City. The tension showed on the face of every player.

Matt Busby, however, seemed to be oblivious to the dire consequences of the outcome of the ninety minutes, but it was simply a demonstration of one of the many the management skills that he possessed. Turning to his players as they prepared to leave the sanctuary of the dressing room, he told them, 'Don't worry about relegation. Put it right out of your minds and just go and play football. I would rather see you all in the Second Division trying to play football than have you stop up by strong-arm methods.'

In the opening minutes, with thousands locked outside, United looked threatening, but Dobing soon took control and forced Gaskell into making a save at full stretch. Foulkes then blocked a shot from Harley, before Charlton completely miskicked in front of goal.

But it was City who took the lead in the ninth minute. Dobing once again broke away and, as the United defence waited on what looked to be an obvious pass to Hayes, the City inside-forward switched the ball to Harley and his shot squeezed past both Gaskell and the post.

The goal did nothing to calm things down, as the game teetered on a knife edge and tempers became more and more frayed. In the twenty-second minute, it looked as if the dividing line had been overstepped and Harley was sent off following a tackle on Herd, which ripped the United man's sock and cut his shin. Referee George McCabe seemingly pointed towards the tunnel as he booked the City player, but it turned out that he was only making a point as to any further misdemeanours.

A similar warning was handed out to Crerand and Wagstaff just prior to the interval, as they followed Harley into the referee's notebook, the result of an incident in front of the main stand. The warnings, however, went unheeded, and violence once again broke out in the tunnel moments later as the players left the pitch at half-time.

Looking back, David Wagstaff clearly remembers the game and the incident: 'This thing with Paddy Crerand,' recalled Wagstaff. 'I must have upset him or something and we're walking up the tunnel and he's still in a rage. But I didn't think he'd turn round and thump me one! We were walking up the tunnel and he was about 3 yards in front of me. I had my head down and I don't know what was going through his mind but he must just have thought, "I'll hit him!" He turned round and did. I thought "what's all that about?" I didn't get it. I'd been involved with a few altercations on the pitch as you do, but I think he just lost it. I certainly never expected it.'

According to Crerand, Wagstaff swore at him as they walked up the tunnel and he simply thumped him one, before threatening to do the same to the intervening City trainer. An irate Matt Busby, hearing of the incident, stormed into the dressing room and confronted the United wing-half, who denied knowing anything about it.

Speculation was rife that Crerand had actually been sent off for his involvement in the tunnel incident, as he did not appear alongside his teammates for the restart, but much to the relief of the red contingent, he eventually reappeared a few seconds after the second half commenced, pulling on his jersey.

City almost increased their lead in the fifty-first minute when an opportunist strike from Joe Hayes was blocked on the line by Nobby Stiles, and the United half-back was again in the thick of things as tempers continued to boil over when he became entangled with Dobing following a tackle. The two players wrestled on the ground before being separated and shaking hands as if nothing had happened.

By now, actual instances of football were few and far between. Players were given little time to settle on the ball, as no sooner had they gained possession than they were knocked to the ground by a reckless, or indeed ruthless challenge.

The only real moment of concern that City faced had seen Bobby Kennedy clear a David Herd header off the line, and they had little else to contend with until Law, with around twenty minutes remaining, suddenly decided that it was time to step up a gear and attempt to pull the carpet from below City's feet to save United's season.

Thrice, Dowd in the City goal dived at the Scottish international's feet to deny him a scoring opportunity, but with eight minutes remaining and United's First Division status slowly ebbing away, the two came face to face again.

For some unexplainable reason, David Wagstaff attempted to pass the ball back to his 'keeper from all of 30 yards out, unaware of the lurking Law. Sensing something of a half-chance, Law darted forward as Dowd rushed from his line and dived at the ball. The 'keeper seemingly got a hand to the ball, palming it away from Law's feet, but at the same time he became entangled with the United man, thinking that he had regained possession, unaware that the ball was rolling to safety.

Law went down and the referee immediately pointed to the penalty spot. Dowd, injured in the collision between the two, hotly disputed the referee's decision after receiving treatment, but the official was unmoved, and Quixall placed the ball on the spot for the most important kick of his career.

Silence enveloped the ground, as the United forward stepped back from the ball. Law, crouched facing the opposite goal too nervous to look, was depending on Cantwell to provide a running commentary.

Quixall made no mistake, placing the ball firmly into the left-hand corner of the net.

City, although having enjoyed the majority of the game, still had time to salvage something as the minutes ticked away, but the penalty award, and subsequent goal, had knocked all the fight out of their system. They were simply resigned to the fact that they would be playing Second Division football in a few months' time; something that, although it had still to be confirmed, looked more than certain.

Following the highly charged ninety minutes, with the much-debated ending, the man at the centre of the controversy, Denis Law, said, 'It was a penalty. The goalkeeper had hold of my legs, but I would never have scored! I was going away from the goal and had lost the ball. It was a lucky break for us.'

Harry Dowd, the City goalkeeper, on the other hand was obviously going to have a much different opinion: 'It was never a penalty. I scooped the ball away from Denis's feet and sent it out of play. I can't remember holding his feet, but I did get a kick on the head. I may then have caught hold of him, but the ball was out of play by then and I'm sure the linesman was signalling for a corner.'

Another City player, Fred Eyre, who gained recognition as being the club's first-ever apprentice, watched the action unfold from a seat in the dugout. 'I didn't have a ticket and it was the only space that was really available,' he recalled.

'The atmosphere was electric that night, especially towards the end of the game when it looked as though City were going to win. Then came David Wagstaff's 30- or 40-yard back-pass. You just could not believe it.

'Was it a penalty? No. But then, Harry should never have rushed out of his goal. He should only have come out a little bit and forced Denis wide. He was too impetuous.

'I remember that it was a long time before the spot kick was actually taken as everyone was going mad. Albert Quixall had already placed the ball on the spot and was standing patiently waiting to take the kick, while all around him was mayhem.

'As I was sitting in the dugout, I was also in the tunnel area at half-time and witnessed the Wagstaff/Crerand incident, and I can remember the City trainer Jimmy Meadows chasing the United player and having the visitors' dressing room door slammed in his face.'

But did Fred Eyre think United would get relegated that season instead of his beloved City? 'To be honest, no. We were certainly hoping so, but no, you just never imagined that Manchester United would ever be relegated. They had too many good players at that time, like my hero Denis Law, Bobby Charlton, Pat Crerand, Johnny Giles and Maurice Setters. The problem they had, however, was that they just couldn't gel together.'

This particular 'local derby' fixture also saw football violence raise its somewhat youthful head. For one United supporter, Altrincham-born John Hewitt, who had first watched United as an eight-year-old in the 1954 FA Youth Cup final against Wolves with his father, it was the first time that he had witnessed actual fighting on the terraces.

'In the late 1950s, early 1960s, matches between United and City were obviously very keenly fought, with United mainly enjoying the upper hand results-wise,' recalled John. 'I remember the rival fans being boisterous, but didn't see any signs of violence. Like United, City were not a consistently good side, as it was the end of an era for the likes of Trautmann, Ewing, Barnes, Hannah and Hayes.

'In that crucial and tensely fought relegation battle, the referee awarding the penalty and Quixall ultimately scoring from the spot set off spasmodic fighting and scuffles on the Kippax.

'There had always been something of a keen, respectful rivalry between United supporters and those of other sides; the likes of Tottenham Hotspur, who at this time were undoubtedly one of the top sides.

'Inside Old Trafford, in the early part of the sixties, security for supporters inside the ground, or outside for that matter, did not seem to be a problem. I can remember standing on the Stretford End for an FA Cup tie against Sheffield Wednesday in February 1960 and a few yards away were quite a large group of Wednesday supporters, loudly supporting their team, with one of them holding a large cardboard owl on a long stick!

'I can also remember on various occasions during the early part of the decade, when large hardcore groups of opposing fans would change ends at half-time, walking round to the other end to stand behind the goal their team were attacking. Segregation was not an issue, but things were soon to change.'

Both City and Birmingham had one game remaining and they both sat on thirty-one points. United on the other hand had thirty-two points and two games remaining. All that was required was for United to defeat the already relegated Leyton Orient at Old Trafford three days after their bruising encounter at Maine Road.

The long-term relegated London side put up a spirited performance as they bade farewell to the top flight; so much so, that the Old Trafford crowd subjected the home players to whistling and slow hand-claps, with Giles and Charlton the main targets, in a first half that failed to impress or give any insurance as to First Division safety. Indeed, as the teams went in at half-time, the visitors were a goal in front via a Dunmore back-header in the ninth minute.

Resiliently, Orient held on, but were finally overcome in the fifty-third minute when Quixall won the ball, moving it out towards Giles, who in turn found Charlton. The latter's cross into the area was headed past his own 'keeper by the unfortunate Stan Charlton.

At the open Warwick Road end of the ground, the towering scoreboard showed that City were losing 4-0 at West Ham, as United sought the winner, while at the same time attempted to quell the threat of Gibbs, Dunmore and Bolland.

With nine minutes remaining a huge sigh of relief enveloped the ground, as Orient goalkeeper George failed to hold the ball and Law pounced to give United the lead. Four minutes from time, Charlton – Bobby this time – scored a third for United. They remained a First Division side for another twelve months at least.

The result was something of a confidence-booster for the trip to Wembley, even though the final League fixture, against Nottingham Forest, was lost 3-2. But even without that victory over Leyton Orient, First Division safety was guaranteed as City lost 6-1 at West Ham. Birmingham had also managed to finish their campaign on something of a high, beating Leicester City 3-2.

Against Nottingham Forest, Matt Busby had made a handful of changes to his starting XI, bringing Shay Brennan back into the fold albeit at left-half in place of Maurice Setters, who had been carried off against Arsenal and taken to hospital for an X-ray on a badly sprained ankle, but had surprisingly returned to the side for the game against Orient. Frank Haydock and Denis Walker also made appearances, stepping up from the Central League side to replace Bill Foulkes and Bobby Charlton. Johnny Giles moved from inside-right to inside-left, while Stiles moved from half-back to inside-forward.

For Stiles, the Forest game was to bring disappointment, as he aggravated a thigh injury, which all but forced him out of the forthcoming Wembley showpiece. However, following treatment and a light training session, alongside other recent treatment-table occupants – Bill Foulkes, Bobby Charlton, Denis Law and Maurice Setters – the diminutive wing-half refused to be ruled out, although his chances of playing were certainly remote.

Busby refused to be drawn about the possibility of Stiles making the Wembley starting XI, telling reporters lingering around Old Trafford in the hope of picking up any scraps of information in relation to the big day, that 'no decision can be made yet, about announcing the team'.

United left the cauldron of pre-final atmosphere in Manchester for the relative peace and tranquillity of Weybridge in Surrey for the final couple of days in their build-up to the Wembley showpiece; however, along with Nobby Stiles, two others in the travelling party were there simply for the ride.

Over the past month, Busby had gone with the following line-up: Gaskell, Dunne, Cantwell, Crerand, Foulkes, Stiles or Setters, Quixall, Giles, Herd, Law and Charlton. Shay Brennan had played every League game at right-back, up until the Sheffield Wednesday defeat on 1 May (although he had not played in the semi-final), before losing his place to Tony Dunne, who had only recently returned to the side at left-back. David Gaskell, who had begun the season as first-choice 'keeper, was another who had only recently returned to side, taking over from Harry Gregg against Wolves the week before the semi-final. He had also experienced something of a torrid afternoon against Forest in that final League fixture of the season, punching what was to be the winner for the home side into his own net, so his selection was another that Busby had to give much consideration to.

With the United players and officials only a few miles from the twin towers, the supporters, now gripped in cup fever, were beginning to filter out of Manchester and head south to London. At Piccadilly station, ticket touts were finding it difficult to offload whatever tickets they still had, asking £5 10s for £2 5s tickets, or £6 for £3 ones, while at Oxford Road station, supporters awaiting the 12.15 a.m. 'cup-special' eagerly sought any spares.

But as those United supporters journeyed south, Busby had decided on his Wembley XI, leaving out Harry Gregg and Shay Brennan and settling for Gaskell, Dunne, Cantwell, Crerand, Foulkes, Setters, Giles, Quixall, Herd, Law and Charlton. There was obvious disappointment for both players, as they had formed part of the United defence in the first four rounds of the competition, and it was only in recent weeks that they had found themselves omitted from the first team.

Rumours were rife that Gregg, who had injured a hand in the reserve match the previous Saturday, had sought a showdown with Busby, having set his heart on a return to Wembley following the disappointment of the 1958 final. The United manager, however, simply said that 'Harry has taken it well'.

Having finished in fourth place in the First Division, Leicester City were firm favourites to lift the cup, with the newspaper journalists seemingly split 50/50 in their opinions, although they were quick to point out that United were simply a team that you couldn't trust, with so many 'ifs' and 'buts' surrounding them. Matt Busby, however, had the belief and confidence that his team would succeed at Wembley where his previous two (or perhaps that should read 'one', as the 1958 appearance was in reality Jimmy Murphy's), had failed. This was in fact his sixth cup final appearance, having played in two for Manchester City.

'We have been playing cup-tie style, full-pressure stuff ever since the freeze and the relegation danger that threatened. Now the tension is off,' said the United manager, while adding, 'we have a fit team of top-class players who will be all out to win. Take it from me; we will be having a go.'

So, the scene was set, with Wembley ready to rake in record gate receipts of around £85,000, with the cheapest tickets 7s 6d (less than 40p) and the dearest 63s (£3.15p). As Busby went round his team, giving last-minute encouragement, he was to find only ten of his players in the dressing room. Missing was Pat Crerand, with the wing-half, wishing to savour the occasion to the full, having wandered out to the mouth of the tunnel to listen to the singing of the traditional cup-final anthem, 'Abide With Me'.

With Crerand having returned to his teammates and the last notes of the famous hymn drifting off into the warm north London air, it was time to leave the confines of the dressing room and let the football decide who was going to walk up the steps to lift the FA Cup.

Leicester City attacked almost from the kick-off, hoping to catch United cold, knowing full well that confidence was perhaps something that their rivals would have to build during the course of the game, and if they could establish an early lead, then the trophy might well be theirs. But by the end of the ninety-minutes, it was a lethargic Filbert Street side who trooped, heads down, off the Wembley pitch, totally outplayed by a rampant United side thanks to a 'treble Scotch' of Pat Crerand's masterly midfield performance, Denis Law's amazing dexterity and David Herd's decisive eye for goal.

Although starting brightly, Leicester were soon on the back foot, as United settled down, casting aside the opinion that they were a team of individuals incapable of producing the teamwork and the blend necessary to produce success.

Midweek rain had softened the pitch, making it ideal for the football that United produced, and reducing Leicester to also-rans in every department, incapable of playing the type of football that they had displayed throughout the past season. To many their overall performance was a great disappointment. Even if they had performed to their capabilities, they would have been unable to live with United that afternoon, as they had nothing to match Busby's tartan trio.

Early on, a misheaded attempt to clear by Crerand caused Gaskell a problem and the ball wobbled dangerously around the United 6-yard area before it was properly cleared. Meanwhile, at the opposite end, Banks had to be alert to save at the feet of the onrushing Law as Giles sent an inviting pass into the area.

Leicester were well regimented in defence, often playing six across the back in an effort to stem the red waves that were expected to surge up the Wembley pitch, and relied on quick counterattacks, but they often neglected the midfield, an area of the vast Wembley pitch where the game was won for United, mainly through the industry of the impeccable Pat Crerand.

While Crerand controlled the middle of the pitch, Denis Law teased and tormented the Leicester defence, like a matador with the bull, but instead of an ear, the devilish Scot was to secure a more valuable trophy.

It was Law who had created the first clear-cut chance of the game, sliding the ball through towards Quixall, but on this occasion he failed to reach it and Leicester broke away. Crerand and Dunne failed to prevent Stringfellow's run and the Leicester outside-left's inviting ball across the face of the United goal was turned away by Cantwell at the expense of a corner. Nudged awake by this near miss, United suddenly took control of the game and seldom let go.

Giles had already missed from close range and Charlton had shot into the open arms of Banks as the game hung on a thread. Suddenly, United sprang into life. Herd found Law standing on the penalty spot with a short pass and the ball was swiftly turned into the path of Charlton, but Banks in the Leicester goal blocked and held the shot, before quickly clearing.

The 'keeper's clearance proved to be a little too hurried, as Gibson just failed to reach the ball and it was pounced on by Crerand, who pushed forward from midfield and from the left side of the penalty area sent a square pass to Law. The noise of the crowd seemed to quieten, as the United No. 10 deftly controlled the ball with a single touch and, although having his back to goal, turned and shot past Banks into the left-hand corner, restoring the volume, certainly from the red contingent, to full blast.

Having gained the advantage, there was now only going to be one winner, although throughout the game, David Gaskell must have given his teammates, United management and supporters heart failure, as he treated the ball as if it were red hot, fumbling the easiest of shots and crosses. But thankfully, Leicester did not put him under pressure too often, or United's superiority might have been tested a little more severely.

Within five minutes of taking the lead, United were almost 2-0 in front. Law evaded an Appleton tackle near the halfway line and dashed clear, leaving two bemused defenders in his wake. Glancing sideways, he spotted David Herd and flicked the ball into the path of his centre-forward, who casually took the ball in his stride before rounding Banks and slipping the ball towards goal. Unfortunately, both Norman and McLintock were on hand to clear the danger.

Leicester began the second half looking like a different team, and for a brief spell they did enjoy most of the play, although they did not have the hunger or indeed the ability of their opponents. Their attacks were competently dealt with by the United defence, except on one occasion when Gaskell dropped Gibson's cross and, as the goalkeeper looked anxiously for the ball, Cross shot past the post.

Twelve minutes into the second half, however, United increased their lead. The fumbling Gaskell for once held a Gibson cross cleanly and cleared upfield to the feet of the elusive Giles on the right. The Irishman in turn swung the ball out to Charlton who, unchallenged, fired the ball towards the Leicester goal. Banks dived, but could only manage to push the ball out to the feet of Herd, who was certainly not going to miss from 4 yards out.

Two goals in front and certainly not looking in any danger of losing the game, United grew in confidence, pushing the ball around the vast Wembley pitch in a sometimes casual manner. Giles and Quixall combined in an often telepathic relationship, while Law strutted like a blond-headed peacock, and Crerand pulled the strings.

Rather surprisingly, United eased up and, with the effectiveness of Herd temporarily reduced due to a knock, they paid the ultimate price with ten minutes still to play. Following a save, Gaskell was penalised for taking too many steps with the ball and, from the resulting free-kick, Keyworth, in a packed goalmouth, threw himself at McLintock's centre to head home.

Were the performances of the previous weeks and months about to return and haunt Busby's team, the game about to slip out of United's grasp, having held the initiative for so long?

Leicester pushed forward again in search of an equaliser, more in hope than anything else, but their fate was soon sealed, as United had no intentions of allowing their opponents the opportunity to draw level, never mind snatch the cup from their grasp. Just as casually as they had lost the goal, United simply slipped up a gear, and with five minutes remaining a Giles cross was dropped by Banks who, like his United counterpart, had not enjoyed the best of afternoons. He had been more than fortunate when a Law header flashed past him, hit the post and rebounded into his arms but, having fumbled the ball, could only look on in agony as Herd snatched his second of the afternoon and sealed victory for United.

As the final whistle echoed around Wembley, the red-shirted players embraced one another in joyous celebration, with Matt Busby hurrying onto the pitch to share in the moment and salute his players. Celebrations continued in the confines of the Wembley south dressing room following the presentation of the trophy and the customary lap of honour, where Matt Busby said, 'It was a wonderful game from our point of view. Only once during it did I have any qualms and that was for five or ten minutes after half-time when we lost our way a little. But I didn't feel we were in serious trouble any time afterwards, not even when Leicester got a goal back.

'We had a feeling we could beat them after our two meetings in the League over the Easter holidays. We got only one point from those two matches, but my players felt Leicester were inclined to leave big, open gaps which we could work with profit on the vast Wembley pitch.'

Although he declined to pick out any individuals, he did say, 'Our half-back line did terrific work. Crerand and Setters really took a grip on things in midfield.'

Perhaps Busby was not prepared to select a Man of the Match, but most were of the opinion that there was one player amongst the twenty-two whose performance stood out: Denis Law. The Aberdonian had come a long way from the day of an impromptu kick about in the Huddersfield Town car park, when manager Bill Shankly called out all his office staff to admire the teenage genius at play.

Although he was not referring to the 'King of Old Trafford', when W. S. Gilbert wrote *Iolanthe* and penned, 'The law is the true embodiment. Of everything that's excellent. It has no kind of fault or flaw,' he might well have been writing about Matt Busby's No. 10.

As the champagne corks popped and the music played, with three security guards babysitting the cup, amid the noise and clamour of United's celebration party at the Savoy Hotel in London, the praise of Law continued, with teammate Maurice Setters adding, 'Denis was fabulous. Once we saw him play like the ace he is, it was a pushover.' Setters also had another reason for celebrating: 'I never had any doubt of the result. In fact, I gave £200-to-£1 two weeks ago that we would win.' Not far from the official celebrations, jubilant United supporters thronged the West End of the capital, giving the bars and clubs bumper Saturday-night takings.

United returned to Manchester the following day on a special train that carried not just the cup-winners, their wives and the rest of the United management and staff, but also 100 bottles of champagne, several hundred bottles of beer and fruit juice, and 200 lamb cutlets – at least it did when it was given a rousing departure from London's St Pancras station. Even the station announcer got into the swing of things, with the loudspeakers echoing, 'Three cheers for the Manchester team.' The front of the train carried a special placard of red letters on a white background: 'Manchester United FA Cup Winners 1963'.

The food and drink was enjoyed by 250 or so on board as it travelled towards Manchester, where an estimated 200,000 awaited to give the FA Cup winners a tumultuous welcome. The crowds began gathering in the city centre some three hours before the train was due to arrive at 8.30 p.m. Their wait, however, was extended by some twenty-five minutes, as the engine ran out of steam, ironically at Leicester!

Having eventually arrived back in Manchester, the players climbed aboard an open-top bus for the crawl through the city streets, where more than 400 were injured, 10 seriously, while another had a heart attack. A fleet of ambulances ferried the casualties to hospital. Many of those hurt suffered foot injuries, having been pushed under the hooves of the mounted police horses. In Mosley Street, the crowd managed to break through a crash barrier and a wall of policemen, cutting off the team coach from the rest of the six-coach party.

As the parade drew closer to the town hall, the scenes became more chaotic, with policemen pushed to the ground as the crowds surged forward. From the huge new Piccadilly Plaza Hotel, which was still under construction, workmen threw streamers, while outside the town hall, many climbed the Albert Memorial for a better view and a huge roar erupted as the triumphant team left the coach for the official welcome home from the Lord Mayor.

The coach driver was later to admit, 'This has been the most frightening drive of my life. Half the city must have turned out.'

Following that Wembley success, Matt Busby proclaimed, 'We are back in Europe. We are back.' True enough, but there was still a long way to go, as surely not even Matt Busby and his trusted assistant Jimmy Murphy could take Manchester United from the jaws of relegation to the peak of European and domestic football in such a short space of time.

Or could they?

5

THE ONLY WAY IS UP

Had United performed in a similar fashion over the previous ten months as they did under the twin towers of Wembley stadium, then there would have certainly not have been any nail-biting finale to a season which brought the first piece of silverware to Old Trafford since the League championship of 1956/57. Many performances had been dire to say the least, but how did the season slip into such disarray, with almost fatal consequences?

Matt Busby professed that the team were 'knitting together', which is true, although in the post-Christmas period the only 'new' face was that of Pat Crerand. But there were hints that the problem was more underlying, with unrest in the dressing room and complaints as to how and what was and was not being done while training. Obviously everyone, including the players, had their thoughts on why things were going wrong, although there was little in the way of direct finger-pointing. But with tempers becoming frayed on the training ground, and harder than normal tackles by some players on others that they felt were not pulling their weight, it was obvious that something was wrong.

Training fell into the hands of Jack Crompton, an old-school gentleman, assisted by John Aston, one of his teammates from the 1948 Cup final side. Jimmy Murphy, having rescued the club from oblivion and provided relentless support for the recovering Matt Busby, had stepped out of the spotlight and returned to the coaching of the younger club employees. Busby, however, was apparently seldom seen prior to matchdays.

Crompton's training methods were debated and complained about, but Busby rightly stood by his man, while a finger was also pointed at captain Noel Cantwell for trying to disrupt the dressing room. The Irishman had moved north from the deep-thinking footballing school of West Ham, where after training some of the players would meet in a nearby café to discuss tactics and the game in general over a pot of tea, using sugar cubes, along with salt and pepper pots, to plan out moves for future games. The United manager had no problem with either player or trainer and allowed the problems to simply fizzle out.

There was also another factor to be considered in why there were numerous poor performances and surprising results: match fixing.

Players, unlike those of today, were not paid a fortune, and any source of extra money was certainly looked into and always appreciated, as only the very top stars could possibly earn extra from any off-the-field endorsements. So when three Sheffield Wednesday players – Peter Swan, Tony Kay and David Layne – were given the opportunity of earning some additional income, after one of them met up with Charlton Athletic's Jimmy Gauld, the named ringleader, they placed £50 each on their team to lose at Ipswich Town on 1 December 1962. Wednesday duly lost 2-0.

It wasn't until January 1965, following exposure from the *People* newspaper which led to the case being taken to court, with those involved convicted and jailed, that it was revealed that such irregularities had been taking place since 1959.

At Old Trafford, there was also more than a hint that such underhand goings-on had been taking place in 1963, and even before for that matter, with those involved simply fortunate that they were not, like those mentioned above, caught in the act. Had the quartet, or perhaps even more, found themselves under investigation, then the history of Manchester United today might have looked slightly different. Perhaps their involvement conjures up yet another possibility as to why things were not as they should have been at this particular time.

Harry Gregg spoke of the subject in later years, writing in his book, *Harry's Game*, 'Yes, match-fixing went on at the biggest club in the world. They know who they are and the shame will haunt them for the rest of their lives.' The goalkeeper also claimed that Matt Busby was aware of the goings-on, but was powerless to do anything about it. 'If he had blown the whistle, everything he had stood for, and the work he had put into the club following the Munich air crash, would have been undone,' Gregg was quoted as saying. 'His instinct would have been to expose them but he put the club first.'

So, was the odd defeat more than simply a poor team performance? We will never know, as those involved would never admit to such an involvement.

There is, however, something of a strange postscript to the match-fixing episode, if we move to July 1966 and a letter to the *Times*, signed by Matt Busby, his Manchester City counterpart Joe Mercer, Malcolm Musgrove – chairman of the Professional Footballers Association, the Association's secretary Cliff Lloyd, and three others.

The open letter asks for some consideration to be given to the players who had been jailed for their involvement in the match fixing, as in most professions where suspension follows, it is possible for the guilty person to rehabilitate and get back into everyday life after a short period of time. It also mentions that 'some of them were quite clearly duped and misled by stronger and more vicious personalities'. The bans were eventually lifted in 1972 following further approaches from Matt Busby and a Member of Parliament.

Back at Old Trafford, to their credit, any differences that the players had were put to one side and they showed that they could gel together when the need arose or the big occasion beckoned, turning Wembley into a launching pad for better things.

Matt Busby was confident that his team had turned the corner so to speak, and said, 'We are looking forward optimistically to the coming season. Last season's League results were disappointing. I'm not denying that many times in League matches the side didn't play well. But there were other occasions when they did – yet lost games and points. We didn't get going last season until Wembley.

'Even when things were going wrong – and quite frankly I was worried – I was certain that the talent was there. We found the blend at last – and we are all hoping to start where we left off last season. If we can repeat that form we must do well and I'm certain too that the present staff are more than good enough. Yes, I think we have the resources to take us towards our double objective of the League title and so entry into the European Cup.'

The European Cup was certainly Busby's main objective, driven on by demons which still haunted him, along with the determination to take United to the pinnacle of European football. However, one other reason offered up for the poor performances during, not just season 1962/63, but those of the previous couple of years, by those who stood on the terraces and sat in the stands, was quite simply that the players were not good enough.

This statement, and not the manager's previously mentioned opinion, was certainly a justifiable one, and something that was confirmed on the afternoon of 13 August at Goodison Park, Liverpool.

Pre-season fixtures had consisted of a mere three games. The first, ninety minutes in Glasgow where they lost 2-1 to the Glasgow Select, and another outing seven days later in Germany, against Eintracht Frankfurt, where they they could certainly claim 'they were robbed' – but this was only in the dressing room, with the on-field action ending in a goal apiece.

The third game was a few miles along the East Lancs Road where, as FA Cup winners, they contested the FA Charity Shield in the usual domestic pre-season curtain raiser facing League Champions Everton. But it was ninety minutes that saw United thrust back towards the substandard play of the previous campaign.

By the second half, the home side were arrogantly strutting around the familiar Goodison Park pitch, displaying little in the way of charity to their visitors. United's suspect defence had long since crumbled, and as the game progressed their tempers became frayed, with the sometimes robust tackling annoying the home crowd.

Despite Everton's undoubted superiority, it was not until three minutes before the break that they took the lead after Jimmy Gabriel got on to the end of an Alex Young–Alex Scott move to slide the ball past Gaskell.

United had kept their game tight, with close-knit passing, but showed little urgency and in the ninth minute of the second half fell two behind in somewhat bizarre circumstances.

Vernon, Everton's captain, was racing through on goal, only to be fouled inside the United penalty area by Setters. Immediately, referee Crawford pointed to the spot. Vernon himself stepped up to take the kick, but suddenly stopped and feinted simultaneously, with David Gaskell diving sideways in anticipation of the shot. Suddenly Noel Cantwell rushed forward, waving his hand angrily in protest, due to the Evertonian not having taken the kick.

The referee subsequently booked Cantwell and, amid the uproar, Vernon eventually took the kick, but saw it brilliantly stopped by Gaskell. Failing to hold the ball, it rolled out towards Gabriel, but once again the United 'keeper managed to stop the Everton player's shot. Further scenes of mayhem were created by a linesman, waving his flag and pointing at Cantwell, who he considered to be standing inside the area when the kick was taken.

So, the referee ordered the kick to be taken for a third time and, on this occasion, Gaskell was left helpless and the home side found a 2-0 lead.

Law was poor, while Charlton received little support on the wing, and before long United were 3-0 behind. A Vernon pass found Stevens, who dribbled past both Setters and Dunne to beat Gaskell with ease in the seventeenth minute. Temple rubbed in Everton's superiority with a fourth, following a foul on Vernon by Law, for which the Scot was booked.

On Merseyside, Busby had sent out his cup-winning side, but following the disappointing encounter against Everton, he decided to make changes for the opening First Division fixture against Sheffield Wednesday at Hillsborough, bringing Harry Gregg back into the fold and giving the forward line a youthful makeover, with the introduction of Ian Moir, Phil Chisnall and David Sadler.

Moir had last featured in the first team back in September 1962, having begun the season at outside-left, while Chisnall had featured only six times during the previous campaign, the last of those appearances in April and the 2-0 home defeat by Fulham. For Sadler, it had been something of a whirlwind few months, stepping up from the amateur ranks and non-League football to being thrust into the First Division spotlight as a £40 per week professional. This was a decision he had made following much thought as he had set his heart on playing for the Great Britain Olympic team in the 1964 competition.

Having learnt their trade under the watchful eye of Jimmy Murphy, the youngsters did not let their master or Matt Busby down, but with only twelve minutes gone, it looked as though the decision to cast fate to the wind was going to cost United dearly, as Wednesday took a 2-0 lead.

A scrambled Quinn goal and a McAnearney penalty, awarded for an unnecessary tackle on Holliday by Moir, put the home side in front. As it began to look as though the game might slip away from United, Moir made up for his previous mistake in the twenty-seventh minute when he burst down the middle, chasing a pass from Crerand, before whipping the ball past Springett in the Wednesday goal.

United now had something to fight for, and thanks to the youthful enthusiasm of the three youngsters and the grit of Setters and Law, Wednesday were going to have to fight for their expected two points.

Charlton put United level twelve minutes into the second half with a thunderbolt from 25 yards, but the home side thought that they had regained the upper hand and the scent of victory in the sixty-sixth minute, when Holliday nodded home a deflected Finney cross.

Last season, perhaps United would have succumbed to the Owls, but despite the trouncing at Goodison, they looked to have added something extra to their game, and in the seventy-eighth minute Charlton claimed his second, this time from a mere 20 yards, and United had claimed a point.

'Fire in their bellies,' claimed James Mossop of the *Sunday Express*, while Alan Thompson of the *Daily Express* decided that United had shown 'little cohesion and much petulance'. No matter what, it was a well-earned point and what could be considered an ideal start, one that certainly pleased the supporters.

It didn't, however, please everyone connected with the club, as Johnny Giles and Albert Quixall, unhappy at being left out of the team for the opening-day fixture, put in transfer requests, which were granted by the United board a matter of days after the season kicked off. David Herd, the other player left out, simply shrugged his shoulders and got on with it, saying that he realised that he had not been playing well. He added, 'Any talk of me following Johnny Giles and Albert Quixall in asking for a transfer is so much rubbish. There are forty-one matches left and I think I should get into a few of them.'

Quixall, having reconsidered things, withdrew his transfer request, much to the delight of Matt Busby, but Giles stuck to his guns and within a matter of days was banished from Old Trafford, heading over the Pennines to join Leeds United in a £32,000 deal.

Blackburn Rovers had made the first move for Giles, while at the same time expressing an interest in Quixall, but were caught out by the speed of Don Revie's approach. The suddenness of the move surprised many, but Giles himself wasn't totally shocked and suggested that it was not simply a poor performance at Goodison in the Charity Shield, but went all the way back to another under-par outing in the FA Cup semi-final against Tottenham in April 1962. He also said that he didn't think that he had been totally forgiven and had been criticised by both Matt Busby and Jimmy Murphy.

After joining Leeds, Giles talked about his departure from United, pointing out, 'There was not a good team spirit there at the time, which indeed, explains why the club struggled in the relegation zone for most of last season. The players lost confidence and directed their frustration at each other, forcing Busby to hold a crisis meeting with the players.'

As for Giles saying that he had been criticised by Jimmy Murphy, this could simply be little more than newspaper talk, as Jimmy Murphy Jnr was quick to point out that Giles was 'one of his (*Jimmy Murphy's*) boys, a golden apple'. He went on to say, 'Giles had played at outside-right in 1963 Cup final; at inside-right was Quixall. Giles wanted more regular football in his favoured position of inside-forward and had a meeting with Matt. Matt favoured Quixall (*he had paid £45,000 for him in August 1958*) so Giles asked for a move.

'Jimmy on the other hand favoured Giles, but Matt's view prevailed and Giles moved to Leeds United.

'I always maintain Giles is unique in that he is the only homegrown player to better himself on leaving United.

'So, who was right, Matt or Jimmy?

'Quixall was thirty and a talented player but was prone to "up and down" performances. Giles was twenty-two, gifted with foresight and two good feet; good passer both long and short. He cost Leeds £32,500 and would develop into one of the best midfield players of the 1960s, going on to win two championships and two UEFA Cups.

'Events would prove Jimmy knew what he was talking about.'

Had the sale of Giles not been so sudden, then United might have obtained a much higher price for the sought-after inside-forward, as Blackburn Rovers admitted that they would also have been interested in signing him and would also have paid a higher fee to secure his services. Unfortunately, they were taken by surprise at the speed of the whole transfer.

So Giles was gone and his presence was certainly not missed, as United suddenly found the right blend and stormed to the top of the First Division, beating Ipswich 2-0 at Old Trafford, gaining more than revenge against current Champions Everton with a 5-1 win, again at Old Trafford, and in the return match with Ipswich at Portman Road, stating their intentions for the months ahead with an emphatic 7-2 victory.

The Old Trafford victory over Ipswich was inspired by a superb Denis Law performance, with a Harry Gregg penalty save thrown in for good measure, while the turnaround against Everton was down to more than a gritty fight for two points, as there was some hurt pride to restore, as the smirks and mickey-taking that accompanied the Goodison Park side's Charity Shield win were hurled back into the Merseysiders' faces. It had been many years since Old Trafford had witnessed such a clinical performance.

'I suppose we asked for this,' admitted Everton right-half Jimmy Gabriel. 'We took the mickey a bit in the Charity Shield, and it put them in this mood for today. You could see they wanted revenge – and they certainly took it.'

Busby, while happy with the sudden transformation, made it more than clear to his players what was expected of them, stating, 'From now any player who feels he cannot give 100 per cent for Manchester United, whether he is a great name in the first team or an unknown in the junior side, must get out now.

'Perhaps one of the best things I have done for this club was to tell Albert Quixall and Johnny Giles they could get out as fast as they liked when they asked for a transfer after being dropped.

'The result was that every other member of the staff knew they were playing for their jobs as well as their places in the first team.

'The youngsters in particular were impressed by my decision and these are the boys I so very much want to get the idea that the club comes before everything else.'

The promotion of those young players, however, was very much down to Jimmy Murphy rather than Matt Busby. 'It was more or less 95 per cent Jimmy's decision,' his son revealed. 'David Meek has written "Jimmy would say that player 'A' is ready and Matt would put him in." This, you must remember, was the era of the majority of games being on a Saturday. If Matt was at, say Spurs, the Reserves would be at Old Trafford, or if the first team was at home, the reserves could be at somewhere like Bolton. Matt would rarely or perhaps never see some of the Reserves play, unless they were playing during the week.

'The coaches would meet each Sunday for lunch at a pub near to Old Trafford and report on each team's performance from the previous day.

'Matt was in charge of the first-team members and Jimmy the remaining twenty-four, or however many pros, and all the amateurs and juniors. Along with Bert Whalley, he would work two nights a week with these younger players.

'Remember, in those days, there were no substitutes, you either played or you didn't, this is why Jimmy's judgement was crucial. He was vital in his role and luckily for Matt, he was a genius in his ability with young players.'

Jimmy Murphy was also very much involved in the arrival of most of the young players at the club, while at the same time had a big say in who would be released. As most of them were youngsters, it would be Jimmy who gave them the bad news.

The transformation to table-toppers was as swift as that of the decline that saw them become relegation fodder, catching the most staunch supporter along the 'Popular Side' on United Road, or behind the goal on the Stretford End (now becoming the heartbeat of the club's vocal support) by surprise. They were not, however, going to be drawn into a false sense security, with an instant feeling that the First Division championship was suddenly about to make a triumphant return to Old Trafford. The past couple of seasons were still firmly etched into the memory.

The headlines, however, were now completely positive: 'New Boys Power A Merciless Revenge', 'Busby's New Babes Give Champions Taste of Their Own Medicine', and 'Youth To The Fore at Old Trafford Again' provided the introductions in the reports following the victory over Everton, while 'Right Blend Found by Manchester United' and 'Ipswich Baffled by United's Skill', proclaimed the *Daily Telegraph* and the *Guardian* respectively following the 7-2 victory in East Anglia.

Jimmy Murphy's youth academy had once again come up trumps, although Moir and Chisnall had long vacated the junior ranks, but the lessons had been learnt and their goals – two for Aberdonian Moir and three for Stretford-born Chisnall – had gone towards achieving top spot. But perhaps the main reason behind the dramatic change in fortune lay behind the return to form of Denis Law, who was leading the pack on the goal front, having scored against Ipswich (at home), followed by a double against Everton and then a hat-trick against Ipswich at Portman Road. It had taken the Scot the opening sixteen games of the previous season to get near to that figure.

Once at the top, everyone wants to knock you off that summit, or at least deny you victory, and at a rain-soaked St Andrews, Birmingham City stemmed the recent flow of goals and stole a point off the leaders with a goal fourteen minutes from time. However, United's football in those opening fixtures gave out the clear message that they had blown away the cobwebs, reclaimed the flare and panache, and it would indeed require some sterling performances from the other clubs if someone was going to deny Manchester United the championship.

Blackpool were beaten 3-0 and could have returned home on the end of a much heavier defeat had it not been for the heroics of goalkeeper Tony Waiters, while three days later on 14 September West Bromwich Albion arrived at Old Trafford unaware that they were about to take part in a game that would be written into the annals of Manchester United.

Up until now, Busby had only made one change to his line-up, Stiles replacing the injured Setters against Everton, but with Denis Law and Ian Moir both failing late fitness tests prior to West Bromwich Albion's visit, he was forced to recall Stiles to take over from Law, the half-back being equally at home as an inside-forward. As for replacing Moir, instead of recalling the experienced Quixall, he decided to introduce the relatively unknown seventeen-year-old Irish schoolboy international George Best to the first-team set-up.

Best was well known in and around the confines of Manchester 16 and also by those who followed the fortunes of United's reserve and youth teams, but to the vast majority of the footballing public, he was simply just another name coming off the United conveyor belt of young players.

West Bromwich Albion had also enjoyed a favourable start to the season and could be found one point behind United at the top of the First Division, so the fixture promised to have something of an edge to it, and no one would have questioned Busby if he had taken a safer route and gone for experience. But following talks with Jimmy Murphy, it was decided to throw the Belfast youngster in at the deep end. And deep end it certainly was, with sharks circling in the form of the tough and highly experienced full-back Welsh international Graham Williams, whose eyes ventured down the pitch to the waif-like Belfast boy tugging at his sleeves as the referee's whistle got the game underway.

If United's attacking options had been somewhat reduced by the absence of Law and to a lesser extent Moir, their defence stood firm, as the visitors, despite their lofty position, did not possess the guile to exploit any slim advantage that they may have had. While the game as a whole lacked the sparkle and entertainment value of the previous half-dozen fixtures, and turned into something of a scrappy and ill-tempered affair, it was an uneventful encounter, marred by petty fouls, and shots at goal being something of a scarcity.

The young Irishman wasn't the only one making his League bow, as West Bromwich Albion had a debutant in the form of nineteen-year-old full-back Crawford, against whom George Best might have enjoyed a more productive afternoon and certainly a less physical ninety minutes than he experienced against Welsh international Graham Williams. The red-shirted youngster was given a first-hand beginner's guide to First Division football, with the Albion defender showing little in the way of compassion to the mop-headed teenager. Indeed, he seemed to relish the confrontation and the derision heaped on him from the United supporters crowded along the touch line, smiling and blowing kisses in their direction after he had shaken the youngster with yet another crunching challenge.

A heavy, over-robust tackle by Williams on Best did not simply subdue the debutant for a while, but also set the tone for the majority of the ninety minutes, as both sides resorted to unnecessary pettiness when it came to physical contact. On one somewhat mysterious occasion, Fenton was left flat out on the pitch with play fully 30 yards away, an incident missed by everyone, including the referee.

Both sets of half-backs outmanoeuvred the inside-forwards of the opposition. With Stiles, for once, finding it difficult adjusting to his forward role and Chisnall completely out of the game, United's thrust and productive play was somewhat stifled and the attack disjointed.

Charlton did much to lift the game and cause a threat to the West Bromwich goal, especially in the lacklustre opening forty-five minutes, moving across the front line in search of an opening, but it was akin to a soloist attempting to lift a complete orchestra out of mediocrity. Faced with the Albion debutant Crawford, he would have been better off remaining on the left and putting the youngster under constant pressure, which would surely have been more productive.

Due to Charlton's wanderings, however, Best was able to seek refuge on the left flank when the going got tough on the right, away from the grinning Williams, but after a breather away from the Welshman's studs and harassment, he returned to show his determination and spirit as he took the ball to, and sometimes past, the experienced defender.

Best's play was often of a high quality and showed the definite hint of promise underneath the immaturity, although he would certainly have been more than happy to have been involved in what was to be the only goal of the game.

Following the goal-less, totally forgettable opening forty-five minutes, with the only real threat of a goal coming when Stiles slammed the ball against the upright as he ran on to a Charlton through-ball, it was still looking as though a 0-0 draw was going to be the outcome. However, in the sixty-fifth minute, Best pushed the ball inside to Stiles, who in turn squared the ball across the face of the Albion penalty area to the unmarked Sadler. Potter moved off his line, but Sadler kept a cool head and directed the ball, left-footed, past the advancing goalkeeper.

Play did improve slightly as the second half progressed, but West Bromwich showed little capability of denting the United defence, while United themselves showed nothing but odd flashes of what they were certainly capable of, putting the visitors' goal under threat on far too few occasions. Towards the end, the game faded rather disappointingly and the spectators began to make their way towards the exit gates before the referee bothered to look at his watch and blow for full-time.

Best failed to make the starting line-up for the following match against Blackpool at Bloomfield Road, the No. 7 shirt going to David Herd, and as the illuminations brightened the promenade a few hundred yards down the road, United's sparkling start to the season dimmed as the home side, second from the foot of the table, snatched a surprise, yet deserved, 1-0 victory.

Having missed two games through injury, Law returned to the fold, but his reappearance against Arsenal at Highbury made little difference to a team that Albert Barham in the *Guardian* considered 'were curiously inconsistent and disappointing. Their form was a throwback to the unpredictability of last season.'

Losing by the odd goal in three, United left the marble halls of Highbury feeling rather hard done by, as with the score at 1-1 and half-time approaching, Charlton, having moments earlier almost shattered the crossbar, saw a volley seemingly carried over the line by Arsenal 'keeper McKechnie, only for the ball to be cleared upfield with no notice paid to the cries of the United players and support by the referee.

As it was, Arsenal snatched a second eight minutes from time to send United home empty-handed and no longer in pole position, Nottingham Forest having claimed top spot with a one-point lead.

If there was one thing that might derail United's championship hopes, it was discipline. There was a strong aggressive streak running through this United side, not that it was a totally bad thing, as the challenge ahead was as physical as it was mental, and without a strong backbone, teams who lacked the skill factor to compete against Busby's team would simply brush them aside by brute force.

Players such as Bobby Charlton were not known for their physical strength, but when the going got tough Noel Cantwell, Pat Crerand, Maurice Setters, Denis Law and even goalkeeper Harry Gregg came into their own and never shirked a challenge. Unfortunately, there was also a downside to this, with any bookings and sending-offs incurred leading to suspensions, while on occasions, as was seen in the Arsenal game, Law (booked for the fourth time this season) and Crerand took their minds off the matter in hand to get involved in petty feuds.

In his report for the *Sunday Times*, Brain Glanville wrote, 'Law, the eternal, incorrigible "*enfant terrible*", covered his usual acres of ground, and as usual interspersed moments of sheer inspiration with moments of hot temper which got him into trouble with the referee. At one point – such is the unsentimentality of football – he was chased and brought down by Baker, with whom, less than two years ago, he was sharing a flat and playing in Turin.'

Having won the FA Cup, Matt Busby had regained a foothold on the European football ladder, albeit in the Cup Winners' Cup rather than the more prestigious European Cup, and although the ultimate dream was to get back into the latter competition, its lesser relation would certainly do for now. This was a stepping stone of which Albert Barham of the *Guardian* wrote, 'It has taken Matt Busby five years to rebuild a side shattered at Munich. They are not yet nearly as good as the "Busby Babes" of the fifties but, if they learn as they go along, they could become serious contenders for this trophy.'

The first-round draw paired United with Dutch side Willem from Tilburg, a small-time Second Division outfit made up of part-time players, who prior to the game would have acclaimed anything smaller than a 5-0 score for their visitors as a victory. On the night, they were certainly not overcome by nerves, and indeed gained more than their hoped-for moral victory with a creditable 1-1 draw.

In the build-up to the game, the Willem players, who earned around £300-500 a year and played in front of average attendances of around 8,000, stepped up training to four evenings a week, experimenting with a 'British style' 4-2-4 formation. But on the night, the visitors failed to put their hosts to the sword in the Feijenoord Stadium. They looked lazy and uninterested, playing disjointed football, with the sending-off of David Herd, ten minutes from time, adding to a dismal evening in Rotterdam.

The home side surprisingly took the lead in the ninth minute, when Koopal took a lucky rebound off a United defender before squaring the ball to Louer, who blasted the ball high into the roof of Gregg's net. But within three minutes, United were level through Herd, who walked the ball into the net following good work from Setters.

Law thought he had given United the lead when he had the ball in the net prior to the interval, but it was disallowed for offside, while in the opening throes of the second half, the same player missed a simple opportunity from a Herd centre. The United No. 10 also hit the post with a header fifteen minutes from time, but amid the sighs of relief from the United players were the boos from the Dutch support when the referee failed to award a goal after a Koopal effort was thought to have crossed the line.

Herd's dismissal for a retaliatory foul on Willem captain Brooymans with ten minutes remaining simply rounded up United's evening, despite many feeling that the decision was a harsh one.

The Dutch FA defended the United player and notified UEFA that they considered the punishment given to Herd as being too heavy: 'We are saying that we are very sorry and upset, and that under the circumstances Herd was very badly punished.' Willem captain Jan Brooymans also echoed his support of his alleged assailant, saying, 'It was a mistake for Herd to be sent off. All the boys thought as I did. It was not a foul I would call serious. I am a hard-tackling man, and understand a player's reaction in the heat of the game.'

Despite their support and the feelings of UEFA regarding the matter, Herd was automatically banned for the second leg.

Back on home soil and League business, last season's cup final opponents Leicester City were once again beaten 3-1, with Herd getting over his unfortunate experience in Holland by netting a double with Setters grabbing the other. But a 1-1 draw at Stamford Bridge on 2 October saw United hauled off the top of the table by Tottenham, who had a one-point advantage as well as a game in hand. This, however, was only for three days, as a bruising, mediocre 1-0 victory at Bolton restored them into top spot on goal average above the Londoners.

Willem arrived in Manchester for the second leg of their Cup Winners' Cup tie and were caught on the night like a rabbit in a car's headlights, as United tore them apart, rattling home six goals to their visitors' one, with Denis Law claiming his second hat-trick of the season. Charlton, Chisnall and Setters claimed the others, with two more disallowed.

United's current form, which was normally entertaining, free-flowing, attacking play causing the opposition innumerable problems, also had its plus points for those clubs who struggled to match the star-studded red shirts, as it brought in additional revenue from crowds who flocked to the grounds to witness what was being called the rebirth of Busby's team.

A fortunate 2-1 win at the City Ground, Nottingham, with the winning goal coming from a Quixall cross that floated lazily into the net, kept United on top, but suddenly the storm clouds appeared on the horizon and West Ham United, who played almost half the game with only ten men, left Old Trafford with both points on 26 October, following their 1-0 victory. Two days later Blackburn Rovers snatched a point from the United citadel with an eighty-ninth-minute equaliser, securing a 2-2 draw. Then, the opening fixture of November ended in a 2-0 defeat at Wolverhampton, leaving United in third place, two points behind new leaders Sheffield United. Had the bubble burst?

Perhaps it hadn't exactly burst, but in Matt Busby's eyes it had become a little deflated, losing five points in three games, which did little to appease the manager. Although he wasn't exactly renowned for diving into the transfer market without just cause, more often than not allowing any of his out-of-form players to play their way back into things, when he did decide to open the cheque-book, those transfer dealings would materialise out of the blue, catching everyone, which often also included the player targeted, completely unaware. Such was the signing of Chelsea's twenty-two-year-old Welsh international forward Graham Moore.

A telephone call to Stamford Bridge late on the Monday night following the defeat at Wolves set the deal in motion, and after the player discussed the move with his wife, the £35,000 (or £38,000 depending which paper you read) transfer was given the green light. Moore had been dropped by Chelsea during the previous month, but had returned to their team that weekend. But it was now obvious that he was surplus to requirements at Stamford Bridge. manager Tommy Docherty believed that the Welshman should have been scoring more goals, with his return of fourteen from sixty-eight outings not considered good enough, hence his decision to release the player. Busby on the other hand saw Moore as more of a playmaker rather than a goalscorer.

'We have been interested in him for some time,' explained Busby. 'We see him as the ideal link man. He will occupy one of the inside-forward positions in our League game against Tottenham next Saturday.'

Moore had cost the London club around £30,000 when signed from Cardiff some twenty months previously, and the speed at which the deal was completed caught the player totally by surprise. 'I was shaken when I heard that United were interested in me,' he said. 'I went home and told my wife Rita and she agreed it would be a good move. I've always thought United were a great side, but never expected to play for them.'

Moore's signing also showed Busby's sometimes ruthless side, as the transfer coincided with Phil Chisnall's error which lead to Wolves scoring their second goal. The youngster, instead of booting the ball clear from the edge of his own area, elected to pass back to goalkeeper Harry Gregg, unaware that Ray Crawford was lurking nearby, presenting the Wolves forward with the simplest of scoring chances.

Despite his five League goals during the current campaign and having been a regular in either of the inside-forward positions, the England under-21 international now found himself back in the Central League side.

Moore made his debut against Tottenham Hotspur at Old Trafford on 9 November, a dress rehearsal for the forthcoming European Cup Winners' tie between the two First Division giants, taking the No. 8 shirt from Chisnall. Busby also recalled David Herd after a two-match absence, during which Albert Quixall had shown that he still had what it took to be a Manchester United player, scoring both of the goals in the 2-2 draw against Blackburn Rovers.

With the London side sitting in third place, a point better off than United although having played a game more, they had a reputation as being an excellent footballing side, one that contained the likes of Greaves, Blanchflower, Mackay and White. It was little wonder that the game was eagerly looked forward to, with supporters outside the ground prior to kick-off paying touts £2 for a 7/6d (38p) ticket.

As well as being something of a 'top-of-the-table clash' and a confidence-booster for the forthcoming cup tie, it also gave supporters, not just those of United and Tottenham, but across the country, the opportunity to compare arguably the two best strikers in the English, or indeed the European game, in Denis Law and Jimmy Greaves.

By the end of the day, there would only be one winner.

Graham Moore wasted little time in acclimatising to the Northern air, displaying a wide array of talent, in particular his precise passing which began many an attacking move. But despite his more-than-promising debut, receiving an eight in the 'Form Report' in the *Sunday People*, he was pushed to the side in the Man of the Match ratings by teammate Denis Law, who gave the Tottenham defence a horrendous afternoon.

Fresh from scoring four for Scotland against Norway forty-eight hours previously, Law almost bettered that performance. Instead, he could only claim a hat-trick, with the linesman's upraised flag denying him twice and other opportunities narrowly missing the target.

Few teams could have lived with United as they set about their visitors with a clinical precision that shook Tottenham, and as they headed back to London, they could have little complaint in their 4-1 defeat, perhaps relieved that it was not in fact more. Even their goal was a United effort, Harry Gregg punching the ball into his own net!

Both sides had missed chances before Law gave United the lead five minutes before half-time, heading the ball over the line while lying on the ground. Tottenham protested loudly, for both handball and offside, but to no avail. Five minutes on the other side of the interval, Law thought he had made it 2-0 as he raced through with the linesman's flag remaining down by his side. Rounding Brown in the Spurs goal, he flicked the ball home, but the noise of the crowd had obliterated that of the referee's whistle, who had over-ruled his assistant, deciding that Law was indeed offside. A decision that a Tottenham defender later suggested was wrong.

There was, however, no controversy regarding the second, twelve minutes into the second half, when the revitalised David Herd drove a powerful effort past Brown.

Tottenham pulled one back in the seventy-second minute, but two further goals from the Lawman in the eighty-second and eighty-fifth minutes sealed the points. Both goals came from poor back-passes by Tottenham defenders, with the ever-alert United forward pouncing on the ball before steering it past his Scottish international teammate in the Tottenham goal.

If there had been a debate between the prowess of Law and Greaves prior to the game, there was little doubt as to who could claim the crown as 'Britain's greatest attacking footballer', with

Jimmy Murphy claiming that he was 'the greatest footballer in the world – and that includes Pele and Puskas'. But the hat-trick hero did not dwell on such accolades and was quick to praise his new teammate, saying of Moore, 'He was great. I didn't have to drop back at all.' As in previous games, he had been not only expected to score goals, but to also combine this role with that of a midfield schemer. 'Every time I turned round, Graham was there. I couldn't help but score. I just have to stay up and wait for it. And I didn't have to wait long.'

Moore himself was more than happy with his performance, saying, 'I have never enjoyed myself so much on a football field. I was allowed to play the way I have always wanted to play, do just what I've always felt I should do.

'Nobody told me to watch this or watch that, fit into this plan or that plan. I just went out and played. They set me free.'

Many had questioned Busby's recent purchase, wondering why he had indeed been signed. After this performance, they were left in little doubt as United, who had struggled in recent weeks, took their game up a couple of notches, adding a bit more in the way of control to the middle of the park, while the Welshman's presence also gave some additional support to the front men, in particular Denis Law.

It is said that through every genius there runs a very slight flaw, a small switch that can be monetarily flicked 'on' to plunge the bright shining light into sudden darkness; or perhaps more accurately, the golden rays of sunshine being quickly shrouded in red mist.

An away fixture at Villa Park followed the 4-1 victory over Tottenham and, with the Midlands side fourth from bottom, more of the same was expected from United. But even though Busby was able to field an unchanged side, the United manager could only sit and watch as his team went from sublime to mediocre.

United were caught cold, with Hateley scoring after only thirty-five seconds, but this should only have been something of a minor setback, with the visitors more than able to step it up a gear and haul their way back into the game, and indeed go on to secure a victory.

Law almost equalised straight from the restart following a brilliant move with Charlton, but the game was suddenly put further out of United's reach in the seventeenth minute, when Deakin shot past Gregg from 30 yards. It could, however, quite easily have been three, as Hateley had earlier sent a header crashing against Gregg's crossbar, with the 'keeper well beaten.

With United clearly on the rocks, needing two goals to simply draw level, their game was sent into complete disarray, as was their main source of securing those goals, when Denis Law was sent off in the thirty-third minute.

Deakin, the scorer of Villa's second goal, went in with a sliding tackle, clearing the ball from Law's feet and, as play moved to the opposite end of the pitch, there was something of a scuffle which left the Villa player on the ground injured. Players from both teams converged on the scene, pushing and shoving and, as the referee forced himself into the midst of it all, the Villa player received treatment for a facial injury. Quickly, the referee pulled Law to one side and, following a brief lecture, pointed towards the tunnel as the home support shouted 'off, off, off'. A bottle was thrown from the crowd in the direction of the departing player.

Reduced to ten men, it was an uphill struggle for United and one that they failed to master, going on to concede a further two goals in a performance which came in for much criticism, not just for the sending-off of Law.

In the *Daily Express*, Alan Williams was critical of United and the way that some of their players had been performing, writing, 'I have now seen Manchester United's last three away matches and their form and general discipline has deteriorated each time. There are too many players who seem to be playing with chips on their shoulders.

'I am prepared to believe the players' view that certain referees are apt to clamp down quicker on them than some offenders, but it was most noticeable that when United were on top at Forest a few weeks ago there was never any suggestions of temper.

'But when things are going against them, United appear to get much too ragged for a side of their capabilities.'

Busby professed not to have seen the Law incident, as did Villa manager Joe Mercer, with both claiming to have been 'watching the ball', while the offender, who left Villa Park just after the interval as he had a plane to catch to Scotland from Manchester Airport, told reporters, 'It is hard to say anything at the moment. But there was a scrimmage – and the referee sent me off.'

Law's sending-off also sparked accusations from some of the Villa support regarding the behaviour of sections of the United following, with the *Daily Mirror* publishing details of the accusations under the heading 'Manchester Fans Admit "We Sang Dirty Words"'. In the article, which was printed four days after the match, Bill Goddard, secretary of the Manchester United Supporters Club admitted that 'United fans sang obscenely after Denis Law was sent off at Villa Park', following the accusation made by a Mr F. Salmon, an Aston Villa supporter, who went as far as to send a letter to the Football Association about the United supporters' conduct.

He alleged that 'a large block of Manchester United hooligans spent nearly the whole of the second half bawling obscene words about the referee, Mr J. Carr of Sheffield, to the tune of "For He's A Jolly Good Fellow"'. In his letter, he wrote, 'For all the women and more particularly, the hundreds of small boys, to be subjected to this thing is absolutely unthinkable. As the father of a ten-year-old boy I dread to think of the harm a repetition could add to that already done.'

Daily Mirror reporter Charles Harrold wrote that he had been at the game and that the singing had begun after the referee had disallowed a goal by Quixall, who had been in an offside position when he headed the ball into the net, with the vocal abuse coming from a section of United supporters, among whom were several women and girls, in the middle of the Holte End. He added, 'I recognised the tune they were singing but only once did I catch the words – "for he's a horrible bastard".

'I have never known such an atmosphere of hate or abuse on any ground, as in the minute or so between the incident that ended in Law being sent off and his disappearance from the field.

'There was fighting later on the Holte End terrace and eight policemen went into the crowd to deal with it. Soon afterwards a man was carried from the terrace with his head bandaged after being hit by a flying bottle.'

The United Supporters Club secretary admitted that he had also had complaints from Leicester, Wolverhampton and Birmingham about the conduct of some of the fans and added, 'For the sake of Manchester United they ought to pipe down and behave in a better manner. This sort if thing only does a disservice to a club they ought to be proud to support. Genuine supporters can only be deeply upset about hotheads who drag United's good name into the mud.'

In 1963, it was announced that England was to host the 1966 World Cup finals, and the United directors were honoured when Old Trafford was selected as one of the stadiums where fixtures in Group C would be held. The stadium had changed little over the years, the covering of the Stretford End and the seating in that same area being the largest development undertaken. However, being given some of the prestige World Cup fixtures prompted the board to put their plans for further ground development into motion, and it was announced in December that the club were to build a £250,000 cantilever stand along the United Road side of the ground. 'New Trafford – as it will be after the £250,000 investment in soccer's future,' proclaimed the *Daily Mail* of 18 December with a *Sportsmail* artist's impression of the new stand superimposed onto an aerial view of the present ground.

Although prompting enthusiastic comments from the United support, the illustration of the architect's drawing, which had appeared in the *Manchester Evening News and Chronicle* the previous day, made the new construction look even more imposing. Alongside this, David Meek, the newspaper's United correspondent wrote, 'Manchester United are to have an elegant, £250,000 cantilever stand at Old Trafford. Work will start at the end of the season on what will be the longest and most advanced stand in the country.

'It will go up opposite the main stand in place of the old covering over the terracing. There will be 10,500 seats and covered standing room for 10,000 more.

'The cantilever roof will project to the front of the terracing where it will be 48 ft high. It will be suspended from steel tubes retained from concrete yokes projecting 30 ft above the rear of the stand. All seats will have a clear, uninterrupted view of the game.

'The architects, Mather & Nutter, of Manchester, have prepared a preliminary scheme and are starting ground investigation immediately. Building will start next summer and be completed in fifteen months, they hope, for the start of the 1965/66 season.

'This will give United use of the stand in good time for the World Cup in 1966. It is, in fact, the plan for this new stand that clinched Old Trafford as a choice of venue for the World Cup in favour of Maine Road.

'The stand, which will be 660 ft long, will run the whole length of the ground and will turn at the corners. At the Streford end it will link up with the existing stand extension, though there will be a slight gap for the floodlighting pylon. At the Streford End, the corner will also be included in the stand.

'The new development will not mean a reduction in the capacity of Old Trafford. New techniques will be used to take the stand further back so that spectators will be sitting over the entrances.'

The building of this new stand was a matter of careful consideration and not something to be rushed into, as it left no funds for strengthening the playing squad, which obviously took priority over any structural matters. Manager Matt Busby, however, felt that his squad was strong enough to challenge for the game's honours and gave the go-ahead for the money to be spent on the stand instead of being left in the bank in case he wanted to make any new signings.

Returning to League matters, following the excitement of the stadium developments being announced, there was plenty of aggression in the following match against Liverpool, who had adapted well to First Division football following a creditable first season back in the big time, in a game practically free from fouls. But United could not complement their endeavour with goals, having been dealt a cruel blow when Harry Gregg was carried off with a broken collarbone as half-time beckoned.

A Thompson corner curled into the United area and, as attackers and defenders challenged for the ball, Yeats, Gregg and Setters collided. Gregg hit the ground, and as the ball bobbled around the area, Setters booted it clear before he also collapsed at the foot of the post. The United wing-half was able to continue following treatment, but Gregg had sustained a broken collarbone and was carried off to hospital.

For the remaining seconds of the first half and as play resumed for the second, David Herd donned the green 'keeper's jersey, performing admirably in holding the visitors at bay, with one of his many saves truly outstanding: diving full length to keep out a shot from Melia.

While forming a strong defensive wall in front of their rookie goalkeeper, United also found the opportunities to press forward despite being a man short, with Quixall causing the Liverpool defence numerous problems. One of the outside-right's efforts was deflected towards goal by Ferns, only for Lawrence to pull off an astonishing save. The Liverpool 'keeper was later fortunate when a Crerand goal-bound header bounced off Moran and away from danger.

Despite being reduced to ten men, United held out until the seventy-fifth minute, when a Callaghan corner was met firmly by Yeats, who brushed everyone aside and powered the ball past a helpless Herd.

The return of Harry Gregg in the dying minutes sent a buzz around the ground, as the goalkeeper, with his right arm strapped up below a red shirt, took up a position wide on the right purely to make up numbers and attempt to cause something of a distraction as the game moved towards a close. The Irishman professed to being 'fed up' watching his teammates struggle. But his appearance was to little avail, as Liverpool held on to their lead and returned to Merseyside as First Division leaders.

Gregg had to return to the treatment table as his shoulder had popped out again during his brief reappearance.

Following the crowd problems at Villa Park the *News of the World*, never a publication to miss out on some of the action, even back in the sixties, despatched journalist Bob Pennington to the terraces rather than the press-box for the Liverpool fixture. But both reporter and newspaper were to be disappointed in their findings, as the headline of 'Hooligans? They're So Friendly' proved.

'The one act of violence of the Old Trafford terraces to which I can testify was a tweak on the bottom of a pretty brunette as we were fighting our way to the exit,' opened Bob Pennington's article. He continued, 'By the tightness of her jeans and the squeal of appreciation that followed this salute from a Merseyside masher this was not the first time this had happened to her on a football ground.'

Pennington then went on to cover what he was paid to do and wrote, 'My return to the 3s enclosure realism after fifteen years in the rarefied atmosphere of the press boxes left me with nothing but admiration for two much maligned sets of supporters.

'Not one apple core, let alone bottle, was thrown by Liverpool fans rated No. 1 trouble-makers by the Football League.

'Not one obscene song was heard by me from a United throat after the disgraceful singing at Villa Park last Saturday.

'My three young daughters might have accompanied me without asking too many awkward questions.

'Maybe I met them all on a good day. Maybe the appeals for soccer sanity have worked.

'All I know is that it won't be another fifteen years before I go back again.'

Gregg's injury, confirmed as a broken collarbone, was a major blow to United, as the first leg of the Cup Winners' Cup second-round tie beckoned, leaving Busby with only one fit goalkeeper in Ronnie Briggs, as David Gaskell, Gregg's usual replacement, was also on the injured list with his wrist in plaster. He was even fortunate to have Briggs, as the 'keeper had been allowed to leave Old Trafford in the summer, but was then rather surprisingly re-signed.

Briggs, forever shackled with the nightmare of being hit for seven against Sheffield Wednesday in that cup replay, admitted that the defeat 'doesn't cause me to lose sleep any more. I've come to live with it.'

'Sure I've got butterflies after hearing that Harry is out for Wednesday and that I am in,' he continued. 'But they're not the butterflies caused by any memory of Sheffield Wednesday. They're from the natural excitement of playing for the first time in the European Cup Winners' Cup.

'I'm not worried about Spurs, Jimmy Greaves, Bobby Smith or anyone. I'm just thrilled to be playing for Manchester United's first team again.'

Not only was Busby without his preferred goalkeeping choice for the European tie, he also had a major fitness doubt surrounding Bobby Charlton, who was rated simply '50/50' due to an ankle injury. But luck was to be very much on the side of the United manager, as the fixture never got underway due to heavy fog reducing visibility to virtually nil.

The postponement gave Busby a little breathing space and he was able to recall David Gaskell in goal against Sheffield United at Bramall Lane, a mere twenty-four hours after having the plaster removed from his broken wrist. As they had done back in September, United put their two previous defeats behind them, and bounced back with a 2-1 victory over the early League leaders, with Denis Law scoring one in each half, silencing the critics who were beginning to offer the opinion that the performance at Wembley was little more than a one-off.

So, United made the journey south to London once again to face Tottenham in the Cup Winners' Cup, and as the evening unfolded, they could do little more than wish that the fog could once again descend and envelope the White Hart Lane ground in a shroud. There had been much prematch debate as to United's tactics on the night, and they did try to simply absorb every Tottenham attack, while attempting to gain whatever advantage possible with retaliatory breaks.

The home side rose to the occasion, backed by a noisy, partisan crowd, and put the United goal under pressure right from the offset, but Gaskell was in fine form despite his recent break and equal to anything that Tottenham sent his way. For over an hour, United stood firm, coming close themselves only when an arcing leap by Brown denied Law a goal. Then, with sixty-seven minutes gone, Jones flicked the ball back into the path of Mackay, who shot past the defiant Gaskell.

And so it stood until the dying minutes and, as many had decided that they would see no more goals on the night, Dunne slowly rolled the ball back towards his 'keeper, Dyson nipped in and from 6 yards out slid the ball into the net.

Busby was disappointed at losing, saying, 'I am disappointing that we lost 2-0, especially after that second goal. It was a fast, hard game – a man's game. But we are not beaten yet, we still think we have a chance.'

Noel Cantwell was equally adamant that the tie was far from over, adding to his manager's opinion, 'Naturally we are disappointed but any team who has played at Old Trafford knows what the roar can do to them. We would still be firm favourites if we had only lost 1-0.'

Dunne's mistake was little more than a momentary lapse by the normally reliable defender, but it was one that would perhaps cost United dearly, although there was the possibility that the outcome of the tie might be decided away from the muddied Old Trafford ground in the Griffin Hotel in Leeds.

It was here that the FA Commission was due to meet and decide the fate of Denis Law, following his recent sending-off against Aston Villa, but in anticipating a ban, Matt Busby approached the European Football Union to see if his star forward would be available to play in the Cup Winners' Cup return leg against Tottenham. It was something of long shot, but certainly worth a try.

In their reply to Old Trafford, the Union secretary, Hans Bangerter created a small chink of light, saying that there would be no objection from the Union as to Law playing against Tottenham unless the Football Association intervened.

Following the meeting, the outcome – a twenty-eight-day suspension – was announced as follows: 'Aston Villa *v.* Manchester United, League, November 16th. D. Law of Manchester United was suspended for 28 days for kicking an opponent. In arriving at the penalty imposed the committee took into account the player's record of previous misconduct on the field of play.'

Not only would he miss United's domestic fixtures, he would also have to sit out the second leg of the Cup Winners' Cup encounter with Tottenham.

Law had not been sent off before, although he had served a seven-day suspension back in season 1960/61 as a Manchester City player, following four bookings over a short period of time, so the punishment was considered somewhat harsh and was the longest since Oscar Hold of Norwich was banned for six weeks in 1947. Hold had lost some £60 in wages, but Law, with the possibility of earning ten times that, found himself in further dispute with the Football Association and the Football League – through no fault of his own it must be added – when his teammates announced that they would be setting up a 'suspension fund' in order to make up the financial loss due to be incurred by their colleague.

Bill Foulkes, speaking about the plans said, 'We think it is a savage sentence. Denis is not a quarter as bad as he is painted.

'It will be left to each player to decide how much he gives. Denis has not asked for this, but the boys feel we should keep up the tradition.'

The Football Association said that they considered such a move as 'misconduct' and although Noel Cantwell admitted that the players found it 'a ridiculous stand to take' they would abide by it – in public at any rate!

Law accepted his punishment, having decided not to ask for a personal hearing, but regretted his actions, admitting that 'it was a terrible thing that I did and I know that now. I am disappointed in myself and I'm sorry. But not just for myself.

'I am sorry that Deakin got hurt and I am sorry for the bad publicity it has brought Manchester United. That is the last thing I ever want to do.

'But I won't have it that I tried to kick Deakin deliberately, as people are saying. It happened so quickly that even I still don't know why I did it ... and I know that it wasn't deliberate.

'I am the one who really knows that I was not trying to kick Deakin.

'He had tackled me after the ball was away and I turned and shoved him off with my leg. It all happened on the spur of the moment.

'I can't complain about being sent off. And I am not trying to make it look as though Deakin was responsible. The man who retaliates is wrong, and I retaliated.

'That's why I am disappointed in myself. I know I have a wee bit of a temper and I am trying to control it.

'I wish this hadn't happened. But it did, and I have got to face up to it. This is the first time I have ever been sent off (*he had been booked thrice already this season*) and it was a terrible feeling.

'I am glad that Deakin wasn't badly hurt and I believe he knows I was not trying to injure him.

'I feel worse of all about the accusations that United are a dirty team. In fact everyone knows that the other Manchester men who have been sent off this season have outstanding reputations as clean players.

So, following Law's dismissal, were the United side of this time in danger of being tagged a 'dirty team'? Were they indeed bad losers? Or did they simply mix their sublime talents with a hint of hardness in their quest to become a successful team?

Law's sending-off had indeed provoked some members of the press to reopen the debate that United were a dirty team, far removed from the previously crafted Busby sides. In the *Daily Express*, Desmond Hackett was quick to voice his opinion, with his article headed 'Law is bringing shame to a great club'. Hackett wrote, 'Manchester United may be riding high in the football championships, but after years of glowing triumph they stand today marked as a team who bring discredit to the sport.

'Football has been exposed to lashings of rebuke because of the misdeeds of crowds and players. When Denis Law was ordered off in the Aston Villa fracas on Saturday he became the fourth Manchester United player to be dismissed from a game this season.

'Ahead of Law in this sorry procession were Noel Cantwell, Albert Quixall and David Herd. This record brings nothing but disgrace to a team whose name and reputation were once among the highest in the land.

'The team became the idols of young boys, an inspiration to them to play with the sporting spirit and bright courage of their heroes.'

He continued, 'It is difficult even to conjecture that Manchester United's well loved chief Matt Busby condones the tantrums of this turbulent young man Law who, at £116,000, represents the highest soccer investment in the land.

Hackett went on to write of how Matt Busby's team were 'admirable ambassadors' at home and abroad before continuing: 'But in this year of soccer shame their players have become noted for their vigour, and for their defiance of the laws of the game.

'If Matt Busby still has that shining affection for his club he should be the first to rebuke his erring players by sacking them from the team until they learn better manners.'

He rounded off his article by saying, 'Unless this regrettable trend is severely checked the best loved club in England will become the most hated and despised.

'No matter what honours Manchester United may win with their powered play, they will never be able to accept them with pride.'

Strangely, Hackett was a Lancastrian, but of the old English school, instantly recognisable due to his brown bowler hat, and was noted and renowned for 'making up more fairy tales than Hans

Christian Andersen', while also being part of a Fleet Street brotherhood of sports columnists whose 'pens were often dipped in poison'. He seemed to have a hankering for the celebrity that followed the footballers of the day, often paging himself at airports so that he had to walk through a gapping crowd to take the call for 'Mr Hackett of the *Daily Express*'.

His piece on United, while thought-provoking, caused little concern in Manchester and was soon confined to the local chip shops to wrap their fare in. Matt Busby knew and trusted his players, aware of their faults, but he was even more aware that he had a team on the verge of greatness, and without their mixture of traits that success would be much further away.

Others, however, latched on to Hackett's words, creating a form of jealousy against Manchester United, a love-to-hate relationship spawned in the sixties, but carried on to the present day.

Law was free to play against Stoke City at Old Trafford the day after he was suspended and went out with a bang, scoring four in United's 5-1 win, one for every week of his suspension, while also creating United's opening goal in the fourth minute for David Herd.

Five minutes later, Law opened his own account, but strangely neither goalkeeper was beaten again until the seventieth minute when Stoke pulled one back through Ritchie, a goal that suddenly turned the game on its head, as the visitors suddenly looked as though they were capable of causing something of a minor upset. But within the space of thirteen minutes, they were to find themselves completely deflated by the brilliance of Denis Law.

They did, to their credit, snatch a second six minutes from time, with United leading 4-1, but even with Stanley Matthews in their side, the veteran winger could do little to change the course of the game, and his side were fortunate not to concede a sixth goal to Law, as his overhead kick crashed against the crossbar with Leslie beaten.

The headlines in the press were all dominated by one word, 'LAW', such as the *Telegraph*'s 'Irresistible Law Goes Out In Four- Goal Triumph'. But another in the *Daily Mail* painted something of a wider picture, and one that was more worrying to the United support: 'Four-Goal Law Leaves Busby A Worry'. Ron Crowther wrote, 'Behind him, after this rich feast of goal-getting skill, he left manager Matt Busby a worrying question. Who is to step into his boots in United's next six vital games?

'For Law, as live and lethal as a panther on the prowl, had laid low Stoke almost single handed.'

Former United idol Dennis Viollet, the man whom Law in effect replaced in the line-up, was amongst those quick to heap praise on the United No. 10. 'He's fantastic,' enthused the Stoke man. 'There's only one thing wrong with his suspension – it should have started on Friday.'

Indeed, without Law, United were a different team altogether. They certainly were not a one-man outfit, but Law's unique brand of individualistic football clearly unsettled the opposition and could unpick the tightest defence, while he also had the uncanny knack of being in the right place at the right time to conjure a goal out of nothing.

So, with the visit of Tottenham for the second leg of the Cup Winners' Cup tie, Busby did indeed have a problem. Not only was he without Law, but recent signing Graham Moore was also ineligible to play, forcing the United manager to reintroduce Phil Chisnall at inside-right and opted for David Sadler to fill the gap left by Law's suspension.

With Tottenham holding a 2-0 first-leg lead, the game suddenly swung United's way with a double blow to the visitors in the space of sixty seconds. With only seven minutes gone, a poor free-kick by Henry was seized upon by Chisnall and, after running unattended for almost 20 yards, he passed to Sadler. After beating Baker on the edge of the area and drawing Brown from his goal, the United centre-forward flicked the ball inside to Herd who threw himself forward and headed the ball home.

Less than a minute later, Tottenham were dealt a second blow. As the United defence attempted to clear the ball, it broke between Noel Cantwell and the oncoming Dave Mackay. As the white-shirted No. 6 attempted to shoot, the United captain turned in an effort to block the ball and the pair collided as the ball flew out of play for a corner. Silence enveloped the ground, as it was obvious that the Tottenham man was in trouble, and he was carried off the field on a stretcher having suffered a broken leg.

Although reduced to ten men, there was no immediate effect on Tottenham and they almost drew level, when Norman headed a Greaves corner past Gaskell, only to see Cantwell clear the ball off the line. Greaves put Gaskell under pressure with another well-placed corner and then shot narrowly over from 20 yards out. United on the other hand squandered numerous opportunities.

Slowly the home side gained the upper hand. Charlton, accepting a pass from Herd 20 yards from goal, sent Brown scampering across his line as the ball flew just wide of the post, and then Setters hit the bar with a shot from all of 35 yards. Minutes before the break, Sadler just failed to get on the end of a Herd pass, while at the other end Crerand made a timely challenged on Jones as the Tottenham man prepared to shoot.

Still a goal behind and needing only one to force a third match at Villa Park, United found themselves pinned back in the early stages of the second half, as Tottenham made a sterling attempt to put the game beyond their reach. But their heroic efforts came to nothing and they were finally pulled back to level terms in the fifty-seventh minute.

A Quixall corner on the right produced something of a goalmouth scramble, and as the ball broke loose to Herd, he made no mistake in driving it past Brown from close range. The advantage, however, was only momentary, as no sooner had the cheers of the United support died down than those of the Tottenham support echoed through the Manchester evening air.

Not for the first time in the game, the United defence appeared slow to react in the face of danger, and Jimmy Greaves, having managed to evade the shackles of Setters, rose to a John White cross and headed firmly past Gaskell.

It was soon ten against ten, as Setters left the field with a cut head, and with twenty minutes remaining, as the ball moved around the pitch as if on a pin table, Greaves left Cantwell in his wake as he surged forward, but his pass to the unmarked Smith was just a couple of inches too far in front of the centre-forward. However, no sooner had Setters returned to the fray than Charlton drove over the bar.

Even with United back to full strength, Setters holding a sponge to his bloodied forehead, which had required four stitches, Tottenham stood firm. With only ten minutes remaining and the game still precariously balanced, a decisive goal materialised when a long through pass from Crerand caught out Norman and Charlton hooked the ball past the helpless Brown to give United a 4-3 aggregate victory.

The suspended Law had taken a seat just above the tunnel and behind Matt Busby, but had endured only eight minutes of the all-British encounter, slipping back to the confines of the dressing rooms to comfort his Scottish international teammate Dave Mackay as he waited to be taken to hospital. Even after Mackay's departure, Law remained below the stand, content to follow the game via the roars of the crowd.

'I can't stand to watch football matches,' he was to say at the end of the ninety minutes.

It was a goal that deflated the visitors, and with only a couple of minutes remaining, the tie was put beyond any doubt when Crerand and Herd combined to set Charlton free to score United's fourth.

Four days later, the Law-less (and also Albert Quixall-less, due to his suspension for a sending-off in a Central League game against Manchester City) United machine rolled on, beating Sheffield Wednesday 3-1 at Old Trafford, David Herd taking his goal tally to six in three games with a hat-trick that pushed thoughts of Denis Law to the back of the mind for ninety minutes at least.

But Law's absence was clearly noticeable four days before Christmas, with the visit to Goodison Park, where Everton, sitting three places and two points behind United in eighth place, repeated their Charity Shield triumph with another 4-0 victory. One report claimed that it was the 'worst display by a United forward line since the bad old days'.

As they had done in the season's curtain raiser, Everton taunted and toyed with a lacklustre United side, embarrassed in the end by not simply the scoreline but by the chants of 'Easy, Easy' which enveloped the ground. It was certainly a far cry from the performance that produced the 5-1 victory over the Goodison Park side back in August.

It took the Everton forwards only ten minutes to secure their victory, scoring three goals between the fifty-fifth and sixty-fifth minutes and leaving United a depleted shell, with a fourth goal coming in the seventy-eighth minute as Maurice Setters, the driving force behind United recent resurgence, played a deep-lying sweeper's role while finishing the game limping badly.

For those who considered the Everton result as nothing more than a one-off, a wake-up call, they were badly mistaken, as Boxing Day at Turf Moor, Burnley, brought everything crashing down to earth with a bang that would certainly have registered on the Richter scale.

Never the most enjoyable of venues for United, they certainly toiled on the wet, slippery surface and often looked disjointed as eighteen-year-old Scottish schoolboy trialist Willie Morgan taunted their defence with a superb display of individual skill.

It took Burnley only seven minutes to open the scoring, Lochhead beating Gaskell with ease, and the visitors were fortunate not to be two down three minutes later, as it was only a linesman's flag that denied Towers. Miller then shot over, before appeals for a penalty after Setters had handled were waved aside.

Twenty-two minutes had passed before United managed their first shot of the game, but on the half-hour, they drew level through Herd, who ran on to a Charlton through-pass to fire home off the body of goalkeeper Blacklaw.

United then enjoyed a greater percentage of the play, but it was little more than the lull before the storm, as three minutes before the interval Lochhead restored Burnley's lead. As the second half got underway, the United goal was fortunate to witness several astonishing escapes.

It was indeed something of a surprise that the home side did not score again until the sixty-sixth minute, when Morgan forced the ball home for his first goal in the claret and blue. Four minutes later, Lochhead claimed his third of the afternoon with a header from a Morgan cross, and in the final eight minutes Morgan claimed his second and Lochhead his fourth of the afternoon, going through with a pass from Towers before leaving Gaskell stranded.

By then, however, United had been reduced to ten men, as Crerand had been sent off with thirteen minutes remaining following an incident with Towers. As Burnley continued to put the United defence under pressure, there had been a number of petty fouls and Crerand's temper got the better of him: he appeared to elbow Towers in the face, leaving the referee with little option than to send him off.

The defeat bewildered Busby and, having reshuffled his forward line for the trip to Turf Moor, bringing in Brennan at outside-left, Quixall in at outside-right and switching Charlton to centre-forward in place of Sadler, he decided to make further changes for the return fixture with Burnley at Old Trafford two days later, bringing in sixteen-year-old apprentice professional Willie Anderson at outside-right for his League debut, and recalling seventeen-year-old George Best from his Christmas break in Belfast to wear the No. 11 shirt.

Burnley almost continued where they had left off, with Lochhead putting the United goal under immediate pressure with a couple of attempts and Pointer hitting the ball straight at Gaskell when he should have done better.

But with eleven minutes gone, it was United who took the lead: Elder, the Burnley left-back, uncharacteristically placed the ball to the feet of Herd, half a dozen yards from goal, an opportunity that the United No. 10 was not going to miss.

Two minutes later, Blacklaw dropped a corner at the feet of Moore and United were two up and from then on the visitors knew that there was unlikely to be a repeat victory.

Crerand set up the third for Best, who initially lost the ball, then reclaimed possession, before beating Blacklaw. Charlton disposed of Elder to set up Moore for the fourth and Crerand supplied Herd for the fifth. Lochhead claimed a consolation goal for Burnley four minutes from time.

Many of the plaudits fell at the feet of the two teenagers, Anderson and Best, although the latter was considered more of a prospect by the inhabitants of the press box, with the 'special correspondent' of the *Daily Telegraph* writing, 'George Best, aged seventeen, playing in his second first-team game, was the hero of the Old Trafford crowd. He gave a tremendous display of speed and artistry and rounded it off with a twenty-fifth-minute goal.'

Best's performance, not entirely unexpected by those in the know at Old Trafford, was something that gave Busby much satisfaction. He had seen his beloved 'Babes' destroyed at Munich, but now, almost six years on, Jimmy Murphy's production line was once again producing players who were capable of taking Manchester United towards greatness, stepping from the junior ranks to the First Division with ease, and taking the game by the scruff of the neck while entertaining the vast expectant support.

But what did Busby do now?

Next up were Southampton in the FA Cup third round, a tricky tie at the Dell and a repeat of last season's semi-final, offering an early opportunity for the South Coast club to gain revenge. But did Busby retain the services of his new teenage sensations, or take the more precautionary route of limiting their first-team appearances, introducing them into the world of top-class football gently?

Deciding to 'go for it', Best and Anderson made the journey to the South Coast as United set about defending the FA Cup, and at half-time, Busby might well have been having second thoughts about the youngsters' inclusion, as Southampton led 2-0 and the rousing chorus of 'When the Saints Go Marching In' echoed around the Dell. Neither of the teenagers had shown the same panache that had tantalised Burnley in the previous game, although the United defence had only crumbled in the final two minutes prior to the interval.

Hoping that the mist swirling around the ground would develop into a dense fog despite the cost involved in travelling south, the United support settled down for what they foresaw as a long, drawn-out forty-five minutes, but they were pleasantly surprised a mere six minutes after the restart, when Anderson crept out of his shell, released by Crerand, and his centre was headed home by Moore.

Ten minutes later it was level pegging. Setters found Herd with a free-kick, as goalkeeper Godfrey floundered in an attempt to reach the ball. The United No. 10's goal-bound header, however, was blocked on the line by Traynor. But the groans from the United support were soon stifled as the left-back, in his attempt to clear, only succeeded in turning the ball into his own goal.

The Saints were no longer marching, reduced to a crawl as the United support spurred their team towards a possible late winner, and they were indeed rewarded with a goal eight minutes from time, but only after a Southampton appeal for a penalty fell on deaf ears and Gaskell saved superbly from Paine. Crerand accepted a pass from Anderson, and brushed past three supposed defenders, before beating Godfrey, slipping the ball into the corner of the net to ensure United's passage into Round Four.

Twelve months had seen a dramatic change in the fortunes of Manchester United, as they had gone from the throes of relegation to the euphoria of challenging for the leadership of the First Division, playing some of the best football seen at Old Trafford and beyond for a considerable number of years.

11 January saw the return to the fold of Denis Law, fresh from his prolonged Christmas break courtesy of the Football Association, and with the team fresh from its enthralling fight-back at the Dell. The visit of Birmingham City to Old Trafford was looked forward to more than the usual fixtures between the two sides.

Birmingham had been knocked out of the cup in one of the shocks of the round, losing to Port Vale, so their expectations of achieving any success in Manchester were practically nil, especially with Law itching to get back into the swing of things again. But by 4.45 p.m. there was a mass exodus of disgruntled red-and-white-clad supporters, shaking their heads in disbelief at Birmingham City's surprising 2-1 victory.

Despite his long lay-off and the expectancy surrounding his reappearance in the red shirt, Law turned in something of an 'ordinary' performance, unable to inspire his teammates to victory – something they perhaps considered a mere formality prior to kick-off.

Alex Harley, a former Maine Road resident, gave Birmingham City the lead with a fourth-minute strike, taking a pass from Auld on the halfway line before racing through a sluggish and hesitant United defence, and rounding Gaskell before slipping the ball into an empty net.

Slowly, United regained something of a foothold on the game, and in the twenty-eighth minute Law chipped a Setters free-kick towards the Birmingham goal and Sadler volleyed home from 10 yards.

There was a hint of rustiness surrounding the returning Law, as he missed several opportunities that he would have normally put away. He was not, however, the only guilty party, as his fellow forwards also shunned opportunities, chances that allowed Bullock, on his Birmingham debut, to snatch what was to be the winner, two minutes into the second half.

Law and United were only human after all!

The defeat at the hands of Birmingham City saw United remain in sixth position with thirty points from their twenty-six games, but they were now five points behind leaders Tottenham, who had played a game less, while second-placed Liverpool had two games in hand over United, and were four points better off.

Yes, Law was indeed only human, but he was soon to prove that it was due to his extensive lay-off that his performance against Birmingham lacked something of its usual sparkle, as he was soon retuned and back amongst the goals, scoring two against another Midlands side, West Bromwich Albion, in a 4-1 win on an icy Hawthorns pitch, before notching up a hat-trick in the fourth-round FA Cup tie against Bristol Rovers.

Albion, undefeated in their previous nine games, were no match for an on-form United, while Third Division Bristol Rovers arrived at Old Trafford on a day which saw Law and Charlton produce the type of form that elevated them into the ranks of the world's best.

Charlton, England's regular outside-left, who up until the 5-1 victory over Burnley had filled a similar position for United, now found himself playing an entirely different role for his club, having taken over the No. 9 shirt that had until recently been shared by David Sadler and David Herd.

Busby had viewed Charlton's recent inconsistency as something of a problem, hence the switch, and prior to the Bristol Rovers cup tie, as the United players relaxed during a three-day stay at Llandudno, the United manager told Derek Wallis of the *Daily Mirror*, 'We are hoping to keep him at centre-forward subject, of course, to the way things go.

'He has been playing very well, particularly at West Brom on Saturday, and as far as one can foresee these things he will stay there.

'He is an adaptable player. After all, he started as an inside-forward.

'He himself seems happier there.'

Charlton himself said, 'Centre-forward suits me fine. I enjoy playing a double spearhead with Denis. Naturally, this calls for me to stay upfield most of the time, but if I feel I want to go forging ahead I can.

'When you are on the wing you're only getting in the game in flashes. At centre-forward you're in it all the time.'

But it was Law who shattered Bristol Rovers' cup dream with a devastating display. He reacted instantaneously to give United an eleventh-minute lead, racing 40 yards to head home a Charlton centre, and added a second in the twelfth minute before completing his hat-trick with another header six minutes from time. A Crerand own goal had given Rovers and their 8,000 travelling support some form of consolation with twenty minutes remaining, but when Herd had put United 3-0 in front fifteen minutes after half-time, it was already game over.

Pat Crerand's sending-off against Burnley on Boxing Day brought a seven-day suspension with the loss of around £100 in wages, but despite this setback – also losing Noel Cantwell through injury for the visit of Arsenal on 1 February – Matt Busby had adequate replacements in Nobby Stiles and Shay Brennan, with the 3-1 victory keeping the dream of First Division, FA Cup and European Cup Winners' Cup success alive. Even the surprise 3-2 defeat at Leicester City seven days later – a result decided by an over-enthusiastic linesman declaring that Denis Law was offside when Best headed the ball past Banks two minutes from time, when he was clearly behind the Irishman and had only followed the ball into the net – was considered little more than a temporary blip.

With a backdrop of slag heaps, Third Division Barnsley provided little resistance in the fifth round of the FA Cup, where a Best double and one apiece from Law and Herd nudged United towards another Wembley appearance. Success on three fronts remained more than a possibility following the 5-0 thrashing of Bolton Wanderers at Old Trafford, the 3-1 win over Blackburn Rovers at Ewood Park and the 4-1 European Cup Winners' Cup quarter-final first-leg success over Sporting Lisbon.

The global appeal of the club, something upon which great emphasis is placed today, was still in its infancy and just beginning to rear its head. Although they could not command fees similar to those that would entice Real Madrid out of Spain for a mere ninety minutes of football, the name Manchester United was certainly not unknown around the globe, although this was perhaps more to do with the Munich air disaster than their sojourns into the competitive world of European competitions. America, Scandinavia and Germany had all been visited on more than one occasion since football had returned to normal following the Second World War, but more recently, overtures had been made to the club inviting them to more exotic locations – invites that were unfortunately turned down.

At the directors' monthly meeting for September 1963, the board had discussed an invitation to play a match in Cairo in January 1964, but had been unable to accept. However, at the same meeting they had looked into the possibility of a tour to Hong Kong and Tokyo in the summer of 1964. The following month, there were also offers from Canada and America, South Africa, and to take part in the International Soccer League in New York to be considered, but the matter was then deferred until further information regarding calls on the players for international duty was obtained.

Having said that, there was the possibility in the summer of 1964 of a ground-breaking trek for the club – something that is actually commonplace today: a tour of Malaysia and the Far East. Much of the negotiations had been carried out by Sir Stanley Rous, the president of FIFA, and following talks with the Malaysian Football Association, agreement was obtained for United to be paid £1,000 per match.

The proposed Hong Kong leg of the tour had been abandoned in November, when it was decided at the directors' monthly meeting that due to the dates being announced for end-of-season international fixtures, and the likely call-ups for United players, it would not be possible to accept the invitation. It was February before the board got round to discussing the Malaysian tour, but this also bit the dust after it was decided that, owing to the lack of a full itinerary and the shortage of time, it was not possible to go ahead with the arrangements.

The eight goals in two successive League fixtures were certainly pleasing to everyone, but what made it even more satisfactory was the fact that those goals were spread between five different players – Best (2), Herd (2), Law (2), Charlton and Chisnall – demonstrating clearly that Manchester United were not simply reliant on the goals of Denis Law in order to claim success.

But it was Law who crushed Sporting Lisbon under the Old Trafford floodlights with an inspired, demonic display of artistry as United took a 4-1 advantage into the return second leg against the Portuguese.

Sporting had come to Manchester with manager Anselmo Fernandes claiming that his side 'could not hope to contain United by a defensive game' and that they 'must go out for as many goals as we can get', but once the game got underway, his team were more than happy to play a cautious, yet highly dangerous offside game, content to do little more than attempt long-range efforts at the United goal. However, they were not a team that United could simply dismiss, as the eighteen-time Champions of Portugal had a formidable record against foreign opposition. Their players also had the added incentive of a £100 bonus to beat United.

Within the opening four minutes, the United forwards had been caught out four times, with the five-man Portuguese defence pushing as near to the halfway line as they could get. But it was a ploy that did not always work, due mainly to the lightning reflexes of Denis Law. Without him, United would have struggled.

In the twenty-second minute he raced on to a Charlton pass before steering the ball around a defender and the goalkeeper and slipping it into the yawning net. Seven minutes later, he returned the favour and Charlton's drive from the edge of the area spun out of the goalkeeper's grasp and into the net. It could well have been six, but the two goalscorers, along with Stiles and Setters, were all guilty of failing to make the most of excellent opportunities.

Osvaldo and Morais both forced Gaskell into making notable saves early in a second half, which was shown live on ITV, confirming that the visitors were not simply there to make up the numbers and that the offside trap was not the only thing included in their repertoire. Law missed another easy chance, when he somehow managed to head the ball out from under the bar instead of down and into the net. But with an hour gone and as the crowd began to think that those missed chances would cost their team dearly, Stiles raced through on goal, only to be unceremoniously upended by Hilario. The resulting penalty allowed Law to increase United's lead to a more acceptable total.

Osvado reduced the arrears six minutes later with a superb 25-yard drive, but within five minutes United had restored their three-goal advantage with a second penalty, this time awarded for a foul on Charlton. It was a decision which annoyed the visitors, as it appeared that the United forward had indeed lost control of the ball when the incident occurred. Law again beat Cavalho with ease.

As the game moved to a close, United continued to shun the opportunities that came their way, but with a three-goal advantage, progress into the semi-finals should have been assured.

The Lisbon officials were far from happy with the penalty awards, with manager Anselmo Fernandez saying, 'They were very bad. In the first case, Stiles was outside the 18 yards. It was not a penalty either, because Alfredo played the ball not the man.

'In the second case, Figuetredo chased Charlton into the penalty area. The ball was out of reach when Charlton fell over him.' Centre-half Baptista was equally annoyed at the referee's decisions. 'The penalties did not exist,' he said. 'The first one was not a penalty because it did not happen in the penalty area. The second was not a foul. It did not exist. We were stolen.'

Matt Busby rather diplomatically steered away from discussing either of the two penalties, but said, 'The lads realise they have played better than this, but a three-goal lead is a pretty good performance and should be enough to see us through to the semi-finals.'

It was straight from one cup tie into another, with Second Division Sunderland travelling to Old Trafford three days later for a sixth-round FA Cup tie: a pulsating ninety minutes and a game that swung back and forth with much regularity, keeping the result in doubt until the last blast of the referee's whistle.

As leaders of the Second Division, Sunderland were never likely to present United with an easy passage into the semi-finals, and reflecting on the ninety minutes as a whole, they were unquestionably the better of the two teams on the day, giving those who had paid £4 for a 9s 6d ticket or £5 for a 30s one value for money.

Law found himself shackled by centre-half Hurley, a well-built, no-nonsense figure, whose close attention was later to frustrate the United captain, leading to some stern words from the referee. Backed by a strong vocal support, the visitors enjoyed a fair percentage of the play, causing the United defence numerous problems before taking the lead four minutes prior to the interval.

Usher crossed the ball from the right, Gaskell came out to gather it, but misjudged it completely and the ball drifted over his outstretched arm towards the far post where Mulhall, standing almost on the goal line, beat Dunne to the ball and headed home. Three minutes earlier, Law had scooped the ball over the bar from close range, for what was to prove a costly miss.

Four minutes after the break, it was 2-0. Herd robbed Setters in midfield and through Usher the ball found Crossan, who set off down the left and, after beating Crerand, cut inside along the 18-yard line, drifting past three United defenders before hitting a superb drive past Gaskell from 20 yards out.

As the 'Blaydon Races' echoed around Old Trafford, United, playing in all-white, attempted to grasp ahold of a game which was clearly slipping away from them. Charlton came close on a couple of occasions before they eventually managed to pull a goal back in the fifty-fifth minute. It was a goal practically out of nothing and a disappointment for the rock-like Hurley.

Crerand lobbed the ball forward, with Setters in hot pursuit, but Hurley managed to get there before him, and as he attempted to head the ball back to his goalkeeper, he could only watch as the ball bounced out of Montgomery's reach and into the net.

Although a disappointment and a bad goal to lose, the Wearsiders' heads did not drop, and before United could put any further pressure on their visitors, Sunderland scored a third in the sixtieth minute.

Crossan chased a ball down the touchline and as he beat Crerand, the ball appeared to many on that side of the ground to have gone out of play. With no raised flag from the linesman and the United defence having momentarily stopped, expecting the referee's whistle, Crossan continued his run. As he moved into the penalty area, he was brought down by Brennan and the referee immediately pointed to the spot. Crossan himself took the spot-kick, sending Gaskell the wrong way to put Sunderland 3-1 in front, and in the eyes of their supporters, into the semi-finals.

Not content to sit on their laurels, Sunderland continued to pressurise the United defence and only Gaskell, with a superb save, denied Herd, the visitors' No. 8, from extending that lead further. With many of the home support resigned to defeat as the minutes ticked away, it did look as though the dreams of a domestic double were about to crumble. Law missed a chance, a Charlton effort flew straight at Montgomery, while the eighteen-year-old 'keeper knew little about a Law header that smacked him full in the face before being scrambled clear for a corner.

Best curled the flag kick into the goalmouth, and with Montgomery still feeling the effects of Law's powerful header, Charlton rose to nod the ball home. With only four minutes remaining, could Sunderland hold on, or would United find some hidden reserve to find an equaliser and take the game to a replay?

With the referee paying as much attention to his watch as he did the actual play, Crerand sought out Best. The young Irishman controlled the ball with ease and then, as many on the still-packed terracing stood open-mouthed, fired the ball through the smallest of gaps and past Montgomery for what was indeed a last-gasp equaliser. It was a goal that not only kept United in the cup, but helped increase the seventeen-year-old's weekly wage packet from his basic £12 to almost £100 thanks to bonuses.

The dramatic fight-back obviously enthralled the 63,700 supporters, but it was a totally dejected Sunderland contingent who trudged off the Old Trafford pitch and made their way back to the North East, wondering why they were not in the FA Cup semi-finals.

Johnny Crossan, in his first full season as a Sunderland player, found himself up against Pat Crerand that afternoon and looking back said, 'As an attacking midfielder Crerand was brilliant, but defensively he had very little and on the day I gave him a torrid time. George Mulhall gave us the lead in the first half, I weighed in with a couple in the second and with only minutes remaining we were leading 3-1. The referee that day was Arthur Holland and I remember asking him how long was left to which he replied, 'Don't worry Johnny, there's only a couple of minutes to go – you're home in a boat.' But amazingly, right at the death, they scored twice to force a replay – it was heartbreaking.'

Another of those Sunderland players who left Manchester in a state of bewilderment that afternoon was Nicky Sharkey. 'We thought we were home and dry,' recalls Nicky, 'until an unfortunate injury to our keeper, Jimmy Montgomery, allowed United back into the game. He was knocked unconscious while diverting a Denis Law shot for a corner and instead of taking a few minutes to recover, he was up almost immediately. When the corner was floated in, Monty was clearly still in trouble as Bobby Charlton scored with a simple header and then, in the last minute, George Best nipped in to grab the equaliser.'

The need for a replay on 4 March cancelled out United's second-leg European Cup Winners' Cup tie in Lisbon, with a shaken United side heading for the North East instead of Portugal and yet another dramatic evening of cup-tie football.

Busby considered a couple of changes for the Roker Park replay, due to some of those who played in the first encounter being clearly off-form, with the possibility of bringing in Phil Chisnall in place of Nobby Stiles and replacing David Gaskell with Harry Gregg. Only the former of those proposed selections was to happen.

Gregg had been unfortunate with injuries over the past few seasons, with a dislocated shoulder and a broken collarbone added to his medical records, the latter against Liverpool in November which resulted in a six-week absence. But following a handful of reserve-team outings, Busby decided that despite the long lay-off, his experience could prove beneficial to United's progress in the competition.

Driving home on the night of the Old Trafford Sunderland cup tie, Gregg, who was later to tell of his drink being spiked at a party, hit a lamp post and was thrown out of his car. In a state of panic he managed to get a taxi home, but ended up in hospital with numerous injuries, obviously curtailing his proposed comeback.

Throughout the day of the replay, supporters converged on Roker Park, with many queuing at the turnstiles as early as 9 a.m., and by kick-off there were frantic scenes around the ground with an estimated 68,000 inside and a further 50,000 outside. Such figures have to be taken with a pinch of salt, but from eye-witness accounts, those figures quoted were not too far removed from the truth.

When the gates opened, there were half-mile-long queues streaming from every turnstile and many, impatient and caring little for those at the front, bore down on the admission areas. With more than an hour to kick-off and the terraces already bulging, it was decided to lock the gates.

Some trudged dejectedly away, causing an immediate build-up of traffic in the area, but most of the estimated 50,000 thronging the streets around the ground stampeded towards the turnstiles, crashing against two exit gates which buckled under the force, leaving hundreds injured and two dead. The latter, however, died as the result of heart attacks while on the way to the ground, with many of those injured coming under the attendance of ambulance men, who had set up a makeshift first-aid station in a nearby house.

'Hooligans surged forward when the gates were closed,' said a woman caught in the mayhem who ended up with neither shoes nor handbag. 'About five of us were swept off our feet. My legs were badly trampled and I blacked out.' While another supporter caught up in it all said, 'I was so scared that I fought my way out of the crush.

'It was just as difficult to get away from the turnstiles as it was to get to them.

'Children were crying and people were picking them up and passing them overhead to safety. I got there at 5.30 p.m., two hours before kick-off, and the crowds were immense.

'The policemen I saw were helpless against the crowd.'

A police spokesman said, 'We were snowed under. Hundreds got over and into the ground', while stating that there had been around 120 officers on duty, but soon after the game got underway, reinforcements were brought in from Durham County, Newcastle-upon-Tyne and South Shields, who were mainly employed in clearing the crowds outside the ground.

As the United team coach made its way to the ground, stones were thrown at its windows and it became bogged down by the volume of bodies. Sixty United supporters who had flown to the North

Morris - Austin - Wolseley
Riley - M.G.
Consult the
B.M.C. Retail Dealers

E.E.Brown&Co
(Smethwick) Ltd.
ST. PAUL'S ROAD, SMETHWICK
SME 1138 - 9

Evening Despatch

NIGHT FINAL

2½d.   No. 20,746   BIRMINGHAM   Thursday, February 6, 1958

MANCHESTER UTD. PLANE CRASHES: 28 DEAD

Numbing blow...

CHARTERED AIRLINER CARRYING THE MAN-CHESTER UNITED FOOTBALL TEAM HOME FROM BELGRADE CRASHED SHORTLY AFTER TAKE-OFF FROM MUNICH TODAY.

Reports from Munich said that 28 of the 40 people on board were killed when the plane crashed into houses and exploded.

The B.E.A. said the plane took off and rose to a height of about 60 feet, then

TODAY, British football with its millions of followers is plunged into deepest possible mourning, writes DICK KNIGHT.

The sport has lost many of its most brilliant performers, belonging to a club which after uncertain post-war years had helped to put our football firmly on the map.

The big football centres of the country have their own pets and fancies, but the exploits of Manchester United have attracted unanimous praise. I say this. No soccer fan in the country felt anything but pride that they had for the second year running entered

suppose you can have crashes just as easily travelling by rail or road."

Aston Villa manager Eric Hiughton said: "I was afraid this would happen one of these days. That is why we never flew to Paris during the close season."

Mr. J. Howley, of Wolves, said: "It is the greatest shock I have ever had in football. Obviously, I do not know it

will affect our match at Old Trafford on Saturday."

George Noakes, Wolves chief scout: "This is the greatest shock I have ever had. Manchester United are our greatest rivals. But this has knocked the bottom out of all of us at Wolverhampton."

Vic Buckingham, West Bromwich Albion manager: "It's just ghastly. What more can anyone say!"

★✦★✦★✦★✦★✦★✦★✦★✦★✦★

FINAL CLEARANCE

Above: 1. The Munich air disaster makes the headlines in the *Evening Despatch.*

Below: 2. The wreckage.

Above: 3. The gym at Old Trafford where the bodies lay overnight upon their return from Munich.

Below: 4. The funeral of United captain Roger Byrne at Flixton parish church.

Above left: 5. Gregg and Foulkes head home from Munich accompanied by Jimmy Murphy.

Above right: 6. The playing squad after Munich.

Below: 7. Duncan Edwards' death makes headline news.

Daily Mirror

FRI FEB 21 1958

2½   FORWARD WITH THE PEOPLE
No. 16,855

EDWARDS OF UNITED DIES

THE DUKE FACES A BARRAGE!

DUNCAN EDWARDS, Manchester United's international left half back, died in hospital in Munich early today.

For a fortnight German doctors had battled to save Edwards's life after the Munich air crash which killed seven other United players.

His death brings the full death roll in the disaster to twenty-two.

Edwards had multiple injuries which included leg fractures and badly damaged kidneys.

Eight days ago an artificial kidney apparatus was taken 200 miles from Freiburg to Munich to cleanse his blood.

His courage had amazed doctors. Since the B.E.A. Elizabethan crashed on take-off the 21-year-old "Busby Babe" had been on the brink of death.

Edwards's parents and his fiancee, Miss Molly Leach, have been staying in Munich to be near him. They were told of his death at their hotel today.

The famous left half back played eighteen times for the full England side.

At the age of 18 he was the youngest player ever to appear for England.

His death is a great blow to England's chances in the coming World Cup series. He was almost an automatic choice since his first game against Scotland at Wembley in 1955.

Early today the hospital said the condition of Johnny Berry, United outside right, and pilot Captain Kenneth Rayment was unchanged.

Matt Busby, United's manager, was given new glasses yesterday—but not allowed to read newspapers.

● *A Boy Who Played Like a Man—*
Page 24.

Robin to see

Above: 8. The start of season 1958/59.

Below left: 9. Bill Foulkes leads United out for their first game following the Munich air disaster against Sheffield Wednesday in the FA Cup fifth round.

Below right: 10. Matt Busby unveils the Munich memorial plaque at Old Trafford.

Above left: 11. Brennan's corner drops into the Wednesday net in the first match after Munich.

Above right: 12. Viollet meets the Duke of Edinburgh prior to the 1958 FA Cup final.

Below: 13. Bolton's first goal in the 1958 final.

Above: 14. The 1962/63 squad.

Below: 15. George Best, European Football of the Year.

Above: 16. The 1963 cup final.

Below: 17. The 1963 FA Cup winners.

Above: 18. 1965 Champions.

Below: 19. League Champions 1964/65.

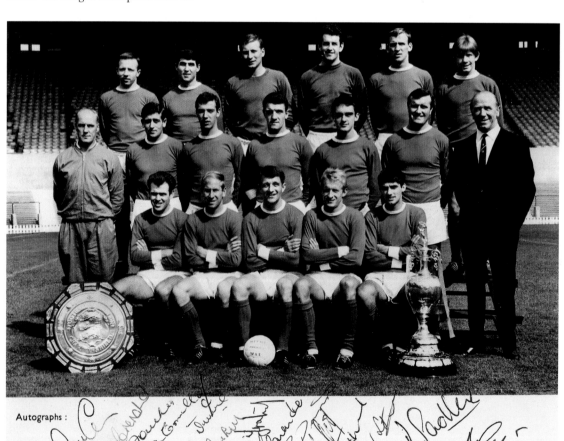

Autographs :

Above: 20. The 1964/65 team, flanked by Matt Busby and Jimmy Murphy.

Below: 21. The team of season 1965/66.

Left: 22. 1967 Champions.

Below: 23. Players on the pitch at Gornik, 1968.

Above: 24. George Best's goal is disallowed in the Benfica match.

Below: 25. Foulkes scores United's third in Madrid, 1968.

Above: 26. European Cup final, 1968.

Below: 27. European Champions, 1968.

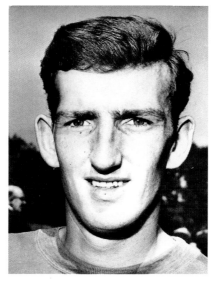

Above left: 28. Albert Quixall, signed by Matt Busby for a British record fee of £45,000 from Sheffield Wednesday in September 1958, as he began rebuilding his shattered team. Quixall had captained the Sheffield Wednesday side in that FA Cup tie at Old Trafford immediately after the crash.

Above middle: 29. Alex Stepney, an important piece of Busby's third great team. The former Chelsea goalkeeper cost £55,000 in September 1966.

Above right: 30. Alex Dawson, former England schoolboy international. His hat-trick in the 1958 FA Cup semi-final replay took United to Wembley.

Right: 31. Bill Foulkes, whose goal took United to the European Cup final.

Below left: 32. Matt Busby, 'the Boss'.

Below middle: 33. Bobby Charlton.

Below right: 34. Colin Webster's goal against West Bromwich Albion in the 1958 FA Cup sixth-round replay took United into the semi-final.

Above left: 35. David Herd played for Stockport County alongside his father. He was signed from Arsenal in July 1961 for a fee of £35,000, going on to form a formidable partnership with Denis Law. He scored twice in the 1963 FA Cup final.

Above middle: 36. Duncan Edwards.

Above right: 37. Ernie Taylor, Jimmy Murphy's first signing following Munich. The diminutive inside-forward cost a fee of £8,000 from Blackpool.

Left: 38. Dennis Viollet, who scored 32 goals in 36 games during 1959/60.

Below left: 39. George Best.

Below middle: 40. Jackie Blanchflower had to retire following the Munich disaster and the injuries he received.

Below right: 41. Jimmy Murphy.

Above left: 42. Johnny Berry, who also had to retire following the Munich disaster.

Above middle: 43. Kenny Morgans.

Above right: 44. Mark Pearson.

Right: 45. Harry Gregg, the hero of Munich.

Below left: 46. Nobby Stiles, the scourge of Benfica's Eusebio.

Below middle: 47. Jimmy Nicholson.

Below right: 48. Pat Crerand, the final piece of Matt Busby's jigsaw, as he completed the rebuilding following Munich. Signed from Celtic for £56,000, in February 1963. Crerand was a major force in the FA Cup victory over Leicester City.

Above left: 49. Stan Crowther, signed from Aston Villa for £18,000, just over an hour before the Sheffield Wednesday FA Cup tie, the first game after Munich. He had already played in the FA Cup for his former club, but was given special permission by the FA to turn out for United.

Above middle: 50. Shay Brennan.

Above right: 51. Denis Law, arguably Busby's best-ever signing. Cost a British record fee of £110,000 in August 1962, but more than repaid the outlay in the years that followed.

Left: 52. Noel Cantwell with the FA Cup.

Below left: 53. John Aston.

Below middle: 54. Warren Bradley, the amateur Bishop Auckland player, was signed following Munich simply as back-up, but went on to play over 60 games for United and also represented England.

Below right: 55. Tony Dunne.

East, paying £6 10*s* each for two chartered flights, were also caught up amid the confusion half an hour before kick-off. Hundreds of other travelling reds were locked out. 'It was fantastic,' said one. 'Absolute and utter chaos. Just a great mob of people out of control.' Another who had travelled North, a sixteen-year-old female, said, 'The queues just collapsed and I was pushed aside. I've never seen anything like it'.

There was also some concern for supporters travelling from Manchester by train on the afternoon of the match, when around 100 could not get on board due to trains being full and British Railways announced that they were not going to put on any extra carriages. Many decided to go home, but two coaches were commandeered from a local company and around forty went off by road, arriving in Sunderland with fifteen minutes to spare. Relieved to be at their destination, they were suddenly confronted with the chaos outside the ground and only two of those late arrivals managed to gain admission.

The game, surprisingly, was not all-ticket, with Sunderland chairman Syd Collings saying, 'There was no time to get them printed. People don't work on Saturdays or Sundays, so how could we get them done in forty-eight hours?' Supporters without tickets clambered over the turnstiles as their operators stood by helpless.

As for the game itself, it was as frantic as the scenes on the streets around the ground and, once again, United had to fight all the way to avoid defeat. At one point they were within two minutes of being deprived of a fourth consecutive semi-final appearance.

Play surged from end to end with neither team able to make any definite breakthrough, but ten minutes prior to half-time, Sunderland almost gained the initial foothold on the game. Setters was caught in two minds and robbed of the ball by Usher. Best slipped and tried to challenge, but fortunately for United Usher hit the ball against the leg of Dunne and it rebounded into the arms of Gaskell.

Five minutes later, that first crucial goal finally materialised when Foulkes headed clear, but only as far as Sharkey. With the ball at waist height, the Sunderland forward sprung into mid-air, connecting with the ball and sending his scissor-kick flying past a helpless Gaskell. Onto the field charged hundreds of jubilant youngsters and it was several minutes before play could be resumed.

That lead was almost doubled when Charlton, helping out his defenders – or at least attempting to – passed the ball rather too casually back towards Gaskell only for it to be intercepted by Crossan. Grateful for the gift, the Sunderland inside-left proceeded to walk the ball round the United 'keeper, but slipped on the muddy surface, and before he could regain possession, the ball had been seized by Gaskell.

United were given something of a lifeline in the sixty-second minute, again courtesy of the Sunderland goalkeeper, when Montgomery appeared to kick more of the ground than the ball while taking a goal-kick, and the ball bobbled straight to the feet of Denis Law. Taking a handful of steps, he pushed the ball wide of the helpless and mortified 'keeper and into the net.

As the frantic pace continued, the home side seemed to tire, but United still could not snatch that winning goal and the match crawled into extra time.

With less than a minute of the additional thirty played, Sunderland took the lead, Setters, trying to bring the ball under control, only succeeded in putting it into his own net. In the 107th minute, Law hit the bar, and eleven minutes later it was again all square. David Herd made up for earlier misses by crossing to Charlton who headed home from close range.

It was certainly another of those never-to-be-forgotten ninety minutes, and one still fondly remembered by Nicky Sharkey, who revealed that it wasn't just the United team who were caught up in the Roker Park mayhem. 'The Sunderland team had spent the afternoon at the Roker Hotel, and we were totally oblivious to the chaotic scenes outside until we set off on our short walk to the ground just after six o' clock. As soon as we came out of the hotel it was apparent that there were problems and when we reached the New Derby pub on Roker Park Road all we could see in front of us was people. We were trying to tell the fans who we were so we could get through, but their initial reaction was "get lost – wait in the queue like everybody else". Then they suddenly realised we actually were the Sunderland team and it was like the parting of the waters, although it still took us ages to force our way through to the players entrance.'

'The atmosphere was unbelievable,' he continued. 'The crowd were almost sitting on the touchline and the noise was incredible. I remember glancing at the United lads as we ran onto the pitch and you could see they were petrified. In fact, I was talking to Nobby Stiles recently, and although he didn't actually play that night, he was with the United party and he described the atmosphere in their dressing room before the match as one of absolute fear. He recalls a terrified George Best sitting in the corner with his head under a towel for a full hour before kick-off.'

Speaking of his goal, Sharkey said, 'It was just one of those instinctive things, as I saw the ball floating towards me I just decided to have a go. Nine times out of ten they end up over the bar but I caught this one perfectly and it gave the 'keeper no chance. It was far and away the best goal of my entire career. The thing I always remember about that goal is that my dad had travelled down from Scotland to see the game, and whenever he'd watched me previously I'd always played badly. At last I'd managed to show him what I was capable of. The mood in the dressing room was almost as bad as the Chelsea match the year before; we just couldn't believe we'd let them off the hook again when the game was effectively won. We were desperately disappointed.'

Rather surprisingly, in the First Division fixture at Upton Park three days later, United carved out a 2-0 victory, a win that offered them a psychological advantage over West Ham United, should the two teams meet in the forthcoming FA Cup semi-final, as well as keeping them within touching distance of the leaders Tottenham. Although they were four points behind with a game in hand, Matt Busby was forced into making five changes: 'All are genuinely injured. If they (*the Football League*) want they can have medical evidence,' said the United manager.

Out went Foulkes, Setters, Charlton, Law and Best and in came Tranter, Stiles, Anderson, Sadler and Moir, with the changes considered advantageous to the Upton Park side, but it was not to be and goals from Sadler and Herd secured the two precious points.

In the continuing saga of the ongoing FA Cup sixth-round tie against Sunderland on 9 March, this time in Yorkshire at Leeds Road, Huddersfield, Wilf Tranter continued at centre-half, but the other injured quartet returned to the United line-up. It was an additional game that United could well have done without and one that the Roker Park side might well have considered they were unfortunate to still be involved in, having twice had victory within their grasp.

Heavy rain in the Huddersfield area on the day of the game made conditions underfoot less than ideal, and it pushed the Leeds Road ground staff into some strenuous overtime, forking the sodden pitch until minutes before kick-off. The Sunderland players certainly did not find the conditions to their liking, and were actually unhappy that the game went ahead. There was also no repeat of the prematch chaos at the turnstiles, as the Huddersfield officials had the foresight to make the game all-ticket. Indeed, the only prematch problems involved the members of the press corps, as there were not enough seats in their allocated area to accommodate all who had been despatched to record the evening's events. The matter was solved by some divine intervention when the local vicar supplied thirty chairs from his Sunday school.

The defining moments of the whole encounter came within the fifth hour of actual play, when three goals in a frantic ninety-second spell decided who would meet West Ham United five days later in the semi-final.

The Roker Park side had been more-than-able opponents in the previous two games, but as this third meeting got underway, United for the first time in the tie looked the more purposeful of the two sides. With only twenty seconds gone, Best almost opened the scoring, running on to a pass from Law, back on familiar territory, only for Hurley's leg to deflect the ball out for a corner.

Sunderland quickly slipped into gear and forced five corners in the opening fifteen minutes, although Gaskell was never actually troubled, and slowly the momentum of the game began to build.

Law just failed to stretch to a centre from Best, but then brought Montgomery to his knees with a shot from 20 yards. Soon afterwards, he was again denied by the Sunderland 'keeper, who dived at his feet to smother the ball.

At the opposite end, with seven minutes to go until half-time, an Ashurst free-kick was headed on by Hurley, but was cleared off the line by Foulkes, with Crossan sliding menacingly towards the ball, after the bounce had beaten Gaskell.

They were all square at the interval, but within minutes of the restart the game exploded. United surged forward, and David Herd fired the ball past Montgomery, but the goal was disallowed for offside. Suddenly, Sunderland were on the attack. Thwarted unfairly, Ashurst again found the head of Hurley and the ball was directed to the feet of Crossan, who in turn picked out Sharkey. The Sunderland No. 9 shot past Gaskell to put his team in front for the sixth time in the three games.

The goal, however, was akin to showing a red rag to a bull, as it galvanised United into an instant reaction. Straight from the kick-off they surged forward, and Herd's shot was stopped by Montgomery, but he could not hold the ball and it broke to Law who side-footed it into the roof of the net.

With the clock still registering the forty-ninth minute, United quickly regained possession after Sunderland restarted the game, and Chisnall weaved his way through the Wearsiders' defence to put United 2-1 in front, the first time that they had held such a position in 259 minutes.

Two minutes later, Sunderland's brave fight was all but over when Hurley up-ended Herd inside the area, allowing Law to make it 3-1 from the penalty spot.

Slowly the fitness of a United team, which had 'rested' five of its personnel the previous weekend, began to tell. Law scored again in the sixty-first minute and Herd rounded the goal spree up six minutes later, although the action was far from over.

As the game moved towards full-time, Hurley turned on Charlton when the latter's boot accidentally caught Harvey amid a goalmouth scramble and the Sunderland captain had to be again restrained after Herd was thrown to the ground in a goalmouth melee. Fortunately for all concerned, the referee failed to see what actually happened and so took no action.

Having been so close on two occasions, defeat at Leeds Road was particularly hard for the Sunderland players to accept, but in the end they had no excuses. 'Basically the pitch was a mess and certainly didn't suit our style of play,' recalled Nicky Sharkey. 'As well as that, United had rested a number of players in preparation for the game whereas we'd played an important League game on the previous Saturday. Having said that, we more than held our own for the first forty-five minutes, then within a couple of minutes of the restart I slotted one in from close range to give us the lead. Looking back, it was probably the worst thing I could have done because it seemed to spark United into life. Denis Law equalised almost immediately and moments later Phil Chisnall put them in front for the first time in the tie. To be honest, after that we just couldn't live with them and they ended up putting five past us. We were all totally gutted after the match, not just because we'd taken a hammering, but because we had the tie won on more than one occasion and let it slip.'

Johnny Crossan was equally deflated after coming so close to victory on two occasions, saying, 'We are disappointed of course. But it was great while it lasted. I think we have proved – more than proved – that we would be capable of holding our own in the First Division.

'Bobby Charlton, on the evidence of our three games with United, is a far greater player than Denis Law. For most of our games Law has been remarkably quiet. Charlton has been tremendous throughout.

'United will win the cup now. They have got over the hardest hurdle.'

Thankfully, there had been no need for extra time, thirty strength-sapping minutes, and Busby spent the following few days preparing his team for their third consecutive FA Cup semi-final, before heading back to Yorkshire, and Sheffield Wednesday's Hillsborough, where West Ham United and Wembley's twin towers beckoned.

Many felt that despite the need to take Sunderland to three games in order to claim that semi-final spot, United, considering that they had beaten West Ham with something of an under-strength side, would be appearing in the final for the second consecutive season. However, Eric Todd of the *Guardian* was not completely convinced, writing, 'In assessing Manchester United's chances it would be as well to take into account their narrow escapes against Sunderland – and they were escapes – as well as their eventual rout of those opponents. If Manchester are as dilatory as they were in those first two matches, West Ham have every hope of success; if Manchester reproduce the form they showed in the second half at Leeds Road on Monday, West Ham almost inevitably will be beaten.

'A great deal, if not everything, will depend on whether Crerand and Setters can reach comparable heights. When they are no more than ordinary, the whole team suffers; when, as at Huddersfield, they are in top form, Manchester become a ruthless machine which tolerates no interference. In those circumstances, Law is a match-winner in his own right, as West Ham know full well.'

Todd rounded up his observations by saying, 'Yet I feel that Manchester's determination to reach the final for the second successive year and to obviate another postponement of their European Cup Winners' Cup game in Lisbon are in themselves sufficient incentives, and I do not think they will be disappointed.'

Wednesday's pitch was little better than that of Huddersfield Town's, oozing mud from end to end, which was not ideal for one of the showpiece games of the season, and unfortunately for United, it was the Hammers who adjusted best to the underfoot conditions. How poor and difficult to master those conditions were is perhaps best illustrated by an incident in the seventy-fifth minute when Standen, the West Ham goalkeeper, dived at the feet of Law, only for his face to sink into the black mud, knocking out all his senses. The United forward quickly helped him to his feet as his trainer rushed to his aid, with teammate Sissons running behind with a bucket of water as they struggled to clear his nose, eyes and mouth.

By then, West Ham were 2-0 in front courtesy of Ronnie Boyce, notching his first ten minutes into the second half and the second seven minutes later. Many felt that Gaskell should have stopped the first, but the United 'keeper had little chance with the second.

Few had given West Ham much of a chance in reaching their first FA Cup final since 1923, but as the game progressed, United looked tired, with the exertions of the past couple of weeks beginning to take their toll. The Londoners, with Bobby Moore practically running the game at his leisure, along with his fellow defenders, kept the United danger men at bay. Eric Todd's observations relating to Crerand and Setters proved to be spot on, as neither of the United half-backs could stamp any degree of authority on the game.

Best hit the bar prior to half-time, and moments after the restart Herd should have given United the lead, but it was not to be.

Boyce scored his first in the fifty-seventh minute with a drive from 25 yards, and this was followed by a headed second, but with twelve minutes to go, and Standen still recovering from his mud-pack facial, Burkett took a goal kick and placed it right to the feet of Chisnall, who quickly returned it goalwards where Law was ideally placed to head home. So, was the 65,000 crowd about to witness yet another dramatic Manchester United comeback?

On this occasion, the answer was no. With three minutes remaining, Bobby Moore beat Charlton and then Crerand wide on the touchline and, as he moved halfway into the United half, he cut the ball inside to Hurst who sent a low left-footed shot past Gaskell. United's Wembley dream was most definitely over.

There was, of course, still the possibility of League and European success, with United heading to Lisbon four days after the Hillsborough disappointment, confident of progressing to the semi-finals of the Cup Winners' Cup thanks to that 4-1 first-leg advantage.

Their defeat in Manchester, despite the two somewhat controversial penalty awards, did little to boost the confidence of the Sporting club, and prior to United's visit, they were held to a home draw in their Portuguese League fixture by bottom-of-the-table Olhanense, prompting a two-hour after-match protest by thousands of supporters in front of the main stand, demanding the sacking of manager Anselmo Fernandes, while a threat to force entry into the club offices was only prevented by police.

Such events caused the Sporting directors much concern, but also saw a story leaked that when United arrived in Lisbon, Matt Busby would be offered the job as manager, with a salary of around £200 per week. Money was no object, as their players were already on £300 a man to win, compared to United's meagre (and FA-restricted) £30.

Following the ninety-minute encounter, the Busby scenario never raised its head again.

Sporting had certainly learnt from their mistakes in Manchester, and straight from that first whistle attacked the United goal, clearly realising that they had little to lose and if they were to go out then they would do so fighting.

Their decisive plan paid immediate dividends, and with only ninety seconds on the clock, a ball into the United penalty area was handled by Tony Dunne, leaving the French referee with little option but to point immediately to the spot. Although inside-right Silva Osvaldo shot directly at Gaskell, the 'keeper had already decided to dive and had little hope in stopping the ball.

So, before they had even broken sweat, United found themselves under unnecessary pressure, but slowly managed to cause some concern in the Lisbon defence when Setters came close with a header. A further couple of raids proved equally fruitless, as the visitors struggled to find any sort of rhythm, and ten minutes after going behind they conceded a second.

Morais collected a through-ball, cut inside a centre quickly into the United area, finding Osvaldo at the far post, and the inside-forward forced the ball home.

United managed to contain Sporting during the remainder of the first half holding, however limply, to the one-goal advantage, but even that was only thanks to the referee, who disallowed a Mascarenhas long-range effort for handball. But it was an advantage that they were not going to have for much longer.

One minute into the second half, it was 4-4 on aggregate, Geo putting his side level with an opportunist's goal. Five minutes later it was 4-0 on the night, a cross from the right driven home by Morais. United were well and truly down and most certainly out. This was confirmed in the fifty-fourth minute, when Osvaldo claimed his hat-trick, scoring with a direct free-kick.

Surrendering a three-goal advantage was a humiliating experience, and had Law's left-footed shot on the turn, following a delightful lob over the head of Batista, beaten Carvalho instead of hitting the post, then the story of the game could have read differently. But it was not to be. United were disjointed, roundly booed and whistled at as they directed their humiliation at their opponents' bodies rather than their goal as the minutes slowly ticked away.

'We were outplayed, out-thought and out-run,' said a disappointed Matt Busby. 'There can be no argument, Sporting were the better side. I was very disappointed. We never recovered from the penalty early in the game and it appears that the heavy programme over the past few weeks has taken its toll.'

'My boys left so much of themselves at home. The three matches against Sunderland took a lot out of them. And the semi-final against West Ham on that terrible mud at Sheffield finally drained them mentally and physically. They were far more affected by those games than we thought.

'All the lads are sick with the shock of this defeat. The last four days have been a nightmare.

'I certainly do not blame individuals. We failed as a team and I still say it was the heavy programme of matches that pulled us down.

'The team is tired physically and mentally.

'Now I hope that we will step back very soon into a winning vein. But it is always difficult to solve a problem like this because it can only be tackled by rest and relaxation. The tremendous pressure on the team has been too much for us.'

Denis Law echoed some of his manager's thoughts. 'It was disastrous,' he said. 'I have never been so choked in all my life. It was the goal that came just after half-time, the third one that killed us off. It's laughable to say I'm disappointed. We were just a disgrace.'

The Portuguese were equally as critical and strangely made a point which is still very much debated today. 'This wasn't Manchester United. This was a tired bunch of men sent to us by the antiquated League system in England.

'No other country in Europe expects her teams to squeeze international games in the odd space between domestic fixtures.'

The United players arrived back in their Estoril hotel looking like chief mourners at a funeral, as the Portuguese press penned their obituaries. The sports columnist of the *Diaro de Noticias*, Lisbon's largest daily newspaper, wrote, 'Many supporters went to the Alvalade Stadium to see Manchester United but Sporting stole the whole limelight. The tactics, flexibility, speed, scoring power, accuracy and ball control in passing and defensive placing were all to be found on the home side. Sporting had the lot. If Manchester have all this, they must have left it behind, like lost luggage, in England! Sporting dominated in all phases and sectors of the game. United did not live up to their reputation. Foulkes and Crerand were the best in defence and Setters tried hard. Law was a disappointment – like the rest of the team.'

'Who could have expected such a tremendous surprise? Who could foresee that Sporting Club of Lisbon would produce such a wonderful performance? Who could guess that Manchester United, the famous team managed by the big Matt Busby, would lose in Lisbon the advantage of three goals got at Old Trafford,' wrote Mr J. M. Salema, the director of the *Sporting* newspaper.

Having previously commented he felt that United's first-leg advantage was fortunate due to the two penalty awards, while adding that had they not been given then the visitors would have indeed have been fortunate in leaving Manchester only one goal down, he was stunned to have seen Sporting Lisbon overcome United and progress into the next round: 'Even after the first half, with the score 2-0, the bet I really expected was the prospect of meeting again those fine people of United in Madrid for a replay match.

'But the Sporting forwards had decided to play the match of their lives (when Osvaldo is inspired, our attack is really dangerous), and three more goals in the first few minutes of the second half turned the happy dreams of United reaching the semi-final into a tremendous nightmare.

'Someone tried to find an excuse for such an unexpected event, and suggested that the English players were tired. This of course, would be a reasonable excuse, providing they did not win the following match with Tottenham in London.

'From my own point of view, the United players lost the match and the tie on account of the good job performed by the Sporting defence.'

United's defeat at the hands of Sporting Lisbon rewrote the record books, as no club in any of the European competitions had ever relinquished a three-goal lead over the course of ninety minutes, but it was hoped that they would manage to shake off such a disappointment and get back on track against Tottenham Hotspur at White Hart Lane.

United flew directly to Heathrow, with David Sadler and Graham Moore, who had both escaped the embarrassment of Lisbon, travelling south from Manchester to join up with their dejected teammates and taking their places in the United line-up, replacing Chisnall and Herd.

With the game twenty-five minutes old, it looked as though United's nightmare was about to continue when Bill Foulkes, on his knees inside the penalty area, pushed the ball away from the feet of Jones with his hand. Strangely, the referee waved play on as the howls of anger cascaded from the terraces. Had he awarded the spot-kick and it had been converted, then United may well have struggled given their previous performances.

The Tottenham players and support felt even harder done by three minutes later, as play swung to the opposite end of the pitch. Charlton allowed a pass from Best to run through to Law, and from an acute angle a yard from goal, the deadly Scot managed to slip the ball between Hollowbread and the goalpost to put United a goal in front. It was, however, a lead that was short lived, as two minutes later Laurie Brown put the home side level, running on to Mullery's pass as the United defence stood looking for an offside decision.

Within a ten-minute spell, the game was suddenly turned on its head. Crerand slung a pass towards Moore and the inside-forward put United 2-1 in front. Mullery stopped a Best effort on the line, but the visitors had their tails up and a third goal wasn't long in materialising. Charlton manoeuvred down the ball some 40 yards towards the Tottenham goal, inter-passing with Moore, before smashing the ball home in customary fashion.

From then on, Totttenham rarely looked like making any dramatic fight-back despite Brown heading against the post, although they did reduce arrears two minutes from time when a lacklustre Jimmy Greaves scored with a penalty after Sadler had handled; a decision that was as incorrect as the one in the first half.

United's victory kept them in the championship race, and what was now their only hope of silverware. Although they were four points behind leaders Everton with two games in hand, Liverpool were second, two points in front of United, having played the same number of games.

Chelsea travelled to Old Trafford on 23 March as United continued their drive towards the championship, but their hopes were somewhat derailed in a rather disappointing ninety minutes, due mainly to a resolute visiting defence.

The Londoners almost took a shock lead within the opening five minutes when Bridges jumped over a Murray cross and Upton forced Gaskell into turning the ball round for a corner. The 'keeper had also to be alert in order to deal with shots from Venables and Bluntstone.

Law headed over a Moore centre in the twentieth minute and was denied by Bonetti soon afterwards as United continued their push towards that title dream. Sadler fired over from 12 yards, then shot straight at the Chelsea 'keeper, but with only sixty seconds remaining before the interval, United finally got the breakthrough. Charlton sent the ball into the middle and in a flash, Law, with his back to goal, swivelled and turned the ball past the helpless Bonetti.

United may well have increased their lead, but poor finishing and Peter Bonetti prevented them from keeping it, as the visitors snatched an equaliser in the sixty-fifth minute when Venables centred beautifully, Bridges headed the ball against the crossbar and Murray latched on to the rebound.

United might well have regained the advantage when Shellito went off with a head injury following a mid-air challenge with Law, but it was not to be and they had to be content with nothing more than a share of the points.

A 2-2 Good Friday draw at Craven Cottage against Fulham saw another valuable point dropped, as did a similar scoreline twenty-four hours later against Wolves at Old Trafford. United's failure to hold on to their leads in both fixtures diminished further those outside hopes of winning the title, leaving them in third place, four points behind leaders Everton. Their game in hand, however, gave them an outside hope.

Back on track with a 3-0 win over Fulham at Old Trafford, something of a crunch encounter followed. Liverpool had overtaken Merseyside rivals Everton and claimed the leadership of the First Divison, standing three points in front of United. They had also played a game less. So, if United still held any outside hopes of lifting the championship then, with five games remaining, two points at Anfield was a necessity to say the least.

But they were two points that were not going to materialise, as Liverpool, from the outset, shrugged off United's somewhat tame attempt to wrestle the championship away from Merseyside. For the third time in a matter of weeks Busby's side failed to rise to the occasion and looked something of a distinctly ordinary side as the newspaper headlines were quick to broadcast to the country. 'Manchester are Crushed', 'It's Champagne Liverpool – Poor United Simply Left Flat', 'Manchester United Outclassed' are enough to tell the sad story of that April afternoon.

Throughout the ninety minutes, they failed to have one worthwhile shot on target, and after one or two half-hearted probes in the opening minutes, they were left mainly on the defensive as Liverpool surged forward. Arrowsmith, Hunt and Stevenson all came close before Callaghan opened the scoring with a thunderous drive in the sixth minute after Gregg dropped Thompson's corner under pressure from Yeats.

Apart from a couple of token attacks, it was all Liverpool – even Denis Law was called into defensive duties, clearing a shot from Callaghan off the line six minutes prior to half-time, but the Liverpool man quickly regained possession, centred to Arrowsmith and Liverpool were 2-0 in front.

As the second half got underway, Setters was twice pulled up for fouls on Hunt, while Gregg did well to prevent that same Liverpool player from scoring a third. But it was inevitable that a third goal would come and in the fifty-first minute, with United's defence in complete disarray, Arrowsmith struck after Moran, Hunt and St John created the opportunity.

'Go home you mugs, go home' to the tune of Auld Land Syne echoed down from the Kop at the disjointed visiting side who drifted aimlessly through the remainder of the game. Law did force Lawrence into making a save, but his frustration later got the better of him and he was booked for a foul on St John. Best tried hard, as did Crerand, but without the support they were never going to cause Liverpool many problems.

So it was a dejected team and supporters who made their way back along the East Lancs Road, knowing full well that the First Division title was going to remain on Merseyside, unless there was a major collapse at Anfield. Liverpool sat comfortably on top spot with fifty-two points from their thirty-seven games, while United remained third with forty-seven points from thirty-eight games. Last season's Champions Everton were sandwiched in between, with forty-nine points from thirty-nine games.

A solitary Denis Law goal, in front of the lowest attendance of the season (25,848) gave United a 1-0 victory over Aston Villa, pushing them into second place, in a game ruined by offside decisions – thirty-three in total, with Villa the main culprits.

It was a frustrating ninety minutes for the sparse crowd, with many venting their disapproval in front of the press box at what Terence Elliot of the *Daily Express* called 'one of the most frustrating and low-grade exhibits of football I have seen at Old Trafford this season'. He added, 'Surely at half-time, when it was seen that the game was developing into a farce, something could have been done by those who dictate tactics on the field of play.'

The jeers continued to be heard around Old Trafford seven days later against Sheffield United, sounding loud and clear when the visitors took a twenty-third-minute lead through Jones, pushing the ball home at the second attempt after Gregg had blocked his initial shot.

United had seen eight scoring opportunities scorned in the opening twenty minutes, but it was not until three minutes before the interval that they eventually found the net. With the crowd continuing to vent their displeasure, Charlton hit the post after surging down the middle, leaving Shaw in his wake, and before Hodgkinson could recover Law had nipped in to prod the ball home.

Twenty minutes from time, having endured the wrath of the crowd for most of the game, Ian Moir secured both points for United. Making only his seventeenth League appearance of the season, the young Scot, who had been booed unmercifully throughout the game, took a Charlton pass and moved down the wing. As the crowd prepared to barrack his expected eventual error, he suddenly cut inside the full-back before squeezing a left-footed shot between the goalkeeper and the post. It was a goal that secured United's victory.

There was now only one point separating Liverpool and United, but the Anfield side had three games in hand and United had only two games remaining.

Although United could compete with the best, the defeat at Liverpool and those other disappointing performances had confirmed to Matt Busby that his side was still lacking one, or perhaps two, final ingredients to propel them back to the top of the English game. In Best and Sadler, flitting between first-team and youth-team duties, they had two highly promising youngsters, but Busby was aware that although youth was the future, you also needed experience, something that, while helping the side as a whole, would also be beneficial in the progress of those youngsters.

Not all youngsters could look forward to a career at Old Trafford, as Busby began pruning his junior staff in an effort to allow more of his youth-team players to progress. As well as Best and Sadler, there were also Willie Anderson, John Fitzpatrick, John Aston and the highly rated full-back Bobby Noble, members of a side that were about to emulate those FA Youth Cup-winning teams of the fifties, by bringing that prestige trophy back to Old Trafford for the first time since 1957.

The news of pruning the playing staff caused concern even amongst the senior players as Busby looked to the future, with the season moving into its final few weeks. But while looking to reduce his overall playing staff, he continued to look towards making improvements and stepped into the transfer market, paying out a reported £40,000 for Burnley's England international winger John Connelly, while immediately recouping £30,000 of the fee by selling Phil Chisnall to Liverpool.

The Connelly transfer was typical Busby, coming right out of the blue, although the United manager had been negotiating with Burnley for some time. The Turf Moor side had continuously turned down United's approaches for the twenty-six-year-old, but when Matt Busby and chairman Harold Hardman made the short journey to Burnley on 14 April, taking in the Clarets' match against Liverpool, the United manager made a preliminary enquiry as to Connelly's availability after the game.

With no definite answer, he returned with a firm offer the following Wednesday and, after a half-hour meeting with the Burnley directors, he got his man, as his 'take it or leave it' final offer was considered too high to refuse by the Burnley board. The evening also enabled the United duo to shake hands on the second deal, this time with members of the Liverpool board, rubber-stamping the transfer of Phil Chisnall. Like United's interest in Connelly, the Anfield club had declared their interest in the player earlier in the month despite denials from manager Bill Shankly.

'John Connelly is the type of winger we want,' said Busby. 'I am very pleased. We shall not hurry him over because he will not be eligible for any of the remaining fixtures.'

Mystery, however, surrounded the actual transfer fee, as it was also reported that United had in fact paid £60,000 for the player, £20,000 more than planned. This was mainly due to the interest of another club and that £40,000 was United's initial offer, with the additional sum swaying the deal. To have improved their original offer by so much was very untypical of Busby and United, certainly at this particular time, but it proved that Connelly was a player that the United manager did not simply admire, but one that he felt was a necessary addition to his team.

Upon signing for United, Connelly said, 'I'm sorry to be leaving, but Burnley need the money and if I had been given the choice of clubs it would have been United. It will be great playing alongside Law and Charlton.

'What club has better prospects than Manchester United?

'It was a bolt out of the blue and caught me by surprise,' continued the highly rated winger. 'I knew, along with the other players, that Burnley had to sell to keep going, but I didn't think it would be me.

'Mr Busby convinced me that my prospects would be good at Old Trafford and after a talk with my wife I decided to sign.

'I'll miss Burnley tremendously: both the club, who have been really good to me, and the town.

'My two regrets are that I couldn't stay to see Burnley hit the high spots again and that I wasn't given a chance at inside-forward this season.'

'We're very sorry to have to part with Connelly,' said Burnley chairman Bob Lord, 'but we decided to accept United's offer. I think our supporters realised our position.' A position that must have indeed been quite serious, as Lord was certainly far from being a signed-up member of the Manchester United fan club.

The transfer did indeed cause much anger and indignation within the support of the Lancashire club, but in the harsh daylight, Burnley, despite their reasonable success a couple of years or so previously, had to sell to survive; even if it did mean doing business with their much-despised neighbours.

It had not been the happiest of seasons for the goalscoring winger, who had been filling the No. 11 shirt at Turf Moor, as he felt that he could have enjoyed things a bit more had been given the opportunity to play at inside-forward or in his old position of outside-right – the one he thought was his best and the one where he was to be deployed by his new club.

Despite now being a Manchester United player, Connelly was unable to play in the remaining fixtures due to the lateness in the season of his signing. With the former Burnley player sitting on the sidelines, United's slender grain of championship hope dissolved completely on 18 April at the Victoria Ground, Stoke, when the home side, fourth from the bottom and continuing their crawl from the grasps of relegation, inflicted a 3-1 defeat; a victory engineered by former United favourite Dennis Viollet.

Indeed, it was Viollet who scored Stoke City's second goal in the twenty-fifth minute, after Palmer had given them the lead seven minutes earlier, although many judged Dobing's throw-in prior to the goal as a definite 'foul-throw'. There was, however, little argument about Viollet's effort, a close-range header from McIlroy's corner.

Nine minutes before half-time, Charlton pulled United back into the game, but any hopes of a fight-back were completely destroyed when Ritchie made it 3-0 in the seventy-sixth minute after more poor defending.

The only hint of some Mancunian aggression came from the terraces, with several policemen having to move into the crowd in an attempt to quell outbreaks of fighting, as the title challenge, which most had known for a few weeks was little more than a dream, disappeared for another twelve months at least.

Nottingham Forest were beaten 3-1 in the final game of the season at Old Trafford, but it was simply a case of what might have been, as Liverpool lifted the title with four points to spare.

So, no League championship trophy for the Old Trafford boardroom, but thousands of supporters, amongst a crowd of 25,563, surged onto the hallowed turf on the evening of 30 April to celebrate the success of United's youth team, who lifted the FA Youth Cup, a trophy that was once the personal property of the club, with a 5-2 aggregate win over Swindon Town.

The likes of Duncan Edwards, Bobby Charlton, Eddie Colman and David Pegg had all plied their trade in the tournament, with the 23-0 victory over lowly Nantwich on 4 November 1952 setting a benchmark that would never be matched, but in the latest batch of hopefuls – three of whom had already graced the First Division stage, one even a full internatonal – gave everyone hope for the future.

In the wake of the Munich disaster, the United youth team had failed to reach the heights of their predecessors who had won the trophy for the first five seasons following its inauguration. Seasons 1957/58, 1958/59 and 1959/60 had seen them fall one step from the final, but into the new decade, they stuttered somewhat, with few of the players showing the necessary talent and ability to make the step up towards the first team.

The crash had taken its toll on every inch of the club, with the youngsters in the junior teams no exception. 'Jimmy (*Murphy*) was the Youth Cup,' explained his son Jimmy Jnr. 'He scouted, recruited and coached all the future stars. He was ably assisted by his "team", especially Bert Whalley. After Munich Jimmy was busy with first-team duties, Bert was dead, as was Tom Curry. Arthur Powell moved up to the professional team, while John Aston moved up to youth-team and reserve-team duties. John, who of course played in the famous 1948 cup-winning side, would prove to be a good coach but he just wasn't Bert!

'Due to the pressure surrounding the first team in those post-Munich days, it was several seasons before Jimmy returned to his more regular role with the youth team, and when he did, John became his right-hand man.

'The effect on the youth team of 1958 was severe, both physically and mentally, as they had lost their idols and role models in the first team. One such youngster was Nobby Stiles, who was fifteen at the time and an apprentice. One of his jobs was to clean boots of senior players, one of whom was Eddie Colman. Nobby would, like me, have watched Eddie playing for the reserves and youth team before progressing to the first team. Eddie would have given Nobby tips, both on football and monetary, and also given Nobby a "bonus" at Christmas. Can you imagine how Nobby felt after the crash? He lost a hero, a colleague and a friend that day, and was to later recall that he was "devastated".

'There would be all the other apprentices of Nobby's time who would have been in a similar position.

'Players were promoted too quickly and the higher grade of football was too much for some. The team reached the semi-finals in 1958 but lost, with the likes of Alex Dawson and Mark Pearson unable to play due to first-team duties. They were the two best players at this time, and in Dawson you had the record goalscorer in the history of the FA Youth Cup.

'You can sense the disappointment that this group of players would have suffered, as they wanted to succeed for "the boys". Confidence in some players would also have dipped.

'The fifteen-year-old boys joining in summer of 1958 and 1959 would not have received the grounding from Bert which was so essential to their start at United. The seventeen-year-old (new) professionals would not be receiving Jimmy's words of wisdom, be they of encouragement or criticism.

'I am certainly convinced that quite a few players would have been released as "not good enough", but who otherwise might have made it with Bert and Jimmy backing them. Both men had twelve years' experience of developing youngsters; this was missing from some of the later crop of youngsters' start at United.

'I would also mention "burn out" for some players after their efforts in February, March, and April 1959. There were many matches to play with some players playing too much. The likes of Johnny Giles, who I would regard at that time as a reserve-team player, was possibly involved in helping out to fulfil the backlog of fixtures. If John, then probably others, and it possibly caught up with some players, with a lasting effect.'

That was until the current season, when a new batch of youngsters hit the conveyor belt.

Goals had been something associated with United in this competition, and although they never got near to matching the twenty-three against Nantwich, they did notch eleven against Bexley Heath, nine against Plymouth, eight against Newcastle and in the 1963/64 competition, fourteen against Barrow. Strangely enough, nine of the goals against Barrow were scored by players who would never see the first-team dressing room – Morton, who scored five and McEwan who hit one less – but despite the deluge, it hadn't been all plain sailing, as Blackpool were only beaten by the odd goal in five and Wolves held a one-goal lead for almost an hour in the fifth-round tie, in front of just over 14,000 spectators. Two goals from David Sadler, however, secured victory.

A 1-1 draw in the first leg of the final at Swindon set up a entertaining ninety minutes in the Old Trafford second leg, despite George Best only flying in from Belfast on the morning of the game, following his fourth competitive fixture in six days – his latest ninety minutes an international for Northern Ireland against Uruguay. Such things mattered little to the impish Irishman who set up a hat-trick for David Sadler in United's 4-1 win. Another youngster with aspirations for the first team, John Aston, scored the fourth.

The future was indeed rosy, but only the sight of silverware of a greater importance would pacify both the support and the management of Manchester United.

6

ENDING THAT EIGHT-YEAR WAIT

Although the disappointment of being unable to land the First Division championship crown lasted throughout the summer – despite an end-of-season 5-3 victory over City at Maine Road, which did bring a trophy to the Old Trafford boardroom in the form of the Duke of Edinburgh Trophy, along with victories over Roma, Livorno and Juventus in the close-season tour – there was cause for much optimism as the dawn of a new season broke across the horizon. A considerable number of those within the media were tipping United to finish the forthcoming season in top spot for the first time in seven years. At one point, however, many of the supporters felt that their team would once again be chasing the leaders, as a huge, dark cloud drifted across the Manchester skyline, with the city buzzing to the rumour that Denis Law had refused to resign and was holding out for a £10,000-a-year contract. Thankfully it was little more than a rumour, as United's most valuable asset returned from holiday and put pen to paper on a new two-year deal, with an option of an additional year, that would see him guaranteed £150 per week, an increase of around £45, although this would be topped up with various bonuses. It was money that United could well afford, as they reported a profit of £44,887 on last season, while also increasing ticket prices for the campaign ahead, which would boost the coffers.

It has to be remembered that any money made by clubs in those now distant days was generated solely through the turnstiles, and mass marketing was something that no one had as yet clocked on to. United, fortunately, due mainly to the talents of Denis Law and Bobby Charlton and the up-and-coming prospect of George Best, could rely on better crowds than most. With their pulling power they could generate improved gates for many of their First Division stablemates, although the games against the Italian clubs at the end of the previous season had failed to attract above 20,000 crowds.

Pre-season had been favourable, with John Connelly settling in nicely with two goals in the 3-1 win in Hamburg. Only an injury to Law in the 4-2 win over Shamrock Rovers in Dublin gave Busby any cause for concern as United prepared to face West Bromwich Albion at Old Trafford on the opening Saturday of the 1964/65 season.

While Law was certainly guaranteed his place in the line-up, unless he was injured or indeed suspended, others could not always be certain of being in favour with Busby. Club captain Noel Cantwell, who had started twenty-eight League games last season, had attracted interest from his old West Ham United teammate, Malcolm Allison, at Plymouth Argyle, while former captain Maurice Setters, who had started thirty-two games in the 1963/64 campaign, found himself debating his future as he was uncertain of regular first-team football. Ian Moir was another who was uncertain of his United future, as Busby sought a greater efficiency from his players.

Maurice Setters, however, was given something of a shock call-up for the opening fixture of the campaign against his former club West Bromwich Albion, at the expense of Pat Crerand. The former

Celtic man, who had played an influential part in the United set-up since his move south, found himself kicking off the new season in the Central League side. 'Pat is going through a slight spell out of form,' declared Busby.

The United manager usually watched his team from the elevated position just above the player's tunnel, but for most of the second half of that opening fixture he was down on the trainer's bench, a sure sign that he was dissatisfied with the way his team were performing on the other side of the touchline.

West Brom stunned the 50,000 crowd by taking a thirteenth-minute lead through Brown, the eighteen-year-old nipping in front of Gaskell to turn a Foggo cross into the net. They continued to harass the home defence and certainly looked more than capable of increasing their lead until Law headed a Connelly cross past Potter for the equaliser in the twenty-second minute.

A 25-yard Charlton drive gave United the lead seven minutes from the interval, but within three minutes, the visitors were back on level terms, when Clark beat an offside trap and his shot cannoned off the legs of Foulkes and past Gaskell.

United seemed to get bogged down in midfield, but the crowd turned their frustration towards David Herd, with the centre-forward booed by sections of the crowd two minutes from the end, after missing a glorious opportunity to secure an opening-day victory for United.

Herd would have numerous other opportunities to atone for that miss and regain the support of those on the terracing, but one man never had an opportunity to regain favour, and carried a much heavier burden on his shoulders than that of simply missing a goalscoring opportunity.

James Thain had been blamed and sacked from his job as an airline pilot in 1960, following the Munich air disaster six years ago, but he was now cleared of all blame by an Aviation Ministry report. Although not issued publicly, the report stated that no matter who had been at the controls of the ill-fated BEA Ambassador, the plane would not have taken off.

An investigation by the German authorities laid the blame fairly and squarely on Captain Thain for not examining the top of the plane's wings for ice prior to take off, but following the new report, the Germans were advised in a strongly worded letter to reopen investigations.

For Captain Thain, although a weight off his shoulders, it did not ease the pain that he had suffered over the years, the recurring nightmares, and he was to remain bitter for the rest of his life (he died at the age of fifty-four in 1975), as the German authorities failed to recognise the findings of their British counterparts.

Two days after the opening-day draw against West Bromwich Albion, the supporters who decided to put money on United lifting the First Division championship must have thought that they would have been better off spending it in their local pub, or indeed giving it to their wives, as a trip to Upton Park saw West Ham United trounce United 3-1.

There was always the possibility that, if some of those who had backed United were also travelling supporters, they might indeed have saved some of their outlay in London's East End, as a considerable number of people clambered over the stadium walls to gain illegal entry into the Hammers ground.

West Ham, in their first home game since winning the FA Cup, were fully aware that United would be out for revenge for their semi-final defeat, but were prepared for the onslaught and stunned their visitors with two early goals through Byrne in the fourth minute and Sissons in the twentieth.

As early as the third minute, United's sloppiness in defence was evident and both goals were the result of poor defending. When Maurice Setters was carried off twelve minutes into the second half, they really had an upward battle on their hands. Frank McGhee, in the *Daily Mirror*, reckoned that United played better with ten men than they did with eleven, and in the seventy-ninth minute, Denis Law pulled a goal back. But it was s comeback that started too late, and one which barely raised any concern within the solid Hammers defence. Instead of being forced back, they were allowed to attack almost at will, and four minutes from time added a third goal through Hurst to round off a miserable night for Busby's team.

Five days later, at Filbert Street, Leicester, it was little better, as United stuttered along for long periods of the game. Leicester took the lead in the ninth minute through Keyworth and it was not until the seventy-first minute that Sadler headed home the equaliser from a Best centre. Six minutes from time, Appleton nudged the home side in front once again, but they were to be denied victory with only two minutes remaining, when Law made it three in three games, blasting yet another Best centre past a wall of blue-shirted defenders, before strutting down the field acknowledging his loyal followers.

It had certainly not been the ideal start to the campaign, with only three points from three games, and certainly not one that Matt Busby and the United support had expected. However, with United, nothing could be guaranteed as they could flow from sublime to mediocre as quickly as it took the ball to go from one end of the pitch to the other. A 3-1 victory in their next fixture produced not simply two valuable points, but sweet revenge.

West Ham travelled north knowing that they had nothing to fear from ninety minutes at Old Trafford, and although Booby Moore and Ken Brown were both in superb form at the heart of the Hammers' defence, United finally shook off the cobwebs and clicked into gear straight from the kick-off. Law and Charlton created an opening for Best, who beat Bond before crossing into the area, where Sadler missed the ball, but Connelly didn't and the ball flashed past the helpless Standen.

A Nobby Stiles own goal five minutes later allowed West Ham back into the game, and they began to push the ball around with their usual aplomb, but once again it was down to Denis Law to release United from the threatening stalemate.

Almost on the half-hour, he snatched the opportunity when Standen failed to hold a shot from Connelly, and suddenly the game changed completely. No longer were West Ham allowed to play their normal tight and controlled game as United took command. Best missed two great chances before scoring United's third in the fifty-eighth minute, but in the end they should have certainly won by more than two goals, as in the opening twenty minutes of the second half alone they missed twelve scoring opportunities.

Strangely, it wasn't a victory that got the season back on track, as despite the two points against West Ham, a visit to Craven Cottage saw the defence continue to capitulate under pressure, while the forward line failed to find any resemblance to a balanced outfit, despite the addition of the talented Connelly. The Londoners sent United back to Manchester pointless. Once again, in a game full of niggling, petty fouls, it was a goal scored late in the game that decided United's fate in the 2-1 defeat.

Although it had been something of an unconvincing start to the season, Busby reduced his first-team squad by one, in early September, when he allowed Albert Quixall, his record £45,000 signing from Sheffield Wednesday, to join Oldham Athletic for the cut-price sum of £7,000. Quixall had not featured in a United starting line-up since the 6-1 defeat by Burnley on Boxing Day 1963, although he had been the travelling reserve for the match at Craven Cottage. Despite being one of Busby's favourite sons, he had been available for transfer for some time, and almost six years to the day since he put pen to paper on his record-breaking move to Old Trafford, he departed for the less demanding pastures of the Third Division and Boundary Park.

'Obviously it is a wrench leaving after six years,' a disappointed Quixall said. 'But I want first-team soccer and I haven't really been part of United's first-team plans this season. So when I heard Oldham Athletic were really keen, I was glad to join them.

'Soccer has helped me achieve all my ambitions. I've played for Sheffield Wednesday – my favourite club. I've played for England five times and I've just got a cup medal.'

It was something of a revolving door, as no sooner had Quixall departed the scene than another player was stepping into the first-team limelight. Signed early in May, for a fee of £10,000 from Shamrock Rovers, goalkeeper Pat Dunne suddenly found himself thrust into the hustle and bustle of the First Division scene at Goodison Park, a ground not entirely unfamiliar to him. The twenty-one-year-old, who had spent six weeks on trial with United as a fifteen-year-old, had also been on Everton's books for three years, before returning to the Emerald Isle on a free transfer after breaking an arm.

The inclusion of Dunne, at the expense of Gaskell, could not give United their second victory of the season, and despite the debutant making a handful of memorable saves to keep his team in the game, United once again threw it all away by conceding a goal late in the game, while leading 3-2.

United took a 2-0 lead with goals from Law in the fourth minute and Connelly on the half-hour mark, but after the interval they allowed the home side back into the game with goals from Pickering in the fifty-first and fifty-sixth minutes.

David Herd, back in favour after missing three games, restored United's lead in the seventy-fourth minute and with only six minutes remaining. However, with both points looking secure, United's defence allowed their concentration to slip and Alec Young drove home the equaliser.

It was result that left United in fifteenth place, but it could have had more severe consequences than a dropped point, as Denis Law escaped serious injury by inches when he somersaulted over a concrete barrier, landing head first on the opposite side, following a first-half attempt on goal.

The minor knocks received were enough to keep Law out of the next game against Nottingham Forest which, strangely enough, United won 3-0 in a rather one-sided encounter. Four days later he was back in the side as large as life, scoring United's second, as they made it two wins on the trot, with a 2-1 home win against Everton.

The corner finally seemed to have been turned and, in a thrilling encounter against Stoke City at the Victoria Ground, a 2-1 win was enough to keep the momentum going. Those three successive victories could not have come at a better time, as not only did it push United up the First Division table to a more respectable seventh position, but also gave them the ideal platform to get their European campaign on the road.

Playing in the Inter-Cities Fairs Cup and drawn against Swedish side Djurgardens, United travelled to Stockholm for the first leg of the opening round against a strong, workmanlike outfit. In the 50,000-capacity stadium, sparsely populated with a meagre crowd of only 6,537, the visitors returned to their slipshod worst and struggled for long periods against the part-timers. It was yet another dismal performance on the Continent, having struggled in Rotterdam against Willem, thrown away the three-goal advantage in Lisbon, and failed to create anything like the reputation that they were beginning to gain on home shores despite that indifferent start to the season.

The Swedes took only eight minutes to break down the United defence, but in a complete reversal of their early season performances, with the game slipping away from them, David Herd headed a goal three minutes from time, salvaging a draw, and set up an interesting second-leg confrontation in Manchester.

Perhaps United were slightly over-cautious, but with their array of attacking players they should have performed much better, although Busby was relatively happy with the result: 'We played better in the second half and it is always pleasing to get a draw away from home in this kind of tie.'

Noel Cantwell, on the other hand, pointed out that the lack of atmosphere within the vast stadium did little to lift the players: 'It was like sitting in a half-empty theatre – no atmosphere and no excitement. It was as bad for the players as actors, trying to perform to a handful of people in a huge theatre.'

Returning to the domestic scene, the seemingly couldn't-care-less approach was nowhere to be seen, abandoned somewhere over the North Sea, much to the regret of Tottenham Hotspur, who were thumped 4-1 at Old Trafford on 26 September. Four days later, Tommy Docherty's table-topping Chelsea received a similar treatment, relinquishing their unbeaten opening run to the genius of George Best and Denis Law.

Stamford Bridge had yet to achieve the accolade of a hostile environment, with the supporters who frequented 'the Shed' going on to become some of the most feared amongst the gangs that were soon to bring mayhem and destruction to stadiums and streets. But at the end of ninety minutes which saw their favourites completely outplayed, they stood, sportingly, and applauded the bewitching display of George Best.

The touchline wizardry of the nineteen-year-old Irishman was simply the icing on the cake of a superb United performance, with the 2-0 victory taking them to within two points of the leaders.

Best had given United the lead in the thirty-second minute, nipping in to snatch a half-chance as McCreadie attempted to pass the ball back to Bonetti. Then, fifteen minutes from time, he set up the second for Law.

The rigours of First Division football took its toll on even the most experienced professional, but for the likes of Messrs Law and Best, skilful, match-winning individuals, there was the added threat of uncompromising defenders determined to block out the danger to their team by any means possible, bringing the risk of injury with every goalward movement.

Following the countless crude tackles that came his way, Best simply got up, sought the ball and took out his retribution on the offender by beating him time and time again. Law on the other hand was not so placid in nature and was just as likely to get up and lash out, incurring punishment from the referee despite being the originally innocent party.

Those bookings and sending-offs would deprive United of their star striker and debatably their main man, as would injuries from the attention he attracted, but there were also injuries to other individuals that would threaten the overall strength of Busby's title chasers. So, there was every need for a strong squad, but with the team in fine form and the manager loath to alter his team selection from one week to another, other than for injury or poor form, there could be long spells on the touchline for some players.

Falling into this category were the likes of Maurice Setters and last season's acquisition Graham Moore. Setters, who had started the season in the No. 4 shirt, had only made four appearances, and his absence from the United first team attracted the attention of numerous suitors.

Stoke City were first to show interest in the player and actually agreed terms for the powerful midfielder, offering £30,000, but after taking five days to make up his mind, he turned down a move to the Potteries, as his wife did not want to move from her Manchester home and the player felt that the daily travel involved would not be fair either to the club or himself.

'It's a very hard decision to make,' Setters was to admit when the opportunity of a move first arose. 'I've loved playing for United, I like Manchester, I like Manchester people.

'A move like this means a whole new life and it's something I can't decide on in two or three days.'

Before he had made that decision, Wolves stepped into the picture, a club who had been interested in the player when it was hinted that he was prepared to leave Exeter City, but no sooner had the news broken that Setters had given Stoke the cold shoulder than Manchester City were being linked with the player.

'There were many things to consider,' said the burly wing-half. 'My prospects at Old Trafford against those at Stoke, my family, because my little girl had just started school, and my wish to continue living in the Manchester area.

'What's the point of deciding quickly and then regretting it after a couple of games? That does not do any good, neither to the player nor his club.'

Moore, on the other hand, had only been at Old Trafford a matter of months, but following a good run in the side, appearances soon became spasmodic. Swansea made an approach in the hope that they could attempt to take the player back to his native Wales with a £25,000 deal, which was only £10,000 less than what United had originally paid, but despite the offer of first-team football, Moore rather surprisingly declined the offer and remained at Old Trafford.

Ian Moir was another starlet who had broken into the side, but found it difficult to live up to the demands of life at Old Trafford, while also keeping the 'boo-boys' off his back, and so asked for a transfer in the search for regular first-team football. It was a transfer that was refused, despite the interest of Cardiff City, Aberdeen and Hull City. None managed to persuade the player to leave Manchester, nor persuade United to part with him, and it was not until later in the season that he finally moved, joining Blackpool.

Getting into the United first team was far from easy, even for the most experienced individual. Few could match the experience of goalkeeper Harry Gregg, but in recent seasons, the Northern Ireland international had endured more than his fair share of injuries and not all suffered out on the pitch.

A car accident back in April had kept Gregg out for five months, but outings with the United 'A' team, as he fought to regain his fitness, had brought him back into the picture. Playing in public parks was not the type of venue where you would expect to find a player of Gregg's calibre, and the sight of the big 'keeper chasing a misplaced ball onto nearby pitches was a sight to behold. Even stranger, and an example of how Gregg eventually treated such outings, came on 17 October at Tranmere, when he stood by his post listening to the Northern Ireland–England international match on a radio. So engrossed was he in the events taking place elsewhere, he ignored a cross by the home side and even the header that flew past him into the net. Thankfully United were winning 3-0 at the time!

United's run of five consecutive League wins stuttered to a halt at Turf Moor, Burnley, a venue that had, in the past few seasons, caused them much grief. On this occasion, however, referee George McCabe ruled the game with an iron glove, and a lack of penetration from both sides saw a ninety-minute stalemate and a 0-0 draw.

Victories over Sunderland at Old Trafford (1-0) and Wolverhampton Wanderers at Molineux (4-2) kept United hot on the heels of Chelsea, while the following four fixtures confirmed that the rather substandard start to the season was little more than rustiness and the quest and challenge for the championship was more than simply a pipe dream.

Aston Villa left Old Trafford on 24 October, having been soundly beaten 7-0, run ragged by four-goal Denis Law, which edged United to within a point of leaders Chelsea, who had only managed a draw at Tottenham.

Bill Fryer in the *Express* commented that 'a great fight looms to decide second and third place in the League championship stakes – behind Manchester United'. Clearly, he didn't see early leaders Chelsea as championship material, but considered even at this early stage of the campaign that the four-point gap between United in second and Everton in third was a significant difference.

The 7-0 victory, United's biggest win since they trounced Villa by a similar scoreline in March 1950 (when Charlie Mitten scored four, three of which were penalties), was watched by a meagre crowd of 35,807. This was the smallest of the season at Old Trafford and almost 16,000 less than had watched the open-day fixture against West Brom. Over 13,000 less than had watched the 1-0 victory over Sunderland. There was certainly no reason for the drastic drop in attendance as results had been favourable, and in any case, those who stayed away certainly missed out.

Surprisingly, United were only 2-0 in front at half-time. David Herd opened the scoring in the seventeenth minute and Law added the first of his quartet three minutes later. Law made it 3-0 five minutes after the restart, and then clinched his hat-trick with the best goal of the game six minutes later. Another, in the sixty-fourth minute made it 5-0. Herd scored his second of the afternoon in the seventy-seventh minute before Law rounded off the scoring in the final minute.

Even the referee was impressed by Law's performance, and indeed by the man himself. As when the two captains met the official on the centre circle prior to kick-off, Peter Baldwin handed Law a half-crown to toss up, telling him that it was the only one he had. The United captain in turn told the referee that he should invest it in his book, *Living for Kicks*, which was on sale at the ground, but the match official replied that he couldn't afford it on a referee's pay. Following Law's destruction of the Midland side, there was a knock on the referee's changing room door and a messenger handed the surprised official a signed copy of the book.

'Considering the trouble Denis has had with men in the middle, I thought it was a nice gesture. I will certainly treasure it,' said Baldwin. 'Every time I look at it I'll remember the greatest display of individual soccer skill I have ever seen. He was magnificent.'

The ninety minutes did indeed produce a sublime performance from Denis Law, and it was followed three days later with a hat-trick against the Swedes of Djurgardens, who despite their 1-1 home draw were no match for a rampant United side who scored four in a ruthless ten-minute display, before running out 6-1 winners. At nineteen minutes to nine it was 1-0. At ten minutes to nine, it was 5-0. Such was the devastation of United's play that Law and Bobby Charlton scored five between them.

Denis Law always came in for the close attention of opposition defenders, but the recent glut of goals would find him more closely marked than ever before. Although the physical side of the game did not deter the Scot, as he could certainly handle himself, many neutral observers and those on the Old Trafford terracing were now of the opinion that he was becoming something of a marked man, with opposition defenders 'out to get him'.

Each game seemed to produce another handful of bumps and bruises, and if injuries did not remove him, and the threat he posed to the opposition, from the First Division front line, then it was hoped that the verbal assault from the terracing and the odd off-the-ball niggles would push him into retaliation, bringing the added threat of suspension.

Law himself did not admit to there being some sort of vendetta against him, but teammate Pat Crerand did comment on the fact that he was coming in for much closer attention than before, while Bobby Charlton suggested that the tackles that often caught Law occurred due to the fact that his teammate was so quick that the tackles looked worse than they actually were.

Seventeen goals in three games, with Law claiming nine of those, was superb form, and as far as the betting men were concerned, United could order the championship flag whenever they liked. Hopefully those who had placed their bets early in the season had not torn their slips up in frustration due to the indifferent form of the opening couple of weeks, as the odds being offered now were only 7-4, with more than a possibility of them being shortened further. Chelsea were 7-2 against, while Everton were 5-1.

The last day of October saw United travel the relatively short distance to Anfield, a more-than-suitable venue and fixture where they could test their title credentials against last season's Champions and a team who, it will be remembered, hit their title aspirations firmly on the head with their 3-0 victory in April.

As it is today, the meeting was an intense affair, and on more than one occasion during the ninety minutes threatened to boil over both on and off the pitch. But United kept their heads and took a thirty-sixth-minute lead through David Herd, who fired the ball home as it bobbled around the penalty area after Law's shot had hit both Yeats and Byrne.

Having gained the advantage, United had to weather the storm and did so admirably, especially goalkeeper Pat Dunne who was subjected not just to a volley of abuse from the Kop at his back, but also a constant barrage of objects thrown in his direction.

A rare Pat Crerand goal, a lob over the head of goalkeeper Lawrence in the fourteenth minute of the second half, gave United a two-goal advantage and eventually both points, but they had to work extremely hard to keep the home side at bay.

A last-gasp intervention by Stiles prevented Hunt equalising Herd's early strike. Law and Crerand both cleared shots off the line, while the whole defence, expertly marshalled by Bill Foulkes, gave the excellent Pat Dunne all the back-up cover that he needed.

There was also an uglier side to the game, as well as the intimidating Kopites, with Ron Yeats headbutting David Herd in an off-the-ball incident and Denis Law clashing with the Liverpool centre-half in an afternoon-long duel.

Those two points lifted United into top spot, due to Chelsea's unexpected 1-0 home defeat by Burnley, and although the goal deluge became a trickle in a 1-0 win over Sheffield Wednesday, the momentum was maintained throughout November with victories against Blackpool (2-1), Blackburn Rovers (3-0) and Arsenal (3-2).

At Bloomfield Road, Blackpool, United almost came unstuck. Herd opened the scoring in the fifth minute, but Oates equalised twenty-three minutes later. Four minutes into the second half, John Connelly headed what was to be the winning goal past Waiters, but for the remainder of that second half it was akin to Custer's Last Stand for United, as the Seasiders surged forward time and time again, against a visiting side that had been reduced to ten men two minutes prior to the interval.

Law and Ball challenged for the ball and, as the pair locked horns, the referee awarded a free-kick to Blackpool. Clearly annoyed with the decision, Law subjected the referee to a volley of words, which left the official with little else to do but book the United No. 10. Even then the Scot would not let up and continued his debate with the referee who, to the amazement of everyone, pointed towards the dressing rooms.

All hell then broke loose as the baying United support sought retribution in whatever form they could. An open-bladed pen knife hit a police inspector on the back and a small air pistol landed on the track surrounding the pitch. A policeman had earlier been hit by a pellet from a similar type of weapon. Fighting broke out on the terracing forcing police to wade into the mass of bodies to split up rival fans, and a dozen red-and-white-clad youngsters were evicted from the ground. One female supporter was taken to hospital with a fractured skull, having been hit on the head by a bottle.

'This was the most unruly crowd we have ever had here,' said Blackpool's Chief Constable Stanley Parr. 'They were ten times worse than those from Everton. We had trouble with them even before the match started.

'Well before kick-off they went on the promenade and threw seats into the sea. This set off a series of 999 calls. We dealt with those and then the fans got onto the ground.

'Some were on the fence on the railway side singing songs such as "Blackpool Tower's Falling Down" and goading Blackpool teenagers to fight.

'We had a feeling there was going to be real trouble. These youths were a big problem, even without the Law incident.

'Some youths got onto the railway coal sidings outside the ground. They hurled lumps of coal over the stands onto the heads of the crowd in the ground.

'Then we discovered a hard core of troublemakers on the Kop – about 400, mostly teenagers.

'When the teams came out, a great shower of toilet rolls and other missiles were thrown. There were so many and of such quantity that police had to set to and clean up the paper to make the ground fit to play on.

'As the trouble was getting worse, a few policemen sailed into the crowd and got a few hooligans out of the ground.

'Most of the United supporters were behind the goal on the Kop.

'Several police saw a bottle flying high in the air from the back of the Kop. It fell short of the ground and hit an innocent fourteen-year-old girl. She has a depressed fracture of the skull.

'Thank god she is recovering. Just imagine if she had died. How could we hope to set about getting evidence on an incident like that?

'The Law and the referee business set up more trouble from these hooligans in fancy hats and after the game there were between 400 and 500 outside the players' entrance waiting and chanting, "We want the ref." We cleared them out without mercy. That enabled myself and another plainclothes officer to walk out with the referee.

'If we had escorted him out with uniformed men, he would have been recognised and probably mobbed and then we would have had some ugly trouble.

'How can we control people who throw things from the crowd? Altogether we had about fifty police in the ground. Thirty were in uniform and the rest were plainclothes men who mingled with the crowds.

'Some hooligans took their own weapons inside, so people unthinkably ask why we don't search people before they go in. How could we possibly search 30,000 spectators?

'We have men at the turnstiles. They look for any sign of missiles such as bottles or knives. Apart from a magic eye beam which would detect metal on persons passing through the turnstiles, it would be impossible to find if anyone had anything under his coat.'

Following his dismissal, Law declared his innocence, saying, 'I was involved in a bit of a foul with Alan Ball. He was pulling at me and I resented this.

'The referee called me over to tick me off. I think he would have told me to watch it and that would have been that, but Pat Crerand chipped in with "Don't be a silly ****". I then turned to him and said, "don't you be a silly **** either". That was what the referee heard and he said "I think you'd better go and get changed, don't you?"

'I was so stunned that I couldn't say a word. I just turned and walked away.

'I know the referee thought I was talking to him, but I swear that I was not.

'It was all a terrible mistake, a misunderstanding.'

Crerand supported his colleague, as could be expected: 'I said something to Denis and he turned round and swore. It was all a terrible mistake. Swearing on the field is like using an industrial language. It doesn't mean anything. I wanted to explain, but Bobby Charlton pulled me away.'

But the referee was adamant that there had been no misunderstanding whatsoever. 'You can assume that I was not intending to send him off for a foul,' said Peter Rhodes, the official caught in the thick of things. 'You can also assume that he was sent off for something he said.' This left everyone on tenterhooks as they awaited the result of the referee's report sent to the Football Association.

Before leaving the seaside town, Matt Busby clamped a 'No Talking' ban on his players as regards the incident, nor would the manager be drawn into conversation regarding it. All he would say was 'Until I know what the referee's version of the matter is, I have nothing further to say. When we do get his report we will discuss the matter with the players concerned. And then we will decide on what we think is the appropriate action.'

It would be early December before the Football Association Disciplinary Commission met to discuss Law's case, and those seeking to prosecute the striker were dealt an early blow when referee Peter Rhodes was informed that he could not use photographic evidence as some kind of corroboration of events. Although both linesmen were also present, they were both were well out of earshot during the exchange of words on the Bloomfield Road pitch, as was anyone else that the referee might call as back up, leaving everything down to his word against Denis Law's.

The following day, Law was informed of his fate by Matt Busby, with the FA statement reading, 'The commission has decided that Law be suspended for twenty-eight days from December 14th and fined £50.

'In deciding the penalty to be imposed the commission took into account the player's previous record of misconduct on the field of play.'

The statement also read that Law 'was guilty of using foul language to the referee and that the referee was justified in sending him off the field'.

It was a decision which sent shockwaves throughout the game, with the Professional Footballers' Association threatening legal action due to the inconsistency of the verdict. Len Badger of Sheffield United had been fined only £25 for striking an opponent, while Sandy Brown of Everton was suspended for fourteen days for a similar offence. Johnny Haynes of Fulham was suspended for fourteen days for swearing, with City's Bert Trautmann given a £50 fine for doing likewise.

Cliff Lloyd, secretary of the PFA, said, 'There is no doubt in my mind that the football authorities set out to make an example of Law because of his big name.

'In this case, nobody was endangered physically, yet there is a heavy punishment.

'I consider it highly objectionable that club directors should sit in judgement on the players of other clubs.'

As he left Old Trafford upon learning the verdict, Law simply shrugged his shoulders and said 'that's life', with a forced grin, knowing that he would also have to pay the costs of the commission, as he had asked for a personal hearing.

There was no appeal against the verdict, from the PFA, the player or the club, leaving Matt Busby to maintain United's title push without his goal machine.

Sandwiched in between the 1-0 victory over Sheffield Wednesday and the away day along the Golden Mile at Blackpool, was the small matter of a trip to Germany to face old foes Borussia Dortmund in the Inter-Cities Fairs Cup, but the Germans fared little better than Djurgardens and were demolished 6-1, leaving little need for a second leg back in Manchester.

For once, however, it was not the name of Denis Law which captured the headlines, as despite the scoreline, the Scot failed to get on the score-sheet, with the goals coming from Herd, Best and a Bobby Charlton hat-trick, giving the hundreds of British servicemen in the crowd a night to remember.

The performance was hailed as the best by any team in Europe, with Frank McGhee of the *Daily Mirror* going as far as to say that 'this was a performance no other Manchester United team has ever topped'. It was one that left the recent leaders of the German National League humiliated and most certainly outclassed, with George Best giving an out-of-this-world display of tantalising brilliance. Such was the Irishman's display that he was carried from the pitch shoulder-high by an invading force of British and German supporters.

But while the football world was full of praise, Matt Busby felt that there could be further improvement from the team that had scored forty-one goals, conceding only eleven, in the unbeaten fifteen-game run. 'I think we can become even better,' he warned. 'There is no secret about it. It is simply that the lads are playing together well as a team. We have begun to find the blend we have always sought.'

The Maurice Setters transfer saga came to an end in mid-November, when he finally moved to Stoke for a fee of around £30,000. It was a move which some at Old Trafford looked upon as a blessing in disguise, as it allowed them the opportunity to step from the shadows and fill the vacated position left by Setters.

Jimmy Nicholson was one such candidate, but he was also soon to move to pastures new, with a £7,500 transfer to Huddersfield Town. Others were Bobby Smith, Eamon Dunphy and John Fitzpatrick, who all coveted a first-team place in the United engine room, but the opportunities for breaking through were few and far between.

Denis Law had a month before his suspension began: four weeks in which to ensure that United remained, if not in pole position, at least within touching distance of the First Division leaders. The previously mentioned victories over Blackburn Rovers and Arsenal certainly ensured that.

Borussia Dortmund arrived in Manchester knowing that they had no chance of overcoming United's 6-1 advantage, but were determined to go down fighting. Any lingering hopes that they may have entertained in salvaging something from the second-round tie were extinguished within fifty seconds when United increased their advantage to 7-1, through Bobby Charlton.

Further goals from Connelly and Law along with another from Charlton gave United a 4-0 victory, causing concern amongst the other clubs left in the competition, all of whom were hoping to avoid a confrontation with Busby's on-song team. But one club had to come out of the hat alongside them and, by a strange quirk of fate, it was First Division stablemates Everton, allowing the rest of Europe to breath a huge sigh of relief.

On Merseyside, there were cries of 'Fix', but this was related more to the fact that the Goodison Park side had gone eight games without a win, compared with United's nineteen without a defeat, than that there had been some underhand work carried out on the Continent, with none of the foreign clubs wanting to come face to face with the rampaging United. Everton had also made a staggering fifty-three team changes in twenty games and, on current form, their only hope of success was in the fact that the tie would not be played until sometime in January when there was the possibility of United being off the boil.

The 3-2 win over Arsenal left United in top spot with thirty-two points from their twenty games, three points in front of second-place Chelsea and four in front of Leeds United in third, but this advantage was pegged back when the Yorkshire side crossed the Pennines on 5 December.

On a wet, foggy, dismal Manchester afternoon, the First Division newcomers, cheered on by 10,000 supporters, frustrated United with their defensive tactics. But it was perhaps a rib injury to George Best, which in effect reduced United to ten men, that swung the game in the Yorkshire side's favour.

As the second half got underway, the fog began to thicken and players began to drift in and out of view like phantoms, with the action at one end of the ground only recognised at the other by the noise of the crowd. There was, however, no doubt as to what had occurred ten minutes into the second period when Cooper collected a Bremner cross before finding the diminutive Collins whose shot evaded the outstretched arm of Dunne to give Leeds the lead.

United lost their way as the noise of the Leeds support echoed eerily around the stadium, but a slender glimmer of hope flashed through the thickening mist when, twelve minutes from the end, referee Jim Finney called a halt to the proceedings and took both teams off the pitch. For seven long, tense minutes, the completion of the game was in the balance, but after inspecting the shrouded ground, dressed in his overcoat on top of his playing kit, the referee disappeared down the tunnel to bring the teams out again to complete the ninety minutes.

There was little change in the play as the game resumed and Leeds held on to their slender one-goal advantage to claim both points, pushing them closer to the leaders, with only two points separating the top three sides.

Denis Law had one game left to play before his extended holiday in Aberdeen, an away fixture at West Bromwich, and the Albion's biggest crowd of the season turned up to say their farewells. Law didn't disappoint, but his fourteenth-minute goal was not enough to give United victory, as Kaye grabbed an equaliser eleven minutes before the interval. It was a goal that was also enough to knock United off the top of the table, as they had scored one less than Chelsea, while also conceding one more.

The disappointment of surrendering the top spot was to last only four days, as another 1-1 draw, this time against Birmingham City at Old Trafford, saw the positions reversed. A solitary Boxing Day George Best goal earned both points at Sheffield United, but when the Yorkshire side visited Old Trafford two days later, they left with a point from an admirable 1-1 draw. United remained on top of the pile, holding off the challenge from Chelsea and Leeds United mainly due to points dropped by both of those title rivals.

January brought the usual diversion from the rigours of League football with the third round of the FA Cup. Much to everyone's relief, the draw was more than favourable to United, pairing them with Fourth Division Chester, although the likes of Hartlepool United, Workington, Bristol Rovers and Walthamstow Avenue had all caused red faces around Old Trafford in the past. Chester, despite their lowly status, were keen to exploit United's strange fallibility on such occasions and came close to registering a major shock.

To the astonishment of the majority of the 40,000 crowd, Chester took a ninth-minute lead when Humes scored with a diving header at the far post, a goal which in fact could well have been their second, had Ryden's shot not hit the underside of the crossbar before being hastily cleared to safety.

Although United pressed forward, forcing goalkeeper Reeves into making a few outstanding saves, Chester were not simply content to sit back and soak up whatever United threw their way while also causing considerable concern within the home defence.

Having held their own for the first forty-five minutes, Chester only survived for ten minutes of the second half before United managed to snatch the equaliser, with Charlton and debutant Albert Kinsey creating the perfect opportunity for Best.

It was Kinsey who rounded off a dream afternoon by scoring the winner, but the outcome was in doubt until the very end, as Chester mastered the heavy conditions underfoot and almost snatched a replay when, for the second time that afternoon and with only five minutes remaining, they were denied a goal by the United crossbar.

There was no fanfare of trumpets, just the biggest League crowd of the season at the City Ground, Nottingham, to herald the return of 'the King'. Despite the lashing rain and gale-force wind, 43,009 flocked to Nottingham, but due to the vast numbers set on witnessing Law's return from his twenty-eight-day suspension, many missed his third-minute opening goal as they were still outside queuing to get in.

Following a foul on Best, Charlton tapped the ball forward to Herd, who in turn squared it to Law, whose shot beat both full-back and goalkeeper to give United the lead.

Forest replied in the fifteenth minute through Hinton, and the same player gave the home side a 2-1 lead eight minutes later. Play swung from end to end and on the half-hour mark, Law struck with his second, darting out from a ruck of players to divert the ball past Grummitt after the Forest 'keeper had initially blocked Herd's shot from a Best corner.

Try as they might, United could find no way through for a winner, although Law did have the ball in the net for a third time, only to see it disallowed for handball. 'I thought I had got away with that,' he quipped to the photographers behind the goal.

The long-awaited 'Battle of Britain' Inter-Cities Fairs Cup third-round tie took Everton to Old Trafford for the first leg on 20 January, with the visitors gaining something of an advantage with a 1-1 draw. Despite both goals coming from defensive errors – Foulkes' miskick in the fourteenth minute allowing Wright to send Pickering through to score, and a lazy back-pass by Gabriel in the thirty-first minute being seized by Connelly to push the ball into the unattended net – United had the bulk of the play and should have won with quite a bit to spare. However, Everton battled bravely and owed a considerable debt to goalkeeper Gordon West, who deserved his standing ovation for keeping the tie alive.

But three days later, Stoke City threw United's championship aspirations into disarray with a 1-1 draw at Old Trafford, in what was a dress rehearsal for the forthcoming FA Cup fourth-round tie between the two clubs.

Behind to an Alan Bloor goal in the tenth minute, United were once again grateful to Denis Law for pulling them out of the mire with an equaliser in the twenty-first minute. But in a tough, untidy, but totally absorbing ninety minutes, United were to once again to rue their missed opportunities, as the dropped point for the second consecutive fixture saw them drop to third, behind Leeds United and Chelsea, two points off the top.

Although the First Division clash grabbed the attention of many, with over 50,000 packed into Old Trafford, there was considerable interest in the Central League fixture between the two clubs at the Victoria Ground, where around 2,000 watched in awe as Sir Stanley Matthews, a week before his fiftieth birthday, strutted his stuff in his first competitive game of the season, with one eye on a return to first-team football in the fourth-round cup tie.

On a snow-covered pitch, Matthews rolled back the years, displaying astonishing stamina in the 1-1 draw, but there was to be no step up to the senior side and a head-to-head against the young pretender to his crown – George Best.

A bus drivers' strike and the weather threatened the Stoke cup tie, while the firm underfoot conditions put paid to the Matthews dream on the morning of the match. Both of the former threats failed to materialise, as did the goals, although there was plenty of action to satisfy the craving of the full house at the Victoria Ground.

In his match report in the *Daily Express*, Eric Cooper suggested, 'If the battle of the Victoria Ground resumes at Old Trafford on Wednesday where it left off here, then I'll be surprised if twenty-two players are on the field at the end of the replay.

'So far, referee Leo Callaghan has earned full marks for tolerance, but it is a wonder that Manchester United didn't talk themselves out of the cup in this display of disorganisation, distaste, and dishonour.

'It shocked me that United should be arguing with the referee almost continuously in view of the recent events involving Denis Law.'

Maurice Setters kept his old teammate Denis Law under control, but George Kinnell and John Connelly became engaged in their own private war, with a truce only called when, following the flailing of both sets of legs in the Stoke penalty area, both players found themselves booked, with tempers overtaking talent on numerous other occasions. However, the general view of the proceedings was that United had much more to offer and would overcome the resilient Stoke to progress into Round Three.

The replay was certainly not for the purists, as Stoke arrived in Manchester with one plan only – to prevent United from scoring – and it was a plan that worked for all of seventy-five minutes. The ball was seldom out of the Stoke half, but with an eight-man defence, United failed to find a way through in order to trouble Leslie in the visitors' goal.

It was another of those mist-shrouded Old Trafford evenings and another ninety-minute encounter that was not for the faint-hearted, with the referee halting play on a regular basis to speak to players on both sides. Even former teammates Setters and Law were hauled to one side for a ticking off.

Many were resigned to a second replay, as some of the players happily kicked out at each other rather than the ball, but as the game moved into its final quarter of an hour, a centre-cum-shot by Tony Dunne was deflected by David Herd past Leslie and into the net. The solitary strike was enough to send United through.

Back on First Division business, United suddenly found themselves slipping behind their two adversaries, Chelsea and Leeds, following a 1-0 defeat at Tottenham, but they continued to make progress on the European front with a 2-1 victory over Everton in the second leg of their Inter-Cities Fairs Cup tie.

The inconsistency of their recent League outings was pushed to the side, and it was the Manchester United of old that tormented and tantalised the Goodsion Park side. An increase in admission prices, agreed by both sides following the draw, saw around 12,000 empty spaces around the ground, but they missed a superb cup tie, worthy of a final never mind a third-round tie, with a dazzling display from John Connelly, who was to give United a sixth-minute lead.

United switched from defence to attack with prolific regularity, something that Everton were unable to counter, although they did manage to create a number of scoring opportunities that they failed to make the most of. Neither had they someone with the brilliance of Denis Law, who swung the game United's way with two moments of magic, setting up both goals.

United thought they had gone 2-0 in front early in the second half, but referee 'Tiny' Wharton, who actually measured up at 6 foot 4 inches, disallowed Connelly's effort for a handball. No one disputed the decision! Soon afterwards, Everton equalised through Pickering, after Stiles had been penalised for a foul on Vernon, but any hopes of snatching the tie from United's grasp disappeared fifteen minutes later when Connelly's shot was only parried by Gordon West and Herd was left with the simple opportunity of slipping the ball into the net for an easy goal; one that would put United into the fourth round.

While goals from Best, Herd and Charlton were securing a 3-2 win against Burnley at Old Trafford on 13 February, there was high drama a few miles up the road at Turf Moor, where the two reserve teams were meeting in a Central League fixture.

With the game moving into its final fifteen minutes and the score at 1-1, Noel Cantwell clashed with Burnley centre-forward Blant and, as the referee had already booked the United captain for a foul on the same player earlier in the game, he was left with little alternative but to send Cantwell off. Surrounded by protesting players, the referee suddenly also sent off Harry Gregg and the melee continued with trainer Wilf McGuinness also becoming involved, as David Sadler prepared to take over in goal.

'Obviously Gregg said something,' was all the official would say after the game.

The 3-2 win over Burnley was something of a dress rehearsal for the FA Cup meeting between the two the following Saturday, and again it was only by the odd goal in three that United secured victory. On this occasion, the visitors stretched their hosts to their limits, only crumbling in the final six minutes of the game.

Burnley had snatched a sixteenth-minute lead when a Bellamy corner was headed towards his own goal by Foulkes and Pat Dunne palmed the ball against the crossbar, with Lochhead pouncing to head the rebound home.

Stiles was booked and Best shot straight at Blacklaw, as United pressed for the equaliser, but none would materialise and as the game progressed, it looked as though a cup exit was on the cards. But with only six minutes remaining and many heading for the exits, the drama unfolded.

Having lost his boot in an earlier challenge, George Best lobbed the ball towards goal with his stockinged left foot. Despite being heavily marked, Law sprang into mid-air and, with his back to goal, slammed the ball home with an acrobatic overhead kick.

In the rush to get the game restarted and press for a winner, Best continued to play with his boot clutched in his hand. Again the ball was worked out towards him and he dribbled forward before crossing for Crerand to hit the winner.

Best's bootless performance was much of a talking point as the dramatic, late winning goals, with three 'neutral' officials saying that the United winger should have been told to put his boot back on. Referee George McCabe later admitted that perhaps he should have done this, but said, 'The first thing I noticed was Best bending down on one knee as if to replace the boot. I assumed that was what he would do and my attention immediately went back to the game, which was in a very tense state.

'It was some time later when I noticed that Best was carrying his boot. I looked at my watch and it was nearly full-time.

'Looking back, I suppose I should have ordered him to put the boot back on, but the game was poised in such a state that I could not relax for a second.'

Best himself admitted that he had tried to get rid of the boot by dropping it over the touchline, but a ball boy gave it back to him.

A struggling Sunderland side left United three points adrift of the top two with a 1-0 victory at Roker Park, as the sparkle slowly began to dull on what, until now, had seemed to be a season that promised so much. Law had not scored a League goal since late January and it was put to Matt Busby that his suspension and subsequent loss of form had much to do with the forward, and the team's, poor showing of late.

'Yes we have lost that spark,' admitted Busby. 'We are waiting for it to come back. And it will come back.

'Denis is out of touch at the moment. But he is only human like the rest of us, you know. He is entitled to a lean spell the same as anyone else.

'I don't think it has anything to do with his suspension. I cannot be positive about this of course, but I feel it is simply that he is just off-form for the moment.'

United worked their way out of the rut that they found themselves in with a 3-0 home victory over Wolverhampton Wanderers, but many were still unconvinced as regards their championship aspirations, or indeed their assault on a coveted League and FA Cup double.

By a strange quirk of fate, the top three First Division clubs – Chelsea, Leeds and United – were all in contention for both trophies, with the Londoners, like United, also having the added interest in a third, although unlike United, for whom the Inter-Cities Fairs Cup was a welcome distraction, the third possible trophy in Chelsea's sights was only the Football League Cup. Obviously, the prestige in winning any of the game's major honours was great, but with the possibility of a double or even triple success coming into the equation, there was also much to gain from a financial point of view.

For the United players, on top of their weekly wage, there was £10 first-team appearance money. Depending on the Old Trafford attendance, there was the added bonus of £1 per 1,000 for a gate between 34,000 and 40,000, and then double that for every 1,000 paying customers over 40,000. (Only three of the fifteen home League fixtures to date had been watched by under 40,000 and one under 30,000.) If the team was in the top three, as it had been for most of the season, then that £1 gate bonus was doubled and the additional £2 per 1,000 became £3. This would be payable for all competitions, so obviously there was a bigger financial incentive to progress in the cup competitions.

Should United shake off their current indifferent form and claim the League title, then a sum of £6,500 would be shared out on a pro-rata basis, with a similar haul on the table for success in the FA Cup. Should the unprecedented treble be achieved then there would be £10,000 to be split amongst the players.

The Chelsea players had been claiming even better rewards, with their agreement seeing them paid £5 if they were eleventh in the League, with each upward move bringing an additional £5. For top spot, they picked up £55 each.

Thankfully for both players and spectators, the process of building the new cantilever stand along the United Road side of the stadium had little effect on attendances, but the plans had taken on something of a different look, as perhaps the most prominent feature of this new construction – one that was not mentioned in David Meek's article back in December 1963 – would be the installation of thirty-four private boxes, which could each hold up to six people. The reason for there being no mention in David's article was that they were not a feature of the original plans, and it was only after Bill Burke managed to persuade to United directors to visit Manchester racecourse to see a previous Mather & Nutter construction, one containing private boxes, and then view the pitch from the back of the semi-constructed stand at Old Trafford, that the board decided to go along with the idea. Whether the added bonus of each director being given three boxes each swung the matter is not recorded. For those who were interested in the new facilities, centre boxes were to be let at £300 for a season, with those at the side £250. The rental secured admission to all home games and, needless to say, all boxes were over-applied for from the start.

In a rare article at the time, United's secretary at the time spoke of the 'one new and interesting feature which will be the installation of thirty-four private boxes, each of which will hold six people'. Going on to describe the facilities that would be available he said, 'These have been taken up by business houses in the city to entertain their clients in the best possible surroundings – a sort of Soccer-Ascot if you like.

'There will be a waiter service available for refreshments, and a private lift will transfer spectators from ground level to the boxes, which will be approached via a luxuriously carpeted lounge. The boxes will be heated and high-class refreshment bars will be installed.

'When all is done, it will indeed be a far cry from the old-time conception of the football fan standing in the open in all kinds of weather, shouting himself hoarse.

'In fact, it will be the equal of anything that the world soccer traveller will find no matter where he goes.'

Les Olive was also quick to add that there was to be much more to Old Trafford's World Cup facilities than one new stand, continuing, 'When completed, our stand will have cost more than £300,000, but by 1966, we will have spent in all, more than £500,000 over the past fifteen years on improvements at Old Trafford.

'Two corner paddocks have been rebuilt and cover has been erected behind the Stretford End goal. Our main stand has been rebuilt and its design will prove a tremendous boon in accommodating visiting radio, television and press representatives.

'We will have to remove seats to extend the press-box to take at least 400 soccer writers and we shall have to provide them with working and rest rooms.

'We will require at least 300 telephone lines, a communications room, radio and TV interview rooms and platforms for TV and film cameras which will show pictures of matches in all parts of the world.

'Luckily, we have sufficient space in which to erect these temporary structures on the first-floor level underneath our 'A' and 'D' stands.'

The United secretary mentioned a cost of more than £300,000 for the new stand, but an early estimated cost for the construction was £175,000. A closer examination then took the figure up to £250,000. The final cost, however, was nearer to £320,000, and with only around £75,000 in the bank at this time, it was a major undertaking, putting the club well into the red, although most of the costs were eventually paid by the Development Association.

So, United moved into a four-day period which could make or break both their season and their bank balances, kicking off with a visit to Molineux in the FA Cup, although they had to wait an additional four days to play the tie, as heavy snow forced the postponement on its original date.

Bottom-of-the-table Wolves cast their threat of relegation to one side and shocked United by taking a 2-0 lead within the opening fifteen minutes through Hugh McIlmoyle. It was a lead they managed to hold until the fifty-first minute, when they were finally pegged back by a defiant United.

The visitors had been caught cold in the third minute, when Woodruff's 35-yard throw-in to the United area was knocked down and Woodruff himself followed through with a shot at goal. This was blocked by McIlmoyle, who quickly turned and fired the ball past Dunne to give the home side the lead. Despite protests from the United players that the Wolves No. 9 had handled the ball, the goal stood.

The second saw Foulkes too slow in attempting a pass back to his 'keeper and McIlmoyle was in like a flash, robbing the centre-half before sliding the ball past a helpless Dunne. It was a superb start by the Midland side and one that remains in Hugh McIlmoyle's memory. 'It is still a game I remember and not just for the two goals,' recalled the Wolves No. 9. 'But what I remember vividly was after scoring the second, as I ran back to the centre circle, there used to be this big clock on the roof of one of the Molineux stands and I remember looking up at it and it was only about 7.45 and I thought 2-0 – game over sort of thing.'

Denis Law reduced arrears a minute before the interval, heading home a Connelly corner, and six minutes into the second half, the game was suddenly opened up when Herd snatched the equaliser at the second attempt.

On the hour, after constant pressure on the Wolves goal, Best took a corner and, as goalkeeper Davies jumped with Law and Herd, the ball swung untouched into the net. It was goal that knocked the heart out of the Wolves challenge and it was no surprise that United added to their total, with a fourth from Crerand in the sixty-seventh minute and a fifth from Law fifteen minutes from time. Knowles grabbed a third for Wolves with nine minutes remaining, but by then, the result was a foregone conclusion.

Hugh McIlmoyle was clearly disappointed ending up on the losing side after going two goals in front, but took his hat off to United: 'They were a team you always looked forward to playing and they would bring a good crowd down from Manchester. It was always the biggest game of the season.

'They were certainly difficult to play against. You would often come up against a team who had one or perhaps two outstanding players, but with United, you had three world-class players to contend with.

'George Best, a fantastic dribbler, Denis Law who was deadly in front of goal and Bobby Charlton, whose name speaks for itself.

'They were a difficult side to play against due to having those three players alone. Three forwards, who were very difficult to play against.

'United, however, weren't a really "great" side at this time. They were certainly a good side, but not yet a great one, as they were still finding their feet after Munich. Still rebuilding, but their comeback in that cup tie was certainly an incredible performance.'

When it was put to him that one of the newspapers of the day suggested that there was a possibility that both his goals could have been disallowed for handball and a foul, Hugh, with a laugh, asked, 'which one, the *Manchester Gazette*?'

If United were going to claim the League championship crown then their next fixture, at home to leaders Chelsea, would be one of those defining ninety minutes, when victory would indeed keep them in contention, while defeat would present them with something of an uphill struggle, casting them seven points adrift with ten games remaining.

'We would be happy with a draw,' said Chelsea manager Tommy Docherty. 'But we are going for full points. It is the only way we can be sure that Leeds do not narrow the gap. We have gone for a win in every away game so far, and we are not changing our approach now.' Such tactics had certainly proved successful, as the Stamford Bridge side had accumulated more away points (23) and more away goals (34), than any other team.

Fingers, however, had been pointed throughout the United team in past weeks and it was hinted that the early season magic had disappeared, along with the sparkle and the goals. In some quarters the question was being asked if it would actually return.

When such questions were put to Matt Busby, the United manager admitted that those facts were indeed correct. 'Yes, we have lost that spark. We are waiting for it to come back. And it will come back.' Busby also admitted that his star striker, Denis Law, was out of touch at the moment, but did not think it had anything to do with his recent suspension, saying, 'He is only human like the rest of us you know!'

Rival manager Tommy Docherty did not consider his top-of-the-table side to be under any form of pressure or strain, but Busby admitted, 'It is difficult to enjoy your football at times like these. But doing so is one of the secrets of easing the strain. Being natural is another. There is not much else you can do in these circumstances. Don't worry about us. We will be alright.'

If Docherty wasn't under any strain or pressure, he certainly was following the 13 March meeting between the two sides, as the sparkle that had been missing from United returned with a vengeance.

'Chelsea relegated to second fiddle – United call time and tune', proclaimed the headline above the report in the *Guardian*, with Eric Todd penning, 'Manchester United who, according to pernickety observers "do not always press home their advantage", beat Chelsea 4-0 at Old Trafford on Saturday. Thus they completed the double over the League leaders, and brought their harvest of goals to nine in two consecutive matches. So much for negligence.'

He continued: '*Roget's Thesaurus* itself stands in danger of being denuded of adequate adjectives with which to describe this United side, whose members delight in blasting criticism sky high. Let it be whispered that the backs are too slow and inexperienced, and Brennan and A. Dunne excel themselves as they did on Saturday. Let it be suggested that Crerand's passes are inconsistent, and he dominates the whole proceedings. And if the slightest hint be dropped that when Law is comparatively subdued United's attack is no more than ordinary, study the reactions of Herd, Best, Connelly and Charlton. United can make fools of everyone, except themselves.'

'Leaders Get A Crushing', stated another report, with the opening line telling the reader that 'League leaders Chelsea were thrashed! The great battle between their young soccer machine and the individual genius of Manchester United was won quickly, easily and magnificently by Matt Busby's United men.'

Tommy Docherty's side were caught cold in the fourth minute. Wide on the right, McCreadie, finding himself under pressure from Best, decided against playing safe and putting the ball out of play. Attempting to clear instead, he only succeeded in kicking the ball against the United winger and, as the ball was charged down, he then tried again unsuccessfully to dribble around him. In desperation, McCreadie then attempted to prod the ball back towards his goalkeeper.

It barely rolled 2 yards on the muddied surface, and as the roar of the crowd began to erupt from the packed terracing, Best was on to the ball in a flash. McCreadie could only look on in anguish as the winger indolently curled the ball over the head of Bonetti and into the net from a tight angle some 20 yards from goal.

A couple of attempts from Charlton came close, as did another from Herd, but it was not until the last minute of the half that Chelsea mustered their first worthwhile attack. By then, however, they were 2-0 behind; Stiles having picked out Herd, standing alone inside the penalty area, leaving the centre-forward with little more to do than pick his spot.

Any half-time pep talk in the visitors' dressing room had been a waste of breath and time, as within three minutes of the restart United were 3-0 in front. Best, more in hope than anything else, returned a headed clearance into the Chelsea area, but it fell to Herd, who managed to deflect it past Bonetti.

With thirteen minutes remaining Chelsea surrendered a fourth, Best setting up Law for his first League goal in six games.

It was an important victory and one which kept the title race wide open, but it still failed to please some people, leaving Matt Busby incensed by the criticism which followed the 4-0 win. He admitted that more than one person had approached him after the game and said that United had won simply due to Chelsea playing badly, while a letter had been received in which the writer proclaimed that United would still fail in the title race and would fail to win anything for the second successive season.

Busby was also annoyed by critics who said that his team 'played it off the cuff and lacked in teamwork', quickly springing on to the defensive: 'I do not know what playing it off the cuff means, but I give the benefit of the doubt and admit that I still have much to learn.

'After our fight-back from 1-0 down to a cup win in the last minute against Burnley, another after being 2-0 down in the cup cauldron at Wolverhampton, and this latest show against Chelsea, who were being written up as virtually unbeatable, I am left wondering what teamwork is if we haven't got it.

'Manchester United are a club wherein, on the pitch and at meetings between the players and me, the team are encouraged in self-expression.

'We plan alright, but I am very strong in encouraging to the hilt the special individual talents of great players who, if those talents don't come of in a match are as unhappy as the rest of us.'

'But unlike the people to whom Manchester United are allowed blacks and whites, but no greys, I shall not now say that we can always beat Chelsea, that Chelsea are not great challengers for the championship.

'I shall not say that we shall win the League, the FA Cup, and the Inter-Cities Fairs Cup.

'I shall not say that we will win even our next match.

'But I will repeat something I said when criticism of United was at its height. Only a hasty man will rule us out of any or all of them.

'Meanwhile, one at a time, please. There are no easy games. We are going to be busy indeed. Fatigue beat us last year. I hope it won't this year.

'I recommend patience. It has not served me badly for the past twenty years or so ... in trial, tribulation ... and triumph.'

If there was a difference in the United team of this season compared to last, it was having a more settled side. During the 1963/64 campaign, the longest Busby went with an unchanged team was three games (on three occasions, in September, November and February), with no individual managing to play all forty-two games. Crerand and Foulkes managed forty-one, while Dunne and Charlton appeared in one less. The next highest was Setters with thirty-two. But during the current season, Brennan, Dunne, Connelly and Foulkes had played in all thirty-two to date, with Stiles, Charlton and Best had only missed one, Crerand two and Herd three. Such consistency had certainly played a major part in the success to date.

Following the defeat of his Chelsea side, manager Tommy Docherty held his hands up and accepted the defeat, but was quick to state, 'Don't worry. We'll still be there at the end of the season.'

An unchanged side against Fulham at Old Trafford, two days after the victory over Chelsea, again notched up four goals, although on this occasion the visitors managed one in reply. It was also a victory, not simply for United, but for the ethics of teamwork the Matt Busby way, as not for the first time in recent weeks, his team had to come from behind to secure victory after Fulham took a sixth-minute lead through Marsh.

Despite the victory, the recent 1-0 defeats by Tottenham and Sunderland ensured that United continued to cling on to the shirt tails of Chelsea and Leeds, with the Yorkshire side more or less saying 'anything you can do we can do better', after defeating Burnley 5-1 that same night.

It was, however, tight at the top, with only one point separating United, Leeds and leaders Chelsea. If it was of any encouragement, United did have the better goal average, but they were soon to find themselves three points adrift of Leeds due to a shock 1-0 defeat against Sheffield

Wednesday in the driving sleet and clinging mud of Hillsborough, a ground where a United victory was something of a rarity in recent years. A waterlogged Stamford Bridge prevented the London side from playing that same night, while Leeds continued to go from strength to strength, with a 4-1 win over Everton.

A 2-0 win over Blackpool at Old Trafford got things back on track, but only just, as the Seasiders' goalkeeper, Tony Waiters, was blamed for both goals. However, this still didn't disperse the doubts hanging over United's ability to maintain their three-pronged challenge. What made it even more worrying was the fact that waiting on the horizon was an FA Cup semi-final confrontation with Leeds on that same haunted Hillsborough pitch, and following the floundering display against Sheffield Wednesday, few gave them much hope of success.

'Prepare yourselves Manchester for slaughter on Saturday,' wrote the reporter who had covered the Wednesday fixture for the *Daily Express*. 'Leeds will not defeat you if you turn in a similar performance on this muddy ground in the semi-final. They will massacre you.' He continued: 'Much of United's title hopes went crashing in this game on the ground where they have lost their last two semi-finals.

'The tragedy of this game lies in the scoreline. It suggests that Sheffield struggled, that Manchester lost heroically and narrowly. And nothing could be wider from the mark ... 4-1 or 5-1 would have justified the play.'

Dawn broke in Manchester and thousands prepared to make their way over the Pennines for the Battle of the Roses. Police notices outside the ground warned supporters to 'beware of pickpockets', but this was perhaps one of the few crimes that were not committed in a dour, ugly encounter, which exploded on the hour with a mass brawl. It was never expected to be a meeting for the faint-hearted, as there were too many players on both sides who many considered relished a confrontation and would certainly not shirk a physical challenge.

Conditions underfoot were difficult and exasperating, with the pitch resembling little more than a ploughed field, while a strong downfield wind, which United faced in the first half, helped matters little, becoming an additional opponent to master.

Dunne in the United goal looked nervous early in the game, but he rode his luck, and with Leeds and the wind kept at bay in the opening forty-five minutes as well as having shown more imaginative use of the ball just prior to the interval, and Law coming close, many sensed that the second half would produce a Mancunian victory. But it was Leeds who took control after the break, if only for a short while, as the actual football soon disintegrated and the 65,000 crowd went back to counting the free-kicks for entertainment.

Throughout the game the underlying tension had threatened bubble over amid the niggling confrontations, and so it came as no surprise when the game suddenly exploded.

On the hour, a clash of sickening intensity between Denis Law and Jackie Charlton in midfield saw both players tangle, and as the grappling continued, another half-dozen players from both sides dived into the melee. Strangely, the referee was more than content to stand back and let the incident fizzle out, before rather bizarrely, booking Crerand and Bremner, who although involved in the scrimmage, could be considered to have taken on more of a peacemaking role.

The game resumed with a free-kick to Leeds with Law now wearing something of an off-the-shoulder look in playing kit, but the free-for-all attitude continued, with Stiles booked for a blatant body check on Johannsen, and Law, never far from the thick of the action, for whipping the feet from under Bell. Neither team, however, could make the breakthrough in terms of goals, with United failing to take advantage of the wind, forcing the game into a replay and another battling ninety minutes.

If United failed to gain the victory that would have taken them to Wembley, they at least had the upper hand in free-kicks, with a total of twenty-two awarded against them, compared to eight against Leeds. Such totals may be minimal compared to the present-day game, but it was enough to raise eyebrows and cause much debate at the time.

Writing in the *Sunday Express*, James Mossop perhaps paints the perfect picture of the afternoon in Sheffield, with his report coming under the heading 'Ugly clashes turn Hillsborough into a soccer hell'. He wrote, 'The vulgar thumpings of the game's lowest tactics wrecked what would have been a soccer symphony. There was kicking, butting, punching, shirt tearing, and every other evil football action to make Hillsborough hell.

'Briefly, Manchester United conceded twenty-two free-kicks for dirty play; Leeds eight. United's Denis Law and Nobby Stiles were both booked. Referee Dick Windle shared the blame for the hiatus, and Leeds deserved to win.

'Not that anyone would want to claim much credit from this slow-motion, ill-tempered, man-baiting maul. It was a tie 65,000 people had been dreaming about since the draw. Nightmares may well follow.'

Many felt that much of the physical play could have been avoided had the referee stepped in with a booking early in the game when Collins and Charlton tangled in the opening minutes, but he had allowed things to continue and indeed get completely out of hand, creating much unneeded tension in the build-up to the replay at the City Ground, Nottingham.

Following the head-to-head in Sheffield, neither manager got involved in the rights and the wrongs of the afternoon, with Leeds boss Don Revie simply saying, 'It was a very hard game. I'm not going to be drawn.' All Matt Busby would comment was a simple 'hard game in difficult conditions'.

There were concerns, however, that the replay would develop into something more sinister and, indeed, steps were taken to ensure that both sets of players were under no illusions and that they had to play by the rules. FA Cup Committee chairman David Wiseman said on the eve of the game, 'It is wrong to say that the players have been "warned" about their conduct. What they will get is better described, I think, as an instruction.

'We have the utmost confidence in referee Windle and we have been in touch with him. What has transpired must be a private matter. But we are not warning anyone.

'The players know the tensions that are always seen in these ties with so much depending on the result. But I feel that with time to cool off the players themselves will be determined to wipe the slate clean and give us a game of football in the best British traditions.'

Leeds were brimming with confidence, having felt that they had enjoyed more of the play in the first game, with Don Revie saying, 'I think we are in with a great chance.' Matt Busby, on the other hand, kept his cards a bit closer to his chest and would only say, 'We shall be all out to play good football from the first to last minute. We know that in the end, it is the side that plays the best football that should win through. We feel that side will be Manchester United.'

In Nottingham, the ninety minutes were a marked contrast to that of four days previously, with the game almost stuttering into life, and neither side quite wanting to be the first to commit any indiscretions.

Herd put one shot past the post, while testing Sprake with another. At the opposite end, a 35-yard free-kick from Collins caused the United goal little concern, but with fourteen minutes gone they did breath a sigh of relief, when a Peacock header was cleared, but only as far as Jackie Charlton, who headed against the bar. Pat Dunne managed to scoop the ball away as the Leeds players protested that it had crossed the line.

United continued to enjoy the superiority, but the Leeds defence stood firm, prompting their forwards into sporadic raids on their opponents' goal, although they seemed more than happy to adopt something of a kick-and-hope approach.

There was little to be seen of the tactics that had marred the previous meeting, with only odd, rather nondescript incidents, and as the second half got underway, United continued to have the upper hand. Herd shot against Sprake and then fired into the side netting, before proceeding to miss an excellent opportunity from 10 yards out, one that he could usually be relied upon to score blindfolded.

Sprake then saved a header from Best, as United piled on the pressure, with the Yorkshire side's good fortune extending further when Bell turned a back-pass towards Sprake, only to find the 'keeper nowhere to be seen and the ball rolled out for a corner.

Leeds slowly clawed themselves back into the game and forced Pat Dunne into making a series of excellent saves that kept United in the game. Twice he saved from Bremner, then another following a corner from Collins. He then fisted a volley from Cooper over the bar as the game moved agonisingly close towards extra time.

With a minute to go, a free-kick was awarded against Stiles for obstruction near the centre circle. Giles sent the ball into the United goalmouth and Bremner, one of the smallest players on the pitch, jumped to head the ball backwards past Dunne.

The red-headed Scot took off like a man possessed as the United players hung their heads in despair, knowing full well that they had little hope of securing an equaliser that would put the game into extra time. Moments later the full-time whistle confirmed their fate.

As the whistle sounded, thousands clambered over the barriers onto the pitch, and amid the mayhem, the referee was struck by a spectator and fell to the ground. As he lay unconscious, within yards of the tunnel, with one of his linesmen watching over him as hundreds of feet pounded the turf around him, a policeman chased and caught his assailant, hauling him to the ground before leading him away.

Following treatment from the ambulance men, it was a dazed-looking referee who was helped from the pitch to the safety of the dressing rooms.

Again, United had triumphed in the free-kick stakes, nineteen to five, but they felt as dazed as the referee as they left the pitch, somewhat uncertain as to how they had lost a game in which they had enjoyed so much of the play. It was a game they should most certainly have won.

Busby now had a job on his hands in raising his players for an away trip to Blackburn Rovers three days later, ensuring that they did not dwell on the cup defeat and concentrated on the remaining seven First Division fixtures, and also the forthcoming Inter-Cities Fairs Cup ties against Strasbourg, as failure on all three fronts was unthinkable.

Prior to the match with Blackburn, something of an unusual event took place, with the two captains, Denis Law and Ronnie Clayton, along with referee Jennings, emerging from the tunnel earlier than usual and moving out onto the pitch to toss the coin to choose ends. They then went back to the dressing rooms and the ground announcer notified the crowd as to who would be kicking what way, allowing supporters to change ends and get behind the goal that their team would be attacking in the first half.

Whether or not the recent crowd problems on the Flyde coast prior to and during the Blackpool game had any bearing on the rather unusual event which preceded that Ewood Park fixture is not recorded, but the likelihood is that it did. It didn't however, prevent any trouble, as fighting broke out behind the goal where most of the United fans were congregated and a youth was helped out and had to receive first aid. Another supporter was arrested for assaulting the referee and was later fined £5 and bound over with the sum of £50, not to get into trouble for twelve months.

There was also trouble at half-time, as inevitably, the supporters of both clubs wanted to change ends, and as some of them were doing so along the side of the pitch, large numbers of United supporters charged down the pitch itself. A policeman quickly positioned himself on the centre line and attempted to trip up any of the supporters who came near him. Eventually he made contact with a passing United supporter, who immediately sprang to his feet and punched the constable, to the approval of many, before running off.

United had struggled through a goal-less first forty-five minutes, producing only one co-ordinated movement, but within three minutes of the restart, Bobby Charlton opened the floodgates with the first of a hat-trick. Goals from Connelly and Herd then gave United a 5-0 victory to restore confidence and get the show back on the road.

There was no getting away from Leeds United though. They stood between United and Chelsea at the top of the First Division and, having just dumped United out of the FA Cup, Don Revie was on the telephone to Matt Busby looking for a favour.

Like United, Leeds were obviously pushing for success on two fronts, but Revie was concerned about his strength in depth, or more to the point, his lack of goalkeeping cover. So, in something of an audacious move, he asked Busby if he could sign out-of-favour goalkeeper Harry Gregg. Gary Sprake was obviously his confirmed No. 1 choice, despite his often calamitous failings, but the only cover available should the Welshman get injured was a seventeen-year-old.

Newcastle had rebuffed an approach for their Welsh international 'keeper Dave Hollins, so Gregg had fallen under the spotlight, but even if the United man did sign, he would only be available for the FA Cup final due to the transfer deadline having passed.

The proposal, however, came to nothing.

12 April saw leaders Chelsea lose 3-2 against West Ham United at Upton Park, while two Alan Peacock goals gave Leeds victory at West Bromwich as well as top spot. United kept tabs on their rivals with a solitary goal victory over Leicester City at Old Trafford, but they were still three points behind as the games became fewer.

Five days later, the hectic Easter programme, with two games in three days, could go a long way in deciding the championship crown; more so, as the first of the two saw United travel to Elland Road Leeds. Coming so soon after the dynamic and controversial FA Cup encounters between the two sides, the outcome of the ninety minutes was unpredictable and, as once again so much hinged on the result, there were fears as to what might develop.

Conditions at Elland Road were far from ideal, as a strong wind blew dust clouds across the ground, turning the game into something of a lottery, as well-intended passes flew into the crowd rather to the feet of the intended player. Law won the toss, which was a victory in itself, forcing Leeds to face both United and the wind, and it brought the advantage of a fourteenth-minute goal from Connelly. Tony Dunne swung the ball deep into the Leeds half and Law continued the forward thrust by prodding it through to Connelly, who drove hard and low into the net. Prior to this, Herd had dithered and wasted two opportunities, while Connelly had seen two shots saved.

United failed to threaten again and re-emerged for the second half prepared for an onslaught from Leeds, the continuously blowing gale and the wrath of the Yorkshire support. Having contained United for much of the first half, the former felt confident that they could overcome the Lancastrian visitors for a second time. Soon, Collins and Greenhoff were holding the ball and managing to work it skilfully along the ground, creating chances for their attacking teammates.

There were, however, few threats on the United goal. It took Leeds sixty-five minutes to force their first corner and a further five to produce a worthwhile scoring effort. When there was a definite threat on the United goal, poor finishing cost Leeds dearly. As Dunne misjudged a centre, Peacock flicked the ball back for Bell, but the full-back lobbed the ball wide of the empty net. Peacock himself was guilty of another miss, again with the goal beckoning.

Charlton and Crerand often earned United some breathing space, but without the suspended Bremner Leeds lacked a leader, and United were often content to drag nine men back behind the ball. Leeds grew desperate, pushing Charlton and Bell forward to add some height and strength to their attack, but still a goal would not materialise, United hanging on for two very valuable points.

On their return to the dressing room, a jubilant United discovered that it had been an even better afternoon, as Chelsea had dropped a point at home to West Bromwich Albion. Only one point now separated the top three, with the Londoners having played a game more than either United or Leeds.

United travelled to relegation-threatened Birmingham City two days later, but with less than half an hour to go, found themselves 2-1 down to the bottom of the table side.

Matt Busby had been forced into making a rare change to his starting line-up, one that left the rank-and-file support wondering what was going on, as club captain Noel Cantwell vacated his usual role as a full-back with the reserve team and made his first appearance of the season wearing the No. 9 shirt, replacing David Herd

George Best had headed United into a thirteenth-minute lead, but Thwaites put the home side level soon afterwards. Then, in the sixty-first minute, Vowden left United and their support shaken, as he turned a Thwaites cross past Pat Dunne to give Birmingham the lead.

Within a minute, United were on level terms again, Best chesting down a Crerand pass before firing home from 15 yards. The momentum was suddenly picked up and three minutes later Charlton made it 3-2 as jubilant United supporters invaded the pitch.

There was still time for Birmingham City to come back, but the game was put beyond their reach with fifteen minutes remaining, when Noel Cantwell headed a Connelly centre past the outstretched hand of Schofield for United's fourth.

At the precise moment Cantwell's header hit the back of the net, the players of Leeds United and Chelsea were walking dejectedly off Hillsborough and Anfield respectively, both teams having lost: Leeds 3-0 to Sheffield Wednesday and Chelsea 2-0 to Liverpool. Former United player Phil Chisnall scored one of those Liverpool goals.

Cries of 'Champions, Champions' filled the Midlands air as the full-time whistle sounded at St Andrews. United had clambered into first place with fifty-seven points from their thirty-nine games. Chelsea were second with fifty-six from forty and Leeds third, with fifty-six from thirty-nine. The bookmakers quickly responded accordingly, making United 8-1 favourites, while Leeds were now 6-1 and Chelsea considered well out of it at 50-1.

The Yorkshire side now faced Sheffield Wednesday at home, Sheffield United away and Birmingham City away, while Chelsea had to travel to Lancashire for their two remaining games at Burnley and Blackpool. United, while still having their Fairs Cup games to contend with, had Liverpool at home, Arsenal at home and Aston Villa away to overcome if they were going to lift the title. All three games would be played in a space of five days.

Last season's Champions Liverpool travelled to Manchester on 24 April and, with one eye on the following week's FA Cup final, surrendered rather weakly to goals from Law in the twentieth and fifty-ninth minutes, and another from Connelly eight minutes from time, giving United a 3-0 victory. The only downside to the ninety minutes was a knee injury to Denis Law, who although having not played well in previous weeks, was still a vital ingredient to the United side.

Leeds continued to put the pressure on United, following up their 2-0 win over Sheffield Wednesday with a 3-0 success over Sheffield United. But they had now only one game remaining, whereas United had two. Chelsea confirmed the bookmakers' opinion by losing 6-2 at Burnley.

51,625 supporters clicked through the Old Trafford turnstiles on the night of 26 April for a nail-biting evening, when two points against Arsenal would ensure that United would indeed be crowned First Division Champions.

The suspense could be cut with a knife, as an unusually nervous United struggled for supremacy against a dour and determined Arsenal side. It was a night of clock-watching and hope. Hope that further south, Leeds would falter against Birmingham City.

7.37: Law, with bandages covering two stitches on his right knee moved in from the left to pick up a pass from Connelly. Beating Howe, he could find no teammate to pass to, so beat Howe for a second time before finally finding Best, who calmly controlled the ball before hitting it firmly past Furnell. 1-0 United.

7.52: News filtered through that Birmingham had taken the lead, but United were still looking far from comfortable.

8.25: Birmingham were now 2-0 in front, but still an eerie sense of foreboding hung over Old Trafford.

8.38: 3-0 to Birmingham and suddenly the spell was broken.

8.39: A Stiles free-kick drops invitingly for Herd, but his header is palmed onto the bar by Furnell. As the ball rebounded at hip height, Law pounced and slammed the ball high into the roof of the net. 2-0 United.

8.47: Twenty-three minutes left and a penalty to Arsenal for a foul on Baker by Crerand. Pat Dunne parries Eastham's kick, but couldn't stop the rebound. United 2, Arsenal 1.

9.02: A groan envelopes the ground as a loudspeaker announcement Birmingham City 3, Leeds United 2.

9.04: Furnell tips a Law header over for a corner.

9.05: Best fires in a low, hard corner, and Furnell misses the ball completely and it rolls to the feet of Law to score United's third.

9.10: Final whistle.

The crowd was already swarming onto the pitch when the crackle of the loudspeaker practically stopped them in their tracks: 'Here is the final score from St Andrews.' Silence all but enveloped the ground.

'Birmingham City 3, Leeds United ... 3.

What few players failed to find the sanctuary of the dressing rooms were enveloped in a sea of humanity, as the shirts were torn from their backs by the jubilant supporters. Policemen had their helmets knocked off trying to subdue the surging crowd, who covered almost every inch of the pitch, making for the mouth of the tunnel in the main stand, in the hope that their heroes would return to take a bow.

Waving their red-and-white scarves and the fragments of red shirts torn off the backs of the players, they chanted 'We want Matt' and 'We've won the League', as Busby and his men congratulated each other in the crowded confines of the dressing room.

Amongst the first people into the dressing room as the party got underway were the Real Madrid stars Puskas and Di Stefano, who were in Manchester prior to playing in a testimonial match for Stanley Matthews. It was party that continued into the boardroom and lounge, interrupted only by a telephone call from Leeds manager Don Revie, offering his congratulations, and by a policeman who announced that traffic was being held up outside the ground due to two cars on the forecourt. One belonged to Bobby Charlton, the other to Nobby Stiles, neither player felt like leaving to move them.

For Matt Busby, it was a golden moment. 'I am proud of these lads who have won the championship for Manchester United,' he said. 'Every single on of them.

'It has been a long, hard road. It has been a long, hard season. There have been tremendous setbacks. We had our share of injuries. And we lost Denis Law for a month.

'There have been times when we just could not seem to find the blend. But not for the first time I have found that patience is a virtue. I have always felt that we have the right quality of players at Old Trafford to do the job. They had shown earlier in the season what they were capable of, and I was fully confident they would do so again.

'But blend or no blend, in every match they have given me the lot. No manager, no club, can ask for more. Gradually, they have found that blend and, happily, gradual though the process was, it came at the right time – the psychological moment if you like.

'It has been a splendid job of teamwork from boardroom to backroom boys, right down to the ball boys, exactly as I have said of Leeds United, the team we have so narrowly beaten to it, and who have had such a wonderful season.

'But now, delighted though we are, we shall not simply stand and preen ourselves. We have more things to do. From experience with our other teams in the past, we know it is hard at the top.

'Finally, I could not be more pleased that the loyalty of our large band of supporters has been rewarded.'

Those celebrations could well have been somewhat premature, but only if the final game against Aston Villa was lost 19-0!

Strangely, Busby only made one change from the team that defeated Arsenal for that final League fixture of the season at Villa Park, giving John Fitzpatrick his second first-team outing. Villa, although in the bottom half of the table, were unbeaten in their last seven games and rounded off their season by making it eight, with a 2-1 win over the newly crowned Champions. So, instead of lifting the title with a distinct point's advantage, they had to be content to lift the title courtesy of a superior goal average.

Although space was being cleared for the League championship trophy to sit proudly in the Old Trafford boardroom, United's season was far from over. Due to the domestic campaign becoming so congested, as the season reached its crescendo, the Inter-Cities Fairs Cup had to take something of a back seat. But now it was time to return to the European front, travelling to Strasbourg for the first leg of the quarter-final.

On the banks of the Rhine, United left the French in no doubt as to why they were Champions of England, with a devastating display, scoring five without reply.

John Connelly opened the scoring in the twentieth minute and David Herd added a second five minutes before the interval, as United, inspired by Crerand and Charlton, who had a hand in every goal, practically toyed with their opponents. Law headed a third on the hour, then Charlton scored the fourth with ridiculous ease in the seventy-third minute. It was left to Law to round off the scoring a minute from time: five goals that Strasbourg had no hope of overcoming in the second leg back in Manchester.

At Old Trafford seven days later, it was party time, but it was something of a strange May evening down the Warwick Road, as the second leg against Strasbourg attracted a crowd of only 34,188. Only two League fixtures had attracted less, but the Fairs Cup second-round home leg against Borussia Dortmund had only attracted 31,896, following the high-scoring 6-1 first-leg victory. This left many to debate whether it was actually worth paying out their hard-earned cash to witness a game that had already been won.

There was, of course, the prematch presentation of the League championship trophy, worth the admission money alone, and for those who did click through the turnstiles, they were determined to make the most of the occasion. The terraces were ablaze with a myriad of red-and-white banners and balloons as the sun shone from the cloudless Manchester sky, making it something of an unusual setting for a football match.

Having already gone through their repertoire of songs, the crowd cheered as the League championship trophy was brought out onto the pitch some twenty minutes before kick-off, followed by the Football League president, Mr Joe Richards.

'Manchester United are fully deserving of their championship,' Richards declared. 'They have proved themselves the best team in the First Division and possibly the best team in the country. I wish them every success.'

The volume was turned up considerably as Denis Law strode forward to receive the trophy, and the cheers followed like regulated cannon fire as each member of the team took the short walk from the tunnel onto the pitch to receive their medals. There was a slight pause and the noise subsided after George Best received his, but it suddenly enveloped the ground again, even louder than before, when Matt Busby made his entrance.

With his teammates standing to one side, Denis Law was again summoned forward, but this time it was for a personal award rather than a team one, although one would not have been possible without the other. Law had been voted European Footballer of the Year and was presented with the Golden Ball by Max Urbini, editor of the *France Football* magazine.

Speaking in French, Monsieur Urbini said to the United talisman, 'You follow many famous players, from Stanley Mathews to Lev Yashin, as outstanding European Footballer of the Year. I am very happy for you, for Manchester United, and of course, for your manager, Matt Busby.'

Clad in red tracksuit tops, the United players proceeded with a lap of honour before the game finally got underway. Ninety minutes that was to prove to be something of an anticlimax, to say the least.

Strasbourg provided little entertainment, taking forty minutes to muster a shot on goal – their only one of the game as it turned out – while United stumbled along, trying frantically to achieve at least a couple of face-saving goals. Slowly, the impatient, frustrated crowd replaced the prematch cheers and applause with boos and slow hand-claps.

At times it looked as through there had been more action in the lap of honour, with Nobby Stiles and his running battle with inside-left Szepaniak creating most of the entertainment, and it was no surprise that many of the crowd drifted off before the full-time whistle.

If the performance did little to satisfy the support, it also did little to concern Ferencvaros, United's semi-final opponents, who were certainly made of sterner stuff than the French. There were, however, twelve days between that semi-final stalemate and the game against the Hungarians, but on a raw, cold night, the visitors stunned the Old Trafford crowd into silence, as they took the lead in the twenty-third minute, after Tony Dunne brought down Varga just outside the area and Novak blasted home the free-kick.

Even at this early stage of the game, tempers were frayed, and Crerand and Rakosi tangled in midfield, as did Best and Varga, while Albert became involved with the linesman. It took a goal from United in the thirty-fifth minute to restore some kind of sanity. Crerand took a short corner from Best and his perfectly judged cross found Law, whose header was palmed out by full-back Horvath. Law placed the ball on the spot, sold the 'keeper a dummy as he feinted on his run-up and, as Geczi dived one way, the ball was despatched into the opposite corner.

The second half resumed in a more-subdued fashion. Herd burst past Matrai, chasing a Charlton pass and, having drawn Geczi from his goal, was dismayed to see Horvarth block his shot on the line. As the half progressed, it was Charlton who was running the show, and in the sixty-first minute supplied the perfect pass for Herd to give United the lead.

With United on top, the evening of skill and high drama was spoiled by the throwing of missiles from behind the Stretford End goal, with the referee having a warning broadcast, which threatened the completion of the game should the unsavoury incidents continue. Things, however, soon returned to some normality in the sixty-ninth minute, when Herd claimed his second of the night. Law moved towards the byline, before cutting the ball back into the path of the big striker, who accepted the opportunity.

Sadly, all this good work was somewhat spoiled, as United became a little relaxed in defence, and with thirteen minutes remaining, allowed Rakosi to emerge from a ruck of players to beat Dunne for the Hungarians' second goal. Although United still held the advantage, it was a goal that they could have done without losing, making the job in the return leg that little bit harder.

Having played that first-leg tie on the last day of May, it was 6 June before the United players ran out to face Ferencvaros on Hungarian soil, a time when it was normally sand under their feet rather than a football pitch. Playing until the end of May was unusual enough in itself but into June was unheard of for a competitive fixture other than the likes of the World Cup. Indeed, the only previous occasion that United were involved at this time was back in 1940, when they played Everton at Old Trafford on 1 June in what was War Regional League Western Division fixture. What makes this particular fixture even more interesting is the fact that the United line-up was something of an all-star cast, with the likes of Stanley Matthews, Peter Doherty, Raich Carter and Alec Herd, David's father, all included in the forward line.

Delving further back into the history books, United would certainly be happy with a similar scoreline to that of their first encounter against Ferencvaros when the recently crowned First Division Champions recorded a 7-0 victory. They would, however, not be wanting a repeat of the scenes that accompanied that resounding success.

Due to the match official's lack of English and a misunderstanding as regards to the different interpretations of the laws of the game, the referee wanted to send three United players off for an infringement of the rules. As the United players surrounded the official in an attempt to explain, one or two of them placed their hands on the referee's shoulders, an action that some of the spectators took to be an attempt to attack him.

Stones suddenly began to be thrown from the crowd, several hitting the United players, and mounted police were forced to intervene and escort the United players away from the ground. Upon the police leaving the players, the crowd once again began throwing stones, before the United team managed to get away to safety.

In Budapest's NEP Stadium, it was a United side, unchanged from the first leg, that ran out attempting to reach their first European final, but they would have to master not just the Hungarian players, but also the conditions, as heavy rain for most of the previous week had left the surface in something of a treacherous condition.

Although there was no change to the visitors' line-up, the match official did differ from that of the first leg, although much was being made of the fact that the controversial Belgian official Hubert Burguet, who had been the man in the middle, had not been withdrawn due to his handling of the feisty first leg: a match that had threatened to get out of hand towards half-time, when a linesman had to run onto the pitch to separate Crerand and Rakosi. Busby also played down the furore over the new appointment, saying that it was common practice to switch referees for the second leg.

Ferencvaros, having secured those two goals in Manchester, knew that there was more than a possibility that they could overcome their opponents and attacked from the first whistle; indeed, they were unlucky not to be two in front in the opening few minutes.

First, Fenyvesi, the elder of the brotherly wing combination, tripped over the ball with the United defence at sixes and sevens, and then Tony Dunne upended the other Fenyvesi brother inside the area and was relieved to see the referee wave play on as the crowd bellowed for a penalty.

As the United players struggled to keep their feet, Pat Dunne pulled off a couple of excellent saves as the momentum against them slowly increased, with the volume of noise from the local support becoming ear-splitting in the twenty-ninth minute, when Stiles impeded Albert inside the penalty area. Again, the referee was reluctant to award a penalty, giving a free-kick instead, and it was ten red and one green shirt on the goal line that kept the ball out.

The Hungarians, although having most of the play, managed few shots on goal from inside the area, while United's first-half efforts were limited to a David Herd header. But with only a minute remaining until half-time, the visitors fell behind. Having just seen a Rakosi shot hit the bar and fly over, another Ferencvaros attack saw Stiles adjudged to have handled the ball, and this time the referee had no hesitation in awarding the spot-kick, which Novak converted.

The second half, with the aggregate score now level, was always going to be a cauldron of fire, with Stiles – who else – verbally abused from all corners of the ground. Pat Dunne kept the glimmer of hope alive with a handful of excellent saves, as United tried to ease the stranglehold that their opponents had on the game, but Matrai, Horvath and Novak stood firm.

As in the first leg, the tempestuous side of the game once again reared its ugly head and Stiles had his name taken as players wrestled and squared up to one another, while Connelly received a bloodied nose from the referee, who knocked him over as Rakosi moved in to lash out.

With fifteen minutes remaining, both teams were reduced to ten men. Crerand and Orosz flew at each other like alley cats after the Scot appeared to have been body-checked. Both players hit the ground amid a hail of punches, and when the Hungarian aimed a kick at Crerand, the referee, linesman and trainer Jack Crompton all moved in to offer some protection. Other officials soon became involved and after some five minutes, the French referee ordered both players off: Crerand limping off while holding his head, Orosz requiring more than a little persuasion to leave the field. Busby's prematch warning of 'Whatever you do, keep your heads' had gone unnoticed.

There were no more goals, leaving the aggregate score at 3-3 and the need for a deciding third match. At the end of the game, Denis Law was summoned to the referee's room, where Monsieur Kitabjian tossed a French franc, having told the United captain that if it came down one way it was Manchester United and if it came down another way it was Ferencvaros. Tossing the coin into the air, it spun and the referee allowed it to fall to the floor, where it bounced, before it rolled tantalisingly out of sight and under a chair.

Matt Busby was unable to look as the chair was moved in order to find the coin, and said to Jimmy Murphy, 'You look Jimmy, I couldn't win an argument.' To him and to everyone else connected with United there was disappointment, as they lost the toss, which meant that they would have to return to Hungary for the deciding ninety minutes. When asked if he would have preferred to decide the actual match in such a fashion, he replied, 'When I saw how the coin had fallen, I suppose I certainly thought that it would have been better that way.'

But Busby rallied his troops, and the play-off ten days later found United in better form than on their previous visit, but they still fell below the standards that they had set upon winning the First Division title.

In the week prior to the play-off in Hungary, United chairman Harold Hardman passed away; with Matt Busby commenting that he had lost 'a great friend' in the former England amateur international, who had been at the Old Trafford helm since 1951. As a player, Hardman had seen service with Everton, Bradford City, Blackpool, Stoke and the Northern Nomads, appearing in successive cup finals (1906 and 1907) with the Goodison Park side, and becoming only one of three amateurs to win FA Cup winners' medals in the twentieth century. With the Toffees, he also won four full England caps. The United manager added, 'He was a great little man and a great character and he will be sadly missed at Old Trafford and in football generally.' He would soon be replaced at the club by Louis Edwards.

Returning to Hungary, United flew to Vienna, before making the four-hour coach journey to Budapest where, upon arrival, they discovered that the hotel they had originally booked into – the Grand on Maigit Island – was unavailable due to the rising level of the River Danube, forcing them to seek alternative accommodation. It was certainly not the best of prematch preparations, while the game itself had far from a normal opening forty-five minutes, as it was halted for two minutes to pay tribute to the late Harold Hardman, a seemingly Continental trend.

In the opening half, United coped well and there was more than a distinct possibility that they could achieve victory and travel back to Manchester to face Juventus in the final. But with a minute remaining before the interval, Karaba shot from 30 yards out and Pat Dunne was too slow in moving to cover the shot; the ball grazed the bar and flashed into the net. It was a bitter blow for United and they were to find themselves two behind nine minutes into the second half, when Fenyvesi met a Karaba cross 12 yards out, leaving them with a mountain to climb.

United pushed forward, with little to lose, but chance after chance went astray as Busby, sitting on the touchline, threw his arms up in the air in despair. Charlton fired over when in a good position, Best drove wide from close in and Herd missed an even easier chance when he shot past the post.

Ten minutes from time, the only show of bad temper saw Crerand booked following a clash with Rakosi. With four minutes remaining, United scored through Connelly after goalkeeper Geczi had parried a shot from Herd. It was, however, too little too late and it was a dejected United who left the field to the polite applause from the sporting Hungarians.

The Hungarian newspaper *Nepsport* praised the United players for their sporting behaviour, but was quick to point a finger at Pat Dunne for both Ferencvaros goals, adding, 'In defence, Stiles saved a lot, but he was rough again – just as before. Crerand covered a tremendous area, Charlton was the conductor of the front line, Best, especially in the first half played well and was quick and Law made a much briefer show.'

It is worth noting, if the play-off had ended all square, then a coin would be tossed to decide who would face Juventus in the final.

So, the United players could finally throw their boots to one side and set off for a well-earned break, knowing that despite the disappointment of failing in the Inter-Cities Fairs Cup, they still had the League championship trophy at Old Trafford, and with it, the opportunity to make amends in the European Cup the following season.

7

LIFE ON A SEE-SAW

With the World Cup being hosted by England in the summer of 1966, Old Trafford, as one of the selected stadiums, was undergoing something of a major face-lift. This had begun the previous season and it was now almost ready to host those elite fixtures. The new cantilever stand, with its state-of-the-art executive boxes, swept from one end to another along the United Road side of the ground, providing a superb backdrop for United's own Football League fixtures.

Even in those somewhat distant days of the mid-sixties, United were considered the 'richest, most skilled and adulated club in the land' and on the eve of the new season, Matt Busby insisted, 'We are the Champions. Only the very best is good enough for us. There must be no scrimping and saving. Our supporters must be given every possible consideration at all times. We must make progress.' It is strange reading such words some forty-odd years on, when part of one statement has stood the test of time, while part of the other falls considerably short of the mark in the opinions of many.

In the previous season, they had made a profit of £48,700, the third highest of the post-war era, even though costs were up £27,000 in wages, while bonuses went up to £131,000. It is also worth noting that the United Development Association had handed over a sum of £34,823 towards the cost of building the new cantilever stand.

But it 1965, United were the trailblazers, the yardstick for others. They were rising to a position that few would ever be able to reach. The forty glass-fronted boxes at the rear of the new cantilever stand were innovative, bringing a football stadium up to a standard only previously expected at the likes of Lords, Ascot and Epsom.

'There has been a tremendous rush for the boxes,' said Busby. 'They represent a pretty fair investment at £300 a centre box and £250 a wing box for all the matches other than the World Cup.

'We thought carefully about this project for a long time. We feel it provides big businessmen in Manchester with an opportunity to give their overseas customers a good day out – and of course it is a fine advertisement for the club.'

'We could sell many more boxes.'

Such facilities were only for the select few, with the ordinary man in the street paying between £8 8s (£8.40p) and £12 for a season ticket, between 7s 6d (38p) and 12s 6d (63p) for a seat in the stand, and either 4s (20p) and 5s (25p) to stand on the terracing. Travelling to the ground by public transport would cost you 8d (less than 5p) for the ten-minute ride by bus from the city centre, or 1s 3d (7p) by train to the station outside the ground. Those with a car could park for 1s (5p) within 500 yards of the stadium.

So it was at a sun-kissed Old Trafford that the 1965/66 season got underway, as United and FA Cup winners Liverpool contested the FA Charity Shield, with just short of 50,000 – around 8,000 of those taking their places in part of the new cantilever construction – witnessing an enthralling encounter. Many had made their way down the Warwick Road via the 'other' Old Trafford where Lancashire were entertaining Northamptonshire, returning at full-time following the 2-2 draw which saw each club 'owning' the trophy for six months each.

It was seven days later on Saturday 21 August, that United's title defence got underway, and the red-and-white-clad supporters piled off the buses and trains and through the turnstiles in the hope of a flying start against Sheffield Wednesday, despite being without the injured Denis Law, who had limped off in the draw with Liverpool, and having youngsters Willie Anderson and John Aston on the flanks.

Such changes made little difference to United, as despite a distinct lack of goals, they put on a superb display, with glimpses of near-perfection opening the season with 1-0 victory.

Two away fixtures followed, against Nottingham Forest and newly promoted Northampton Town, and suddenly, the hints of a promising start hit the buffers, with Forest becoming not simply the first side to beat the newly crowned Champions, but the first side to put four past them for almost a year. New boys Northampton didn't quite match the performance of Forest, but on the strange cricket-cum-football pitch, they kept United at bay, frustrating their superior opponents into giving away needless free-kicks, and leaving the Champions in the lower half of the table following the 1-1 draw.

Such a position was not exactly something that gave Busby sleepless nights, as they were only three games into the new campaign. What did worry the United manager was, in the weeks and months ahead, the number of games that his players would be called upon to play.

'It is never easy when you are at the top,' he proclaimed. 'And we realise it is going to be very difficult to make a real European Cup challenge.

'But now we realise everything is going to be tougher than ever with so many extra commitments and so many international calls to meet.

'It may be all right for some clubs who are not very much troubled by international games, but we are always having to release players.

'The problem is the World Cup preparation. England want matches each month and Ireland and Scotland are going to seek their players.

'I know we have plenty of ability in the reserves, but having key players away so often is bound to increase our problems and affect our planning.

'A middle-of-the-road team without international calls will have a much easier time. It will be able to develop rhythm.

'But I would not have it any other way at Old Trafford.'

Law had returned against Northampton, and this allowed Busby to field his first-choice side for the following five games, although he had dropped Pat Dunne following the defeat at Forest, bringing David Gaskell back between the sticks, while at the same time telling Harry Gregg that he could leave the club, after the Northern Ireland international had handed in a transfer request.

'I must get back into top League football,' Gregg insisted. 'I am tired of sitting around. I have had only four games in the past nine months. And I have been fit all that time.

'I played in the reserves a couple of times and then was out again. I got fed up and asked for a transfer and have been told that I can go.

'I am not leaving with any hard feelings. It is a great club, but I feel I have to get away now. I don't mind where I go, as long as I can return to the game.'

It was, however, a transfer that would never materialise, as Gregg would not only remain at Old Trafford for a further twelve months, but would reclaim his place in the first team.

As Gregg kicked his heels on the touchline, his teammates struggled to find that winning formula, with consecutive home draws against Nottingham Forest (0-0) and Stoke City (1-1). The goalkeepers of both clubs – Peter Grummitt of Forest and Lawrie Leslie of Stoke – pulled off numerous superb saves to keep United at bay.

Having already struggled against newly promoted Northampton, it was with some trepidation that United travelled to the North East to face the other promoted side Newcastle United. However, goals from Herd and Best, although they did concede one near the end, gave them a 2-1 victory, their first in five games. It was not, however, a victory that began the start of a long, unbeaten sequence, as three days later they made the short journey to one of their bogey grounds – Turf Moor, Burnley – where United had to play second fiddle for all but fifteen minutes of the opening half.

Burnley went in front through a Harris free-kick in the sixth minute, and it wasn't until the half-hour mark that United sprang into life, ironically around the same time that the tension that had been simmering away on the terracing also erupted into violence, with the police making the first of what were to become regular forages into the crowd to deal with unruly spectators.

Law rounded Talbut and flicked the ball past Thomson, the oncoming Burnley goalkeeper, towards the empty goal. But to his dismay, Angus ran back and cleared the ball, almost off the line, for a corner. Best then dallied too long on the ball when set up by Charlton and it was to prove costly, as Burnley took the play to the opposite end. From Morgan's centre, Latcham turned the ball back to Harris, who beat Gaskell without much of a problem.

Irvine should have added a third soon after, but it wasn't until the final minute that the home side did in fact add to their total, when Elder scored from the penalty spot after Foulkes had fouled Latcham.

The game, however, was somewhat overshadowed by the behaviour of a considerable number of United supporters, who were beginning to cause the club much concern. At Burnley, many of those congregated behind the Burnley goal in the first half had 'chanted slogans and obscenities to various players and the police had moved in to drag one long-haired idiot out and escort him out of the ground'.

Fireworks were thrown from the rear of the terracing into those standing in front, whether they were fellow United fans or not, and at full-time, following countless disturbances throughout the second half, supporters of both clubs surged onto the pitch where, according to one report, 'they fought like animals'. Willie Morgan and referee Kevin Howley were also attacked.

United, dismayed by such scenes and the conduct of many others, took the first steps in an attempt to eradicate them, by banning eight supporters from the ground after they had been arrested for obscene chanting during the Stoke game, while a further six, who had been arrested at Burnley, were also banned.

'We have taken this drastic action because we cannot have a minority spoiling things for everyone else,' said a disappointed Matt Busby. 'They damage the reputation of both the club and the majority of decent supporters.'

'Following the obscene remarks chanted at the referee during the game against Stoke, eight youths, aged from fifteen to twenty-one, have been banned from entering the ground for the rest of this season and the directors wish it to be known that they are prepared to take these and other measures if the young fans at the Stretford End will not co-operate.

'They must be made to realise that they are a disgrace to the club they pretend to support and if they cannot behave as true supporters they are not wanted in the ground.'

Many agreed with the United manager's comments, calling the unruly supporters 'morons', but there were others who were not prepared to allow those comments to pass without some form of reply, as letters to the *Manchester Evening News* were to show.

Sue, who signed herself as a Stretford Ender wrote,'The majority of people who go to the Stretford End go because it is the only part of the ground where they can give United vocal support instead of being told to be quiet.

'If you stand in any other part of the ground and start to cheer, you are told to either be quiet in an impolite manner or to go and join the so and sos in the Stretford End.' While, 'Still Proud Red' penned, 'In support of the "morons" behind the Stretford End goal, if it wasn't for the majority of these "morons", United would be without encouragement. Supporters in other sections of the ground seem embarrassed to open their proud red mouths.'

A 'Hopeful Reds Fan' wrote, 'I am what the person might call a "moron". Is it because I pay my four shillings to watch United play. I want them to win, so I shout and cheer.

'Matt Busby asked the crowd to cheer, but it got him nowhere. Let's have everybody cheering on the reds. They need it at this point in time.'

If the behaviour of the supporters frustrated Matt Busby, the performances of his team did likewise, although he stressed that while he was 'disappointed' he was not 'worried': 'The forwards are getting bothered and over-anxious. Their lack of scoring in the past couple of weeks is worrying them. But it is in the tradition of Manchester United to start seasons slowly. We have done it many times, last season for instance. We seem to develop staying power and then come on to the scene near the end. That is what will happen this season, though at present we do not seem to have found any sort of stride.'

Attendances, like the form of the players, had also dropped. When questioned about the rather poor attendances, Busby was quick to divert the reason away from his team's performances, saying, 'I do not believe the crowds are deserting us. You should have seen the rain in Manchester just lately. People are just staying at home.' This was certainly arguable, as gates had fallen. The opening fixture of the previous season had attracted some 52,007, while the corresponding fixture of this season saw only 37,524 click through the turnstiles.

The visit of Newcastle to Old Trafford on 15 September could also be taken as something of a yardstick in the argument, as almost twelve months previously 53,058 had watched the 4-1 win over Tottenham Hotspur, while a disappointing – rain or not – attendance of 30,401 was attracted by the Geordies' visit, a game that produced the fourth draw of the season, even though 70 per cent of the play was in the visitors half.

'Manchester United lack punch' was the headline preceding Brian Crowther's match report in the *Guardian*, with the correspondent writing, 'Manchester United have almost lost the game's most basic and crucial skill – they have the gravest difficulty in getting the ball in the goal. Last night at Old Trafford, though they clearly played the better football, they could only draw 1-1 with Newcastle United. And their goal came only five minutes from time even though probably 70 per cent of the play had been in Newcastle's half.'

Newcastle surprised the majority of the crowd by taking the lead three minutes prior to the interval, when Stiles was adjudged to have held back Bennett as he broke through, and the referee pointed to the penalty spot, with McGarry giving Gaskell no chance with his kick. It wasn't until the final five minutes of the game that United managed to rescue a point, with Stiles redeeming himself for his earlier misdemeanour, driving the ball past Marshall, following good work from Law and Charlton.

While mentioning the latter, the United legend, whose career was to span some three decades was, according to most sources, only booked once, in the 1967 FA Charity Shield match against Tottenham Hotspur, but the referee had not reported the caution, as he realised United had been losing 3-2 at the time. However, the myth that Bobby Charlton was never booked is now broken, as he had his name taken by referee Ken Stokes during the match against Newcastle, just after they had scored, for something that he said to the official.

Having scored a meagre eight goals in their opening eight fixtures, the second-lowest total in the First and Second Divisions, Busby decided to wield the axe, dropping George Best and bringing in John Aston for the visit of Chelsea.

Once again groans enveloped Old Trafford as United went behind, with Venables giving Chelsea the lead in the twenty-third minute. The Londoners' lead, however, was short-lived, as eleven minutes later Aston centred and Charlton drove home to put United level. The whole course of the game suddenly turned.

As if sparked into life, United regained much of their lost confidence and, sixteen minutes into the second half, Charlton sent Connelly clear and from the winger's cross, Law leapt above Shellito to head the ball down into goal. Twelve minutes later, another Connelly centre saw Law's head once again meet the ball and it flew past the outstretched hand of Bonetti to give United the lead.

Chelsea, something of a shadow of last season's title-chasing side, showed no enthusiasm for a fight, and in the seventy-eighth minute, Law claimed his hat-trick with yet another header. The victory could not have come at a better time, as League fixtures were put to one side and the quest for success in Europe took prominence.

Drawn against HJK Helsinki in the preliminary round, United travelled to the Finnish capital in a confident mood despite recent results on the domestic front. Busby attempted to boost the confidence of his players by declaring that he rated his current side the equal of the one who had last competed in the European Cup back in 1958.

'I believe we are ready to take on any club in Europe and beat them on a home and away basis. But, we still have to prove it,' Busby told the press prior to the game, as United trained under the watchful eye of 2,000 local youngsters in Hameenlinna. However, he was quick to point out that victory over the Finnish Champions, minnows in such a prestige competition, would prove nothing, as his team were expected to win and win it well.

Such expectations proved to be rather misguided, with Busby's claim that his side were ready to beat the best looking a little exaggerated. United struggled against the amateurs and were certainly a little fortunate not to be facing a deficit for the return leg.

A goal in front through David Herd after only thirty seconds, extended to 2-0 by John Connelly in the fifteenth minute, and United seemed to be on course for the expected avalanche of goals. But a mistake by Gaskell allowed Pahlman to reduce the leeway in the thirty-fourth minute, giving the Finns a hint of hope, only to be brought back to earth again within three minutes, when a Law goal regained United's two-goal advantage.

Gaskell redeemed himself with a number of fine saves as the match suddenly swung on its axis and, in the opening twenty minutes of the second half, United found themselves on the ropes. Without playmaker Pat Crerand, United clearly struggled, although his replacement, eighteen-year-old John Fitzpatrick, certainly did not let the team down. When the predicted tiredness of the HJK players failed to materialise, a hint of panic suddenly became evident in United's play.

There was also, at times, a rather relaxed look about United's play, and for this they paid the price when seventeen-year-old Peltoniemi, playing only his second first-team game, drove the ball past Gaskell for Helsinki's second, with thirteen minutes remaining.

It was a result that gave Busby much to think about on the journey home to Manchester, having told the travelling members of the press, 'We thought they would be sure to tire in the second half. Instead, they improved and played really well. Needless to say, I was disappointed with our display.' Also on Busby's mind was the forthcoming Saturday fixture at Highbury against Arsenal: ninety minutes that took on something of an edge, even at this early stage of the season, as both sides had got off to something of an unsteady start to their League programme and were placed uneasily in mid-table.

Sadly, in north London, United continued to look out of sorts, jaded and disjointed, despite taking the lead from a Charlton header in the twenty-fifth minute. By half-time, they were to find themselves 2-1 behind, following goals from Baker and Radford.

Armstrong hammered a 20-yard drive past Dunne seventeen minutes into the second half to make it 3-1 and United were on the ropes. However, an error of judgement by Furnell in the Arsenal goal allowed them back into the game, when he dived at a rather feeble Aston effort and knocked it into his own goal.

Stirred by this piece of good fortune, United managed to raise their game, and in one promising attack, Connelly surged past McCullough inside the penalty area and, as he moved forward, the Arsenal defender grabbed his jersey, pulling him back amid the cries of 'penalty' from the United players and support. The referee waved play on after looking across at his non-committal linesman.

Had it been given, and converted, it would have been 3-3, but instead, within ten minutes it was 4-2. Baker crossed from the left, Radford headed the ball back across goal and Eastham coolly headed past Pat Dunne as his defenders looked on.

United remained in thirteenth, four points behind the leading trio of Burnley, Leeds United and Sheffield United.

In the modern-day game a manager could quite easily have found himself under pressure following such results, even out of a job altogether, but this was the sixties and although such things did occur, they would certainly not happen to Matt Busby, who was not simply unsackable, but untouchable. If any one person was bigger than the club who employed them, this was the man. Not only was he manager of Manchester United, he was now the club's third-largest shareholder, after being given 500 ordinary shares, valued at £15,000, which also made him the holder of one-ninth of the whole club.

But while Busby was in total control of things, certainly at team level, the United board had one eye on the future. Having been at the helm for some twenty years, he was not always going to be there and it might come as some surprise that plans were being put in place for him to stand down as team manager at the end of the season, moving up into the boardroom as chairman, replacing Louis Edwards who was reportedly ready to step aside.

Was it however, a cunning piece of manoeuvring by Edwards? Yes, he was going to step aside, but he was also planning to take a step up and become president of Manchester United, a title that held a bit more clout than that of chairman.

'Matt is Manchester United,' professed the current chairman, 'and he has made a tremendous contribution, not only to the club, but to British football.'

'We have repeated our invitation for him to become a director at any time he wishes. It is there for him when he is ready.'

But he was not ready, stating, 'All this came as a complete surprise and it is a gesture by the directors I greatly appreciate.

'The horizons are wide open for Manchester United. We are back in the European Cup and this of course is the competition I have always wanted to try and win.

'I am quite happy at the moment, playing my part in trying to face up to the tremendous challenge in front of us.'

Not only had the United directors discussed the elevation of Busby from manager to the boardroom, they had also gone as far down the road as to discussing his immediate replacement, and apparently had only one candidate in mind: former club captain Johnny Carey, currently manager of Nottingham Forest. However, everything would hinge on one thing – success in the European Cup. Busby would then feel that his job had been done.

Such a success looked a long way off, if current form was anything to go by, but the return leg against Helsinki offered something of break from First Division matters and also brought the deluge of goals against the amateurs that everyone had expected when the draw had been made.

Despite the 6-0 scoreline, it took United a while to get into the swing of things, but they looked invigorated by the return of George Best to the starting line-up. Indeed, it was the nineteen-year-old Irishman who put United 2-0 in front a minute before half-time, after Connelly had given them a fourteenth-minute lead.

After the break, it was practically one-way traffic, with Pat Dunne in the United goal not having one single save to make, after only two in the opening forty-five. Connelly added a third a minute into the second half. Best, with a half-volley, made it 4-0. Charlton, from all of 35 yards, added a fifth on the hour mark and Connelly rounded off the scoring with a sixth.

This six-goal victory, albeit against somewhat poor opposition, seemed to give United something of a lift, while also persuading the Manchester public to leave the comfort of their firesides and make the journey towards the Salford docks, as 58,161, the biggest crowd of the season by just over 9,000, filled the ground for the visit of Liverpool.

Not all, however, were there simply for the ninety minutes of football. Indeed, a few would not even see that, as the malignant head of troublemakers manifested itself in Manchester 16 that particular afternoon.

Numerous reports, while extolling the reader with the 'graceful subtlety of Best', the 'raidings of Hunt, Thompson and Strong', the 'foresight and authority of Crerand' and 'the brilliant headed passes of St John' were equally quick to pick up on the darker side of the occasion.

'What we remembered most vividly was the deplorable misbehaviour on the field and on the terracing,' wrote Hugh McIlvanney in the *Observer*. 'There was fighting and missile-throwing – Stiles appeared to have his arm gashed near the finish – behind the United goal, and on the pitch there were dreadful fouls. It was indeed a sordid second half.'

A fellow scribe, Brian Glanville of the *Sunday Times* also found cause to devote some of the lineage within his summary of the afternoon's entertainment to the non-footballing side of things, penning, 'It all got rather rough now, perhaps in response to the violent goings-on on the terraces behind the goal, which led to the usual stream of Liverpool (and, perhaps, some Manchester) supporters being hauled away by police. Towards the end, a youth even ran onto the field, and later still, Stiles, who had been booed from the first whistle by the Liverpool throng, appeared to be hit by an object thrown from the terracing.'

Eric Todd in the *Guardian*, having slightly longer to dwell on his thoughts than his press-box colleagues, opened his report with 'Manchester United beat Liverpool 2-0 on Saturday at Old Trafford in the presence of 58,161 spectators. Perhaps 58,150 would be nearer the mark by the time the local constabulary had finished its reaping.

'The "arrests" while necessary were regrettable as was the smashing of several windows on the United premises as the crowd squeezed its way home. Appearances in court will reveal the miscreants' identities and home addresses if any; until then judgement must be suspended because supporters of both sides favour the same colours. It did seem unlikely that United's followers would express their pleasure with the result by throwing stones at anybody or anything.

'In spite of everything, it would be wrong to assume that there was no discipline at all on the field – where the overall behaviour was good until near the end – or off it. Reports of "ugly scenes" or "riots" often are so much exaggerated nonsense and serve merely to incite the more hot-blooded to further indiscriminate behaviour at a future date. Mercifully this lunatic fringe is in the minority and I am sorry it is necessary to publicise its activities at all.'

On the field, United should have scored early on, but did not take the lead until the nineteenth minute. Yeats had actually put the ball in the United net, but was given offside, and the ball was quickly despatched downfield, where Smith and Charlton flattened each other in a challenge. Yeats, having managed to get back into his own half, knocked the ball back to Lawrence, who did appear to have it in his hands. In a split second, however, Best headed the ball away from him and then prodded it into the empty net.

Seven minutes from half-time, Law made it 2-0 and that was that. United seemed content simply to play the second half out at their own leisurely pace, with Liverpool failing to offer anything in return.

As the crowds headed for home, a number of Liverpool supporters congregated outside the directors' entrance and a pint mug was thrown through Matt Busby's office window, covering the carpet in glass splinters. Another bottle shattered the window of chief scout Joe Armstrong, and bottles and stones showered on the boardroom windows. Directors of both clubs had to leave their private room and guests in the lounge hurriedly drew curtains for protection. During the game, a dart had landed beside United 'keeper Pat Dunne.

'The birch is the only answer,' said Liverpool chairman Sidney Reakes. Little did he know how this problem would escalate over the years, with his own team as much at the fore as any other.

With eight goals in two games, many hoped that, at long last, the corner had been finally turned and Matt Busby could celebrate twenty years as manager of Manchester United with his team pushing their way back to the top of the pile. The sun was certainly high in the sky, shining down on White Hart Lane on the afternoon of 16 October, but a dark cloud was soon to envelope United.

Law went off injured, not something that was as much a major factor as in the past due to his indifferent start to the season, with only five League goals to his name, but now United crumbled in front of a lock-out 58,000 crowd, conceding five before Charlton grabbed a seventy-fourth-minute consolation. There were now seven points between United and leaders Sheffield United, as hopes of retaining the title began to slowly disintegrate, with less than a third of the season gone.

Len Noad of the *Sun* offered an interesting perspective of the season to date when he wrote:

To even suggest that Manchester United won't win the League, the cup, the European Cup, or indeed, all three, is, I feel, akin to writing rude words on the headmaster's wall. Or to be accused of being a rabid City fan. But can one justifiably say that about a side who have been notoriously bad starters through the years and in late October still give the impression of being tied up in the tapes at the starting gate?

This lethargic start to a season has become so commonplace through the years that even an outstanding manager like Matt Busby, even if he has been concerned about it, has never shown it. With an air of quiet confidence he has answered the 'What's wrong Matt' questions with complete aplomb and an assured 'It'll all come right. You'll see. We have far too much talent for the team not to succeed.' And, of course, inevitably all has come well as their incomparable record since 1945 informs us so accurately in the record books. They have had only two indifferent seasons in the last nineteen. A record that not even the brilliant pre-war Arsenal side could match.

But one cannot disagree that the side have turned in some Jekyll and Hyde performances this season. They came back with a bang against Liverpool – and the Merseyside club's ultra-enthusiastic manager, Bill Shankly, has all along rated United as the biggest barrier to the League championship going to Anfield – yet a week later Tottenham Hotspur slammed the Old Trafford pin-up boys by five goals to one. That put United seven points behind the leaders with a third of the season gone and their match performance as jagged as a twisted seam.

There used to be a theory that United didn't play well until the heavy grounds sorted out the men from the boys and the skilful from the runners. Certainly, I feel this was true of the first post-war side. But since then changes in personnel have occurred, both inevitably and tragically, and such a yard-stick to my mind no longer gives accurate measure.

The fact is that the United defence have conceded more goals than the forwards have scored. And last season it was their goal average, vastly superior to that of Leeds United, which gained them the title and re-entry into the Champions Cup.

But so far this season I feel that neither wing-half, both of whom achieved such masterly a year ago, have hit their best form. This can also apply to the attack where Denis Law has been troubled with injury since the season's opening game; David Herd has been left out and George Best switched to inside-forward. Goalkeeper Gaskell, too, replaced by Pat Dunne at one stage. This suggests that Busby too has been concerned at the team's inability to find that streak of consistency which is essential for League honours. His new forward formation, first tried against the amateurs of Helsinki in the European Cup, worked like a dream. But the Finns were like a Victor Sylvester lesson with the quick bits left out.

Without seeking cheap excuses, the reds this season have often outplayed the opposition but failed to apply the winning touch, Goalkeepers have played blinders; sitters have been missed; final passes have gone astray. The players come off the field asking each other – 'What have we to do to win?'

The answers from Busby will always be the same. 'Keep playing your football lads. There is no other way.'

The exertions of last season, which had the team still playing when the rest of the soccer world were sunning themselves on sundry beaches at home and abroad, may have been a valid excuse by the die-hards a few weeks ago. But even they will agree that they should have been back in harmony at this stage. Maybe Matt Busby will make one of his rare but shrewdly-timed and dramatic excursions into the transfer market and buy one player to revitalise the team. For obviously, something is lacking. Time is running out and that coveted League championship is slipping away. The cup of course, is still to come. And that ancient trophy has re-juvenated far less talented sides than the reds in the past. This obviously, is now their best chance to remain in European competition next season. For although they have another comparatively easy draw in their second-round European Cup match with the East German side Vorwaerts, they have done nothing to suggest they will be a match for the big sides like Inter and Benfica later in the competition.

Although on paper, a side can appear to retain the skill which took the honours, history shows that the magic touch can disappear almost overnight. When one surveys the playing staff at Old Trafford, however, that appreciation of the present situation would be a dismal one indeed. Busby believes, and the whole history of the game supports him, that skill must tell in the final analysis.

I learned something a long time ago. That it is extremely dangerous to 'write-off' a side like United.

If United were going to recover from their perceived slump in form, then Busby would need all the guile and experience that he had accumulated throughout the highs and lows of his twenty years at the helm, pulling his team from the jaws of adversity and blending them into one of Europe's best. Such was the adroitness of the United manager and indeed the football club as a whole, it was of little surprise to many that seven days after conceding five against Tottenham, they scored four against Fulham at Old Trafford, before claiming a further two points at Bloomfield Road, Blackpool. Many, even the most biased United supporters, felt that the visitors were more than fortunate to claim both points in the latter fixture and that Lady Luck had more than a helping hand in the result.

Blackpool had outplayed their guests in the opening forty-five minutes and were in front at the interval through an Alan Ball goal. It was a lead that they held until the seventy-fifth minute. Three minutes earlier, the course of the game was altered when the home side lost their goalkeeper, Tony Waiters, with a head injury, right-half Turner taking over between the sticks. The stand-in 'keeper had no chance of stopping Herd's equalising goal.

Having relaxed slightly prior to the goal, Blackpool were roused into action, but failed to breach the United defence as the minutes slowly ticked away. Due to the injury to Waiters, the referee added an additional four minutes, and with only two of those remaining, David Herd burst through between two Blackpool defenders, running on to a Nobby Stiles through-ball. Immediately cries went up for offside, but they were ignored by referee Crawford and Herd continued towards goal, rounding the 'keeper before tapping the ball into the empty net.

'It was not only my opinion, but the linesman's opinion also that Herd was on side when the pass was made,' said Crawford after the game.

'It looked like another of those time-wasting gestures,' wrote Bob Russell in the *Daily Mirror*. 'Herd did not even perform the usual joy-dance. Nobody congratulated him ... not until referee Crawford turned and pointed to the centre circle. Even if the referee was right – and I very much doubt it – Manchester United's win was still a hollow one.'

United rode their luck for a second consecutive Saturday afternoon when Blackburn Rovers, bottom of the First Division, visited Old Trafford on 6 November, and for those who made the habit of leaving the ground early, they missed a finale completely different to any that had been witnessed previously within the red-brick walls of the stadium.

United were moving towards a single-goal victory over their Lancastrian neighbours, a win that would have taken them up to joint-eighth in the table, and with seven minutes remaining, they looked more than capable of keeping their visitors at bay. Suddenly, however, the floodgates of excitement and emotion were opened.

Blackburn won a corner on the left and, after Harrison's kick had been comfortably cleared upfield, it was noticed that their centre-half, Mike England, who had challenged for the ball with Harry Gregg, was lying flat-out on the ground. The action suddenly swung from one end to the other, as the United penalty area became a mass of players, all surrounding the referee.

No one seemed to know what was going on until a minute or two later, when it became obvious to all that Gregg was being sent off and Blackburn had been awarded a penalty. Slowly and rather dejectedly, the big Irishman removed his green jersey and handed it to David Herd, whose first involvement between the sticks was to face the spot-kick. Gregg crouched on the touchline, a towel draped over his shoulders, as Harrison blasted the ball past the stand-in custodian.

Gregg disappeared from view, as did United's two points. Down to ten men, United attacked like men possessed and Law, back in the side following a two-game lay-off, restored United's lead. But with the extra-man advantage, Rovers decided that it was now all or nothing, and with sixty seconds of the game remaining, they were awarded a free-kick just outside the United area when Byrom was fouled. Harrison took the kick, and as the ball moved towards goal, Crerand stuck out his leg in an attempt to block the shot, but he diverted it past Herd and into the net, giving Blackburn a share of the points.

For Harry Gregg, it was a disappointing afternoon, as he had only returned to the United first team against Blackpool, following eighteen months out. He had also come under a barrage of glass and stones from Blackburn supporters behind his goal, which held up the game for a short period while the debris was cleared off the pitch. His sending-off also stoked up considerable ill feeling and a form of retaliation from United supporters, including girls, who stoned the Blackburn team coach, smashing a window.

Gregg, suspended for seven days and fined £25 after being sent off in the reserve game against Burnley in February, received some sympathy from the Blackburn players after the match, as they thought that referee Clements had acted a little harshly. Even Mike England told the United 'keeper 'We'll give evidence on your behalf'. This, however, led to a confrontation between the Ewood Park club and the Professional Footballers Association.

Although the Rovers players were happy to give evidence when Gregg was summoned to appear before the disciplinary committee, the club's management refused to let the players take the stand. This forced PFA secretary Cliff Lloyd to say that the ban had created a 'grave situation' and he questioned the right of any club to do such a thing, adding, 'How can a man expected to prove himself innocent if witnesses are denied the right to give evidence on his behalf?'

For his latest misdemeanour, Harry was given a fourteen-day ban and a fine of £25. But more worrying for the goalkeeper was the threat of either David Gaskell or Pat Dunne claiming that No. 1 jersey.

The ban didn't take effect for a couple of weeks, allowing Gregg to keep his place in the United line-up for the League fixtures against Leicester City at Filbert Street and Sheffield United at Old Trafford, as well as the European Cup first-round, first-leg tie in East Germany against ASK Vorwaerts.

At Filbert Street, against a Leicester side who had won their previous three games, United conjured up the sort of form that had eluded them all season, playing with a machine-like precision that the home side found hard to contain. The home side were a goal down in eleven minutes and never really recovered from this early setback, allowing United to score a further four without reply through their own inefficiency.

On the day prior to the game against the East German Army side, United were unable to practice in the Walter Ulbricht Stadium, due to the lack of time and the frost-bound conditions. But it was to cause little concern, as despite the rather bleak conditions – the surface was treacherous in places, with patches of black ice – it was an achievement to remain standing, never mind achieve a victory.

In the hours leading up to the game, Denis Law was doubtful, due to a heavy cold and only regarded as having a 50/50 chance of playing. Thankfully Matt Busby took the gamble in playing the Scot and the player considered himself fit enough to endure the fourteen degrees below zero conditions. With the game drifting towards a stalemate and only seventeen minutes remaining, Law leaped above centre-half Unger and headed home David Herd's cross. Eight minutes later, the United No. 8 set up John Connelly for goal number two.

A few of the travelling members of the British press would normally have criticised United for their agonisingly out-of-touch start to the game, but in view of the conditions they considered that any finger-pointing was totally unjustified.

'Conditions were atrocious,' said Busby. 'The lads were troubled by the cold for quite a while, but in the end it was a great triumph of teamwork.' The United manager did, however, confess that he would have been 'more than happy to settle for a goal-less draw. We set out to hold them and come out and play when we could and we did remarkably well.'

It was a result that would practically ensure a place in Round Two, while a similar two-goal spurt, in the thirty-fifth and thirty-seventh minutes, from Best and Law, was enough to kill off Sheffield United, after the Irishman had given United an eighth-minute lead and Jones had equalised on the half-hour.

The return against Vorwaerts went as planned and David Herd secured United's place in the next round with a well-taken hat-trick in the 3-1 win, a match that, despite the scoreline, did little to boost United's credentials on the European front. Nor did it enthral the 30,000 crowd, displeased with the speed of the game, who reverted to slow hand-clapping after the Germans scored in the eighty-second minute to make the score 2-1. It was not until the final seconds of the game that Herd secured possession of the match ball.

United's European honeymoon was now over, as the whipping boys were now out of the competition, leaving hardened, experienced possible opponents in the form of Sparta Prague, Partizan Belgrade, Inter Milan, old foes Real Madrid, Anderlecht and Ferencvaros. None of them, however, followed the name of Manchester United out of the hat. Instead, it was Portuguese Champions and twice winners of the competition Benfica who were to provide the opposition.

'We're right back in the big time again. Things will be booming at Old Trafford. It's a terrific draw,' exclaimed Busby. 'One that reminds us of the days when we felt on top of the world. We will be playing a great side and it is our opportunity to show Lisbon how much better a team we are now than when last we were there.'

The United manager may well have thought that his team were indeed back in the big time, but three days after their success over the Germans they had to suffer the wrath of their supporters during the game against West Ham United at Old Trafford, as it drifted into an aimless lethargy early in the second half, with a backing track of 'why are we waiting' from the full-voiced Stretford End. And wait they continued to do, as a 0-0 draw was certainly not what they had paid their money to watch, especially on a cold, wet, winter afternoon.

There were more audible groans of discontent the following Saturday at Roker Park, with the hardcore travelling support wincing as Sunderland's Neil Martin gave his side the lead after only five minutes. But true to form when those two clubs came head-to-head, the game against the North East side exploded into life ten minutes later, when Best equalised before putting United in front twenty minutes later.

Sunderland were reduced to ten men for the last half-hour, after a crunching tackle from Foulkes led to Moore being stretchered off and United took advantage of this with a third goal, scored by Herd. But still the home side did not give up, with Martin scoring his second of the afternoon to pull it back to 3-2. Fortunately for United, an equaliser was just out with Sunderland's grasp.

The two points at Roker Park, along with a further two against Everton at Old Trafford in a 3-0 win – as George Best once again grabbed the headlines with a superb display to which the visitors had no answer – took United from eighth to third in the table, five points behind leaders Liverpool, who had played a game more. The gap was closing.

Something had certainly clicked within the Old Trafford camp, as United made it eleven goals in three games in the run-up to Christmas, with a revenge 5-1 hammering of Tottenham Hotspur at Old Trafford on 18 December. On their day, few could match Manchester United in full flow, with the men in the press box scrambling for adjectives to describe another sublime performance.

Perhaps the pen of Brain Glanville in the *Sunday Times* sums up that emphatic victory over Tottenham best: 'At Old Trafford today, Manchester United lit up the damp and lowering afternoon with a display of coruscating virtuosity. When their attack is under full sail it is a formidably impressive sight. The forwards shuttle in and out, back and forth, like a loom weaving a giant red carpet.

'Positions are secondary; the right-winger turns up on the left, the left-winger on the right; Charlton is now deep and distributing, now up and striking, while Law, shirt hanging out, hair slicked by the rain, mud obscuring the number on his back, stabs and darts into space no one else would notice.

'Crerand, never happier than when moving up behind his forwards, and Herd, a rampant second spearhead, were equally troublesome to a Spurs defence drained of all its confidence after Charlton's first, phenomenal goal.'

It was that goal, already rated as the season's best, fired past Jennings with tremendous power from 35 yards out, that opened the floodgates. An own goal, one from Herd and a Denis Law double saw off Spurs, who managed one in reply just after the interval, as the new Old Trafford anthem of 'We Shall Overcome' echoed around the ground.

Brian Glanville brought his report to a close with 'Once more United had shown us that on their day they are incomparably the best team in the country. One hopes that they have two such days against Benfica.'

But this was Manchester United. A team that could go from the sublime to the mediocre in a matter of minutes despite the riches that Matt Busby had at his disposal. The inconsistency that had submerged them in recent seasons returned like a fast-flowing ebb tide.

Three 1-1 draws, against West Bromwich Albion, Sunderland and Leeds United, in the following four fixtures were enough to bring their title hopes crashing down around them. With a 2-1 defeat at League leaders Liverpool, sandwiched in between the home games against West Bromwich Albion and Sunderland, doing little to offer any encouragement to players and spectators alike.

Denis Law, however, felt otherwise, saying, 'Manchester United are playing really well – well enough to retain the championship.' He did add something of a postscript: 'Mind you, it is going to be very tough. There are some great teams still in with a chance.'

A chance they certainly had, but it was more a case of relying on Liverpool slipping up, as the New Year's Day defeat at Anfield left United in fifth position and once again struggling seven points behind their rivals from along the East Lancs Road, although they did still have two games in hand.

United had silenced the Kop with a goal from Law after only ninety-five seconds and should have grasped the initiative, but time and again Herd was caught offside. Liverpool equalised seven minutes before the interval and snatched the winner with five minutes to go, leaving team and supporters alike to wonder if Milne's late strike would be pivotal come May.

A solitary, twenty-eighth-minute goal at Craven Cottage on 15 January gave United their first win in five League outings and got them back on track, although any increase in momentum was halted by the third round of the FA Cup, where they were drawn away at Second Division Derby County.

Coasting at 3-0 with only twenty-five minutes played, following goals from Law and a George Best double, complacency suddenly set in and United found themselves pegged back to 3-2 before half-time. It wasn't until the final fifteen minutes of the game that they finally managed to overcome a plucky Derby side.

A fifth draw in eleven games, goal-less this time against Sheffield Wednesday, was not the ideal warm-up for the visit of Benfica to Old Trafford as the European Cup campaign resumed following its winter lay-off. It was, however, a game that Matt Busby felt would be the yardstick against which he could measure how far his current team had come, or hopefully, how near his team were to regaining the standards set by the pre-Munich side.

Looking back before the visit of Benfica, Busby reminisced:

I think the team we had would one day have won the lot. No, I am sure of it. Came Munich and we were nothing, or nearly nothing. We were broken. We were heartbroken.

Miraculously I was spared, but there were times in those awful early days when to myself I cried: 'Enough.' It was the end. With memories that could never leave me. I could not face the prospect of building again.

Then it came to me that I *must* try again. The players left behind, some of them very young, were my responsibility. They had left parents and homes to go to Old Trafford. I had become a parent to them.

And I felt I owed much to the club itself, the people in it, and the people who so loyally supported it.

So, backed wonderfully by the chairman, the late Harold Hardman, the present chairman Louis Edwards, and the rest of the board, we started off again.

We had to buy players where our policy largely had been to breed and nurture them. We couldn't wait five or six years for youth to mature, especially since youth is by no means certain to mature. The club had to maintain its quality.

I bought fearlessly, always with splendid support from the board. I stood by my own opinions. I was ready to be judged by them, whether they turned out right or wrong.

Now I think we are ready again.

We at Manchester United have always aimed to be with the top clubs of the world. That's why went into Europe. Because that was the avenue to progress, the avenue to the future.

Look to the future or vegetate. That is the choice. We made our choice years ago.

Strangely there was no mention of the man who did so much in Busby's absence, the current assistant manager, Jimmy Murphy!

The feeling in the national press prior to the visit of the Portuguese Champions was that United, if they hoped to continue making progress the European Cup, would need a commanding lead to take into the second leg. An unnamed reporter in the *Daily Mail* suggested that they 'cannot afford to go to Lisbon on 9 March with a lead of less than three goals', while in the *Daily Express*, Desmond Hackett went as far as to suggest that United would actually win by three goals. Albert Barham in the *Guardian*, however, was a little more cautious, merely suggesting that 'so much depends on how much they (*United*) apply themselves, and on their determination to win'.

United did in fact score three. Unfortunately, Benfica managed two in reply.

Straight from the first blast of referee Dr Karol Galba's whistle United surged towards the Benfica goal and may well have gone one in front within the opening five minutes. Best was fouled by Cruz, and as the free-kick floated into the Benfica area, Herd nodded the ball forward past the static defence, but it struck the post and rebounded into the arms of the goalkeeper before being cleared to safety.

Costa Pereira saved from Charlton and Herd before scrambling across-goal to thwart Herd yet again, pushing the ball round the post for a corner as United sought that all-important breakthrough. They didn't exactly throw caution to the wind, but in surging forward, they did leave themselves vulnerable to the counter-attack and were caught out on the half-hour.

Having pushed forward, the Portuguese won their second corner of the night and Eusebio curled the kick tantalisingly towards the United goal. Augusto flew through the air to meet the ball firmly and it flew past Gregg and into the net. The silence was deafening.

Twice Law was through within 10 yards of goal, but his usual cool assurance eluded him on both occasions, but eight minutes before the interval, United were level. Best whipped the ball away from Torres and passed to Crerand. The cultured half-back threaded the ball through towards the oncoming Herd, who hit it low and hard past the right hand of Pereira.

The crowded terracing swayed in time to the tempo of the game and they were looking forward to a relaxing ten-minute break as much as the players, but with only sixty seconds remaining before the interval, they were once again whipped into a frenzy.

A weak corner from Best was partly cleared, but the ball was soon picked up by Charlton, who skilfully turned and sent it back towards the Benfica goal. Law pounced, bringing the ball under control with one foot, before hammering it home with the other.

The second half saw United surge forward with even more determination, stretching the ageing Benfica defence, with even right-back Tony Dunne pressing forward, forcing Pereira into something of a panic-stricken save. Law began to look more confident; Best produced numerous tricks from his ever-expanding repertoire, while Charlton conducted the whole affair from the middle of the pitch.

Two minutes short of the hour mark, Benfica conceded yet another free-kick, which were becoming more numerous as the game went on, when Germano impeded Connelly and, as Cantwell floated the ball into the area, Foulkes suddenly dived through a crowd of red-shirted defenders to head past Pereira.

Just as everyone's hoped-for goal target was within United's grasp, they dropped their guard and, in the seventieth minute, allowed Benfica back into the game. Eusebio, forever a source of danger, won the ball out on the left and his curling speculative cross should have been easy meat for a goalkeeper of Gregg's experience, but uncharacteristically, he failed to either catch or push the ball over the bar to safety. Instead, he pushed the ball up in the air and suddenly, as it dropped, Torres was there to knee it over the line from 2 yards.

It was a totally unnecessary goal, but its importance was only too visible on the faces of the players of both sides as they trudged off the pitch twenty minutes later. United, heads down, shoulders sagged and faces showing little in the way of expression. The Portuguese, however, were all smiles and almost skipped off the pitch while waving to a dejected and disappointed Manchester crowd.

Disappointing it certainly was, to both spectator and player alike, with Noel Cantwell speaking for the latter: 'We are all disappointed. We know we should have finished with a two-, maybe a three- or four-goal lead, but the way we are looking at it, we should get the breaks next time. Benfica got them this time.' Matt Busby spoke in a similar vein, saying, 'A one-goal lead isn't a lot to take to Portugal, but seeing what I saw tonight, I know we are a better side and the better side usually wins.'

If the United camp was confident of success in the return leg, what of Benfica? 'This was a magnificent game,' exclaimed their coach Bela Guttman. 'The 64,000 crowd had good value for money.

'Manchester United are a wonderful side and, even though we have a fine record in European Cup matches, I consider we have only an even chance of pulling back this one-goal deficit.'

Despite the disappointment behind the Benfica result, the performance, as a whole, was satisfying, with the confidence gained from the closely fought encounter carried forward into the League meeting with this season's new arrivals on the First Division scene, Northampton Town.

Harry Gregg, who retained his place in the side despite numerous fingers being pointed in his direction as being at fault for Benfica's two goals, had something of an easy afternoon, as his fellow teammates ran riot, making Northampton's first visit to Old Trafford on 5 February one to forget. Had United enjoyed a little more luck and their finishing been slightly more accurate, a new First Division scoring record might well have been made. As it was, the only record that United could claim that afternoon was achieving their 1,000th League point in post-war football with the 6-2 win.

The game was all over in the opening half-hour as United swept in to a 4-1 lead, opening the scoring as early as the fifth minute, but the visitors played their part in an entertaining afternoon's football, never giving up until the final whistle and being rewarded with two goals for their sterling effort. One of the Northampton goals came from former United player Graham Moore who, due to his prolonged stints in the Central League side, had moved to Northampton in a £12,000 transfer only a couple of months previously.

Seven days later, the Old Trafford attendance leaped from 34,986 to 54,263, with the additional 19,000 hoping to witness another deluge of goals, this time with Second Division Rotherham United becoming the whipping boys. But as Scotland's national poet, Robert Burns, wrote in his classic ode 'To A Mouse', 'the best-laid schemes o' mice an' men gang aft agley' (the best-laid plans of mice and men often go awry). The underdogs on the day were never overawed by the occasion and fully deserved a second opportunity against United, holding them to a 0-0 draw.

A victory might well have been within the visitors' grasp had it not been for the sterling efforts of Gregg making up for his misdemeanours against Benfica, along with fellow defenders Tony Dunne and Bill Foulkes in the heart of the United defence, and all at Old Trafford knew that the midweek trip to Millmoor for the replay would not be straightforward either.

The mismatch of mainly local junior recruits, put together at a cost of around £24,000 (their oldest player was only twenty-two), once again raised their game in front of their own supporters and gave the all-international £300,000 United XI countless nerve-wracking moments on the tight, muddied pitch, with the overlooking slag heaps offering an unusual backdrop.

Rotherham matched United for long periods and deserved full credit for taking the tie into extra time, but in the end, the efforts of the home side were overcome by the extra pace and stamina of the experienced United players, with thirty minutes' extra time finally catching up with them.

The home side's best spell was just before the end of the first half, but once the game moved into the additional half-hour, it was all United and with the Second Division youngsters now more content in holding out for a draw and a second replay. With only five minutes remaining, Stiles left his defensive duties, moving forward and sending a square pass to the feet of Connelly, who shot right-footed into the roof of the net from 15 yards to ensure victory for the visitors.

Back on League business at Stoke on 19 February, United surrendered a 2-0 lead and collected only a point in a 2-2 draw, a result that kept them ten points adrift of leaders Liverpool, with hopes of retaining the title now all but gone. Burnley were then beaten 4-2 and there was little time to catch a breath and recover from any niggling knocks, as Wolverhampton Wanderers were sitting in wait in the FA Cup fifth round, seeking revenge for their sixth-round defeat twelve months previously.

With the trip to Portugal for that all-important European Cup second-leg encounter only four days away, Matt Busby could have been forgiven for casting rules and regulations aside and fielding an under-strength side at Wolverhampton, but it was something that the United chief was loath to do. In any case, this was the 1960s and your first team was more or less that, not a squad, but usually no more than fifteen players and, unless you were injured, suspended or had the ignominy of being dropped, you played. So, it was essentially take life as it comes and United's often carefree attitude served them well, especially when they found themselves behind to two penalties at Molineux.

In the second minute, Hunt gathered the ball from Wagstaffe, turned into the United penalty area and instantly hit a wall of defenders. Colliding with Crerand, the winger fell to the ground and referee Howley rather generously pointed to the spot, despite the protests of the penalised playmaker. Wharton hammered the ball wide of Gregg's right hand.

Seven minutes later, a clearance rebounded from Wilson and Foulkes, caught a little off balance, stuck out his hand at the awkward, bouncing ball, leaving the referee with little option than to once again point to the penalty spot. Once again, Wharton got the better of Gregg.

Had United decided that fate was against them and their interest in the FA Cup was nearing its conclusion, then no one would have argued with them, but as history had shown, and would continue to show in the months, years and decades ahead, this was Manchester United, a far from ordinary football club.

Following the two rather harsh penalty decisions, that some might consider self-inflicted, many teams would have accepted that this was not going to be their day and plodded away for the remainder of the game. But United simply shook themselves and set about regaining a foothold on the cup tie. Pulling a goal back in the twenty-second minute, a typical header from Law from inside the 6-yard box, gave United the encouragement that they needed and from that moment on, there was only going to be one winner.

In the three minutes immediately after the interval, McLaren in the Wolves goal had been forced into making three notable saves, including one from Herd, tipping a rasping 30-yard drive over the bar. However, play continued to swing from end to end, with Wolves reminding United that they could easily fall further behind if they erred in the face of caution.

The pivotal moment in the game came in the sixty-second minute, when Gregg ran from goal to deny Holsgrove what looked like a certain goal. Play suddenly switched to the opposite end and Knowles rather lazily aimed a back-pass in the direction of his goalkeeper, only to see Connelly dash forward, latch on to the ball and, as McLaren moved from his goal, calmly cross it to the head of Law for United's second.

Gregg was forced to dive full length to stop a McIlmoyle header at the foot of the post, but in the seventy-third minute, United once again broke away. Flowers lost the ball to Best in the centre circle and the Irishman, evading the close attention of three defenders, exchanged passes with Herd and set off towards the Wolves goal. Drawing McLaren from his line, he slid the ball past the advancing 'keeper to give United the lead. With four minutes remaining, Charlton and Best combined to create the opening for Herd to score a fourth and his 101st goal for the club. United were in Round Six.

Eight goals in two games set United up nicely for their European Cup second-leg tie in Lisbon on 9 March. Conceding two in each fixture gave a slight cause for concern, but more so due to the Portuguese Champions' impressive record against European opposition, where they had played fifty-four games, winning thirty-nine and drawing eight, overall scoring 108 goals, while conceding only forty-nine. Impressive indeed!

United's last visit to the city ended in tears, when their 4-1 first-leg victory against Benfica's rivals Sporting was overturned and ended in a 5-0 defeat. It was a game they had been expected to win comfortably, but one that still haunted Matt Busby, who shuddered at the memory, claiming it was one of the blackest nights of his long managerial career.

With the daytime temperature hitting the seventies, the United players were warned to keep out of the sun and, with the game scheduled for a 9.45 p.m. kick-off, Busby took his players to the stadium at 9 o'clock the night before in the hope that they would get the feeling for what lay ahead. 'It would be foolish to let Benfica get the initiative, especially here,' said the United manager. 'We shall defend when necessary and attack when we can, for to play defensively would be foolish for us. We shall play to the usual policy, which won us the championship last year, and we shall have four forwards just when we want them.'

Daily Express correspondent Desmond Hackett on this occasion refused to be drawn into making any forecasts, writing, 'I fear Eusebio will be at his most menacing because before the match he will receive a golden football to mark his election as European Player of the Year by French sports writers.

'But I refuse to make any forecast. I am prepared to stand up and cheer one of the greatest British soccer achievements if Manchester United, with a slender lead of one goal, can win their way into the semi-finals.

'If they do that, I say right now they will win the European Cup.'

Prematch was utter pandemonium, with all roads to the ground jammed. Even the referee was delayed in getting there. Multicoloured rockets lit up the evening sky as the crowd cranked up the noise. But in the humid atmosphere of the impressive Stadium of Light, with the visitors urged on by a smattering of red-and-white-scarved Mancunian supporters, the 70,000 passionate Portuguese were stunned into silence as United scored thrice in the opening twelve minutes, after the kick-off had been delayed for a quarter of an hour due to Eusebio's presentation. A ploy perhaps by Benfica, to keep United on edge, but one that certainly did not work.

Pinto fouled Charlton in the sixth minute and, from the free-kick out on the left, Best rose above the Benfica defence to head the ball past Costa Pereira and give United a shock lead. Benfica only offered a couple of half-hearted attacks in response, with Eusebio showing only the briefest of hints as to what he was truly capable of.

Twelve minutes gone, United went further ahead. A long clearance was headed towards Best by Herd and the Irishman took the ball in his stride almost on the halfway line. Running forward, he weaved his way past a trio of mesmerised Benfica defenders, before smashing the ball under the body of Pereira and into the far corner. A minute earlier Best had a goal chalked off for offside.

Only two teams had ever managed to score twice when facing Benfica on their home turf.

On song, there was no stopping United who made it 3-0 in the sixteenth minute. Best, again in the thick of the action, combined with Connelly to set up Law and put United 6-2 ahead on aggregate.

'Easy, Easy,' chanted the United contingent, something that was totally alien to ears of the home support, as the pace began to slacken following such an effervescent opening, but United still looked the most dangerous side when on the attack and in the twenty-eighth minute, Best should have completed his hat-trick, but his shot went narrowly wide.

Eusebio hit the outside of the post in the closing stages of the first half and Gregg showed his bravery, diving at the feet of the oncoming Torres, before fisting the ball away as Torres again threatened.

United survived a few anxious moments as Benfica opened the second half strongly, but they finally conceded a goal when Brennan, under pressure from Eusebio, lobbed the ball over the head of Gregg as he attempted to pass the ball back to his 'keeper.

Herd tested Pereira from 20 yards, while at the opposite end Gregg saved from Torres. But any hopes that Benfica held of salvaging the tie were totally shattered in the seventy-eighth minute when Crerand stormed into the penalty area to make it 4-1. With two minutes remaining, Charlton added a fifth amid scenes of disbelief and total euphoria.

Benfica were gracious in defeat. 'Manchester played better, and won by a margin which explains everything. I congratulate them,' said their captain, Coluna, while their coach, Bela Guttmann, also praised United: 'Do not feel sorry for me. Manchester United are a great team and deserved to win. We lost against a team who were much better than us.'

La Bola, the Lisbon sports paper, christened George Best 'El Beatle', while writing, 'Whatever causes one seeks, one sole reason stands – the extraordinary, almost unique class of Manchester United.

'We were convinced that the team, guided and trained by the famous Matt Busby, is the greatest club team that European football ever produced after the fabulous Real Madrid.

'Now, after seeing the repetition of the marvellous performance at Old Trafford, it is not only a conviction, it is a certainty.'

Another newspaper, *Diario De Noticias*, carried the following: 'Manchester United were really fabulous in all that is most beautiful, artistic, athletic, imaginative and pure in football.

'Their attack had an unsurpassable firmness in which the personalities of Denis Law and Bobby Charlton could hardly be excelled.'

Even the Italians were gripped by the performance, with the front page of the *Corriere Dello-Sport* proclaiming, 'Manchester showed itself as the great star of European soccer. Benfica was surprised. The only thing they did was watch how this collection of goals was scored.'

Basking amid the tumultuous wave of adoration, Matt Busby was quick to respond, saying, 'I have always believed that a great team is built on blending the skill of great players.

'I have never been convinced that great tactical systems and playing by numbers is a guarantee of success. And certainly not of entertainment.

'At Old Trafford we have placed our faith in real football and this was a glorious vindication of that policy.'

Manchester United had never been a club short of strong individual players, characters who could ignite a game as if on the flick of a switch, conjuring up some form of magic to mesmerise the opposition and secure another victory for their team. Now there was another name to add to the on growing list: George Best.

Playing in only his third season of League football, the scrawny Irishman, whose talents had been obvious for some time, was now the talk of not simply English football, but that of Europe as well.

Following his two outstanding displays, against Wolves in the FA Cup and Benfica, Matt Busby declared the nineteen-year-old as 'world class'.

But Best could have been lost to the game, or at least to Manchester United, as having crossed the Irish Sea as a fresh-faced schoolboy, two days in the industrial sprawl of Manchester was enough and he hot-footed back from whence he came. Only the understanding of Dick Best, the player's father, and Matt Busby, persuaded him to give it another go and return. Slowly he settled in to the new way of life and blossomed on the pitch, becoming a rare precocious talent.

When he made his debut against West Bromwich Albion, back in September 1963, he was earning £12 per week, but within three years, that figure had risen to nearer £5,000 a year, thanks to both his off-the-field charisma and on-the-field ability. The latter was something that United were slowly beginning to depend upon.

Chelsea manager Tommy Docherty had bumped into the United party as they arrived back in Britain, and congratulated Matt Busby on his triumph, but upon seeing the sombrero-wearing Best, he called out, 'Hullo there Pancho. That was a great performance in Lisbon. Do me a favour and don't repeat it against Chelsea tomorrow.'

Strangely, the Irishman seemed to heed Docherty's words, as both he and his United teammates looked jaded and tired against the Londoners at Stamford Bridge, and failed to make any impression in the 2-0 defeat, with the two Chelsea goals coming within the opening four minutes and United 'keeper Harry Gregg blamed for both. It was a stunning start that presented United with a major challenge and one that they were unable to meet, as they contributed little to something of a disappointing ninety minutes.

Perhaps the delay of the kick-off for twelve minutes was something that unsettled the visitors, as they were already out on the pitch warming up when the referee summoned them back to the dressing rooms, as hundreds of youngsters had spilled off the terracing and onto the greyhound track surrounding the pitch. Police, however, were instructed by Chelsea officials to move them back onto the seething terracing, where some 60,296 were already packed, with an estimated 20,000 outside.

It was a game that United desperately had to win if they were to maintain something of a statistical challenge to Liverpool, but by teatime they were ten points behind the Merseysiders, with two games in hand. But even if those additional fixtures materialised into victories, there was still something of a mountain to climb in order to get a fingerhold on the championship.

Back on track with a 2-1 victory over Arsenal at Old Trafford, a much more comfortable victory than the scoreline actually suggested kept United ticking over, although Eric Todd in the *Guardian* suggested that some of Matt Busby's players were beginning to feel the strain of having to compete on so many fronts. The door to European Cup and FA Cup success was still wide open, even though the opening to the First Division championship was now nothing but a mere crack.

If the United players were indeed suffering from over-exposure, then they could have certainly done without having to visit Deepdale and face Preston North End in the sixth round of the FA Cup, as there was no way that the Second Division side were going to bow out of the competition without a fight against their more illustrious opponents.

In the run-up to the rather precarious cup tie, Matt Busby spoke of the visit to Deepdale as being a venue where United might just receive their fourth FA Cup fright in a row. 'Preston have not won a League game since 11 December,' said the United manager. 'But a team who can beat Tottenham (2-1) as convincingly as they seem to have done, are capable of beating anyone on their own ground. Preston in fact, are a different team altogether in the cup.'

The unfolding ninety minutes is perhaps best summed up by Hugh McIlvanney in his report for the *Observer*, who wrote, 'Preston and Manchester United fought relentlessly and sometimes bitterly, and in the end any other result was scarcely conceivable.

'It was a classically grim draw, with the initiative switching frequently from one side to the other, but never with sufficient emphasis to suggest that the tie was about to be decided.'

United were certainly impressive at times, equalising Preston's fortieth-minute goal three minutes into the second half, but they failed to threaten the home defence for sustainable periods, and losing the effectiveness and possible match-winning ability of Best with a leg injury saw them fail to conjure up an all-out attack as the game moved into its final minutes, adding yet another ninety minutes to an already packed fixture list.

Four days later in the Old Trafford replay, things were little different, with the cup favourites – United that is, not Preston – once again caught struggling against their lesser opponents, with former United players Alex Dawson and Nobby Lawton doing everything in their power to register something of an upset.

United, without the injured Best, took the lead on the half-hour, Law pouncing as the ball rebounded towards him after Herd had forced Kendall into making only a partial clearance, kicking the ball almost out of the hands of his own goalkeeper. It was a lead that they held, perhaps a little unconvincingly, until the seventy-first minute, when Singleton, whose only other goal for Preston had been the one that took them to Wembley in 1964, headed a corner from Lee past Gregg. It was little more than the methodical, hardworking visitors deserved.

Extra time now looked certain as the game staggered along, but with only three minutes remaining, Aston, on the side in place of Best, swung a corner towards the Preston goal, where it looked as though the whole United team were encamped. Foulkes rose high above everyone and nodded the ball further into the danger area, Herd giving it a little more momentum, before Law managed to nudge the bouncing ball over the line.

It was an unkind blow to Preston, and before they could regroup for another assault on Gregg's goal, Aston raced down the left, and crossed into the Preston area where the ball was missed by Barton, presenting Connelly with an easy scoring opportunity to put United into their fifth consecutive FA Cup semi-final. It was a far-from-convincing display, but one perhaps on par with many of United's performances throughout this particular season.

United were struggling, despite beating Preston and Arsenal in recent games, and without George Best, United looked a completely different side, although they were far from being forced to rely upon the Belfast Boy to inspire them to victory. Those days were still to come, while Matt Busby had been fortunate to date in being able to select basically the same eleven players week in, week out.

This, however, changed for the visit to Villa Park on 6 April, when the United manager was forced into making alterations to the side that had struggled against Preston in the cup. Injuries, sustained either in the cup tie or the previous weekend's Scotland–England fixture, forced Harry Gregg, Nobby Stiles, Bobby Charlton, David Herd and George Best onto the sidelines.

Into the team came David Gaskell, out of the first-team limelight since September; John Fitzpatrick, making his first start since the final fixture of the previous season; ironically enough at Villa Park, Willie Anderson, whose last start was on the opening day of the season; and Noel Cantwell, once again called into the side as a stop-gap forward. John Aston replaced the injured Best.

Both teams took a long time to settle and the paying public could well have complained at being short-changed during a rather uninteresting 1-1 draw. This was a claim that could also have been made three days later, when an even more mismatched United XI ran out at Old Trafford to face Leicester City: a game they were to lose 2-1, displaying their mixture of assorted brilliance and inexplicable ineptitude, and one that signalled a definite end to any lingering hopes that the League championship could still be snatched from the hands of Liverpool, as it left them thirteen points adrift, with the three games in hand now meaningless.

One of the reasons for what were considered to be rather poor showings was mooted by club captain Noel Cantwell: 'From 26 March, the cup sixth-round tie at Preston, the team seemed set to face a gruelling programme of eight matches inside twenty-eight days. Then came a gesture that will long be appreciated by all at Old Trafford. Aston Villa, expecting two Easter matches against the reds which could have been safely guaranteed to get the turnstiles clicking merrily at both grounds, readily agreed to rearrange their fixtures. They did it to allow us the opportunity of fitting in its European programme at suitable spaced times, quite obviously appreciating the importance of United being allowed to make careful preparation for these semi-final matches against Partizan of Belgrade. They did it too, in the full realisation that the loss of such an Easter crowd-puller could clip their finances rather badly.'

Cantwell felt that United faced more than the difficulties provided by the opposition teams and 'if they were to achieve their ambition and sweep out of this season as the first English club to win the prized European Cup, it will be a performance that has defied the most impossible odds. For the simple truth is that the English football season is not designed to give advantages to any of its clubs that may want to attempt the conquest of Europe. Of all the countries involved in this international tournament, I would claim that none has a harder task of making progress than an English team.'

In Busby's mind, the League was something that, if it could be won, was indeed a bonus, or perhaps even a miracle. However, four days after the visit from Leicester City, there was a more-important ninety minutes to be played, with United having to make a return trip to Belgrade, a city of memories, for the first leg of the European Cup semi-final.

Against Leicester, Busby decided to make changes, rather surprisingly recalling Nobby Stiles, Bobby Charlton, David Herd, Harry Gregg and, even more surprisingly, George Best. David Sadler at centre-half and debutant Bobby Noble at left-back were the only really new faces. Why force players who were carrying slight knocks into playing something of a meaningless fixture when the most sought-after prize was glistening on the not-too-distant horizon? Only the United manager knew.

Playing George Best in particular against Leicester was a big gamble, as the Irishman was still carrying the effects of a knee injury received in the cup tie against Preston. A prolonged rest would have been more beneficial than ninety minutes of football, and as United trained in the Red Army Stadium on the eve of the match in Belgrade, he wore a protective knee bandage, which he would continue to wear during the match itself.

Busby and his assistant manager knew the risk they were taking in gambling with the Irishman, as they could well find themselves with ten men should the injury flare up. But with the Holy Grail dangling in front of him, the United manager was perhaps blinkered by his desire to win that ultimate prize, rather than attempt to keep the scoreline in Yugoslavia at a manageable level and preserve his talisman for the return leg in Manchester.

'I know it is a calculated risk,' he admitted. 'But I feel I must take this chance. I am playing the lad because I feel we have a chance of making a bit of history by winning the European Cup and the FA Cup in one season.'

Having beaten Benfica so convincingly, hopes were high on progressing to the final itself, but the Yugoslavs were an outfit more than capable of causing United problems, as their quarter-final result against Sparta Prague demonstrated – coming from 4-1 down in the away first leg to win 5-0 on home soil. Should they win, there was also the added bonus of having negotiated a third of the gate money, which was expected to be around £10,000, shared amongst the players depending on how they performed over the two legs.

Back in the dressing room at the end of the ninety minutes of that first-leg encounter, the Yugoslavs were already planning what to do with their share of the £10,000, as a few yards down the corridor the United players sat slumped in disappointment and disbelief following their 2-0 defeat.

United should have been well in command within the opening twenty minutes, but both Best and Law squandered easy opportunities, while they were also unfortunate not to go in front in the thirty-eighth minute, when Law headed a Best cross against the bar. Such opportunities would later be reflected upon as defining moments in the game, more so when the home side scored twice in the opening fourteen minutes of the second half.

Within two minutes of the second forty-five minutes getting underway, Jusufi moved down the wing and, from his cross, Hasanagic headed firmly past a somewhat badly positioned Gregg. The second, in the fifty-ninth minute, followed a foul by Crerand, with the free-kick swung across the pitch to the unmarked Vasovic. The left-half quickly played the ball into the path of the oncoming Becejac, who controlled the ball with his chest before shooting into the corner of Gregg's net.

Between the two Partizan goals, an offside decision robbed Connelly of what many thought was the equaliser, but United were clearly a shadow of themselves. Despite conceding two goals, Gregg kept United in the game with some fine saves, but against a team playing in their first European semi-final, the visitors clearly struggled and their hopes of making the final, something that Peter Lorenzo in the *Sun* still felt was more than a possibility if 'they played with something approaching their normal form and flare', were dealt a severe blow twelve minutes from time when Best became little more than a passenger, after wrenching his right knee going up for a high ball. He had, in fact, been ineffective for most of the game, having twisted it minutes earlier when stretching for a pass from Charlton.

Busby's gamble had failed to pay off, and his decision now left United's season hanging by a very thin thread.

The injury to Best and the subsequent visit to a specialist upon his return to England confirmed that he would have to go into hospital for a cartilage operation, which would rule him out for the remainder of the season, while causing much debate as to whether or not he was actually fit to play in the first place.

'I'm satisfied that I was fit. The decision to play was mine and I stand by it. My knee went during the game,' he declared, adding, 'After a wonderful season the team has been having it almost breaks my heart to miss out just when it looks as though we can win the European Cup and the FA Cup.'

Fit or not, there was nothing that could be done, United were without their talisman for the remainder of the campaign, which still had ten fixtures to be completed – eight in the First Division and one each in the FA and European Cup.

On 16 April, United travelled to Bramall Lane, Sheffield, four days prior to the return leg against Partizan Belgrade. Busby, well aware of the importance of the forthcoming tie, made a handful of changes in preparation for the visit of the Yugoslavs. Fitzpatrick came in at right-half instead of Crerand, Cantwell at left-back in place of Tony Dunne, Willie Anderson at inside-right for Denis Law, David Sadler at centre-forward in place of Bobby Charlton and John Aston took over from Best on the wing, with Connelly switching from left to right.

Despite such juggling and rearranging, United put up a spirited performance, although they continued to be rather slack at the back, something they had become common in recent weeks. This allowed Sheffield United to record a 3-1 victory, although it could quite easily have been more, while at the same time giving little indication as to how the European semi-final tie would unfold.

The loss of Best was United's biggest problem, pushing the onus onto the feet of his fellow front men Law and Charlton, while victory also hinged on Crerand delivering the type of match-winning performance that he was truly capable of. Two goals on the night would see a play-off, but many felt that United were indeed capable of scoring at least three.

European veteran Bill Foulkes was certainly confident that United could turn it around. On the eve of the game he said, 'We can beat Partizan in tomorrow's semi-final second leg. We feel we have a much easier job than when we faced Real Madrid. Being two goals down to Partizan on the home leg isn't as difficult as when we had to play Bilbao under the same handicap.'

But starting the match two goals behind created something of a mental obstacle, and United began, not in the swashbuckling style that surfaced in Lisbon, but ultra-cautious and anxious. The determination was there, perhaps in greater abundance than had been obvious in the first leg, but it was overshadowed by the lack of cohesion and at times the intelligence of their play. On the other hand, Partizan, with their advantage, could well afford to be relaxed and happily allowed United to come at them, soaking up such attacks with ease.

The failure of any United individual to stamp their authority on the game was another significant factor that hindered any progress being made, although Law buzzed around like a hyperactive bee, giving away three fouls in the opening seven minutes, and causing moments of panic in the

Yugoslav defence when he burst through and kicked the ball straight at goalkeeper Soskic, before Rasovic kicked off the line. Other opportunities arose, but none could be converted, either due to the exceptional form of Soskic or the poor finishing of a United player.

Two of the Partizan defenders had been booked in the first half for overzealous challenges by the sometimes ultra-efficient Swiss official, but as the game progressed, anxiety and tempers rose, bubbling over completely in the sixty-fifth minute when Crerand and Pirmajer become involved in a nasty scuffle and were sent off.

Finally, in the seventy-third minute, United scored. Stiles pushed further forward than normal, took a short corner to Connelly and, taking the return pass, swung it more in hope than anything else towards the Belgrade goal. Soskic, for the first time in the game, misjudged the flight of the ball and somehow managed to push it into his own net.

Awoken, the crowd filled the night air with chants of 'United, United', hoping to spur their team on to snatching the last-gasp equaliser that would see a play-off materialise. Herd, Connelly and Law all failed to connect with a tantalising bouncing ball in the Partizan box as the crowd stood transfixed and open-mouthed.

The visitors were now close to panic. No doubt the thoughts of their £10,000 disappearing from view flashed through their heads, especially when the ball fell to Anderson with the goal at his mercy, but he sliced his shot wide. The storybook ending and the hero worship were not to be.

Had United scored fifteen, or perhaps even ten minutes earlier, then there might have been the possibility of a second goal materialising as the Yugoslavs panicked, but for the third time in a decade, Matt Busby's team fell at the final hurdle, with a place in the European Cup final within sight.

In the *Daily Express*, Desmond Hackett, never one to mince his words, insisted that United had become drained of inspiration, while lacking their old spark and fire, and failed to respond to the vocal support from the packed terraces. There was just no response,' he wrote. 'United just kept playing across field or tossing the ball on to the heads of the best disciplined defence in European football.

'The saddest thing was to see the manner in which United tamely accepted this defeat; the way their shoulders sagged as they trailed wearily off the field.

'They looked like a team which has seen too much football and had lost the flavour for international action.

'They tried desperately hard but the staleness was evident in almost every player apart from the industrious, explosive Nobby Stiles.

'I feel sorry for them. I also very deeply regret the heartbreak that manager Matt Busby must be suffering.'

Despite heartbreak and disappointment, there was barely time for any regrets or to show any remorse while tending cuts and bruises, as the FA Cup semi-final against Everton at Burnden Park, Bolton, was three days later, a record-equalling fifth successive appearance, making United the first team to do so since Oxford University in 1877.

Busby was able to field the same XI that lost against Partizan Belgrade, but on a sodden pitch – what was it about semi-final day and pitches in poor condition – their misery was completed as their search for success on three fronts crumbled. United without Best and Everton without Pickering took away some of the spectacle of the occasion, and in the opening half United worked steadily, but failed to create many opportunities or trouble their opponents' defence.

Their best opportunity, not just in the first half, but in the match as a whole, came ten minutes before the break, when Law met Brennan's cross with the back of his head, throwing the Everton defence into chaos. Brown miskicked and Connelly hooked the ball towards goal, but West dived across his goal to push it past for a corner.

In what seemed to be something of a common occurrence, tempers slowly became frayed as the game progressed. Crerand on Scott, Stiles on the same player, and Brennan on Temple showed a hint of panic in United's play, and with twelve minutes remaining, their season crumbled around them.

Temple left Foulkes in his wake as the pair chased a Young back-header and, showing superb control, the Everton winger turned the ball inside towards Harvey, alone some 12 yards from goal, and quickly despatched the ball into the net past the outstretched left arm of Gregg.

The final ten minutes were akin to an old Keystone Cops movie, with play moving quickly around the pitch. Dunne fell over the ball, presenting Trebilcock with a one-on-one with Gregg, but the big Irishman made a superb one-handed save. Trebilcock also set up Young, but the Everton centre-forward's shot hit the outside of the post and rebounded back into play.

Law, with the clock fast approaching full-time, just failed to connect with a Stiles cross after the United No. 6 found space at the corner of the 6-yard box, but had he scored, the general opinion was that a draw would have been a result that United did not deserve.

As the disconsolate United players contemplated the misery of defeat in the hunt for both domestic and European honours, thunder boomed around the ground and lightning flashed across the sky, a fitting backdrop.

It is worth noting that Everton had fielded a complete reserve side against Leeds United the Saturday prior to the semi-final, losing 4-1 and, although they found themselves in front of a Football League enquiry after claiming that their first-team players were all carrying injuries, a fine was small punishment, as they were now going to recoup any such costs from their cup-final appearance.

Matt Busby should have made a similar decision prior for United's fixture against Leicester City. Had he done so, then he would most probably have found himself managing a team who were about to play in two major finals. Instead, Busby now had to pick his players up for the final League fixtures of the season, seven games that would determine if they would collect the consolation prize of a place in the Inter-Cities Fairs Cup. They were currently fifth, with forty-two points.

There was a chance for a form of instant revenge as United's first opportunity to get back to winning ways and end their season with some respectability was against Everton at Goodison Park, but a goal-less draw in a rather drab encounter did little to raise the spirits.

Blackpool were beaten 2-1 at Old Trafford, lifting United to fifth, but a 3-2 defeat at Upton Park against West Ham United and a 3-3 draw against West Bromwich Albion at the Hawthorns saw them drop to seventh, with the consolation prize of the Fairs Cup now slipping out of their grasp. The six-goal thriller at the Hawthorns marked the debut of another youngster from the Old Trafford conveyor belt, Jimmy Ryan.

Ryan was born in Stirling in May 1945, and like almost all youngsters came to attention of scouts from senior clubs at an early age: 'I was playing junior football in Stirling and I had been approached by a few clubs and had played a couple of reserve games for Dundee, and for Falkirk. I was playing a game one day when, after it was over, I was approached by a guy who asked me if I fancied going down to Manchester United. I went down for trials and then eventually signed for them.'

Leaving his family home and venturing south was something of a daunting experience for the newly signed United apprentice. 'Well you must remember that people didn't travel as far in those days, and it was a major journey for me to travel down by train,' explained Jimmy. 'When I got there of course, the accent was completely foreign to me as I'd never been out of Scotland. I was just sixteen and had never been anywhere. So all that was strange, but was very, very exciting, and of course they were the one English team then who had a massive image in Scotland, simply because of the "Busby Babes", and the fact that Matt Busby was a Scottish manager.'

Although a Manchester United player, Jimmy seldom saw Matt Busby, as the manager's priority lay with the first team. The only face-to-face conversations took place when contract negotiations were due: 'He talked to me when it came time for him to offer me a contract. He took me in and talked to me about building up my strength. I was quite skinny and weak I suppose when I was younger, but I had some ability. So he explained that they were going to try and build me up, and in fact they made me do a period of weight training when I went back home during the summer to Scotland. I was still a novice then.'

But during those fledgling days of his United career, the young Scot came under the tutorage of a man who was to play a big part in shaping his career: 'Well, I know that there was one guy who had a massive influence, although I didn't realize it at the time, and he was John Aston whose son played for the team as well. I didn't really realise it at the time, but I went through a very rough period after I was at the club for six months or so. I started to struggle to play very well, and I found out subsequently that he was constantly backing my ability.'

John Aston Snr was certainly justified in backing Jimmy, and the coach and player were rewarded when the team sheet was pinned on the dressing room noticeboard for the fixture against West Bromwich Albion on 4 May, a call that although hoped for, but still came as something of a surprise: 'To be honest, I had been playing very, very well in the reserves, and the lads that I was playing with kept saying that I'd get a game in the first team soon. You kind of don't believe it, but think I'm playing okay now but keep focused, and keep playing. Then they just told me that I was going to West Brom with the first team, and I kind of thought that maybe this was it. But they never told me until an hour or so before the game.'

But there was to be something of a flourishing finale, with eleven goals in the final three games. Blackburn Rovers were beaten 4-1 at Ewood Park and Aston Villa hammered 6-1 at Old Trafford in front of a miserable crowd of 23,034, while the final ninety minutes of a disappointing season, against First Division runners-up Leeds United at home, brought a 1-1 draw and fourth place in the table, above Chelsea on goal average.

'I could weep. But there is no time to weep. We must pick ourselves from the floor,' declared Matt Busby. 'In four days the world tumbled around us. Nobody is more disappointed than the players.

'Nevertheless, I congratulate them on a fine season. Yet this is not good enough for Manchester United. But it is not the end of the world. Our theme is try, try, try again, as I have said often before.

'There must be something lying beyond and we must attack it. Attack, indeed, we will.

'Our collapse started in Belgrade in the first leg of the European Cup semi-final, when we lost 2-0. We let ourselves down there and we never recovered our composure.

'George Best's injury was a tremendous blow.

'Now everything must be geared to making a decisive bid to get back among the big boys of Europe. This, of course, we shall do.

'I am personally determined that this will happen, and we will be making the necessary preparations as from now.'

Such preparations included making additions to the playing squad, and speculation had the club linked with Blackburn's Welsh international centre-half Mike England, Blackpool's inside-forward Alan Ball (both of whom had £100,000 price tags on their head), Millwall's young England goalkeeper Alex Stepney, and Celtic's robust winger-cum-centre-forward John Hughes.

Competition for England and Ball would be stiff with Stoke City, Leeds United and Everton all sniffing around the Blackpool player, who had been offered £10,000 signing-on fee and wages of £100 a week by the Seasiders if he stayed. With Blackburn Rovers relegated, they would be unlikely to hold on to their prized asset, despite numerous clubs keen to take him off their hands.

England was Busby's main target, or perhaps that should read as being Jimmy Murphy's favoured transfer target, as the assistant manager felt that his fellow Welshman would be a tremendous asset to the club. In any case, the United manager flew home early from a holiday in Jamaica in order to try and clinch the deal, making an offer within hours of arriving in Manchester, which was reported at first to be £100,000 for the now transfer-listed Welshman. It was later to turn out to be only £85,000. Rovers dropped hints that they would prefer a player-exchange deal, but Busby was intent on building a strong squad in order to remount his First Division and European challenge, and said, 'We have made a cash offer and so far have heard nothing. Blackburn seem to be more interested in players than in cash and I certainly have no players to offer them. Our bid is a case of cash only.'

The Blackburn centre-half turned down the offer of £100 a week to stay with the relegated Ewood Park club, making him slightly unpopular with their supporters, but his supposedly long-standing ambition to join United failed to materialise, as Tottenham came along and offered Rovers £95,000. Busby was quoted as saying that he would not pay an outrageous fee for England, but perhaps dropped out of the race to sign the player too quickly, or indeed felt that the attitude of the Rovers management was forcing him away from signing the player.

The wages offered to the player were also far superior to what United would be prepared to pay and, taking into account that a first-team place at White Hart Lane was ready and waiting for him due to the retirement of Maurice Norman, whereas Bill Foulkes still had a grip of the red No. 5 jersey at Old Trafford, the move to London was the one he chose.

The failure to add Mike England to the Old Trafford payroll also surprised former Tottenham Hotspur captain Danny Blanchflower, who was now earning respect as a journalist. He recalled a taxi ride with Matt Busby, when the conversation centred around two topics. One was George Best, who was due a cartilage operation, but had visited a 'magic' muscle manipulator in Belfast who had spoken of his doubts as regards the planned surgery, much to his manager's concern. The other was Mike England.

Blanchflower considered Mike England to be an obvious player for United, but sensed that although Busby wasn't against the transfer, he wasn't exactly enthusiastic about it. He felt that there was something that he couldn't put his finger on, but knew that Busby had a good reason, direct or indirect, for not signing the player he regarded highly.

Looking back at the transfer that failed to materialise, Jimmy Murphy Jnr reflected, 'There is no doubt Jimmy regarded Mike England as a top centre-half, one of the best in the leagues. He would certainly have loved to have seen Mike wearing a red shirt at Old Trafford.

'Jimmy had lined him up to join United but Matt had other ideas as he thought that Mike was "injury prone" and later went for Ian Ure. As with Quixall *v.* Giles, so England *v.* Ure. Jimmy was proved right again as thirty-year-old Ure played only sixty-five games for United in his brief spell with the reds, the last of his eleven caps coming two years before joining United.

'England would have joined United at age twenty-eight and played for Spurs from 1966 until March 1975, winning a bundle of international caps for Wales.

'Wrong time, wrong nationality!'

It must be remembered that at this time, United, along with Liverpool, thanks to managers Busby and Shankly collaborating, were the two lowest-paying clubs in the top flight. Wages and actual transfer fees were to cost United dearly in the years ahead.

Matt Busby had returned from holiday five days early in the hope of signing new players, but upon going through the mail in his Old Trafford office and opening one letter in particular, he was stunned at its content and had to read it for a second time in order to take it in. The letter came from Denis Law, and in it the Scottish international explained that if he didn't receive a new contract with vastly improved terms when his new deal came to an end, along with a signing-on fee, then he would prefer to leave Manchester United. The club had an option on his current deal for two more years.

If Law thought that his ultimatum would bring him the financial rewards that he had requested, then he was in for a shock, as Busby, after speaking to his directors, announced that the club were not even prepared to consider the player's demands. The name of Denis Law would be placed on the transfer list and United would listen to offers.

'It came as a shock to me,' proclaimed the United manager. 'I was upset that he didn't come to see me to discuss the matter. I realise that, with his wife expecting a baby, he has his problems. But at least he could have 'phoned me. As it was he left the letter with one of the staff.

'I have had no problems before with Denis. There is no question that he is a genius; but, I repeat, we cannot accept an ultimatum.'

It was rumoured that Law had asked for a signing-on fee of £20,000, with Busby saying, 'The signing-on fee will destroy the game. A fee to a player before he has served a reasonable length of time (*Law had been at Old Trafford four years*) is getting the reward before it is earned – like getting a pension before it has been worked for.

'Signing-on fees do not encourage loyalty to a club. There will be no loyalty the way things are going.

'Players who are due for rewards are those who have served a club and its supporters loyally over a long period.'

Despite his brief sojourn in Italy prior to joining United and Law proclaiming that he had not enjoyed his time there, as soon as the news broke that he had handed in a transfer request, Italian clubs were quick to express an interest in the player, with a fee of £150,000 being quoted as what it would take to obtain his signature. Those same Italian clubs were, however, banned from playing foreign players until June 1967, but the likes of Juventus, Inter Milan, AC Milan and Genoa, who had all hinted at being interested in Law, could sign the player and then lease him to a club in either England or even Spain for a year.

Law, in the meantime, had quickly left the goldfish bowl of Manchester, off to his old haunts in Aberdeen, leaving Busby to field the press with his usual expertise, although with considerable doubt as to what the days ahead would bring. Contemplating the situation at length, the United manager decided that there was to be only one outcome and that was to put the player on the transfer list.

The official club statement read, 'The club are not prepared to consider these demands and have decided to place Law on the transfer list. They are now open to offers for him.' Brief and certainly to the point.

Following the announcement that Law was for sale, Matt Busby spoke to respected journalist Ken Ashton of the *Daily Mail*, telling the scribe, 'No one is greater than Manchester United. Not Matt Busby. Not Denis Law. Not Anyone.

'This situation left me with no alternative but to let Law go. I couldn't agree to his request.

'It (*Law's written transfer request*) stated conditions and said if those conditions were not met, he wanted a transfer. What could I do? I had to decide between the club and the player. With me, the club always comes first.'

He continued, 'I have always taken Denis's side and we have always had an understanding. But we have never talked about this matter. He merely left me a letter which I found on my return at the weekend.

'I know Denis has had a bad season by his standards (*at one point he was dropped from the Scottish international squad*), but he is still a great footballer and soccer's greatest genius. You don't part with men like that lightly.'

In Aberdeen, all Law would comment was 'I cannot say anything until I have made a few phone calls and have spoken to my agent in Huddersfield.'

It was not just clubs on the Continent who were quick to show an interest in the unsettled player, with millionaire Birmingham City chairman Clifford Coombes saying, 'Obviously it would take a substantial amount of money, but we have some very wealthy directors and we are determined to go places. I would think it will be the sky's the limit to try to get the right men. It's Stan Cullis's (*the Birmingham manager*) prerogative to negotiate for players and he is on holiday at Hove until next Wednesday, but to me the news is out of this world. I don't like interrupting holidays of course but there is only one Denis Law and he doesn't go on sale every week. I am hoping Stan will contact me when he reads about the Law situation.'

Busby left the Law situation behind when he flew to Lisbon in an attempt to negotiate a place for United in the following season's Inter-Cities Fairs Cup, something that had been taken for granted due to finishing fourth in the First Division. But they suddenly found themselves on the outside looking in, when the place that they considered to be theirs by right was given to the Football League Cup winners West Bromwich Albion. No amount of protesting could alter the situation.

While in the Portuguese capital, the United manager received another surprise: two telephone calls from none other than Denis Law. Busby missed both calls, most likely through being out on the golf course, but was given the message that the player wanted to talk to him as soon as was convenient.

Unable to speculate as to why Law had made contact, he told British journalists that he would now not be entering into any discussions with other clubs regarding the player's future and would speak to Law within the next few days.

Busby returned to Manchester disappointed that his team would not be playing in Europe during the season ahead and prepared for his meeting with Denis Law, who had also returned to the city from his Aberdeen sanctuary.

In the confines of the manager's office, the two Scots sat facing each other, but from the moment Law had delivered his transfer request to Old Trafford there was only going to be one winner, and the genial Busby was confident about the outcome of the meeting as his player explained his reasons for putting pen to paper.

After listening to Law, Busby opened his desk drawer and pulled out a pre-written letter and pushed it towards the puzzled player who, upon reading it, discovered that it was a typed apology from him which his manager explained he would be reading to a packed press conference later that day. He then produced another typed page. This time it was a new contract, and he pushed a pen in front of the bemused Law for him to sign with, which he did without any hesitation.

'I am delighted that Denis has been big enough to express his regrets,' said the United manager. 'If he can be big, then it is up to us to be big as well and so we are pleased to regard the matter closed.'

As for the player, he admitted that he was 'in the wrong. I never wanted to leave United. I'm so glad it all ended happily. I wish now that I had taken the advice of Mr Busby or our union secretary Cliff Lloyd before I made the move. Then this would not have arisen.

'I did it all on the spur of the moment. I thought at the time it was permissible to ask for a re-signing fee.'

Although he had lost out on Mike England, and was also to miss out on Alan Ball (apparently paid a signing fee of £10,000 by Everton), he had made an important signing in Denis Law and one that would pay dividends in the weeks ahead. Busby had won again.

There are, however, two small points surrounding the signing of the new contract.

Firstly, in his most recent autobiography, Denis states that the contract he signed was for the terms that he had been seeking (£10 per week), but without the signing-on fee. However, a newspaper article from the time tells a different tale, with a quote from Matt Busby reading, 'Denis Law visited Old Trafford today and had an interview with me at which he expressed regret for his recent demands for special signing-on fees.

'He has now accepted the terms which had previously been offered to him and requested that his name be taken off the transfer list.

'This, the board of directors and myself are happy to do. He has now signed a two-year contract and the matter is regarded as closed.'

There is also another quote from Law, a number of years earlier than his recent publication, where he says, 'We did a deal which nobody knew about. He told me that if I apologised in public for the trouble I'd caused he'd give me half the rise I'd asked for.'

So, did he get the additional £10 per week? Was it half what he had asked for and something that Busby kept quiet at the time? Or was there no increase at all and it was mentioned so that no one would lose face and it was clear that the iron fist was still seen to rule Old Trafford?

8

AIMING FOR THE TOP

For those who were around in the sixties, it was a magical time, carefree and memorable, especially towards the middle of the decade with the 'getting back to normal' post-Second World War days now nothing more than a distant memory. Throughout the country, there were numerous changes in everything from music to politics, and of course in football.

1966 saw England win the World Cup, defeating West Germany in extra time beneath the twin towers of Wembley. Despite United's Bobby Charlton and Nobby Stiles playing a vital part in the success, with another red, John Connelly, taking something of a supporting role, their teammates Pat Crerand and Denis Law cared little and certainly did not join in the euphoria which swept the country. For the Scots, it was a foreign country that had lifted the Jules Rimet trophy, and one that they had little interest in except for earning their livelihood.

Lifting that small golden trophy had, however, enthralled most of the nation, and as the dawn of a new season touched the horizon a new wave of excitement swept through the national game and attendances were ready to rise.

Despite the forty-one points that separated the top and bottom clubs at the end of the 1965/66 season, there was little to choose between the twenty-two teams that made up the First Division, as each club had a handful of quality players who would be eagerly snapped up by a rival should they become available. Some, like United, did have more quality than others, and the words of the 'United Calypso' from the previous decade, 'Whenever they're playing in your town, be sure to get to that football ground', were never to be more appropriate than for the season ahead, with crowds flocking to see the team that had something special all others lacked. Certainly attendances rose the length and breadth of the country following the World Cup, especially when Manchester United were in town.

Season 1966/67 did not get off to the best of starts, however, or perhaps that should read that the preparations for the months ahead did not get off to the best of starts.

For the first of the pre-season warm-up fixtures, United remained in Britain instead of venturing overseas, and made a relatively short journey beyond Hadrian's Wall to take on Scottish Champions Celtic at Celtic Park. The euphoria that had swept England only weeks before did not stretch as far north as Glasgow, as the friendly took on the mantle of a Scotland–England encounter. The red-shirted visitors were despised as if they were simply the 'Auld Enemy', having changed from their usual white shirts to red.

Around 60,000 squeezed into the Parkhead ground, voicing their opinions of the visitors in no uncertain terms, and despite the presence of two World Cup winners alongside the other eight full internationals in the United line-up, they were no match for the green-and-white hoops, who played some excellent fast-flowing football which, in the opinion of many, left United fortunate to finish the game with only three goals separating the two sides.

Any latecomers into that cauldron in the east end of Glasgow could well have missed three of the afternoon's five goals. Indeed, if they were fifteen minutes late in squeezing onto the packed, seething terracing then they would have missed four.

Celtic wasted little time in setting out their stall, with Bobby Lennox opening the scoring after only eight minutes. A cross from Auld was collected by Chalmers and almost immediately whipped into the goalmouth, where the lightning-quick anticipation of Lennox outfoxed the United defence, and the Celtic forward blasted the ball past Gregg.

Three minutes later, it was 2-0. Chalmers, again in the thick of the action, pushed the ball out to the right towards McBride, but a neat dummy saw the ball roll to Johnstone whose inviting centre was thundered home by the advancing Murdoch.

Before the jubilant cheers of the Celtic support had died down, United had pulled a goal back. Straight from the restart, Charlton passed to Sadler, who in turn pushed the ball back to Crerand. The former Celtic favourite in turn squared the ball to Law. A long pass through the green-and-white-hooped defence allowed Sadler to volley the ball into the roof of Simpson's goal.

The goal brought the home support and their team back down to earth with a bang, but the silence and the setback was only momentary, as within three minutes the two-goal advantage was restored. A 25-yard drive from McBride found its way into the corner of Gregg's net.

The voracious home crowd were soon back in full cry, taunting the United team and Stiles in particular, with chants of 'go home' and 'Ea-sy, Ea-sy'. They were perhaps a little too unappreciative of United's football at times.

The second forty-five minutes failed to live up to the first in terms of both goals and excitement, but United certainly did their best to reduce the two-goal deficit, with Sadler hitting the bar and Ronnie Simpson pulling off a trio of superb saves from Denis Law. At the opposite end, Harry Gregg, who could have done better with McBride's goalbound shot in the first half, made four crucial saves – three from Lennox, and the other from Chalmers – to keep United in with a shout of salvaging some pride.

But as it was Celtic added a fourth in the sixty-third minute, or perhaps to be more exact, an own goal from Bill Foulkes gave the home side a three-goal advantage. As McBride charged into the United penalty area, Stiles attempted to clear and, to his dismay and the delight of the baying crowd, the ball cannoned off Foulkes and past a totally surprised Gregg.

That, as they say, was that and United failed to produce anything that might have created panic in the Celtic defence or even something of a further consolation goal, with their only real goalmouth action coming in their own area when Stiles and Gregg were involved in a rare argument.

Four days later United, although still somewhat shell-shocked from their defeat in Glasgow, were off on their travels, with one game in Germany against Bayern Munich followed by another in Vienna against FK Austria. If they had hoped, or indeed expected, their pre-season preparations to gather momentum from the moment the referee's whistle got the match against Celtic underway, then they were certainly struggling to find some crumbs of comfort, along with some form of inspiration following a 4-1 defeat at the hands of the Germans.

There was little for the United management to take encouragement from, with only brief flashes of skill from Denis Law and odd moments of true form from the likes of Crerand, Best and Stiles. But on the whole, it was an evening that most would simply want to forget, with the forward line showing little punch and the likes of Stiles and Brennan frequently moving up to try and bolster the attack.

In defence, where Harry Gregg was at fault for two of the four goals, and at centre-half with Bill Foulkes in somewhat-hesitant form leaving Matt Busby to contemplate not having signed Mike England, there was much need to tighten things up, while the forwards showed a distinct lack of enthusiasm, although goalscoring opportunities were in rather short supply.

In his summary of the game, a *Sportsmail* reporter penned, 'unless their (*United's*) defence is tightened considerably and the attack becomes a lot busier and sharper, a similar fate probably awaits them in their third pre-season game, against FK Austria in Vienna on Friday.'

He obviously had access to a crystal ball, as the *Daly Mail* correspondent was 100 per cent correct in his prediction, with United indeed suffering their third successive pre-season defeat as FK Austria went one better than Celtic and Bayern by scoring five.

As if a third defeat was not enough of a problem for Matt Busby, the match in Vienna produced yet another headache for the United manager, with the dismissal of Nobby Stiles. The tough-tackling defender was already walking something of a disciplinary tightrope, as the Football Association had received a letter from FIFA following England's World Cup tie with France – a game in which Nobby had been booked – which said that if the United player was reported to them again, then they would take 'serious action'.

The flashpoint had come in the eightieth minute, with United heading for defeat and Nobby having already had the disappointment of scoring an own goal, as well as being booed throughout the game. Denis Law had rather needlessly pulled down Sara midway inside the United half, and as the Austrians jostled around the fiery Scot, Stiles stepped into the fray in an attempt to defend his captain. Moving to the edge of the pushing and shoving melee, closely followed by Austrian winger Kodat, Nobby appeared to be struck by his opponent, but when the referee stepped in to try and restore some sort of order, it was the United player who was sent off.

Prior to leaving the pitch Stiles, who had earlier been involved in an incident with outside-right Parits after being fouled by the Austrian, performed something of an impromptu strip-tease, removing his shirt and offering it to the referee.

Amid a backdrop of whistles and boos, United trainer Jack Crompton and reserve goalkeeper David Gaskell ran onto the field to escort the dejected Stiles away from the mayhem on the pitch towards the safety of the dressing rooms.

Harry Gregg, who had raced 60 yards from his goal to become involved in the pushing and shoving, had been at fault for the Austrian's opening goal in the third minute, but despite their early advantage, it was not until the deflected Stiles own goal, fourteen minutes after half-time, that they scored their second.

Rather surprisingly, two David Herd goals levelled the scores, but Parits made it 3-2 in the seventy-fourth minute, with Binder and Heisl adding a fourth and a fifth after the Stiles sending-off.

So the dejected United party headed back to Manchester and the drawing board, with Busby not only hoping he could reinstall some form of confidence into his team before the League programme got underway, but that Nobby Stiles, who had become an integral part of the United team, would avoid punishment for his misdemeanour in Vienna. Thankfully, a £50 fine, plus costs, was all that he incurred when the FA Disciplinary Commission met to review the case.

Scorching heat and humidity greeted the opening First Division fixture of the season, with West Bromwich Albion visiting Old Trafford on 20 August. Rather surprisingly, the crowd was a paltry 41,343. Those present, however, were treated to an exhilarating afternoon's football, with United taking the lead after only forty-five seconds, adding a further four within twenty minutes.

Fully recovered from his end-of-season cartilage operation, George Best gave United their early lead, with Nobby Stiles driving home the second from all of 40 yards in the eighth minute. Sixty seconds later, Hope gave the visitors a glimmer of just that, but Law restored the two-goal advantage in the fifteenth minute with a header, while a minute after that, Herd, in an effort to outdo the effort from Stiles, blasted the ball past Potter from 25 yards.

Law added a fifth and had another effort disallowed for offside, but it mattered little, as the game was by now over as a contest and the second half paled into significance despite West Bromwich scoring two minutes after the restart. Such a scintillating pace could not be maintained throughout the ninety minutes. Their third, a minute from time, was like the first of the afternoon, missed by many as they were off home, content with what they had witnessed. United were back on song.

The 5-3 victory over West Bromwich Albion not only kicked off a successful start to a new campaign, it also saw United recognise a milestone in the career of a former Albion player, with assistant manager Jimmy Murphy having notched up twenty-five years' service at Old Trafford. Having been thrust into the limelight in those dark, dismal days following Munich, Murphy was now away from the glare of the spotlight and content to be back working with the kids, giving Busby support whenever it was required; his role in the regeneration and ultimate survival of Manchester United Football Club was sometimes forgotten.

It wasn't, however, forgotten for a few short minutes prior to the Albion match, when he was presented with a silver coffee set, coffee table and canteen of cutlery, and in a short speech admitted unabashed that United was his whole life and only love.

There was an early opportunity to avenge the previous season's FA Cup semi-final exit at the hands of Everton, with a visit to Goodison Park three days after the opening-day victory and a sultry, sometimes impetuous ninety minutes. United, through two typical Denis Law goals, earned both points, coming from behind with the winning goal in the dramatic final seconds.

If the possible close-season transfer target of Alan Ball had caused United problems with his new club Everton, it was Old Trafford old boy Johnny Giles who was behind the defeat of his former employers at Elland Road in the third game of the season. It was United's first post-war defeat at Elland Road, and despite the 3-1 scoreline they could consider themselves unfortunate to make their way back across the Pennines with nothing to show for their afternoon's endeavours.

Gaskell's hesitancy gave Leeds their opener, while the defence as a whole could be faulted for the second. The third, twelve minutes from time, came from a highly debatable corner. It was, however, still early days. But for the United 'keeper, it was enough to see him dropped.

The post-World Cup boom in attendances did not reach as far as Old Trafford on the opening day of the season, with the crowd a rather disappointing 41,343 on what was a glorious Saturday afternoon. Rather strangely, Everton's visit to Manchester on the evening of 31 August saw almost 20,000 more click through the turnstiles, as the 61,114 was 500 more than had watched the first of the double-header eight days previously. Certainly, the visitors would have brought a bigger travelling support than West Bromwich, the delay of the kick-off for fifteen minutes going as proof of this, but it was a midweek fixture and you would have expected more to be in attendance for a Saturday kick-off, especially the season's opener. Was there still disappointment in the air from last season?

If there was and those supporters had decided to stay away, already writing off United's chances in the campaign ahead, then they should have heeded the words of Eric Todd in the *Guardian*, who wrote, 'Those people who had "written off" United prematurely thus must revise their opinions. On the other hand, we should wait and see whether or not last night's form is maintained before rhapsodising overmuch.'

Pushing the defeat against Leeds to one side, United got back on their winning ways, with a 3-0 win over Everton, after taking the lead a minute before the interval through Foulkes heading home a Connelly cross. Skirmishes during the half-time interval cleared large gaps on the Stretford End, as infiltrating Everton supporters clashed with home supporters, keeping the police and paramedics fully occupied. Because of this, numerous supporters missed United increasing their advantage ten minutes into the second half, when Connelly pounced on the ball after an effort from Law had been inadvertently blocked by Herd. Five minutes later came one of those memorable Denis Law goals, when the blond head connected with a powerful Herd cross that looked destined to go out of play. Lurking at the far post, he somehow managed to leap and twist his head towards the ball for a header past West.

Such were the off-field activities that they managed to make the front page of the *Times*, a newspaper whose football coverage, more often than not, could certainly not match that of its broadsheet stablemates the *Telegraph* and the *Guardian*.

'Fans Hurt' was the headline, followed by 'Football match fight. Six people were taken to hospital with serious injuries and several arrests were made after fighting broke out among the 61,000 crowd at half time during the Manchester United home game with Everton last night.

'Police said afterwards that two men from Liverpool had been charged and would appear in court today.'

The win kept United a point off the leaders, but the 3-2 home victory against Newcastle United took them level on points with the early pacesetters in Sheffield Wednesday, Burnley, Chelsea and Tottenham Hotspur.

Just as quickly as United strode towards the top, they were plummeting back down again following successive defeats at Stoke City (3-0) and Tottenham Hotspur (2-1). Strangely, in the latter of the two defeats United were the better side, with Jimmy Greaves claiming that Tottenham had indeed 'robbed' the visitors and that 'you don't have to be an expert to know that United were far the better team'. Perhaps a more honest view was that United threw the game away, as they were leading 1-0 with only five minutes remaining. Mike England became the second Busby close-season target to bring embarrassment to the manager, with a sterling ninety minutes (Alan Ball having been the other).

Missing from the team that lost at White Hart Lane was John Connelly, something that he did not take too kindly to, as he felt he was being treated rather harshly and made something of a scapegoat.

'We were beaten and we did not play well, but I did not think I was any better or worse than the rest of the team,' complained the disappointed winger. 'Any time things go wrong, I am one of the players who has to pay for it.

'I think I could have settled to play well this season, but it seems I shall have to fight my way back the hard way.'

But would the player ask for a transfer? 'I am under contract' was all he would say when asked. His days, however, were numbered.

Even with the season in its infancy, there were one or two fingers being pointed United's way, with Danny Blanchflower, the former Tottenham captain, now journalist with the *Sunday Express*, wondering if Matt Busby had lost something of his desire to play the game as it should be, the emphasis now being on defence rather than attack, forsaking what he had built over the years.

Perfection had always been United's yardstick, but this was, and indeed had to be, pushed to the side as the team was rebuilt after Munich. It was a team that could no longer rely on attacking flare to see them through, but needed to fight to achieve the heights that they craved so much. The pre-Munich side were certainly no shrinking violets and few would mix it with Byrne, Foulkes and Jones, or indeed Harry Gregg. But now, according to Blanchflower, there seemed to be more aggression within the ranks, more fouls committed and players sent off. There was more desperation in their play.

Blanchflower wrote, 'Now the club (*United*) have banned the supporters carrying banners and flags. It seems a pity. Being proud of a cause and carrying a banner or flag to wave in its honour is part of the fun. But these banners have become some sort of antagonistic weapon in the hands of some of the holders.

'I watched United at White Hart Lane the day they went over to defensive football. It was a sad day for me. I felt Matt was deserting the cause he had fought so nobly for these last years.

'You could make excuses for him. United were giving away a lot of goals and it was time for concern. Yet they have always been slow starters to a season and they have started this one as good as any before.

'So I felt that Matt was getting a bit too edgy.

'Perhaps he's just tightening up at the back until he has a breather. But I don't like the signs. I hope it is not happening yet. It would be too choice a capture for those terrible hounds of time.'

Blanchflower's comments were read by Busby and the United manager was 'astonished' and replied by saying that the game had not changed. He certainly had not adopted any new method and that the difference was more simple: 'It is that where the game in some positions was static, it is no longer so. There are no sleepers now. Every man plays all the time. The game is more mobile. The players have to be more versatile.

'We at Manchester United believe we have creative players. It would be a foolish waste of such talent to harness it to some inflexible task.

'Such players create something from nothing. They play an overall pattern – sweepers, strikers, etc. But they all do other things besides when the situation calls for them.

'We still feel that getting goals or creating chances for goals is what football should be all about. But we know that we have to defend too.

'But we at Manchester United shall aim first at creation, whatever people like to call it.'

Matt Busby, however, had recognised something of a failing within the ranks, having already used two different goalkeepers in the seven fixtures to date, with his team having conceded fourteen goals over the course of those games.

After losing out on centre-half Mike England, whose name continued to haunt the corridors of Old Trafford, Busby was now reportedly interested in Alan Stephenson of Crystal Palace, something of a raw talent and certainly a cheaper option than the former Blackburn defender. At the same time, he was also reportedly in the market for a goalkeeper, despite having three experienced men on the books.

His attention was now focused on Chelsea's reserve-team goalkeeper, Alex Stepney, a player he could have signed a couple of months earlier, as the twenty-four-year-old had only moved to Stamford Bridge from Millwall for £50,000 in the summer. But it had been a move that was to falter, for the time being at least, as a meeting with Chelsea manager Tommy Docherty failed to secure the 'keeper.

Busby and Jimmy Murphy travelled to London in the hope of persuading Docherty into releasing Stepney and recouping his original outlay, but the Chelsea manager said, 'I told Matt that I could not possibly part with him, particularly as Peter Bonetti is on the injured list.

'I explained that if the position changed in any way in the future. I would give him first refusal on Stepney. There was no talk about Bonetti and Manchester United.'

So, the United pair had to return home empty-handed, with Busby adding, 'I have not bid for any other player. I am disappointed I have not signed Stepney, but I am happy with the promise of the first option on him from Tommy Docherty.'

There was considerably more embarrassment to follow, with United's defensive failings further exposed in the midweek Football League Cup tie at Bloomfield Road, Blackpool. It was a competition that United entered only due to the absence of European football from their fixture list, and on reflection it was something that they should have avoided, enjoying a break from the game altogether.

With the illuminations shining brightly down the Golden Mile, a few hundred yards from the seafront on a dismal wet evening, a United side which saw Charlton rested, Law out injured and Gaskell, who had returned to the side against Tottenham, once again out of favour and replaced by Pat Dunne, was emphatically beaten by the First Division's bottom club; a club that had only earned one point from their opening seven fixtures, scoring a mere four goals in the process.

Against United, however, they raised their game, scoring five to the visitors' one, a memorable victory and one that gave United something of a wake-up call. But even before the defeat, Matt Busby had decided that changes were necessary if his team was going to have any say in the outcome of the game's honours in a few months' time.

Changes were certainly made and Alex Stepney made the surprise journey north to Old Trafford, only days after an apparent deal monetarily falling through. The meeting between Busby and Docherty had indeed taken place, but what had not been leaked at the time was the fact that the goalkeeper's transfer had been agreed there and then.

'I have known that I was going to United since Thursday but I was sworn to secrecy,' said the world's most expensive goalkeeper two times over. 'I'm thrilled to bits about the move. United is the club I have always wanted to play for.

'Chelsea have been fair with me all the time and in a way I'm sorry to be leaving so quickly. United is the only club I would consider going to from here.'

Lifting the lid on the move, Tommy Docherty revealed that Stepney had originally been bought as something of an insurance policy, as he had been convinced that his regular number one, Peter

Bonetti, would be leaving Stamford Bridge, possibly for Old Trafford, in the summer and therefore he had signed Stepney from Millwall for £50,000 as his replacement.

'Busby came in for Alex last Tuesday,' said Docherty. 'But Peter Bonetti was injured at the time and so I asked Matt to leave it until after the weekend.

'United is the only club I would have sold Alex to. I have a great respect for this great man (*Busby*) and I am glad to sell him the second-best goalkeeper in the country.

'I think Peter is just that bit better at the moment. But Alex has great potential.'

Stepney's career at Stamford Bridge lasted all of 112 days and took in three pre-season tour matches, three reserve games and one First Division outing. Although inexperienced when it came to top-flight football, Matt Busby had no qualms as regards throwing the 'keeper in at the deep end, telling his new signing that he would be making his United debut against Manchester City at Old Trafford.

The banning of banners and flags within Old Trafford that Danny Blanchflower mentioned previously was something that United had recently addressed and something that would come into force for the home fixture against Manchester City.

It was a craze which had come more to the fore during the World Cup finals, and in a club statement United said, 'The club have decided that supporters carrying banners or flags on poles will not be admitted to the ground at future matches.

'Complaints have been received from spectators being struck in the face when these have been waved and as they are being brought along in increasing numbers they have become a source of danger and are spoiling the enjoyment of many other spectators.

'The police have been asked rigidly to enforce this ban, and the co-operation of supporters of both clubs attending the "derby" match on Saturday is requested.'

United needed to get back on track following their heavy League Cup defeat at the seaside, and this they did, at least if you go by the score alone, defeating neighbours City 1-0. With no banners or flags, there was certainly a lack of colour about the occasion until the end, when the Stretford End held their red-and-white scarves aloft as some sort of response to the ban.

In the first meeting between the two clubs since May 1963, when a 1-1 draw at Maine Road had sent City down to the Second Division, there was strangely enough little in the way of excitement, with Stepney having something of an uneventful debut.

Law was by far the most dangerous player on the field and was indeed fortunate to still be in it ten minutes after kick-off, never mind come full-time. Having taken a free-kick, which was blocked, he ran head-on into City's defensive wall, lashing out blindly as the ball rebounded. Oakes hit back and suddenly a scuffle evolved which lasted for at least fifteen seconds, but surprisingly went unnoticed by the referee, as he was following the ball which had been cleared upfield. Summerbee dragged Law away before things turned really nasty. Even the raised flag of his linesman failed to attract the match official's attention.

Pardoe stabbed the ball past Stepney, but saw his effort disallowed for offside, as United slowly increased their pressure on the City defence, before taking the lead five minutes before the interval. Charlton found Law with a superb pass, the United inside man moving forward before exchanging passes with Aston and dribbling through a trio of light-blue shirts around goalkeeper Dowd before slotting the ball home.

Summerbee rolled the ball just wide of Stepney's goal immediately after the restart, before avoiding a couple of bottles thrown from the crowd, but City's opportunities were few and far between, as were United's, and the game faded into obscurity.

The sight of one of the girls in the Kerry Pipers Prize Band from Middleton fainting in the centre circle as they played prior to kick-off and then getting carried off by two bandsmen added to the action, as the did the touchline confrontation which almost led to City coach Malcolm Allison being thrown out of the ground.

Constantly up from his seat on the trainer's bench, shouting and gesturing from the touchline, it wasn't the referee who was forced to speak to the more-vocal half of the City management team, it was the police, with an inspector issuing him with an ultimatum: 'Sit down, shut up, or get out.' Both of the latter events were remembered by many for longer than the actual ninety minutes of football.

Munich was always only a thought away, and on 19 September came the announcement that the second inquiry, held in Bonn, into the events of 6 February 1958 had come to the conclusion that the crash was indeed caused by ice on the wings of the plane.

It was stated that if there had been no ice on the wings of the plane, the state of the runway at the time would have allowed the plane to reach the speed needed for a successful take-off. It also added, 'The unclear command relationships aboard the plane could also have had an unfavourable influence on the take-off.'

Missing from the ranks for the visit of City was John Connelly, who found himself dropped following the Blackpool defeat, having been previously omitted against Tottenham, even though he had scored twice in two of his other three first-team outings. It was a decision that disappointed the winger, who admitted, 'I just don't seem to suit the boss.'

His absence from United's starting XI did not go unnoticed, with Arsenal and Blackpool both contacting Matt Busby to ask about his availability, but Connelly himself was in no hurry to rush into anything, despite having spoken to the United manager about his future. 'I am on quite a good contract here and it would take one at least as good to get me away. I think it would be better in the long run if I did move.

'I am certainly interested but it's a big step and I shall take my time. I shall think about it over the weekend and possibly into next week before deciding.

'But from the way things seem to be going it would be in my benefit to move.'

The World Cup winger certainly gave Busby options for his wing berths, but as well as George Best the manager had the options of playing the emerging John Aston and Jimmy Ryan. Connelly, however, did have the experience and most certainly the ability, but if the player was not willing to play something of a bit part, then there was little point in him staying.

Despite not exactly being flavour of the month at Old Trafford, Connelly was selected for the Football League against their Irish League counterparts and turned in an outstanding performance in their 12-0 victory, scoring twice and making six, which stirred up further interest from possible suitors, including his previous club, Burnley,.

'Since arriving back from the Football League match at Plymouth I have been interviewed by three clubs – Blackpool, Blackburn and now Burnley,' the in-demand winger declared. 'All I want to do is get some sleep, but I should think that I will sign for one of the three tomorrow.

'I am going to think very, very carefully about this move. I have had a long chat with Blackpool manager Ron Stuart and the terms he offered me this morning have been very attractive.'

A return to his old club was certainly another interesting option, conjuring up the possibility of making his Burnley debut at Old Trafford, but with all three clubs offering United £40,000 for his services, where he plied his trade in the weeks and months ahead was entirely down to the player himself. In the end, his choice was not Turf Moor, but Ewood Park and a step down into the Second Division.

'It's a good move,' said Connelly. 'Last time I was transferred it was a rush job, and this time I wanted to make sure it was the right move.'

It was therefore a Connelly-less Burnley that arrived at Old Trafford on 24 September on a sun-kissed afternoon, with the Turf Moor side sitting second in the First Division, behind leaders Chelsea, thanks to a superior goal average over Stoke City and Tottenham Hotspur. United were to be found in ninth spot, one of half a dozen teams with ten points, two behind the leaders.

It was a game that would see United claim the scalp of the unbeaten Burnley in an enthralling ninety minutes of football; a game that would produce one of those iconic Old Trafford goals.

Having begun strongly, United's pressure on the visitors increased as the game progressed, but it was not until the thirty-ninth minute that they broke the deadlock. Herd pushed the ball forward towards Best, who squirmed his way past two defenders, and as Blacklaw advanced the winger turned the ball across the face of the goal. Suddenly, with his back to goal, Law launched himself into mid-air and somehow hooked the ball over his head and into the Burnley goal.

The goal was typical of the Scottish striker: a flash of individuality, with Law having something of an uncanny ability to hover, as if suspended, in mid-air before executing such a goal or flashing a header past a helpless goalkeeper.

Burnley equalised a minute before the break, when a defensive mix-up allowed Lochhead to head the ball past Stepney, but United regained the advantage within five minutes of the second half getting underway.

Having had strong appeals for a penalty turned down when it looked as though Harris had handled, United were soon back on the attack. A through pass from Charlton found Herd and, outpacing the Burnley defence, he drove the ball past Blacklaw from the edge of the penalty area.

United lost Law due to injury, but his absence did little to sustain the pressure around the visitors' goal, or indeed give Burnley any increased hope of snatching something from the game, as despite putting up a brave fight, further goals from Crerand and Sadler gave United a 4-1 win.

The victory kept United within two points of leaders Chelsea, but United were the masters of inconsistency, and seven days later crumbled to a 4-1 defeat against Johnny Carey's Nottingham Forest at the City Ground.

Carey, the former United captain and a strong contender to take over the United managerial reigns from Matt Busby when he finally decided to call it a day, allowed his team to 'play by ear', a tactic employed by his former boss. But on this occasion it was the 'pupil' who gained the upper hand over the 'master', although United were also the creators of their own downfall, with some poor defensive play. This latest performance made the failure to sign Mike England all the more puzzling.

Forest opened the scoring in the first minute when Baker won a corner and took it quickly, finding Crowe unmarked, who headed past Stepney at ease. Despite being without the injured Law, United were soon pushing forward in search of an equaliser, with Best creating openings, as only he could, for both Herd and Aston, but neither could add that final touch.

They were opportunities that were to be regretted, as Wignall made it 2-0 in the twenty-seventh minute, following a run down the right by the roving centre-forward Baker, which left Stepney and Dunne lying on the ground after the pair collided in an attempt to get the ball. Four minutes before the interval, it was 3-0, Baker again involved with another run and cross which Stepney came for in an attempt to punch clear and missed completely, leaving Crowe as easy a headed goal as he was ever going to get.

The second half was always going to be something of an anticlimax, although Forest went 4-0 in front in the fifty-fifth minute when Baker beat Stiles, but suddenly found himself upended inside the area. Crowe completed his hat-trick with a spot kick going in off the post.

United's afternoon went from bad to worse, as Stepney misjudged yet another high ball and Stiles became involved in a prolonged argument with the referee when he thought he should have had a penalty. Much to their relief, Forest took their feet off the pedal as the game wore on, and although United pulled a goal back through Charlton with eighteen minutes remaining, there was no way back and it took a superb save by Stepney from Baker to prevent Forest from adding a fifth.

It was a defeat that saw United drop down three places in the First Division, making the trip to Bloomfield Road, Blackpool, where they had already lost 5-1 in the League Cup – not something that was looked forward to, as confidence was not exactly flowing through the side at this time.

Prior to the game, United fans, rapidly getting a bad reputation but not enough as yet to put towns across the country totally on red alert when the red hoards were visiting, broke through a padlocked gate and held an impromptu kick about on the pitch. Strangely, the ground was unmanned and the turnstiles were opened with the 500 or so still inside, making it a hopeless task for the ground staff and police to remove the interlopers.

The defensive frailties which blotted the ninety minutes in Nottingham gave Matt Busby some cause for concern and prompted the United manager into making a couple of changes in order to ensure that such problems would not be ongoing. Out went Shay Brennan and Bill Foulkes, the latter having endured a miserable afternoon beside the Trent after being constantly caught out of position – according to one journalist, 'far too slow nowadays to operate' – and in came Noel Cantwell at centre-half and Bobby Noble, for what was only his third League outing, at left-back; Tony Dunne switched to right-back.

Blackpool were propping up the table with only two points from their ten games, but a visit from Manchester United was inspiration enough for any team, and the Seasiders reacted accordingly, taking a third-minute lead through Charnley.

United managed to draw level in the twenty-third minute, but the goal had more than a hint of good fortune about it rather than some well-planned and highly skilful effort. Best snatched at a pass from Crerand and moved forward, attempting to go past Hughes. However, he almost lost the ball and rather half-heartedly attempted a shot at goal which, despite having little pace, struck Law on the leg and beat Waiters.

On another day, Blackpool might have built on their promising opening and simply pushed the lucky equaliser to one side, but on this particular October afternoon fortune did not smile on them, as they lost centre-half James on the half-hour mark, forcing them to remove the robust Charnley, who had given Noel Cantwell much cause for concern in the opening stages of the game, to take up defensive duties, with substitute Craven taking over up front.

They did, however, plod away, stretching the United defence at times, but to little avail, and when it looked as through their sterling efforts would be awarded with a most-welcome point, disaster struck with two minutes remaining. Charlton headed the ball forward towards Best, who was fouled by Hughes as he moved in on goal and, from the resulting penalty, Law made no mistake.

Two fortunate points for United, but it kick-started their season, assisted by a 2-0 victory over Fiorentina in Florence on 12 October. With the season barely underway, Matt Busby rather surprisingly took his team to Italy for this one-off fixture, a match organised as part of the 'British Week' celebrations. Although competitive, the game lacked any real enthusiasm for the 15,000 present, which was reflected in the 0-0 half-time scoreline. But after the interval United took the initiative, and goals from Charlton and Best were enough to give United victory, along with something of a lift for the visit of First Division leaders Chelsea to Old Trafford three days later. With the return fixture at Stamford Bridge rather strangely only a fortnight later, these were two fixtures that United could certainly not afford to lose if they wanted to maintain something of a challenge for the title.

Local tradition always made out that United apparently kept their most outstanding displays for the best opposition, cranking up the prematch build-up and atmosphere for the visit of the Stamford Bridge side to Old Trafford. Unfortunately, for once, tradition crumbled and United looked 'lethargic' and like a 'jaded and scrappy side of misfits' according to one journalist, while Brian Glanville in the *Sunday Times* wrote that United 'relied on individual achievement rather than collective endeavour'.

Prematch entertainment was to take on the form of the constant removal of unruly individuals from the packed terraces, reducing considerably the given attendance of 56,789 and the number that actually witnessed the ninety minutes; for example, the announcement for a gentleman from Stretford to 'go immediately to his place of employment and release a man who had been locked in'. Did the unfortunate internee suffer a further ninety-minute wait before securing his release?

Chelsea showed their championship credentials with some fine play, utilising the spacious Old Trafford to their advantage, but it was their finishing that let them down; otherwise they may well have had the game sewn up in the first forty-five minutes. But it was United who came closest to opening the scoring, two minutes before the interval, when Charlton, tightly marked on the edge of the area, worked the ball across the face of the Chelsea defence before hitting a drive that Bonetti could only parry. Sadler rushed forward, but with the goal gaping in front of him, could only hit the foot of the post and as the ball rebounded Best ballooned it over the bar.

The second half was only seven minutes old when the visitors gained the advantage. Boyle was almost on the touchline in the middle of the field when he hooked the ball over the head of Stiles before setting off down the wing. His cross over the face of the United goal was low and hard, and as Crerand stuck out his foot in an effort to deflect the ball wide, he only managed to divert it past Stepney.

An injury to full-back McCreadie three minutes short of the hour mark lifted United's hopes of snatching something from the game, but it was not until eleven minutes from time that the equaliser came.

Bonetti, under pressure, knocked down a rather awkward lob from Best; Charlton then drove the ball against the Chelsea 'keeper's body and Law pounced to sweep the ball into the net for a point that left United still in sixth place, three points adrift of leaders Stoke City.

Against Arsenal fourteen days later, United stumbled to a 1-0 victory with a lacklustre performance. However, the following Saturday, in the rather swift return fixture against Chelsea, with the Londoners now sitting at the top of the First Division, it was a completely different United who captivated the 55,000 plus Stamford Bridge crowd, despite being without the injured Denis Law, Noel Cantwell and Tony Dunne.

In the build-up to the game, Busby warned his charges that the next ninety minutes was 'the key match of the season and could decide the title.

'This is an absolutely vital game for us. Who knows, the championship could rest on this result.

'I am not underestimating our task. Chelsea are a fine young team and it will take a brilliant side to knock them off the top of the table.

'But I think we are on our way to finding our peak form. We hope to prove this against Chelsea tomorrow.'

The United manager had to go into the top-of-the-table clash without Denis Law, who was injured, but pledged to retain his belief in attacking football. He accepted the contradictions in his statement, as a few weeks earlier his team had adopted a somewhat defensive approach a few miles across the capital at Tottenham. 'We had to do it then,' he said. 'The circumstances were different. We didn't let on but we had a goalkeeper who wasn't really fit to play. We had to protect him and I felt the way to do it was to pull back on defence and try to get a point.'

The game turned out to be a connoisseur's feast of football, led by the player who captured all the headlines in the following two days of press coverage – George Best, an individual who was beginning to emerge as the jewel in Manchester United's crown. He was a player who epitomised Matt Busby's style of football, and of who the United manager was to say, 'Each generation throws up one or two great footballers – Stan Matthews, Tom Finney, Pele, Eusebio, Denis Law, Bobby Charlton, and so on.

'With normal luck young George Best promises to join them.'

Although full of praise for the Belfast youngster, Busby was still not convinced that his player was the finished article: 'George's fault at the moment on the road to maturity is his very love for the ball, or in soccer parlance – "overdoing it".

'But as one of his famous colleagues said, "You might be cussing him one moment for not parting after beating three men or beating one man three times, and then the next moment he is liable to do the same thing again and win the match."'

Win the match he certainly did, with some of those headlines proclaiming 'Chelsea Outwitted By Genius Best', 'Best Caps Brilliant Move With Wonder Shot' and 'Best Scores One In The Law Class'. Others highlighted the difference between the teams as being more than simply one individual, with 'Chelsea Outclassed by Man Utd', 'Superb Manchester Utd Find Chelsea Flaws' and 'Chelsea Finish Lengths Behind'.

The result was indeed a blow to Chelsea's title aspirations, but despite the 3-1 defeat they remained in top spot, one point in front of Stoke City and Everton and two in front of United. The latter, however, did have a game in hand.

On a wet afternoon in south London, there was little excitement until the twenty-third minute when Bonetti saved a header from Sadler, but from then on the game slowly rose from its slumber.

Sadler shot a foot wide, Bonetti rushed from his goal to clear from the oncoming Best and, at the opposite end, a deflection off Brennan was pushed over the bar by Stepney, before the deadlock was finally broken three minutes before the interval.

Crerand burst through from midfield, having taken the ball off Boyle, and held off two attempted tackles. From just inside the penalty area he tried a low shot which Bonetti could just palm to the side. Aston, following up, stroked the ball almost effortlessly into the net.

Within sixty seconds of the restart United had came close twice to increasing their lead. Stiles had forsaken his defensive duties, and from his cross, Sadler just failed to connect, while seconds later, it was Sadler again, this time denied by Bonetti, who pulled off the best save of the match, pushing the United player's rasping drive round the post for a corner.

Stepney denied Boyle who had latched on to an excellent through pass from Baldwin, but play swiftly moved to the opposite end. Best found fellow lodger Sadler in the area and the ball was quickly returned towards the feet of the oncoming Irishman. It looked, however, that the winger only had a 50/50 chance of reaching the ball, but somehow, as the Chelsea defenders closed in, Best managed to surprise Bonetti into thinking that he was going to hit the ball with his right foot, before sending it soaring into the roof of the net with his left.

Ten minutes later, the home side pulled a goal back with a Hollins shot-cum-centre, which flew over the heads of the United defence, whose number also unfortunately included Stepney, and the ball hit the inside of the post, going into the net.

Any thoughts of a Chelsea comeback were extinguished within three minutes. Best had a shot blocked by Bonetti, but once again the 'keeper failed to hold it and, as it had done earlier in the game, the ball broke to Aston, who coolly took it inside Kirkup before sliding it beyond the reach of Bonetti to ensure United victory.

The performance itself was acclaimed by Busby as his team's best of the season, while in the *Sunday Mirror*, reporter Ken Jones waxed lyrically with regards to George Best's second goal of the afternoon. 'It was one of those moments that not even the tricks of memory can polish into something more marvellous,' penned the respected scribe. 'It was there to see, to savour, to enthuse over – the genius of George Best, Manchester United's Irish international.

'For seconds that must have seemed an age to Chelsea full-back Eddie McCreadie, he was still, his body keeled over at an incredible angle, his right foot poised like a wand over the ball.

'Then Best was away, sprinting for a return to the pass he had stabbed to the feet of David Sadler.

'An incredible shot, hit off the wrong foot, swept past a bewildered Peter Bonetti, and a capacity crowd at Stamford Bridge were suddenly living lavishly with the greatness of it all.

'It was more than a great goal. It was absolute proof that in the ultimate it is the magic of the individual that makes the game live.'

Having performed somewhat indifferently during the opening three months of the season, the victory at Stamford Bridge acted as a form of inspiration, a confidence booster, as it propelled United into a run of five consecutive victories, something that they had not managed to achieve in the League since April 1965. Sheffield Wednesday were beaten 2-0 at Old Trafford, Southampton 2-0 at the Dell, Sunderland thumped 5-0 in Manchester and Leicester City 2-1 at Filbert Street.

The victories against Sheffield Wednesday (2-0) and Southampton (2-1) saw United move to within a point of leaders Chelsea with a game in hand, while the 5-0 triumph over Sunderland not only boosted the goals for table, but pushed them into joint top spot. Squeezing themselves in beside Chelsea did, however, have an element of good fortune about it, although even without the rub of the green the Roker Park side would have undoubtedly crumbled against the in-form United.

Law had set up Herd for the opening goal in the twenty-seventh minute following an amazing 50-yard run, but four minutes later disaster struck, when a collision between goalkeeper Jim Montgomery and Tony Dunne reduced the visitors to ten men. From then on, the game slowly slipped away from them.

Centre-half Charlie Hurley wemt between the sticks, attempting to keep United at bay, if only until the interval in the hope that the 'keeper would be fit to return, but he was soon beaten as Herd claimed his second. Substitute Park replaced Hurley in goal after the restart, the centre-half hoping at least to block United's route to goal. But reduced to ten men, Sunderland were always chasing the game and Herd continued his one-man assault on the Roker goal, claiming not simply two further goals, but the distinction of scoring against three different goalkeepers in the same game. Law scored United's other goal in the 5-0 trouncing.

The five-goal victory over Sunderland was followed by a five-star display in the 2-1 victory against Leicester City, the Filbert Street side's first home defeat of the season and a win that took United into first place, two points ahead of Chelsea, with the press exalting the praises of the new leaders.

In the *Daily Mail*, Brian James wrote, 'The seat of Champions was taken last night by Manchester United in the style of Champions.

'They defeated Leicester with football that soared above the ordinary in a match that must stand high in a season already distinguished for great games.'

Thousands were locked out of the compact Midlands ground, but two entrances were forced open by some of those determined to gain entry by fair means or foul, and a considerable number did get into the ground, although they were quickly rounded up by gatemen and police. Once they had paid their admission money, they were allowed to remain on the inside.

Scrambling onto the already heaving terracing, they were just in time to see Law opening the scoring in the twenty-third minute. After rising and dipping as it flew towards Banks in the Leicester goal, the ball skidded in the mud in front of the England 'keeper, who was unable to prevent it from entering the net. Banks had previously countered United's brisk opening, denying both Law and Charlton, with his teammates, after that initial setback, clawing their way back into the game and keeping the United defence on their toes.

Spectators were still being herded around the touchline as the second half got underway, but most had settled down by the time United increased their advantage in the fifty-fifth minute. Some 30 yards from goal, Best began a cross-field run, shrugging off attempted tackles for the blue-shirted Leicester players and the persistence of Ritchie Norman, before unleashing a shot from 25 yards that flew past the helpless Banks and high into the net.

In the final few minutes, Law missed three easy chances to increase United's lead, but the only other goal was a consolation effort from Gibson three minutes from time.

The Filbert Street fixture restored United to pole position, rekindling the dream of championship success come May. It could also have rekindled another dream, resurrecting the career of one United player who had thought his first-team days were over.

Wilf McGuinness had suffered a broken leg seven years previously, but had made a surprising return to United's second string on 16 September against Manchester City, having been given the all-clear by the United medical staff and following talks with the club's insurance company. He was named as substitute for the match against Leicester.

'I don't know whether I shall get a game, but even to come into the reckoning like this makes everything worthwhile,' declared the enthusiastic McGuinness. 'I have dreamed of hearing a big crowd roar again and am ready if United need me.

'I have dreamed of playing ever since I broke my leg and this season I decided to try and do something about it before it got too late.' Unfortunately, however, the dream failed to become a reality, as his services were not called upon and a reappearance in the First Division never materialised.

Back at the start of season 1956/57 United began issuing tokens in the official programme the *United Review*, an idea that was meant to ensure that the regular match-going supporter would be guaranteed a ticket whenever an all-ticket match came around. This was not entirely foolproof, as you could purchase as many programmes as you wanted for friends who were unable to get to a certain match, but it did have its advantages.

With many supporters travelling to away fixtures when tokens were being issued at selected reserve or youth-team games, the club then decided to extend the 'token system' to include the cover of away programmes. It was a move that led to untold problems.

Away games were volatile enough, with countless reports of supporters running amok, but now there was even more irresponsible behaviour as gangs of United followers attacked programme sellers outside away venues, stealing their stock and their cash. Such scenarios were brought to the fore after an elderly seller was beaten up at Southampton and his 500 programmes stolen, but it was revealed that similar incidents had occurred at Tottenham (on 3 September) when another elderly seller was attacked and robbed of not only his programmes but also his walking stick.

At Nottingham Forest (on 1 October), programmes had been snatched from the seller's hands, while at Chelsea (on 5 November) two sellers were manhandled and robbed of their stock. At that same game, a man also went to the club office with £30 and asked for 1,200 programmes. Clearly a black market was developing.

Those attacks had certainly not gone unnoticed around the country, as sellers at the Leicester City fixture had demanded police protection and were told to pick a spot near to where police officers were on duty. Despite the problems, the programme token scheme was to continue.

Like the career of Wilf McGuinness, all good things must come to an end, and United's recent run of victories came to a sudden and abrupt halt at Villa Park on 3 December, not through the brilliance of the home side, but due to the inept performances of the usually articulate United forwards. It was this undistinguished display of shooting, with Herd, Charlton and Aston the main culprits, that cost United victory.

On at least four occasions in the first half and eight in the second, when the home goal was practically under siege, United scorned every opportunity that came their way, courtesy mainly of George Best, but it was not until fifteen minutes from time that they finally managed to put the ball past Withers in the Villa goal.

The home side had taken the lead in the twenty-first minute, when Scott forced the ball home in a crowded goalmouth after Stepney had blocked a shot from Roberts, but from then on it was practically all United. Law had a goal disallowed for offside as United hit back, but the ball went everywhere except into the back of the net.

When Herd scored with a quarter of an hour remaining, many expected the visitors to snatch a late winner. Few, however, expected them to surrender the point they justly deserved. But lose it they did in the eighty-first minute, when Scott broke free and his pass found Chatterley who blasted the ball past Stepney.

One man who wasn't at Villa Park on that December afternoon, or indeed at Old Trafford playing for the United Central League side, was goalkeeper Harry Gregg. The Irishman, the hero of Munich and a major part of the recovery programme following the crash, had been unfortunate in recent seasons with injuries, but although he had managed some twenty-six League appearances last season, he found himself down the pecking list this time around with only two outings prior to the signing of Alex Stepney.

Due to those limited opportunities and the belief that he still had something left to offer, he asked for a transfer, which was granted, with United allowing the 'keeper to leave on a free. Interest was shown by Swansea Town and Chester, with the former making a firm offer, but it was Stoke City who won the race for his signature. United secretary Les Olive said, 'In view of the length of service and because we wanted to help him find a new club, there was no transfer fee involved.'

'I hadn't had any other offers,' said the big goalkeeper. 'But I was very keen to get into the coaching side of the game and it was part of the agreement I had with Tony Waddington, that as soon as John Farmer, who was out injured at the time, returned to full fitness, then I would step down. An agreement which stood.'

Despite the defeat at Villa Park, United remained in top spot, as only Liverpool and Leicester in the top six managed to record a victory that same afternoon, but there was something of a down-side as, during the tense finale to the game, Stiles was involved in an altercation with Chatterley, which left the Villa player with a bruised eye. Both players were booked by the referee, but the involvement and ultimate booking of the United wing-half saw him hauled in front of the FA Disciplinary Committee and suspended for fourteen days.

Following the committee's decision, a statement read, 'The Disciplinary Committee, at a meeting held in Nottingham considered a report from referee L. Callaghan of a caution administrated to N. Stiles of Manchester United FC in a match against Aston Villa on 3 December.

'In view of the player's previous misconduct on the field of play, and a warning given on the occasion of a previous caution, the committee decided that Stiles be suspended for twenty-one days from Monday, 26 December.'

The suspension, no matter when it came, would have been a blow to United's title-chasing hopes, but to fall at this particular point was something of a double punishment, as Stiles was scheduled to miss five games, due to the increased number of fixtures over the holiday period. It was a particularly harsh decision, which should have seen the fixture list consulted, as earlier in the season Alan Gilzean of Tottenham had received a fourteen-day ban, but missed only one fixture.

However, the club and player could not really have any complaints, as this was the second time this season that the hard-tackling wing-half had found himself in trouble with the game's top brass. He had been fined £50 and warned as to his future conduct following the sending-off against F. K. Austria in a pre-season friendly.

Stiles did seem to show some remorse as to his misdemeanours, saying, 'I can't explain it. I am trying hard, you know. I am trying all the time. I just can't explain it to myself. Oh yes, you get a lot of provocation, you know. Nobody notices it.' Meanwhile, Matt Busby, like Stiles' international manager Alf Ramsey, stood firmly behind him. 'He's no trouble here,' said Busby. 'You very, very seldom hear his voice. On the field he's this tremendous will to win. I think he erupts at times. One thing I always say and I've said it before, I've never seen him kick a player or hurt a player sufficiently for him to go off the field for the rest of the game. He's very upset when it happens. He gets so full of the match. He's winning and losing – he's fighting for his life.'

Influenza forced Stiles out of the top-of-the-table clash with Liverpool at Old Trafford, as an injury did to Law, a match that brought together the reigning Champions with the title pretenders and a fixture that hinted to just as much action off the pitch as on it. Fortunately, the former failed to materialise, as the club had stepped up its efforts to cleanse the terraces of those who did so much to spoil the match-going experience of others, by installing a closed circuit television system, with a special squad of policemen scattered around the ground and linked by pocket radios.

On the field, the action was non-stop, with Liverpool bouncing back from a midweek 5-1 European Cup defeat at the hands of Ajax, to share the points in a 2-2 draw that saw all the goals coming in the opening forty-five minutes.

It was the visitors who took the lead in the thirteenth minute, St John racing round Sadler to beat the advancing Stepney, after Milne intercepted a lazy pass from Brennan that had already bounced off Stevenson. But it was a lead that the visitors could only maintain for three minutes, when a defensive error returned the compliment and allowed United back into the game.

Strong, under no pressure, directed the ball to the feet of Herd, who in turn sent Best striding for goal. Avoiding the close attention of Yeats, he managed to send the ball wide of Lawrence and into the far corner. Best once again got the better of Yeats, but his pass to Herd saw the usually dependable centre-forward miss from only 8 yards out. But it was only moments later that United took the lead, when a Best throw-in was returned to him by Charlton and the Irishman in turn sent a long, cross-field ball to the feet of Ryan. Playing a one-two with Herd, the winger found himself inside the penalty area and bearing down on goal, but before he could shoot he was upended by Yeats. From the spot-kick, Best smacked the ball against the underside of the crossbar, but much to his relief the ball bounced over the line before coming back into play.

It was also much to the relief of the United No. 7 that the referee allowed him to stay on the field for the remainder of the game, following a swing at the much-more-solid figure of Yeats, which left the Liverpool player flat on his back. An earlier incident had seen him pull down the even-more-intimidating Smith; bravery indeed. The referee had taken no action in relation to the earlier incident, but following the collision with Yeats, the official was left with little choice but to book Best, although the United player could consider himself to be fortunate that he was allowed to stay on the pitch, with a booking the only punishment.

In the final minute of the first half, Liverpool equalised; St John, with his back to goal, spinning to send a Thompson corner past Stepney.

The second half began slowly, but by the end of the second forty-five minutes the score could easily have stood at 5-5. Sadly there were to be no further goals, only near misses. Dunne, who had begun the game in the totally unfamiliar No. 6 shirt, went off injured, replaced by the more attack-minded Anderson, the United defence was stretched at times, but there was always Best to keep the visitors on their toes. One run-in especially took him past four challenges before passing to Ryan, who in turn found Aston, only for the winger to finish a wonderful move with the anticlimax of a tame shot.

United did get a sniff of victory, when Ryan was upended by Strong just inside the penalty area, and while the Liverpool trainer attended the injured Yeats, Crerand placed the ball on the spot. Once the Liverpool captain had recovered, however, the referee surprised everyone by stepping forward and picking the ball off the spot and placing it further back for an indirect free-kick.

Thompson outfoxed Noble, the United full-back, having earlier found himself on the receiving end of a brutal foul by Stevenson, for which the Liverpool player was booked, but having made room for a shot, he squandered an ideal scoring opportunity.

The visitors had no answer to the brilliance of Best, but were more than content to head back along the East Lancs Road with a point that kept them within touching distance of the First Division top spot, hanging on to the dream of retaining the title.

As the year moved into its final couple of weeks, United continued in their search for the championship, although they were to find that not every side could be steamrollered out of the way. At the Hawthorns on 17 December, an exhilarating ninety minutes produced seven goals, four of them in United's favour, but Boxing Day at Bramall Lane saw Sheffield United manage to repel the marauding Lancastrians and record a notable 2-1 success. It was, however, a result that only provoked retaliation twenty-four hours later, when goals from Crerand and Herd gave United a 2-0 victory, returning them to the top of the First Division, a position that they had relinquished to Liverpool the previous afternoon.

The Battle of the Roses continued on New Year's Eve when Leeds United travelled over the Pennines, taking home a point from a 0-0 draw in a hard, uncompromising match. But United went into the New Year as leaders, determined to hold on to their advantage in the second half of the season.

Law was missing for the visit of Tottenham Hotspur, an entertaining 1-0 victory for United, as he was for the trip across Manchester to Maine Road, which would have ended with a similar result had Stiles not had the misfortune to head the ball past Stepney with a minute remaining.

A diversion from the rigours of the First Division dog fight came as always with the January intervention of the FA Cup, with the third-round draw pairing United with Stoke City at Old Trafford. Having already beaten their hosts 3-0 back in September and sitting a mere four points behind them in the table, Stoke were certainly no pushovers, but as the afternoon unfolded, they provided little in the way of opposition and, by the end of the ninety minutes, despite enjoying the better of the early play, they had no further interest in the competition.

Slowly, United clawed their way into the game and took the lead twelve minutes before half-time, with Best teasing the Stoke defence before sending a right-footed centre to the far post, where Law was lurking to nod the ball home.

United continued to raise their game, reaching a height that Stoke had no hope of matching, and although they held out admirably, it came as no surprise when they finally conceded a second goal with seventeen minutes remaining. Herd caught Farmer completely unaware with a strong right-footed drive from all of 30 yards, which flew into the net via the post.

The game was now over as a contest, with Best continuously toying with the Stoke defenders, who left the field grateful at having not conceded more than two goals. Indeed, such was United's performance in those final stages that Arthur Hopcraft wrote in his report for the *Observer*, 'In the last twenty minutes of this fine game, with the clear lead secured and Stoke's defence left skeletal by the urgent call for reinforced attack, Manchester's forwards flowered into that burgeoning talent that no other League side can match.'

A second consecutive League draw, 1-1 against Burnley at Turf Moor (a team who had won only one game in their last eight), was enough for Liverpool to knock United off their high perch. However, the knowledge of having a game in hand was enough to keep alarm bells from ringing, and with half a loaf being better than none, players and supporters alike trudged back towards Manchester knowing that there would be days ahead when a similar ninety minutes would produce the goals and also both points.

Nottingham Forest's visit to Old Trafford on 11 February brought together the second- and third-placed sides in the First Division, tussling to keep a grip of Liverpool's shirt tails, and it was only through the brilliance of Denis Law that United secured victory. This stretched their lead above their third-placed rivals to three points, while remaining only one behind the Merseysiders.

Attendances, in comparison to those of the previous season, were now back to what was expected at Old Trafford, with the 62,727 who watched the ninety minutes against Nottingham Forest only 1,736 fewer than the aggregate for eleven games in the Fourth Division. Indeed, the 41,343 that had watched the opening-day fixture against West Bromwich Albion was the smallest of the season to date, with the above crowd for the Forest game turning out to be the highest barring the fixture that was to follow.

The chase for the First Division title took something of a back seat on Saturday 18 February, with the FA Cup taking preference for those who had managed to avoid a third-round exit. Second Division Norwich City made the journey north to Manchester as lambs to the slaughter in the eyes of many. None of the green-and-yellow bedecked travelling supporters, nor the Old Trafford faithful, however, had forgotten that the East Anglian side had created a major cup upset at Carrow Road back in January 1959, turning the form book upside down by recording a memorable 3-0 third-round victory; a result that ignited a memorable cup run for the Canaries, which came to an end with Wembley only one step away.

That 1959 defeat had come on the back of eight consecutive United victories, so considering that in the run-up to this particular cup tie they had won four, drawn three and lost one, there was a distinct possibility of a similar upset being witnessed by the 63,405 crowd who made their way to Old Trafford that cold February afternoon. Few, however, expected the ninety minutes to unfold in the manner that it did, although Norwich manager Lol Morgan had his own ideas.

'We must be in with a chance,' he declared. 'Because this is a game played by men, not machines. We know, as professionals, and so do Manchester United, that there are players who will sometimes play above themselves and others who will not reach their true ability.

'This is one of those unpredictable factors which underline what football is all about. It is the constant possibility that the unexpected may happen that makes the game so appealing.'

Form and divisional status is thrown out the window for any cup tie, and Norwich came to Old Trafford with little to lose but plenty to gain. However, it was not so much the skill, stealth and craftsmanship of the visitors that turned this particular game on its head; rather it was more the defensive indiscretions of the home side that were to cost United the game.

Stepney was seldom troubled, as Norwich were more than content to settle for a defensive game plan and hope that an odd upfield venture might produce the possibility of a goal, with a clear hint that keeping United at bay might produce a replay back in East Anglia. So, they stretched their defence across the 18-yard line and their hard tackling prevented United from gaining any form of momentum. This was equally helped by Messrs Best, Crerand, Charlton and Herd all electing to have an off day at the same time, allowing Morgan to enjoy a smug smile from his touchline seat.

Twice in the first few minutes Stiles had to cut out hopeful through-balls from Bryceland and Heath, while his teammates struggled to put two passes together and, with twenty-six minutes gone, they paid for their rather shoddy play when Norwich gained the advantage.

A long downfield pass from Bryceland was chased by Heath and, as the United defence stood aimlessly looking for an offside decision which never materialised, the Norwich inside-forward gathered his wits, realised the position in which he found himself and proceeded to sidestep Stepney before pushing the ball into an empty net.

The goal seemed to awaken United from some sort of slumber and slowly they began to show some form. In the thirty-fourth minute they grabbed an equaliser. Herd sent FA Cup debutant Jimmy Ryan down the right wing and the youngster swung the ball into the Norwich penalty area, where Law coolly flicked the ball left-footed into the roof of the net. It was a goal that roused the crowd, but failed to inspire the red-shirted players. Chance after chance went amiss while the first half drew to a close and second half got underway.

Twenty minutes into the second half Norwich once again found themselves in front, thanks again to United's inability to defend.

Bolland, more in hope than anything else, booted the ball upfield, with Stiles and Dunne in pursuit. The latter attempted to pass the ball back to Stepney, but somehow made a complete hash of things and it rolled well out of the 'keeper's reach, into the path of the oncoming Bolland, who had little more to do than slip the ball into a vacant goal.

If Norwich had been considered defensive in the previous hour, then the final thirty minutes saw them even more resilient at the back in the determination to hold on to the lead. But United were never likely to rally for an equaliser, never mind a winner, as it was simply one of those afternoons when nothing went right and mistakes were well and truly punished.

'Thank heaven we won,' said Norwich captain Terry Allcock. 'It has been like living under a shadow for eight years. I was in that team and proud of what we achieved in 1959. But the trouble is the fans have never let us forget those famous victories. Everything we have tried since then has been compared with those days and always the present players have suffered.

'It's a terrible feeling, being told always and no matter what you do, that somehow it is never quite good enough. It can easily destroy the confidence of players and the team's belief in itself.

'Let's be honest. In that last victory over United we caught them on an icy pitch and ran them to defeat. Everything went for us.

'But this time we went to Old Trafford and beat them on a perfect surface. Which is the greater feat? I don't think you need ask.

'Now perhaps the fans will forget the past, look at us as we really are. We can stand on our own.'

Gordon Bolland, the hero of the Carrow Road support, revealed that in his half-time team talk the manager told his players to 'lob the ball over Sadler's head because United were leaving gaps. And it worked.' He added, 'As for my goal, it was already going into the net, but I followed up to make sure.' Meanwhile, a jubilant Lol Morgan said, 'We looked in trouble for the first ten minutes, but then got to grips with the game. Anyone will do in the next round ... if you can beat Manchester United you can beat anyone.'

As for United, the players trudged off the Old Trafford pitch with heads down and faces as red as their shirts, but they simply had to put the disastrous ninety minutes behind them and get on with their quest for the First Division title. 'Of course it is disappointing to lose to Norwich again,' declared Matt Busby. 'It is always heartbreaking to be beaten by a side from a lower division, but we didn't play well today.

'Now we have got to put it behind us and get on with the other job of trying to win the championship.'

Sales of the *Manchester Evening News* were certainly down on that particular Saturday night, as the United faithful had no intention of being reminded of what they had witnessed. However, the actual drop in sales wasn't too severe as countless Norwich City supporters pounced on the street-corner sellers to see the actual scoreline in print, proof indeed that it wasn't a dream, while one or two United supporters who had been unable to attend the match did buy copies, but only to read about how their heroes had failed.

Not only did the FA Cup defeat at the hands of Norwich have an effect on the sales of the *Evening News*, it had an even bigger influence on the numbers that passed through the Old Trafford turnstiles seven days later for the visit of Blackpool on Football League business, as the attendance was some 16,247 fewer. It was a considerable drop, and one not simply brought about due to the Seasiders being at the foot of the table, nor the heavy rain and wind around Salford.

It took United a full half-hour to cast their embarrassment aside, and by that time they could well have been a goal behind, but Suddick, having evaded the attention of Stiles and with only Stepney to beat, shot wide. It was a miss that was soon regretted, as a chip into the Blackpool goalmouth by Aston saw Law race forward some 10 yards as the visitors' defence stood still, and a flick of the blond head saw the ball flash past Waiters.

The greasy surface was making good football difficult, and with only four minutes of the second half played, Waiters lost his footing as he moved out of his goal in an attempt to prevent the ball from reaching Law. Stranded and with the ball running clear to Charlton, there was little the 'keeper could do as the World Cup hero sent his shot bouncing over his body and into the unguarded net. Strangely, this was Charlton's first goal for more than three months, with his performances taking something of a dip following his exertions of the previous summer.

Despite having the upper hand and the game practically won, United still stuttered along and it was only with an element of luck that they increased their lead as Law's shot hit the post and then the body of Hughes before crossing the line.

Charlton seemed to have been revitalised by his goal and he slowly began to flourish, his confidence boosted, with tactics that had previously failed starting to work for him; so much so that he added a fourth for United ten minutes from the end. Best sent a cross-field pass half the length of the pitch to Law out on the right, and almost immediately the ball was pushed through towards Charlton, who drove the ball home from the edge of the penalty area in familiar fashion.

It was a victory that put United back in top spot, albeit only on goal difference, while it also gave something of a boost to the confidence that was so severely dented by the cup defeat. However, it would be another couple of weeks before the machine was back in full running order.

United's trip to Highbury on Friday 3 March was rescheduled due to the Football League Cup final – the first to be played at Wembley – taking place the following afternoon between Queens Park Rangers and West Bromwich Albion. The match threatened to blast the Football League attendance record right out of the water, although the exact figure, which turned out to be 91,423, would never make it into the actual record books. Rather ironically, the record Football League attendance – 81,962 set at Maine Road on 17 January 1948 – was between the same two clubs.

On that particular afternoon, almost two decades ago, everyone was at the same stadium, but on this occasion, they were divided between North London and Manchester, as the fixture was beamed live to Old Trafford via closed circuit television, the first time that such a screening had taken place.

In Manchester, the images from Highbury were projected onto seven screens measuring some 40 feet wide by 30 feet high, situated around the pitch, giving the 28,423 spectators a panoramic view of the match in London. Opinions on the night's viewing were varied, especially as one of the screens was blown down, but the quality of the camera work was acceptable, and on the night the crowd soon became involved in the game, which gave the sponsors encouragement for the future.

It was a game that many wanted to see, creating chaos from King's Cross to Highbury Hill, and leaving countless supporters battered and bruised as they fought their way through the turnstiles and onto the overflowing terraces where 63,363 were packed, giving Highbury its highest attendance since

October 1963 and the visit of north London rivals Tottenham. The problems in gaining admission were soon forgotten as the crowd became wrapped up in an absorbing encounter.

Arsenal, a team renowned more for their obsession with the past than the future, started the game strongly, pushing United onto the defensive. Dunne was pinned back by the ebullient Armstrong, while Sammels kept Stepney on his toes. At the opposite end, Furnell only touched the ball four times in the opening half-hour – one back pass, two goal kicks and a corner – such was the lack of forward thrust from the visitors.

For all their attacking, Arsenal could find no way through the United defence, marshalled supremely by Foulkes, and if a goal was to come for either side it would be because of an individual mistake. With four minutes remaining until half-time, that mistake materialised, when Law, back helping out his defenders, tripped Sammels inside the area and the referee immediately pointed to the spot. Sammels himself took the kick and his shot went in off the upright.

Often at their best when behind, United slowly gained the advantage and thought that they had levelled the scoring six minutes into the second half when Best, having been impeded, curled the free-kick past Furnell. The Irishman, however, was completely unaware that the kick was indirect.

Three minutes later, they were indeed level, with Best once again in the thick of things. Slipping ghost-like past two defenders, he curled the ball towards goal, and just when it looked as though it was safely in the hands of Furnell, it was suddenly seen to be bobbing precariously near the Arsenal goal line. Quickest to react was John Aston and the United winger dashed forward to prod the ball over the line. In London and Manchester, the reaction of the United supporters was identical.

McLintock was injured and replaced by Court, but back came Arsenal, only to be denied by Stepney when it looked a forgone conclusion that Graham would score after fine work by Armstrong. The United 'keeper was soon called upon to perform similar heroics in order to deny Sammels.

But soon it was all United. With tempers becoming frayed and tackles became harder, Graham and Law found themselves on the receiving end of lectures from the referee. The latter's was slightly more prolonged than that of the Arsenal man, and despite their second-half supremacy, the visitors, or the home side if you were back in Manchester, just could not breach the Arsenal rearguard, although both Crerand and Stiles forced the best out of Furnell with shots that the Gunners' 'keeper did well to tip over.

Despite the loss of a point, United remained in top spot, a point in front of Liverpool and four in front of third-placed Nottingham Forest.

George Best was by now becoming the focal point of the United side in more ways than one. On the field, he terrorised opposing defences. Off the field, he was terrorised by female fans. His undoubted footballing talent and good looks were adding a distinct new dimension to not simply Manchester United, but football as a whole.

Avoiding the attention of an overzealous full-back was something that came naturally to the impish Irishman, but evading the attention of his female fans was an entirely different matter. Having purchased a soft-top convertible and left it one matchday, as usual, on the Old Trafford forecourt, he returned to find that some female had scrawled, in indelible lipstick, 'I love you, George' across the roof. A Sunday with a bucket of soapy water would not shift it! From then on, he would drive his car to a nearby garage and arrange for a taxi to take him to and from the ground.

At this particular time, he was also receiving more fanmail than the rest of the team put together, and would send out around 300 signed photographs each week. It had been hinted that he had his signature duplicated, but he replied, 'It takes two afternoons a week to sign all the photographs and books, but if the fans take their trouble to write to me then the least I can do is send them my own signature and not a carbon copy.'

On the field, Best had been receiving some stick of late and admitted himself that there had been a couple of bad games. 'I played terrible against Norwich in the Cup,' he confessed. But on other occasions, he had been brilliant, although the critics were quick to pounce on him for those two underachieving ninety minutes.

But it was not simply stick from the men of the press that he was having to deal with; there were also the intense man-marking jobs that many teams employed when facing United, with Peter Storey, a renowned 'hard-man', marking George so closely in the Highbury encounter that it often gave the impression that they were wearing the same pair of boots!

A 0-0 draw at Newcastle did little to enhance United's title credentials, although it did keep them narrowly in front, albeit on goal average. But apart from the four goals scored against Blackpool, Busby's all-star forward line had failed to score more than once in the League since 27 December, nine games previously. Perhaps thankfully, the defence had been in a rather selfish mood during that period, conceding only three goals; a major factor in the position that they held at the top of the First Division.

Pent-up frustration will always be released at some point, and although it was perhaps only the Stretford End and their fellow Old Trafford inhabitants that were experiencing it, with their team's failure to turn chances into goals and draws into victories, the United forward line suddenly exploded from their hibernation with a five-goal blast against Leicester City. But it was to come at a price.

On an afternoon of thoroughly entertaining football at a sun-kissed Old Trafford, the usually solid red-shirted defenders almost destroyed their back-to-form front men, but as had often happened in the past and would certainly do so in the future, it was Manchester United's unpredictability that captured the 53,813 crowd, keeping them on their toes for the whole ninety minutes.

The game was only ninety seconds old when United took the lead. Sent through by Law, David Herd latched on to the ball, sending it wide of Gordon Banks, while at the same time he was sent crashing to the ground under a heavy challenge from Graham Cross. The crowd erupted as the ball crossed the line, but Herd, waving away his celebrating teammates, lay in agony, his left leg broken.

Replaced by David Sadler, equally at home in attack or defence, although preferring the latter, United continued to attack the Leicester goal and were two up within ten minutes. Charlton, having been presented with the European Footballer of the Year award prior to kick-off, scored with a 20-yard drive after Best had been allowed to run some 50 yards unchallenged before setting up his colleague. Banks appeared to be preoccupied by the close presence of Law, but as the United No. 8 was not interfering with play, the goal was allowed to stand.

Leicester managed to hold their own until three minutes into the second half, when a Crerand free-kick found Sadler, whose shot hit Law on the back and then rebounded to the feet of Aston, who whipped the ball home.

Now well in command, it was soon 4-0. Law, moving forward, noticed that the route to goal was blocked by Banks and two defenders, so with little to lose and always one to attempt the unexpected and the extraordinary, he sidestepped Cross and chipped the ball over the head of Banks and his startled teammates into the net inches below the crossbar.

The crowd were now in full voice, celebrating Leicester's predicament, but within ten minutes they were silenced as the visitors reduced the leeway by two goals. With over twenty minutes remaining, the outcome might well be far from predictable.

For both goals, Stringfellow broke down the left and his crosses were turned past Stepney by Sinclair, but they were to be little more than a reward for Leicester's contribution to an entertaining game, as United, shaken from their visitors' umbrage, regained the momentum and with four minutes remaining scored a fifth. Charlton swung a corner into the Leicester goalmouth, which Banks managed to miss completely, allowing Sadler the simplest of tasks to head the ball over the line.

Despite the victory, many felt that the loss of David Herd could prove pivotal in the quest for the championship, as the Scotsman was United's second-top scorer on sixteen goals, two behind Denis Law. With ten games remaining, the onus now fell at the feet of others and it was hoped that the goal drought of a few weeks previously would not materialise again.

The injury to Herd cemented David Sadler's place in the side, but rather surprisingly, the England under-23 international had been poised to have a meeting with Matt Busby as regards his future with the club.

Despite having played in all but the opening half-dozen fixtures, playing mainly as a centre-forward although he did take on a more defensive role for nine mid-season fixtures, the former Maidstone United man had found himself dropped following the 0-0 draw against Newcastle United, something he did not take too kindly too. The injury to Herd, however, pushed any thoughts of looking for first-team football elsewhere to the back of his mind.

Sadler, like everyone from one end of the East Lancs Road to the other, now had his mind firmly fixed on the game that would possibly be the most crucial ninety minutes of the season – United's visit to Anfield on Saturday 25 March. The League table on the morning of the match showed that United held the upper hand, with a two-point advantage and a superior goal average over their Merseyside rivals. Third-placed Nottingham Forest were four behind on forty-one points, and Chelsea, in fourth, could be considered out of the equation with thirty-seven.

Over the previous weeks, Liverpool's grasp of the First Division championship trophy was being slowly loosened finger by finger, and this rather disappointing ninety minutes prised apart the Merseysiders' rather uneasy grip just that little bit more, despite the goal-less stalemate.

Such encounters are fraught with tension both on and off the park, and this one was little different. Within minutes of the kick-off Yeats had fouled Best and then enjoyed a brief altercation with Law, with brawn rather than brains becoming the order of the day. The physical side of the game slowly subsided, despite being liable to resurface at the flick of a boot. The real violence of the afternoon was, however, reserved for behind the United goal in the Anfield Road End, where a huge space developed as a series of vicious fights broke out.

Charlton and Aston, not renowned for their physical prowess, were little more than names on the match programme, and it was left to Crerand to orchestrate United's attempt at victory. As the game progressed into its final stages, however, even he was employed more in a defensive role in order to cling on to the point that the lack of goals was going to provide.

Liverpool showed more authority in the second half, with efforts from Hunt and Yeats blocked by Dunne and Stiles. Stepney, injured in preventing St John from scoring, did well to keep out Hunt and Yeats, while at the opposite end Best was subdued and a wild shot from Law somehow landed at Sadler's feet, but Lawrence did well to smother his effort.

As the minutes ticked away the momentum also decreased, with United more than happy to play the game out with the guarantee of a point that would secure their position at the top.

Easter was always regarded as a make-or-break stage of the season, when hopes of championships, promotions and relegation could take on a completely different outlook, with three often-crucial games played over the course of three days. In 1967, there were no twenty-five-man squads, no changing personnel in order to give players a rest and retain freshness. This was a period when the first team was simply that – your best eleven players. Changes were made simply because of injury or loss of form, never fatigue. If players had to play, often carrying injuries, twice in a week, never mind three games in four days, they did so without complaint, always giving 100 per cent. Those who came into consideration for first-team duty when the opportunity arose were certainly match fit, due to having played regularly in the Central League and not having spent most of the season sat in the stand. Skill-wise they might not be up to scratch, but they had been brought up in Jimmy Murphy's school of hard knocks and were more than capable of rising to the occasion.

United were in a jubilant mood as they travelled to London for the Easter Monday fixture against Fulham, confident of maintaining their foothold on the race for the title, and on the journey south Busby debated on his team selection for the first of the double-header against the Craven Cottage side, with slight knocks to Law and Dunne crucial to his eventual team selection.

The XI who earned the precious point at Anfield – Stepney, Dunne, Noble, Crerand, Foulkes, Stiles, Best, Law, Sadler, Charlton and Aston – were joined by Cantwell, Fitzpatrick, Brennan, Ryan and Burns, with a new name added to the list of travellers, that of seventeen-year-old Brian Kidd. Busby, however, was to stick with the XI who had drawn with Liverpool.

Fulham's biggest crowd since the war, 47,290, descended on Craven Cottage, where they witnessed the home side shock the League leaders by twice going in front, only to be pegged back by a resilient United XI. Charlton hit the post early on, before Clarke gave the home side an eighteen-minute lead, with the Fulham goal having another narrow escape when Aston saw his effort thud against the crossbar.

With ten minutes remaining until half-time, United drew level, Best sending a Law pass through a forest of legs and past Macedo. But they were only on level terms until the fifty-third minute, when Barrett restored the home side's lead seconds after Cohen had lobbed the ball against Stepney's bar.

Urged on by an away support that seemed to match those who were egging on the white shirts, United surged around the Fulham goal and were rewarded for their efforts seven minutes from time, when Stiles, having suddenly become the visitors' centre-forward, headed the ball home after Sadler and Crerand did the leg work.

Twenty-four hours later, the action swung to Manchester and once again Fulham put up a brave fight, not surrendering both points until the final minute, although they found themselves under seemingly constant pressure.

Charlton again hit the woodwork, while Best waltzed round four players before finding a fifth just a step too far. United mounted one attack after the other, although they failed to turn their efforts into goals until the sixty-ninth minute, when Stiles headed the ball past nineteen-year-old stand-in 'keeper Seymour.

Thirteen minutes from time, Sadler miskicked and substitute Earle nipped in to snatch an equaliser and a goal that Fulham thought had earned them a point. But they were to be denied in the final minute, when a Crerand centre found Foulkes in the Fulham penalty area and the United centre-half headed home to maintain United's two-point-advantage at the top.

Having got the hectic Easter period out of the way, the finishing line could be seen in the distance, with only seven hurdles to be overcome successfully if the League championship was indeed going to find a resting place at Old Trafford. But it wasn't simply a case of getting the name of Manchester United engraved once again on the championship trophy. Busby, as he had for a decade now, set his sights much higher, with that elusive and formidable target of the European Cup being his inevitable goal. In order to achieve this, however, the challenge of Liverpool and Nottingham Forest had to be overcome and title success assured over the course of those fixtures that still remained.

Matt Busby was well aware of the pressure that was now mounting and the strain that was being heaped upon the shoulders of both himself and his players: 'There is no such thing as an easy game for United. You have to be in this position to appreciate how exacting it can be. Still, it's the only position we want to be in.

'At this stage, not only do you have the constant tension of your own match but you are looking over your shoulder to see how your rivals have got on. You are not proud of your feelings but you are elated when your rivals lose, disappointed when they win.

'These days, of course, it must be appreciated that games are far harder to win, goals are more difficult to get and no team is a pushover.

'Everything is on the move now and naturally we must be expected to win our home matches.

'I am happy about the way the lads are playing now. They pleased me more in their two matches against Fulham than for quite some time.

'I was really happy about their more fluid approach to midfield play. And, most vital of all, they are now showing no real signs of tension.'

The visit of West Ham United to Old Trafford would still leave half a dozen fixtures remaining, but it was seen as something of a pivotal ninety minutes as the campaign began to reach its crescendo, mainly due to the fact that United had won only two of their last six, with their forwards having scored only once in the last three. Comparitively the Hammers had taken maximum points from their last three games.

With the crowd still settling down, the Hammers' 'keeper was beaten by Charlton, after Best robbed Moore as he prepared to take a pass from Hurst. The United winger moved away from the England captain and his inch-perfect through-ball set up Charlton to score. Despite taking this third-minute goal and continuing to play with panache and something of an arrogant elegance, they simply could not conjure their supremacy into goals. Stepney was something of a spectator, while Standen, his opposite number in the West Ham goal, endured a somewhat hectic ninety minutes.

Aston headed a Charlton centre on to the bar, while the Hammers' 'keeper did well to palm away another centre from Stiles. He was then beaten by Law, but a linesman's flag denied the Scot as the one-way traffic continued. Thirteen minutes after the interval, Charlton was brought down inside the area by Bovington, but to everyone's surprise the referee decided to award a free-kick on the edge of the box. And so it continued: plenty of action, but no goals, with Stiles having two unbelievable misses. As the minutes ticked away, the supporters began heading for the exits, convinced that the solitary strike was all that they were going to witness that afternoon.

For those preferring the early departure to the game's final five minutes, they chose the wrong option, as the referee was soon to atone his earlier decision when he considered a Charles challenge on Best worthy of a penalty. Law beat Standen from the spot, but his kick smacked against the post and was quickly cleared. Once again, the seats in the stands clattered as their occupants decided to head for home, but a minute later they missed Standen being beaten once again. On this occasion there was no obstacle and Best's shot flew past the 'keeper and into the net.

With sixty seconds remaining, Best's cross-field pass was misheaded by Moore towards Law, who brought the ball under control before shooting past a helpless Standen. Another vital three points were in the bag.

Nine days later, Sheffield Wednesday's Hillsborough ground witnessed its largest crowd for five years, with 51,018 enjoying an entertaining ninety minutes that saw United's title aspirations take something of a dent. Two Bobby Charlton goals, in the thirty-sixth and thirty-eighth minutes, put United in front and by all accounts left them looking likely to clinch yet another victory. Best ran the Wednesday defence ragged, but somehow they managed to stand firm against the red tide.

Having been knocked out of the FA Cup the previous Saturday, Wednesday were determined to repay their supporters with a sterling performance against the would-be Champions. United were taken by surprise by a dramatic comeback, which saw the home side put the ball past Stepney on three occasions, but much to their relief, only two counted.

The point gave United a three-point advantage over Forest, but they had now played one game more than the team hot on their heels. Liverpool were four points behind, but their title challenge was soon to disintegrate, with only one win in the final five fixtures of their League programme.

On 18 April Southampton left the rather spartan surroundings of the Dell and made the long journey north to Manchester and the grander structure of Old Trafford, where the leaders spent most of the first half frustrated and often near to panicking while their visitors fought for the points, in what for them was becoming something of a fight for survival due to their precarious position towards the foot of the table.

Despite the rather unappealing guests, the fixture marked Manchester United out as the country's 'must-see' team. By the time the attendance against Southampton had been totalled up, they would have attracted more than a million spectators through the Old Trafford turnstiles to watch their nineteen First Division fixtures this season. It was a figure already passed, if the two FA Cup ties and the closed circuit televised game were taken into consideration, but in League games alone, United stood on a pedestal. It was only the third time that United had notched such a figure since the war, with the others coming in the immediate post-war boom of season 1947/48 (when of course they were lodgers at City's Maine Road ground) and in the first post-Munich season of 1958/59.

Held to a goal-less first half, only thanks to Bobby Noble clearing a Ron Davies header from a Terry Paine corner off the line, and Stepney saving a Davies shot after Paine had once again created the opening, United required only five second-half minutes before taking the lead. A misjudged pass from Paine was intercepted by Law and the United No. 8 teed up Charlton who blasted the ball past Martin with unstoppable force.

Southampton did offer some resistance, but on the hour mark they found themselves further behind after Charlton lofted the ball forward and Law, after shrugging off Knapp's attempted rugby-style tackle, placed the ball wide of Martin for United's second.

'When United are in this form it seems an understatement to call them League leaders. They look the only conceivable Champions,' wrote R. H. Williams in his report for the *Daily Telegraph*. As the game progressed, Southampton were no match for their visitors, with United subjecting their defence to a miserable evening.

Having witnessed United's rather out-of-form performance against Sheffield Wednesday, Eric Todd penned in his *Guardian* report, 'There are few teams who can transform themselves so suddenly and so effectively as United. It may be some private whim or else sheer cussedness. But once Law and Charlton "click" simultaneously no opponents have a hope of competing with this terrifying alliance. Not that those two were alone in their glory last night. Their improvement, or change of heart, call it what you like, inspired the rest of the side and if Best, Foulkes, and Dunne also are given special mention it is no reflection on the rest of this most accomplished outfit.'

With ten minutes remaining, Sadler scored a third, sending a glancing header wide of the outstretched arm of Martin, and restoring United's three-point advantage over Nottingham Forest. It was an advantage that they would continue to hold twenty-four hours later, when Forest failed to take advantage of their game in hand, losing 1-0 to Sunderland at Roker Park.

By a strange quirk of fate, Roker Park was United's next port of call: a crucial match with only four games remaining. Its importance was highlighted through the ultra-cautious approach of the League leaders, demonstrating that they could, when the occasion arose, curb their attacking, swashbuckling style. Also strangely, it was United's eighth consecutive away draw in the First Division, undoubtedly a record, while also giving strength to the age-old belief that if you won your home fixtures and drew your ones on the road, then you would end up within touching distance of the title.

Not only was it goal-less, but it was also a game devoid of goalmouth action until the final few minutes, when both sides seemed to come to the conclusion that they had failed to provide the 43,000 plus crowd with any real value for money.

George Best, that tormentor of defences, almost cost United both points, when he attempted to dribble the ball out from his own penalty area, only to be robbed by Gauden. The Sunderland outside-left quickly centred and Suggett's shot cannoned off the crossbar, rebounding to Martin who, much to the Irishman's relief, fired narrowly over.

Best was suddenly under further pressure, this time from Stiles, who subjected him to a torrent of abuse for his lack of thought and concentration. At the opposite end, in what were the dying seconds, Charlton squandered a golden opportunity to grab both points when he hesitated in front of goal after Law had forced his way past two defenders, allowing Montgomery to block his first shot and then grab the rebound before the United man could react.

That point at Roker Park did not guarantee United the championship, as there were still only three points separating them from Nottingham Forest with three games remaining, but it certainly edged them closer to clinching that sought-after piece of silverware, with the players returning from the North East in high spirits. But less than an hour after returning to the familiar surroundings of Trafford Park, the dreams of one United player were about to be shattered.

Bobby Noble said cheerio to his teammates and climbed into his Triumph Herald before heading down Chester Road towards his club-owned house in Sale. A mere 100 yards from home, a Mini turned across in front of him and he could do little to avoid smashing into the side of it.

The former Youth Team captain, who had come into the side and was now on the verge of England international honours, later recalled, 'I remember nothing until I woke up in hospital about four days later. The doctors reckoned I had a 50/50 chance of survival.'

His wife Irene was hosting a party at their home and had heard the bang, but thought nothing of it until a policeman appeared on the doorstep two hours later to break the news of the accident.

The United full-back, who had made his debut during the previous season, had made the left-back spot his own following his call-up at Blackpool in October. Although one of the poorest-paid individuals in the squad, earning £35 per week with a further £10 appearance money, he was on the verge of stepping up to £100. He did, however, receive his championship medal, along with £25,000 in damages, but despite attempts at a comeback over the following two seasons when he trained with the kids, his career was shattered and the offer of a job in the United Ticket Office was turned down.

'It was a struggle to come to terms with not playing anymore,' said Noble, who recalled how he was never allowed to play against George Best in practice games. 'I never liked people taking the mickey and George loved to do that. I had a chip on my shoulder, even as a kid. I wasn't too happy with the glamour boys.

'United knew I'd have kicked George out of the following week's game. I was quite sharp and inclined to be a bit naughty.'

Without the services of Bobby Noble, Busby brought Shay Brennan back into the fold at right-back, switching Tony Dunne on to the opposite flank. For Brennan, it had been a long and disappointing season in the Central League side, although the quiet-spoken defender had begun the campaign as first-choice right-back before disappearing from view following the 4-1 defeat at Nottingham Forest. He managed only three further outings in November and December, but had the experience to see both himself and his teammates through the crucial final trio of fixtures.

Busby had endured few selection problems during the past months, with the team virtually picking itself, and it was the experience within the ranks that the supporters hoped would carry their heroes towards that championship success.

Aston Villa, precariously placed only three points away from second-bottom club West Bromwich Albion in the First Division table, supplied the opposition in the penultimate home game of the season, helping to create one of the most bizarre ninety minutes of the season, although the 3-1 victory edged United to within touching distance of the title.

Amid chorus after chorus of 'Relegation to You', Villa closed their ears to the taunts and thumbed their nose at the baying terracings, taking the lead in the fifteenth minute through United old boy Willie Anderson. Stobart beat Foulkes with surprising ease and his pass to Anderson left the former United player with the simple task of placing the ball wide of Stepney, who was rooted to his near post.

It was a lead that Villa held for forty minutes, during which time Denis Law was at his infuriating worst, doing little to contribute towards grasping an equaliser or considering the rather adverse effect that his actions were having on his team's title assault. He was petulant, argumentative and arrogant, acting appallingly towards a linesman, and that was just in the first forty-five minutes. Why he was not sent off by referee Davies was one of the season's mysteries.

Early in the second half, Aston crossed into the Villa goalmouth and Stiles headed home what he thought was the equaliser, only to see it disallowed after a conversation between the referee, who already given the goal, and his linesman, who considered that a red shirt was in an offside position.

Minutes later, the same linesman once again had his parentage questioned by the majority of the home crowd, after he once again raised his flag for an offside decision against United. Law, on this occasion, reverted to his footballing skills and beat Withers, only to have the goal chalked off by the linesman's decision, even though three Villa defenders stood between him and the goalkeeper. Such was the ferocity of Law's complaint against the decision that he was booked by the referee for his verbal assault.

In the fifty-sixth minute, United finally broke down the Villa defence, whose play at times was little more than desperate, when Best took advantage of Aitken's slowness, before finding Aston, who drove the ball through a crowded goalmouth and into the net. Stiles, Chatterley, Crerand and Aitken were all spoken to by the referee, as United awoke from their slumber, realising that if they were to claim the First Division crown, this was a game that they would certainly have to secure both points from.

With half an hour remaining, a run from Charlton produced a corner and, from the flag kick, Law rose to head the ball past Withers via the underside of the crossbar. Ten minutes from time, victory was indeed secured when Best moved down the right before unleashing a left-footed shot from the corner of the penalty area, which swerved viciously before flying past the helpless Villa goalkeeper.

Law, who was fortunate to finish the game, spent the last few minutes wandering around with both boots tucked under his left arm.

Neighbours Manchester City failed to do United a favour, losing 2-1 at the City Ground, Nottingham, on 2 May in a game that saw two booked, one sent off and the referee assaulted. It was a result that left Forest three points behind with an inferior goal average, placing considerable emphasis on the following Saturday's fixtures, which took United to London to face West Ham United and Forest to the South Coast to face Southampton.

In reality, United were a point off the title, and prior to the game in East London, Matt Busby looked upon the FA Cup defeat against Norwich City as a game that gave his team the necessary nudge towards the title.

'Being knocked out of the FA Cup this year has helped us towards the championship,' admitted the United boss. 'Until Norwich came up and beat us, we had our eyes set in two directions.

'Once the shock wore off, we saw we were left with one thing to go for: the title. The lads haven't let up for a match. The determination has been unbelievable.'

West Ham, who only a few weeks ago were on something of a roll, had failed to win any of their previous five games, while United's recent point away from home saw the championship being clinched at Upton Park as more than a possibility.

Few who flocked to Upton Park that Saturday afternoon realised what they were about to witness, both on and off the park, with the gates locked three quarters of an hour before kick-off and a post-war record crowd of 38,424 packed inside.

Although the game did not in effect clinch the title, United went in front within two minutes of the kick-off. Law and Stiles combined to sweep the West Ham defence aside as they drove forward, with the latter shooting for goal only to see his effort blocked. As Burkett moved to clear the ball, Charlton was on him in a flash, snatching the ball off the startled defender's feet before beating Standen.

Three minutes later, there was no doubt as to where the championship was heading. Aston ghosted past Burkett before sending a high cross into the West Ham penalty area, where Crerand headed past the unfortunate Mackleworth, playing in only his third First Division fixture, for United's second. Then, with the clock showing that no more than ten minutes had actually been played, Foulkes rose alongside the novice 'keeper, challenging for an Aston corner. Mackleworth dropped the ball at the feet of the centre-half and a mere tap was all that was required to put United 3-0 in front.

Of all the white-shirted players, the performance of Charlton was nothing short of sublime, surpassing not simply the party tricks of Best, but also his superb performance against Portugal a handful of miles further north in last summer's World Cup finals. One move saw him outwit seven West Ham players as he ran the midfield, commanding his troops, urging them on to victory.

Best, who had been scythed to the ground twice in the opening five minutes, snatched a fourth in the twenty-fifth minute from a Stiles pass, and although there were fleeting glimpses of the West Ham attack, the superiority of the Champions-elect shone through. World Cup brothers-at-arms Hurst and Peters, on occasion, took the Hammers to within sight of the United goal, but they achieved little more than that, as Sadler and Dunne were indomitable in the visitors' defence. Although a goal from Charles in the opening minute of the second half, beating an unsighted Stepney, gave the home side a smattering of pride, it did little to dull matters.

A rather harsh penalty award brought the fifth for the Champions-elect in the sixty-third minute, when Charles was adjudged to have pushed Law in the back. The United man made no mistake from the spot. Law also claimed a sixth, ten minutes from time, following through to stab the ball into the net after Mackleworth failed to hold a Best shot.

As the referee blew his whistle to bring the game to an end, the ragamuffin red-and-white battalions surged onto the pitch in an act that was as much in defiance as it was in celebration, saluting their heroes and calling for Matt Busby to take a bow.

'We were boys against men' was how one West Ham United player summed up the afternoon.

It was an afternoon, however, blighted by the behaviour of a minority of the United following. Behind the West Ham goal in the first half, vicious fighting broke out, with the police and ambulancemen kept constantly busy, removing countless individuals, delinquents and bloodstained alike, from the terraces. A large gap was soon to appear, like a no man's land, and the fighting abated somewhat. After the match, Upton Park was left, according to Brian James of the *Daily Mail*, 'looking like a disaster area, with a sagging crossbar and glass-littered terraces.'

He continued, 'Only loyalists would have trekked south in sufficient numbers to see West Ham's ground packed to capacity ninety minutes before the start. But only lunatics would have felt it necessary to try and bash a neighbour's nose in appreciation of their team's talents.

'The throwing of bottles, the wielding of barbed sticks, the wrecking of the goal at the end added a sour note. United will enter grounds all over England and Europe in the coming year as representatives of the best of English soccer. They do not need such thugs among their following.'

It was unfortunate that United's championship triumph had to walk hand in hand with the reports of their supporters' scandalous behaviour at Upton Park, but headlines such as 'Twenty Injured as Soccer Crowd Starts Riot' and 'Soccer Fans Hurt in Brawl' painted an unsavoury picture. The former, in the *Sunday Express*, told of 'fighting with bottles, razors and sticks' with the brawls breaking out after every United goal. The 'Brawl' report told of train services on the District Line between Whitechapel and Barking being stopped for eighty minutes after emergency handles were pulled and couplings damaged as police chased people jumping from the train onto the line.

The mood of the afternoon is perhaps captured best in the *Guardian* by Susanne Puddefoot, the Women's Editor and daughter of former Hammers player Syd Puddefoot. She wrote, 'the significant thing was the air of high tragedy that had hung over Boylen Ground since before dawn; the Manchester supporters, who had been waiting since 4 a.m., went off and smashed windows in the market before coming back to pack the stands at ten.

'It was evident, even from outside the ground, that tension was already near breaking-point. The red ranks waited silent and sinister until the home team ran out. Their appearance raised a wall of booing. Already the razors were out in the stands, the blood was being drawn.'

Following Charlton's goal she continued her narrative: 'And the support for the Champions was organised in a manner almost crypto-fascist in its thoroughness. The chanting, the scarf flourishing, the banner waving and hand-clapping were produced relentlessly as if from a machine of aggression.'

And as the game came to a close: 'Afterwards in the boardroom, over the scotch and caviare (*sic*), as well as in the corner pub over the pints, the conversation was the same. Why, everyone was asking, why? Why the massed, vindictive hostility that insisted on fighting the battle off the field as well as on? What was the hidden force that had driven these hordes south of the Trent, a living demonstration of the "two nations" theory?'

Amid the furore, disruption and devastation, United were indeed Champions for the fifth time since the war, their seventh in total, equalling the record set by Arsenal and Liverpool. It was claimed that since becoming manager of Manchester United, Matt Busby had inherited a team, built a team and bought a team. A fair-enough argument! However, it would take a brave man to judge the best of all. Many would still go for the unfulfilled potential of the 1956–58 side, but then, who could ignore the trio of Best, Law and Charlton, superbly assisted by Crerand and Stepney. The debate as to the answer lingers on.

In his hour of glory, Matt Busby reflected on his club's title success, saying, 'Pride, relief, excitement, and, most of all, gratitude. Those are my feelings at this moment, now that Manchester United are Champions again, and have proved themselves the best in the land.

'Gratitude to the players for a start. I have had a feeling since before the season began that they were determined to win this championship.

'They wanted to win the FA Cup. Have no doubts about that, and they could not have felt more frustrated at being knocked out of it by Norwich.

'But I felt that they had set their sights on the League whatever happened.

'Professional footballers are proud people. I think we should have won the European Cup last season. But so did the players, and they were as disappointed as I was when we lost to Partizan.

'So I am grateful that they have worked, and run, for me, for the club, for themselves, for the public.

'They have not been perfect in every match. Which man is at his best in any profession all the time?

'But they have won this championship well, and the First Division championship is the hardest contest in the world to win.

As United trampled over West Ham, their nearest rivals, Nottingham Forest, had stumbled to a 2-1 defeat at Southampton, rendering the 6-1 hammering little more than just another result. However, it had emphasised the quality that Matt Busby had at his disposal, putting Manchester United on a pedestal above the rest. The plaudits, the accolades and the distinction of being First Division Champions was all very well, but there was still one mountain to climb, one title that Matt Busby and his team coveted above all others: to become European Champions.

'We have a great team,' said the United manager. 'But to do well in Europe you need more than just a team. I want more players but they have got to be our sort of players. I believe the present team is good enough, but obviously if the right player comes on the market we shall buy.'

Busby had bought only once during the campaign and that was to add Alex Stepney to the squad, but it turned out to be an inspired signing, with the United manager quick to praise his goalkeeper. 'I don't think we would have won the championship without him,' he declared.

With an apparent transfer chest of £150,000 to spend, who fitted that criterion was open to question, as many would argue that it was not simply a player's ability that would define any possibility of a move to Old Trafford – much could also depend on the size of the proposed transfer fee, with the sum mentioned a greatly exaggerated figure that was never likely to be spent.

But with the United manager having spoken about requiring at a minimum of eighteen players for his assault on Europe, it was widely speculated that a defender and a forward would be top of any shopping list.

Two players who were thought to be subject of an approach from United were Sheffield Wednesday's Scottish international Jim McCalliog, the twenty-year-old having just been granted a transfer by the Yorkshire club, and the Crystal Palace defender Alan Stephenson, with a bid already rumoured to have been made. Such a move was denied by the Palace manager Bert Head, who said that his club had not heard from United, and in any case they were well down the queue in the race for the defender's signature, as West Ham had first option on the player following an approach two years previously. Others who were considered as possible recruits were Southampton's thirty-nine-goal Ron Davies and Fulham's highly rated Alan Clarke. Both individuals were, however, tied to contracts with their clubs. Another, a candidate for the defensive role and a replacement for the ageing Bill Foulkes, was Arsenal's Ian Ure, but he had recently signed a new contract with the Gunners following a dispute.

Strange how three of the above were to end up at Old Trafford at a later date!

Despite the transfer rumours and amid the championship celebrations, there was still another ninety minutes to be played before the season finally came to a close, with Stoke City due to bring the curtain down at Old Trafford on 13 May.

Despite the drizzle, Old Trafford was abuzz from early morning, and with a couple of hours still to go before kick-off, there were already around 20,000 in the ground, many carrying bottles of champagne and brown ale.

The Old Trafford choir were soon in full voice, rising to a crescendo when the United players, dressed in red tracksuits, emerged from the tunnel, passing through a guard of honour of the Stoke City players. Out on the pitch sat the championship trophy, along with past Football League president Mr Joe Richards, the League's assistant secretary Eric Howarth, United chairman Mr Louis Edwards and Football League president Len Shipman, who presented the trophy to captain Denis Law.

There was then something of a lull, as the ninety minutes of football took over; an unwanted distraction as far as many were concerned, as they simply wanted to party. The ninety minutes were practically uneventful, an anticlimax compared to those that had passed in the previous weeks and months.

A goal-less draw ensued, with the crowd only really coming to life in the seventy-ninth minute when Peter Dobing fouled Pat Crerand. The United man quickly retaliated, before becoming involved in another unsavoury incident with Tony Allen. Crerand and Dobing were fortunate to escape with a booking. Had it not been the final game of the season, both would have surely enjoyed the pleasure of an early bath. The final few minutes saw an attempt by United to secure victory, sensing a debt of honour to their support, but it was not to be.

With the players having left the pitch prior to a final lap of honour, around 200 supporters managed to invade the pitch in one corner of the Stretford End, but an announcement warned that unless they cleared the pitch, the players would not reappear. The pitch was eventually cleared, and the police regaining control, allowing Denis Law to lead the players back onto the pitch for their lap of honour. Stopping in front of the Stretford End, the players and manager saluted the heartbeat of the United support, but around them, the police were fighting a losing battle, as a number of supporters began to gain access to the pitch. If the players had to beat a hasty exit, the fans were determined to stretch the occasion out for as long as possible.

The numerous toilet rolls that had been thrown onto the pitch during the game were launched back from whence they had come by the invading youths, while others swung from the Stretford End crossbar. The police knew there was little point in attempting to clear the pitch, as every youngster they removed would be replaced by another half-dozen, so they simply stood back and waited for the invaders to become fed up and head for home.

Following the long and arduous season, there was little time for relaxation, as the first few weeks as newly crowned First Division Champions were spent on an energy-sapping tour that took in the United States, Australia and New Zealand, where they were to play a total of twelve fixtures against opposition that ranged from the likes of Benfica and Dundee to Christchurch and the Victoria State XI. This just about left enough time for the United players to enjoy a brief holiday before reporting back for pre-season training.

9

IT'S NOW OR NEVER

Matt Busby's dream of Manchester United becoming the first British team to conquer Europe was not to be, as dear friend and fellow Scot Jock Stein claimed that accolade when his Celtic side, made up entirely of not simply homegrown players but individuals who had all been born within 30 miles of Glasgow, triumphed over Inter Milan in Lisbon. It was perhaps fitting that it was a Scottish club who achieved this success, as it had been another green-and-white-clad XI, Hibernian, who had first taken up the European challenge on behalf of Britain in 1956. The Scottish Football League and the Scottish Football Association showed none of the reluctance of their English counterparts.

Despite the expectations at the end of the previous campaign that there would be new faces at Old Trafford in an effort to mount yet another challenge on the European Cup, Matt Busby failed to make any moves on the transfer front during the rather limited close-season break. Nor was he to do so in the weeks and months ahead, relying on the players who had lifted the League title to push for that illusive European crown.

With David Herd still to return from his broken leg and Bobby Noble something of a long-term casualty, Busby was certainly taking a great risk in not adding to a squad that could be considered reliant on experience, and more so their exalted trio of Best, Law and Charlton, who between them had scored forty-five of United's eighty-four League goals. Herd had notched sixteen before he was injured, six less than the other half-dozen scorers added together. Clearly, any injuries to those match-winners could prove fatal.

Looking at the professional squad as a whole, it was certainly lightweight. Consisting of thirty-eight players, twenty-one of whom had no first-team experience, it was indeed a gamble by the manager not to bring in a couple of additions, especially with the sojourn into Europe.

Despite the lack of new faces, expectations were high around Old Trafford prior to the start of the 1967/68 season, but as always with Manchester United, there was the unexpected, catching you completely unaware, making you scratch your head in wonderment, and not believing what you had just witnessed. It only took eight minutes of the FA Charity Shield curtain-raiser against Tottenham Hotspur for one of those moments to occur.

United found themselves a goal behind to the FA Cup winners as early as the third minute, when Bill Foulkes sliced his clearance, which fell to the feet of Jimmy Robertson, who beat Stepney with ease. Five minutes later came that mouth-opening moment.

Best brought down Mackay and Mullery tapped the ball back to Jennings in the Tottenham goal. With his back to the baying Stretford End, the big Irish 'keeper took a couple of steps before kicking the ball downfield, hoping to launch another assault on the United goal. The ball soared towards the Scoreboard End, bounced twice on the edge of the 18-yard box, and from the second of those spun off the wet surface and over the head of the advancing Stepney. Stranded 15 yards out of his goal, caught out by the speed and flight of the ball, the United 'keeper could do little more than watch in utter amazement, like everyone else in the ground, as the ball landed in the net.

By the twenty-first minute, United were level when two Bobby Charlton left-footed drives had Jennings diving for cover rather than the ball. But in between those two superb efforts, Tottenham should have increased their advantage through Saul, but the opportunity went amiss. He did, however, make amends three minutes after the interval, when he out-jumped Foulkes and Stiles to head home via the post.

The highly entertaining curtain-raiser continued to provide the 54,106 crowd with value for money, but they had to wait until the seventy-first minute for the sixth goal of the afternoon and the United equaliser, when Denis Law latched on to the ball after Jennings had failed to hold yet another tantalising effort from Charlton.

The goal by Pat Jennings was certainly a major talking point as the spectators made their way home and in the pubs later that night, but there was another name on the lips of the United supporters: Brian Kidd.

Born in the Collyhurst district of Manchester, following in the footsteps of a certain Nobby Stiles, Busby and Murphy had again nurtured a diamond. Having sprung to prominence during the prolonged close-season tour, scoring ten goals in ten outings, the eighteen-year-old was possibly the reason behind Busby's decision not to purchase a replacement for David Herd. But it was a decision which was soon to once again be debated as the opening fixture of the new season saw the Champions crumple to a 3-1 defeat at Goodison Park.

'How did you win the League,' taunted the Everton support, as United stuttered through the ninety minutes, the reliance on their triple spearhead blunted by the home defence. Charlton managed only one shot on goal, Law none at all and Best was subdued for most of the afternoon by a strong and confident defence. The novice Kidd persisted bravely against the odds, but his teammates were a far cry from the side that only weeks before had been crowned Champions.

Back on home soil, the chastening experience on Merseyside was nudged to the side, although far from forgotten, but the solitary goal victory over Leeds United at least got the show on the road. The two points against the Elland Road side were hard-earned as always, but for once, the malice associated with such fixtures remained under the surface.

A point from a 1-1 home draw against Leicester City three days later still failed to give the supporters, or the media in general, any hint that this was a United side who were going to defend their championship crown, or even make any kind of progress once the European Cup got underway. This wasn't simply due to a poor team performance from United, it was more to do with the fact that Leicester had been handicapped somewhat in the first half, when goalkeeper Shilton injured his left ankle, and yet still managed to keep the United forward line at bay.

Ten minutes from time, Shilton injured his right leg keeping out a close-range drive from Best, and this time it was impossible for him to continue. He was carried off and replaced by right-half Roberts. But even against ten men and a novice goalkeeper, United failed to make any leeway.

Shilton's injury created something of an opening for out-of-favour United goalkeeper David Gaskell, with Leicester keen to sign him as a replacement. But just when it looked as if a deal was in place, Gaskell turned the move down, as he didn't want to sign a one-year contract. The Leicester game did, however, create an opening for another United player, and one that he was to grasp with both hands.

Glenboig-born nineteen-year-old Francis Burns had come to prominence during the close-season tour, having made his debut in the 8-1 victory over Auckland, and a couple of years later he would carve his name into the United history books, an entry that will most probably stand forever, as United's most-used substitute in one game! In 1970, against Eintracht Franfurt in Los Angeles, he began the game in the No. 6 shirt, but was replaced by Steve James. He then came on for Paul Edwards, before being replaced again by Willie Watson. His involvement in the game wasn't over, however, as he once again entered the fray replacing Pat Crerand. At Upton Park, he put in a sterling performance, while being well protected by the more-experienced players around him, as United claimed their second victory of the season with a 3-1 win.

But on 2 September 1967, following United's somewhat erratic start to the season, Shay Brennan found himself omitted from the team that travelled to Upton Park, his No. 2 shirt claimed by Tony Dunne, switching over from his usual left-back berth, with the No. 3 jersey given to Burns for his League debut.

The appearance of Brian Kidd, John Aston and now Francis Burns in the first team helped strengthen the rather fragile-looking squad, and their youthful enthusiasm also added considerably to the team's overall performances. However, they were something of a dying breed, as the conveyor belt of youth to first team had slowly became a thing of the past.

Following Munich, Jimmy Murphy had promised Busby that he would deliver another FA Youth Cup-winning team, which he did in 1964, but after that he had taken something of a back seat in regards to youth, junior and reserve-team affairs, with a greater emphasis put on his duties as a No. 2 at first-team level. Hence it could be seen that the youth team fell into disrepair, although this is certainly not pointing a finger at the ability of Wilf McGuinness, who was now in charge of this end of the United production line.

It had only been seventeen weeks since United last visited the east London ground, but the memory lingered on, not just in relation to the emphatic performance that clinched the title, but also the violence that marred the fixture, forcing United to publish a warning in their programme for the Leicester City match, that any supporters travelling to the London should keep away from rival fans. They also warned that West Ham had banned flags and banners on poles from the ground.

It was a plea that went unheeded, as numerous reports mentioned trouble at the game. The *London Evening Standard* reported that 'Police ejected over a dozen spectators, most of them young Manchester United fans, before the match at West Ham began today. Some were searched for offensive weapons and several were put straight into police vans in the car park.'

The *Sunday Times* mentioned that the interval brought its customary quota of arrested fans in red and white, while the *Guardian* reported that for once the spectators could enjoy the occasion as the would-be agitators were pounced upon before the start of the game, with two of them being 'a couple of ten-year-olds'.

On the field, Bernard Joy of the *Evening Standard* considered United 'ragged and disjointed', but they were still too good for their hosts, although it was not until nine minutes into the second half that they managed to gain the advantage as Brian Kidd volleyed home his first League goal. Sadler made it 2-0 four minutes later and, although Peters struck back twelve minutes from time, Ryan secured victory for United in the eightieth minute.

Despite the 3-1 victory over West Ham, there was still no consistency to be achieved. The journey up to the North East to face Sunderland at Roker Park produced a point from the 1-1 draw while Burnley's relatively short trip to Old Trafford saw them take a point back to Turf Moor following a 2-2 draw. At one point, it did look as though United's unbeaten home record, stretching back to April 1966, was about to be broken, as the visitors were leading 2-0 with only four minutes remaining. This was only salvaged thanks to Francis Burns – his first senior goal – in the eighty-sixth minute, and Pat Crerand's ninetieth-minute equaliser.

It soon became a hat-trick of draws, as seven days later a point was once again snatched from the jaws of defeat at Sheffield Wednesday, thanks to George Best's seventy-fifth-minute goal. It was a point that kept United in ninth place, three points behind Liverpool, but with a game in hand.

It was certainly not the most promising of starts, but sprinting out of the starting blocks was not a trait that Manchester United were renowned for. What was a major concern, however, was the fact that the European Cup was about to make an entry into the fixture list, and for many, this sojourn into a competition that had now grasped the attention of everyone, a far cry from its humble and suspicious beginnings, was now regarded as the Holy Grail. For many of the players within Matt

Busby's first-team squad, this could well be their last opportunity in attempting to snatch that ultimate crown.

Fortunately for United, the first-round draw paired them with one of the minnows of the competition, the unknown Maltese side Hibernians: a mismatch of amateurs and part-timers coached by Father Hilary Tagliaferro, a local priest.

The Maltese contingent arrived in London *en route* for Manchester and proceeded to lose one of their players, seventeen-year-old Francis Mifsud, who decided he wanted an ice cream, left the team's hotel and became lost. Somehow, he managed to find his way to Manchester, and his team hotel, by train and the help of a fellow passenger, but was subsequently left out of the starting line-up at Old Trafford, as he was considered to still be suffering from the experience that he had endured.

On the night United were met, rather predictably, with a ten-man defensive wall. The visitors, who knew they had no chance of winning, simply attempted to keep the scoreline down to as little as possible, in an effort to attain some form of credibility.

It took United only twelve minutes to breach the Hibernians' defence, but the expected avalanche of goals failed to materialise despite their overwhelming dominance, and a David Sadler strike along with another from Denis Law were the sum total of the opening forty-five minutes.

United would have undoubtedly have been expected to run up double figures against their £4-per-week opponents, who were experiencing playing not simply under floodlights for the first time, but also playing on grass. However, careless finishing and the determination of the Maltese left the crowd irritated and restless.

Sadler and Law scored again in the second half, with the four goals looking ample to see United through to the next round. On occasion Hibernians did show some promising football, but they were never going to conjure up a goal, never mind a shock result.

Inconsistency had been a major factor of United's season to date and looked certain to continue against Tottenham Hotspur at Old Trafford on 23 September where, in similar circumstances to three days previously against Hibernians, United's all-star forward line failed miserably in front of goal, despite their overall superiority.

Tottenham took the lead in the fourth minute through Gilzean, then sixty seconds later Law hit the post with a penalty kick after Charlton had been upended. It was only a brief let-off for the visitors, as United equalised in the sixth minute, Knowles failing to cut out Charlton's through-ball, allowing Best to run through and score.

Law produced gasps of disbelief from the packed terraces as he rose to send an overhead kick past Jennings, only for his effort to be disallowed for offside. But, as the game progressed, it was frustration that took over, as the home support became disenchanted by the failure to take advantage of the opportunities, with yet another dominant display failing to produce the goals that could ensure victory.

With seven minutes remaining, it looked as though Tottenham were to secure a point, but then a corner from the right found the head of Foulkes, who directed his header down to the feet of Law to blast home. Sadler then missed an easy opportunity to secure victory, but that moment came with a mere two minutes to play, when Best snatched upon an opportunity after Jennings had beaten out Kidd's close-range shot.

Having clawed out a victory from the depths of despair, the question on everyone's lips was, had United finally turned the corner, following the somewhat indifferent start? The answer, however, was certainly not forthcoming from the European Cup second-leg tie in Valletta's Gzira Stadium, where, on a hot, humid afternoon, on a pitch totally devoid of grass and covered in sand and gravel, United were rather surprisingly held to a 0-0 draw in front of 25,000 spectators.

How many of that 25,000 actually supported the home side is debatable, due to the United following on the Mediterranean island, but those with an affiliation to the visitors would have been left disappointed as United failed to increase their overall advantage, and once again squandered numerous scoring opportunities. Kidd could have done better in the fifteenth minute, while Dunne and Charlton both hit the woodwork. The biggest surprise came five minutes into the second half, when tempers became frayed following a foul by Stiles on Privitera. Thankfully the Italian official managed to quieten things down and normality resumed.

If the crowd were disappointed, Matt Busby on the other hand was simply content to get this particular fixture out of the way. The 0-0 draw, however, was an achievement for the home side, and coupled with preventing United from scoring amounted to a victory in the eyes of Father Tagliaferro and his Hibernians players.

From Malta, the action suddenly swung to Maine Road for the sixty-seventh Manchester 'derby' since United abandoned the Newton Heath title of their forefathers. On current form, the match could have gone either way, with City two places above their cross-town rivals, although United had a game in hand. Since the war, United had won thirteen of the thirty-two Maine Road fixtures and drawn twelve, with City's last victory at home over their one-time tenants back in season 1959/60. They could, however, claim a victory at Old Trafford in 1962/63.

It wasn't a game for the purists, or indeed those seeking something of a spectacle. Nor was it a game for those of a light-blue persuasion. 'The point would hardly be acceptable in the pubs around Maine Road, but as the second half spluttered and faltered in a raggle-taggle mixture of ill-temper and weariness, it was plain enough that this City side did not know nearly enough to win,' wrote Arthur Hopcraft in the *Observer*.

Bell gave City the lead after only five minutes, but having enjoyed much of the opening quarter of the game, they suddenly found themselves behind following two defensive errors that allowed Charlton to score in the twenty-second and thirty-fifth minutes: two goals that gave United not simply a victory over their old, local rivals, but something of a confidence booster and perhaps a launching pad to finally get their season off the ground.

Stepney kept the City forwards at bay, while the referee helped United's cause by denying the home side two penalty claims. However, in the *Guardian* Eric Todd wrote that 'United's defenders failed to convince collectively and more than once their gesticulations denoted lack of confidence in each other' and 'the fact that City did not score again was due as much to their own shortcomings as to any improvement in United's security arrangements'.

The usual bitterness which simmers to the surface when the two sides come face to face was always there, and on the pitch it resulted in blows being exchanged between the eighteen-year-old Bowles and Kidd. The referee would have been justified in sending both off, but with the game drawing to a close and upon the intervention of their more mature teammates, he did little more than take their names.

It had taken nine First Division fixtures to achieve back-to-back victories, but Eric Todd was certainly not the only one still to be convinced by the Champions' current form, despite having to come from behind on both occasions to claim maximum points. The decision not to buy still rankled many, as did the defensive failings that were apt to appear at some point during each ninety minutes. There was also an edge to the side that many felt was not in keeping with the Manchester United image: a darker side to their game, with a blue touch paper that required only the slightest of sparks to ignite it, throwing a game into disarray, breaking concentration while the possibility of vital points and victories was cast into the wind.

While chasing silverware, or indeed attempting to fend off relegation, there is usually a defining moment or two during a season that, when looked back upon, can be identified as the point when the fine line between success and failure was crossed. For the Manchester United side of season 1967/68, their defining moments were still to come, but in the opening couple of months of the campaign, there were two incidents that could well have proved fatal, even at this stage of the season, and might well have costed United a second consecutive League title, had it not been for the strength and resilience of the current side. The first of those came on Saturday 7 October, with the visit of Arsenal to Old Trafford. The other materialised across the Pennines seven days later.

A solitary John Aston goal in the seventy-sixth minute, a rarity in itself, was enough to secure both points for United against the Gunners and give them their third successive victory, but it was a goal that would be erased from the memory seconds after the ball hit the back of Furnell's net, as this was a game in which unsavoury and irresponsible incidents would linger in the memories of those present for much longer.

Arsenal arrived in Manchester, in the words of James Mossop in the *Sunday Express*, 'determined to show a ruthless professional face and determination to snatch any reward – particularly a point.' They were ideally situated to make something of a challenge towards the top spot in the First Division, sitting third, only two points behind leaders Liverpool, and set their stall out accordingly, with the towering blond-headed Ian Ure given the job of shackling his fellow countryman and a player who could conjure a goal out of nothing, Denis Law.

What Ure's specific instructions were from his manager, Bertie Mee, are unknown, but man-marking Law was certainly one of them, with the former Dundee centre-half taking his manager's prematch team talk perhaps just a touch too literally. Having obeyed his manager precisely, while showing the defensive traits that persuaded Mee to pay £62,500 for his signature three years previously, his attention to Law was at times just too personal, and with just over twenty-four minutes played, one foul too many saw the United No. 10 retaliate, giving referee George McCabe little option but to book both players.

The booking of players in the immediate post-war period was something of a rarity and often documented in the match reports as if it were something of a major scandal. Even in season 1967/68, taking an individual's name was often seen as something of a last resort. Ure and Law had both crossed that dividing line and, as the game progressed, others like Kidd and McLintock, Pat Crerand and Peter Simpson were fortunate not to join them. Likewise George Best, who was guilty of swinging a punch at Peter Storey. Only Bob McNab, for a foul on Kidd, forced the referee into once again producing his notebook and pencil.

A foul by an Arsenal defender in the first minute set the tone for the afternoon, although there was also some good football on view from both sets of players. United created two clean-cut scoring opportunities, but shunned both, while Furnell in the visitors' goal had luck on his side on several occasions: once when an Aston shot struck him on the knee as he dived, and again when an effort from Kidd hit him on the hand and bounced to safety. It was Arsenal, however, who had the best scoring opportunity, when a back pass from Dunne was misplaced, leaving Stepney at the mercy of Simpson, but the defender, employed in something of an attacking role, blasted the ball instead of taking his time placing it, allowing the United 'keeper to pull off an excellent save.

With a share of the spoils looking likely and only fourteen minutes remaining, play swung towards the Arsenal goal. A Kidd pass picked out Crerand, and from his cross Aston, the calmest player on the pitch during this feisty encounter, dispatched his header past Furnell.

There was still time for an Arsenal equaliser, but the game was soon to spiral out of control in the eighty-third minute when the simmering feud between Law and Ure finally boiled over. Law, who had been clearly unsettled by the close attention of the Arsenal defender throughout the game, tackled Ure from behind. A kick was then aimed in the direction of the red No. 10 shirt as he tried to get up off the ground, and soon the two players were struggling violently with each other, leaving the referee with little option but to send them off.

Law's previous misdemeanours left him clearly at the mercy of the Football Association's Disciplinary Committee, and having suffered two lengthy periods of suspension in 1963 and 1964, a third was now most certainly on the cards, soon to arrive in the form of six weeks on the sidelines. Probably also taken into consideration was his sending-off during the club's final match in their post-season tour of Australia, when he was dismissed against Western Australia in Perth for using abusive language and fined £20. It certainly wasn't the best of summers for Law, as he was more than a little fortunate not to have been sent off in one of the other so-called friendlies, against Representative XI in Sydney, when he headbutted one of the opposition's players!

Ure admitted afterwards that he 'should have known better', as indeed should Law, but counting to ten was not in the latter's mentality and his six-week suspension, which could quite easily have been more, was to see him miss seven games.

It was not only the booking of players, or indeed the sending-off – both commonplace in today's game – which makes the football of the sixties seemingly from a different planet at times. Eric Todd in his superb match summary of the Arsenal encounter for the *Guardian* wrote, 'It is time, too, that more managers put their own houses in order beginning with an instruction to their players to behave less like consenting males when one of them scores. If they want to kiss and cuddle, let them seek some dark alley. Or does the law insist on the privacy of a house?'

Todd also shared his views with his multitude of readers on the sending-off, dismayed that while some of the United support booed Ure off the field, they serenaded Law with his theme tune of 'We'd walk a million miles for one of your goals, our Denis'. He added, 'Spectators are ejected for fighting. Footballers deserve the same treatment as, belatedly, Law and Ure received this day. Magistrates have been advised to be stricter in dealing with hooligans. The FA Disciplinary Committee must set an example and for "hard" cases the term of suspension should be measured in terms of months, not weeks. With a fine, increased by £100 each time, for every dismissal.'

Law clearly had some making up to do prior to his suspension coming into force, having only found the back of the net once during the domestic campaign. As it turned out, United would win two of the three fixtures that he was available for prior to his suspension, with his only goal coming from the penalty spot, while during his seven-game penance on the touchline there would be four wins, two draws and one defeat. So was the 'Lawman' still the force of old, capable of turning a game on its head, or was he a luxury that United, at times, could do without?

A 3-0 victory over Sheffield United at Bramall Lane did much to confirm that United had indeed found, at last, some form of consistency; as did the equally convincing 4-0 thrashing of Coventry City at Old Trafford. John Aston, scoring once at Sheffield and twice in the latter fixture, made it four goals in three games, doing much to erase the memory of Denis Law for the time being at least.

The Coventry fixture was a poignant return to Old Trafford for former club captain Noel Cantwell, who had taken over the manager's seat at Highfield Road the previous week. His appointment, taking over from Jimmy Hill, had ended days of rumour and counter-rumour.

Cantwell had been appointed as manager of the Republic of Ireland side the previous week, taking over from another former United captain Johnny Carey, having recently turned down an approach by Aston Villa to become their new coach. But then Coventry City came along, dangling a £7,000-per-year carrot in front of him, and the man who led United to their FA Cup success in 1963 admitted, 'I did not apply for the job. The offer came out of the blue. I had little hesitation and Mr Busby said, "Go. This is a fantastic chance for you and I know you can do it." When someone like Mr Busby says this you must take notice.'

But Cantwell's return to Old Trafford could not prevent United from extending their unbeaten run to eleven games, coupled with an unbeaten home League run of thirty. The 4-0 victory edged United into joint-top spot along with Liverpool and Sheffield United on eighteen points.

But all good things come to an end, and the journey to the City Ground, Nottingham, saw a beleaguered United beaten 3-1, a victory masterminded by another former United captain Johnny Carey.

Law, playing his last ninety minutes before his six-match ban came into effect, was a shadow of his former self according to David Lacey in the *Guardian*: 'Poor Law; he dragged his heels as he led United onto the field and looked as though he dreaded the game's start, let alone its end. There was none of the old fire about his play and, having gone through the motions for ninety minutes, he walked off with his head bowed. Few would quarrel with the length of Law's suspension but it was a pity that the wretched business should have coincided with a fixture that usually produces a close contest in attacking styles.'

So, Law's imminent suspension was considered as much to blame for United's defeat as that of the overall team performance, but perhaps a more important factor in the defeat, and indeed how the team would perform at home and abroad in the coming weeks, was the omission of Nobby Stiles, injured against Sheffield United and soon to be diagnosed as requiring a cartilage operation that would sideline him for seven weeks.

'The loss of Stiles is a stunning blow to United's championship and European Cup hopes,' wrote Steve Curry in the *Daily Express*. It was an opinion echoed by Matt Busby. 'It really is grim news,' said the United boss. 'We cannot expect Nobby to be fit for at least six weeks, one week more than the period Denis still has to serve under suspension. A terrible blow. It really could not have happened at a worse time for us.'

Having lost at Forest, there was a hint of desperation surrounding the visit of Stoke to Old Trafford on the first Saturday in November, but a solitary goal from Bobby Charlton was enough to snatch both points from a Stoke side, who were in Manchester with the intent of obtaining a share of the spoils.

At a fog-shrouded Elland Road four days later United slumped to their second consecutive away defeat, and with 11 November taking United to table-topping Liverpool, there was every possibility that it could well become three in a row. But even without Law and Stiles, with Best having moved from the right wing to Law's inside-left spot, Jimmy Ryan being given the No. 7 shirt, and the versatile David Sadler taking over from Stiles, Busby's team shrugged off their two previous away reversals and showed a packed Anfield, and later that night an enthralled *Match of the Day* audience, why they were in the European Cup, and Liverpool the Inter-Cities Fairs Cup.

Neither of the missing United duo were, to put it simply, missed. Best, the scorer of both United goals in the 2-1 victory, caused more than enough problems up front as Liverpool struggled to hold on to their unbeaten home record, while behind him Dunne controlled the threat of Thompson, with his fellow defenders equally secure despite the home side enjoying most of the attacking play.

United took the lead from their first corner. Aston floated the ball into the area, and Best managed to reach it as goalkeeper Lawrence came out in an attempt to punch clear, heading it past a helpless Byrne on the line. Five minutes before the interval, Best struck again, stroking the ball into an empty net after a slip by Lawrence, as the 'keeper misjudged a through-ball from Crerand.

Despite Liverpool pulling a goal back through Hunt, the grit and determination of the United players, backed by the Mancunian chorus of 'Champions of Anfield', proved that there was never any possibility of their one-goal advantage being surrendered, nor the one-point lead they now held at the top of the First Division.

Crowd trouble and football-related hooliganism had again reared its ugly head in recent weeks, with a sixteen-year-old Liverpool supporter stabbed at Anfield. The United 'football-special' trains were cancelled indefinitely due to a series of train-wrecking incidents. But it was on-the-field trouble that was about to come Manchester United's way.

If the Maltese side Hibernians were something of an unknown quantity, then equally unfamiliar were the second-round opponents, the Yugoslavians of Sarajevo. Situated at something of a crossroads between Europe and the Middle East, the city's main claim to fame, or perhaps notoriety, was because it was where the Archduke Ferdinand and his wife Sophie, Duchess of Hohenberg, were assassinated in June 1914; an incident which was to spark off the First World War. Its imposing architecture, including the eye-catching Bey's Mosque and the Old Orthodox Church, were certainly lavish in comparison to the city airport, approached through thick woodland with deep gorges on either side. As Rex Bellamy in the *Times* explained, there was a chance that poor weather could cancel this mode of transport altogether, and in any case the landing would have put off even the most experienced of travellers, as the plane had to land on a strip down the middle of a grassy field, with a ploughman at work on one side and sheep grazing on the other.

Matt Busby had once again done his homework and decided against gambling with the weather, as well as the nervous disposition of his players, taking the United party to Sarajevo on a near twelve-hour torturous journey.

Leaving Old Trafford on the Monday prior to the game at 7.45 a.m., they flew from Manchester on a British Eagle flight at 9 a.m., arriving at the more palatable Dubrovnik Airport at 12.55 p.m. Half an hour later, they were on their way to Sarajevo by coach, a six-hour, 178-mile journey, winding through the wild mountain side. It was a route decided by the United manager, as he considered it more suitable than the one he had taken when he came to watch his opponents, which involved travelling by train from Zagreb. It was certainly not the best of preparations for a European Cup tie.

Following their sometimes rather traumatic journey, the United players and officials received a warm welcome from the Yugoslavs – but then so did the Archduke!

Sarajevo were a far cry from the side that had lifted the Yugoslavian League title for the first time last season, as since then they had lost six players and their coach. Their form was bordering on the indifferent, with five defeats in the last seven games, and having won only four of their eleven games during the current campaign.

Far from being hapless amateurs, their players were on a basic wage of £40 per week, compared to the average Yugoslav wage of £8 per week, but they were not expected to cause United any major problems. Indeed, one of the Sarajevo directors, Milivoj Stekovic, a wartime friend of Busby's who he met while stationed at RAF Wilmslow, proclaimed, 'It would be folly to think we have a chance against United.' But in common with countless opponents before them, the Yugoslavs managed to raise their game against their illustrious visitors.

Stekovic's words galvanised the Sarajevo players on the night and perhaps went some way towards the tactics that they employed, deciding that if they could not match Manchester United for skill, then they would use their physical strength in an effort to achieve a favourable result.

The game opened briskly, with little hint of what lay in store. United adopted something of a safety-first tactical plan, with only Kidd employed upfield. As early as the seventh minute, Sarajevo showed that they were indeed capable of causing something of a minor upset, when Stepney was forced to make a fine save from Antic. Shortly afterwards, he was again in the thick of the action, tipping a 30-yard drive from Prljace over the bar.

Luck was certainly with United in the twenty-second minute, when Prljace slipped the ball through to Musemic, who confidently rounded Foulkes before shooting. Stepney managed to partially stop the ball, but it rolled tantalisingly towards the line, and the 'keeper grabbed it at a second attempt. Many, including members of the British press corps, considered that the ball had indeed crossed the line before Stepney managed to recover, but neither the referee nor linesman agreed with the protesting Yugoslavs, who were enraged even more when the referee awarded United a free-kick 10 yards from where Musemic had shot.

Sarajevo were reduced to ten men in the thirty-fifth minute, when Prodanovic was forced off with a leg injury, but still United could not force a worthwhile chance. Angered by the disallowed 'goal', along with the problems of playing a man short, the Yugoslavs blotted their copy-book severely with countless rash challenges, blatant fouls and body-jarring challenges, although they had been guilty of underhand tactics throughout the game. Busby, as always, had warned his players of their responsibilities, which they thankfully adhered to a tee, the only blemish being a booking for John Fitzpatrick following his challenge on Siljkut.

United, while never looking like scoring in the Kosevo Stadium, controlled the game towards the end, calmly playing the ball around, content to see the minutes tick away and take the goal-less scoreline back to Manchester for the second leg, along with the numerous bumps and bruises, from a game described by Bill Foulkes as 'the worst I have ever experienced'.

Matt Busby, seldom one to complain, made his feelings known to all and sundry, proclaiming, 'It was the most disgraceful exhibition I have ever seen. I am only pleased that the boys kept their heads under extreme provocation. All I could tell them at half-time was "Keep your heads, because this treatment is going to continue."

'I thought they kept control of themselves wonderfully well under extreme provocation. In such difficult circumstances I am delighted with the result.'

It was therefore rather surprising, considering the rigorous and uncomfortable return journey from Yugoslavia, not to mention the physical ninety minutes the players had to endure, that both points were secured in a 3-2 home victory over Southampton three days later.

There were few signs of rustiness or hints of fatigue in the United play. Indeed, Busby fielded an unchanged team, but the visit of the unfashionable Southampton failed to persuade many of the United support to part with their hard-earned cash, with the fixture producing Old Trafford's smallest crowd of the season: 48,732. What many of those who could not afford to spend much of their loose change on football had decided, was they would rather spend their cash to watch United's European Cup second-leg tie against Sarajevo than on the South Coast also-rans.

They did, however, miss something of a pulsating encounter, with United perhaps more than a little fortunate to grab both points. Two goals in front through Aston and Kidd, the visitors should have drawn level with goals from Chivers and Channon, had Davies not allowed himself to be caught offside. However, when they did pull a goal back, with Davies finally managing to stay onside, United simply upped a gear and scored a third through Charlton. A second Southampton goal was not enough to unsettle the home side, although the visitors' tackling at times almost did.

Before that European Cup second-leg tie, there was a visit to Stamford Bridge: ninety minutes that should have been of little concern to United, as Chelsea had somewhat fallen from grace of late and were actually seventeenth in the First Division, one place below Southampton and nine points behind their table-topping visitors. It was also a venue considered by United as something of a home from home, having suffered only four defeats in their previous ten visits.

George Best had missed the midweek Northern Ireland–England international fixture with a knee injury, sustained against Southampton, but much to the relief of the United following and manager Matt Busby, he travelled to London, pronouncing himself fit only an hour before kick-off. Whether or not there was more than a footballing reason behind his rather swift recovery is uncertain, but the Irishman was now an icon of immense proportions, with a bevy of females as large as his more football-knowledgeable supporters.

He had also found time to pen his memoirs to date, in a book entitled *Best of Both Worlds*, but this fell foul of the club's standards on its players putting their thoughts down on paper, forcing the winger to scrap two chapters. Out had to go 'The Nasties Eleven' and 'The Girls Eleven', as in the former he was going to name names, with one full-back in particular being referred to as being 'fair' and 'dedicated', but one of the most 'charming killers' that he had played against. Was he referring to the man he would come face to face with at Stamford Bridge?

Best's presence at Stamford Bridge added a considerable number to the attendance, with the gates closed a quarter of an hour before kick-off and 54,712 inside. However, many of those among the home support were not appreciative of the Irishman's talents and booed his every touch. Equally as unappreciative was Ron Harris, who showed little in the way of respect to his opposite number, and was eventually booked for his overzealous tackling on the United inside-forward. The treatment of Harris on Best was considered by Albert Barham of the *Guardian* as 'hard, but often unfair, cruelly so'.

Two minutes after his thirty-third-minute booking, Best turned the tables on his marker, backheeling the ball into the path of Dunne, who in turn found Crerand, the wing-half's far-post cross being headed home by Kidd to equalise Chelsea's twenty-first-minute opener.

United were indeed unfortunate not to grab a winner, but with Best once again having wormed his way towards the Chelsea goal, he was unceremoniously hacked down from behind by Hinton when a goal looked more or less a certainty.

So it was back to Old Trafford and the visit of Sarajevo, with the United players now well aware that should they progress to Wembley and actually lift the European Cup, then the largest cash inducement ever offered to a United team – some £30,000, working out around £2,000 per man – was theirs for the taking. New contracts were drawn up, after permission was given to do so by the Football League, putting on offer the biggest single cash incentive for any British team. Their visitors, on the other hand, had a £500-per-man carrot dangled in front of them to progress in the competition, with their coach, Ibro Biogradlic, confident that his side could pull off something of a surprise.

'We shall attack because we must,' he said following a training session under the Old Trafford lights. 'But we intend to leave a good impression of the occasion of our first game in England.' Sarajevo committee member Zendravko Pudaric added, 'We're here to win by playing an open game. Psychologically, we're in a better position than United. We have nothing to lose and nothing short of world fame if we pull it off. I realise United could and should have played better than they did in Sarajevo, but we have been picking up form dramatically since their visit, and I'm sure player for player we're just as good.'

Matt Busby, on the other hand, was looking forward to a good sporting game: 'Win, lose or draw, I hope the players of both sides come off shaking hands. I hope also that the crowd will enter into this spirit. Please encourage the lads, but let us all keep our heads.'

The responsibility of keeping order fell on the shoulders of French referee Monsieur Roger Machin who, when asked by David Meek of the *Manchester Evening News* if he regarded himself as a strict referee, and whether he had read any of the reports on the first leg, replied, 'I am severe if the players do not follow the rules. I heard it (*the first leg*) was a draw and a little difficult for the referee. It is difficult to say what will happen in the second match. I must react depending upon how things go.'

Unfortunately, the hopes of both coaches failed to materialise, while referee Machin had an eventful evening during which his two years of experience on the FIFA list were severely tested.

United took the lead as early as the tenth minute, John Aston quickly latching on to the ball after Muftic had blocked a point-blank, seemingly goal-bound header from Best after Kidd had superbly beaten Blazevic on the right. It was a lead they held on to, often rather shakily, as the Yugoslavs late tackled, body checked and made a nuisance of themselves, without threatening the United defence to any great degree. However, had Antic taken his two early chances, then the result might well have been entirely different.

The possibilities of Sarajevo snatching a goal, or even a shock victory, were always a threat, although they continued to let their guard slip with some unnecessary challenges, and the tone for the second forty-five minutes was set soon after the restart, when Aston was callously fouled by Jsenkjvic. Slowly, the simmering undercurrent boiled over in the fifty-eighth minute, surprisingly brought about by the actions of George Best. As could have been expected, the winger had been tightly marked all evening and it could be suspected that a considerable amount of frustration had been building up as numerous mazy runs bore no fruition. Having seen a header palmed out from under the crossbar, the Irishman collapsed in dismay on the goal line. Sportingly, Sarajevo goalkeeper Muftic tried to lift Best back onto his feet, but suddenly, and certainly needlessly, the United player aimed a back-handed blow with his clenched right fist to the head of the surprised 'keeper, who immediately collapsed somewhat dramatically. The referee rather surprisingly gave Best nothing more than a talking to, unsuspectingly lighting the blue touch paper.

The Yugoslavs were now hell-bent on revenge for their assailed 'keeper, with Best a hunted man, and it was Prljaca who claimed his scalp, although paying the price by getting himself sent off for his deliberate and blatant kick at the Irishman, amid rather violent and unnecessary protests from his aggrieved teammates.

Play had no sooner resumed than Best was in the thick of the action again, but this time it was for all the right reasons. From the free-kick, which led to the sending-off, Crerand passed to Aston, who lobbed the ball first time into the crowded goalmouth. It was met by the head of Foulkes, but the ball crashed against the crossbar and looked to be going out of play, before being controlled by Burns who hooked it back to Best to fire home.

The goal immediately signalled another round of protests from the visitors, the players backed by three officials who had made their way down the touchline, surrounding the linesman who had failed to support their claim that the ball had gone out of play. Such was the extent of the protests that policemen had to move in to protect the under-threat official.

Reduced to ten men and with less than half an hour remaining, the odds were now stacked against Sarajevo, and as the game went on, despite the names of Fazlagic and Jesenkovic going into the referee's notebook, a sense of calm seemed to prevail. With three minutes remaining and United satisfied with their evening's work, Delalic headed home something of a consolation goal for the visitors.

The action, however, did not simply come to an end with the full-time whistle as there was further trouble in the tunnel at the end of the game as the players left the pitch. Muftic, still upset from his earlier involvement with Best, struck out at Matt Busby. The incident, however, was quickly snuffed out and no complaint or report was made.

'A wee bit of a skirmish' was how Busby referred to the incident, going on to praise the performance of his team. 'I was delighted with the way we played, particularly in the first half which I thought the lads played awfully well.

'And never mind the question of whether it was a goal or not, I thought we were well worth victory.'

United were into the last eight, but they could put the European Cup to the back of their minds and concentrate on domestic matters, as it would be February before they would have to make plans to face further foreign opposition.

West Bromwich Albion travelled to Old Trafford on 2 December, and a George Best double, in the space of five minutes, was enough to kill off any threat from the Midlands side, whose seventy-fifth-minute strike was little more than a consolation. The victory kept United two points in front of Liverpool at the top. However, six days later, it was reported that a cat managed to do what the Albion defenders, and countless others for that matter, had failed to do – get the better of George Best.

Travelling back to his lodgings in Aycliffe Avenue, Chorlton-cum-Hardy, in the early hours of the morning after 'playing cards with friends', the winger reported that a cat ran out in front of his white 3.4 Jaguar while he was travelling down Victoria Avenue in Blackley, forcing him to conjure up a swerve that would have sent any defender in the opposite direction. Avoiding an oncoming defender is one thing, but attempting to miss a stationary vehicle is another and the United forward collided with the car.

The impact of the collision caused Best to hit his head on the windscreen, while his knee cracked against the underside of the dashboard, and he staggered from his car feeling a little worse for wear. But following hospital treatment for a facial injury, he was allowed to return home, and the following morning the United club doctor declared him fit to travel to Newcastle. 'The doctor said I was alright to play,' said Best. 'I am used to taking a few knocks.'

When club secretary Les Olive was asked by reporters if there was a possibility of Best being disciplined by the club in regards to the incident, Olive replied, 'I don't know what will happen. This is a matter for Mr Matt Busby, the manager, to decide.'

At the first board meeting following the incident the matter was indeed brought up, with Busby reporting 'that player G. Best had been involved in a car accident at 4 a.m. on the 8th Dec. resulting in facial injuries and shock. He had travelled to Newcastle later that day and had been able to play in the match on 9th December'. The directors, having had sufficient time to consider the matter, expressed their concern at what they considered to be a breach of training regulations and decided that the player be fined a sum of £25, as well as being severely censured and warned as to his future conduct.

Surprisingly, when the player appeared in front of Manchester City Magistrates' Court charged with driving without due care and attention, the cat had mysteriously disappeared and the truth suddenly unfolded. According to his counsel, Best had failed to see the parked car, which apparently had its parking light on, until the last minute and when he turned away, putting his foot down in an attempt to avoid it, he misjudged everything and collided with the rear of the parked vehicle, sending it some 30 yards down the road. As a result of the accident, the brakes on Best's car could not be tested, but his car was considered to be in good condition.

With no other choice than to plead guilty, he was fined £25 and banned for six months, with £2 4s to pay in costs. This was mainly due to the fact that he had been fined £3 in March 1966 and his license endorsed for speeding. In November of that same year, he again had his license endorsed and was fined £8, again for speeding. This year had already seen him fined a further £10 for driving without due care and attention.

On a St James' Park pitch resembling a skating rink, Best looked none the worse for his late-night escape, but could do little to prevent the home side from taking a two-goal lead. However, once again, United relished the challenge, and knowing title rivals Liverpool had been leading Leeds 2-0 at half-time, they showed tremendous character and determination by snatching a point from the jaws of defeat.

Brian Kidd pulled a goal back six minutes from time, after Best picked him out with a superb pass and, with only sixty seconds remaining, Tony Dunne's hopeful centre towards the Newcastle goal suddenly materialised into a shot, with the ball going in off the far post.

That United were crowd pullers was of little doubt, but few would argue that it was not the likes of Shay Brennan, Tony Dunne, David Sadler and Francis Burns that crowds rolled up to see, although the importance and contributions of that quartet, like all the other individuals who pulled on the red shirt, can never be doubted. However, it was the extraordinary talents of George Best, Bobby Charlton, and of course Denis Law who were the real five-star attractions. This is clearly illustrated by comparing the Old Trafford attendances for the fixtures against Southampton (48,732), West Bromwich Albion (52,568) and that for the visit of Everton on 16 December, which marked the return of 'the King' from exile, with 60,736 clicking through the Old Trafford turnstiles to salute his return. There was even a pipe band to welcome him back!

Lost points may well have been avoided had Law been present, but there was nothing that could be done with regards to that. He was now back in the fold and about to make up for lost time. Sadler gave United the lead in the fifth minute, but having used the opening forty-five minutes to ease himself back into the swing of things, Law came to life in the second half. His fifty-second-minute shot was only parried by Gordon West, and Bobby Charlton was on hand to slip the ball home. Thirteen minutes later he controlled a Charlton pass with ease and slipped past two defenders before whipping the ball past a helpless West. Everton pulled a goal back fifteen minutes from time, but it was too little, too late. United had both points in the bag and Law was back.

With the European Cup due to commence in February, Matt Busby and chairman Louis Edwards travelled to Zurich on the Monday following the victory at Goodison Park for the quarter-final draw, with United going into the pot alongside the likes of the unfamiliar Sparta Prague, Vasa Budapest, Eintracht Brunswick, Gornik Zabrze, the Italians of Juventus and old foes Benfica and Real Madrid.

Aware that to win the coveted trophy, he would have to prime his side to beat anyone who came their way, the United manager was desperately keen to avoid the Polish side Gornik, a team of part-time miners, who had stunned Europe by defeating Dynamo Kiev, the team that put out holders Celtic in the previous round. But, as luck would have it, Manchester United and Gornik Zabrze were the last two names out of the hat, with the first leg scheduled for Old Trafford.

Two days before Christmas, Law was again on the score-sheet, making it two in two games, notching the opening goal in a rugged 2-2 draw at a saturated Filbert Street, Leicester. It was a point that kept United ahead of the pack, although they were now only too well aware of a new shadow at their shoulder in the form of neighbours City.

Back in August, with less than a handful of fixtures completed, both clubs could be found in the lower half of the table following something of an indifferent start. By the end of September there had been a steady improvement, with United now in fifth and City a mere one point behind in seventh. Four weeks later, there were now three points between them and two places: United in second behind Liverpool.

All eyes had been on Liverpool, as the team United would have to best if they wanted to claim a second consecutive championship, but City, continuing to plod away and obtain favourable results – including a 1-1 draw at Anfield on 16 December and a 4-2 victory the following Saturday against Stoke City at Maine Road – found themselves nudging the Merseyside club out of second spot. They were now breathing heavily down their neighbour's neck, with only one point separating them, while having a better goal average of thirty-two courtesy mainly of having scored fourteen more goals at Maine Road than United had at Old Trafford.

United, however, gained something of an advantage on Boxing Day, clawing back the goal difference with an emphatic George Best inspired 4-0 victory over Wolves at Old Trafford, while City slumped to a 3-2 defeat at West Bromwich Albion. It was a defeat that saw them pushed back into third, with Liverpool now clutching at United's shirt tails.

Matt Busby's team were now at their vintage best, and four days after the four-goal victory over Wolves, they put a further three past the Midland side in the return fixture at Molineux. That Wolves hit two in reply was of little relevance; United were on a high and seeing the old year out in a style that the name Manchester United was synonymous with.

'No other team can play football the Manchester United way,' proclaimed Derek Wallis in his report in the *Daily Mirror* following the five-goal encounter on the edge of the Black Country. Wallis continued, 'Other teams may challenge United from time to time. Other teams may beat them from time to time. But I doubt whether any other team can match them for sheer entertainment value.

'Entertainment is often forgotten in the cut-throat world of football. Too many sides try to play as if the whole thing has been rehearsed.

'Too many teams *do* rehearse their matches by analysing the opposition down to the last detail, by drumming into their players the importance of a particular strength or weakness so that the whole exercise is inclined to become monotonous.

'But Manchester United rarely seem to forget that football is, unlike the theatre, an unrehearsed entertainment: that the unexpected is often the most entertaining and the most lethal in terms of goalscoring.'

United went a goal behind after only thirty seconds, but on a dull, wet afternoon in the Midlands, they simply allowed Wolves to enjoy their moment of glory, a twenty-minute first-half spell, when the home side directed the play as if the League positions had been reversed.

Less than a minute after the interval, however, it was all square. Law pushed the ball forward to Charlton, who then ran some 25 yards before sweeping past a couple of hapless defenders and flicking the ball with the outside of his left foot past Williams.

Four minutes later, Charlton's pass sent Best off on one of those mesmerising runs, leaving Thompson in his wake, and the Irishman, who had frustrated his teammates on more than one first-half occasion when he chose to go it alone instead of passing to a teammate, picked out Law inside the area. Law's shot was blocked by Williams, but Aston was on hand to blast the ball home with a fierce left-footed shot.

It was now all United, and Kidd added a third in the sixty-first minute from another Best/Law move. That Wolves scored a second five minutes later mattered little, as a chance for the home side to equalise was unlikely to materialise; they were constantly pegged back on the defensive, with their crossbar rattled twice and another effort cleared off the line as United countered with something akin to a bombardment.

It was not only Derek Wallis in the *Daily Mirror* who considered United a notch above everyone else, as Alan Hoby of the *Sunday Express* was of a similar opinion, and in an article entitled 'Can anyone stop Busby's boys?' he plumped for United, 'showbiz in soccer boots – the greatest club in English football', to lift the crown.

Hoby questioned the championship credentials of the leading pack and lamented that Tottenham required more strength and toughness, while Chelsea were as unpredictable as ever. Arsenal, he felt lacked 'blasting power' in attack. Liverpool, however, were one team that he felt might stop United from driving unchallenged to a second successive title, but he had a strange feeling that one other team 'who might stop majestic United are their neighbours Manchester City'.

He went on to reveal that 'Manchester City are the most athletic team in soccer. Nearly every week Derek Ibbotson, the former sub-four-minute miler, slims them down on slogging runs through woods and fields'. He did, however, feel that the only thing that went against City was their small professional playing staff, and if injury struck, then they might well find themselves struggling. Only time would tell.

Sixteen goals in the last six fixtures, or twenty-two in the last nine if that reads more impressively, saw United end the year three points in front of second-placed Liverpool, with recent challengers Manchester City having slipped to fourth and now five points behind. Strangely such statistics seemed to matter little to Eric Todd of the *Guardian* who, on the morning of the visit of West Ham United to Old Trafford, was of the opinion that the Hammers could snatch a narrow win!

The seasoned Todd should have known better, as United in their current form were untouchable and swept West Ham aside with a 3-1 victory. Bobby Charlton crowned his 400th appearance for United with the opening strike after twelve minutes. Fourteen days later Sheffield Wednesday were overwhelmed 4-2 as Busby's machine rolled on, with James Mossop in the *Sunday Express* proclaiming that the title race was all over and the trophy would stay at Old Trafford.

If United could be derailed, then the FA Cup could well be the competition in which to see it happen, although having the home advantage for their third-round tie against current holders Tottenham Hotspur did weigh strongly in their favour, as it had been thirty-seven League games since they had last tasted defeat at Old Trafford. However, there had been one setback during that period, twelve months previously against Norwich City in the FA Cup.

'Sure Manchester United have, in Denis Law, Bobby Charlton and George Best, the best forward set-up in the world,' said Tottenham captain Dave Mackay. 'They know this too. Maybe they know it too well and will try to get cocky. It is to our advantage they have had such a long winning run.

'We have a few useful forwards like Jimmy Greaves, Alan Gilzean, Martin Chivers and Cliff Jones. And I reckon our defence can take on the best.'

So it was a confident Tottenham who journeyed north; confidence that was given a tremendous boost as early as the fourth minute, when the visitors took the lead. Burns, one of three United youngsters making his cup debut – Fitzpatrick and Kidd the others – brought down Mullery, and England's free-kick was partially headed clear by Fitzpatrick. It fell to Robertson, whose low shot was stopped by Chivers, and the tall Tottenham forward calmly switched the ball from his right foot to his left before blasting it high into the top left-hand corner of Stepney's net.

Within two minutes United were level. Jennings took a short goal kick to Kinnear and, as he attempted to clear the ball upfield, Best quickly moved forward to block the clearance. In an instant he had despatched the ball into the vacant goal. Despite protests for a raised foot by the Irishman, the goal stood.

Best was thwarted by Jennings, having left Knowles stranded, but Tottenham continued to show signs that they were there to do more than make the numbers up to twenty-two, and on more than one occasion Stepney was called upon to make decisive saves.

With fifteen minutes remaining, United scored what many imagined to be the goal that decided the tie. An Aston corner saw Crerand shoot towards goal, but his effort struck Kidd and, fortunately from United's point of view, rebounded to the feet of Charlton, who blasted it back towards the packed goalmouth, where it cannoned off a defender and past Jennings into the left-hand corner.

Few made for the exits as the minutes ticked away, sensing that the tie might still conjure up some last-minute drama, and with four minutes remaining there was another twist to this compelling game.

England centred from the left and Gilzean, at the near post, turned the ball back towards Chivers, who smacked it right-footed high into the net. As the Spurs players celebrated, the United defenders urged referee Jim Finney to consult his linesman as to the validity of the goal, as the latter had raised his flag prior to the shot from Chivers. With the crowd momentarily hushed, a brief conversation between the two officials ensued, but the end result remained in the visitors' favour. They still had one hand on the trophy and could now look forward to contesting the outcome of the tie on their own backyard.

Four days later another all-ticket full house assembled, this time in north London, for what everyone hoped would be an equally compelling ninety minutes, as the two heavyweights met to slug it out for a place in the fourth round.

United had been without the injured Foulkes in the first encounter, his experience missed against the robust Chivers, and Busby had to consider if he should take a gamble with his centre-half's damaged knee and throw him into the fray. 'Foulkes has certainly improved,' said Busby in the run-up to the game. 'We will just have to wait to see how he is.'

The United manager, however, had another decision to make: whether or not to include long-term absentee David Herd in his line-up. Herd had been away from first-team action for ten months and had suffered a muscle strain during a comeback against Wolves' reserves. 'This has been a frustrating time for me,' said the forward. 'I am very happy to be in the party (*that travelled to London for the replay*), and even if I don't play I can feel I've made a real start to my comeback.'

Herd made the United starting line-up, replacing the injured Law, but Busby refused to take a double gamble, leaving Foulkes up in the stand.

Tottenham had sold 36,000 tickets in two hours for the replay, many of their supporters heading straight to White Hart Lane upon their return from Manchester, and they would shift another thousand in the hours running up to the game due to United's failure to sell their allocation. Despite this, there would still be some 14,000 United supporters packed into the ground to urge their heroes on.

With one side never having lost an FA Cup replay at home since 1911, and the other never having gone out of the competition at this early stage for nine years, it was always going to be something of a titanic struggle, with the 57,300 packed into White Hart Lane guaranteed to get value for money.

Such was the tightness of the game that United only had one real opportunity to snatch a goal in the opening half, but Aston met Best's curling corner with his shoulder, rather than his head, and the ball went wide. Moments later, Gilzean found himself in the clear, but rushed his shot and put it past the post. Had he taken his time, United would have certainly found themselves behind. As it was, like the opening exchanges in a game of chess, one move would cancel out the other, with scoring chances continuing at a premium.

Tackles were hard, but fair, despite the simmering undercurrent that was always going to be present in such an important game, as one team tried to outwit the other; however, fourteen minutes into the second half, the game suddenly and unexpectedly erupted.

Kinnear broke down the right, beating one red-shirted defender before reaching the United penalty area. He was then pulled down by Fitzpatrick, but with the Tottenham players and the majority of the crowd screaming for a penalty, referee Jack Taylor surprisingly waved play on.

As play continued, and United moved menacingly forward, Kinnear sprinted back to his defensive position angrily waving his arms and, catching up with Kidd, took his frustration out on the United forward. Both players fell to the ground, their legs entangled. Kidd was first to get to his feet and, as Kinnear attempted to get up, was knocked unconscious with a forceful punch to the jaw. Referee Jack Taylor was left with little alternative than to send both players off.

Perhaps rather strangely, both sides immediately forgot the incident and got on with the game, seeking the breakthrough that failed to materialise during the normal ninety minutes. The closest a goal came was when Mackay hit Stepney's right-hand post and Greaves shot narrowly wide, although United continued to pass the ball confidently around and looked capable of snatching victory.

In the first fifteen minutes of extra time, Jennings did well to save at the feet of Best after the winger had been picked out by a long pass from Charlton. Trying to take the ball wide and round the 'keeper, his Northern Ireland teammate pounced to block the danger.

One minute before the end of that first half of the additional half-hour, the breakthrough finally materialised. Greaves took a corner and sent it high into the United area. Up jumped England, practically on top of Stepney, creating a clear shout for obstruction, and the centre-half headed the ball against the bar. As the ball dropped, Robertson, amid a scrum of bodies, forced the ball home.

As the game moved towards its conclusion, United threw caution to the wind, with practically the whole team surging forward at times in search of the equaliser, and the opportunity to take the game to Villa Park for a further ninety minutes. But it was not to be, and Tottenham earned the right to play Preston North End in Round Four.

Defeat is never easy to take, and an appearance at Wembley in the cup final a moment to cherish, but if it was any consolation to Matt Busby's team, it allowed them to concentrate more fully on their main objectives, the European Cup and retaining the League title.

The Manchester United players did not have to wait long for an opportunity to extract revenge on Tottenham for their FA Cup exit, as the two teams were scheduled to meet just three days after the cup replay at White Hart Lane.

Worrying for United was a knee injury to Denis Law, picked up in the first of the two cup ties, and although Law travelled to London with his teammates, he was bound for Harley Street to see a specialist and not White Hart Lane. The pain in the back of the right knee had been troubling the Scot since October and had hindered his acceleration during games, hence the real reason behind some of the underpar performances.

Busby's other injury worries before the third clash with Tottenham in eight days were Crerand with an ankle injury, Best with an ankle and a leg injury, Kidd with calf injury, and Sadler with a groin strain, but all passed late fitness tests after enjoying something of a get-away-from-it-all at Weybridge, instead of travelling back to Manchester and then returning south a day later.

The rest did seem to have done the United players good as they gained their revenge with a 2-1 victory in a game described by Hugh McIlvanney in the *Observer* as 'a match of exhilarating pace and recurring brilliance which swung late, but deservedly, to the most creative team in British football.

'Such a result, so splendidly earned, confirms United's right to keep the League championship and only bigots, or spendthrifts, will bet against them now.'

United's victory could have been even more emphatic had Charlton, rather uncharacteristically, not missed a first-half penalty. But neither Tottenham, nor anyone else for that matter, could live with United in this form.

Charlton atoned his fortieth-minute miss from the penalty spot with a goal which, if it didn't make the actual headlines above the match reports, was enthused over in the opening paragraphs, as indeed was the game itself.

'The goal that caps a series to remember,' preceded the *Daily Mail* report by Brian James, with the journalist writing, 'The marvellous thing about Bobby Charlton's goal was not the run that made it possible nor the shot that made it count. But rather that it brought to 300 minutes of outstanding football a conclusion that was exactly right.

'These three matches between the sides – they must stand together as a series – gave a huge audience deep pleasure and both teams the reward that each prized most.'

As for Charlton's goal, James wrote, 'There was inevitability about Charlton's scoring. This became apparent with twenty minutes to go. The match was beginning to fade. The demands on these teams' stamina, answered without question during the previous four hours' football, were now being denied.

'There was a mood of resignation, an acceptance of deadlock. Charlton, keeping his head when all about him were hanging theirs, alone said "No".

'He ran and shot and ran again. He nearly scored, cursed his miss, and called aloud for another chance. It came with a pass in his own half. He sidestepped Mullery to begin his run, swerved away from England and Beal to end it, and shot left-footed for victory.

'After his victory somersault, after drumming his heels on the turf he had conquered and after a shower that should have been in champagne, he told me, "I think it was my most important goal for United ever. If we had lost this game we may not have done it ... but now ...'"

Tottenham had taken the lead in the third minute through Chivers, with Best equalising seventeen minutes later in a United-dominated first half. In the second forty-five minutes, after the home side enjoyed the early stages, United slowly took over, but failed to turn their opportunities into goals. 'Oh for Denis Law,' their supporters sighed. But with only three minutes remaining, up stepped Bobby Charlton.

'I didn't even see what I was aiming at,' said Charlton. 'I knew the net was somewhere over that way and I kept my head down and let go.'

The goal was also a fitting tribute to the memory of those who had perished at Munich ten years previously. Since that unforgettable Thursday afternoon, United had lifted the championship trophy twice, been runners-up once, won the FA Cup, lost another, got to the last four on a handful of occasions, as well as making the semi-finals of both the European Cup and the Inter-Cities Fairs Cup: all achievements that many teams would have been proud to have accomplished. Many, however, felt that the current crop were on the verge of greatness, within touching distance of emulating what the 'Babes' had set out to do. That was certainly the opinion of Donald Saunders of the *Daily Telegraph*, who wrote, 'Now, despite frequent injuries this season to key players, they possess what I believe to be their most accomplished side for ten years and can draw on a reserve pool of greater strength than at any time in their history.'

United were now three points clear with a game in hand, over Leeds United who had edged their way into second place above Liverpool and Manchester City. But following a blank Saturday due to their elimination from the FA Cup, although Leeds United did play and took two points from West Ham United to narrow the gap, United were brought back down to earth with a crash of Richter-scale proportions at Turf Moor, a ground where they had only won once on their previous five League visits.

The defeat was worsened by the fact that United had taken the lead through George Best in the eighth minute, but decided to attempt to stroll through the remainder of the game. It did little to help matters when Burnley were reduced to ten men with twenty minutes still to play, Casper receiving his marching orders following a retaliatory right hook to the head of Burns. However, their complacency was hit a shattering blow midway through the second half, when two goals within six minutes from O'Neil and Dobson left them struggling to secure even a point.

Missing from the line-up for the trip to Turf Moor was David Herd. Having returned for the cup replay against Tottenham and retained his place, in the absence of Denis Law, for the League fixture against the north London club, he was disappointed to find himself omitted for the Burnley fixture.

'I am very disappointed about losing my first-team place,' the one-time regular-choice No. 9 said. 'I had enjoyed my return to the first team and quite honestly felt that I had reasonable matches. Now I shall watch how things go over the next two weeks and will consider my future.'

Sadly for Herd, his days at Old Trafford were now numbered.

With Gornik loitering on the horizon, United travelled to Highbury, and it was something of a blessing that Denis Law had just returned from injury, because if he had been fully fit then his presence would have been required north of the border, at Hampden Park, coming face to face with teammate Bobby Charlton. Strangely, there was no place in the Scotland line-up for Pat Crerand, or in the English line-up for Nobby Stiles.

Arsenal also had more pressing concerns, with a League Cup final date with Leeds the following week and injuries to Law's sparring partner Ure, along with Radford and Neill. Only the latter was to face United.

The Gunners had no answer to George Best, who always seemed to revel in visits to the capital, and who scored United's second. With the assistance of a Peter Storey own goal, United stretched their advantage over Leeds United to three points. Liverpool were five behind, while Manchester City were six. The latter two did, however, have a glimmer of hope with a game in hand, although both still had to visit Old Trafford in the weeks ahead.

Gornik flew into Manchester with thoughts of their last competitive visit to these shores in the back of their minds – an 8-1 thrashing at the hands of Tottenham Hotspur in season 1961/62, in what was their first experience of playing under floodlights. The men from the coalfields of Silesia had obviously improved considerably since then, both in experience and overall playing strength, and although they had featured in the European Cup on six occasions, this was the first time that they had progressed as far as the quarter-final stage.

Due to the severe Polish weather causing their season to be suspended, Gornik, not having played since November, had prepared for their ninety minutes against United with a couple of friendlies against Belgian and Hungarian sides. But despite the lack of playing time, the Poles were still confident, with their coach, former Hungarian international assistant manager Dr Geza Kelocsai, saying upon his team's arrival in Manchester, 'Whoever wins this tie will take the European Cup.

'United have better individualists than us. Men like Best and Charlton could win the tie on their own. But I think we play together as a team.'

Kelocsai, however, was not overly impressed by United, having watched them in action against Sheffield Wednesday and considering them to be 'less than brilliantly organised tactically' and that he could devise a plan to cope with any threat that they threw up.

If United were to progress in the competition, then they would certainly be required to take some sort of advantage to Poland for the second leg, as their opponents were not to be taken lightly and were indeed an experienced side, with their travelling party of fifteen being able to amass a total of 159 caps between them. But United had their problems, as Charlton, so important in recent games, had picked up a knock playing for England against Scotland at Hampden, while Denis Law was out of contention altogether due to his continual knee problem.

Having been at the Cliff training ground the day prior to the match, in order to give his knee something of a test with a few laps around the ground, Law was dismayed to find that it began to swell following the work out. In an attempt to play, he was given a pain-killing injection, but it had something of a reverse effect, and the swelling increased.

He was ordered to remain at home and rest the knee, with a hospital appointment made for the morning after the Gornik match. It was felt that a complete examination into the problem, which was coming from behind the right knee, was needed – the knee that he had a cartilage operation on as a youngster with Huddersfield Town. The injury in the past had been simply described as 'mildly arthritic'.

The Gornik match, however, was no simple European Cup tie, as so much depended on the outcome. United should have clambered on to the top of the rostrum two years ago, having left every European side quaking in their boots following the 5-1 demolition of Benfica, but then there was the surprising capitulation to Partizan Belgrade. There could be no failures this time around.

Had it not been for Huber Kostka, a twenty-seven-year-old mining engineer, then United's progress into the semi-final of the European Cup would have been assured in the first leg. But the Polish goalkeeper thwarted United throughout the ninety minutes, with a series of superb saves that frustrated the home side and its supporters time and time again.

Within ninety seconds United had forced two corners, and by half-time had won a further twelve to Gornik's none, such was the one-sidedness of the opening half. Aston came close in the twelfth minute with a header which went just wide, while a minute later Sadler could only watch as Kostka tipped his 30-yard drive over for a corner.

Despite being constantly deployed in or around their penalty area, Gornik did show numerous neat touches and were dangerous on the break, coming close in the fourteenth minute when Stepney did well to save from Lubanski.

Burns hit the post and Kostka saved from Kidd, but still that crucial opening goal would not come, and so it continued into the second half, with another Gornik break eight minutes after the restart, from which they won their first corner, keeping United on their toes.

But on the hour, United got that goal they so desperately craved. From a Crerand lobbed pass, Best beat two men in superb fashion before shooting into a crowded goalmouth. Florenski, in an attempt to deflect the ball away from danger, did little more than push it beyond Kostka and into the net. Although there was much relief on the United bench and from the packed terraces, the Gornik heads did not drop, nor did panic set in, and they continued to defend magnificently while maintaining their attacking threats.

United continued to press forward, but it did begin to look as though the solitary own goal was going to be the only advantage that they would be taking to Poland for the second leg. However, with two minutes remaining and many of the crowd already heading for home, Jimmy Ryan, replacing Law in the United front line, hit a shot, more out of hope than anything else, towards the Gornik goal. With Kostka unsighted, the ball bobbled, Kidd stuck out his foot and the ball struck his heel and bounced over the line.

'Yes, I was kind of involved in it,' recalled Jimmy Ryan. 'You know, I sort of mishit a shot which went right across the face of the goal. In fact a few of the other players thought that I had scored, to be honest, I didn't even see where the ball went, so I had no idea who had scored. I was surprised because I knew that I hadn't hit it particularly well. But it is a game that I remember very well, because I never felt so exhausted in a game in my life, and we had to work very hard to beat that team.'

It was a goal that perhaps gave United the edge towards progressing into the semi-finals, although an equally tough ninety minutes was still to be played out in Poland a fortnight later, but they had triumphed on the night, a victory that would have been achieved with considerably more ease had it not been for Kostka in the Gornik goal. Such was his play on the night, with saves, punches and overall excellent handling, that at the end of the ninety minutes the United players lined up at the mouth of the tunnel and applauded the 'keeper from the pitch.

It was not just the performance of Kostka that caught the eye, but also the manner in which the game was played, with Donald Saunders writing in the *Daily Telegraph* 'United and Gornik proved during the first leg of their quarter-final at Old Trafford that sportsmanship and entertainment are still possible in this much-criticised game, no matter how great the strain or how high the stakes.

'In recent years, international soccer, once famous for the exciting football produced by the likes of Manchester United, Real Madrid, Bilbao and Benfica, has become notorious for brawls on the pitch and riots on the terraces.

'Sportsmanship has been replaced by gamesmanship, entertainment has been overwhelmed by a determination not to lose and keen competition has developed into violent nationalism.

'Far too often we have been excused because the players were under great strain. Well, United and Gornik were subjected to tremendous tension and each club is desperately anxious to become the first to take back the European Cup to its country.

'Yet, a statistically minded observer assures me that the referee had no need to whistle for a foul during the first twenty-two minutes of a match that contained its full share of physical combat.

'Moreover, although Gornik pulled eight men back into their own half, they employed defensive tactics with such skill and flair that there was never a dull moment during ninety memorable minutes.

'Now both clubs will carry an additional burden when the battle is resumed at Katowice on Wednesday week. Discipline and entertainment of the highest order will be expected of them.'

Before Matt Busby could devote his thoughts to plotting Gornik's downfall in the second-leg quarter-final tie, there was a simple matter of Chelsea's visit to Manchester to contend with first.

They started the match according to Michael Wale in the *Sunday Times* 'as arrogantly as they left off in the European Cup on Wednesday, employing at once the lesson they learned from that match, the low hard ball into the goalmouth'. But this was not Gornik, not European opposition, but Chelsea, a familiar foe and an opponent who were equally knowledgeable of United's faults as they were of their skill factor. The League leaders were made to pay for their apparent arrogance by a determined, hard-running and aggressive-tackling Stamford Bridge side, as well as, it must be added, a rather poor referee.

United had not lost at Old Trafford since April 1966, some thirty-seven games ago, but Chelsea tossed that record aside with creditable performance, a rude awakening that no one around Manchester 16 either wanted or believed would actually happen. Even the 'if' brigade – 'if' that had not happened or 'if' this had happened – could argue about the overall outcome of the game.

The game had barely started when Birchenall brought down Best, a clear indication that the Irishman was the main danger and he would be stopped at all costs, but moments later, the United No. 7 eluded Harris and Thompson and, as Bonetti dived, the ball hit the 'keeper's body. Another early effort was just a little too high.

But like his teammates, Best slowly faded from the forefront of the action, and all the match reports were in agreement that United slipped languidly, showing exhaustion in both mind and body as the game progressed.

Following those early threats from Best, Chelsea soon recovered and stunned the packed Old Trafford by taking the lead in the eighth minute. Webb pounced on Burns and robbed him of the ball. He then beat Kidd, before finding Cooke who, gathering the ball almost on the centre line and moving forward, sent over an inviting cross as two red shirts closed in. Tambling, lying in wait, steered the ball past Stepney and in off the post.

Six minutes later, further disaster struck United, as Stepney sustained a thigh injury jumping for a high ball along with Baldwin and Stiles. By the end of the game, he was really struggling, hobbling practically on one leg, with the injured thigh heavily strapped.

On the half-hour Osgood scythed down Burns, but brought little more than a few words in his direction from the referee, with this moment of apparent leniency not going unnoticed by the visitors, who began to take their tackles and challenges to the very limit.

Eight minutes after the interval, United equalised with something of a sloppy goal. Ryan crossed from the right and the ball bounced towards Kidd who bundled it rather awkwardly past Bonetti. The goal did little to inspire the rather lacklustre United side, despite the Stretford End bursting into their own version of Manfred Mann's 'Mighty Quinn', with 'You ain't seen nothing 'til United win'. On the hour, as petty yet sometimes cynical fouls blighted the game, they allowed the visitors back into the game when Webb sent Baldwin scurrying down the wing, scoring with a superb effort from the edge of the area, as the United defence chased back while appealing for offside.

United should have been level again within four minutes, as Baldwin tripped Burns inside the area and the referee was left with no choice but to point to the penalty spot. Best, however, blasted the ball high over the bar. It was a miss that they were to pay dearly for, as eleven minutes from time Chelsea, in something of a rare breakaway, scored a third through Osgood, as Stepney struggled in an attempt to get across goal and reach the ball. Had he been fully fit then there is little doubt that he would have saved it.

The defeat, although putting a minor dent in United's title challenge, did not knock them off the top. They still held that three-point lead over Leeds, as the Yorkshire side didn't play. City moved within four points and, like Leeds United, had the advantage of a game in hand over United.

Despite his contribution in the goals against Gornik and Chelsea, Jimmy Ryan could do little to cement a place in first team, with the likes of George Best and John Aston maintaining the type of form that made it difficult for Matt Busby to leave them out of his starting XI. So how difficult did the stand-in find life at Old Trafford at this particular time, and did it affect his confidence in his own ability?

'Probably. Not getting a run in the team, or each time I went into the team, or I was on the bench, or came on for some periods, you were still feeling that you were trying to prove something. That makes it a little bit more difficult to really come out and play really well.'

As well as the worry over the loss of form against Chelsea, which he hoped was simply a blip, and something to be expected along the way, Matt Busby had the added worry of Denis Law's injury problems. Having missed the defeat by Chelsea and the victories over Gornik and Arsenal, Law was now ruled out of the trip to Poland.

United's sojourns to foreign fields have, from time to time, been anything but straightforward, with Matt Busby's first overseas trip as manager of Manchester United fraught with problems from start to finish, and this must have cast a doubt in the minds of the United directors as to whether anything similar in the future would be worth the trouble.

The match against a BAOR Combined Services side in Hamburg in March 1946 had seen the plans for the United party to fly from Manchester's Ringway airport two days prior to the game cancelled at the last minute, because the plane they were due to travel on had not been through its planned overhaul. The departure was then scheduled for twenty-four hours later.

They eventually took off the following day but, as fate would have it, their Tuesday flight encountered problems, being forced to land at Celle, around 70 miles from Hamburg, due to poor flying conditions. The two motor lorries which had been arranged to take them to their intended destination then broke down, forcing the United players and directors to spend the night at a local RAF station at Celle.

Wednesday morning saw alternative transport arrangements made – an RAF 3-ton lorry – and it was a rather tired and fed-up United team that arrived in Hamburg a mere two hours prior to the intended kick-off time. On their arrival, they were then informed that they would have to make their return journey to England by rail and sea, as no planes were available as had been originally agreed.

It is little wonder then that Matt Busby's team failed to get the better of their Rhine Army opponents in a rather uninspired match, which was played before a crowd of around 25,000 servicemen inside the stadium and a considerable number of interested Germans who claimed various vantage points overlooking the ground.

As the events on the field progressed, high-ranking army officers tried unsuccessfully to charter a special plane to take the United players and officials back to England. As it was, they had to travel to Baddenhaussen by road and then catch a train for Calais, using a special-duty train normally reserved for brigadiers and colonels.

Matt Busby told Tom Jackson of the *Manchester Evening News*, 'I spoke to a major-general after the game and told him that plans for our flight back to England had broken down. He was very concerned and said he would get in touch with Rhine Army Headquarters and try to arrange a Stirling Bomber to take us back. However, he was not able to do this and we must return by the longer route.

'League clubs have fixtures to fulfil at home and it is very unfair and very unsatisfactory that we shall get back only a few hours before we are due at Bradford on Saturday.'

The United manager did add, however, that the Army arrangements for the visit were very good, but an unfortunate series of events had marred the trip.

Due to the change in arrangements, there was indeed every possibility that the United party would not manage to reach Bradford in time for their Saturday afternoon fixture, and the Football League were duly informed, with secretary Fred Howarth saying, 'The responsibility so far as we are concerned rests with Manchester United. If the match is postponed, then United will have to pay compensation to Bradford. Clubs will probably think twice about going to play matches on the Continent if they meet difficulties like this.'

Luck was finally on United's side, as they arrived at London's Victoria station on Friday afternoon after a long sea trip. The party was then rushed across the city in special transport to Euston, where they caught the 1 p.m. train to Manchester, arriving back at the familiar London Road station around 6 p.m., with thoughts of their own comfortable beds more to the fore than ninety minutes against Bradford a few hours later.

A club tour of the United States in the close season of 1952 produced a friendly against Mexican side Atlas in Los Angeles, with the 2-0 victory throwing up unruly scenes, as play was held up for fifteen minutes, with the referee being attacked by spectators, and a similar incident at full-time which simmered on the edge of a riot.

The trip to Bilbao and a far-from-sunny Spain for the European Cup tie of January 1957 saw the United players assist in the sweeping of snow from the wings before the flight home, while May 1958 brought the week-long journey to Milan and back.

Then there was Munich.

Poland in March 1968 also had its problems as the United party made the journey to the industrial sprawl of Katowice in two stages, flying to the snow-covered Krakow airport two days prior to the game and then setting off over treacherous conditions for the final 50 miles by coach, where the over-night temperature was a sub-zero -6 degrees.

'This is what I was dreading,' said Matt Busby, as he watched the snow sweeping past his hotel window. 'The conditions were similar when I came here to watch Gornik play a friendly match a few weeks ago. There was a hard crust of snow on top of the pitch.'

The weather may have been dreadful and cold, but there was certainly warmth in the hearts of the locals, who gave United a tremendous welcome, with hundreds of supporters awaiting the team's arrival at their hotel, and their appearance creating scenes resembling something accorded to popstars.

Busby was fearful for the conditions at the stadium on the night of the game and told the press corps who had made the journey with his team that he would examine the playing surface carefully when he took his players training on the eve of the tie: 'If the conditions are bad, I shall make representations to the referee, Mr Lo Bello. This match is far too important a game for United and, for once, we are not up against time. We have come here to play football and after the great first match at Old Trafford it would be sad indeed if the return were reduced to a travesty of football. However, we must wait to see what the conditions are like on Wednesday although with things as they are at the moment I would expect the referee to be here tomorrow.'

Twenty-four hours prior to the game, considered United's most important of the season to date, there was a 3-inch covering of snow on the Chozow Stadium pitch, and as his players trained warily, Busby was a shade happier than he had been the previous day. 'If they leave the carpet of snow and there is no more to come, the pitch will be playable,' he admitted to reporters. 'But even a severe frost overnight could make some of the ruts rather dangerous.'

The Gornik officials were well aware of United's concerns and their visitors' suggestions that they would seek a postponement if the playing conditions were not to their liking, but their president Frantiz Gladyck made it quite clear that no matter how strongly United protested about the pitch, the match would be played. He did, however, admit that the pitch was indeed dangerous, but said, 'We shall put salt on the pitch and sweep away the snow and it will be perfectly playable. We admit it will not be perfect even when we have tidied it up. Conditions will be more difficult than normal but Silesian teams are used to playing on pitches like this at this time of year.'

Gornik club secretary Adolf Kaminski added, 'The snow is soft and powdery and there is no ice coating underneath. The ground will not be as soft as under normal conditions, but we are doing everything to keep it in as good trim as possible.'

Busby still had his doubts: 'If the pitch is not good tomorrow (*the day of the game*), it will probably not be much better on Thursday. We are willing to come to Silesia again next Monday, or if conditions are still bad, next week, or whenever appropriate.'

In the exposed stadium, the United manager had watched his players go through their paces as best they could. They were able to turn on the pitch, which was still covered in 3 inches of snow, but he was still not entirely happy about gambling his team's European future on a lottery of a pitch, and despite what the Gornik secretary said, Busby told the reporters that there were patches of ice beneath the snow, making the conditions dangerous: 'Players could so easily break their legs. If the snow is removed the match cannot be played. I hope it does not freeze again, for then the ruts we made in training will certainly make the pitch unplayable.' Surely they were all accidental!

Despite the conditions, the United players maintained an excellent team spirit and, well aware of what they were travelling to, they came prepared. Roommates Alex Stepney and Pat Crerand had left room in their luggage to bring a kettle, an electric ring, tea, dried milk and cans of soup, with Crerand admitting, 'At times, it was like Sam's café in our bedroom. Most of us are great tea drinkers and you cannot get a good cuppa in these Continental countries. So we make our own.

'We had a brew-up after every meal, and there was always a can of minestrone if anyone fancied it. Alex and I took turns at being chef.'

If the United players and officials thought that they had it tough, what about the supporters?

Travelling abroad to watch United in the sixties was a far cry from what it is today, when an away fixture in Europe will see around 3,000 or so head off to a destination on the Continent to cheer on their favourites. Holidays are saved and overtime worked to ensure a place on the plane.

But when it was the likes of Best, Law and Charlton who fired the imagination, European holidays were only for a select few, never mind trips abroad to watch a football team. However, there was one individual who must be considered a pacesetter for the modern-day Red Army footsoldiers: John Camm.

John, born and bred in Nottingham but supporting Derby County from the age of four, can recall watching the likes of Peter Doherty and Raich Carter. He was a goalkeeper for Notts County, playing in the FA Youth Cup in 1955 at the same time as Bobby Charlton was making a name for himself in the same competition. Fate and personal circumstances resulted in John moving to the Manchester area and becoming an honorary Mancunian. He made his first visit to Old Trafford in September 1959 and very soon he became an enthusiastic red, following United around the country, enjoying the weekly diet of domestic fixtures. But suddenly, a taste of adventure and excitement overtook trips to the likes of Highbury, Bloomfield Road and Anfield, and he packed a bag and headed for foreign shores.

The temptation to visit Strasbourg in 1965 for the grand sum of nineteen guineas, and Lisbon to watch the rout of Benfica a year later whetted the appetite, so with United once again chasing the elusive European crown in season 1967/68, John and his faithful travelling companion Arthur Littlemore (who he had met on the trip to Strasbourg) had the passports at the ready.

John and Arthur vowed to attend every game that season, but Arthur was prevented from going to the sunshine island of Malta for the first-round game against Hibernians due to his daughter's wedding the following Saturday – some wifely threats have to be taken seriously. John visited Malta for the game as an independent traveller where he met and made many friends on the island with whom he remains on friendly terms forty-five years later.

The next-round draw was against Sarajevo, but a commercial trip was not possible, nor was an independent trip, being completely ruled out due to political and geographical problems.

The draw for the following round conjured up a trip to the Polish city of Katowice to face Gornik Zabrze, and initially it looked as though it was another away leg that would have to be missed.

'We heard nothing from our usual travel agency, Mancunia Travel, so I phoned the boss, Gerry MacDonald, who told me that problems had arisen and it was most unlikely that a trip could be arranged,' explained John. 'The nearest airport was in Krakow but this was not equipped to receive international and commercial flights and the Polish authorities insisted on the proposed flight being made to Warsaw and then we were expected to transfer to one of their own planes for the transfer to Krakow.'

'Gerry told me that the price for such a trip was about treble what he would expect so he made further enquiries. He found a loophole which permitted an individual person to charter a plane (as opposed to a commercial entity) and fly directly into Krakow. He made the application in his own name but the authorities rumbled his plan. My phone call arrived at just at the time he was considering his next move, so the obvious outcome was for me to volunteer to charter the plane in my name.'

Filling a coach to an away match in the Midlands was one thing, but a plane to freezing Eastern Europe was something else. But slowly the seats for the 33gns flight, two nights' accommodation and a ticket began to fill; thanks partly to around a dozen Polish immigrants in Manchester taking the opportunity to visit their homeland. Finally, the capacity of 118 seats was filled.

On the morning of the outward leg of the journey into the unknown, fog in Luton caused a delay to the flight, but 118 hungry passengers were compensated by a 'free' three-course lunch in the Lancaster Restaurant, and the 11 a.m. flight eventually took off at 2 p.m.

John had decided to supplement the cost of his trip by taking a holdall full of United souvenirs, badges, pennants and the like, which he intended to sell on the plane. This would also fund any additional expense once in Poland as currency regulations only permitted each passenger to take £15 sterling out of the UK. By the time he reached his destination, he had more than £100 in his pocket. Some passengers used more conventional methods by concealing an extra £10 in each sock.

It was after 5 p.m. by the time the pilot told us we were approaching Krakow and we were apprehensive as we knew the weather was bad with heavy snow during the previous days. We were told to expect very cold and well below-zero temperatures, so we were well prepared with undergarments and top garments. It was in our minds that we were going behind the mysteriously named Iron Curtain, and we had been warned by Polish friends to expect some restriction of movement, how little we knew in our innocence.

It was a strange sight as we landed, snow-covered everything and in the plane's lights we could see snow falling horizontally so the wind was strong. On neither side of the plane could we see buildings or lights and the apprehension brought out nervous jokes indicating that the pilot had landed in a field. When we had taxied for at least fifteen minutes, it was suggested that we were doing the last 100 miles by road.

After another five minutes, we heard voices at the front of the plane telling those of us at the back that a light had been seen and sure enough the plane came to a stop about twenty-five minutes after landing. All we could see was snow on one side, snow on the other side with a single-storey building on the left side. How the pilot found the landing strip was a tribute to his skills and radar.

Arthur and I were right at the rear of the plane, but when the door at the front-left side was opened, we felt the cold immediately. By the time we reached the door we were cold and when we emerged the cold air took our breath away. Rushing down the steps we found a path had been created in the snow to the building door, through which we entered expecting the interior to be warm. Not so, the building's roof shape confirmed that we were in nothing more than a Nissan hut type of outbuilding with few lights, but we could see more lights at the far end with some semblance of humanity.

After about ten minutes, two large doors opened; the cold-air rush was followed by a tractor pulling open trailers upon which were our snow-covered bags and suitcases. The driver jumped down and literally threw or pushed our bags onto the concrete floor and we had to find our own before joining the queue for immigration. Arthur and I were right near the end of the queue, which stretched for some distance, to what appeared to be a couple of desks and a roped entrance. We could see two immigration officers who began to see one individual at each desk and progress was slow. Someone came from the front end of the queue and told us that each clearance was taking five minutes, so a quick calculation suggested we could be in for a two-hour wait.

After about ten minutes, we were sitting on our suitcases, still at the chilly end of the Nissan hut, when I heard my name being called from the front of the queue. I stood up and saw Gerry MacDonald our travel agent and leader calling and waving for me to go forward and 'bring your bags'. I had a suitcase plus the large holdall containing the residue of my Manchester United badges, rosettes and pennants.

So I wandered forward and Arthur came with me at my suggestion. My only thought was that as the flight was registered in my name, my presence was required, after all I had been in the country less than half an hour so there had been no time to commit a misdemeanour, let alone a felony.

What happened next was like something out of a television programme.

Approaching passport control, John was told that his presence was required by the chief of police, and he and Arthur were escorted to his office, where they were met by an officer in full uniform with an impressive array of medal ribbons. With no idea what to expect, John and Arthur, who had tagged along more in support of his friend than anything else, were welcomed with a salute and a firm handshake and perhaps even more surprisingly a glass of first-class brandy.

'If that wasn't enough to stun us,' recalled John, 'we were even more so when our host spoke for the first time – "You have ze souvenirs of Bobbeee Charlton?" His eyes gazed fondly at my holdall and it began to seep through my frozen brain cells that he wanted some of my stuff. I gave him three enamel lapel badges bearing the faces of Bobby Charlton, George Best and Denis Law and his face lit up like a beacon and I almost saw a tear in his eye. The man was ecstatic and his dignity diminished as he returned to his schoolboy world.

'I gave him a Manchester United rosette with a cheap cardboard imitation of the European Cup in the centre and he received these items into his cupped hands as though he was taking Communion. He marched across to a door, had opened it to reveal a full-length mirror on the inside, in front of which he stood proudly as he affixed the badges and the rosette on the right side of his tunic, incongruous compared with the rows of medal ribbons on the left side.

'More brandy followed, as did a plate of sandwiches, but at a price. "I hav also zee son who likes Bobbee Charlton. I hav also zee brother who likes Bobbee Charlton," uttered the chief of police, so it was back to the holdall.

'I worked it out later and based on my wholesale prices, items worth about £2 were gifted to the chief of police,' said John, 'but I would most probably have given him the rest of the holdall's contents had he asked.'

Just as John and Arthur decided it was about time to leave and get back to the rest of the party, who would no doubt by now be wondering what salt mine they were heading for, the chief of police picked up his 'phone and, after shouting some instructions down the line, a 'large female officer, with immense thighs of which Duncan Edwards would have been proud' appeared and escorted John and Arthur outside to a waiting large, black Mercedes car which had flags and emblems on all four corners and on the roof. She proceeded to drive them to their hotel, where she left them in the hands of the hotel manager, obviously passing on her chief's instructions to him. 'As a result, the manager escorted us to an upgraded suite on the highest floor and he even carried our suitcases right to the room', thus bringing to an end an unbelievable episode.

Gornik had resumed their domestic season with an emphatic 6-0 victory over Odra Opule on a heavy, muddy pitch, maintaining third place in their League, and welcoming outside-right Wilczek back to something like his best form, which had been so obviously missing during the first leg in Manchester. United, on the other hand, still had a doubt hanging over Alex Stepney, who was continuing to feel the effects of his knee injury, along with David Sadler, who had an ankle knock. However, as kick-off approached, Busby decided to gamble with both, while springing something of a surprise by recalling David Herd and playing him on the left of a juggled forward line.

Despite being exposed to the freezing cold, the 100,000-seated Slaski Stadium, on the outskirts of the Katowice, was full to capacity, many having been inside at least an hour prior to kick-off. Having braved the weather, they were treated to an excellent ninety minutes of football, played in atrocious conditions, making their presence felt with a cacophony of horns, with fireworks exploding round the pitch adding to the earsplitting backing track.

The game began amid a raging blizzard, and the already snow-covered pitch took on an extra blanket, with the red lines being obliterated within minutes of the kick-off. Had the snow continued, then even the most partisan Pole would have had no complaint if the referee had called the proceedings to a halt.

As early as the first minute, with the United players still finding their feet, Gornik almost took the lead. Lentner found himself with a clear run down the left, but his cross into the United area was cut out by Sadler, immediately justifying his manager's decision to include him. Moments later, Latocha sent Musialek away, but with the goal almost at his mercy, he hurried his shot which went wide. The threat of the rejuvenated Wilczek came to nothing, as Fitzpatrick, his flowing locks treated as some form of amusement amongst the Poles, reduced his involvement in the game with an early challenge that left the Polish international limping. It was an incident that had fatal consequences for the Gornik player's mother, who collapsed and died as she watched the incident on television.

The visitors continued to find it hard to adapt to the conditions underfoot, and a miscalculation by Stepney almost cost a goal. The United 'keeper attempted to roll the ball out to a teammate, rather than kick it aimlessly upfield, and was horrified to see it stick in the snow, allowing Lentner to pounce, but again the opportunity was scorned with a shot wide of the goal.

Gornik attempted something of a long-range bombardment of the United goal, but with the visitors rigidly adhering to their 4-4-2 formation, the route to goal was more often than not blocked. A foot injury to Dunne caused some concern, but even with it heavily strapped, his play was still efficient and determined.

The snow of the opening half had drifted away after the interval as United began to find their feet better, gaining in confidence, with Best coming close with a rising shot. Seven minutes after the break, Crerand opened up the Gornik defence with a beautifully directed cross-field pass to Herd who, rising above the Polish defence, headed the ball towards goal. Kostka fumbled the initial save, but managed to recover quickly enough to save at the feet of Best.

With twenty minutes remaining, the game suddenly changed. Having gathered the ball following another failed Gornik attack, Stepney was penalised for either carrying the ball too many steps, holding on to it for too long, or for a nudge on a Gornik forward. In any case, it was a free-kick to the home side, almost on the penalty spot. From the kick, with almost the whole United side strung along the goal line, Kuchta drove the ball forward. Blocked by the red wall, it rebounded to the right and was recovered by Kuchta, who lofted it towards the opposite side, where it was flicked on to Lubanski who shot past Stepney.

From something of a relaxed, comfortable feeling on the United bench, there was now an air of tension, but as the minutes continued to tick away, the United defence stood shoulder to shoulder with a 'they-will-not-pass' motto, happy to clear the ball wherever and ensure that the one-goal advantage from the first leg remained in their favour.

They were now, yet again, one step away – or to be more exact, 180 minutes away – from the European Cup final: the pinnacle of Manchester United's footballing aspirations, where only victory would suffice.

'A marvellous performance,' exclaimed Busby. 'One of Manchester United's greatest nights. We came here to do a job, to contain them, and we did that job really well, although the conditions were all against us. Surely after that, we deserve to get to the final at least.

'We defended magnificently; especially the younger players. Take Francis Burns for instance. Several times he had the ball and I found myself on the edge of my seat saying "Kick it, son, kick it."

'But no, Francis showed the coolness and assurance of a man who had been playing in such an atmosphere all his life and kept proving me wrong by calmly playing it away down the line with comfort.'

Busby's opposite number, Dr Kalocsai, was not overenthusiastic in his praise for the victors, complaining that 'Manchester refused to do anything but defend'. But one of his defenders, Oslizlo, was more appreciative, saying, 'We hope Manchester win the European Cup. It would be nice to think we were put out by the Champions.'

In the restaurant of the Hotel Katowice, long after the final whistle, the United party, along with the travelling journalists who had endured an equally memorable evening perched high above the action on a wind-whipped tower of a press stand accompanied by the swirling snow, enjoyed a few drinks with choruses of song for entertainment.

'I Belong to Glasgow', although geographically a few miles out, was a salute to the Orbiston-born Matt Busby. But amongst the celebrations, there were certain worries and fears surrounding the two semi-final ties.

'I hope it doesn't turn out the way it did after Benfica,' shuddered Nobby Stiles, back to his best following weeks out with injury. 'It was all champagne toasts and singing that night in Lisbon, but we were banged out by Partizan in the semi. What a let-down that was. I couldn't stand another one like that.'

At another table Bobby Charlton spoke of the importance of playing in the European Cup and the pressure involved: 'Each time we have to play one of these ties it is in our minds for weeks. We go to sleep thinking about it and wake up thinking about it. A lot of people in the game talk about treating each match as the same. It's a nice idea but how could it apply in this case? We want to win anything we can but nobody has to ask what we want to win the most.'

In his *Sunday Times* column, Hugh McIlvanny wrote, 'All the evidence indicates that from now on very few goals will get past Manchester United's defence in the European Cup. We all know what their attack can do and there must be real hope that they are about to land the big prize at last.'

For John Camm and company, if their outward journey, or at least the final part of it, had been eventful, then the return trip to Manchester also had its moments, as due to problems with currency and fuelling the plane, the chartered flight had to touch down at Vienna and Amsterdam before landing at Manchester six hours later.

United, as McIlvanny suggested, might not concede many more European Cup goals, but the respected Scottish journalist mentioned nothing as regards the battle for supremacy in the First Division of the Football League, in which, three days after the success in Poland, United travelled to Highfield Road, Coventry, where they conceded two without reply.

Having boosted their ranks with transfer-deadline signings in Chris Cattlin and Ernie Hunt for a combined fee of £135,000, Coventry took United apart following their week in the frozen waste of Silesia. It was a defeat that saw them knocked off their long-held top spot, albeit on goal average, overtaken by neighbours City, who that same afternoon gave hapless Fulham a 5-1 hiding.

Twelve days prior to this encounter, the first at Highfield Road in the League since a Second Division fixture in 1937, fire swept through the main stand, forcing the installation of temporary seating for supporters, directors and press alike. But on the pitch there was nothing makeshift in the performance of former United captain Noel Cantwell's team.

Inspired by another ex-red, Maurice Setters, determined to put one over his former teammates, Coventry, struggling for their First Division survival, took the lead in the thirty-second minute, with a 25-yard drive from Machin finishing off a criss-cross movement by Carr and Hunt.

United did not appear unduly troubled by the setback, but eight minutes into the second half, when Setters headed a Hannigan centre past Stepney, they at last seemed to awake from their slumbers.

Aston replaced Kidd just after the hour and had a shot palmed away by Glazier. Herd hit the post, and with three minutes remaining Brennan hit the bar. Despite Glazier being on his knees as Herd latched on to the rebound, he somehow managing to punch the ball away. In between it all Charlton could only look at the referee in amazement when he failed to award a penalty after being upended by Machin.

Thus the leadership was lost.

United had been the first to qualify for the semi-finals of the European Cup and were joined twenty-four hours later by Benfica, who overcame Vasas Budapest with relative ease. It wasn't until 20 March that the other two semi-finalists were known, Juventus requiring a play-off before squeezing through with a solitary goal victory against Eintracht Brunswick, and Real Madrid going through with a 4-2 aggregate win against Sparta Prague.

Four days after the disappointing defeat at the hands of Coventry, Busby was in Prague, taking in the Sparta – Madrid match, mainly out of curiosity, while also making mental notes should his team draw the winners of that particular tie. The following morning it was off to the city's Park Hotel where the draw for the semi-final of the European Cup would take place. At twelve minutes past twelve, in the conference hall of the imposing hotel, the red phials containing first the name of

Manchester United and then that of Real Madrid were drawn from a champagne ice bucket. Busby's ninety minutes in the Prague stadium had not been wasted.

Following the draw, Matt Busby looked across the packed hall, picking out the familiar figure of Antonio Calderon, the Madrid manager, and they moved slowly across the room, meeting in the middle, where the old friends greeted each other with unabashed hugs.

What then, were the United manager's thoughts on the draw? 'As it happens this trip has been a good thing because it's also given us the opportunity of watching Real away from home. The draw came out very well for us. We were the last team into the bucket and the first team out.

'I would have preferred to play Real in the final at Wembley but I am not complaining.'

Calderon was equally pleased: 'This match will capture the imagination of all Spain. We shall charge 350 pesetas and sell out the stadium.'

It was difficult to contemplate what made the Spaniard happier, the thought of playing United, or the fact that his club would make a considerable amount of money from their second-leg tie, as the proposed ticket price was the equivalent of around £2 2/- (£2.10p) in British money and half a week's wages for many Spaniards!

Negotiating the dates for the semi-final in Calderon's hotel bedroom was far from straightforward, although the first-leg date of 24 April was agreed within thirty seconds. The date for the second leg was the one that created a problem and it was to take more than an hour to come to a compromise. Room No. 222 was abandoned for the hotel bar and Andres Ramirez of the Spanish FA, Denis Follows of the English FA and UEFA representative Hans Bangerter were all called into the discussions. Finally, over a few glasses of beer the date of 15 May was agreed. Should a third game be necessary to decide the winner, then it would take place in Lisbon on 17 May.

With countless United supporters contemplating travelling to Madrid, a play-off did not bear thinking about, as it would prove extremely costly and nigh impossible to get back from Madrid to Manchester and then out to Portugal for the replay.

Whether it was the euphoria of reaching the European Cup semi-finals or the thought of coming face-to-face with old adversaries Real Madrid, the rather dismal League form of late, a mere two points from the last eight, was shoved to one side and Nottingham Forest were comprehensively beaten 3-0 at Old Trafford. Forest were not short of opportunities, and had Stepney's instinctive reaction to Baker's goal-bound effort in the eighth not diverted the ball against the crossbar, then the outcome might have been entirely different.

It was in midfield where United won the game, with Fitzpatrick and Stiles in excellent form, and the former fitted into the side superbly, turning up wherever the action occurred. But it was Stiles who rather inadvertently created the opening goal in the fifteenth minute. Scheming his way into the Forest penalty area, his attempt to score from Charlton's pass saw the ball hit a defender's leg, but it was to break to David Herd who marked his first game at Old Trafford in over a year with a goal.

Shay Brennan scored a rare goal in the twenty-ninth minute for United's second, while another unfamiliar name to be found on the score-sheet, Francis Burns, added a third with twenty-one minutes remaining, sewing up the game in United's favour.

The result kept United in second place, but it was now Leeds United ahead of them – although only on goal average and having played a game more – following their 2-0 Elland Road victory over Manchester City, who were now two points behind, making the Manchester 'derby' four days later of major importance to the title aspirations of both clubs.

With six of their last ten League fixtures at Old Trafford, the ball was very much in United's court. City had the opposite, with half a dozen of their final ten fixtures away from home. Leeds, who were perhaps the most consistent of the trio, had taken eighteen points since Christmas, whereas City had taken fifteen and United thirteen, but the Yorkshire side had the added distractions of the FA Cup and Inter-Cities Fairs Cup ties to contend with.

Matt Busby considered the 'derby' was indeed a 'four-pointer' and still considered that his team were capable of lifting the title despite the recent setbacks.

'Of course our defeat at Coventry was food in the mouths of the dismal jimmies. The fact that we have lost two League matches immediately following European Cup clashes with Gornik suggest the old bogy ... too much on the plate.

'This theory, however, refers to physical strain and I am not prepared to accept that as the reason in our case.

'Our failure against Chelsea and Coventry was, I believe, a mental reaction after two tense and difficult cup clashes with the Polish team.

'Unless you have been a professional player I couldn't blame you for not understanding the failure to turn on top-class performances week after week.

'The argument is that there is incentive in money, medals and honour for which no effort should be spared.'

So, Manchester City made the short journey across town on the evening of 27 March for the most decisive 'derby' fixture in five years, when that vital point in the 1-1 draw at Maine Road more or less sent City tumbling down into the Second Division. This time around, the fortunes of both clubs had changed dramatically and it was now the threat of missing out on the championship that haunted the losers.

As the supporters made their way to the ground, the red-and-white factions were loud and brash, high in their expectations, while the light-blue neighbours were in a more subdued mood, scarves tucked out of view. Even in the ground they were a mere whisper compared to the ear-splitting noise bellowing from the Stretford End and United Road.

Missing from the United line-up was Brian Kidd, who had been given a fourteen-day suspension for his sending-off against Tottenham in the FA Cup, and as well as missing the crucial ninety minutes against City, he would have to watch the forthcoming fixtures against Liverpool and Stoke from a seat in the stand.

Many were still either clambering up the stairs towards their chosen advantage point, or were still outside, pushing and shoving their way to the already overworked turnstiles, when the evening air was abruptly broken by an explosion of noise, as United took the lead after only thirty-five seconds. Fitzpatrick played a throw-in square to Stiles, who sent a rather innocuous ball forward towards the City penalty area. Book hesitated momentarily, allowing Best the seconds he required to slip round him before flashing the ball past Mulhearn from just inside the penalty area.

Although shaken by this early setback, City did not shrink from their task, and within seventeen minutes they were back on level terms. Bell took a pass from Young, playing on the inexperience of Fitzpatrick, before driving the ball well wide of Stepney's right hand. Whether the Birkenhead shopkeeper, summoned over the loudspeakers to return to his premises as two of his employees were locked in, witnessed the goal is unknown, but the light-blue half of the city rejoiced.

Summerbee and Lee both shunned good scoring opportunities early in the second half, but they were soon forgotten when the visitors took the lead in the fifty-seventh minute. Fitzpatrick was again harassed by Bell and fouled the City player. From the free-kick Coleman floated the ball into the United area with fine precision and Heslop jumped to head home his first League goal with Stepney stranded on his line.

With City now in front, the tempo increased, as did the ferocity of the tackles. United took off the rather ineffective Herd and replaced him with Aston, hoping for more direct penetration of the light-blue defence from down the flank, but City stood firm. Their considered vulnerability in the air was rarely challenged, even by Law, who was back in the United line-up having missed the last three League outings through injury, although clearly lacking in match practice.

United looked nothing like potential Champions, despite the confident start to the game, as that early confidence disappeared by the minute, replaced by desperate lunges on one of the pretenders to the crown. As the minutes ticked away, so did United's hopes, and as Bell, with his left knee heavily bandaged from previous close encounters with United boots, attempted to go round Stepney, he was unceremoniously upended by Burns. The probable goal became a definite penalty.

From the spot-kick, Lee made no mistake and moments later the final whistle blew. City had leapfrogged their local rivals, albeit on goal average. The Manchester duo and Leeds United were now all on forty-five points and all had nine games remaining.

The ninety minutes were instantly forgotten by the red faction of Manchester, but one Yorkshireman, *Manchester Guardian* journalist Michael Parkinson, something of a closet red, was enthralled by the game, writing, 'Sometimes in sport that rare thing happens and a game is burned in the brain.

'Those of us who were present at Old Trafford on 27 March 1968 will not easily forget all that we saw. Those who tell you that football isn't the game it used to be, that the modern player in no way compares with the heroes of the past, should have been at Old Trafford to have their theories destroyed by plain and simple fact.

'Was there ever a more original genius than George Best? Could any players of the past have matched the strength and speed of Bell, the cunning and durability of Summerbee on this perfect evening? Which team could have come back against all the odds as City did and win so convincingly against a side which even when off colour is still a long way from being a pushover? Was there ever a game which stirred the spectators more than this?

'The answer to all those questions is probably yes, and if that is how you feel then all I can say is that I was there and you were not.

'It could easily have been so different. If the players had caught the hysteria so expertly stoked by the newspapers, the match would have needed coverage by a crime reporter and not a sports writer.'

Assessing the game, Parkinson thought that the early United goal looked to be too much for the visitors, but then 'City began to destroy the pattern and the rhythm of United's play. They looked sharper, fitter, altogether more determined. Doyle at wing-half began directing his forwards towards the United goal and Bell, driving from deep positions with awesome speed, started creating problems for the United defence which were never solved. In the end they were the better team, not slightly better, but overwhelmingly so.'

He completed his lengthy article with 'what is also undeniable is that at present, it is City and not United who are cock-of-the-walk, and the City supporters, a hitherto-despised minority, have a new pride and reputation.

'And for those who were present will never forget. It was simply more than a game.'

For the United support, it was indeed 'simply more than a game'. They had lost two points and given their greatest rivals not simply a boost in confidence, but also the impetus to make a serious assault on the championship itself. Losing the title was one thing, but losing it to City was something else altogether. So much so, that when George Best went to his boutique, he found the door draped in black crepe!

Stoke away was the next hurdle for Busby's confidence-hit side, but no sooner had the ninety minutes in the Potteries got underway than United were a goal in front. George Best lifted his teammates out of the doldrums with a goal that showed all his trademarks. Grasping at Crerand's pass, the Irishman headed towards the Stoke goal line and, just inside the 6-yard box, with Banks expecting the ball to be pulled back to an in-running teammate, Best suddenly spun it past the bemused goalkeeper from a seemingly impossible angle.

Although stunned by this early setback, Stoke were level within six minutes. Crerand and Sadler failed to clear a Bloor free-kick and Eastham was on hand to score his first goal of the season. They were, however, only on level terms for a further sixteen minutes, and Alan Gowling repaid his manager's faith in him with a goal on his League debut. The nineteen-year-old Economics student, who was still an amateur and had already claimed twenty-three Central League goals, snatched a half-chance after Banks had pushed a Charlton effort against the crossbar.

Stoke once again fought back, Dobin equalising eight minutes before half-time, but if they thought that they could perhaps capitalise on United's recent failures in the second half, then they were sadly mistaken. Had they harnessed the irrepressible Best then they might well have had a chance, but with twenty minutes remaining, the United No. 7 crossed from the left, and as Banks scrambled for the ball, Aston ran in to turn it into the net. Four minutes later he forced his way through the middle of the Stoke defence and, as Banks attempted to dive at his feet, the ball bounced out of his reach, allowing substitute Ryan to lob the ball into the empty net for United's fourth and the final goal of the afternoon. It was a victory that restored them to top spot with a two-point advantage over City and Leeds. They had, however, played that one game more.

Gowling was the third teenager to be introduced into United's League line-up this season, with Francis Burns and Brian Kidd making up the trio, and the line-up against Stoke City showed eight players who had come from the Jimmy Murphy school of hard knocks. Eight games remained: eight vital games with victory and failure balanced precariously on a knife edge. Those youngsters would have to grow up quickly, learn from their more-experienced teammates and remember the players in whose footsteps they were treading.

Despite three consecutive 1-1 draws at the end of December, Liverpool continued to sit on United's shoulder as 1967 blended into 1968, only three points behind on the same number of games. By 12 February, they had slipped to third following consecutive defeats against Everton and Chelsea, and had been overtaken by Leeds, with the further handicap of having played a game more than their Lancashire rivals.

By Saturday 6 April, when they made the short 30-odd mile trip along the East Lancs Road to Manchester 16, they had been nudged further down the pile to fourth, but were now only four points behind. However, due to their added interest in the FA Cup, they now had the advantage of two games in hand, and by the end of the afternoon looked more of a championship side than their tired-looking opponents.

Liverpool were more businesslike, more resolute and more composed, and although the Stretford End bellowed 'We are the Champions', it sounded somewhat less creditable in the wake of the recent defeats. Those defeats had showed United to be far from immune against setbacks and imperfection, and despite Best catching the Anfield defence cold in the second minute, the visitors, like Manchester City, clawed themselves back into the game, snatching a valuable victory which further dented United's championship aspirations.

More or less straight from the kick-off, Charlton obstructed St John, but Yeats made a complete hash of the free-kick, the ball barely rising off the ground and going straight to the feet of the offending Charlton. Quickly, he curled the ball out towards Best on the right and, despite Hughes looking to have the ball covered, was soon left lying on his back as the Irishman controlled the ball and sped for goal before hitting the ball firmly past Lawrence for his twentieth goal of the season.

Yeats was to redeem himself in the eleventh minute, rising to head a St John free-kick to the far post. As it rebounded back across the face of the United goal, Lawler attempted to score as Dunne and Sadler stood rooted to the spot, but missed, only for Yeats to lunge forward and stab the ball home.

A further seven minutes on, Liverpool were in front. Sadler over-hit the ball towards Crerand who, failing to control it, lost possession to St John, who in turn sent Hunt away. A one-two with Hateley caught the United defence flat-footed and Hunt had sufficient time to control the ball before placing it beyond the reach of Stepney.

With the wind behind them, United, despite now being behind, played some exciting football inspired by Crerand and Charlton, but were denied by the handling and, on occasion, the bravery of Lawrence in the visitors' goal.

The inexperience of Gowling shone through just before the break, when Best slid the ball forward to the nineteen-year-old just inside the area, but he did not have the guile of Law to beat the Liverpool 'keeper. It was on occasions such as these that the presence of the Aberdonian was sadly missed.

United missed several opportunities to snatch, at the very least, an equaliser; the most notable of those coming fifteen minutes from time, when Crerand chipped a free-kick over the defensive wall and Best shot on the run, but he was denied by Lawrence, who dived and held the ball at the post.

Liverpool, who were noisily barracked in the final ten minutes for time wasting, also had the opportunities to increase their advantage, but were more than content to see the game played out with no further scoring.

Across the Pennines, Leeds United had romped to a 3-0 victory in the Yorkshire 'derby' against Sheffield United, with the two points allowing them to leapfrog United into top spot on goal average, as well as having played a game less, while Manchester City had also slipped up, losing 1-0 at Leicester.

With three games spread over the four-day holiday period, Easter was always a crucial part of the footballing calendar, especially when it came down to the search for silverware. If your club was not one of those at the top end of the table, it was a period when the threat of relegation could either become more of a reality or completely subside.

Good Friday saw United travel to Craven Cottage, where they brushed aside both the disappointment of the defeat by Liverpool and a Fulham side who propped up the rest of the division, with a mere twenty-one points from their thirty-four games.

For those inside the quaint Thames side ground before kick-off, they were to witness what surely must be something of a record; one that will, I'm sure, stand the tests of time. For their fourth consecutive League fixture, not only did United take the lead within three minutes of kick-off, the scorer of all four goals was none other than George Best.

Against Manchester City on 27 March, it took the lad from the Cregagh estate in Belfast thirty-five seconds to get on the score-sheet, while three days later, it was eighty-five seconds further into the game before he got the better of the Stoke City defence. Against Liverpool, it was again two minutes after the first blast of the referee's whistle when Best breeched the opposition defence, and now, against Fulham, the Good Friday fixture was only seventy seconds old when he latched on to a loose ball, as Crerand's cross bounced away from the lackadaisical Fulham defence, to prod the ball past goalkeeper Macedo.

Fulham, more or less already relegated, surrendered a further two goals in the opening forty-five minutes, although they did give a better account of themselves than in the second half, when they looked in complete disarray yet conceded only one.

A rock-hard pitch and a swirling wind could be given as an excuse for United's failure with 'missing chances – enough to account for all their fingers and a few toes as well' according to Bryon Butler of the *Daily Telegraph*, who also considered United to have had 'a poorish game by their own standards', but no matter what, it was still two points.

Best added a second ten minutes from the interval, flicking the ball off the feet of Callaghan before turning and hitting a left-footed shot past the helpless 'keeper, while Kidd made it 3-0 five minutes later after Macedo dropped a Best corner invitingly at his feet only a couple of yards from goal.

Fulham stumbled along throughout the remainder of the game and somehow managed to concede only one other goal five minutes into the second half, through Law, who was far from being match fit. In playing him, Busby took something of a gamble. Charlton saw Macedo block two stinging efforts, while Best and Law put each other through for scoring opportunities, but neither accepted the chances.

The victory took United back to the top, the fifth time in a month that the leadership had changed, as Leeds lost 2-1 a few miles north at Tottenham's White Hart Lane, their first loss in twenty-seven games. Manchester City, however, kept up their title challenge with a hard-earned home win against Chelsea, courtesy of a solitary Mike Doyle goal. Liverpool, the other member of the quartet at the top, slipped up at home, losing 2-1 to a steadily improving Sheffield United.

They were still two points ahead of Leeds and City, although both title rivals still had that game in hand.

Injuries to Law and Stiles kept them out of the trip to Southampton the following day, with the Scot's knee injury giving the United management something of a continual headache, but even without the duo, United were expected to secure both points as their hosts' defensive qualities were considered equally as poor as Fulham's.

In front of the South Coast club's biggest gate of the season (30,079), however, United found themselves 2-0 down at half-time, Southampton taking full advantage of the rustiness and lack of match fitness in Bill Foulkes, playing his first senior game since 30 December, with goals from Paine in the thirteenth minute and Davies twenty minutes later. The latter's goal seemed to give United something of a jolt, and with Southampton feeling a little smug at taking a two-goal lead against the League leaders, they were caught out when a Burns free-kick was headed on by Sadler and, as the defence dithered, Charlton lunged at the ball to score.

With the seconds ticking away towards the interval, Best conjured something out of nothing, whipping a right-footed shot past Martin which went in off the post. It was a goal that made the half-time scoreline something of a parody of the play.

Having managed to pull themselves back into the game, it looked as if United had scented blood, and they immediately swung into action when the second half resumed. Martin made a brilliant one-handed stop from a Kidd header, while Sadler volleyed against the bar. At the opposite end, Davies hit the post, but that was as close as it got and there was to be no further scoring, with United content to be returning north with a point, their position at the top intact.

The third match of the Easter period saw Fulham arrive at Old Trafford, and with neither Leeds or City playing until twenty-four hours later, it was crucial that there was no slipping up against the Londoners.

Injury once again forced Busby's hand, and at such a crucial stage of the season these bumps and bruises were becoming something of a concern to the United manager. His latest casualty was goalkeeper Alex Stepney, throwing twenty-year-old reserve-team 'keeper Jimmy Rimmer into the fray for his League debut.

As the sun shone, the 60,465 crowd (the eleventh time that over 60,000 had clicked through the Old Trafford turnstiles), were somewhat subdued throughout the entirety of the ninety minutes, with many dismayed that United once again failed to take advantage of their opponents' poor form and reap a more substantial harvest than the scoreline showed. At Craven Cottage they should have doubled their four goals, and here they should have again been more cynical, often allowing their visitors to pass the ball around unabashed.

Eric Todd in the *Guardian* simply dismissed United's performance as 'adequate for the occasion', even with Law and Stiles back in action, writing that there was 'no fuss, no toughness. A match against opponents who had little to offer.'

Despite Fulham again having little to offer, United only scored thrice – Charlton in the eighth minute, Best on the half-hour and Aston five minutes from time – leaving the support slightly dismayed, as they knew full well that championships can be won or lost on goal average, something that seemed to be completely ignored by the players.

With five points from a possible six, United were firm favourites for the title, especially when twenty-four hours after their 3-0 win over Fulham neighbours City lost 1-0 to Chelsea. Leeds maintained their challenge with a 1-0 home win over Tottenham the following night, but many felt that their demanding schedule of League, FA Cup and Inter-Cities Fairs Cup fixtures would prove too much of a burden to carry and they would falter at some point.

The European Cup semi-final first leg against Real Madrid at Old Trafford was now firmly entrenched in the minds of all connected with United, forcing Matt Busby to make some serious decisions in relation to his team to face Sheffield United at Old Trafford four days prior to the visit of the Spaniards.

An injury to any of his 'main men' would certainly give the Spaniards an advantage, so leaving out George Best or Bobby Charlton was very much in Busby's thoughts, as was omitting Denis Law, whose appearances in recent weeks had been blighted by injury. On the other hand, however, anything other than a victory against the Yorkshire side could certainly cause problems in the retention of the First Division championship.

In addition to the above, there were also slight concerns about the fitness of Alex Stepney (damaged ribs), Francis Burns (sprained ankle), and Nobby Stiles (strained thigh), but in the end, Busby decided to risk everything on a victory over Sheffield United, making only three changes from the game against Fulham: replacing Jimmy Rimmer with Stepney, Nobby Stiles taking over from Sadler, and the versatile defender replacing Bill Foulkes. All the big guns remained in place.

Rather strangely though, the United players seemed happy to conserve as much energy as they could against a Sheffield side, who in recent weeks had shown some excellent form, but on this particular afternoon they scorned numerous opportunities, enough in fact to have won 5-1 at least.

Denis Law gave United a five-minute lead, and from that moment on, United were simply content to hold on to that slender advantage, often playing with eight defenders, but at times the action in front of Stepney left the crowd biting their nails and longing for the final whistle.

Woodward and Reece were the main culprits when it came to missed opportunities by the visitors, with Currie not too far behind on an afternoon that the *Sunday Express* journalist Richard Bott wrote that 'they couldn't have hit a barn door from handshaking distance'. Bott's report also brought some comfort to his United-supporting readers, confirming the Law was back to his best: 'a racing, rampaging warrior seeking to be at the heart of the action all the time.'

But like most of his teammates, he failed to make any impression upon the game in the second half, other than bringing the Stretford End to life as they emerged from the tunnel in a change of shirts – red, short sleeves, with a v-neck – producing chants of 'sexy'. However, as the game, which was anything but a turn-on, moved towards its final ten minutes, Busby made his way from his seat in the stand to the touchline bench, eager to enforce the importance of concentration upon his players as the Yorkshire side pushed forward in search of at least a point.

In Spain, Real Madrid had prepared for their trip to Manchester with a 2-1 victory over Las Palmas, a victory that ensured they retained the Spanish title, and if United sought for any crumb of an advantage it was in the suspension of Amancio, the leading scorer who had taken an eighth-minute hat-trick in his team's home leg against Sparta Prague. But a push to the chest of West German referee Rademacher saw him sent off and automatically banned from the first-leg tie.

Busby and his assistant Jimmy Murphy had watched Madrid in Prague and acknowledged that the Spaniards would be difficult to beat, having preferred to meet them in the final instead of over two legs, but Real were a far cry from the team of old, having rebuilt over the years. Gone were the likes of Di Stefano, Santamaria, Del Sol and Puskas, although Gento, the sole survivor from that first final and who had appeared in all eight, was still a formidable threat even at the age of thirty-four. Despite those magical names of old no longer appearing on the team sheet, United would still have their work cut out and it was widely considered that they would need at least a two-goal advantage to take to Spain for the second leg.

'United will need at least a two-goal lead to take to Madrid on 15 May,' wrote Donald Saunders in the *Daily Telegraph*, while Ronald Crowther in the *Daily Mail* told his readers that 'an international TV audience of 150 million, the biggest for any club game in Britain, will see Manchester United hell-bent for a three-goal lead over Real Madrid tonight.

'No score short of that would serve as a margin for the return game in Madrid. United, committed to the effort of a lifetime to fulfil Matt Busby's dream of European conquest, know that their place in the Wembley final depends on a supreme effort tonight.'

Busby himself was more than aware of what the ninety minutes meant, both to him as a person and to the club as a whole. 'After Munich I was very conscious of the fact that we had to keep our name as a club to the fore,' he said. 'We asked them (*Real Madrid*) to come to Old Trafford and play a friendly. They were such wonderful friends that they charged us less than 50 per cent of the price they could normally command for games all over the world. Our sense of mutual regard has continued ever since.

'This Old Trafford game could be a football epic. I only hope the tremendous tension does nothing to spoil it.'

The United manager, however, was a little concerned about his side's recent form, saying, 'During the last three or four League games we have not played as well as we should have. But so often we have come back when something big is at stake. I am sure that tomorrow night the team will give a display in keeping with Manchester United's tradition and reputation.'

Around Old Trafford, with a 63,200 crowd inside, there was the merest whisper of a breeze, with the setting sun conjuring up a glow across the Mancunian sky, as the backdrop of noise rose to a crescendo with the emergence of the two teams from the mouth of the tunnel.

The classic encounter that had been hoped for, but one that few had dared anticipate, failed to materialise, such was the tension surrounding the ninety minutes, coupled with the impressive and organised defensive display by the visitors, which saturated United's attacking brilliance.

The two-goal lead that most had recommended could have been achieved, with just a little good fortune, within the opening three minutes. Firstly, Best weaved his way through the Madrid defence, leaving Zoco and Pirri in his wake, before curling a tantalising centre across the face of the goal. Aston rose and headed the ball down towards the foot of the post, but Betancort was alert to the danger, diving across his line to push the ball round the post for a corner. From the resulting kick Law snatched at the ball on the byline, when the Spanish defenders thought it was going to run out of play, and from his pass Crerand struck the foot of the post with a superb effort from 20 yards out.

So Madrid breathed a sigh of relief, but remained under siege as United attempted to prise open the compact defence without much luck, although Best came close with a shot on the turn, while a Charlton special flew harmlessly over. But it was the visitors who had the best chance in those opening exchanges, when a Gento free-kick in the thirty-first minute found Grosso in front of goal, but he mistimed his effort and the ball was cleared. Other than that, Stepney was rarely called into action.

Ten minutes prior to the interval, United finally managed to break down the wall of white shirts. A long pass from Kidd found Aston, who broke down the left, stumbling momentarily before regaining his footing and beating Gonzales. Cutting the ball back from the byline in front of the swaying Scoreboard End, the winger crossed towards an unmarked Best, loitering around the penalty spot. Pulling back his left leg, he struck out at the oncoming ball and it exploded goalwards, past Betancort and into the net.

The second half, like periods of the first, was predictable. Sanghis kept closer to Best than countless blondes in a nightclub, while Pirri was seldom far from Law. Zunzunegui stifled any attempts by Kidd to get involved in the action. But despite such close attention, United continued to push and probe in an effort to gain further advantage.

Law controlled the ball with his chest, but could not get in that final shot, while a flick of his blonde hair had the 'keeper scurrying across goal, before Stiles blasted high over the bar. Amid those half-chances, the visitors almost snatched an equaliser when Sadler allowed Perez to get the better of him, but his blushes were spared by his alert teammates. Charlton toiled away in midfield, but the Spaniards had done their homework and as the game moved towards its conclusion, they were more than content in taking the one-goal deficit to Madrid for the second leg.

With nine minutes to go, they were almost caught out when Kidd squandered an opportunity that could have been seen as costly. The ball broke to him 15 yards from goal, but in the red-hot cauldron with the pressure surrounding the youngster, he slammed the ball widely over.

So, the two- or three-goal advantage that many had considered a necessary safety net to take to Spain failed to materialise. 'It's Not Enough Matt', proclaimed the heading above Peter Lorenzo's report in the *Sun*, while the *Daily Mail* carried 'United miss the two-goal target', with Brian James writing, 'Manchester United last night beat Real Madrid and 50 million at their TV sets know that justice was done. But today, as the glow of fine match dies, those 50 million must share United's dread that victory was merely a prelude for defeat.'

In the *Guardian*, Albert Barham penned, 'Can this slender lead – the same as they took to the Stadium of Light in Lisbon – be turned into another triumph as it was against Benfica? There can be no mistaking the apprehension which must lie over United until the second match in three weeks' time.'

Although having had a poor game by his standards, Pat Crerand was upbeat with regards to the outcome of the tie, saying, 'Real are not as good a side as Gornik. They certainly didn't play as well here as Gornik did.

'We are not the least despondent because at least we are one up and they know they have got to score in Madrid. That means they have got to come at us and it will leave us more room in attack. We are very confident.'

Despite the failure to conjure up more than the one goal, Matt Busby was happy with the result. 'The boys played well,' he said. 'I know we only scored one goal, when we would have liked two, but I thought we were the better side and we will prove it in Madrid.

'We didn't get the breaks even though we were always in the ascendancy.

'They will have to come and play on the attack in Spain. Tonight they came to contain us.'

Equally content was Miguel Munoz, the Madrid coach. 'The return in Madrid will be just as difficult, but I am happy with the result. With Amancio back we will create more offensive moods in the return leg.'

For now, Real Madrid could be forgotten about. There were still three First Division fixtures to be completed, and on the evening of Monday 29 April, United travelled to the Hawthorns to face West Bromwich Albion, as crucial a ninety minutes as any. Manchester City were also in action, at home to Everton, with the outcome of both fixtures having an impact on the League table.

Prior to kick-off, United stood in first place, with fifty-four points from their thirty-nine games and a goal average of 1.68. Leeds United were second, a point behind and with a goal average of 2.09, with City were third on fifty-two points and a goal average of 1.97.

Busby made only one change from the team that faced Madrid, bringing in Burns for Brennan, with Tony Dunne switching flanks, but against a side who had reached the FA Cup final only days before, with their manager Alan Ashman making three changes, even the inclusion of Brennan, giving United an extra-man advantage, was unlikely to make any difference to the outcome of such a compelling ninety minutes of football.

Over the ninety minutes, United created two chances for every one by Albion, but they were totally lethargic, both in defence and in attack, squandering countless opportunities while gifting the home side enough chances to win two or three games.

With only nine minutes gone, West Brom took the lead, a goal missed by many latecomers who were still squeezing through the turnstiles and then winding round the pitch side before finding places on the crowded terraces. Dunne made a complete hash of an attempted pass back to Stepney and Astle, evading a heavy challenge from Law, hooked the ball into the roof of the net.

Rather surprisingly, it was the thirty-eighth minute before the second goal materialised, again from a defensive error. Burns attempted to trap the ball, but missed it completely, allowing Rees to run through and beat Stepney.

Even 2-0 down, many expected United to recover and snatch a result, but when Law squandered two of the easiest scoring opportunities of his career – one, four minutes before the break, from a mere 2 yards out with not even the goalkeeper to beat – it began to look as though the writing was indeed on the wall. Law, in his disgust, walked some 20 yards away from the scene of the crime with his head held low.

Ten minutes into the second half, United were 3-0 behind. Stiles brought down Rees on the edge of the penalty area and the referee pointed to the spot amid furious protests from practically every

United player. Those protests were soon increased a few notches when Stepney saved Brown's spot-kick and the referee ordered it to be re-taken as a linesman, who had his flag raised even before the kick was taken, considered the 'keeper to be guilty of not remaining on his line. Brown made no mistake from his second attempt.

Then, just prior to the hour mark, Tony Dunne fouled Rees, forcing the Albion outside-right to leave the field and, from the resulting free-kick, Bobby Hope found Astle's head and the ball again flashed past a helpless Stepney.

Within sixty seconds United were awarded a penalty, when Fraser hacked down Kidd, and Law found it easier to score from 12 yards with a 'keeper in front of him than he had done previously; once again conjuring up belief in the hearts of the United support that something could be salvaged from the game despite Albion's three-goal advantage. There were hopes that the home side's cup semi-final and United's Saturday off might prove advantageous.

Such dreams and expectations were shattered in the seventieth minute when seventeen-year-old Asa Hartford, enjoying a huge amount of space courtesy of the spread-eagled United defence, scored his first goal in senior football. Even then the drama wasn't finished, nor was the generosity of the United defence, as five minutes later, Astle struck again, heading home a Lovett cross to make it 6-1.

Despite having seen their defensive colleagues disintegrate, the red-shirted forwards continued to push forward, and were rewarded with too-late goals from Kidd in the eightieth and eighty-second minutes.

With Manchester City beating Everton 2-0 at Maine Road, United had thrown their opportunity of securing their second consecutive championship to the wind. The defeat at the Hawthorns cracked the championship wide open as their blue cross-city rivals leapt into prime spot on goal average with two games remaining.

Leeds were still hanging on, one point fewer than their Lancastrian rivals, but with a game in hand. United had the advantage of having two home fixtures, against Newcastle United and Sunderland, while City had to travel to Tottenham Hotspur and Newcastle.

If the 6-3 defeat wasn't a big-enough blow to the Old Trafford faithful, the news that Denis Law was out for the rest of the season left them contemplating what those final few weeks of the season could conjure up. Law, whose mobility had been severely restricted during the past few weeks, had been suffering from a knee injury for some time, and it was inevitable that he would come under the surgeon's knife sooner rather than later. However, it had always been hoped that he could be patched up to survive until the end of the campaign, adding his presence, even in some minor part, to United's ongoing search for silverware.

A saddened Matt Busby said, 'He has tried to ride the injury. We thought it would get better in time, but it wasn't to be.

'I feel there's a bit of a shadow in the knee and that it will have to be opened up.

'It's a tremendous blow to our European Cup and championship hopes, but I am still quite confident.'

There was also a major scare over not simply the fitness of George Best, but of his well-being in general, as word spread through Manchester that the Irish genius had been killed in a car crash. Newspaper offices, police stations, telephone exchanges and hospitals were flooded with calls from people of all ages desperate to know if the rumours were indeed true.

Best himself was oblivious to those rumours as he sat chatting with his girlfriend of the moment – or should that read the hour – in one of his boutiques, with his white S-type Jaguar standing outside, only finding out when his girlfriend's father burst through the shop door, breaking down in tears when he saw the couple.

'Just some nut-case I suppose,' was the reply when asked who he thought was behind the rumour, and it was soon forgotten when it was announced that he had been named as the Footballer of the

Year, amassing some 60 per cent of the votes. Although still only twenty-one, the youngest player to receive the accolade, Best admitted that he could 'retire tomorrow and have no financial worries' for the rest of his life. 'Money doesn't have the same significance for me as it did. I have just paid £45 for a suede coat and I might never wear it again. My dad, a Belfast shipyard worker, would think I am bonkers. A pound is still a lot of money to him.'

Thankfully Best was fully fit, but there was some concern over the fitness of Nobby Stiles who, like Law, was encountering problems with his knee despite having a cartilage operation. The England man was left out of the side for the visit of Newcastle United in the penultimate fixture of the campaign. Also missing was Francis Burns, dropped, with Shay Brennan returning to the fold.

Having failed to secure the lead that was determined as essential against Real Madrid due to something of an indifferent performance, coupled by the total collapse in the Midlands against West Bromwich Albion, a victory over Newcastle United on 4 May was of utmost importance, not simply to maintain the championship challenge that had taken such a massive dent following the debacle at the Hawthorns, but to keep the overall team performance at a level that could quite possibly secure a favourable result in Madrid.

During the ninety minutes against a totally ineffective Newcastle side, there was arguably just as much excitement off the pitch as there was on it, with the majority of the near 60,000 crowd just as interested in the goings-on at Elland Road, where Leeds were up against Liverpool, and at White Hart Lane where Manchester City were the visitors.

United took ten minutes to gain the advantage, Crerand's throw-in finding Gowling, and the gangling forward sidestepping Clark before he chipped the ball into the Newcastle goalmouth. Kidd rose to head past McFaul, and then came the first hint of high drama.

With a quarter of an hour gone, news filtered through that Leeds United had taken the lead against Liverpool. Any nervousness around the Old Trafford terraces, however, was soon forgotten eight minutes later, when the newly crowned Footballer of the Year beat McFaul from outside the penalty area after Crerand had headed on a Charlton corner.

It was still all square at White Hart Lane when Best put United 3-0 in front, scoring from the penalty spot after Robson upended Kidd as he was about to shoot. Things were looking good down by the Salford docks, but something of a dampener was put on the proceedings five minutes before the interval when the news came through that Colin Bell had given City the lead. There were still forty-five minutes to go, so anything could happen.

Many were still finishing their half-time refreshments when they found out that Bell had made it 2-0 to City, and the evening took on a completely different atmosphere.

Best made it 4-0 in the fifty-fourth minute, again from the penalty spot, after he was knocked to the ground by Winstanley, and Brian Kidd claimed his second, again with a header, making it 5-0 on the hour mark. David Sadler made it six four minutes later, finishing off a Gowling – Charlton move.

It could well have been more, as Gowling missed three good opportunities, and despite claiming his first hat-trick for the club, Best could well have had seven – goals that could have boosted their average beyond comparison.

Suddenly, it was 3-0 to City, then Greaves pulled one back with a penalty for Tottenham. Did they have the time, or more to the point, the necessary to claw back another two? 'We now have another score flash,' crackled the transistor radios. 'Leeds United 1, Liverpool 1.' Barely had the announcer's voice faded from the night air than he was back on telling his avid listeners that Liverpool had just scored a second.

No matter what materialised in the next four minutes at Old Trafford, United had their two points, but there was no further news, or it turned out scoring, from White Hart Lane, so what was the League table looking like now? Could the six goals they had witnessed, without reply, be enough to push them back into top spot? Sadly not; City had a goal average of 2.05, while United were on 1.66. Both had fifty-six points.

Although rejoicing in their team's victory over Newcastle, the United support had witnessed the visitors looking jaded, utterly dispirited and totally disorganised, and there was little conviction, from what they had seen, that even on home turf they could re-man the battlements and repel City in seven days' time.

So, after forty-one games, it was down to ninety minutes to decide the First Division championship. This game would decide if the famous old trophy remained in the Old Trafford boardroom, or made the short yet hurtful journey across Manchester to Maine Road for only the second time in history. On only three occasions since the war had the title been decided on goal average: in 1950, when Portsmouth piped Wolverhampton Wanderers; then three years later, when Arsenal snatched it from Preston North End; and in 1965, when United themselves had managed to grab the trophy from the clutches of Leeds, whose defeat by Liverpool had pushed them out of the reckoning.

But having said that, if by some strange quirk of fate United and City both lost their final fixture, and Liverpool defeated Nottingham Forest at Anfield and then overcame Stoke City at the Victoria Ground, then the championship would move some 30-odd miles down the East Lancs Road. It was, however, highly unlikely that both United and City would succumb to defeat, so close were they to success.

Newcastle, although having lost only once at home in the League during the present campaign, had lost 1-0 in front of their own supporters to Carlisle United in the FA Cup and failed to win any of their last five home fixtures. Indeed, they had won one of their last eleven fixtures full stop.

On paper, and according to the bookmakers, United had the easiest challenge – Sunderland at Old Trafford. Despite the Roker Park side having enjoyed numerous favourable results in the immediate post-war years, they had failed to achieve a victory in the past sixteen years.

Newcastle made changes to the side that lost heavily at Old Trafford, adding the strength and experience of McNamee and Iley to their defence, but retaining McFaul in goal. Sunderland on the other hand included six of the players who had experienced defeat at the hands of United in that epic cup tie of 1964. Revenge was certainly an inspiration and motivation.

A correspondent in the *Guardian* on the morning of that final day suggested that Sunderland's thirst for defeat would not be quenched, and indeed, if United did not once again score six goals in front of their fanatical support, then they could go very close to doing so. Close enough to snatch the championship?

Needless to say, a full house assembled at Old Trafford for those defining ninety minutes on Saturday 11 May, with Sunderland having travelled south as the proverbial lambs to the slaughter. Prematch superstitions were observed precisely and anything relating to a 'lucky charm' was taken through the turnstiles in the hope that good fortune would favour those in red shirts.

All such pagan rituals were to prove fruitless, however, as even the most pessimistic amongst the United following could not have anticipated the abysmal performance from their favourites that was about to unfold.

More accurately, what unfolded at Tyneside on Salford Quays would determine the destination of the championship trophy, and within fifteen minutes of the kick-off, a black cloud could be seen slowly moving across the Mancunian skyline.

Sunderland had almost stunned United by taking the lead in the opening minute through Mullhall, but with only thirteen minutes gone at St James' Park, Mike Summerbee pushed the advantage City's way, giving them the lead and a grip on the championship trophy.

That grip was strengthened a minute later when Colin Suggett rocked Old Trafford by giving Sunderland the lead. A long ball out to the right by Harris, followed by a looping cross from Stuckey, saw Suggett hooking the ball past Stepney at the near post. Having Dunne off the field receiving treatment to a head injury certainly contributed to the failure of the home defence to clear the danger, but it was a goal that was always going to materialise.

Newcastle levelled the scoring, installing a faint glimmer of hope into Busby's team and supporters, but in the thirty-third minute of the Old Trafford drama George Mulhall emphasised Sunderland's superiority when he headed past Stepney after both Foulkes and Brennan had jumped and missed the ball. Five minutes prior to half-time Neil Young restored City's lead in the North East, only for Newcastle to level matters prior to the interval. Around the same time George Best created a glimmer of hope in Manchester, scoring with a 30-yard drive. Kidd then hit the bar with a header. Could there still be light at the end of the tunnel?

United had looked anything but potential Champions, disintegrating into a shadow of their former selves, looking tired with their nerves brittle to the point of actually snapping, while performing worse than they had done against West Bromwich Albion – if such a thing was indeed possible.

The second half had barely got underway when news filtered through to Old Trafford that City were 3-2 in front courtesy of Neil Young, and as the frustration and ill-temper began to rise to the surface on the banks of the Manchester Ship Canal, City's grip on the trophy became an unbreakable hold, when Francis Lee made it 4-2 in the sixty-third minute.

Best was flattened by Ashurst as things turned ugly, and the Sunderland left-back was in turn sent flying by Crerand, with the two assaulted players requiring attention from their respective trainers. Crerand was pacified by Charlton, but a verbal assault on the referee by Best led to a booking. The Irishman was indeed fortunate to escape being sent off, as a wild kick in the direction of Ashurst minutes later missed the Sunderland player as well as going unseen by the referee.

Stiles was also fortunate to escape a caution after he hurled himself wildly at Montgomery in the Sunderland goal as United chased the wind. Busby had left his seat in the stand to try and conjure up something of a miracle from the touchline, and pulled off Foulkes for Gowling in hope more than anything else. The youngster did manage to put the ball into the back of the net, but a linesman's flag ruled the goal out.

Time slipped away, as did many of the United support, and the referee's whistle brought an end to a frustrating League campaign. As the final score from the North East was announced, polite applause echoed around Old Trafford.

Looking back on that afternoon, United supporter Tom Clare recalled, 'Newcastle looked far the harder fixture as Sunderland were way down the League going into that last game. Most people would have backed United to wallop Sunderland and that was what we were expecting that Saturday afternoon. The atmosphere was terrific and the Stretford End was in full voice. It was almost carnival-like. However, a lot had transistor radios with them and were following events up at St James' Park, and we were praying for City to slip up. City just drew, and the title was ours as we thought our two points were virtually guaranteed.

'I don't know whether that mood transmitted itself to the dressing room or not, but we did not play well at all that afternoon. There was a tension about United's play, and Sunderland took the game to them. United found themselves 2-0 down while City's game was yo-yoing up in Newcastle and the fans behind the goal at the Stretford End were giving Stepney updates.

'George Best pulled a goal back for United and that gave us hope, but we knew we just had to win. City were pegged back to 3-3 up in Newcastle and the crowd did their best to lift United, but they just didn't seem to be able to shift up a gear as they battered away at the Sunderland goal.

'Of course when City went ahead 4-3, the news quickly spread throughout the Stretty and it dampened everybody's spirits – we knew then, it was all over. It was a sickening feeling and the atmosphere became muted. When the final whistle went we were absolutely deflated.

'I spoke to Paddy Crerand about the game a couple of years ago and he said they were annoyed with each other in the dressing room after the game because they knew that they had blown it. What really cost them the League though was that they lost two significant home games on the run-in – 3-1 to City and 2-1 to Liverpool. United should have had the title wrapped up before that last game of the season, and Paddy says it still rankles with them today!'

Losing to Sunderland was disappointing and frustrating, especially as it meant the championship trophy going to neighbours City, and in the confines of the Old Trafford dressing room, the United players were annoyed with each other, as they knew they had blown it. But it was not simply the failure to beat the Roker Park side that had cost them the title, as there were numerous incidents and games that could be analysed as the point where it all went wrong.

Was it the injury to Denis Law? 'With a fit Law, I am sure we could have won the championship,' proclaimed assistant manager Jimmy Murphy. Or was it the failure in not having replaced Bill Foulkes with a newer model?

There was little time for tears, for reflecting on where or why it all went pear-shaped, as in four days' time United would be in Madrid, coming face to face with a more-experienced, sterner, hungrier opponent than Sunderland. Matt Busby had to reassemble his troops, rinse away that bitter taste of defeat, and install a belief into his players that they could succeed in the white-hot atmosphere of the multi-tiered Bernabeu Stadium, and take that tentative step towards the Holy Grail.

Jimmy Murphy had worked his magic in the wake of the tragedy at Munich, creating a team out of nothing. Now, alongside Matt Busby, he had a more pressing matter, one that should not create much of a problem for the duo, as the players were already in place. They did, however, need some cajoling, a little bit of reassuring and, above all, their confidence reinstated, or the European Cup dream would come crumbling down around them.

United did at least have that one-goal advantage, a slender lifeline, but one that they would fight to keep a hold of, especially the likes of Bobby Charlton and Bill Foulkes, who saw this as their final tilt at European glory, at reaching the end of their long, memory-strewn rainbow.

Charlton had, like everyone else, been devastated at the title collapse and confessed, 'Last Saturday when we lost the championship I was sick. I didn't sleep much when I went home. I kept thinking about us losing.' Slowly, amid the anguish, his thoughts turned towards Madrid.

'Then I began to see it differently. It meant that so far we had won nothing and that was all the more reason to win this one.

'We know there are no consolation prizes if we lose in Madrid. We can't turn round and say, "Well we won the League."'

Unlike United, Real, who were Spanish Champions for the third successive year, had not been faced with a tension-packed, must-win weekend fixture. Instead, six of the first-team squad faced Second Division side Calvo Sotelo, who they toyed with in a 2-0 win, while the remainder of the squad had a forty-minute kick about two days prior to the second-leg tie.

But despite so much, for both sides, depending on the outcome of the game, there was tremendous respect between the clubs. Busby had spoken of it prior to the first leg; now it was the turn of Santiago Bernabeu de Yeste, Madrid's one-time centre-forward, who went on to become not only club president but after who the monumental stadium is named.

'I want Manchester United greeted and treated and respected as the greatest club in the world,' he said. 'And as our friends for many years nothing must go wrong.

'If we are beaten in the European Cup by Manchester United then we shall have lost to a great team. We have met them on many occasions and it is about time their luck changed.'

Luck United would certainly need.

European travel, certainly for football matches, was still in its infancy, with no mass exodus of supporters as there is today. A few had made the journey to the Spanish capital in 1957, but the sixties saw the doors opening towards travel abroad, for holidays as well as for recreational activities.

'Worried Turkey', who we encountered as a fresh-faced schoolboy, was by now a fully integrated match-going red, and although he had not actually planned to go to Madrid for the semi-final second leg, when the opportunity arose, he grabbed it with both hands.

He recalled:

We were sat in the pub enjoying a darts night when Roy, the pub landlord, received a phone call from one of the lads who was on holiday in Madrid. Real were selling tickets for the semi against United, but we could only have four, 'did we want four?' Six eager heads nodded with delight, but how were we going to split four into six? We thought of everything. Who had been to most matches? Who had been the longest without missing a domestic game? Most money (which immediately ruled me out) and umpteen other suggestions.

In the end we decided to rip a beer mat into six, individually sign a piece then place it onto the bar. We asked the next four people who bought a pint to remove a piece, but to leave face down, we waited nervously. Eventually four pieces lay on the bar waiting to be turned over. The landlord was itching to turn them over, but we weren't. After drinking enough to null any pain we asked Roy to reveal all. Luckily and thankfully my name came out third. I was on my way!

Due to the amount of alcohol consumed we decided to meet the following day at midday to discuss details; the pubs opened at eleven and closed at three in them days. 'Right then, when are we going and how?' Two of the lads were wadded and decided to travel on the Wednesday morning by plane. Tim and I opted for the thumb-and-hope approach!

When the pub closed we went to collect our passports and any money we had or could scrounge. What are mums for? Don't worry, I always repaid money borrowed. And off we set. First stop was the local transport café, and with a bit of luck we were offered a lift to Birmingham, which we gladly accepted. On our arrival at Brum, the driver offered directions to the best tranny café and, after asking around, our luck just couldn't get any better, as we secured a lift straight to Dover and, wait for it, the lad was going to Spain! However, the inside of the cab was full of City stickers … argh … but with a silly smirk we set off. We arrived at Dover well before our Monday ferry set sail, bought our tickets, then Tim, the driver and I went on the drink.

Once we had arrived at Calais we informed the driver of our true destination. We had only mentioned Spain and hid our United scarves in our duffel bag, as we were wary of not receiving a lift. Hooliganism was starting and football fans had earned themselves a bad name. With all the luck in the world he was passing Madrid and, with a grin on his face, said he already knew where we were going due to the United songs the night before in our drunken stupor! Anyway he dropped us off on the outskirts of Madrid and even wished us and United all the best.

We had arrived! Early Tuesday morning, waiting for a game that wasn't due to start for approximately another forty hours. Nowt for it, is anywhere open? What else was there to do?

We decided to go to the stadium on Wednesday afternoon, and what a sight – magnificent. Some stadium, some way of life. The surrounding areas of the ground began to fill and the first sign of football life appeared as United fans came into being. We pulled out our scarves and started to enjoy ourselves. A few beers later and with kick-off rapidly approaching we went in search of our turnstile, which we eventually found after what appeared to be hours.

Inside the stadium United fans had started to come together, unfortunately for Tim and I we were not with them, our tickets had been bought in Madrid … doh! We were so high up the players looked like ants. Just as the game was about to kick off the other two mates arrived, so a band of four stood against the Madrid might – not really, as those around us were a great bunch and the game was off.

Amancio, who had been missing from the Madrid line-up in Manchester through suspension, toyed with United, as the Spaniards set about dismantling the visiting defence in an attempt to snatch the early goal that would put them back on level terms. As early as the tenth minute, he rose to a Perez corner and headed for goal. Stepney was alert to the danger and palmed the ball onto the crossbar. But for half an hour, during which United only created one opening – a curling Crerand free-kick which deceived Betancort but bounced inches wide – red repelled white. It was a vital thirty minutes in the eyes of Matt Busby, although no sooner came the hopes of the storm having being weathered, than the evening suddenly darkened and the game was turned on its head.

With thirteen minutes remaining before the interval Pirri headed home an Amancio free-kick, a goal that had more than a hint of good fortune surrounding it. The ball had gone out of play, with the Italian referee signalling a goal kick. The linesman's upraised flag saw his decision changed, with a free-kick awarded to Madrid for obstruction by John Aston on Perez, 2 yards from the right-corner flag. Taken by Amancio, it flew perfectly towards the near post, where Pirri out-jumped two United players to head firmly home.

The white handkerchiefs fluttered in the evening breeze around the vast, tiered stadium, and the fireworks exploded as Madrid slowly increased the tempo. Ten minutes later, they gained the advantage when Brennan failed to control a long through-ball, and the veteran Gento ran through, evading four fierce tackles before beating Stepney with ease.

Momentarily resting on their laurels, the Spaniards' guards were down, and from the restart Dunne sent a long ball into the Madrid penalty area, more in hope than anything else. As the ball dropped over Betnacort, Zoco stuck out a foot in an effort to claw it away from goal but could only manage to divert it into the net.

United had a lifeline as half-time beckoned.

There was, however, more drama before the interval, as Amancio once again turned the screws on United, controlling a difficult ball with ease before hitting it on the half-volley past a forest of legs and an unsighted Stepney. Moments later Stiles was booked for a bad tackle – certainly not his first – on the goalscorer, amid shouts of 'fuera' (out) from the terraces.

It was a downhearted, dejected collection of red shirts who headed for the dressing rooms, but once in the bowels of the stadium, away from the heat and the neverending noise created by the Spanish support, it was a time for reflection; ten minutes to decide where the following forty-five were going to take Manchester United.

'At half-time I knew I had to say something,' admitted Busby. 'Because the boys looked as though they had just walked in from a funeral.

'So I shouted, "just tighten up your boots and go right at them. They are on their knees and look ready for taking a belting."' The United manager did not believe his own words, but he had to install some new belief into his players.

Pat Crerand also revealed what went on in those few minutes behind the closed dressing room door, saying, 'When we came in at half-time, George Best said, "We're as well losing 10-1 as 3-1. Let's have a real go at them."'

So, they realised that they had nothing to lose, and that if they were indeed to get beaten then they might at least do so with their heads held high and make their hosts fight for that place in the Wembley final. Within three minutes of the restart Foulkes got his head to an Aston corner, but Betnacort did well to save, and as United pushed forward, the Madrid 'keeper found himself under constant pressure. His undoubted ability stood out with a number of fine saves, including an excellent block from Best. However, in the seventy-fourth minute he was beaten and the vast arena was silenced, except that is for a small pocket of Mancunian supporters. A free-kick from Crerand was headed high into the air by Best and, with the ball looking to be going out of play, Sadler chased and managed to get a foot to it, prodding it over the line.

With 3-2 on the night and 3-3 on aggregate, Madrid were stunned, United rejuvenated. The game had been turned on its head and now looked to be heading towards a play-off in Lisbon two days later.

Four minutes after Sadler, a far-from-noted goalscorer, had clawed United back into the game, play once again flowed towards the Madrid goal. Best, who had not enjoyed the most favourable of evenings under pressure from two defenders, chased the ball towards the byline, clawing it back towards the Madrid goal. There was no Charlton, no Kidd or even Sadler in sight, only the veteran defender Foulkes, having for some unknown reason vacated his defensive position and responsibilities, who was now, to everyone's surprise, in front of goal. Three times a losing semi-finalist, United's elder statesman calmly hooked the ball past Betnacort and into the net, with the air of a man who had done it on countless occasions throughout his lengthy career.

It was 4-3 in United's favour, although there were still fourteen minutes to go: fourteen nerve-wracking minutes for United to hold on to the dream. Despite their early dominance, Madrid now looked a completely different outfit, drained of energy and deprived of inspiration and motivation. United's biggest obstacle was maintaining their concentration amid the thoughts that sporadically clouded the mind.

With nine minutes still to play, the result could have been put beyond all doubt, as the ball broke to Kidd 15 yards from goal, but the teenager fired wildly over. On another day, he would have scored, but tonight was an entirely different occasion. Soaked in sweat, at times a cold sweat, exhausted in both mind and body, the United players, and perhaps even more so the management team, were suddenly released from their fears and trepidations as a shrill blast of a whistle pierced the night air. Manchester United were, at last, in the European Cup final.

United supporters somehow managed to invade the pitch, hoisting a tearful Bobby Charlton to his feet – forgetting that some ninety minutes previously some Spanish supporters had snatched a United flag and set fire to it. They were simply eager to congratulate their heroes before they could disappear from the field of glory.

The United dressing room was a scene of utter mayhem: players hugged each other, tears flowed unashamedly, and showers were taken in full playing kit. But in one corner sat the unlikely hero of the hour, Bill Foulkes, who, when asked what was he doing in the Madrid penalty area when he scored simply replied, 'Oh, I saw George set off down the wing and I'd nothing better to do, so I followed him.

'I saw that ball go into the net and I never felt such a thrill in football before. I thought we had had it at half-time.'

Once outside the confines of the away dressing room and heading for the coach that would take them to their hotel, the United players were met with a reception committee of aggressive Spaniards, one of whom attempted to leave a lasting impression on the head of Nobby Stiles with a bottle. As the coach pulled away, Pat Crerand stuck his head out the window and shouted 'Mucho Bollockos' to the frustrated locals.

'Worried Turkey' even made the after-match celebrations: 'The Madrid fans were great afterwards, as drink followed by drink came our way. We even discovered where United were staying and managed to (alongside other United fans) get ourselves inside the Phoenix Hotel and celebrated with the team, which is a memory I will never forget.'

While the British press were in raptures over the United triumph, the Spanish press were quick to point the finger at the Real Madrid defence for losing the game, and had any of the Spanish side's followers bothered to buy any of the numerous newspapers they would have found the likes of the following: *Arriba* led with 'Madrid eliminated from the European Cup; Many mistakes in the second half enabled Manchester to draw', while according to *Ya*, 'Madrid eliminated itself against Manchester.'

In the Wembley final, United's opponents would be the Portuguese side Benfica, winners of the European Cup in 1961 and 1962, who had defeated Juventus 3-0 on aggregate. However, their progress was not overly enthusiastically received by the Lisbon press, with *La Bola* reporting, 'A meeting with Manchester is the worst thing that could happen.'

But as the Manchester United party flew home, the worst thing that could now happen was that they would run out of BEA champagne.

10

THE DREAM BECOMES A REALITY

Travelling to London for the 29 May Wembley final would not cause any problems for the United faithful, with road, rail and even air options available. Tickets, however, would be a different kettle of fish altogether, with only 30,000 available to the Old Trafford regulars.

Having returned to Manchester, where they were welcomed by thousands of jubilant supporters, the players had twelve days to rest and prepare themselves mentally for the task ahead. There would be training to keep them physically tuned, but nothing strenuous and not until the following week, as ten months of football had, in the testing latter stages of the First Division campaign, taken much out of them. With the energy-sapping Wembley turf awaiting their presence, Busby had to ensure that his charges were indeed ready to meet the challenge.

What the United manager did have to ponder over, and indeed give much serious thought to, was which eleven players would be extolled the privilege of representing Manchester United Football Club in the most important game in its history. Some would pick themselves, while others gave the manager sleepless nights.

Denis Law would have been one name quickly pencilled in by Busby as he began his team selection, but the charismatic forward had been out of sorts for most of the year, playing in only nine of the eighteen League fixtures since January, and scoring three goals. He had travelled with the eighteen-man squad to Madrid, but with his persistent knee problem, his chances of playing had been slim. The possibility of him playing in the final was even slimmer, but victory was paramount and even a half-fit Law could perhaps be enough to give United the crown. However, there was also the possibility of the player breaking down and leaving United an uphill battle with ten men.

Another dilemma for the United manager was Bill Foulkes. A veteran from the offset of United's European adventure he had, like Law, missed many games in the latter part of the season, having played only four since the turn of the year. Experience on occasions such as these was something that you could not buy and the centre-half had that by the sackload. Blotting out the threat of Torres for a mere ninety minutes was something that Foulkes could surely be relied upon to manage.

The decision on Law was easily made, as it was in the interest of both player and club that he should go into hospital for an operation to remove what was discovered to be a piece of loose cartilage from his knee, ensuring that he would be fully fit for the following season. He wasn't completely forgotten about, however, as Matt Busby took some time out from his busy schedule to visit one of his favourite sons, after putting the rest of his squad through a light-hearted practice match at Old Trafford, prior to the United party leaving for their prematch headquarters in Egham, Surrey. In that twenty-minute Old Trafford kick about, not only did Nobby Stiles prove his fitness – another lingering worry for Busby due to the player having missed countless games throughout the season – but the United players were kitted out in an all-blue strip, to give them a taste of playing in their Wembley colours. As both sides normally played in red, it was decided that they would both change to alternative colours on the night, with Benfica reverting to all-white.

Following that somewhat impromptu kick about at Old Trafford, Busby, after a brief conversation with Jimmy Murphy, decided on his team for the final, selecting the XI who had lost against Sunderland in that final, instantly forgettable League fixture: Stepney, Brennan, Dunne, Crerand, Foulkes, Stiles, Best, Kidd, Charlton, Sadler and Aston. Allowed to name a substitute goalkeeper, Jimmy Rimmer earned a place on the bench.

As for the players who took part in those earlier rounds – a total of sixteen had been used throughout the competition – three had no expectations of playing at Wembley: Jimmy Ryan, who had played against Gornik at Old Trafford; John Fitzpatrick, who managed two appearances, away to Gornik and away to Sarajevo; and David Herd, whose solitary appearance had also come in Poland. However, there was obviously going to be disappointment for one individual, and that player was Francis Burns.

Burns had been in the side at the start of the campaign and had played in seven of the eight fixtures, only missing the home leg against Sarajevo. He had also played in all but six of the forty-two League games, missing the opening three back in August and three of the last four. His place was taken by Shay Brennan, who had only played in thirteen League games and two European Cup ties, and had only returned to the side due to the somewhat indifferent display by the young Scot in the 6-3 defeat by West Bromwich Albion.

The former Scotland schoolboy international captain was obviously disappointed. He would, however, get a share of the lucrative 'pot' dangling in front of the United players, who had already earned themselves £1,000, a figure that would double if they were to triumph at Wembley. However, he would have been more than happy to give this up in exchange for a place in the cup final line-up.

Busby found himself called upon for countless interviews. All were treated courteously; some reporters, however, were old friends and received more time than others, such as Arthur Walmsley of the *Sun*, who sought his old friend's thoughts on more than the forthcoming final.

Why had he pursued the European Cup with such an obsessive purpose, wondered Walmsley?

'I have always had the conviction that one day Manchester United would win the European Cup – even though it might not be in my time as manager,' came the reply. 'I have no doubt at all that the pre-Munich side would have won it in time.

'All I have done is to try and make that achievement come sooner than later.'

But what of the mental torment of Madrid, and how much longer could he go on bearing the strains of modern soccer?

'The European Cup does involve me in tremendous pressure – but that is because we have not won it yet. If we win it this time the pressure will never be the same again – it will ease.

'I will retire when I feel I can no longer handle the affairs of my club properly. That time has not yet come – but when it does I will need no telling to go. I could never cut myself off from football and Manchester United. The vacuum would be too great to be filled by anything else. Maybe I could take the less-demanding job of general manager.'

In another interview, the United manager was quick to play down the massive tidal wave of confidence that was sweeping the country as the game drew closer. 'The thing that disturbs me most,' he was to admit, 'is that everybody seems to think we are just going along to Wembley to pick up the cup. They don't realise we are playing one of the best teams in the world.

'These Benfica players are all gifted. Genius is the right way to describe one or two of them.

'In this game, you do not win any matches off the field. We can only become European Champions by beating them at football.

'All the lads are fit and happy. There is no apprehension about playing Benfica, but at the same time the thing we must instil into them is that their real task still lies ahead.'

The United manager, accompanied by Jimmy Murphy and Bobby Charlton, had been down to the 'big smoke' the previous week along with George Best for the latter's presentation of the Footballer of the Year award, and Busby's own Manager of the Year presentation. All hopes were now on a hat-trick.

Cup final opponents Benfica flew into London and headed for their team hotel in Harlow, on the edge of Epping Forest. At Wembley they would be joined by around 10,000 supporters, making them seriously outnumbered on the night, something that didn't cause the Portuguese too much concern.

With Busby having announced his team, there was no cat-and-mouse game from the opposition, as Benfica manager Otto Gloria was equally quick to name his starting XI, going as far as to reveal that his team would also take up a 4-2-4 formation, although, with the hint of smile, he admitted to the assembled press at his team's Harlow hotel that 'of course there will be little variations, a little secret, perhaps. But you wouldn't expect me to tell you about that.'

Of United, he added, 'Manchester will play the same way. They can't play with one method all season and then use another for just one game. We have no complex about Manchester United, about Nobby Stiles, about playing at Wembley. This is the fifth European Cup final for us in eight seasons. For Manchester United it is the first. They must surely do the worrying.

'We rest content and we are experienced. We have seen it all before. That is all I can say.'

Since reaching the final, Old Trafford was a hive of industry, with staff working long hours, dealing with the thousands of ticket requests and everything else that went along with taking part in such a prestigious fixture. Their reward, however, was that the entire club staff, along with their wives, were invited to the game, as were two officials, or representatives, of every side United had beaten on their way to the final. None refused.

Cars and coaches filled with Benfica supporters moved across the Continent heading for Wembley. One old car, looking unlikely to make the end of the road, never mind London, contained ten people, while some plans were hit on the head due to a strike at French airports, causing many to divert to Holland. Around 120 travelled from Germany, while a similar number of Portuguese hotel workers crossed the Channel from Jersey. Others travelled from Mozambique and Johannesburg, while the 12,000 or so Portuguese working in London added to the demand for tickets.

Had the Benfica management been aware of the demand, then they would have taken a much bigger allocation, swelling their support, but when asked back in March by the Football Association how many tickets they would require if they reached the final, they had asked for 10,000, citing that they did not know if they would get to the Wembley final as an excuse.

'Although United virtually will be playing at home, we are not all that pessimistic,' said Benfica's Brazilian-born manager. 'It is not the advantages that United will have that concern us, it is the quality of their football.

'I do not think United are perhaps as good as when they beat Benfica 5-1 in Lisbon two years ago, but it is also true to say that Benfica are not as strong.

'At this stage I would say both teams are very similar, both have had hard seasons and both are not in the peak of form.'

The Benfica manager, however, was convinced that the final would be a feast of attacking football: 'I was convinced that the England–Portugal game in the World Cup would be a great match. It was, with only three fouls in the ninety minutes. I am just as certain about Wednesday.'

Two players involved in that confrontation were Nobby Stiles and Eusebio, with the United man coming out on top, and much had been made of the rematch, although the Portuguese star was quick to play it down. 'The result is in the hands of God,' he said, 'not in the hands of Nobby Stiles.'

'I am a professional. This is just another match. I feel no emotion, no nervousness,' he continued. 'I admit I broke down and cried when Portugal lost at Wembley against England in the World Cup. But that was two years ago and is forgotten. Now Wembley holds no terror for me.'

If the two teams were evenly matched on the field – the Portuguese danger-men of Eusebio and the towering Torres cancelling out Charlton and Best – off the field it was a different story altogether, as the Benfica players would not know how much, if anything at all, they would receive for their cup-final efforts.

If they were to win, then there would be no problems, as they could then expect around £700 per man. If they were to lose, then they might receive £500, but this was dependent on how they actually played, as the actual figure would not be decided on by the manager and directors until after the match!

Busby took his United players to Wembley twenty-four hours before the decisive showdown 'for a bit of a canter around the ground', leaving little else to do as he had already spoken to his players about what was expected of them, outlining their individual duties and warning them of the dangers within the opposition ranks: 'When one visualises the terrific double menace of Torres, with his magnificent headwork, and Eusebio, who is one of the world greats of any time, plus the thrusting of Simoes and the generalship and captaincy of Coluna, who could underestimate this team?

'Yet, I feel very confident about the outcome.'

Equally confident of a United win – perhaps more so – was the vast red-and-white army who would follow their team to Wembley, and the additional thousands who would watch the drama unfold on their television screens or listen to the game on the radio.

For the travellers, their cup-final countdown had begun more than seven days previously, when those precious tickets went on sale at Old Trafford. Hundreds of supporters slept under plastic sheeting and huddled together on a cold, wet, Mancunian night waiting for the ticket office to open. Some had to wait for up to ten hours to claim their prize, with friends working something of a shift pattern in order to keep their precious place. There were also many women in the queue, who were doing their piece of matrimonial duty by keeping places for their husbands on that damp Sunday morning.

Police kept an all-night watch on the ever-growing numbers, and by 8 a.m. reinforcements had to be called, as the queues stretched for half a mile along Warwick Road and all other approaches to the ground, forcing the sale of tickets to begin much earlier than the planned 10 a.m.

Amongst the bedraggled supporters in that long and winding procession was a thirteen-year-old Pete Molyneux who, looking back, recalled the excitement and the anguish of an important time in his life:

I'd just become a teenager by the start of the '67/'68 campaign; it was my fourth season watching United. Every home game I'd try desperately to persuade my dad to let me stand with the seething mass of humanity that was the Stretford End. Every home game I failed. His excuses ranged from me being too young, to the devil taking my soul if I mixed with those sorts. So for now I remained 'Scoreboard End Pete'.

United seemed to carry on where we'd left off the previous season, and by Christmas 1967 the reigning Champions led the First Division by three points. At the start of March, Chelsea became the first team to win a League game at Old Trafford in twenty-three months, and only the third in four seasons. But the run-in found us wanting, particularly against our closest rivals. The Chelsea defeat was the first of four in the last eight home matches. On the final day Manchester City nicked the title by two points.

As disappointing as that was, Busby's United had their eyes on a greater prize. The Wednesday after we lost the League United took a 1-0 first-leg lead to Real Madrid in the semi-final of the European Cup. Just like the trip to Benfica two years earlier, we were taking a very slender lead into a cauldron. This time it would be the Bernabeu Stadium, home of the six-time winners of the competition. The sceptics seemed to have called it right as United went in 1-3 down at half-time. With no live TV coverage, radio was still having its finest hour. When either side attacked, the crowd got excited and the commentator was drowned out. Through the fuzzy noise I heard Sadler had scored a second goal for United; we were level on aggregate. The tension was unbearable. With only minutes remaining the commentary went very faint; it mentioned United going forward with Best, then faded and said Foulkes was involved. Bill Foulkes was a veteran centre-half and rarely ventured forward so I thought United's attack had broken down. 'Goal!' screamed the commentator. I was anticipating a 4-2 scoreline when it came through loud and clear that United had equalised and now led on aggregate. I couldn't believe we were so close to reaching the European Cup final; those remaining seconds were like hours. United held on and all hell broke loose across Manchester and a small corner of the Bernabeu.

My dad was at his sister's that night so I phoned him after the game. He was really up for the final. My Uncle Albert, a knowledgeable old red, joined in the conversation and was already speculating about how Best would have a field day on the wide-open spaces of Wembley in the final.

We talked about going to the final and my dad said we should be able to get tickets because we'd collected enough programme tokens from the matches we'd been to that season. I hardly slept a wink that night with excitement.

There were only a couple of weeks between the semi and final and there were two important hurdles to overcome. The first was getting a ticket. So, early on Sunday 19 May we queued with thousands of other supporters hoping there would be enough tickets to go round.

There was no electronic distribution of tickets in those days – that wouldn't come until the mid-nineties. There were no executive members taking priority, no loyalty pot, just 8,000 season-ticket holders who had first choice and were sent their tickets through the post, and then it was open to those who had enough tokens on a first-come first-serve basis.

We got to Old Trafford well before the ticket office was due to open but the queue still went down Warwick Road (*now Sir Matt Busby Way*) to the junction with Trafford Wharf Road and along the railway tracks towards Trafford Park for about a quarter of a mile. My heart sunk when we joined the queue but four nervous hours later a nice man at the office handed my dad two tickets. I was off to the European Cup final at Wembley – or so I thought.

The second hurdle to overcome was getting time off school.

A big stink had been created in the media about whether schoolchildren who had tickets should be given the day off to travel to the final. It started with a story in the *Manchester Evening News* about some schools who would be turning a blind eye to absentees on the day compared with those schools that were taking a hard-line stance and threatening to treat the matter as truancy. Suddenly, because it was a United story, the whole nation had a view.

Ex-majors were writing to the *Times* about the issue and how it was an example of the country going downhill. Questions were asked in Parliament. I couldn't believe it. I know I'm biased but, my God, this was the bloody European Cup final and Manchester United were playing in it! How in anybody's mind that couldn't take priority over one day's education was lost on me.

The grammar schools took the high moral ground initially. My dad got cold feet and said he couldn't risk my future education at Stand for one football match and said I couldn't go. The Suez Canal and Cuban Missile crises put together didn't match the tension going on in the Molyneux household. I kept working on my dad, explaining how much this meant to me and that we may never get another chance to live this dream, but he was a stickler for doing 'the right thing'. I couldn't eat.

With days to spare, common sense prevailed. A few schools broke rank and said that if parents wrote to the Head confirming they had match tickets and requesting absence then it would be granted with no further action taken. The 'resistance' tumbled like a house of cards and the great and the good of Stand Grammar's governors followed suit. Now I *was* on my way, praise the Lord!

Another who had been in that Old Trafford queue was 'Worried Turkey':

It was a tired and hungry (and smelly) lad who arrived home on the 17 May 1968, having just returned (hitching) from the semi-final of the European cup against Real Madrid. As I got through the front door about 9 o'clock at night the smile on my face said it all. We were going to Wembley to face the might of Benfica, a team who had been there and done that '61 and '62. They had the 'Black Pearl', Eusebio, who was a threat, but we had 'Nobby' who had put him in his pocket in the '66 World Cup. As I went to sleep that night I played the semi-final through my head time and time again. Nobody could stop us, could they?

Then a bolt out of the blue hit home – was I going to get a ticket? I was up finding my token sheet … I looked everywhere. Then mam, hearing all the racket, asked what was up. 'Token sheet, token sheet' was all I could say. The dozy mare had put it in a safe place, good woman.

I looked at the token sheet and that season I had attended every home and away League game, courtesy of Bill Foulkes. I used to caddy for him and his money for caddying helped me to a lot of matches, including Gornik Zabrze and, of course, Real away. I unfortunately missed the away fixtures against Hibs Malta and Sarajevo. With token sheet safely at the side of the bed I slept contented, but still with slight doubt.

Tickets for the final went on sale on the Sunday. My mate and I made our way to Old Trafford on Saturday with sleeping bags, butties and drinks packed and we still weren't first in the queue.

By Sunday morning at 6 a.m. the queue went round Old Trafford and along Warwick Road. There was also a strong police presence as the ticket office opened. We edged closer and closer and then it was my turn. My token sheet was inspected and thankfully my ticket was handed over. Where do I put it for the best? Front pocket? No, just in case I was mugged. Back pocket? No, pickpockets always go there. Inside jacket pocket? No, I'm always in there. Off came the shoe and sock; it's going in there!

As we wearily trudged up Warwick Road past queues of supporters, you could feel and see the envy and expectation of those waiting in hope. All of sudden touts came from everywhere offering five, ten times face value for your ticket. Are they that stupid to think that, after all these years and what I and countless others had gone through, we would surrender to their paltry games? It had been ten years of torture. It had been a stone around our necks. We were going to Wembley and come what may we were going to enjoy it. We should have been making this journey a few years ago, possibly in '58 and if not then surely '59. To think you would give your heart's desire away for money then these touts didn't know the strength and feelings of Manchester United's fans! As I arrived back home all places I could hide my ticket were going through my head. In the end I put it at side of my bed so I could look at it every night.

As the date of the final approached my nerves steadily increased. On the Sunday before the big day we decided to travel by coach to London on Wednesday morning. There was one leaving Manny at 6.30 a.m., but being as daft as we were we ended up going on Monday, just to be on the safe side.

So Monday came and we arrived in London for dinner time. Would we be the first there? We stuck to our usual favoured routine and headed for the centre to find the fountains were already bathed in red and white as crowds gathered from all parts of the universe. The atmosphere was unbelievable, people hugging each other just for wearing red and white. We were lucky to meet some students and ended up staying at their place for two nights.

By Wednesday morning the capital didn't know what had hit it as thousands upon thousands of reds were swarming the place. Spurs fans tried trouble and were repelled, while Arsenal fans had a go and were sent packing, and little pockets of Hammers fans bit the dust. It was just unbelievable because everybody moved as one, and as if everybody sensed it was time to go we went on mass as one to the tube. We were on our way to Wembley!

Another supporter who had to queue for a ticket, but ended up being paid to go to Wembley, was Tom Tyrrell who, at the time, was working mainly as the cricket correspondent with the *Oldham Evening Chronicle*, although he had covered the odd United game during the winter months. Prior to the final, he had persuaded his editor that they should produce a special souvenir supplement on the final and would provide a piece on the game from a supporter's point of view (which he certainly was) standing on the terracing behind the goal.

Tom recalled, 'I usually travelled to games with work-mate Warren, my brother-in-law Dave and Jimbo from Chorley, and the four of us queued for tickets through the night when they were due to go on sale. We were actually at the front of thousands.

'We drew lots and worked out a shift pattern. Warren got midnight until 3 a.m., Dave 3 a.m. till 6 a.m., and I pulled out the plum 6 a.m. to 9 a.m. shift, by which time the ticket office would be open.

'Poor Jimbo got the short straw. He got to Old Trafford at teatime on FA Cup final day – 18 May – and spent the evening wandering around the forecourt, gazing up at the clock and no doubt wondering if he was doing the right thing.

'Dave's shift was the third of the four, but as I had to take him there, the four of us met up at around 4 a.m. on a damp Sunday morning, breathing the night before's beer and curry fumes over one another.

'Around us, fans were sleeping under plastic sheets or huddled together to keep warm; others had played football on the pitch! The walls were much lower in those days.

'At dawn there were attempts to trade tokens by those who had not got enough to qualify for the first batch of tickets being sold. We had offers of swaps or cash for any of our surplus, but refused because there was always the fear you could be turned away if it looked as if your token sheet had been tampered with.

'By the time the ticket office opened, the queue went back hundreds of yards and Jimbo took his place in history, buying the first standing ticket for the 1968 European Cup final.'

Those tickets, however, soon became a form of currency, as the scramble for those precious pieces of paper intensified. At their team hotel, the Benfica management were soon inundated with countless requests for tickets, receiving letters containing £5 notes and blank cheques.

In the run-up to the game, 10/- (50p) standing tickets were changing hands on the black market for £7, with £2 seats going for £20, such was the demand. A street newspaper seller in the Piccadilly area, where many of the Portuguese supporters were staying, did a lucrative trade, having made a two-day visit to Lisbon and secured some 120 tickets out of the Benfica allocation by unknown means.

The Wembley Stadium ticket office was not immune to the demand for tickets, as a rumour swept Manchester and beyond that Benfica had returned some 1,800 10s standing tickets. Many travelled south in the hope of securing one and the office was besieged by a 500-strong mob, many queuing from early morning. When the police announced that there were no tickets for sale a number of fans then directed their anger at the reporters and photographers who were in attendance, as a Wembley spokesman announced that if the person responsible for the announcement had been present then he would have been lynched by the mob.

Those unfortunate supporters would have gladly paid more than face value for one of those precious tickets, as many had already done, making the £120,000 figure for gate receipts from the sell-out match a little out – although the balance would go into the pockets of the unscrupulous touts, some of whom were attacked by irate fans prior to kick-off.

Television companies had paid out £50,000 to beam the game worldwide, to an audience of around 250 million, while United, having already earned more than £60,000 from the competition this season, could look forward to around another £45,000. After expenses, the gate receipts would be a record for the European Cup and exceeded in Britain only by the World Cup final two years previously. Those receipts would then be divided four ways – 10 per cent to both UEFA and the Football Association and 40 per cent to both clubs. Television revenue would be equally divided between all four.

As the morning of the final broke, the newspapers offered their opinions, their much-read reporters offering their thoughts and beliefs, hoping that they would not have egg on their faces twenty-four hours later, having had to write an epitaph for Matt Busby's team.

'Manchester United will never have better chance,' wrote Geoffrey Green in the *Times*, while Peter Lorenzo in the *Sun* simply proclaimed, 'United Will Win'. Desmond Hackett of the *Daily Express* was perhaps not so confident, as his heading was nothing more than 'It Looks Like United!' The *Telegraph*'s Donald Sanders predicted that 'United Can Realise Busby Ambition', with Albert Barham's piece in the *Guardian* preceded by 'Manchester United poised to win the European Cup – Matt Busby prepares for his greatest moment'.

But if any of the morning newspapers banished any small, niggling, lingering doubts amongst those making the journey south, or indeed any United supporters in general, it was Brian James of the *Daily Mail*, who wrote, 'Manchester United should beat Benfica in the final of the 1968 European club championship at Wembley tonight. Surely great teams do not come home to die.

'If United were destined to meet defeat again in this fourth attempt on the trophy of trophies, they would have done so in Madrid two weeks ago.

'Then, amid those awful moments of doubt at half-time with Real leading 3-1 and scarcely containing their laughter in the dressing room across the corridor, United spat in the face of the fortune that cost them three other semi-finals.

'They went out to win one of the most astonishing victories of recent times, sustained partly by belief in their own skill, more by the knowledge of how near they were to the European Cup that had eluded them for eleven years.

'This same sense of being about to conquer in a competition in which many of them have exhausted their careers, had even cost some of them their lives, will carry United through before their own folk at Wembley tonight.'

Travelling to the stadium on the United team coach, slowly winding its way through the throngs of supporters, John Aston recalled, 'When we were in sight of the stadium the nerves started and I possibly felt it a bit more than some of the others as I had never been to Wembley before.

'Inside the ground I remember looking around the somewhat Spartan dressing rooms and while in the toilet area I thought to myself that a lot of famous backsides must have sat there and began to laugh. One of the lads asked what was so funny and when I told him everyone began to laugh, which helped to lift the tension a little.'

As kick-off beckoned, there was now nothing more that Matt Busby or Jimmy Murphy could do; the stage was set and the thespians knew the script, and as the United management team made themselves comfortable on the benches along the side of the touchline, the drama began to unfold.

The opening forty-five minutes were disappointing, although United did cause the opposition's defence one or two problems with their rapier-like raids. However, the Benfica manager's prematch prediction of a foul-free encounter soon evaporated into the north London night air. It took a mere thirty seconds for the first free-kick of the night to be awarded, as the game began to turn into a foul-ridden session where brawn was more in evidence than brain. A further twenty-nine free-kicks were recorded in the opening forty-five minutes.

Twice in a matter of minutes, Best, clearly targeted as United's main danger man, was crudely fouled by Cruz. A switch to the right flank produced similar treatment from Humberto, who was to find himself in the referee's notebook after only twenty minutes for one foul too many on the Irishman. The referee, however, was apt to miss the malicious, although seeing and punishing the petty. Even a calculated stamp on Best's head by Graca, as the winger was lying on the ground following a tackle from behind, went unpunished.

But despite their somewhat over-physical approach, it was Benfica who almost gained the early advantage, although on the whole, they attacked only fitfully. A misplaced pass by Best, intended for Crerand, was intercepted by Torres, and the lanky Benfica No. 9 sent Eusebio scurrying away. Evading Stiles, and then Foulkes, the Portuguese forward, 25 yards from goal, whipped the ball against the underside of the United crossbar. Fortunately, there were none of his fellow teammates close by and the ball was safely delivered into the arms of a grateful Stepney.

Best was shadowed everywhere he went, while Charlton was tracked by Augusto, two decisions that were to add to Benfica's downfall, as it allowed the severely underestimated boyish enthusiasm of John Aston to shine through. Twice he sprinted past right-back Adolfo before sending over inviting crosses for his teammates. Kidd nodded one back towards Sadler, but it was little more than an inch too far of his teammate's outstretched foot.

Aston had a shot smartly saved by Henrique and then Sadler missed a golden opportunity in the twenty-ninth minute. This time the defender-cum-forward found himself unmarked as Kidd flicked the ball forward, but with only the goalkeeper to beat, sliced the ball wide before sinking to his knees in despair. Had the opportunity fallen to Charlton or Best, or even Kidd himself, United would undoubtedly have been a goal in front.

In the thirty-fifth minute, the referee, not for the first time, earned the wrath of the vast United support, when he penalised Foulkes for a shoulder charge on Torres. From the free-kick on the edge of the penalty area, Eusebio's powerful shot deflected off the defensive wall, forcing Stepney into making a fine save.

The numerous hard challenges kept the actual tempo of the game down, although it was seven minutes prior to the interval before the first actual flare-up kicked off, bringing the police around the front of the terracing to their feet as the United support became even more agitated. Eusebio ran straight into Crerand, knocking the Glaswegian out. Immediately, Stiles was involved, tapping his old adversary on the head as numerous players jostled and pushed each other before matters were restored.

As the teams walked off at half-time, the sound of boos and whistles echoed around the stadium, aimed at the Benfica players for their rather robust performance, diluting the occasion as a footballing spectacle. It was looking as though it would become a cup final to forget.

There looked to be little in the way of change as the second half got underway, as Cruz once again floored Best, but slowly the mood of the game changed, although it was to take a goal in order for it to do so.

With eight minutes of the second forty-five gone, Sadler, out on the left, flew a perfect ball in towards the near post and up rose Charlton to deflect the ball, perhaps more than head it, into the far corner of the net. An eerie silence enveloped the ground for a split second, before it erupted in a wall of sound and the scorer was enveloped by jubilant teammates.

A minute later, the ball was again nestling in the Benfica net, Best having raced past a defender before firing the ball home. Unfortunately, a linesman's flag ruled the Irishman as being offside.

Charlton's goal, however, had galvanised United. Best, again in the thick of the action, ghosted past three defenders, as only he could do, and from just inside the penalty area unleashed a powerful drive straight at Henrique. The Benfica 'keeper was unable to do anything other than parry the ball and it fell to the feet of Sadler. Once again, the United No. 10 failed in front of goal, his delayed effort hitting the goalkeeper then going wide for a corner.

At that particular time, it was to prove a costly miss for United, for with only ten minutes remaining, Benfica equalised. A deep right-wing cross from Augusto towards the far post found the head of the towering Torres, who nodded the ball down to the unmarked Graca. Unlike Sadler, Graca fired the ball home. The United defenders sank to the ground in disappointment.

With three minutes of the game remaining and the Portuguese Champions finally coming out of their shell to play with a skill and rhythm that had been missing from their game for most of the match, time suddenly stood still.

For more or less the first time in the preceding eighty-seven minutes, the United defence found themselves caught out of position, spread across the vast Wembley turf. Eusebio, chasing a through pass from Augusto, thundered through on goal. Superbly poised and taking his time, he unleashed a shot of tremendous power towards the solitary figure of Alex Stepney.

Unwavering before the sight of the Portuguese striker, Stepney stood his ground and, as Eusebio's shot cannoned towards him, he managed to get his body behind the ball and clutch it to his chest. Eusebio, stunned at the save and obviously disappointed at not scoring what would indeed have been the winning goal, sportingly stood and applauded the green-clad United 'keeper as he got to his feet and cleared the ball upfield to safety.

Extra time now beckoned, with Busby, Jimmy Murphy, Jack Crompton, John Aston Snr and Ted Dalton rushing onto the pitch, along with their Benfica counterparts, using the brief break in an effort to cajole players, get stiffening limbs massaged and prepare them for the vital half-hour that remained.

'We were really gone,' recalled Bobby Charlton. 'None of us could run. It was a terrible, helpless feeling. My legs were killing me, both of them. It wasn't like an ordinary cramp. They just sort of seized up and there wasn't a real stoppage in that last quarter, so that you didn't get a chance to get down and give them a shake to loosen them. It was murder.

'When they scored, it looked on for them, considering the state we were in, but we held on somehow.

'I was too busy getting my legs rubbed to hear much of what was being said before extra time started. We were flopped out there like dead men, but we were ready to go when we had to. The boss said, "Just keep going; you can still beat these."'

Charlton's words were echoed by Nobby Stiles, equally exhausted by the end of the ninety minutes: 'As we got close to the end of the ninety minutes, we got scared of losing. We were a goal up and without really thinking about it we went into our shell. But we were clapped out and could not play a proper containing game. We were playing as two units: a defence and a forward line. Before extra time the boss told us to begin playing as a team again, to go up together and get back together, and to start picking up people in defence.'

'Strangely, Benfica looked in worse shape,' commented Jimmy Murphy, after glancing over at the opposition players lying sprawled on the pitch a few yards away. 'They could scarcely get to their feet to start extra time.

'But one thing that stands out more than anything else was one of Matt's comments to the lads as they got to their feet: "You are the better team. Now go out and prove it. This is going to be our day."'

'A master stroke,' was how Jimmy Murphy described Busby's words, and as the additional thirty minutes got underway, the blue-shirted players rallied to the call.

A Stepney clearance was back-headed by Kidd into the path of Best and, clear from the shackles of either Cruz or Humberto, he wriggled past three bemused defenders and, with a hint of arrogance and mischief, also left goalkeeper Henrique in his wake, before slipping the ball towards the yawning goalmouth. The goalkeeper followed the ball into the back of the net in what was always going to be a failed attempt at preventing the goal.

Two minutes later it was 3-1, Kidd celebrating his nineteenth birthday with a goal he would never forget. A Charlton corner from the left was met by Sadler and headed towards goal by Kidd, but the ball hit Henrique on the face, rebounding out to the nineteen-year-old who headed it over the 'keeper.

But still Benfica posed something of a threat and Best showed some excellent defensive qualities, as well as his undiluted reserve of energy, as he ran back to block a Coluna run towards the United goal.

But despite holding an advantage that now looked unassailable, United continued to press forward and, with twenty minutes of extra time remaining, the game was well and truly wrapped up when Charlton scored a fourth, clipping home a cross from Kidd.

Benfica were by now demoralised, although Eusebio continued to wage a one-man kamikaze war on the United defence. His last-ditch attempt to gain some form of respectability surrounding the scoreline, bursting through the United defence, saw Stepney simply pluck the ball out of mid-air with one hand.

With three minutes of the game remaining, there was more action at the Benfica end of the stadium, as a couple of over-excited United supporters managed to clamber over the touchline barriers and run onto the pitch chased by policemen. One managed to grab the corner flag and run off with it, while the other, with play still going on, attempted to get back into the crowd, but soon found himself rugby-tackled by a policeman and led away.

After the game, a police spokesman said that the United victory was by far the best thing from their point of view, and apart from a few drunks who fell asleep and missed extra time, there was very little to report, with the only real incident being the discovery of over a thousand forged tickets in a hedge beside one of the roads leading to the stadium. Wrapped in a German newspaper, the tickets were for section J53, and they were thought to be the reserve supply of 'brilliant' copies for a gang of forgers, dumped there earlier until the rest of their hoard had been sold. It was believed that, going by the serial numbers, at least 500 had been used by supporters to gain entry. Only a reported two dozen supporters were turned away with forgeries.

Had the forgeries been sold, a Scotland Yard spokesman said they would have earned the touts around £10,000, but as it was, with the kick-off drawing closer, the touts were actually struggling to sell countless unwanted, genuine tickets, in the end more or less giving them away. One mounted policeman had been given thirty, which had been passed on to children.

The unknowing 500 with forged ticket stubs in their pockets celebrated alongside those with legitimate tickets, rejoicing with complete strangers in a mass love-in, as the Benfica players slumped to the ground, exhausted in mind and body, and the United players and staff, oblivious to everything around them, hugged and celebrated their achievement.

As R. H. Williams wrote in the *Daily Telegraph*, 'In the end, this sordid melodrama became an epic, and the heavy-footed United, who somehow survived the punishing time between the eightieth and the ninetieth minutes, achieved a famous victory for dedicated football and sportsmanship, even if the latter is always comparative.

'Ultimately only skill and stamina mattered. There was no longer any point in breaking the laws and there was a moral for Benfica and others in that.'

Back in St Joseph's Hospital, Manchester, Denis Law, recovering from his operation, watched the game with friends and lay exhausted. He had kicked every ball, 'and scored every goal'.

'I was very nervous,' he told a visiting reporter. 'It was worse than playing, but the lads were brilliant. I was nervous because I was restless and not able to have a dig myself.

'I feel marvellous, great, so just imagine how the lads are feeling. It was obvious they were doing it for the boss for they pulled themselves up in extra time to give it a dig again.

'This is what he wanted and they gave it to him convincingly.'

But where was young Master Molyneux? After the 'will I or won't I be there' sleepless nights, did he fulfil his dream?

I wish I could remember every minute of that day, but at that age you don't savour special occasions because you don't appreciate the historical significance or their impact on your life.

What I do remember is it being a glorious day with brilliant sunshine. My dad and I went by Preston's coach from Whitefield. I remember thousands of short-sleeved reds everywhere we stopped on the way down. Outside Wembley there were hundreds of homemade flags proclaiming United's rightful place amongst the elite or supporters' affection for Busby or the players. There was a huge following from Malta, singing and dancing with an enormous banner on the forecourt just under the twin towers.

Inside Wembley it was a concoction of heat, excitement and noise. I got separated from my dad but that was okay. United's all-blue kit for the night looked awesome under the Wembley floodlights and against the deep, rich-green turf. The support was superb with at least 95 per cent of the stadium given over to United's cause.

The first half was niggly and tense, the great Benfica uncharacteristically resorting to Leeds-like antics to stop Best. A goal by Charlton early in the second half seemed to have won it until Jaime Graça equalized with ten minutes left. A few moments later Alex Stepney made a great save from Eusebio that has gone done in football folklore. Those last ten minutes saw United look tired and edgy but that was shrugged off as Busby's boys exploded into action in the first nine minutes of extra time. Best, Kidd and Charlton scored to put United into an unassailable 4-1 lead. There was an outpouring of relief and joy that the European Cup was finally destined for Old Trafford.

It was also one of those rare occasions where your dream game doesn't end as a tense affair, holding on to a slender lead or scrapping to get a winner. We were 4-1 up with over twenty minutes to sing United home, and sing them home we did. Several older fans around me were crying with joy. I didn't fully understand the significance then, but I guess they'd watched United through the early European games, the days of the Busby Babes and the crash at Munich. How poignant was that night for those supporters?

As United went up Wembley's famous old thirty-nine steps, it was difficult to pick out the players in their dark-blue, sweat-stained shirts. Suddenly, a huge spotlight lit up the players amongst the crowd as they climbed to the pinnacle of club football to receive the European Cup. When Charlton lifted the trophy it gleamed like a beacon and it looked massive. I found my dad and we celebrated together. We stayed to watch the lap of honour and join the partying that seemed to go on forever, yet forever wasn't long enough. Manchester United were Champions of Europe; we sang loud and long to let the world know.

Victory was a combined effort by all eleven players and stretched well beyond the 120 minutes at Wembley, but if any individuals did deserve to be singled out for their performances in north London, two stood out above the others: Alex Stepney and John Aston.

It was perhaps Stepney who indeed earned United victory with his save from Eusebio, and looking back, the goalkeeper said, 'The build-up was rather low key. The manager took all the pressure off the players and just left us to concentrate on the game. The first half, in truth, was a bit of a stalemate. It was a case of "you have a look at us and we'll have a look at you". Eusebio hit the bar from a free-kick but there were few clear-cut chances at either end.'

When asked about 'that' save, Stepney replied, 'I came haring from my line when Eusebio broke through because I thought I had a chance of getting the ball. But it was the old Wembley turf which was very spongey and the ball held up on the surface.

'I suddenly realised that I wasn't going to get there and started back-pedalling like mad.

'Eusebio leathered the ball all right but I managed to get to it and, more importantly, hold on to it so that he had no chance with the rebound.

'Extra time was mind-boggling.

'I can remember that I had a hand in the build up to George's goal. I played a little pass out to Tony Dunne on the edge of the box and he gave me it back. I then did the same with Shay Brennan on the other side of the box and he too played it back to me.

'It was then I picked it up and hoofed it downfield. Bestie just latched on to the ball and ran through their defence as though it didn't exist before rounding the 'keeper and stroking the ball into the empty net.

'From then on, it was one-way traffic.'

Many felt that the Wembley stage was tailor-made for George Best and expected the Merlinic Irishman to stand out above all others on that momentous night. However, it was the man on the opposite wing, something of an unsung hero, who went on to outshine his more illustrious teammate.

John Aston had been initially rejected by United as a youngster because he was considered as being too small and came close to joining Everton. But he eventually convinced the Old Trafford management that he had that special quality required to become a Manchester United player and followed in his father's footsteps.

Still somewhat modest about his contribution, he recalled, 'When the team sheets came around, I noticed that the full-back who would be marking me was called Alfonso. I was quite relieved at that.

'We had played Benfica in a friendly in America the year before, losing 3-1 in Los Angeles, and I had been marked by a different player who had made life very difficult for me.

'I didn't know a lot about Alfonso but he looked big and fairly ponderous and that type of player usually suited me because there was one thing I wasn't short of and that was pace.

'This was one of the occasions when being one of the team's lesser lights was a positive benefit. There was obviously a lot of pressure on the stars of the team, like Bobby Charlton and George Best, to turn on the style in a match of this importance being watched by the entire country. But the same expectations weren't heaped on my shoulders, so I was just determined to relax and give it my best shot.

'It was obvious right from the start that I could beat Alfonso for pace and both Pat Crerand and David Sadler spotted it as well. They kept pumping passes down my throat and I lost count of the number of times I got past Alfonso and got a cross over.

'The first half simply flew by and the most vivid recollection of the second was the save that Alex Stepney made from Eusebio.

'I swear my heart stood still when Eusebio broke through and I couldn't believe it when Alex not only saved the shot but held on to it.'

Once the United players and management had finished congratulating each other, Bobby Charlton slowly moved towards the touchline, leading the way towards the steps down to the royal box where Gustav Wiederkehr, the president of UEFA, waited to present the trophy. They had tried, unsuccessfully, to persuade Matt Busby to lead them towards the tall, glistening trophy at the top of the thirty-nine steps. It had taken almost twelve years to reach the foot of those steps; twelve years of toil and tears. But Busby was content to take a step back and let the players who had finally brought the coveted trophy to Old Trafford savour the moment and enjoy the plaudits.

The Portuguese press were complementary in defeat. Vitor Santos, writing in the Lisbon paper *A Bola* penned, 'With unique stoicism and enthusiasm with a break, the Manchester of Matt Busby won a title which had been lacking in English records.

'It was beautiful and thrilling the way United scored a series of goals, impressive for the categoric assertion of vitality, perseverance and determination – that determination of the English when they think of winning.

'What we saw in London was exceptional – Manchester United in crescendo, more and more powerful as time went by, and Benfica in decline and well beaten.

'Those obstinate boys of United, with Best, Charlton and Crerand their great ones, all contributed highly to a victory which soccer of old England will not forget for a long time.'

Even Otto Gloria, the Benfica manager, admitted his team were second best: 'Manchester United are very good and they had a big advantage at Wembley. Some of the Benfica players, like Torres and Coluna, felt some difficulty early on with knocks and could not produce the football they normally would. The title is in very good hands.'

The supporters were as exhausted as the blue-and-white-shirted players out on the Wembley pitch. 'We were shattered too!' recalled Tom Tyrrell. 'We had jumped and chanted, sung and shouted from long before the kick-off. The Wembley terracing vibrated under our feet. It bounced as we bounced! The earth really did move for United fans that night.

'On the final whistle, I remember a flood of tears. It was all to do with reaching the end of the road, and Munich. There was pain in the memories but we were deliriously happy too.'

Having witnessed the cup presentation, the United supporters surged from the ground in a jubilant mood, with many heading for the bright lights of London's West End, determined to start a party to end all parties. In Trafalgar Square, they paddled in the fountains that surrounded Nelson's Column, singing every known United anthem. They then marched up the Strand like an invading army, and at Piccadilly Circus swarmed around the statue of Eros, blocking the road.

Down Whitehall marched an estimated 500, turning right into Downing Street, where they stood outside No. 10 as midnight approached, chanting, 'Wilson out, Busby in' before continuing on towards the Houses of Parliament.

Extra police were brought in to keep the traffic moving, but the hoards quickly moved on of their own free will, constantly swelling in numbers, and headed for the team hotel in Russell Square, where again the traffic was brought to a halt as they thronged around the hotel entrance. Inside the Hotel Russell, the party was in full swing, albeit half an hour behind schedule, but that mattered little.

Every time one of the United players entered the vast room, the Joe Loss orchestra belted out the Cliff Richard's hit song ' Congratulations', but those in attendance did not have to endure it twelve times – once for each of the players and an encore for Matt Busby – as one individual did not make it.

A cup of tea was all Bobby Charlton wanted upon his arrival at the Hotel Russell, and having gone to his room to change, he decided that he didn't feel well enough to go back downstairs to attend the function and told his wife to go on her own. The emotions of the game, the celebratory champagne had all been too much. He was also dehydrated. The party went on without him.

If Charlton missed the party of a lifetime, then others certainly did not and that included one or two uninvited guests.

One of those was John Camm, a private investigator, who began the story of how he came to be at the United party by saying:

It seems impossible now for me to say that during the late sixties when the United team was so successful, I was earning more in a week as a private investigator than any United player other than possibly Denis

Law and Bobby Charlton. I have it on reliable authority that most players were earning less than £100 per week in 1968. I only wish that I could still make that claim...

At that time I was very friendly with a chap called Arthur. We met on a Fairs Cup flight to Strasbourg in 1965 and we began to travel everywhere together and got on very well. At that time he was over sixty and I was a mere thirty. His worldly-wise experience combined well with my youthful exuberance and ability to drive everywhere. At that time I was five years into my one-man business as a private investigator (it lasted for forty-eight years), so I had the confidence to move in such exalted company.

We made a big mistake in 1966, having been to Lisbon to watch United stuff Benfica (yes, I was there!) where we waited for the semi-final draw which would pair United with Partizan Belgrade. So, over a few drinks on the return journey from London, we deduced that United would stuff Partizan and that Real Madrid would stuff their semi-final opposition, so we went ahead and made reservations for flights to Brussels for the final. We then booked a hotel in Brussels for two nights and flights with Sabena, Tuesday out and Thursday return. The entire outlay, paid up front, was just over £50 each.

What we failed to anticipate was that George Best would be injured for the second leg with Partizan and you can guess the rest – Arthur and I spent two days in Brussels to watch Real Madrid vs Partizan Belgrade at the Heysel Stadium! So we were the first people to be able to say, 'George Best failed to turn up for our appointment!'

Undeterred we boldly did a similar deal in 1968, booking a twin bedroom at the Russell Hotel for Tuesday and Wednesday of the European Cup final week, even before the semi-final first leg against Real Madrid.

We travelled to Madrid for the second leg and at half-time we feared the worst. Arthur turned to me and said, 'Will you cancel the Russell or will I?' By the end of the game, we had a different story and our gamble had paid off. Apparently Les Olive booked the entire Russell Hotel for the Monday, Tuesday and Wednesday nights, every room was booked by United, except one – ours!

This of course gave us sole admittance to the hotel on Tuesday and Wednesday and we had a great time before and after the game, meeting people such as the families of the Munich victims and parents and wives of the current team. It was late when we returned to the hotel after the game and it must have been 4 a.m. when we returned to our room. I have the signed menu card for the evening and photographs of Matt Busby arriving with the cup and having a big embrace with his wife Jean on the steps of the Wharncliffe Suite as the team arrived.

I have many memories of that evening, including the eye-popping arrival of George Best with his latest girlfriend – a blonde, name unknown, but she wearing very little, except for a mini dress in the style of a string vest; she was wearing very brief white panties and no bra. Some things you never forget.

The evening is reasonably clear in my memory, despite an abundance of alcohol. A number of my friends from Malta were at the function and had no way of finding a room so, if you promise to say nothing, I slept in one bed, Arthur slept in the other and four Maltese friends were scattered on the floor around the room.

We left the hotel about twelve noon on Thursday, right at the same time as Bobby Charlton, who was going off to join the England party. I had obtained a large match pennant which I intended to hand over to my friends in Malta and I had obtained all the autographs except one. Bobby had spent most of his evening in his room, so he signed the pennant to complete the set and this was picked up by the television lunchtime news. A photograph of Bobby and me holding the pennant aloft appeared in the next edition of the FA News.

Another 'non-United' guest at the after dinner celebrations was Joe Glanville from Malta. But he had to confess that he nearly missed the occasion of a lifetime:

I nearly missed the dinner. At the end of the game, I was sick; winning the trophy for the first time following Munich was too much for me and had to go straight to my hotel. Thankfully, I managed to recuperate and made it. It was a great occasion. The surprise of the night was the menu as it had the result of the game included. This must have been done in a matter of an hour as the game went on extra-time.

I was invited to the dinner, through the club secretary, Les Olive, along with a couple of friends from Malta and our Manchester friends, John Camm and Arthur Littlemore. These two supporters we had met in Malta when United opened their European campaign against the local side, Hibernians. They used to travel all around Europe and were very close friends of Tony Dunne. They were familiar faces with everybody at Old Trafford.

Matt Busby, as expected, was the centre for the whole night. He was in great form and I also managed to meet his mother, Helen, who kindly autographed my European Cup final rosette. These rosettes were purposely made by a tailor and friend of ours from Salford, Alec Goodall. He had appreciated our efforts for travelling from far away to be present for this occasion. I still treasure this item and would never let go for anything. It is autographed by all players and officials.

Jean and the Busby family were in great form and no wonder the party went on till the early hours of the morning. Pat Crerand cut his finger with a glass and my rosette is still stained with his blood. Tony Dunne's father was very close to our table. He enjoyed himself tremendously even though in his old age. Bobby Charlton retired early due to post-match reactions and he also had to join the England party the following morning. The occasion was so great because at that time the club had what we used to call that family belonging, feelings and environment – something that is sadly missing today.

Back in Manchester, the silence that had enveloped the city during the day, and more so during 120 minutes of the game itself, was soon broken as jubilant supporters took to the street in mass celebration, abandoning televisions and radios in a dash to the nearest pub, as there were only twenty-five minutes of drinking time left to toast Matt Busby and his team.

With the 10.30 closing time curtailing the amount of alcohol that could be consumed in that short space of time, many headed instead to the nightclubs, which enjoyed later opening times, and where the champagne flowed long into the night. One such club owner beamed, not because of United's success, but because that success had brought a higher number of people through his doors: 'Usually it's a quiet night on a Wednesday, because few people have any cash left. But tonight everyone has money to spend.'

Even amongst the more serene audience at the city's Free Trade Hall, where Sir John Barbirolli, the conductor-in-chief of the proclaimed Halle Orchestra, was giving his farewell concert, transistor radios were discreetly tuned in. The conductor, well aware that they would be, told those present, 'There will be either ecstasy or misery by the time I have finished' and he was not referring to his own performance. At the end, he cried, 'Caramba – we won!'

The early morning editions of the newspapers were eagerly snapped up by those leaving the city-centre clubs, and around 2 a.m. they were joined by the passengers of the first 'soccer special' returning from London as they spilled down the Piccadilly concourse.

On one of those early trains back to Manchester was Tom Tyrrell, although he remembered nothing of the return journey: 'We had booked our seats for the return journey, as well as the outward one, but when we went to look for the seats we had reserved, we found a dozen people had piled into them and fallen asleep. So what?

'Warren and Dave stood in the corridor talking to Jimbo, but I was shattered. I lay down in the space between the carriage doors, put my head on the rolled up red banner we had made with "We Are The Greatest" on it, pulled the red-and-white-painted bowler hat over my eyes and fell asleep.'

For Matt Busby, the victory was a poignant moment, as he reflected on the long, painful journey that he had taken Manchester United on. A journey that at times he thought was never going to reach its intended destination.

'At last, at last!' he exclaimed. 'We have done it. It is Manchester United's European Cup, my dearest longing for the club. It is the greatest moment of my life.

'After the match I was overcome – with relief, I suppose, at the end of the tension. Certainly with pride at the magnificent heart of the team.

'Here we go again, I said to myself, making it hard work for ourselves.

'When Benfica equalised we were beginning to sink away, it seemed, but Alex Stepney made that tremendous save from Eusebio and if there was a turning point, I think that was it.

'But did I say our boys had heart? Here was more proof. They showed it as they showed it in Madrid, and also they had the ability that raised the team to such a splendid achievement.

'That Stepney save, happening just before the end of normal time, seemed to lift us. From then on I thought it would go our way.

'In the eleven years since first we entered, the first English club to do so, we have tasted near triumph, great disappointment, and disaster which nearly destroyed us.

'Now we are the first English club to have won this most-coveted club trophy.

'My first reaction is a feeling of gratitude to the players for their tremendous effort.

'I am proud of them all. And I would not single out any one. But I would be remiss if I did not say how delighted I am, especially for Bobby Charlton, our skipper, and Bill Foulkes, who have come through the long test of time with me.

'I did pretty well everything I could do as a player, including captaining my country. I had been well-blessed with every success as a manager, including managing my country. There was only this great club championship missing.

'And when I say I am proud, it is pride on behalf of every single person who works for Manchester United.

'This is a team throughout the club. I have always maintained that if club is not right at the top it cannot be right anywhere. It is right at Old Trafford with Mr Louis Edwards and his board.

'Well blessed am I with the whole team, indeed, with Jimmy Murphy, my friend and confidant, with Les Olive, our secretary, who gets on with the job without noise or fuss, and his staff; with Jack Crompton, Wilf McGuinness and John Aston, all old United players who give the benefit of their knowledge and love of the club to our players; with Joe Armstrong, our chief scout; with Ted Dalton, who rubs away our bruises so cheerfully, with so many other people in the place it would fill a page to name them.

'I am grateful too, to the tremendous band of supporters who have cheered us in huge numbers.

'And I am grateful to the clubs and supporters all over Britain who have been on our side in this great battle.

'I must make special mention of the players who did not play, including the "pool" who stood ready for the call. Real club men, all of them.

'When I awaken I am sure I shall shake myself and wonder if it is not all a dream.

'Then I will realise that the dream had a wonderful end. And it is indeed the end of a wonderful dream.'

It was indeed a wonderful dream and a story that Hollywood scriptwriters would have found difficult to write. It would, however, have been a big-screen epic and one that would have undoubtedly have won numerous awards.

But although the victory at Wembley brought so much relief and happiness, it was tinged with immense sadness, as even in the hour of triumph, Munich was still the ghostly spectre floating through the corridors of Old Trafford, and indeed at the celebrations in the Hotel Russell, where those who survived were joined by the families of those who had died.

Who knows what thoughts went through their minds?

The dream, however, had been achieved. On numerous occasions it had ended in little more than a blur, a rude awakening in a cold sweat. But tonight, the dream had continued, and crossed over to become a reality. Manchester United were, finally, Champions of Europe.

Matt Busby would never banish the demons that haunted him from time to time, but on this night of nights he had gone a long way down the road to doing so, and as the night wore on and the celebrations continued, he took to the stage alongside Joe Loss and his orchestra, took a microphone in his hands and began singing 'What a Wonderful World'.

SOURCES

In the writing of this book, I have consulted countless newspaper articles and reports from both my own personal archive and from the Manchester Central Library and the Mitchell Library in Glasgow.

Quotations have been sourced from the following newspapers and I would like to acknowledge the assistance that they have been in the weeks and months that I worked on this publication.

Manchester Evening News
Manchester Evening Chronicle
Daily and *Sunday Express*
Scottish Daily Express
Daily and *Sunday Mirror*
Daily and *Sunday Telegraph*
Times and *Sunday Times*
Manchester Guardian
Observer
Daily Herald
Daily Mail
News of the World
Sunday People
Sun
Empire News
News Chronicle/Daily Dispatch
Daily Record
Sunday Post
Evening Times
Evening Citizen

More specifically, some of the larger quotations have been drawn from the editions listed below:

Page 18	Bristol Rovers manager Bert Tann – *Daily Express,* 8 February 1958
Page 22	United chairman Harold Hardman – *Manchester Evening Chronicle,* 10 February 1958
Page 23	Jimmy Shiels – *Sunday Tribune,* January 2008
Page 38	Stan Crowther – *Daily Express,* February 1958

Page 48	Viv Buckingham – *Manchester Evening Chronicle*, 27 February 1958
Page 54	Bob Lord – *Daily Herald*, 17 March 1958
Page 74	Matt Busby – *Daily Express*, August 1958
Page 75	Jimmy Shiels – *Sunday Tribune*, January 2008 (see bottom on second page)
Page 80	Albert Quixall – various, August 1958
Page 85	Johnny Berry – various, January 1959
Page 89	Matt Busby – various, May 1959
Page 91	Matt Busby – *Manchester Evening Chronicle*, August 1959
Page 111/12	Noel Cantwell – *Manchester Evening Chronicle,* November 1959
Page 136	Matt Busby – various, August 1962
Page 141	Albert Quixall – *Manchester Evening News*, October 1962
Page 147	David Sadler – *Sunday People*, September 1963
Page 169	Matt Busby – *Football Monthly*, September 1963
Page 172	Matt Busby – *Manchester Evening News/Chronicle*, August 1963
Page 183	Denis Law – *Manchester Evening News/Chronicle*, November 1963
Page 201	John Connelly – *Manchester Evening News/Chronicle*, April 1964
Page 206	Albert Quixall – *Manchester Evening News/Chronicle*, September 1964
Page 208	Maurice Setters – *Manchester Evening News/Chronicle*, October 1964
Page 211	Blackpool chief constable – various, November 1964
Page 211	Denis Law – *Daily Express*, November 1964
Page 217	George McCabe – *Daily Mirror*, February 1965
Page 218	Les Olive – *Football Monthly*, 1965
Page 221	Matt Busby – March 1965
Page 227	Matt Busby – various, April 1965
Page 233	Matt Busby – various, August 1965
Page 244	Matt Busby – *Daily Express*, February 1966
Page 255	Matt Busby – *Daily Express*, May 1966
Page 258	Denis Law – *The King*, Bantam Press, 2003
Page 264	Tommy Docherty – unknown, September 1966
Page 276	Terry Allcock – *Daily Mail*, 20 February 1967
Page 281	Matt Busby – unknown, April 1967
Page 287	Matt Busby – *Daily Express*, May 1967
Page 297	Matt Busby – *Daily Express*, 16 November 1967
Page 315	Matt Busby – *Sunday Express*, 17 March 1968
Page 318	Matt Busby – *Manchester Evening News/Chronicle*, 23 March 1968
Page 336	Otto Gloria – *Sun*, May 1968
Page 336	Eusebio – *Daily Express*, 29 May 1968
Page 342	Bobby Charlton – *Observer*, June 1968
Page 342	Nobby Stiles – *Observer*, June 1968
Page 344	Denis Law – *Manchester Evening News/Chronicle,* 29 May 1968
Page 345	Alex Stepney – unknown, May 1968
Page 345	John Aston – unknown, May 1968
Page 348/49	Matt Busby – unknown, May 1968